Readings in Western Civilization

Vere dignum

University of Chicago Readings in Western Civilization
John W. Boyer and Julius Kirshner, General Editors

University of Chicago
Readings in Western Civilization
John W. Boyer and Julius Kirshner, General Editors

5
The
Renaissance

**Edited by Eric Cochrane
and Julius Kirshner**

The University of Chicago Press

Chicago and London

Eric Cochrane, 1928–1985

ἀθάνατος μνήμη
Immortal memory

Eric Cochrane was born in Berkeley, California, in 1928. At the time of his death in 1985 he was professor of history at the University of Chicago. He authored *Florence in the Forgotten Centuries, 1527–1800: A History of Florence and the Florentines in the Age of the Grand Dukes* and *Historians and Historiography in the Italian Renaissance*, both published by the University of Chicago Press.

Julius Kirshner is professor of history at the University of Chicago and an editor of the *Journal of Modern History*.

The University of Chicago Press, Chicago 60637
The University of Chicago Press, Ltd., London
© 1986 by The University of Chicago
All rights reserved. Published 1986
Printed in the United States of America
95 94 93 92 91 90 89 88 87 86   5 4 3 2 1

Library of Congress Cataloging-in-Publication Data
Main entry under title:

University of Chicago readings in Western civilizations.

   Includes bibliographies and indexes.
   Contents: —v. 4. Medieval Europe / edited by
Julius Kirshner and Karl F. Morrison—v. 5. The
Renaissance / edited by Eric Cochrane and Julius
Kirshner.
   1. Civilization, Occidental—History—Sources.
2. Europe—Civilization—Sources.   I. Boyer, John W.
II. Kirshner, Julius.   III. Title: Readings in Western
Civilization.
CB245.U64   1986   909'.09821   85–16328
ISBN 0–226–06934–6 (v. 1)
ISBN 0–226–06935–4 (pbk.: v. 1)

ISBN 0–226–06944–3 (v. 5)
ISBN 0–226–06945–1 (pbk.: v. 5)

Contents

In Memoriam

Eric Cochrane, friend, colleague and coeditor, did not live to see the publication of this volume. He died suddenly during Thanksgiving of 1985 in Florence, the city he dearly loved and whose history he illuminated with brilliant scholarship. A splendid teacher, he guided a generation of students at the University of Chicago over the terrain of Western Civilization. His acerb wit and extraordinary generosity to students and colleagues, which were legendary, will be deeply missed.

He firmly believed, along with the Renaissance historians he admired, "that a knowledge of what men had done in the past could be of use in informing and directing the decisions of men in the future. A knowledge of the past," he insisted, "was not something that could be merely copied and then transmitted. It had to be acquired, with the expenditure of considerable labor, from a study of the remnants of the past that were often nonhistorical in nature and that were frequently incomprehensible to an investigator without very refined philological skills." A man of action as well as of very refined philological skills, he worked many hours, together with Lydia Cochrane, to render into readable English the prose of Leon Battista Alberti, Bernardino of Siena, Niccolò Machiavelli, and other remarkable personages who appear in the following pages. This collection of texts, Eric Cochrane hoped, would delight as well as instruct a new generation of students and would serve to remind them that death is insignificant in comparison to history, which he passionately embraced as a source of life.

Julius Kirshner

Series Editors' Foreword

This series is the result of almost four decades of teaching the History of Western Civilization course at the College of the University of Chicago. The course was founded in its present form in the late 1940s by a group of young historians at Chicago, including William H. McNeill, Christian Mackauer, and Sylvia Thrupp, and has been sustained during the past twenty-five years by the distinguished teaching of Eric Cochrane, Hanna H. Gray, Charles M. Gray, and Karl J. Weintraub. In the beginning, it served as a counterpoint to the antihistorical and positivistic thrust of the general education curriculum in the social sciences in the Hutchins College. Western Civilization has since been incorporated as a year-long course into different parts of the College program, from the first to the last year. It now forms part of the general intercivilizational requirement for sophomores and juniors. It is still taught, as it has been almost constantly since its inception, in discussion groups ranging from twenty to thirty students.

Although both the readings and the instructors of the course have changed over the years, its purpose has remained the same. It seeks not to provide students with morsels of Western culture, nor to nourish their moral and aesthetic sensitivities, and much less to attract recruits for the history profession. Its purpose instead is to raise a whole set of complex conceptual questions regarding the nature of time and change and the intended and unintended consequences of human action and consciousness. Students in this course learn to analyze past events and ideas by rigorously examining a variety of texts. This is in contrast to parallel courses in the social sciences, which teach students to deploy synchronic and quantitative techniques in analyzing society, usually without reference to historical context or process.

Ours is a history course that aims not at imparting relevant facts or exotic ideas but at providing students with the critical tools by which to analyze texts produced in the distant or near past. It also serves a related purpose: to familiarize students with major epochs of that Western historical tradition to which most of them, albeit at times unknowingly, are heirs. The major curricular vehicle of the course is the *Readings in Western Civilization*, a nine-volume series of primary sources in translation, beginning with Periclean Athens and concluding with Europe in the twentieth century. The series is not meant to be a comprehensive survey of Western history. Rather, in each volume, we provide a large number of documents on specific themes in the belief that depth, not breadth, is the surest antidote to superficiality. The very extensiveness of the documentation in each volume allows for a variety of approaches to the same theme. At the same time the concentrated focus of individual volumes makes it possible for them to serve as source readings in more advanced and specialized courses.

Many people contributed to the publication of these volumes. The enthusiastic collaboration and labors of the members of the Western Civilization staff made it possible for these *Readings* to be published. We thank Barbara Boyer for providing superb editorial direction to the project and Mary Van Steenbergh for her dedication in creating beautifully text-edited manuscripts. Steven Wheatley's advice in procuring funding for this project was invaluable. Members of the University of Chicago Press have given their unstinting support and guidance. We also appreciate the confidence and support accorded by Donald N. Levine, the Dean of the College at the University of Chicago. Above all, we are deeply grateful for the extraordinary dedication, energy, and erudition which our late colleague and former chairperson of the course, Eric Cochrane, contributed to the *Readings in Western Civilization*.

We are grateful to the National Endowment for the Humanities for providing generous funding for the preparation and publication of the volumes.

John W. Boyer and Julius Kirshner

General Introduction

The age commonly referred to as the Renaissance has been defined in many ways. One of the earliest definitions was the one given by Giorgio Vasari in the selection printed in this volume: the age in which the fine arts were reborn and brought to perfection. To this original definition the historians of the eighteenth century—from Ludovico Antonio Muratori to Voltaire and William Robertson—added the notion of the perfection of the principal vernacular languages and the flourishing of Latin and Greek scholarship. The historians of the nineteenth century emphasized the recovery of the intellectual and artistic heritage of classical antiquity; and the most influential of them, Jacob Burckhardt, went beyond the phenomenon to the cause, which he found in the particular social and psychological environment of the courts of the northern Italian tyrannies and in the self-conscious, self-contained individuals who inhabited them.

Twentieth-century historians have enriched the definition still further. Renaissance culture, argues Federico Chabod, was the successor to Franciscan piety as the spiritual expression of the merchant class that built the Italian communes; by juxtaposing ancient pagan and Christian moral values, that culture in turn generated its successor, the Protestant Reformation. The greatest achievement of Renaissance culture, declared Bernard Berenson, and many art historians after him, was the development of a technique for exactly representing objects in nature; and the Renaissance ended when the so-called "mannerist" artists consciously abandoned anatomical accuracy and spacial unity. For Hans Baron, the greatest achievement of the Renaissance was a new ethical system and a new historical perspective, one that fully justified the role of the citizen in economic and political activities. For Paul Oskar Kristeller, the Renaissance added several new disciplines, such as poetry, moral philosophy, and historiography, to those that had been taught in the schools of the Middle Ages. For Eugenio Garin, the Renaissance put all these disciplines onto a new foundation: philology. Philological methods, when applied to the in-

1

vestigation of nature, eventually produced still another humanist discipline—the empirical and mathematical sciences. For many of the historians of the various new churches to which the collective name "Protestant" was eventually given, the principal innovations of the age were theological and ecclesiological, and the immediate precursors of the innovators were the biblical and patristic exegetes and the latter-day heirs of the great medieval scholastics.

Recently, the study of Renaissance culture has been supplemented by much more intensive studies of the political, social, and economic milieu in which these cultural innovations first appeared and flourished. Demographers and ethnographers have joined historians trained in the methods and techniques of the social sciences in poring over the abundant archival records. They have drawn attention to many aspects of the age that were ignored by their predecessors and have added immensely to the kinds and quantity of available documentation. Some of these important new documents are published in English for the first time in this volume.

Above all, recent historians have multiplied the number of outstanding questions of interpretation and synthesis. Was the Renaissance simply a continuation of the Middle Ages, as some economic and social historians suggest? Or did a sharp break between two epochs occur sometime in the late fourteenth and early fifteenth centuries, as the historians of literature and the arts insist? Did the various religious reformations of the sixteenth century reject the artistic and literary heritage of the fifteenth century? Or were they products of the same culture? Did cultural forms change notably as they were transported from their original Florentine or Roman base to the other cities of Italy and then to the rest of Europe? And were they transformed by their introduction into different kinds of societies—mercantile republics, princely and ecclesiastical courts, academies, universities? When, finally, did the Renaissance—however it may be defined—come to an end? Or did it not end at all but rather become an integral part of the lasting heritage of Western Civilization?

Faithful to the guiding principles of the course for which these volumes have been designed, the editors have consciously chosen to concentrate on only some of the many aspects of the age that have interested recent historians. Demographic changes are only rarely, and never systematically, referred to. Economic and business history appears only in a few passages of Leon Battista Alberti and Luca Landucci and are thus limited to the particular circumstances of the city of which these writers were citizens. Since plays must be read either in their entirety or not at all, dramatic literature—one of the most flourishing forms of culture in the age of Ariosto and Shakespeare—is omitted, as are lyric poetry, poetics, and classical scholarship. Technology and the natural sciences are omitted because they constitute a major theme in the succeeding volume of this series. Music appears in the form of music theory alone, although applications of the theory can easily be illustrated with recent performance recordings of works by composers contemporary to the theorists.

Even those aspects of the age represented in this volume are narrowly circumscribed in space and time. The important problem of the transition from medieval to Renaissance culture is documented not, for example, by the gradual adoption of classical motifs in basically gothic buildings in France or Germany, but by one jurist, one poet-moralist, and one theologian, all of whom spent most of their lives in the particular circumstances of the northern Italian city-states of the mid to late fourteenth century. Similarly, the quest for a viable political order—one of the most pressing concerns of all Europe at the time—is represented by documents chosen from one city alone. This restriction has not been adopted because the editors believe that Florence was a typical or model Renaissance state. It most certainly was not. Rather, it has been adopted because Florence happens to have produced one of the most influential political philosophers of all times, Niccolò Machiavelli, and because its political evolution can be followed throughout an entire constitutional cycle, from oligarchy to monarchy.

Indeed, part 3 of this volume can be of particular use to those who wish to concentrate on the history of political thought—another area of interest to historians of early modern Europe. They can trace the emergence of Machiavelli's political concepts from the attempts of Leonardo Bruni and Bartolomeo Scala to impose first Aristotelian and then Ficinian-Platonic and Roman juridical categories upon the commercial-industrial city-state described by Luca Landucci. They can appreciate the novelty both of Machiavelli and of his predecessors by comparing them with their pre-Renaissance forerunner, Bartolus of Sassoferrato. They can measure the extent to which Machiavelli's concepts were realized or superseded both in practice, in Scipione Ammirato's account of what happened in Florence after 1537, and in theory, in Giovanni Botero's efforts to overcome Machiavelli's dichotomy between political and Christian morality. Machiavelli the careful observer of contemporary political phenomena and Machiavelli the searcher for definitive solutions to outstanding political problems are abundantly documented both in his personal correspondence and in the selection of chapters from his chief work of political theory, the *Discourses*.

Whoever wishes to emphasize culture rather than its environment can turn immediately from Petrarch's letters to part 4. Two of the documents included in this section are particularly relevant to the visual arts. Vasari presents both a general historical perspective of his age and a theoretical explanation of High Renaissance art. Pontormo presents a similar explanation—one of the very few in existence—of mannerist art. And both authors can be usefully supplemented with slides or photographs of the David, the Sistine Chapel, the Last Judgment, and one or two of Pontormo's well-known paintings.

Marguérite de Navarre provides both an idealization of aristocratic court life and a good example of the humanist principle of *imitatio* applied to another imitable "model," this time a "modern" one, Boccaccio's *Decameron*. The contrast between ancient and medieval literary "models" will be readily grasped by those who, having studied the previous volumes in this series, now compare the chronicler Landucci with the historian Ammirato, whose statements on the principles of humanist historiography are included in this selection. All these texts can be used to test the editors' own definition of Renaissance humanism: the culture created by those artists and men of letters who recognized as normative the literary and artistic masterpieces of ancient Greece and Rome along with those masterpieces of their own day generally held to be equal to those of antiquity, and who followed the forms and standards of those normative models in the hope of surpassing them.

One of the two essays by Montaigne illustrates the way in which the role of antiquity in providing a perspective for critically evaluating the present was transferred to the newly discovered lands overseas. The other essay bears witness to the vast expansion of available reading material, which many contemporary observers held to be one of the chief characteristics of their age. The dialogue by Galilei illustrates the application of humanist principles to the discipline of music. It may also suggest the impropriety of the common, although (in the minds of the editors) erroneous, assumption that the Renaissance vanished in Italy—and in Florence—sometime after the first two decades of the sixteenth century.

The selections in part 4 reflect another dominant theme of current historical research: that religious commitments and a commitment to the reform of religious institutions were integral parts of the age dominated by humanist culture, not its successors or antitheses. They also reflect a current methodological principle: that religious doctrines must be studied not only in themselves, but also in the way they were experienced in the lives of those who heard them. The connection between other forms of humanist culture and the religious reformation is documented in Erasmus's statement of the aims of biblical and patristic scholarship as well as in the bull of Convocation of the Council of Trent. The most concise statement of Luther's principal doctrines—*sola fide*, *sola scriptura*, and the priesthood of all believers—is contained in his *On Christian Liberty*, which, since it is available in an inexpensive edition (Muhlenberg Press), is not reproduced here. The repercussions of these doctrines for contemporary German society is illustrated in the *Twelve Articles*. The impact of the doctrines of the Tridentine reformation are illustrated in the diary of Giambattista Casale. This document may also serve to clarify the attitudes and aspirations of the urban working class. It may even help to dispel another common assumption: that the Tridentine doctrines were imposed by force on an unwilling but impotent population which otherwise would have converted, depending on the preferences of the modern historian, to Protestantism, Scepticism, or Deism.

Select Bibliography

Supplementary Texts

Besides those already mentioned, supplementary texts for subjects covered in this topic are abundant. Humanism in fifteenth-century Italy is well represented in Paul Oskar Kristeller, ed., *The Renaissance Philosophy of Man* (University of Chicago Press); humanism in the sixteenth century by Erasmus's *Ten Colloquies* (Liberal Arts) and Thomas More's *Utopia* (Yale). Many more texts on the various Protestant reformations are contained in John Dillenberger, ed., *Martin Luther* (Doubleday Anchor) and *John Calvin* (Scholars Press), in Hans J. Hildebrand's *The Protestant Reformation* (Harper Torchbooks), and in Steven E. Ozment's *The Reformation in Medieval Perspective* (Chicago: Quadrangle Books, 1971). The selections here on art and art theory can be supplemented by Leon Battista Alberti, *On Painting* (Yale), and by Elizabeth G. Holt, ed., *A Documentary History of Art* (Doubleday Anchor), vols. 1 and 2.

Suggestions for Further Reading

The Classics

Baron, Hans. *The Crisis of the Early Italian Renaissance*. 2d ed. Princeton: Princeton University Press, 1966.

Berenson, Bernard. *Italian Painters of the Renaissance*. Oxford: Clarendon, 1930.

Burckhardt, Jacob. *The Civilization of the Renaissance in Italy*. New York: Paidon Press, 1983.

Chabod, Federico. *Machiavelli and the Renaissance*. New York: Harper & Row, 1965.

Garin, Eugenio. *Science and Civic Life in the Italian Renaissance*. New York: Anchor, 1969.

Jedin, Hubert. *A History of the Council of Trent*. New York: T. Nelson, 1957.

Kristeller, Paul Oskar. *Renaissance Thought and Its Sources*. New York: Columbia University Press, 1979.

Weinberg, Bernard. *A History of Literary Criticism in the Italian Renaissance*. Chicago: University of Chicago Press, 1961.

Recent Scholarship

Brucker, Gene. *Renaissance Florence*. Berkeley: University of California Press, 1983.

Burke, Peter. *Tradition and Innovation in Renaissance Italy*. London: Batsford, 1972.

Cochrane, Eric. *Historians and Historiography in the Italian Renaissance*. Chicago: University of Chicago Press, 1981.

Delumeau, Jean. *Catholicism between Luther and Voltaire*. Philadelphia: Westminster Press, 1977.

Evennett, H. Outram. *The Spirit of the Counter Reformation*. Cambridge: Cambridge University Press, 1967.

Gerrish, B. A. *The Old Protestantism and the New: Essays in the Reformation Heritage*. Chicago: University of Chicago Press, 1982.

Gilbert, Felix. *Machiavelli and Guicciardini*. Princeton: Princeton University Press, 1965.

Hale, John, ed. *Renaissance Venice*. London: Faber & Faber, 1973.

Herlihy, David, and Christiane Klapisch-Zuber. *Tuscans and Their Families*. New Haven: Yale University Press, 1985.

Holmes, George. *The Florentine Enlightenment, 1400–1500*. New York: Pegasus, 1969.

Martines, Lauro. *Lawyers and Statecraft in Renaissance Florence*. Princeton: Princeton University Press, 1968.

Maclean, Ian. *The Renaissance Notion of Women*. Cambridge: Cambridge University Press, 1980.

Miskimin, Harry. *The Economy of Late Renaissance Europe, 1460–1600*. Cambridge: Cambridge University Press, 1977.

Murphy, James J., ed. *Renaissance Eloquence: Studies in the Theory and Practice of Renaissance Rhetoric*. Berkeley: University of California Press, 1983.

Ramsey, P. A., ed. *Rome in the Renaissance: The City and the Myth*. Binghamton, N.Y.: Center for Medieval and Early Renaissance Studies, 1982.

Rice, Eugene. *The Foundations of Early Modern Europe*. New York: Norton, 1970.

Rubinstein, Nicolai. *The Government of Florence under the Medici*. Oxford: Clarendon, 1966.

Skinner, Quentin. *The Foundations of Modern Political Thought*. Cambridge: Cambridge University Press, 1978.

1
From the Middle Ages to the Renaissance

1. Bartolus of Sassoferrato, *On the Tyrant*

Bartolus of Sassoferrato (1313/14–1357), the most celebrated jurist of the fourteenth and fifteenth centuries, began his life as a humble rustic. He was born at Venatura, a village near Sassoferrato in the territory of Ancona. A brilliant, analytic, and far-reaching mind, good fortune—he survived the Black Death of 1348—and excellent training at the Universities of Perugia and Bologna permitted Bartolus to overcome his humble origins. From 1343 onward, he taught at the University of Perugia and produced a vast corpus of work that filled eleven large folio volumes in the Venetian edition of 1602–3.

Bartolus's writings include commentaries on all the principal divisions of Justinian's codification, known as the *Corpus juris civilis*; questions (*quaestiones*) that had been disputed in formal academic settings; and monographic tracts on public, private, criminal, and procedural law. Among the most notable of his works is *On the Tyrant* (*De tyranno*), the first tract dedicated by a jurist to the subject of tyranny. Composed between 1355 and 1357, this tract analyzes the causes and nature of tyranny, a common type of rule in mid-fourteenth-century Italy, and discusses possible legal remedies to be used against the tyrant. Bartolus's writings reflect an extraordinary knowledge of the *Corpus juris civilis*, the interpretations related to the Justinianic compilation, opinions and monographs of other jurists, canon law, customary law, feudal law, and the statutory law promulgated by city-states. This knowledge, combined with

From *Il "De tyranno" di Bartolo da Sassoferrato (1314–1357)*, edited by Diego Quaglioni (Florence: Leo S. Olschki, 1983), pp. 175–213. Translated for this volume by Julius Kirshner.

his mastery of dialectic, permitted Bartolus to arrive at hundreds of novel doctrines and constructions, though without modern critical editions of his work, it would be foolhardy to make extravagant claims on behalf of his originality.

Bartolus's jurisprudence is distinguished from that of his predecessors who believed that human laws were not self-sufficient, and the task of the jurist was to fit a law into a preconceived system guided by the abstract ideal of justice. The jurist performed his task by discovering the *ratio* or just quality of each law—that is, by gauging the law's conformity to natural reason, a metalegal postulate. Where his predecessors' universe tended to be abstract and immobile, and consequently impeded a full accommodation between the Roman law (also known as the *ius commune* or common law) and contemporary practices, Bartolus's universe tended to be open-ended and flexible, responsive to the vexing problems generated by the economic, social, and political convulsions that beset Europe in the mid fourteenth century. He accomplished the accommodation between the Roman law and his society by "updating" the Justinianic compilation in the light of contemporary practice. At the same time he invoked the Roman law to justify, modify, or repress myriad practices that had no counterpart in the Justinianic compilation. This dual process is a defining feature of Bartolus's jurisprudence.

Among the most influential doctrines spawned by this process is Bartolus's teaching that the authority of a city-state (*civitas*) on affairs conducted within its jurisdiction is parallel to that of an emperor. In Bartolus's celebrated phrase, the *civitas* is its own emperor (*civitas sibi princeps*) and does not recognize a superior. He endorsed the city-states' authority to promulgate statutes, to create new citizens, to impose taxes, and the like. Such statutes, he taught, must submit to the universal authority of the common law as interpreted by bona fide jurists.

Bartolus's works were avidly read and reproduced, as witnessed by the thousands of manuscript copies and printed editions bearing his name. His opinions and doctrines were cited as authoritative by judicial officials in Spain and Germany as well as in Italy. Although Bartolus and his followers were attacked by fifteenth-century humanists for barbarizing the ancient Roman law, his preeminence was not diminished and was expressed in the professional maxim that no one was a jurist who was not a Bartolist (*nemo jurista nisi sit Bartolista*).

The translation of the *Tractatus de tyranno* is based on a recent critical edition brimming with details regarding the Biblical, legal, and theological authorities and sources that Bartolus cited to justify his arguments. His tract was addressed to an audience of fellow jurists trained to recognize and understand the significance of these citations as well as the technical jargon Bartolus employed. For the purpose of making his tract readable to an audience not trained in the mysteries of medieval jurisprudence, we have deleted most of Bartolus's citations and have relegated them to the footnotes. Citations have been retained in those passages that would be incomprehensible without them.

The following abbreviations and method of citation are used to refer to the *Corpus iuris civilis* and the *Corpus iuris canonici*, the standard collection of canonical rules, regulations, and papal decrees, as well as the major texts studied in the law faculties of medieval universities.

Corpus iuris civilis, 11th ed., 3 vols., edited by T. H. Mommsen, W. Kroll, P. Krueger and R. Schoell (Berlin, 1963–66):

I.4.18.8 = Justinian's *Institutes*, Book 4, Title 18, *Lex* 8.

D.11.12.1.13 = Justinian's *Digest*, Book 11, Title 12, *Lex* 1, subsection 13.

C.9.14.7 = Justinian's *Code*, Book 9, Title 14, *Lex* 1.

Corpus iuris canonici, 2 vols., edited by E. Freidberg (Leipzig, 1879–81):

Gratian, D.XV, c. 3 = *Decretum* of Gratian, *Distinctio* XV, canon 3.

C. IX, q. 1, c. 5 = *Decretum* of Gratian, *Causa* IX, *quaestio* 1, canon 5.

X.1.6.34 = Decretals of Pope Gregory IX, Book 1, Title 6, chapter 34.

VI.2.14.2 = Decretals promulgated by Pope Boniface IX, Book 2, Title 14, chapter 2.

Clem. 2.11.2 = The collection of decretals promulgated by Pope Clement V, Book 2, Title 11, chapter 2.

Long have I labored now, investigating in many treatises the subjects most pleasing to my tastes. These have totally filled me—heart, soul and body—with relish; but so replete have I become with their savory sweetness that I have lacked the stomach to deal with realities of a more bitter, oppressive, and distressing nature—even more so as I witness the treachery of tyranny swelling its might. Nevertheless, trusting in the protection of that grace which "makes the tongues of infants to speak clearly,"[1] I dare, with the arm of the Lord as my shield, to take up the chilling and horrifying subject of the perverse nature of tyranny—not that I may derive joy and solace therefrom, but that all may be able to rid themselves utterly of the knotting coils of the horrendous evil, namely, the slavery of tyrannical

1. Wisd. of Sol. 10:21.

rule. May God free us from its stern and unbridled governance and preserve us in his own holy, good, and perfect tranquility. May he make us to rejoice together in the sweetness of his liberty. And so will I, Bartolus of Sassoferrato, citizen of Perugia, a most insignificant doctor of laws,[2] before proceeding further to the treatise at hand on the tyrant, set down in brief some questions which we will presently address in the course of our exposition.

First, I ask about the origins of the word tyrant.

Second, I ask how one defines tyrant.

Third, I ask whether one speaks of a tyrant in a neighborhood.

Fourth, I ask whether there can be a tyrant in a household.

Fifth, I ask how many kinds of tyrants of a city there are.

Sixth, I ask who is called a manifest tyrant by defect of title in a city.

Seventh, I ask whether acts performed by manifest tyrants of this type or performed during their administrations are valid.

Eighth, I ask who is called a manifest tyrant by virtue of his conduct.

Ninth, I ask if a duke, marquis, count, or baron who has a lawful title is proved to be a tyrant by virtue of his activity, what should a higher authority do?

Tenth, I ask what shall we say about the things our supreme pontiff, emperor, and their legates have clearly done?

Eleventh, I ask whether actions performed by the aforementioned tyrants, who genuinely have lawful title, are valid.

Twelfth, I ask about the tacit and concealed tyrant.

1

First, I ask about the origins of the word tyrant.

It is derived from the Greek word *tyrus*, in Latin *fortis* (strong) or *angustia* (oppression), wherefore "powerful kings were called tyrants. Later it came about that the word was used to refer to the worst and impious kings who ruled their peoples by unbridled passion and extreme cruelty."[3] According to Huguccio "it is derived from *tyrus*, that is, oppression, because he oppresses and brings affliction upon his own people."[4] That *tyrus* should be understood as I have said is evident from the interpretations of the Bible,

---

2. Although Bartolus had an intimate knowledge of canon law, his doctorate was in civil law.

3. Isidore of Seville, *Etymologiarum sive Originum libri XX*, 9, 3, ed. W. M. Lindsay (Oxford, 1911), cols. 19–20.

4. Huguccio, *De verborum derivatione*, s.v. (under the word) Tyro. Huguccio (d. 1210) was the most important canonist of the twelfth century.

where we read: "*Tyrus* means oppression or tribulation or strength,"[5] all of which are combined evilly in the person of the tyrant.

These definitions will be of use to us when we consider the nature of the tyrant and how he is to be recognized as such.

2

Second, I ask how one defines tyrant.

Gregory, in the twelfth book of his *Moralia*, gives this definition: "A tyrant, in the strict sense, is one who rules a whole commonwealth unlawfully. But it should be understood that every proud person practices tyranny in his own manner. For sometimes one practices tyranny in a commonwealth through the power of an office he has accepted; another in a province, another in a city, another in his own house, while another practices tyranny in his own thoughts through concealed wickedness. The Lord does not consider one's ability to commit evil, but one's desire to commit it; and although one lacks the trappings of power to do what one wishes, he remains a tyrant at heart if wickedness rules him from within. For, even if he does not outwardly oppress his neighbors, inwardly he yearns for power so that he may oppress."[6] Such are Gregory's words which ought to be observed as law.[7] Let us briefly examine them.

"A tyrant, in the strict sense," etc.: Just as a king or a Roman emperor is strictly a legitimate, true, and universal ruler, so if anyone wishes to occupy that office unlawfully he is called a tyrant in the strict sense.[8]

"A whole commonwealth": meaning the Roman Republic.[9]

"One who rules unlawfully": This happens because he lacks a legitimate title, since he was not elected, or unlawfully elected, or elected but then rejected;[10] or else elected, crowned, but afterwards justly rejected. As it is told of king Saul in 1 Kings [13: 13–14], where the prophet Samuel said: "You have behaved foolishly. You have not kept the command laid on you by the Lord your God; if you had, he would have established your dynasty over Israel for all time. But your line will not at all endure; the Lord has sought a man after his own heart and has appointed him prince over his people, because you have not kept the Lord's command." It is therefore evident that a king is deprived of his kingdom through sins and is, consequently, a tyrant because he rules unlawfully.

5. Jerome, *Liber interpretationis Hebraicorum nominum, De libro Iesu Nave* (James 15:24; 19:29) (ed. P. de Lagarde, *Opera*, I, 1).

6. Gregory the Great, *Moralium libri*, 12, 38 (*PL*, 75, col. 1006).

7. Gratian, D.XV, c.3.   8. C.1.2.6 and 16.

9. D.50.16.16.   10. X.1.6.34; VI.2.14.2.

"But it should be understood": Gregory has finished speaking of a ty-rant in a universal sense and now begins to speak of particular ones, who are not tyrants in quite so strict a sense.

"Every proud person": Pride is the root of all evil, and such pride is especially apparent in the case of tyrants. There follows in that passage a discussion of five kinds of tyrants. One is a general tyrant over the whole Roman Republic, another of a province who rules unlawfully, another of a city, another of a household, and another of himself. It must be determined whether there can be a tyrant of a neighborhood, a question that I shall discuss below.

"Through the power of an office he has accepted": This can be deter-mined by what precedes or what follows.

"Another in a province": In a province it is possible for someone to rule unlawfully in the same way that I have spoken of above with regard to the whole commonwealth. So it is another form of tyranny when one is made governor of a province for a fixed term or serves at the pleasure of the appointing power and at the expiration of his term refuses to make way for a successor. Such a person is a tyrant and is subject to the *lex Iulia maiestatis*.[11]

"Another in a city": Our discussion will be chiefly concerned with the tyrant in a city.

"Another in a household": I shall discuss below how this can be.

"Another practices tyranny in his own thoughts through concealed wickedness": It is not for the jurist to consider the tyranny concealed in one's thoughts, because no one can be punished for his thoughts.[12] Yet it must be understood that if one plans and arranges for an action, even if he does not carry it out, he is to be punished as if he had carried it out, in accordance with the *lex Iulia maiestatis*.[13] In the passage of Gregory which follows (the one I have been discussing), reference is made to punishment that occurs after examination by the eternal judge, and therefore I refrain from expounding on this issue, but leave it to the theologians. Nevertheless I have raised this issue as it is useful to us.

"He yearns for power so that he may oppress": It should be especially noted that an act of tyranny consists chiefly in the oppression of one's sub-jects. He is called a tyrant because "he oppresses and brings affliction upon his own people," as has been said. The acts of a tyrant are of many kinds, as will be shown below.

This is enough by way of comment on the passage of Gregory.

11. D.48.4.2.   12. D.48.19.18.
13. D.48.4.3.

3

Third, I ask whether one speaks of tyranny in a neighborhood.

The answer is no, as is evident from Gregory's words, since he did not mention this kind of tyranny. This is proven on the following grounds. The rule of a tyrant is the very worst kind of rule, for it is directly opposed to the rule of a king, which is the best.[14] Yet if the tyrant is he who does not rule lawfully, it is evident that where there is neither realm nor rule, there cannot be a tyrant. But now in a neighborhood there has customarily not been a king or any kind of government with jurisdiction;[15] hence, there cannot be a tyrant in a neighborhood. In fact, a neighborhood is not governed by one person but by the ruler who governs the whole city. Even if certain great and powerful persons oppress others in a neighborhood, they are not considered tyrants but simply more powerful persons[16]—unless, indeed, we suppose that in a neighborhood or in a certain part of the city someone may become so preeminent that the general council can do nothing except what that person wishes (as the nobles in Rome are now doing); such persons are correctly called tyrants in that part of the city.

On the other hand it may be said that any city is generally divided into quarters or parishes, in each of which there are persons called captains or syndics who preside over the affairs of that section of the city.[17] Now it would seem that where there is government, there might be a tyrant.

But I reply that such persons have no jurisdiction even though they sometimes are entrusted with coercive power for the purpose of exacting certain imposts and of denouncing wrongdoings to the authorities. They should rather be called the servants of rulers than actual rulers themselves, for they do not rule but serve rulers. Therefore, they cannot be called tyrants, but only powerful persons who, by virtue of their offices, are able to instill fear among their subjects, and who are thus subject to the constitution *Si per impressionem*[18] and *lex Si simulatio praesidis.*[19]

Furthermore, the wrongdoings of the powerful in a neighborhood can quickly be redressed by those who rule the city; and on this account the powerful are not to be called tyrants. This explains why the blessed Gregory did not mention that there could be tyranny in a neighborhood. By the

---

14. Cf. Aristotle, *Ethica ad Nicomachum*, 8.10.1160, a-b; Saint Thomas Aquinas, *De regimine ad regem Cypri*, 1, 3, ed. J. Mathis (Turin, 1924), p. 4.

15. Jurisdiction (*iurisdictio*) generally designated a complex of supreme judicial, administrative, and legislative rights and powers. It was often defined by medieval Roman jurists as a power publicly introduced with responsibility for pronouncing what is right (*ius*) and enacting what is just (*aequitas*).

16. D.4.7.3; D.1.18.6.2.   17. D.2.14.14.
18. C.2.19.11.   19. D.47.13.1.

same token I say that in villages, towns, and fortified areas situated in the countryside around some cities, where there is no jurisdiction in either law or fact, there can be no tyrant, even though there is one person more powerful than the rest. But if one such place should be strong enough, thus leading someone to rebel and to defend himself against the city, so that wrongdoings could not be prevented there by city officials without great difficulty, he might then be considered a tyrant, according to the *lex Iulia maiestatis*,[20] *lex Quicumque*,[21] and *lex Fideiussor in iudicio*,[22] where it says that it is difficult to bring suit against someone of substance who hails from a well-fortified place or town.

4

Fourth, I ask whether there can be a tyrant in a household.

It would seem that this is not the case, since no jurisdiction is exercised there.

But, as related above, Gregory says the contrary.

In my opinion, the head of the family may be said to possess in some degree the right of a ruler over his subjects in his own house because he declares the law there with regard to his children and his slaves.[23] Likewise, the elder of a family has a certain kind of jurisdiction over his wife, children, and slaves; and even the eldest brother or the paternal uncle has jurisdiction over those in the house who are under twenty-five years of age.[24] If, then, one governs the family contrary to law, he may properly be called a tyrant. Thus if any member of the family should make a contract or any other agreement through fear of that person it would be null and void, just as if it were made through fear of a tyrant, according to the *lex Iusiurandum vicem*.[25] In my lecture on this law, I have discussed how one may prove this kind of fear; and such proof is indicated by Innocent IV.[26] On the other hand, if there is in the house an elder person with a younger brother or brother's son younger than he, but over twenty-five years of age, the elder does not have that kind of power over him, since he ought to govern himself.[27] In that case fear alone is not sufficient, for there must be proof of fraud or a general state of fear, should someone wish to nullify the acts of such a person.

---

20. D.48.4.3.   21. C.11.59.2.
22. D.2.8.2.   23. D.47.2.17; C.8.46.4.
24. C.9.14.1; C.9.15.1.   25. D.44.1.5.

26. Innocent IV, on X.1.39.1. In *Quinque libros decretalium commentaria doctissima* (Venice 1578), fol. 73rb, n.1, s.v. (under the word) "non timore." Innocent IV (Sinibaldo Fieschi, d. 1254) was an important canonist, who became pope in 1243.

27. D.4.4.1.

We may also call the abbot of a monastery a tyrant if he rules unlawfully: either because he is a usurper,[28] or because although his title is
valid, he rules tyrannically, as will be explained below in our examination
of tyranny in a city.

5

Fifth, I ask how many kinds of tyrants of a city there are.

From what has been said, it is evident that a tyrant of a city is one who
rules unlawfully. And just as there are many ways of ruling unlawfully,
there are many kinds of tyrants. Some are open and manifest tyrants,
others concealed and tacit. Likewise, it sometimes happens that one is a
manifest tyrant by defect of title, sometimes by virtue of conduct. So in the
same way a concealed tyrant may be such at times because of defect of
title.

Concerning these distinctions, let us inquire further.

6

Sixth, I ask who is manifest tyrant by defect of title in a city.

He who rules in the city, openly, without lawful title, as is evident from
our previous definition. This can occur in numerous ways. First, if the city
or fortified town which is invaded lacks the right to choose its own ruler, he
who acts there as a ruler is a tyrant because he is ruling contrary to law and
is consequently subject to the *lex Iulia maiestatis*.[29] The same is true if
after his term of office has expired, he remains in it against the will of the
competent authority responsible for that office.

But suppose that the city or fortified town has the right to elect its own
ruler and that the city has given someone jurisdiction, although this was
done under compulsion. Then there can be some doubt whether he is ruling
contrary to law, since what is done through fear is valid, even though it
may subsequently be annulled by the special action *quod metus causa*.[30]
Meanwhile, he is the legitimate ruler, and it cannot be said that he is a
tyrant by defect of title. But the contrary is true, for jurisdiction must be
transferred voluntarily, and if it is done out of fear, it is not legally valid.[31]

---

28. VI.3.4.18.   29. D.48.4.3.

30. Use of duress in order to compel a person to conclude a transaction, to assume an
obligation, or to make a payment is a private crime (*delictum*) which may be prosecuted by
the person who acted under duress by a special legal action, *actio quod metus causa* (for what
was done because of fear).

31. D.5.1.2; D.4.2.21.3.

Now we must consider how violence or fear is wielded against the people.

When an army is led against a city without authorization of a superior, as in the *lex Iulia maiestatis*; or when the city is taken by assault with the help of foreign troops, as in the *lex Iulia de vi publica*.[32] If, however, he procures his election as lord through intrigue or rebellion with help of the people of the city itself, then this question (whether he is a tyrant by defect of title) is more doubtful, because it appears as if the greater part elected him and that this was a greater part (*maior pars*)[33] because he was elected. But it must be said that even in this case, he turns out to be a manifest tyrant who holds office by defect of title and who becomes such through violence and fear.[34] But now suppose that one occupies the fortifications of a city with a small force and that through this occupation a reasonable fear descends upon the people. Certainly he is elected through fear. Or suppose he prevails with the backing of that part of the population only in number, comprising common folk and men of low estate, as generally happens. Certainly in this case he cannot be said to be made ruler by the greater part of the people, since men of low estate ought not to be members of the municipal senate or council.[35] The same is true if he prevails with the backing of people from the surrounding countryside.[36] Or suppose that with a small band of citizens he has led an uprising, when the others were scattered in their houses, for a united few are more than equal to a divided multitude. Certainly this would justify a state of fear among the people. Or suppose that at the outset he has driven out or killed one or more of the worthier citizens with a small band, on which account the people were justly alarmed. For it is written: "I will smite the shepherd, and the sheep shall be scattered (Matt. 26:31)." That the people's fear was reasonable is demonstrated by many examples from history, especially in the book of Judith (14:3; 15:1–7).

And without qualification I say that if a ruler is chosen unlawfully through intrigue or rebellion he is a manifest tyrant by defect of title.[37] Even if later he rules well, he remains a tyrant, unless he is subsequently excused for his misdeeds.[38] That the above argument is true is apparent from this: if at the time of his election he wrongfully expels any citizens,

---

32. D.48.6.3.2.

33. *Maior pars* does not refer to an absolute majority but only a majority of the people qualified to conduct the affairs of the city, thus excluding the numerically superior lower orders of the community.

34. X.2.13.19.

35. C.12.1.6.

36. C.11.54.1.

37. C.1, q.1, c.25; C.XIV, q.5, c.9.

38. X.1.9.10.

those expelled can be said to have been treated despicably and ought to be recalled.[39] If therefore an election is held while they are so treated, it is invalid,[40] and thus he is a manifest tyrant by defect of title.

From what has been said, therefore, the method of determining who is such a tyrant becomes evident.

7

Seventh, I ask whether acts performed by manifest tyrants of this type or performed during their administrations are valid.

This question has several parts.

It must first be determined whether those acts which are performed with jurisdiction are valid. It is certain that the acts performed by tyrants themselves, on the basis of having jurisdiction, are *ipso iure* null and void, as in the *lex Decernimus*, where it says "basically void"[41]; and the *Glossa* explains: "that is, *ipso iure*."[42] And fittingly, for when it says "basically," it is as if it said that these acts are without basis and were never valid. The same is true of the acts of officials appointed by the tyrants themselves and for the same reason.[43]

Yet, in a city where there is such a tyrant, there is doubt regarding the validity of acts performed by other officials who were elected by the city itself without opposition from the tyrant. It seems that these acts are not valid under the aforesaid *lex Decernimus*, where it is said that whatever is done in the time of tyranny is *ipso iure* null and void. For the words of the law refer not only to the acts performed by the tyrant himself but to any acts performed in the time of tyranny; and this argument is grounded on reason. For no act is freely performed where there is a tyrant, and thus it seems that everything is done by the tyrant himself. Authority for this is found in the decretal *Cum vobis*,[44] where it is said that the time elapsing during a schism may not be counted toward the time within which one is allowed to take certain legal actions, by which it means that in time of schism no lawful acts can be performed, or else the time elapsing during a schism would count. Now the period of tyranny can be called a time of schism, since the tyrant breaks away and separates himself from the univer-

---

39. C.10.32.2.   40. X.1.6.28; X.1.6.34; X.1.6.36.
41. C.1.2.16.
42. Glo. "funditus," C.1.2.16 (*Codex*, Lyon, 1612, col. 35). The *Glossa* was the standard and authoritative medieval collection of exegetic comments on the texts, phrases or single words of Justinian's *Corpus*. These comments, written by jurists as marginal or interlinear glosses, were compiled by Accursius (1182–1260) in the early thirteenth century.
43. X.5.8.1; C.IX, q.1, c.5.   44. X.2.26.14.

sal empire. This is clearly so because he is subject to the *lex Iulia maiestatis*, as we said.

On the other hand, as it is not said in the aforementioned *lex Decernimus* that all acts are null, except those made against churches, other acts would therefore continue to be valid. Besides, injustice would be the result, for if in a city tyranny should be greatly prolonged, shall we declare all solemn acts and legal proceedings to be null? This seems harsh.

I do say that legal proceedings against rebels and enemies of the tyrant are *ipso iure* null. For they ought not to appear before a judge openly hostile to them or in a place openly suspicious of them.[45] But certain ordinances as well as legal judgments and proceedings are directed against the inhabitants of the city, in which case there is more doubt about their invalidity. We should compare this case with that of a free man subject to another, who is under the power of the head of a family or a lord, and while in that position performs some conscious act, or what he, in any event, would do. In that event, his act is valid; on the contrary, if he would do otherwise.[46] Thus in the case at hand a once-free people or officials chosen by such a people, now subject to tyrannical power, perform certain acts which they would have performed in any event, even if they were free to act for themselves—as, for example, decisions regarding ordinary legal cases which every tyrant allows to go through the judicial process. Such acts are valid because they are performed voluntarily. There are certain acts which would not have been performed unless there had been a tyrant, and these are not valid because they are performed, not freely but through fear of the tyrant, as shown by the above-mentioned laws. And so says the *lex Decernimus*. For it is certain that measures concerning churches could not be taken by persons other than legitimate ecclesiastical officials if there were no tyrant; and therefore such acts are said to be basically void. We judge these from the character of those performing the acts, as if we were speaking of a minor who has done something which a prudent person of mature years would not have done. I also think that if in legal proceedings injury is inflicted by judges upon persons whom the tyrant has under suspicion, restitution should be made to them in accordance with general statutory provisions regulating this matter.[47] I further think that the time for demanding restitution should run from the termination of the tyranny, just as in other legal situations it runs from the termination of one's absence or minority.[48]

Our second inquiry concerns the validity of contracts. Such contracts arise from many different situations.

45. D.36.1.8; D.32.4.7.1; D.50.7.5; Clem. 2.11.2.
46. D.41.1.19; D.41.1.54; D.29.2.6.1.   47. D.4.6.1; D.36.1.67.2.
48. X.2.26.14.

When the city makes a grant or a concession to the tyrant, such a contract is *ipso iure* null. For just as a promise made by a captive to the person who has thrust him into prison is not valid, so also is a promise or any contract made by the people with the tyrant who holds them captive and, as it were, prisoner. For a tyrant is said to hold the people in servitude.[49] We can also say that such contracts are null.[50] For if contracts of this sort are annulled when made with a just ruler, how much more in the case of a tyrant ruling unjustly.[51]

Sometimes contracts are made between a tyrant and individuals under his power, and it can be said that these are also null. Moreover, it can be said that such a contract ought to be annulled under the constitution *Si per impressionem*.[52] This is especially true if the tyrant causes property to be sold to him by coercion; for in that case he is subject to that constitution, which compels him to restore the property and forfeit the payment. Coercion is proved if the tyrant would not allow the property to be cared for, or if he threatened the possessor should he refuse to sell, or sought other pretexts, or made repeated demands upon one who had nothing to offer for sale. For the request of a superior constitutes a command.[53]

Sometimes a tyrant of this sort makes a contract with foreigners on behalf of the city: if in fact this contract subjects or obligates the city to another person, it is invalid *ipso iure*.[54]

Sometimes he does not subject the city to another person, but makes a different contract: If in fact this contract is advantageous to the city which he rules tyrannically, it still seems to be invalid, just as we say of a possessor in bad faith of an inheritance.[55] A contrary opinion is held by Hostiensis,[56] namely that such a contract is valid in so far as it is favorable to the city, just as we say of a minor.[57] But if a contract is partly favorable to the city and partly unfavorable, and if there are separate clauses, the contract is valid in so far as it favors the city.[58] If, however, the clauses are interdependent, and if the city rejects the contract in so far as it is unfavorable, it cannot likewise accept it in so far as it is favorable.[59] Such is the

---

49. X.3.49.6.   50. C.1.53.1.

51. Auth. 4.18.2.1. This reference is to the medieval collection of the Latin translation of the 134 novels promulgated by Justinian between 535 and 536.

52. C.2.9.11.

53. Glo. "quemadmodum," D.15.4.1.2 (*Digestum vetus*, col. 1583).

54. C.11.53.1; X.5.8.1; VI.1.6.17.   55. D.2.14.17.6.

56. Henry of Susa, on X.5.8.1, s.v. "firmitate" (in *Quintum Decretalium librum*, 1581, fol. 40v). Henry of Susa (d. 1271) was one of the most celebrated canonists of the late Middle Ages and in 1261 became Cardinal-bishop of Ostia, whence his name Hostiensis.

57. C.2.12.14.   58. D.4.4.29.1.

59. D.17.2.23.1; D.4.4.41; D.4.4.24.4.

opinion of Hostiensis. I think his opinion is true enough, and in principle, is applicable to the case of a contracting party who knew that the man was a tyrant. Consequently, he has no remedy under the title *Quod falso tutore auctore*. If, however, we suppose that the contracting party was ignorant of the tyranny, he has a remedy by way of restitution under the same title.[60] But, indeed, how is it possible that anyone can remain ignorant of so notorious an event—as, for instance, that someone is a tyrant by defect of title?

Sometimes the tyrant does not make a contract, but sells off property in separate parcels, receiving directly or through his officials payments owed to the commonwealth. Are those who pay released from their debts? On this point it must be understood that if they are debtors of the city by virtue of a contract made with the tyrant himself, it would seem that they ought to be released from the debt, in accordance with *lex Si urbana*.[61] But that text refers to the case of a contract made with a thief in his own name, while here it is a question of a contract made with a tyrant in the name of the city. Nevertheless it seems that the debtor may be released from his contract as if it had been made with a slave or a son under the paternal power.[62]

Sometimes a debt is payed for which the debtor was obligated to the city in some other way than by an act of the tyrant, and here it would appear that the debtor is not released,[63] as in the said *lex Si urbana*. On this issue, one can allege the excellent opinion found in Innocent IV's commentary on the decretal *Nichil*,[64] where it seems to be said that those who make payments to a usurping official without lawful title are not released.

It seems to me that the above opinions are sound when the debt is paid to a thief, or a usurping prelate, or a tyrant, none of whom are in a position to inspire fear in the debtor or to threaten him with harm—as, for example, were the debtor of another city. If, however, the tyrant can inspire fear, or apply force, or threaten harm by virtue of the jurisdiction he exercises (though this jurisdiction is merely *de facto*), then, since the debtor is subject to him, he is released when he pays the debt to the tyrant or his official.[65] This opinion is also proven by reason. For, through public levies violently imposed upon a debtor, an injury is inflicted upon the city to which he belongs. Here the city itself, on its own account, tyrannizes and the fault seems to lie with it.[66] But when in fact the quantity of goods owed is de-

---

60. D.27.6.1.6. Under Roman law, legal action is allowed against a *falsus tutor*—a person who acts as guardian without having been legally appointed.

61. D.12.6.55.   62. D.2.14.27; D.15.1.56; D.46.3.35.

63. D.12.6.55.

64. Innocent IV, on X.1.6.44. s.v. "ministrent" (in *Quinque libros decretalium*, fol. 33r-v).

65. D.32.1.27.2; D.33.1.21.3.   66. D.19.2.25.4; D.24.3.66.

stroyed through the fault of the creditor, the debtor is released by pleading an exception.[67] If a specific item of property is owed, then there is little doubt that the debtor is released *ipso iure*. For this reason, if a specific item of property owed to one is seized by force, one can allege the *lex Lectos*, *lex Sequenti*, *lex Locum purum*, *lex Lucius*, and *lex Item si verbatim*.[68] The text makes a similar distinction, namely whether force is wielded by someone with jurisdiction or not.[69] Perhaps it may be said that if a tyrant of this sort be of such condition that the payment to him may readily be recovered, the debtor should not be allowed to plead an exception.[70] The reverse is true should recovery be difficult. But, as I think, this distinction applies to the case where violence is used against a person resulting in injury to that person, but not where injury is inflicted upon his creditor, for the reasons stated above. I do not think it necessary for someone to demonstrate the fear put upon him by the tyrant; for this it suffices that the tyrant has enacted a law or given public notice ordering payment to be made. For, if one has made payment on account of such notice, he had good reason to fear violence, and that suffices as the text states (*lex Novissime*).[71] This text serves considerably to excuse debtors who pay under such conditions, for in this case the guardian is compelled (through fear) to inflict injury upon his ward, just as the debtor is compelled to inflict injury upon his city. From what has been said, it is evident that if tax collectors or other officials appointed by the tyrant collect money and later dispose of it in compliance with his orders or hand it over to the tyrant himself, they are not held liable.

Sometimes tyrants of this sort neither enter into contracts nor sell off property in separate parcels but allow the properties of the city to waste away and its rights to be lost by prescription. In this case I think prescription cannot be enforced against the city.[72] I also say that if the tyrant exercises any right or pertinent jurisdiction which properly belongs to the city itself, claiming that his right or jurisdiction is recognized, not by the city itself but by another, then, as far as he himself is concerned, he appears to be using another's right, but, as far as the city is concerned, that is not the case; for by reason of that use, the city retains its right.[73]

67. D.46.3.72. In general, an *exceptio* was any kind of defense applied by the defendant in order to paralyze, peremptorily or temporarily, the plaintiff's claim.
68. D.18.6.13–14; D.13.7.43; D.21.2.11; D.6.1.15.1.
69. D.2.11.2.9.   70. D.2.10.3.
71. D.27.6.7.   72. C.7.33.1; X.2.26.14.
73. D.43.19.1.

8

Eighth, I inquire about someone who possesses a lawful title but is a manifest tyrant by virtue of his conduct, even though he is less properly called a tyrant.[74]

I say that he is a tyrant by virtue of his conduct because he performs tyrannical acts, that is, acts directed not toward the common good, but to his own advantage. And this, in fact, is to rule unlawfully. So that the manner of proof may be made easier, let us come down to specific acts, which, as detailed in the first part above, consist in the oppression of subjects. These acts are clearly enumerated by Aristotle in the fifth book of his *Politics* and Egidius Romanus in his book, *On the Rule of Princes*.[75]

First, it is the practice of a tyrant to annihilate the preeminent and powerful men of the city, lest they rebel against him. We see that tyrants murder even their brothers and kinsmen, a sign of the very worst kind of tyranny.

Second, they eliminate the wise men, lest they reveal their iniquities and incite the people against them.

Third, they put an end to study and education. For they not only eliminate wise men, but also strive to prevent others from being trained, because they are always in fear of being censured through learning and wisdom.

Fourth, they prohibit private associations and public meetings, even lawful ones, through fear of uprisings against them.

Fifth, they have many informers throughout the city. For they know that they are doing wrong and therefore always believe that people are speaking ill of them and plotting against them, and for this reason they gladly listen to such informers.

Sixth, the tyrant strives to keep the city in a state of division so that each faction, by fearing the other, will not rebel against him.

Seventh, the tyrant deliberately keeps his subjects poor, so that they may be fully occupied with earning their living and thus have no time to hatch plots against him.

Eighth, he foments wars and sends his soldiers to fight abroad to prevent them from hatching plots against him since through wars men are reduced to poverty and called away from study, things which a tyrant desires. Also

74. C. XIV, q.5, c.9.

75. Aristotle, *Politics*, 5.11.1313 a-b; Egidius Romanus, *De regimine principum*, 3, 2, 10 (Venice, 1498), fols. 104v–105v. Also known as Giles of Rome (ca. 1243–1316), Egidius was an influential Augustinian theologian, who composed *On the Rule of Princes* while he served as tutor to the young Philip IV of France.

in this way he keeps soldiers in training for his own use when he needs them.

Ninth, he makes up his bodyguard, not from his own citizens but from foreigners, for he stands in fear of the citizens.

Tenth, when there are factions in the city, he always supports one of them and in union with it suppresses the other.

Such are the opinions of the philosophers, and now let us examine them.

First, the annihilation of preeminent persons or brothers is a tyrannical act. This is true unless it is done for a just cause, as in the case of Romulus and Remus.[76] For who can doubt that if any powerful person provokes violence and sedition, he ought to be expelled by any just judge?[77] Therefore, if the cause be a just one, the act is not tyrannical.

Second, the annihilation of the wise men should be understood in the same way, when it is done without good reason, in conformity with the preceding laws.

Third, the termination of study and education: understand this to apply to intellectual activities that are appropriate for the city.[78] If, however, a ruler prohibits such intellectual activities because they are not appropriate for the city, this is not an act of tyranny.[79]

Fourth, that public meetings, even lawful ones, are prohibited unless they occur with good reason. What if a public meeting, even if lawful, commits a wrongdoing? Certainly, it should be dissolved.[80] For I have seen persons congregate under the pretense of religion and throw the city into a state of confusion. We must, therefore, judge by the kind of persons congregating, whether it is an act of tyranny to disrupt these public meetings.

Fifth, the employment of many informers in the city. This may be the act of a just ruler if it is undertaken for a lawful purpose.[81] An upright ruler employs informers to punish wrongdoings and other offences committed in the city. But a tyrant employs them against those who may damage his own position, and he uses all things to his own advantage.

Sixth, that the tyrant strives to keep the city in a state of division. This is absolutely a tyrannical act, since it is the primary duty of a just ruler to preserve the peace among the citizens.[82]

Seventh, that he deliberately keeps his subjects poor. This is also an absolutely tyrannical act, for the upright ruler should accept nothing beyond his due nor afflict his subjects with burdens upon their persons or their property.[83]

76. D.1.8.11.
77. D.48.19.28.3; D.48.19.38.2; D.1.12.3.14.
78. D.27.1.6.2.   79. D. const. *Omnem*, 7.
80. D.49.16.3.9.   81. D.1.12.1.13.
82. D.1.12.1.12; D.1.18.13; Auth. 3.4.2.   83. C.9.27.4; C.9.27.6; Auth. 3.4.9.

Eighth, on fomenting wars. To foment civil wars is absolutely an act of tyranny. Sometimes foreign wars may be just wars, but an unjust war is without qualification an act of tyranny.[84]

Ninth, maintaining his bodyguard of noncitizens may be justified, for a people may be so uncontrollable and so ill-tempered that a lord, even though he may be just, cannot rely upon them. This is especially likely to happen in newly recovered cities, even under just lords. For this reason emperors sometimes expelled all the inhabitants of a city and settled others there.[85] So also we sometimes see just lords build fortifications and strongholds in the city. These are legitimate measures.[86] But a just lord undertakes these measures in response to special circumstances, whereas the tyrant undertakes them indiscriminately.

Tenth, supporting one faction while suppressing the other, is absolutely an act of tyranny, since the ultimate purpose of citizenship, as has been said, is the tranquility and peace of the citizens.

All the above, therefore, are distinguishing characteristics demonstrating the existence of a tyranny, but note especially these two: to keep the city divided, and to impoverish subjects and to injure their persons and property. This is excellently demonstrated in the chapters set forth above.

From what has been said, the manner for demonstrating this sort of tyrant is now evident.

9

Ninth, if some duke, marquis, count, or baron who has legitimate title is proved to be a tyrant by virtue of his conduct, what should a superior do?

He ought to depose him, since lords who act in this manner hold their people in servitude, and it is the duty of a superior to deliver the people from servitude.[87] Likewise it is the duty of a superior to depose tyrants.[88]

But under what law do tyrants fall, and by what law can they be deposed?

The tyrant who occupies his position without lawful title is subject to the *lex Iulia maiestatis*. As for the tyrant who has lawful title but is shown to be a tyrant by his conduct, I say that because he oppresses his subjects in their persons, he is subject to the *lex Iulia de vi publica*.[89] Also, because he keeps the city in a state of division and thus prevents the rendering of legal judgments that are necessary, he is subject to the same *lex Iulia de vi pub-*

---

84. L.F.II.28.1. This reference is to the *Liber Feudorum*, a collection of Lombard laws.
85. C.10.1.4; C.11.55.1.   86. L.F.II.1.
87. C.1.27.1.   88. C.1.27.2.
89. D.48.6.10.

lica. Moreover, by imposing new burdens and new taxes he incurs the penalty of the same law,[90] which is deportation, according to the *Institutes*.[91] Thus he forfeits all rights under the civil law[92] and, as an officially disgraced person, he loses his office and jurisdiction, as explicitly indicated by the *lex Iulia de vi privata*.[93] He is also subject to the *lex Iulia de ambitu* and *lex Vectigalia nova*.[94] He may also be subject to the penalty of death.[95]

I say, further, that if those living under such a tyranny "conspire in whatever way, openly or secretly," against the emperor or his officers they are *ipso iure* rebels of the empire and forfeit their offices, according to a new law of Emperor Henry VII.[96]

10

Tenth, what shall we say about the things which it is clear that our Supreme Pontiff, the Emperor, and their legates have done? Certain persons whom they well knew to be tyrants in lands which they held through such tyranny, they made vicars of the Holy See or the Empire, as did Clement VI at Bologna with the lord Taddeo dei Pepoli and his sons, Iacopo and Giovanni. Our Emperor Charles IV did the same thing with the tyrants of Lombardy, and Egidius of Albornoz, bishop of Sabina and legate of the Holy See, did the same with many tyrants in the March of Ancona.[97]

We must presume that such great lords would not perform these acts without extraordinary justification which can be of two kinds. First, there is some extraordinary and pressing need which they are obliged to satisfy, for as a diligent sailor jettisons his less valuable cargo in order to save the more precious,[98] and as an attentive head of the household selects his more valuable goods[99] [in case of danger], so sometimes a just lord comes to terms with a tyrant and makes him his vicar so that he may first accomplish more pressing reforms. The second reason may be his love and affection for the tyrant's subjects. We see physicians follow nature when a disease cannot be cured without great danger to the patient; they strive to aid nature by preventing the disease from proceeding any further, thereby al-

90. D.48.6.12.
92. D.48.19.17.
94. D.48.14.1; C.4.62.4.

91. I.4.18.8.
93. D.48.7.1.
95. C.10.20.1.

96. *Extravagantes Henrici VII*, 2, *Qui sint rebelles*. Henry VII (ca. 1269–1313) was elected Roman Emperor in 1308. In 1310 he marched into northern Italy, hoping to restore imperial authority, and was hailed by Dante as the deliverer of Italy.

97. Clement VI reigned as pope from 1342 to 1352. Charles IV reigned as Holy Roman Emperor from 1355 to 1378. In 1353 Cardinal Gil Albornoz (ca. 1302–67) was named by Innocent VI as papal legate and vicar general in the Papal States and northern and central Italy.

98. D.14.2.8.   99. D.13.6.5.4.

lowing nature to come to her own aid. Sometimes a just emperor, seeing that a tyrant cannot be deposed without inflicting great damage upon his subjects, makes the tyrant vicar for their sakes, so that being less fearful he will be less oppressive to the people. Meanwhile some opportunity may arise through which the tyrant may be deposed in conformity with justice and without injury to the people.

Despite the legitimacy which is subsequently conferred upon their titles, these tyrants do not cease to be tyrants if they continue to perform the aforesaid acts of tyranny. For such wrongdoings do not enter into the commission with which they are entrusted,[100] but are perpetrated in a manner tantamount to defrauding creditors.[101]

11

Eleventh, I ask whether the actions performed by the aforementioned tyrants, who genuinely have legitimate title, are valid.

I say that either he proceeds against exiles and rebels, in which case the legal proceeding is not valid, since no one is bound to appear before a notoriously hostile judge, as was said above; or else he proceeds against citizens within the city, and then the legal proceeding is valid as long as the tyrant is permitted to remain in office.[102]

But what if the legal proceeding against such a tyrant has already begun: are the acts performed by a tyrant, while the case is pending and before definitive judgment is pronounced, valid?

Should his case be such that declaratory judgment[103] is pronounced concerning a crime for which he would *ipso iure* be deprived of his jurisdiction, or would be declared a slave or an officially disgraced person, then acts performed after the legal proceeding commenced are not valid, as in the end of the *lex Testes servi*, where one reads: "no one up to this time has disputed their legal status."[104] If, on the other hand, his case is such that he would be deprived of jurisdiction only in consequence of the sentence to be pronounced, then his acts are valid, because meanwhile he retains his office.[105]

100. D.12.6.6.   101. D.42.8.12.

102. D.1.15.3; C.7.45.2; C.6.23.1; X.1.3.13; X.2.27.24; Innocent IV, on X.1,3,13 (in *Quinque libros decretalium*, fol. 6rb).

103. Strictly speaking, a declaratory judgment is preliminary, in which the judge or court makes determinations regarding questions of law without ordering anything to be done. Since the tyrant's conduct in this case deprives him of his office *ipso iure*, a declaratory judgment is one which merely declares which law is applicable to the case, judgment then following automatically.

104. C.6.23.1.

105. D.49.14.46.6; D.50.1.17.12; C.10.60.1.

In the same way, if a contract is made or terminated with the tyrant, the agreement is valid, as was observed by Innocent IV in his commentary on the decretal, *Nichil.*[106] But understand that the agreement must not result in the city's subjugation, as I shall explain below.

I say also that if one is under the power of a noble person and has lawful title, even though he is a tyrant by virtue of his conduct, he has nevertheless a privileged position[107] so long as he is allowed to hold office; not so, however, if his title is defective.

I say further that if one having a legitimate title subsequently becomes a tyrant because of his conduct and brings about a certain broadening of his jurisdiction to be granted him by the people, it would not be valid, on the assumption that the people would have made the grant from fear, as was said above.

Also every contract that he may have made subjugating or binding the city would not be valid; for he is not acting as a lord when he deprives the city of its liberty.[108]

12

Twelfth, I ask about the tacit and concealed tyrant, that is, one who under some cover rules over a city unlawfully. This cover may be of two kinds. The first, in which he has a title granted to him; the second, in which he does not allow a title to be so granted.

Concerning the first, in which he has a title granted to him, it should be understood that a tyrant is, strictly speaking, the antithesis of a king, as was said above. But it is the nature of royal power to be perpetual and to have full jurisdiction, as clearly set forth in our previous chapters. Now from these two qualities have come two ways of concealing a tyranny.

First, that one has a certain jurisdiction granted to him for a specific period, and upon completion of that period has the grant reconfirmed so that his rule seems to be that of a judge rather than a tyrant. On this point I say that although he causes such jurisdiction to be granted to him in his own city, his title is invalid, for no person can have a jurisdiction of this sort.[109] This does not apply to the city of Rome where anyone can be *praetor* and senator for not more than one year.[110] The same holds for the

106. See above, note 64.   107. Clem., 3, 15, 1.
108. D.41.4.7.3; X.2.24.33; VI.1.6.17,7.   109. C.1.51.10.
110. C.1.39.2; VI.1.6.17. The praetors were the highest magistrates in the Republic after the consuls and were vested with full imperium and far-reaching authority in military, judicial, and administrative matters. Under the Principate the activity of the praetors was almost exclusively jurisdictional.

defensor civitatis.[111] However, these officials do not have *merum et mixtum imperium*,[112] but only simple jurisdiction. And so what was said above regarding the tyrant by defect of title must be said again regarding the tyrant who would assume an invalid title.

But if we suppose a city in which, either by privilege or custom, the power of the people to make a concession cannot be revoked, even in a doubtful case, a title granted in the first instance would be valid. Now we must consider whether he becomes a tyrant on the grounds that he had himself reconfirmed. That would seem to be the case under the common law because such recomfirmation is not valid; indeed he is subject to the *lex Iulia de ambitu.*[113]

The second cover is that certain tyrants cause some title to be conferred upon them which conveys almost no jurisdiction. For example, they have themselves appointed as standard bearers; or they have the defense of the city entrusted to them; or they have themselves made captains of mercenaries or the militia. Because of these functions some say that they are not tyrants, since a tyrant must have full jurisdiction like a king. He cannot be said to rule who has no or only a limited degree of jurisdiction. Certainly he is not a tyrant by reason of his title. But if through these functions he attains so much power that he administers the affairs of the city as he wishes, and the city's officials obey him as their lord, then I say, if he acts tyrannically or causes others to so act, he is a true tyrant. Indeed he rules in the city because the public officials remain obedient to him; and yet he is not ruling according to law, since he is acting tyrannically, and therefore is a tyrant.

But how can this be proved when a tyrant of this sort keeps himself con-

111. Auth. 3.2.1. The *defensor civitatis* was appointed by the emperor for the first time in 364 for the defense of the poor against exactions by the great landowners and powerful citizens. This office eventually acquired jurisdiction in minor civil affairs and even developed certain police functions.

112. Ulpian's (Roman *jurisconsult*, d. 228) distinction between criminal jurisdiction, *merum imperium*, and civil as well as criminal jurisdiction, *mixtum imperium*, was reformulated in the Middle Ages. For Bartolus, *merum imperium* encompassed those cases which had as their objective the public welfare (*utilitas publica*). Bartolus divided *merum imperium* into six grades. The first grade is the power of making laws. Next, came the right to inflict punishment involving death or loss of members. The third grade covers cases relating to loss of citizenship. The fourth covers cases in which the penalty is banishment without the loss of civil rights. The fifth is the power of the magistrate to coerce anyone who affronted his authority. The sixth covers cases in which the penalty was a fine. *Mixtum imperium* did not have as its principal objective the public welfare. It encompasses legal actions protecting the private interests of individuals, although such actions might indirectly contribute to the welfare of the community.

113. C.9.26.1.

cealed, does not act in person, seldom appears in the town hall, while the public officials obey his written orders and agents?

I answer that proof is difficult, since when things of this sort are done witnesses cannot be called. In consideration of the difficulty of proceedings against powerful men, a decretal addressed to a particular case ordered that a plaintiff should prove by oath (that he was afraid of) someone else's power.[114] But I do not think this principle applies in general. In this case, the plaintiff taking the oath merely obtains the right to have his case decided by a judge outside the city limits. But nothing is decided concerning the person against whom the oath is taken. Therefore I think that proof here must be secured in some other way. It should be understood that although some actions cannot be directly proved of themselves they are still capable of proof, as I have shown in my book on the alluvial deposit.[115] Although the alluvial deposit cannot be perceived while it is forming, nevertheless, from the fact that it has been formed it follows of necessity that the river has formed it. So also, although the conception of a child is not perceptible, it is considered sufficient proof if it can be shown that the child was born of a woman cohabiting in a household with a man.[116] Since the purpose of proof is to enable the judge to have confidence in the facts, the sorts of things just mentioned are sufficient to accomplish this. So it is in the present case, if it can be shown that there is division in the city (perchance one faction has been driven out), that crimes are committed and atrocities occur without punishment, that citizens are greatly oppressed, and that similar things occur that are commensurate with the tyrannical acts of which we have spoken above. Further, if the person who has that title is the most powerful man in the city and if it is a matter of common knowledge that he is behind these acts, then, I say, tyranny is sufficiently proved. For these acts cannot proceed from anyone except that most powerful man. These acts, together with the common knowledge that he is behind them, are enough to convince the judge that he is a tyrant. This agrees with what we have said in the case of one who rules lawfully: namely, that it is sufficient if he is so considered and reputed.[117] For the very same reason one may be considered and reputed a tyrant.

But now, are acts performed during a tyranny of this sort valid?

In reply I give the same opinion as in the case of a manifest tyrant who causes these acts to be performed through officials elected by the city.

114. VI.1.3.11.
115. *Tractatus de fluminibus seu Tyberiadis*, I, *de alluvione* (Bologna, 1571, fols. 21–23).
116. D. 1. 6. 6.   117. D. 1. 15. 3.

This truly happens when the majority of the people are oppressed, or burdened, or kept in a state of discontent. If, however, some are forced to remain in exile or some within the city are maltreated by exclusion from public offices, while in other respects the city is well governed and the public welfare is cared for, then the person having a title of this sort or a similar distinction would not be a tyrant in the plain meaning of the word, since the public welfare is cared for by such a government, which is the direct opposite of a tyranny. But with regard to acts directed against foreigners or enemies of the man thus superior to others, even though he governs the commonwealth well, I think we should regard his acts as those of a tyrant. There is no reason why one should not be called a tyrant with respect to certain persons and a lawful ruler with respect to the community.[118] For this reason it should be understood that, just as one is seldom found who is completely healthy, indeed free from all bodily defect, so it is a rare thing to find a government that is completely devoted to the public good without some of the qualities of a tyranny. It would be more divine than human if rulers had no regard for their own advantage and cared solely for the common welfare. We call it a good government and not a tyranny in which the common and public welfare prevails over the personal welfare of the ruler; the one in which personal welfare is cared for more, we call a tyrannical government. This is stated by Egidius Romanus in his *On the Rule of Princes*,[119] and it ought to be especially borne in mind when we consider proving whether someone is a tyrant.

A third form of concealment occurs when one allows no title to be conferred upon him in the city but administers its affairs in such a manner that everything proceeds according to his will. That such men are tyrants is proved in the way described immediately above, namely that in the city tyrannical acts are performed, that he is the most powerful man on account of having the greatest following, and that it is a matter of common knowledge that he causes the aforesaid acts to be performed. Many things inevitably happen in the course of a tyranny which cannot but lay bare the perverse designs of the tyrant and reveal an easy method of proof.

As for the acts performed during a tyranny of this sort, I hold to what I said immediately above.

Whether there can be a tyrant in a neighborhood or in a certain part of the city or the surrounding countryside, I have already given my opinion.

118. C. 5. 7. 1.   119. *De regimine principum*, III, ii, 11 (fol. 105vb).

2. Francesco Petrarca, *Letters on Familiar Matters*

Petrarca, or Petrarch, was born in 1304 in Arezzo where his Florentine father was living in exile, and he spent his first years just outside Florence. Here he learned the local language that he was to use in the love poems collected in his *Canzoniere*. He then followed his father to the papal court at Avignon, spending his early maturity in permanent residence there or on study tours to the universities of Paris, Montpellier, and Bologna, and vacationing at his modest estate in the nearby Vaucluse. It was there that he acquired the enthusiasm for ancient literature that led him to search systematically for manuscripts—and to inspire several generations of disciples to follow his example until they had recovered almost the whole corpus of ancient literature extant today. This enthusiasm also inspired a long epic poem, *Africa*, composed on the model of Virgil's *Aeneid*, which won him the laureat's crown in Rome referred to in the letters included in this selection. The reading of Augustine's *Confessions* brought about a slow spiritual crisis, one which is described in his letter of 1336 on a climb to the top of Mt. Ventoux and in his dialogue *Secretum* of 1342–43 (revised in 1353 with additional notes in 1358). Following the advice he attributes in the dialogue to Augustine, he spent his later years in the diplomatic service of the dukes of Milan and the princes of Padua or at his retreat house at Arqua, near Padua, where he died in 1374. As the letters Petrarch collected and constantly revised set the pattern for the many other such collections of the Renaissance, so the dialogue form he adopted, in imitation of Cicero, for the discussion of literary and ethical questions, became a standard form of literature.

Although Petrarch himself continued to be spoken of with deference, his many Latin works went out of circulation as soon as his followers surpassed him in his own aim of restoring classical Latin. Indeed, they were first published not in Italy, but in Germany (Strassburg, 1472); and after its appearance as *De Contemptu Mundi* in the Venetian edition of the *Works* (1501–3), Renaissance Italians had to wait for the Basel (1544) edition of the *Works* to read the Latin text of the *Secretum*—which is probably why none of them seems ever to have read it. The most recent critical editions are those of Guido Martellotti, in *Prose* (Milan: Ricciardi, 1958), and Antonietta Bufano (with emendations upon the pre-

From *Francesco Petrarca, Letters on Familiar Matters*, translated by Aldo S. Bernardo (Baltimore: The Johns Hopkins University Press, 1982), pp. 47–50, 193–95, 214–19, 267–70. Some footnotes deleted.

vious edition), in *Opere latine* (Turin: UTET, 1975). Petrarca's vernacular poetry, on the other hand, was revived by the *literati* in the entourage
of Lorenzo de' Medici in the late fifteenth century. After 1524, when the
linguist and critic Pietro Bembo elevated them to the rank of classics of
the genre, the poems themselves were acclaimed as imitable models all
over Europe, and the language they were written in came to be accepted
as the official written, and eventually spoken, language of all Italy.

1.9

To the same Tommaso da Messina,[1] on the study of eloquence.

The care of the mind calls for a philosopher, while the proper use of
language requires an orator. We must neglect neither one, if, as they say,
we are to return to the earth and be led about on the mouths of men. But I
shall speak of the care of the mind elsewhere; for it is a great undertaking
and an enormous labor, though very rich in harvest. At this time in order to
avoid slipping into a subject other than the one that I set out to treat, I urge
and admonish that we correct not only our life and conduct, which is the
primary concern of virtue, but our language usage as well. This we will do
by the cultivation of eloquence. Our speech is not a small indicator of our
mind, nor is our mind a small controller of our speech. Each depends upon
the other but while one remains in one's breast, the other emerges into the
open. The one ornaments it as it is about to emerge and shapes it as it
wants to; the other announces how it is as it emerges. People obey the judgment of one, and believe the opinion of the other. Therefore both must be
consulted so that one will be reasonably strict with the other, and the other
will be truthfully magnificent toward the first. The fact remains that where
the mind has been cultivated, speech cannot be disregarded, just as, on the
other hand, there can be no merit to speech unless a certain dignity is
present in the mind. What good will it do if you immerse yourself wholly
in the Ciceronian springs and know well the writings either of the Greeks
or of the Romans? You will indeed be able to speak ornately, charmingly,
sweetly and sublimely; you certainly will not be able to speak seriously,
austerely, judiciously and, most importantly, uniformly. The reason for this
is that unless our desires first order themselves (and you must know that no
one can achieve this except a wise man) it is inevitable that such disorder

---

1. Petrarca addressed eight other letters (including the preceding letter) to the same Tommaso da Messina, or Tommaso Caloria; but modern Petrarca specialists have not identified
him further.

will be reflected in our conduct and in our words. The well-ordered mind is the image of an undisturbed serenity and is always quiet and peaceful. It knows what it wants, and does not cease wanting what it desires. Therefore, even lacking the ornaments of oratorical skill, it is able to call forth most magnificent and serious words harmonious with itself. Moreover, undeniably the most unusual often emerges when the movements of the mind are composed. But when these are in agitation little of any significance can be produced. The study of eloquence requires much time. If we did not need it, and if through its power our mind could silently display its good traits without the support of words, great toil would yet be necessary for the sake of those with whom we live. For without doubt, our conversations would be of great assistance to their minds.

However, stepping forward, you say, "How much safer for us and more effective for them it would be to exhort them to let us provide for their eyes examples of our virtue. Delighted by the beauty of such examples they would be seized by the urge to imitate. For we are aroused perfectly naturally in much better fashion and much more easily through the stimulus of deeds rather than of words. Through this pass let us advance more readily to the highest reaches of virtue." In truth I am not opposed to this. How I felt about this you were already able to understand just now when I warned that among the first things that must be done is the ordering of the mind. Nor do I think that without good reason the Satirist[2] said: "You owe me first of all the riches of the mind." These would certainly not be first if anything came before them. Furthermore, how much help eloquence can be to the progress of human life can be learned both in the works of many writers and from the example of daily experiences. How many people have we known in our time who were not affected at all by past examples of proper speech, but then, as if awakened, suddenly turned from a most wicked way of life to the greatest modesty through the spoken words of others! I shall not report here what Marcus Cicero said about this matter at considerable length in his books *On Invention*,[3] for what he said there is very familiar, nor would I cite the fable of Orpheus or of Amphion, the former of whom lured huge beasts with his song and the latter plants and stones which he is said to have moved at will, except as one understands that because of their outstanding eloquence both were able to inculcate gentleness and patience in all things, the one into lustful and savage men whose customs make them very like beasts, the other into rustic and rough men who were as unmanageable as stones. Add to this that such study permits us to be useful to those living in distant regions with whom we will never be permitted to

2. Juvenal (Decimus Junius Juvenalis, c. A.D. 60–c. 140), *Satires*, 8:24.
3. 1:1.

socialize but to whom our words may perhaps come. And indeed how much good we will do to our posterity can very well be judged when we consider how much our greater predecessors have left to us.

But once again you remark: "What need is there to work hard if everything advantageous to men has already been written during the past thousand years in so many volumes of a marvelous perfection by god-like talents?" Lay aside this anxiety, I say, and don't ever let it drive you into laziness. This fear was already removed by certain of our great ancients, and I shall remove it from the minds of those who come after me. Let thousands of years flow by, and let centuries follow upon centuries, virtue will never be sufficiently praised, and never will teachings for the greater love of God and the hatred of sin suffice; never will the road to the investigation of new ideas be blocked to keen minds. Let us therefore be of good heart; let us not labor uselessly, and those who will be born after many ages and before the end of an aging world will not labor in vain. What is rather to be feared is that men may cease to exist before our pursuit of humanistic studies breaks through the intimate mysteries of truth. Finally, if no sense of charity toward our fellow men drives us, I would still consider the study of eloquence of the greatest aid to ourselves rather than something to be held in the lowest esteem. Let others hold their own views. I cannot tell you of what worth are to me in solitude certain familiar and famous words not only grasped in the mind but actually spoken orally, words with which I am accustomed to rouse my sleepy thoughts. Furthermore, how much delight I get from repeating the written words either of others or sometimes even my own! How much I feel myself freed from very serious and bitter burdens by such readings! Meantime I feel my own writings assisted me even more since they are more suited to my ailments, just as the sensitive hand of a doctor who is himself ill is placed more readily where he feels the pain to be. Such cure I shall certainly never accomplish unless the salutary words themselves fall tenderly upon my ears. When through the power of an unusual sweet temptation I am moved to read them again, they gradually take effect and transfigure my insides with hidden powers. Farewell.
5 May

4.7

To Robert, King of Sicily,[4] on his laurel crown and against those who praise the ancients while always despising things of the present.

How much the study of the liberal and humane arts owe you, oh glory of

4. Roberto d'Anjou, the grandson of Charles d'Anjou (d. 1343) who conquered the kingdom with the pope's blessing in the late thirteenth century, became king of Naples in 1309. He was also count of Provence and lord of Avignon, where he lived from 1319 to 1324 and prob-

kings, which you yourself preferred to pursue with considerable industry, if I am not wrong, rather than attempt to become more famous through the crown of a temporal kingdom, has been known to the world for some time. Recently you obliged the abandoned Muses with new kindness by solemnly consecrating to them this talent of mine, however small. To this end you decorated the city of Rome and the decaying palace of the Capitoline with unexpected joy and unusual foliage. "A small matter," someone will say. Nevertheless it is something very conspicuous because of its distinguished novelty and because of the applause and delight of the Roman people. This custom of the laurel crown, which has not only been interrupted for so many centuries, but here actually condemned to oblivion as the variety of cares and problems grew in the republic, has been renewed in our own age through your leadership and my involvement. I know many other outstanding talents throughout Italy and in foreign countries which nothing would have kept from this goal except for its long disuse and the ever suspect novelty of the affair. After my personal experience with it I am confident that the novelty will wear off in a short time and the Roman laurel will be vied for through competition. For who could seriously hesitate when King Robert is one of the patrons? It will be of help to have been first in this competition in which I do not consider it to be inglorious even to be the last. I myself would not have been imbued with such a desire feeling so unworthy of such an honor unless your support had provided me with strength and courage. And would that you could have adorned the joyful day with your most serene presence which in fact, as you yourself were accustomed to say, were it not for your age which did not allow it, your royalty would never have stood in the way. I actually felt through many signs that you enjoy testing for yourself certain customs of Augustus Caesar and particularly the one which caused him to show himself not only gentle but friendly and warm to Flaccus,[5] son of a freedman who had previously been an opponent; and not to despise the plebeian origin of his Virgil in whose talents he delighted. An excellent trait indeed, for what is less becoming to a king than to expect an artificial nobility in those of outstanding virtue or talent who actually possess the kind of true nobility with which you yourself could provide them? I am not ignorant of what certain contemporary men of letters who belong to a haughty and lazy group opposed to this would answer. They would say: "Maro[6] and Flaccus are now buried; to waste fine words on them is in vain: distinguished men have long perished and only

---

ably first met Petrarca. This letter was written shortly after Petrarca, with the king's support, was awarded the laureat's crown on the Capitoline in Rome on 8 April 1341.

   5. I.e., Horace, who fought on the side of Brutus against Octavian (later Augustus) at the battle of Philippi.

   6. I.e., Virgil.

the mediocre remain as with wine only the dregs remain at the bottom." I
know what they might say and what they might think; nor can I oppose
them on every count. It seems to me that those words of Plautus applied not
only to his age when a taste for such things had barely begun, but even to
ours. He says, "The flower of poets lived at that time, and they have departed hence for a common abode."[7] We indeed can more worthily complain in such a way, for in those days there had not yet arrived those whose
departure he laments. However, the intention of these men is most suspect,
for they do not say what they do in order to lament the destruction of
knowledge, which they wish to remain destroyed and buried, but in order
to discourage through despair the contemporaries whom they are unable to
imitate. Doubtless the despair which holds them back motivates us, and the
bridle and chains which affect them, are goads and spurs to us so that we
try to become what they believe no one can become except one of the ancients. Although I confess that such men are rare and few, there are some.
And what forbids one to be one of the few? If this very rarity deters everyone, there would be in a short while not a few but none at all. Let us make
an effort, and in keeping our hope alive perhaps we can achieve the goal.
Maro himself says: "They are able because they know they are able."[8]
Likewise, believe me, we too will be able if we truly believe it. What
is your opinion? Plautus deplored his age, grieving perhaps the death of
Ennius or perhaps of Naevius. The age of Maro and of Flaccus was also
not just to such great talents. The one, poet of divine inspiration, while he
lived, was harassed by endless contentions among his rivals who slandered
him as a plagiarist. The other was accused of insufficient admiration for the
ancients. It has always been and always will be true that veneration is accorded the past and envy to the present. About you, however, oh greatest of
kings, worthy to be numbered among philosophers and poets, one can say
with even greater truth, what Suetonius says about Augustus: "He fostered
the talents of his century in every possible way."[9] And you foster the talents
of your century and always favor them with your kindness and indulgence.
And I speak as one who has experienced also what follows in that author:
"You listen kindly and patiently to writers reciting their works, not only
poems and histories but orations and dialogues. But you feel offended that
anything be composed about you unless it is done seriously and by distinguished writers." In all these things you have imitated that same emperor,
and you have turned away from those who are unhappy with everything

7. The Roman playwright Titus Maccius Plautus (c. 254–184 B.C.), in the prologue to
Cassandra.
8. Virgil, *Aeneid*, 5.231.
9. Petrarca calls Suetonius, the author of biographies of the early Roman emperors, by his
first name, Tranquillus, in the original. The quotation is from his life of Augustus, 89.

unless they are attracted by the impossibility of ever achieving it. I have recently been honored by these ways of yours and by your courtesy just as many others have, by mere chance and without deserving it. Not, as I said, would your royal esteem have stopped here if either old age were more distant or Rome closer. This messenger of your majesty, who intervened in your behalf in all the functions, will tell you personally what happened to us either in Rome or after our departure, whether joyful or dangerous. As for the rest, your very last words urging me to return to you as soon as possible shall remain forever in my memory, and as God is my witness, not because I was taken by the splendor of your court as much as by your talent. I expect from you riches different from what are usually expected from kings. Meanwhile I pray that He who is the fountain of life, and the King of kings, and the Lord of lords, prolong the years of your life and ultimately transfer you from this mortal throne to an eternal one.
Pisa, 30 April.

4.15

A controversy with a certain famous man[10] against vaunters of knowledge which is not theirs and against excerpters of literary ornaments.

It is difficult for me to say how much my ears, weary of the rabble, were charmed by your letter which I read over and over again. Although the letter appeared to you too wordy, as I learned from its ending, I myself found nothing wrong with it except excessive brevity. Therefore, I was unhappy to read that you threatened hereafter to be more brief. I would prefer that you would be more lengthy. However, you are free to do as you please. You are the father; it is not proper for you to yield to me, but for me to yield to you. But do you believe that it will all depend on you? Do you not know that the fact is often different from the intent? You will perhaps hear things which, though you are desirous of silence, may compel you to speak. Would you like me to follow through since I seem only to be threatening? I start by saying that I hold the same opinion of you which Macrobius held of Aristotle regardless of whether it was based on love or on truth.[11] I believe that there is hardly anything that you do not know. If anything emerged from you opposed to truth, I surmise that either you gave it too little thought or that you were joking, as Macrobius also says about Aristotle. Of course what you say about Jerome, that you prefer him among all of the

10. A gloss in one manuscript identifies him only as Iohannes Andree, who may be the then famous and extraordinarily prolific Florentine canon lawyer by that name (d. 1348).

11. Cicero in *Somnium Scipionis*, the last part of *De Re Publica* ("On the Commonwealth"), 2.15, 18.

doctors of the church, is not new to me at all; this opinion is quite old and widely known. Indeed, you dispute in vain when you speak of comparisons where superlatives are involved. You cannot be wrong, for whatever choice you make will be the greatest and the finest. I recall having many discussions with your dear friend from Lombez, Bishop Giacomo.[12] He, following your footsteps, constantly preferring Jerome, and I Augustine among Catholic writers. If indeed I were not afraid of offending either you or the truth, I would say, dear father, what I feel. Just as the stars are many and varied and bright, and this one is called Jupiter, another Arcturus, and another Venus, yet is Augustine the Sun of the church. But, as I said, I hardly attach any importance to this since the choice is a safe one and judgments must be left free. But as for what follows, namely, that you prefer Valerius[13] among the moral philosophers, who would not be astounded if it were said seriously and persistently and not for stimulation and jest? If Valerius is first, where does Plato fall, or Aristotle, or Cicero, or Annaeus Seneca whom certain great judges in such matters place before all? Unless perchance that judgment of yours excluded Plato and Tullius[14] as I was greatly surprised to read in that part of your letter where, for some reason, you asserted that they are poets and are to be included in this group. If you can prove this, you will achieve more than you perhaps think, for with Apollo's support and the approval of the Muses, you will have added two inhabitants to the shady peaks of Parnassus. I ask, what moved you to believe that, or to say it when Tullius appears as the greatest orator in his first books and as a famous philosopher in his last ones? Just as Virgil is everywhere a poet so is Tullius never one, since, as we read in his *Declamations*, "Virgil lost all felicity of talent in his prose; Cicero in his poems." [15] What shall I say about Plato when he has deserved the name of prince of philosophy by consensus of the greatest men, and when Cicero and Augustine and many others always except Plato in all of the works in which they declare their preference for Aristotle over other philosophers? Plato might be thought of as a poet if regard is paid to Tullius' account of Panetius' calling him the Homer of philosophers, but this was intended to mean no more than the prince of philosophers, making him among them

12. Giacomo Colonna (d. 1341), of the powerful Roman family of the same name, became bishop of Lombez in the Gascon Pyrenees in 1327 and received Petrarca there for a visit in 1330.

13. Valerius Maximus (first century A.D.) wrote a nine-book collection of "Memorable Deeds and Sayings" that was plundered for anecdotes throughout the Middle Ages (and the Renaissance). The author did not intend his collection as a treatise on moral philosophy, even though the single entries frequently served moral philosophers as exemplars of their theses.

14. I.e., Marcus Tullius Cicero.

15. Seneca the Elder, *Controversies*, 3, Preface, 8.

what Homer is among poets. What are we to reply to Tullius himself who somewhere in his letters to Atticus calls Plato his god?[16] In a variety of ways all of them attribute to Plato divinity of talent, at times using the name of Homer, and, what is even more distinctive, the name of God.

Therefore, availing yourself of this opportunity, and considering the extraordinary pleasure derived from speaking about unknown things, you should plunge deeply into an examination of the great poets. You should discover of each poet who he was, in what period he was born, his particular poetic style, and the status of his reputation. It would take too long to pursue other individual details in your letter, many of which have never been heard of and others which you could have taught all of us in our desire to learn from your eloquent letter. But, if it is permitted to my profession to interject a thought, I marvel at why you are so unfamiliar with the name of Naevius[17] and of Plautus that you thought I was saying something quite strange because I cited them in my letter to you, and you imply, although with concealed admiration, that, as Horace says, I dared "to form a new person."[18] So thoroughly do you dwell on this matter that the only possible answer appears to be that I be condemned for my boldness in introducing upon the stage new and foreign names. You halted your attack, however, and finally felt it best to blame your own lack of knowledge. This you did most modestly and politely. Yet although your words suggest one meaning, your true meaning, unless I am mistaken, seems to be different, once again most surprisingly since you seem to be so familiar with Terence. For he almost at the very beginning of his proem to the *Andria*, recalls Naevius and Plautus together with Ennius in the same verse. And again in his *Eunuch* he mentions Naevius and Plautus, while in his *Adelphis* he makes mention only of Plautus. Both of them were recalled by Cicero in his *On Old Age*, and by Gellius in his *Attic Nights* where he transcribes the epigrams of both in a very ancient language. But what am I doing? Who, may I ask, ever hears the name of poetry without the names of these men? That is why, dear father, I marvel with good grace at your astonishment. I beseech you not to let this fall into strange hands, for where your fame is most acclaimed, there is where it must be guarded most zealously. With me of course you can speak as if to yourself, and, as the learned do among themselves, change and retract what you may have said. But after your words have reached the public, that possibility is gone and you must undergo the judgments of the many. Thus I am returning your letter to you by

16. Cicero, *Ad Atticum*, 4.16.3. Petrarch himself discovered Cicero's correspondence with Atticus in Verona in 1345.

17. Gnaius Naevius (c. 270–c. 201 B.C.) attempted to give the Romans a national epic parallel to those of Homer among the Greeks.

18. Horace, *Ars Poetica*, 125–26.

a trustworthy messenger, and this one along with it, a copy of which I shall be keeping for no other reason than to refresh my memory by consulting it should you decide to answer. You introduce one further unusual and unknown opinion (I speak quite freely since I cannot do otherwise having started this way), when you state that Ennius and Statius Papinius were contemporaries. I ask you, dear father, how you ever arrived at such a chronology? Who ever sought such information from you? Anyhow, check this more carefully. You will find that Ennius flourished under Africanus the Elder, and that Statius, after several centuries, flourished under Prince Domitian.[19] Unless I am mistaken, you now have reasons for wanting to answer and will not be able to do so as briefly as you thought.

By your leave let me add one thing in good faith. I recall having written you what I am about to say some time ago while I was spending my youth somewhere in Gascony, and I did so rather bashfully, as behooved my age, because I expressed my displeasure at the vernacular writings which during that period you had occasionally sent to Giacomo Colonna, whom I mentioned before[20] and whose love attracted me to those lands as it would have attracted me to Ethiopia. But at that time I spoke childishly as one who had scarcely been weaned. The time has now come for my words to be manly, and therefore, as I said, if you will give me leave . . . what are you saying? I believe you are laughing. Fine, you have given me such leave. Listen, therefore, dear father, and observe and take particular care that no outsider intervenes. I am speaking to you, and I desire that you be judge of your writings which, although I seem to attack, I would defend against any detractors. Nor am I unaware that this letter of censure of a son to a father appears too strong and insolent, but love forgives boldness. Just as I wish my reputation to come to me through real worth rather than through unclear popular approval, so was your reputation of particular concern to me since my young years. This is what is compelling me to speak, lest, if I remained silent, you might hear the same from others, or, what is even worse, might be torn to pieces by anonymous critics. Certain unjust judges of such matters would measure your abilities by such small things as you playfully include through the oversight of the wandering mind. I have noticed that in all of your writings you try your very best to be clear. This explains your searching through unknown works so that in borrowing some things from some writers you insert them among your own thoughts. Your

19. Quintus Ennius (239–169 B.C.) also wrote a national epic, which, like that of Naevius (n. 17 above), was superceded by Virgil's *Aeneid*. P. Papinius Statius (A.D. 40–c. 96) wrote poetic narratives of the emperor Domitian's campaigns in Germania and Dacia (modern Romania); he also wrote an epic poem, the *Thebais*, about a quarrel between the two sons of Oedipus, of which the first part, the *Achilleid*, was known to Dante.

20. See above, n. 12.

disciples applaud you, astonished by the countless names of authors and call you omniscient, as if you were an expert on all those whose works you quote. Learned men, however, easily discern what belongs to you and what to others, and even what has been interchanged, what has been borrowed, what has been stolen, what has been drawn in considerable substance and what has been borrowed unconsciously. It is childish glory to show off one's memory. As Seneca says, it is shameful for a man to search for little flowers, for it becomes him to enjoy the fruit and not the flowers. You, who are so venerated in this age and so famous in your profession, and indeed (to soothe your feelings rather than to be constantly stinging) being the only prince without comparison in our time interested in scholarly matters to which you are dedicated; you, I say, for some strange and childish reason went indifferently and blindly beyond your limits into foreign areas, and with the day coming to an end, you wasted your time plucking little flowers. You like to test unknown fields where, often failing to find a path, you either wander endlessly or sink.

You like to follow in the footsteps of those who display their knowledge as though it were merchandise in the marketplace, while in the meantime their home is barren. It is certainly legitimate to strive for what may make of you more than you seem to be. But boasting is always painstaking and dangerous. Remember also that while you may wish to appear great, countless other things occur which not only reduce you to your true size but sometimes even reduce you to inferiority. To the unique mind it is sufficient to deserve the glory of one field of knowledge. Those who pride themselves in being honored in a great number of arts are either divine or impudent or insane. Who among either the Greeks or the Romans can be remembered as having presumed so much? New customs bring new rashness. Such men carry before them glorious titles so that, as Pliny says, "they may deserve recognition, but when you look underneath, dear God how little you find there of any substance."[21] You, therefore, so that I may now end, if you believe me at all, be satisfied with your limits, do not imitate those who promise all things, who deliver nothing, and who, handling all things and, as the comedian says, perceiving all things, understand nothing. There is an old and helpful Greek proverb which says, "Let him who knows some art exercise his skill therein."

Farewell, and I beg you to forgive me if you feel offended.

17 August.

---

21. Pliny (the Elder: Petrarca did not know the difference between the uncle and the nephew, who appears in vol. 2 of this series), *Natural Histories*, preface, 24.

15.7

To Stefano Colonna, Provost of Saint-Omer,[22] concerning the unsettled condition of nearly the entire world.

Either I am mistaken, O noble sir, or whatever you behold in nearly every region of the world is contrary to your own goals and convictions. Consider Rome, our common fatherland, our mother: she lies there—O shameful spectacle!—trampled by all whom she, the conqueror of all lands and seas, once trampled; and if perchance she leans on her elbow as if to rise again, she soon falls, struck down by the hand of her own sons. Therefore either no hope remains for her or, if there be any, I greatly fear that it lies beyond the present century. Perhaps He will have compassion; perhaps He who selected her as the see of His successors, who established her as the temporal head of the world and as the foundation of His religion, will have compassion for this sacred city. Someday He will have mercy on her, but beyond the limits set for our brief lives. There is nothing in her, then, to render joy to your eyes or to your spirit. What shall I say of the rest of Italy, with her cities and states too numerous to list? Let us therefore limit ourselves to her provinces. Cisalpine Gaul, which includes what the public calls Lombardia but the learned call Liguria, Emilia, and Venetia, indeed whatever lies between the Alps, the Apennines, and the Rubicon— the ancient boundary of Italy—is almost totally in all its vastness oppressed by an undying tyranny; even that region looking westward and sitting at the foot of the mountains—O cruel fortune!—has become a passageway for transalpine tyrants. There you will not find one place where a lover of virtue and tranquillity may seek repose, save that most noble city of the Venetians; though she has remained until the present the sole sanctuary of liberty and justice, she is now so shaken by warfare and is furthermore so much more dedicated to merchant trade than to the Muses in order to regain her former well-being, that I doubt whether she could be a pleasant abode for you. Tuscany, once the most flourishing of lands, which had filled all the universe with its renown and wealth, according to Livy, whose success long before the Roman Empire is amply attested to, especially in the fact that, although countless peoples inhabited the lands near the two seas that gird Italy, Tuscany alone with general consent gave to both seas its name, which will endure forever; today, I say, she proceeds with staggering footsteps between an uncertain liberty and a dreaded servitude and knows

22. This Stefano is not the same as either Stefano the Elder, the father of the Giacomo mentioned above in n. 12, or Stefano the Younger, both of them participants in and victims of the brief regime of Cola di Rienzo in Rome in 1347–48. Even Ernest Hatch Wilkins does not further identify him, although his own translation of this same letter appears in Wilkin's *Petrarch at Vaucluse* (University of Chicago Press, 1958), 97–103.

not on which side she will fall. The seagoing Ligurians who dwell, as Florus attests,[23] between the Var and the Magra, whose capital was once Albenga and today is Genoa, are so managing their affairs and their time that, in accordance with their ancient custom, the end of a foreign war means the beginning of a civil one. Would that my recent letter urging them not to let this happen at the present time be as effective as it is sincere! Nevertheless, thus far their stretch of land and the area bordering Illyria on Italy's other shore are raging with the loud thunder of wars and storms of great slaughter; as you know, even today, the Genoese and the Venetians are in battle. And so, in order not to lose any of our ancient ways, we gnaw and are gnawed in turn, tearing each other apart. Every region of the Piceno whose capital is now Ancona but formerly was Ascoli, as Florus again has it, is caught in the ebb and flow of the changeable waves of passions, and the natural fertility of its fine soil spoiled by the nature of the inhabitants. Beautiful Campania, which the great Plotinus once chose as his domicile to enjoy noble leisure where it looks upon the Ernici and Monte Algido, is now not only unsuited to philosophical retreat, but is barely safe for travelers, beset as it always is by roving bandits. On the other hand, where it embraces Capua and Naples and was once called the Land of Labor[24] with much too ominous a foreboding, it now shares a common fate with Apulia, Abruzzi, Calabria, and the entire Kingdom of Sicily: within and without its boundaries, it is shaken and belabored. Once, indeed, that portion of the world had as its sun Robert, greatest of men and kings; on the day he departed the human condition,[25] the sun seemed to have fallen from the heavens, as was said of Plato. If you do not believe me, ask its inhabitants how long the eclipse lasted, how much foulness and sadness pervaded the darkness. I need not say even one word about the city where you dwell, which some call little Rome but which I customarily call the newest Babylon, since it is so well known, not only to its neighbors, but to the Arabs and Indians.

Now bear with me a little longer. All of Gaul and Britain—the very extremity of our part of the world, jutting even beyond its confines—are weakening each other with serious warfare; Germany no less than Italy is sick with internecine riots, burning in its own fires; the kings of Spain have

23. Lucius Annaeus Florus wrote an *Epitome* of Livy's history of Rome, here cited at 1.19.4.

24. Petrarca calls the region (around Naples) Terra Laboris. It is still called Terra di Lavoro in Italian, but the sense of the word is "work," not "labor," hence without the pejorative connotation.

25. See above, n. 4. King Robert died in 1343. The quotation is from John of Salisbury, *Policraticus* (in vol. 4 of this series), 7:6: "Quo die rebus humanis excessit, quod de Platone dicitur sol celo cedidisse visus est."

turned their arms against themselves; the largest of the Balearics has lately
seen its king, first in exile, and shortly thereafter his body miserably beheaded; Sardinia labors under an inclement heaven and a shameful servitude; primitive and squalid Corsica and the smaller islands in our sea have
become notorious and infamous for pirate raids; like fiery Etna, the whole
of Sicily is parched by great flames of hatred, deliberating whether it prefers to be with Italy or with Spain, but meanwhile remaining neutral, in a
wavering state of mind but in a certain and unmerited slavery, except that
whoever wishes not to be free deserves to be enslaved. Rhodes, protector
of the faith, lies inglorious without wounds; Crete, that ancient center of
superstitions, is living with new ones; Greece travels its wandering path
alone, threshes for itself, feeds itself, and poorly ruminating the food of
salvation has deserted our fold; in the rest of Europe Christ is either unknown or hated. Lacking an armed enemy, battered by a weakening and
easy idleness, pleasures, lust, and other ugly enemies, Cyprus is an unfit
abode for a strong man; lesser Armenia fluctuates between the danger of
temporal and eternal death, besieged on all sides by enemies of the cross.
The garden and sepulchre of the Lord, the twofold haven and repose of
Christians, is being trampled beneath the feet of dogs; nor does it have any
secure or easy access for those wishing to visit it, surely an enormous disgrace and perpetual shame for our age. Ought death not to be preferred
over this crime, unless perhaps we are already dead? About all of Asia and
Africa I speak not, although the testimony of histories and of the saints
proves that once they were subject to the yoke of Christ, but the damage
wrought by the passage of time has resulted in dissimulation and contempt,
and what we should have avenged with arms, we have mitigated with oblivion, consoling ourselves with silence. We are more gravely distressed by
nearby evils: who would believe that Genoa's little fleet with its hostile
prows would reach the Venetian shore, and who would believe that Britain
would attack France with a small band of men? Within a very short period
of time we have heard of both. Where, I ask, can one now find a safe dwelling place? Venice and Paris seemed the safest of all cities in our region of
the globe; the former was a fortress for the Italians, the latter for those
beyond the Alps. Recently an enemy easily invaded both these cities, causing profound trepidation. Who would ever have thought that the French
king would be vanquished in a British prison, perhaps even to die there? At
present we are certain of his imprisonment, but in suspense about his end.
Who would have guessed that the British army would reach the gates of
Paris? Now it has happened, although who could be astonished at the king's
imprisonment or the city's siege, unless he be truly ignorant of the course
of history? A Roman emperor grew old in a Persian prison in the most abject servitude; the city of Rome herself saw Hannibal with his army stand-

ing in hostile array before the Porta Collina; she would have borne that shame with greater restraint by comparing it to more serious ones, since many centuries later she was to be captured by the Goths, as she had been many centuries before by the Senones. From all these examples, I draw one conclusion: in mortal affairs there is nothing so miserable that it cannot happen even to those considered most fortunate.

Since this is so, O worthy sir, your course is clear; and therefore I approach you as a faithful adviser, perhaps unneeded, seeking to persuade you to do what I wish I had done long ago. Do then what men accustomed to cleanliness are wont to do, indeed not only men but some white animals that dislike filth; upon emerging from their lairs and perceiving their surroundings covered with dirt, they retreat and remain inside their hiding places. Seeing peace and rest nowhere in all the world, you too return to your room and within yourself; be on guard with yourself, speak with yourself, be silent with yourself, walk with yourself and stand firm with yourself; do not think you are alone if you are with yourself: but if you are not with yourself, though you may be amidst people, you will be alone. Make for yourself a refuge within your mind where you may hide, rejoice, rest without interruption, and live together with Christ, who through the sacred priesthood made you in your youth His confidant and table companion. You will ask, "and with what skills do I do that?" It is virtue alone that is powerful enough to accomplish it all; through her you will be able to rejoice and to live happily wherever you are; no evil can approach you in the midst of evils, for you will choose nothing except what brings you happiness, you will fear nothing except what brings you unhappiness; know, however, that what brings you happiness or unhappiness exists nowhere except in your own heart. What lies outside of you is not yours, only what lies within you is yours; nothing outside of you can be given to you, nothing that is yours can be taken; in your hand alone is found the course of the life you choose. The multitude's opinions must be fled and those of the few followed; with a noble spirit you must scorn fortune, knowing that she possesses more threats than power, that she threatens more than she wounds, that she rages more than she injures, that she has no control over your goods, that her flatteries are not to be trusted, for whatever she gives must be possessed with uncertainty. If you ever assume a higher position, attribute it to divine mercy; if not, note with equanimity that in fortune's realm the good are crushed and the evil exalted, understanding "their final destiny" as the Psalmist says,[26] and recalling that this life is the fatherland of hardships, not of rewards. Farewell.

26. Psalm 72:77.

3. Francesco Petrarca, *Secretum*: Second Dialogue

Augustine: Have we rested enough?

Petrarca: Yes, as you wish.

Augustine: Well, what do you think now, and how much faith do you have? For hope in a sick man is no small sign of returning health.

Petrarca: I have no hope from within myself; my hope is from God.

Augustine: Wisely spoken. Now I return to the matter at hand. Many evils besiege you, many clamour all around, but you yourself still seem ignorant both of their numbers and their strength. . . . When before your eyes, I shall reveal the evil pressing and encircling you on this side and that, you will be ashamed that you were in pain or fear less than was fitting, and you will be astonished that your soul (*animus*), besieged by so many things, was unable to break through the enemies' wedges. You will see clearly how that healthy reflection, to which I endeavor to bring you, is overwhelmed by opposing thoughts.

Petrarca: Indeed, you make me horribly afraid. I have always been aware that my danger was great; and now, in spite of this, you tell me I have greatly underestimated it, and indeed, compared with what they ought to be, my fears have been nothing at all. What hope have I left?

Augustine: Despair is the worst of all evils, to which no one has ever come to except too soon; therefore I would have you know this above all: we must despair of nothing.

Now you can easily understand how paltry are the things in which you take pride. You trust in your intellect (*ingenium*) and the reading of many books; you pride yourself on eloquence, and are delighted by the beauty of your own mortal body.

Yet do you not feel that in many things your intellect fails you? Are not there many things in which you cannot rival the skill of the humblest of mankind? Nay, might I not go further and, without mentioning mankind, may I not say that with all your labor and study you will find yourself no match in skill for some of the meanest and smallest of God's creatures? Go on, let us see you boast of your genius.

As for that reading of yours, what has it profited you? For out of all that you have read, how much has stuck to your soul? How much has taken root and borne fruit in season? Search your heart well and you will find that the

From *Petrarch's Secret or the Soul's Conflict with Passion*, 2d Dialogue, translated from the Latin by William H. Draper (London: Chatto & Windus, 1911), pp. 47–106. Translation revised for this volume by R. J. Wood III based on the critical edition, *Francesco Petrarca Prose*, edited by G. Martellotti et al. (Milan and Naples: Ricciari, 1955), pp. 68–128.

whole of what you have is but a shrunken stream dried by the summer heat compared to the mighty ocean.

And what good is it to know a multitude of things? Suppose you have learned all the circuits of the heavens and the earth, the spaces of the sea, the courses of the stars, the virtues of herbs and stones, the secrets of nature, and then be ignorant of yourself? Of what profit is it? If by the help of Scripture you shall have discovered the right and upward path, what use is it if anger and passion make you swerve aside onto the crooked, downward way? Suppose you have learned by heart the deeds of illustrious men of all the ages, of what profit will it be if day by day you yourself care not what you do?

What am I to say of eloquence except what you yourself will confess, that you have often been deluded by your faith in it? Moreover, what does it matter that others approved of what you say, when you condemn it yourself? For though the applause of those who hear you may seem to yield a certain fruit which is not to be despised, yet of what worth is it after all if in his heart the speaker himself is not able to applaud? How petty is the pleasure that comes from the plaudits of the multitude. And how can a man soothe and flatter others unless he first soothe and flatter himself? Therefore you will easily understand how often you are deluded by that glory you hope for from your eloquence, and how your pride therein rests on a foundation of wind.

For what, I ask, is more childish, nay, more insane than that amidst such great disregard for all things and such great disregard for one's own weakness, to devote one's time to the study of words and with sore eyes never discerning one's own faults, to feel such great pleasure from literary pursuits, like those little birds, which they say, take pleasure in their own song even to the point of their own destruction. . . .

What, therefore, is that eloquence of yours, so narrow, so fragile, which neither embraces all things nor draws together what it has embraced. . . . There is, as you see, a very great controversy on the subject of the primacy of eloquence, not only between you and the Greeks, but among our most learned writers themselves. There are those in our camp who hold for the Greeks, and it may be there are some among them who hold for us, if at least we may judge from what is reported of the illustrious philosopher Plutarch. In a word, Seneca, who is ours, while doing all justice to Cicero, gives his final verdict for the Greeks, notwithstanding that Cicero is of the contrary opinion.

As to my own opinion on the question in debate, I consider that both parties to the controversy have some truth on their side when they accuse both Latin and Greek of poverty of words: and if this judgment be correct in regard to two such famous languages, what hope is there for any other?

Bethink you therefore what sort of faith you can have in your own simple powers when the whole resources of that people of which you are but a little part are adjudged poor, and how ashamed you should be to have spent so much time in pursuing something which cannot be attained, and which, if it could be, would prove after all but vanity itself.

Let me go on to other points. Are you exalted by the goods of your body? "And do you not see what dangers are brewing up. . . ." [1] What pleases you in the body? Is it your good health and strength? But truly nothing is more frail. It is proved by the fatigue you suffer from even little things. The various maladies to which the body is liable: the stings of insects, a slight draught of air, and a thousand other such small vexations all tell the same tale. Will you perchance be taken in by your own good-looking face, and when you behold your smooth complexion and comely features in the glass you have a mind to be smitten, entranced, charmed? The story of Narcissus has no warning for you, and content with gazing only at the outward envelope of the body, you consider not that the eyes of the mind tell you how vile and plain it is within. Moreover, if you had no other warning, the stormy course of life itself, which every day robs you of something, ought to show you how transient and perishing that flower of beauty is. . . .

Unless I am mistaken, these are the things which prevent you, exalted by lofty pride, from considering the lowliness of your condition and from remembering death. Furthermore, my soul also brings me to review other things.

Petrarca: Stop a little, I beg you lest, overwhelmed by such a great mass of things, I may not be able to rise and respond.

Augustine: Well then, say on, I will gladly stop.

Petrarca: You astonish me by casting in my teeth a multitude of things that never entered my head at all. Do you say that I trusted in my intellect? But surely there is no sign of my paltry genius except this one, that I have put no faith in it. Am I to become prouder from the reading of books which, though they have brought me a modicum of knowledge, have also brought an abundant supply of cares? How can you say I have sought the glory of eloquence? I who, as you yourself acknowledged a moment ago, am wont above all things to complain that speech is inadequate to my thoughts? Unless you wish to try and prove the contrary, I may say that you know I am always conscious of my own insignificance, and if by chance I have ever thought myself to be anything, such a thought has come but rarely and then only from seeing the ignorance of other men; for, as I often remark, we must acknowledge, according to Cicero's celebrated phrase,

1. Virgil, *Aeneid*, 4.561.

that "what powers we may possess come rather from the weakness of others than from any excellence in ourselves."[2]

But even if I were endowed as richly as you imagine with those advantages you speak of, what is so magnificent about them that I should be vain? I am surely not so forgetful of myself nor so featherbrained as to let myself trouble about cares of that sort. For genius, knowledge, and eloquence bring little profit, if they offer no remedy for the maladies eating away the soul. I remember lamenting this fact in one of my letters.

Now, as for what you said most earnestly about my bodily goods, that nearly made me laugh; did you imagine that I had put hope in this mortal and fleeting body, when I feel its downfall daily? May God give me better things. As a boy, I confess, I cared for trimming my hair and adorning my face; but this care vanished with my early years. Now by experience I know the truth of that saying of the Emperor Domitian, who writing of himself in a letter to a friend and complaining of the very swift flight of corporeal beauty, said "Know you, nothing is more pleasing, nothing more brief, than beauty."[3]

Augustine: I could wax eloquent against those words of yours, but I prefer that your own conscience inspire you with shame rather than any words of mine. I will not labor the point or wring the truth from you by torture. But like those noble avengers, I merely prefer a simple request that you will continue to avoid what you profess you have avoided hitherto.

If ever the appearance of your face affects your soul, let your soul envision how those same limbs of yours, which now please you, will be—how foul, how sad, how you yourself would have to shudder at them if you should see them; and amidst these things repeat frequently that saying of philosophy: "I was born for greater things than to be the slave of my body."[4] For indeed the highest madness belongs to men who adorn the body and limbs in which they dwell and neglect their real selves. If a man is imprisoned for a little while in some dark, damp, and dirty dungeon, would he not seem to have lost his senses if he did not shield himself as far as he was able from any contact with the walls and soil? And with the expectation of freedom would he not eagerly listen for the footsteps of his deliverer? But if giving up that expectation, covered with filth and plunged in darkness, he dreads to leave his prison; if he turns all his attention to painting and adorning the walls which shut him in in a vain endeavor to counteract the nature of his dripping prison house, will he not rightly be counted a miserable fool?

2. Cicero, *De Officiis*, 2.21.75.   3. Suetonius, *Domitian*, 18.
4. Seneca, *Epistulae ad Lucilius*, 65.21.

Well, you yourself know and love your prison house, wretched as you are. And on the very eve of your issuing or being dragged therefrom you chain yourself more firmly in it, laboring to adorn what you ought to despise. Just as you yourself in your *Africa* brought in the father of that great Scipio saying: "We hate the ropes and the well-known fetters, we fear / the burden of liberty. We love that which we are now."[5] It would be wonderful, if only you said yourself what you make others say. But I cannot disguise from you one word in your discourse which to you seems very humble, but to me seems full of pride and arrogance.

Petrarca: I am sorry if I have said anything with pride, but if the soul is the master of one's deeds and words, then it is my witness that I have said nothing arrogantly.

Augustine: To depreciate others is a kind of pride more intolerable than to exalt oneself above one's due measure; and by far I would have preferred that you exalt others, although you place yourself above them, than, having spurned all, to raise most proudly your shield of humility out of contempt for others.

Petrarca: Take it as you will. I attribute little to myself or others. I am ashamed to tell you what experience has made me think of the majority of mankind.

Augustine: To spurn oneself is very safe; but to spurn others is dangerous and vain. However, let us proceed to what remains. Do you know what else leads you astray?

Petrarca: Say whatever you please, only do not accuse me of envy.

Augustine: Would that pride had done you no more harm than envy. So far as I judge you are free of this charge (*crimen*). But I will mention certain others.

Petrarca: You will not disturb me with any accusations. Tell me freely whatever it is which leads me astray.

Augustine: The desire for temporal things.

Petrarca: Come, come. I have never heard anything more absurd.

Augustine: There, suddenly you are disturbed and forget your promise. There is no question of envy.

Petrarca: No, but of avarice, from which charge no man is more removed than I.

Augustine: You are great at self-justification, but believe me, you are not so clear of this fault as you think you are.

Petrarca: Am I not free from the stain of avarice?

Augustine: Nor even from ambition.

5. Petrarca, *Africa*, 1:329–30.

Petrarca: Go on, press your attack, double it, carry out the accuser's duty. I wonder what fresh blow you have in store for me.

Augustine: Indeed, you call the testimony of your own truth accusation and ill-treatment. For true is the saying of satire: "The accuser will be he who will speak the truth."[6] Nor less true is that saying of comedy: "Flattery begets friends, truth hatred."[7] But pray tell me, what is the use of this irritation and anger that make you so on edge? Was it necessary in a life so short to weave such long hopes?: "The sum of a brief life forbids us from entering into long hopes."[8] You read these things, but pay them no heed. I suppose you will respond that you are compelled by your affection for your friends, and you will find a fine name for your error. But what madness it is, that in order to be a friend to another, you declare war on yourself and treat yourself as an enemy.

Petrarca: I am not so ill-bred or uncivilized to be without solicitude for my friends, especially those whom virtue and merit commend me. For they are the ones I admire, whom I revere, love, and pity. But, on the other hand, I am not so generous, that I ruin myself on account of my friends. What I desire is to manage my affairs so as to have a decent subsistence while I live; and since you assail me with javelins from Horace, let a Horatian shield protect me: "May I have a decent supply of books and enough food for the year, / may my spirits not depend on the hour's caprice."[9] And further my object is, in the same poet's words: "to pass my old age with a sound mind, / with my cithara, and with style."[10] . . .

Augustine: Nothing would be sweeter than such a life, nothing more charming, if you should but live by your own laws and not those of the mad world. Why, therefore, do you torture yourself? If you would measure yourself according to your nature, you were rich long ago. If you measure yourself with regard to the applause of other people, you will never be rich, and something will always be wanting. In pursuing this you may be swept over the precipice of your desires.

Do you remember with what delight you used to wander in the depth of the country? Sometimes, laying yourself down on a bed of turf, you would listen to the water of a brook murmuring over the stones; at another time, seated on some open hill, you would let your eyes wander freely over the plain stretched at your feet; at others, again, you enjoyed a sweet slumber beneath the shady trees of some valley in the noontide heat, and reveled in

6. Juvenal, *Satires*, 1.161. Trans. Loeb Classical Library.
7. Terence, *Andria*, 68.
8. Horace, *Odes*, 1.4.15. Trans. Niall Rudd.
9. Horace, *Epistulae*, 1.18.109–10. Trans. Niall Rudd.
10. Horace, *Odes*, 1.31.19–20.

the delicious silence. Never idle, in your mind you would ponder over some high meditation, with only the Muses as your companions—you were never less alone than when in their company, and then, like the old man in Virgil who "equalled in his mind the wealth of kings, / and coming home in late evening, / loaded his board with unbought delicacies," [11] you would come at sunset back to your humble roof; and, contented with your good things, did you not find yourself the richest and happiest of all mortal men?

Petrarca: Ah, welladay. I recall it all now, and I sigh with the recollection of that time.

Augustine: Why, why do you speak of sighing? And who, pray, is the author of your woes? Surely it is your own soul which has been ashamed for so long to obey the laws of its own nature and has believed that servitude had not broken its bridle. Even now it drags you along like a runaway horse and unless you tighten the reins, it will rush headlong into death. Ever since you grew tired of your leafy trees, of your simple way of life, and society of country people, egged on by cupidity, you have plunged once more into the midst of the tumultuous life of cities. I read in your face and speech what a happy and peaceful life you lived; for what miseries have you not endured since then in your rebellion against the teachings of experience?

And still you hesitate, impeded by the bonds of sin which keep you back, and God allows that, as you passed your childhood under a harsh master, so, though you once became free, you have again fallen into bondage, and there will end your miserable old age. Verily, I was at your side once, when, quite young, unstained by avarice or ambition, you gave promise of becoming a great man; now, alas, having quite changed your character, the nearer you get to the end of your journey the more you trouble yourself about provisions for the way. What remains then, except that on the day of death, which may even now be at hand and certainly not far off, thirsting for gold you sit half-dead poring over your ledger?

For those anxious cares, which increase day after day, must by necessity at last have grown to a huge figure and a prodigious amount.

Petrarca: Well, after all, if I foresee the poverty of old age, and gather some provisions against that time of weariness, what is there so much to find fault with?

Augustine: O for the ludicrous anxiety and mad neglect, to worry and trouble yourself about a time at which you may never arrive and in which you assuredly will not have long to stay, and yet to be quite oblivious of that end at which you cannot help arriving, and from which there is no return once you have reached it. Such is your execrable habit, you care only for

11. Virgil, *Georgics*, 4.130–31. Trans. Loeb.

the transitory, you neglect the eternal. As for this delusion of providing a shield against old age, no doubt what put it into your head was that verse of Virgil: "The ant who dreads a destitute old age." [12] And so you have chosen that ant as your teacher in life and you are as excusable as the satiric poet who says: "The ant has at last taught some of them to dread cold and hunger." [13] But if you have not gone off totally to the following of ants, you will discover that there is nothing more unfortunate or absurd than to ward off poverty one day by loading yourself with it all your life. Do I then recommend poverty? Pray for it least of all, endure it with the highest effort. My opinion is that in every station in life man must aim at the middle way. Thus I do not restrict you to the rules of those who say, "bread and water suffice the life of men; with these none is poor; whosoever has confined his desire to these will rival in happiness Jupiter himself." Nor do I establish "Ceres and water" as the limit to men's life. Such maxims are as extreme as they are troublesome and odious to hear. And so, to regulate your conduct as regards your weakness, I instruct you not to overindulge your nature, but to curb it. What you already have would be sufficient for your wants if you had known how to be sufficient unto yourself. To heap up riches is to heap up cares and anxieties. This truth has been proved so many times that there is no need to argue further. What a strange delusion, what deplorable blindness that the human soul, whose nature is so noble, whose birth is from heaven, neglects heavenly things and covets earthly metals. Think carefully, I ask, and focus the eyes of your mind, nor let the flash of gleaming gold distract them. Each time you come down from your meditations to these base thoughts, drawn by the hooks of avarice, do you not feel hurled from heaven to earth and plunged from the midst of the stars into a bottomless pit?

Petrarca: Yes, I do feel it, and one knows not how to express what I have suffered in my fall.

Augustine: Why, therefore, are you not afraid of things you have experienced over and over?

Petrarca: I strive as well as I can to do so, but since my human condition shakes and unsettles me, I am torn away unwillingly. It is not without reason I imagine, that the poets of antiquity dedicated the twin peaks of Parnassus to two different divinities. They begged from Apollo, whom they called the god of genius, the inner strength of the soul. But from Bacchus they asked for a plentiful supply of external goods. This has been suggested to me not only by the teachings of experience, but by the frequent testimony of wise men whom I need not quote to you. Thus, although a multitude of gods may be ridiculous, nevertheless this opinion of the seers

12. Virgil, *G.*, 1.186.   13. Juvenal, *Sat.*, 5.360–61.

is not devoid of common sense. And in likewise making a twofold supplication to the one God from whom all good things come, I do not think I can be called unreasonable, unless you hold otherwise.

Augustine: I do not deny you are right in your view, but the poor way you divide your time makes me indignant. Once you devoted your whole life to honorable work. If anything compelled you to spend any of your time on other occupations, you regarded it as lost. But now you only devote to honorable things the moments your avaricious zeal has left you.

Any man in the world would desire to reach old age on such terms, but what limit or end will there be? Create a goal for yourself, and when you have reached it, you can stop and breathe a little. You know that saying, which comes from the lips of man, but has the force of a divine oracle: "The greedy are never satisfied; / fix a limit to your dreams." [14] What end will there be to your desires?

Petrarca: Neither to want nor to abound, neither to command others nor to obey them, this is my object.

Augustine: Then you must shed your humanity and become a god if you would want nothing. Do you not know that of all the creatures, Man is the one that wants most? . . .

Petrarca: Now do I repent my undertaking, and I would desire nothing. But I am seized by my perverse habits and I feel something unfulfilled in my breast.

Augustine: This thing (to turn the discourse to our subject) is the thing which turns you away from the contemplation of death. Meanwhile, caught up with earthly cares, you do not lift your eyes to higher things. If you trust me at all, you will cast away these cares as so many destructive burdens upon our souls. Nor will it be a great labor to cast them away, as long as you restore yourself to your own nature, and commit yourself to that end, not to be ruled by the violent passions of the crowd.

Petrarca: I will do so willingly. But I desire to hear at last what you were beginning to say about ambition.

Augustine: Why ask me to do what you can do quite well for yourself? Examine your own heart. You will discover among its faults that it is not ambition which holds the least place there.

Petrarca: It has profited me nothing to have fled from towns whenever I could, to have thought scorn of the world and public affairs, to have gone into the recesses of the woods and silence of the fields, to have proved my aversion from empty honors, if still I am to be accused of ambition.

Augustine: You renounce many things well—all you mortal men; but not so much because you despise them as because you despair of getting them.

14. Horace, *Epist.*, 1.2.56.

Hope and desire inflame each other by their mutual sting, so that when the one grows cold the other dies away, and when one gets warm the other boils over.

Petrarca: What, then, prevents me from hoping? Did all the liberal arts (*bonae artes*) fail me?

Augustine: I am not speaking of the liberal arts. Certainly you did not have those arts which, especially in the present day, enable men to mount to high places. I mean the art of courting the thresholds of great men, of flattery, deceit, promising, lying, pretending, dissembling, and putting up with all kinds of slights and indignities. Lacking these arts and others of the kind, and seeing clearly that you could not overcome nature, you turned to other pursuits. Indeed you acted wisely and prudently, for, as Cicero says, "to contend against the gods as did the giants, what is it but to make war with nature itself." [15]

Petrarca: Farewell great honors, if they are acquired by these arts.

Augustine: Well said. But in my ears you have not yet proved your innocence, for you do not assert your indifference to honors, though you shudder at the trouble of the pursuit. Just as the man did not disdain seeing Rome, who, terrified at the toils of the road, stepped back from his undertaking. Add to this that you have not stepped back from the pursuit of honor, as you persuade yourself and as you try to persuade me. But leave off trying to hide behind your finger, as the saying goes. All of your thoughts and actions are plain before my eyes. And when you boast of having fled from cities and become enamoured of the woods, I see no real excuse, but only a shifting of your culpability.

By many ways can we reach one end, and believe me, though the road you have left is worn by the feet of the crowd, you still direct your step by a side-path toward this same ambition that you say you have spurned. It is repose and solitude, a total disregard of human affairs, which just at present lead you to ambition. But the end is still glory.

Petrarca: You drive me into a corner whence I could escape. Nevertheless, since we have not much time and must make many distinctions, let us proceed to the remaining matters.

Augustine: Follow me, then, as I proceed. There will be no mention of gluttony, for which you have no affection, except sometimes, when indulging friends in conversation over a meal. I have no fear for you on this score for, as soon as the countryside has reclaimed its native son (now snatched away to the cities), all the snares of such pleasures will disappear. When these are removed, I confess I have observed you living in such a way that I took pleasure in your sobriety and moderation, which surpass

15. Cicero, *De Senectute*, 2.5.

that of your friends and neighbors. I also pass over anger, although you are often inflamed by it more than is just. Nevertheless, by the goodness of your gentle nature, you are accustomed to soothe the disturbances of your soul, ever mindful of Horace's advice: "Rage is a burst of madness. Restrain your temper [animus]: it will either heed you or rule you. Keep it in check with bridle and chain." [16]

Petrarca: This poetic saying and other pieces of advice from philosophers of this sort have helped a little, I confess, and even more has the recollection of life's brevity. What madness to spend in hating and destroying our fellow-men the few days we have among them. Soon enough the final day will arrive to extinguish those flames in human breasts and put an end to our hatreds; and if we wish for an enemy nothing worse than death, to grant us this our wicked wish. Why then, seek to take one's own life or that of others? Why lose the best moments of our very brief time here? The days allotted for honest joys and deliberations of our future life (which are hardly enough though one may exercise the utmost frugality), why take them from their proper and necessary uses and turn them equally into instruments of sorrow and death for ourselves and others? This reflection has helped me so that when struck, I did not totally fall, and when I fell, I recovered. But thus far no lesson has been able to protect me so that I am not tossed by gusts of anger.

Augustine: As I am not afraid that this wind of anger will cause you to make shipwreck of yourself or others, I willingly agree that, passing over the promises of the Stoics, who try to root out the maladies of the soul, you content yourself in this matter with the milder treatment of the Peripatetics. Therefore, these things aside for the moment, I hasten to more dangerous matters for which you must diligently take care.

Petrarca: Good God! what is yet to come that is more dangerous still?

Augustine: How much have you been burned by the flames of lust?

Petrarca: Indeed, sometimes so fiercely that I mourned sorely that I was not born without feelings. I would sooner have been a senseless stone than be tormented by so many stings of the flesh.

Augustine: You have, therefore, that which divides you most from the contemplation of things divine. For what else does the heavenly teaching of Plato advise, except that the soul must be guarded from corporeal desires, and false opinions must be rooted out so that the soul may rise up pure and ready to see the secrets of the divine to which the contemplation of its own mortality is bound? You know what I mean and you are very familiar with these things from the books of Plato, to which you have devoted yourself with great zeal lately.

16. Horace, *Epist.*, 1.2.62–63.

Petrarca: Yes, I own I had given myself to studying with great hope and desire, but the novelty of a strange language and the sudden departure of my teacher cut short my purpose. That doctrine which you mention is very well known to me both from your writings and from the writings of other Platonists.

Augustine: It matters little from whom you learned the truth, though authority has great influence.

Petrarca: In my case especially the authority of that man, concerning whom Cicero's remark in his *Tusculan Disputations* made a deep impression on me: "Plato," he says, "even if he were to adduce no reasoning (you see what I attribute to the man), he would subdue me with his very authority." [17] Often in reflecting on this heavenly genius, it seemed to me an injustice that when the disciples of Pythagoras did not require their chief to submit proofs, Plato should be obligated to adduce reasonings. But, not to be carried away from our subject, authority, reason, and experience alike have for a long time so much commended this axiom of Plato to me that I do not believe anything more true or more truly holy could be said by any man. Every time I have raised myself up, thanks to the hand of God stretched out to me, I have recognized with infinite joy, beyond belief, who it was that then preserved me and who had cast me down in times of old. Now, having fallen back from my own weight into my old miseries, I feel what has again undone me with a keen sense of bitterness. I tell you this, that you may see nothing strange in my saying I had put Plato's maxim to the proof.

Augustine: Indeed, I do not think it strange, for I have been present at your struggles and I have seen you falling and rising up again. And now, pitying you as you lie prostrate, I am moved to bring help.

Petrarca: I am thankful for such feelings of pity. But of what avail is any human help?

Augustine: It avails nothing, but the help of God is much every way. None can be chaste except God give him the grace of chastity. You must therefore implore this grace from Him above all, with humbleness, and often it may be with tears. He is wont never to deny him who asks as he should.

Petrarca: So often have I done it that I fear I am as one too importunate.

Augustine: But you have not asked humbly or moderately enough. You have always allowed your passions to creep in and extended your prayers to the future. I speak from experience, this also happened to me. I used to say: "Give me chastity, but not now; put it off a little. The time will come soon. While still in its bloom let my life go its own way, according to its

17. Cicero, *Tusculan Disputations*, 1.21.49.

own laws. It will feel more shame later, when it returns to its youthful folly. I will give up this failing when the course of time itself shall have rendered me less inclined that way, and when satiety will have delivered me from the fear of going back." In saying these things do you not understand that you want one thing, but pray for another?

Petrarca: How so?

Augustine: Because he who prays for a thing tomorrow neglects it today.

Petrarca: With tears I have often asked for it today. My hope was that after breaking the chain of my passions and casting away the misery of life, I should escape safe and sound, and after so many storms of vain anxieties, I might swim ashore in some haven of safety; but you see, alas, how many shipwrecks I have suffered among the rocks and shoals, and how I shall still suffer more if I am left to myself.

Augustine: Trust me, there has always been something in your prayer; otherwise the Supreme Giver would have granted it or, as in the case of the Apostle Paul would have only denied you to make you more perfect in virtue and convince you entirely of your own frailty.

Petrarca: That is my conviction also; and I will go on praying constantly, unwearied, unashamed, undespairing. The Almighty, taking pity on my sorrows, will perchance lend an ear to my prayer, sent up daily to His throne, and even as He would not have denied His grace if my prayers had been pure, so He will also purify them.

Augustine: You are quite right. Nevertheless force your way up, and as men fallen in battle are accustomed, rise up on your elbows and look round at the evils assailing you, lest your limbs give way at the sudden assault of some war engine. And in the meantime, pray directly for the aid of Him who can raise you up again. He will perhaps be present when you have believed him to be absent. Always hold one thing before your eyes. You must not spurn Plato's higher teaching, of which we were speaking just now. Nothing hinders you more from the knowledge of the Divine than carnal desires and burning lust. Reflect on this doctrine yourself. This is the sum of our advice.

Petrarca: To show you how much I welcome this teaching, I have embraced it very eagerly not only sitting in its own halls, but also lurking in foreign groves. And I remember well the place in my soul, where it first came to my attention.

Augustine: I await what you are going to say.

Petrarca: You know how many struggles Virgil led his brave hero through on that dreadful, final night of Troy's sack.

Augustine: Yes, I know. For what is more common to all the schools? He also makes that very man recount his own misfortunes:

That night—what words can render its deaths and disaster?
What tears can rise to the level of all that was suffered then?
An ancient city is falling, after long years of power:
So many motionless bodies prostrate everywhere
Along the streets, in the houses, on the gods' holy thresholds.
Not the Trojans alone paid their account in blood:
There were times when courage returned even though we knew we were
    beaten,
And the conquering Greeks fell. All over the town you saw
Heart-rending agony, panic, and every shape of death.[18]

Petrarca: And what is more, as long as he wandered among the flames of the enemy with Venus as his companion, though his eyes were open, he could not see the wrath of the slighted gods. So long as Venus spoke to him, he understood nothing except the earthly. But after that Goddess left him, you know what happened: it followed immediately that he saw the angered faces of the gods, and recognized the whole danger surrounding him: "Terrible shapes loom up, set against Troy, the shapes of / Heaven's transcendent will."[19] From which I have concluded that contact with Venus obscures the vision of the divine.

Augustine: Clearly you have found light under the clouds. For surely it is in this way that there is truth in poetic fictions. But since we shall return to this question later on, let us save what we have to say for the end of our discourse.

Petrarca: That you may not lead me by unknown paths, where have you promised to return?

Augustine: I have not yet touched of the greatest wounds of your mind, and I have purposely deferred to do so, in order that coming toward the end, they may be more deeply graven in your remembrance. In another dialogue we will treat more fully of the subject of the desires of the flesh, on which we have now just only lightly touched.

Petrarca: Go on then, as you propose.

Augustine: There need be nothing to hinder me, unless you are obstinately bent on stopping me.

Petrarca: Indeed, nothing will please me better than to banish for ever every cause of dispute from the earth. Nothing has ever been so clearly known to me, that I have willingly argued about it. For the differences that arise, even between friends, have a certain character of sharpness and hostility contrary to the laws of friendship.

But continue with those things to which you think I will readily agree.

18. Virgil, *Aeneid*, 2.361–69. Trans. C. D. Lewis.
19. Virgil, *Aen.*, 2.662–63.

Augustine: A certain deadly plague of the soul grips you, which the moderns call *accidia,* and the ancients *aegritudo.*

Petrarca: I shudder at the very name of this disease.

Augustine: No wonder, for you have been plagued long and hard by it.

Petrarca: Yes, and although in almost all the other diseases which torment me there is mingled a certain false delight, in this sad one everything is harsh, miserable, and dreadful. The way to despair is always open, and everything goads one's unhappy spirit to destruction. Moreover, while other passions attack me only in bouts which, though frequent, are but short and last only a moment, this plague grips me so tenaciously that it clings to me and tortures me for whole days at a time. It is not like light or life for me, but like infernal night and bitter death. And perhaps the worst of my miseries is that I so feed upon my tears and troubles with a kind of dark pleasure, that I am unwillingly torn away from them.

Augustine: You know your disease very well. Soon you will know its cause. Tell me therefore, what is it that really saddens you? Is it the chaos of material things? or pains in your body? or some injustice of harsh fortune?

Petrarca: No, not any one of these would be so strong by itself. If I were challenged to single combat, I would surely still be on my feet. But as it is, I am undermined by a whole army.

Augustine: Tell me more exactly what torments you.

Petrarca: When fortune inflicts any one wound on me, I remain undaunted, and recall to myself that I have often come off the victor when I have been grievously struck by her. If soon afterwards she redoubles the wound, I begin to stagger somewhat. But if after the second, a third or fourth blow succeed, I am forced to retreat into the citadel of reason, not in headlong flight, but gradually, step by step. If fortune still lays siege to me there with her whole front line, and if, to assail me, she piles up the miseries of our human condition, the remembrance of past struggles, the dread of those to come, then finally, attacked from all sides and trembling at such a mass of evils, I throw up my hands and moan. Hence arises that grievous sorrow. I feel like someone hemmed in by countless enemies, for whom no escape is open, no hope of pity, no comfort anywhere, but for whom everything is hostile. The war engines are in place, the mines buried beneath the earth, and already the towers tremble; the ladders stand at the gates, the grappling hooks cleave to the walls and fire runs through the roof tops. With the gleaming swords and the menacing faces of his enemies around him, and thinking utter ruin is upon him, why should he not quake and mourn? Even if they allow him his life, the very loss of liberty is a sorrowful thing to brave men.

Augustine: Although you recount these things in a confused manner, nevertheless I understand that your false opinion is the cause of all your troubles which has in the past claimed and in the future will claim innumerable victims. So you think things are bad for you?

Petrarca: Yes, very bad.

Augustine: And on account of what?

Petrarca: Not for one reason, but countless.

Augustine: The same thing happens to you which happens to those men who, because of the slightest offense, remember old quarrels.

Petrarca: No wound in me is so old that it may be destroyed by forgetfulness. The things that torture me are all recent, and if anything could have been abolished by time, fortune renewed her attack with such frequent blows that no scar ever bound the wound. There is, in addition, my hatred and contempt for the human condition. So, oppressed by all these things I cannot help but be very, very sad. Whether you define it as *aegritudo* or *accidia*, or something else, I do not care. We agree on the thing itself.

Augustine: Since, as I see, the disease has deep roots, it will do no good to heal it slightly, for it will soon throw out more shoots. It must be torn out by the roots. But I am uncertain where to begin, there are so many things on my mind. To make the task of dividing the matter easier, I will examine each point in detail. Tell me then, what is it you think is most troublesome for you?

Petrarca: Whatever I see, whatever I hear, whatever I feel.

Augustine: Come, come, does nothing please you?

Petrarca: Nothing, or very few things.

Augustine: If only the more healthy things pleased you. But what especially displeases you? Pray, answer me.

Petrarca: I have already answered.

Augustine: This all relates to that *accidia* I mentioned. All of your affairs displease you.

Petrarca: The affairs of others displease me no less.

Augustine: This too comes from the same source. But so that there may be some order to our words, do your affairs really displease you, as you say?

Petrarca: Stop harassing me with your little questions. They are more than I know how to reply to.

Augustine: Therefore those things that make you enviable to many others seem vile to you.

Petrarca: He who envies an unfortunate man must himself be very unfortunate.

Augustine: But what out of all your affairs displeases you the most?

Petrarca: I do not know.

Augustine: What? If I guess it right, will you confess it?

Petrarca: I will confess it freely.

Augustine: You are vexed with Fortune.

Petrarca: Why should I not hate the proud, violent, blind goddess, who turns around mortal affairs arbitrarily?

Augustine: Concerning everyday affairs, the complaint is common. Let us now pursue your own injuries. What if you complained unjustly? Would you wish to be reconciled with your fortune?

Petrarca: Persuasion is a very difficult thing, but if you will demonstrate what you have said to me, I will give in.

Augustine: You think that fortune is too harsh on you.

Petrarca: No, too greedy, too wicked, too proud, too cruel.

Augustine: There is not one "Grumbler" in comic poetry, but many. You are still one of the many. I would prefer you were one of the few. But since the subject is so old that scarcely anything new could be added, will you allow me to offer you an old remedy for an old malady?

Petrarca: As you wish.

Augustine: Come on then: has poverty compelled you to endure hunger, thirst, or cold?

Petrarca: My fortune has not raged to that extent.

Augustine: But for countless many that is their daily lot.

Petrarca: Find some other remedy, if you can, since these do not help me at all. I am not of those, who, in their own troubles, take pleasure in an army of unfortunate and mourning people around them, and often I mourn as much for the griefs of others as for my own.

Augustine: I do not expect the misfortunes of others to amuse any man, but to console him, and teach him to be content with his own fortune. All the world cannot occupy the first and best place; how will there be a first place, unless there is a second place following it? Be thankful, O mortals, if you are not reduced to the last of all, but have endured only the milder outrages of fortune's many. To those who have endured the utter extremes of fortune we must apply other remedies, of which you have no need. That which casts men into hardships is that each one, forgetting his lot in life, in his mind essays the highest place, which, as I have said, all cannot occupy. Indignation comes over him when his attempts fail. But indeed if men knew of the miseries of the highest position, they would shudder at it. Let me call as witnesses those who by dint of toil have reached the pinnacle, and who no sooner have arrived than they bewail the too easy accomplishment of their wish. This truth should be familiar to everyone, and especially to you, to whom long experience has shown that the summit of rank, surrounded as it is with troubles and anxieties, is only deserving of pity. So it happens that no position in life is free from complaints, since both those who have attained what they desire and those who have been repulsed show just cause for lament. The former think that they have been deceived, the latter neglected.

Follow, therefore, Seneca's advice: "When you see how many people are in front of you, think also how many are behind. If you wish to be reconciled with providence and your life, think of how many people you have surpassed." [20] And in the same place the same wise man says: "Set a goal, which you could not attain, even if you wish."

Petrarca: I established a certain goal to my desires long ago, and unless I am mistaken, a very modest one; but amidst the insolent and shameless manners of my time, what place is there for modesty? It is called slackness and lack of initiative.

Augustine: Can your peace of mind be so easily destroyed by the winds of popularity, which never judge rightly, never call things by their right names? But those winds, if my memory serves me right, you were accustomed to spurn.

Petrarca: Believe me, I have never spurned them more. I make no more of what the vulgar crowd thinks of me than of what I am thought of by the beasts of the field.

Augustine: Well, what bothers you?

Petrarca: I am annoyed that, when not one of my contemporaries has desired more modest things than I, no one has advanced to his desires with more difficulty than I. That I have never coveted the highest place, my witness, the guardian of truth, can attest. Forever seeing into my thoughts she knows how many times in my own human way I have gone over in my mind all the stations and positions of men. She knows that I have never found even in the highest one that tranquillity and serenity, which I place above all other goods; that, shuddering at a life full of troubles and cares I have preferred with sober judgement more modest things. Not only in word alone, but in mind have I approved Horace's advice: "Who values most the middle way / avoids discreetly both the squalor / of the slum and a palace liable / to excite envy." [21] Nor less did the reasoning please me than the dictum: "The gale shakes most the lofty pine, / tall towers fall with the louder / crash and the highest peaks most often / are struck by lightning." [22] Actually, I regret that this middle way has never been revealed to me.

Augustine: What if those things which you think moderate do exist in

20. Seneca, *Ep.*, 15.10–11.
21. Horace, *Odes*, 2.10.5–8. Trans. W. G. Shepherd.
22. Horace, *Odes*, 2.10.9–12.

your past? What if the true middle way has indeed happened to you, and abundantly? What if you left it far behind, and now give many men the means to envy you, if not hold you in contempt?

Petrarca: Even if this were true, nonetheless, it seems contrary to me.

Augustine: Undoubtedly false opinion is the cause of all your troubles, especially this last one. From this whole Charybdis you must flee, as Cicero says, with the help of your oars and sails.[23]

Petrarca: Whither can I flee? To where direct my ship? Of what do you bid me have an opinion, except what I see?

Augustine: You can see where you have directed your eyes. If you should look back, you will see that a countless throng follows, and that you are somewhat nearer to the front rank than to the rear. But the pride swelling in your soul and the singlemindedness of your purpose do not allow you to turn your eyes behind.

Petrarca: But, sometimes I have turned my gaze and have perceived many coming after me. I am not ashamed of my lot in life, but I am annoyed and dissatisfied because I have such great cares. To use a phrase of that same Horace, "may my spirits not depend on the hour's caprice." [24] If this trouble that burdens me could be removed, it would but suffice. I would then say calmly that which the same poet says in this same place: "What, my friend, do you think is my state of mind and my prayer? May I have what I have now, or less, and live for myself what's left of my life (if heaven decides that any is left)." [25]

I am always in doubt of the future, my soul is always uncertain, I take no pleasure from the gifts of fortune. So far, I have lived only for others, which is the most wretched thing of all. Heaven grant me some peace in my old age that I may die in port, having lived among stormy waves.

Augustine: Will you, therefore, in this great whirlwind of human affairs, in this great diversity of fates, and in such great darkness of future things, to speak briefly, placed under the sway of Fortune, will you alone out of all the multitudes of men lead a life free from care? Look what you desire, O mortal man. Look at what you demand. But as for the fact that you complain that you have not lived for yourself, that is a fact not of poverty but of servitude. I may confess that this is a very wretched thing, as you say. Nevertheless, if you look around you will discover that very few men have lived a life of their own. . . .

Petrarca: You have moved my soul, I confess, so that I can no longer complain of either servitude or poverty.

Augustine: Complain rather that you are not wise. Wisdom alone would

23. Cicero, *Tusculan Disputations*, 3.10.23.
24. Horace, *Epist.*, 1.18.110.   25. Horace, *Epist.*, 1.18.106–8.

have provided you liberty and true wealth. But anyone who, while calmly bearing the absence of the causes of those good fruits, complains that he does not have the effects, does not possess sound reasoning of the causes or the effects. Now tell me, what is it that makes you suffer besides what has been said? Is it weakness of body, or some hidden problem?

Petrarca: Of course this body is a burden to me every time I think of myself. But when I cast my eyes on the awkwardness of other people's bodies, I acknowledge that I have a fairly obedient slave. I wish I could boast the same thing of my soul, but that rather commands me.

Augustine: Would that it submit to the command of your reason. But I return to your body. What in it do you find troublesome?

Petrarca: Nothing really, except the common complaints: that it is mortal, that it plagues me with its sufferings, burdens me down with its weight, urges sleep when my spirit is awake, and subjects me to other human necessities which it would be tedious to go through.

Augustine: Calm yourself please, and remember you were born a man, and presently your troubles will cease. If anything besides this torments you, tell me.

Petrarca: Have you not heard of savage Fortune, the stepmother who in one day destroyed with an impious blow my hopes, my riches, my family, and my home.

Augustine: I see the tears in your eyes, and so I go on to other subjects. For you are not now to be instructed, but warned. Thus it will suffice to make this one warning. If you honestly consider both the disasters of private families and the ruins of the most well-known kingdoms throughout history, your reading of the tragedies will profit you such that you will not be ashamed that your modest roof has been razed along with so many royal palaces. Somehow you must keep going. For these few words of warning will inspire you to long meditation.

Petrarca: Who can express the loathing and disgust which I feel every day of my life in the saddest and most confused city of all lands, the narrow and final sink of the earth, overflowing with the filth of the world? Who could rival in words what everywhere stirs nausea: streets full of disease, filthy pigs mixed with rabid dogs, the screeching of wheels grinding against the walls, the four-horse chariots dashing down at every crossroad. So many types of people, the spectacles of destitution, the madness of the rich. The former are transfixed with sadness, the latter are floating about in joy and lewdness. And finally such discordant souls, the diverse arts and endless clamor of their confused voices, the hustle and bustle of people as they jostle each other in the street.

All this exhausts the senses that are accustomed to better things, destroys the peace and quiet of noble souls, and interrupts the pursuit of the liberal arts (*bonae artes*). May God save me from this shipwreck with my craft unharmed, for often, in looking around, I seem to myself to have descended alive into the underworld. 'Go now,' I say to myself, 'and do some good with yourself. Go now and devote your attention to honorable reflections: "Try composing tuneful lines in the middle of that." ' [26]

Augustine: This little verse of Horace reminds me of what you lament most of all. You lament the fact that you are at a place unsuitable for your studies; for as the same poet says: "The poet's company loves the woods and abhors the town." [27]

And you yourself in a certain letter have expressed the same thought in different words: "The woodland pleases the Muses, the city is hostile to the poets." [28] But if ever the inner turmoil of your mind were to find peace, believe me that thundering din around you would indeed strike your senses but would not stir your soul. Not to heap on things which have long been familiar to your ears, you have Seneca's useful letter concerning this matter. You also have the same man's book *On the Tranquillity of the Soul*, and on removing this whole *aegritudo* of the mind, you have the excellent book of Cicero, which he dedicated to Brutus from the *Tusculan Disputations* held on the third day.

Petrarca: You know that I have read each of these works carefully.

Augustine: Well then, did you not profit from them?

Petrarca: Yes, I profited very much while I was reading, but once the books fell from my hands, all agreement with them readily disappeared.

Augustine: It is a common habit of readers, which creates that accursed sight: those shameless herds of lettered men who wander here and there, and though they constantly discuss the art of living in the schools, rarely convert their words into action. But if only you will take notes of the chief points in what you read, you will be well rewarded for it.

Petrarca: What kind of notes?

Augustine: Whenever your readings offer you beneficial ideas that stir or moderate your soul, do not trust in the strength of your intellect, but hide these thoughts in the inner sanctuaries of your memory. Then with much study make them familiar to yourself so that, just as experienced doctors do whenever an urgent malady comes along, you may have the remedies engraved, so to speak, in your soul. For there are certain maladies in the soul, just as in the human body, where delay is so deadly that if you postpone the remedy you take away hope of a cure. . . .

Take note in your reading if you find anything dealing with anger and the rest of the emotions, especially with this plague of which we have been

26. Horace, *Epist.*, 2.2.76.   27. Horace, *Epist.*, 2.2.77.
28. Petrarca, *Epist.*, 2.3.43.

speaking. When something from your reading strikes you, put careful notes on the useful passages (as I have said from the beginning) which, like hooks, will prevent them from flying away from your memory.

With this defense you will stand firm against the other things and against the depression (*tristia*) of the soul, which, just like a pestilent cloud, kills the seeds of virtue and the fruits of genius. This depression, as Cicero says elegantly, is the fount and head of all miseries. But if at the same time you examine yourself and others carefully, if you pass over the fact that there is no man for whom there are not ample causes of lament and ignore that particularly mournful and disquieting thing, the recollection of your own sins (which is the one healthy type of sadness, so long as despair does not overcome you), you will confess that many things have been granted to you from heaven, which, among the throngs of those who complain and groan, may give you much cause for consolation and rejoicing. . . .

Petrarca: Although many things trouble me, particularly that you think it is my decision, and an easy thing, to leave the cities, nevertheless, since in many things you have surpassed me in reason, I also wish here to lay down my arms before I am thrown down.

Augustine: Can you, then, when you have cast aside your depression, be reconciled to your fortune?

Petrarca: I can indeed, if I have a little good fortune. For as you see, there is such great disagreement on this matter between the poet of the Greeks and our poet that, while the former never deemed it worthy to mention fortune in his works, our own poet often mentioned fortune and in a certain place even called her "omnipotent." Of this opinion both that celebrated historian and famous orator approve: Sallust says that fortune holds sway everywhere;[29] and Cicero was not afraid to declare her the mighty mistress of human affairs.[30] As for what I think, perhaps there will be another time and place for me to say. But as far as concerns our purpose, your advice has profited me to the point that, when I compare myself with the greater part of mankind, my station in life does not appear so wretched as it used to.

Augustine: I am glad if I have been of any help to you and I desire to bring you more abundant help in the future. But since our conversation today has progressed far enough, will you grant that the remaining matters be put off to a third day and the end of our discussion be established there?

Petrarca: Indeed the number three I embrace with my whole mind, not so much because the three Graces are contained in it, but because it is held to be most dear to the divine. Not only you and other professors of the true religion have been persuaded of this, for whom all faith is in the Trinity,

29. Sallust, *Bellum Catilinae*, 8.1.   30. Cicero, *Pro Marcello*, 2.7.

but also gentile philosophers, from whom it is handed down that they used the number three in the consecrations of the gods. This my Virgil does not seem to have ignored, when he says: ". . . in an uneven number heaven delights." [31] For what goes before makes clear that he means the number three. From your hands, therefore, I await the third part of this, your three-fold gift.

4. Giovanni Dondi dall'Orologio, *Letter to Fra Guglielmo Centueri da Cremona*

Giovanni Dondi was a disciple of Petrarch who taught medicine at the universities of Pavia and Padua until his death in 1399. His interests went far beyond his academic specialty, at least to judge by his library, which included the works of the Dominican scholastics, of several ancient Roman writers—e.g., Pliny, Cicero, Ovid, Suetonius, and Seneca (upon whose letters this one is modeled)—and, of course, Petrarch, from whose letter to Guido Sette of 1367 he borrowed some of the material in this letter. He was also something of a mechanic: he made improvements on the clock (hence his nickname, "dell'Orologio") and devised a new way of representing graphically the position of the stars. Fra Guglielmo (d. 1402) was a Franciscan who, after studying at Paris, founded the faculty of theology at Pavia. With the support of Giangaleazzo Visconti, Duke of Milan, whom he served as an advisor, he became bishop first of Piacenza and then of Pavia.

What should I do now, distinguished sir and most excellent doctor? For I am indeed perplexed, since you have lately placed me between two opposed and equally suspect courses of action. Since the nature of the opposition compels me to choose one or the other of them, I have hesitated for a long time as to what counsel I should take in this matter. Some time ago it was proposed that I should joke with you, writing in the vernacular, so that your mind, weighed down by the manifold cares of office, could be lifted up by inane trifles, by way of relief, so to speak, from your usual concerns. Meanwhile, my friend, though your mind's burden is not yet cast off or diminished—indeed, if I may speak truly, it is even considerably in-

31. Virgil, *Eclogues*, 8.75. Loeb trans.

From Neal W. Gilbert, "A Letter of Giovanni Dondi dall'Orologio to Fra Guglielmo Centueri: A Fourteenth-Century Episode in the Quarrel of the Ancients and Moderns," *Viator* 8 (1977): 339–46. © 1977 by The Regents of the University of California. Some footnotes deleted. Reprinted by permission of the Regents.

creased by new and important duties—you call me from the proposed jests to serious matters, and you beg me to say something useful. Should I then keep quiet and close my ears to your request, or should I speak, and, having given up the jokes that we used to enjoy, try to say something useful, as you ask? I feel something frightening about both courses. For if I take the first, I fear either that I would be condemned for insolence and arrogance and accused of despising or neglecting your request—although such a failing, if I am not mistaken, has only very seldom characterized my behavior—or, that I should be condemned for excessive cowardice, and although I have no doubt more than enough of that trait (would that it were not so!), still who could fail to see that I should be on guard against this—not from you, best of men, always most concerned for my welfare—but from the teeth of the envious, who lurk everywhere today, as you well know. When they think that they can poison anyone with derogatory words and bring a cloud over another's name, they consider this their ultimate in enjoyment. And hence this is my primary task, this above all else my most diligent concern. I must beware, I say, lest in not obeying you I perhaps keep silent and these people speak more boldly, and ascribe my silence to mere ignorance and inexperience in speaking.

But if I should turn to the other option (or course) and try to expound something useful, as you suggest, I suspect that my intention might be defeated. For who would doubt that whatever emerges from a mind preoccupied and overcast, and from an intelligence almost alienated, so to speak, will be not only not serious but completely ridiculous, empty, and of no consequence as well? And so because as you see, neither course is sufficiently safe for me, if I have hitherto hesitated and the matter has been so long delayed, you must not be surprised or even a little indignant. Rather it is fair to indulge someone who is perplexed and gladly shuns the perils mentioned. But since your authority urges me, I shall come over to your side; and, though I am sure that silence is much safer than foolish talk, I nevertheless propose to say something to you, with more confidence, since I feel that I cannot help but speak well with you. For whatever it is, and of whatever nature, if it comes from a friend, you, I have no doubt, will consider it worthwhile, or I am mistaken as to your humanity and patience.

So that what I am going to say to you will agree with what has been said before, and in order that my present style will follow more decently the former jests, I shall review the upshot of our previous exchange. When then we had amused ourselves on various subjects in vernacular verses, I ended up, still in that style, by deploring with heavy heart the defect and misery of our present age, and at the same time our unhappiness and that of others to whom it has been given to conduct this mortal life in these times; and I made out those of an early age to have been a more fortunate lot, especially during the principate of Caesar Augustus, when the world was almost pacified and the Latin genius flourished to the greatest extent, and when due reward was given to merit. But now you, most sagacious man, if I have sufficiently caught the sense of your words, take the part of our age, nor will you give preference to the memory of Ancient times—since, as you say, those times did not lack in miseries, when men were ambitious of glory and keen on dominating, and hence for that reason were burning with the ardor of conquering, and were always in arms and frequently afflicted with miserable disasters. Thus you and I differ with respect to these matters. I prefer the Ancient times, you defend the Modern. Hence it might perhaps be of some use to discuss this matter thoroughly.

Yet I must advance one proviso to the development of my theme: what I have said in previous comparisons of ages and what I am now going to say do not refer to divine religion or the Faith. I am not so insane, nor do I cling so lightly to the faith of the Catholic religion, that I can ignore or doubt in any way that the dense and black cloud of errors concerning the faith of religion in which the Ancients were immersed, as they wandered from the main path, and which blinded their eyes so that they could not recognize the true divinity, can be compared with the light which our Savior the son of God, Jesus Christ, opened up to us, any more than blindness can be compared with sight, or any privation with possession. And so in this respect I shall deny that we are more unhappy than they, and I shall not claim that Christian times ought to be rated below those; indeed those people who went to damnation along with their benighted leaders were unhappy, and we are rather the happy ones, to whom the true light has been shown, and given to us to know if we so wish, and for whom the way is opened on which we may come to true felicity, if we walk upon it. Here there is no divergence, no quarrel, no disagreement whatever, but complete harmony and total agreement.

But to return our discussion to the point where it began: if we think of the cultivation of virtues, the reward of duties, the robustness and efficacy of minds, and finally of the excellence of minds, I shall not cease to claim boldly that we are greatly outdone by our predecessors, and that Modern times have notably declined from the Ancient. Ah, would that I could demonstrate the opposite! But this seems so easy to understand that it cannot escape anyone who attends to it, and hence does not need any defense to conclude its argument, since it should be clear just by observation of the present times and recognition of the former. The customs of this age are obvious even if we just open our eyes a little. Unless he is blind, there is no one who does not see what cultivation there is now of virtue, and what kind it is. Today everyone recognizes, and I find it disgusting to recall, by what arts the favor of princes is sought, by what merits higher honors and greater riches can be hoped for, and finally who and what sort of men are commonly believed to excel in sense and prudence, which, according to Cassiodorus, is to be preferred above all else, since in a happy (?) man it is found. To such a degree of error has the judgment of mortals declined that this to me is a sign of the senescence, if I may use the term, of human nature, and a sign that it will very soon decline into decrepitude and finally come to nothing, unless perhaps Divine Goodness in its mercy provides otherwise. Now you see everywhere a mankind whose greatest aim it should be to mingle with others socially, to live together and communicate in a civil way, cheating one's neighbor and setting traps everywhere, by means of which any careless or unsuspecting person who walks by may be tripped up. And alas! alas! today this is nearly the only concern of all men, if you observe carefully, this is almost the whole preoccupation, these are the virtues of our Age. A man seems to himself superior, he seems wiser and more prudent, not just to himself, but, what is still more to be deplored, to others as well, who uses whatever mind heaven has endowed him with for the embezzlement of another's wealth, or for the betrayal of a trusting associate. And he who deploys the machinery of the abominable arts more subtly and shrewdly will easily gain the favor of princes, will receive gifts and rewards, and in a short time will gain dominion over those who dominate.

But who and what sort of men those Ancients were, by what customs they lived, what virtues they had, what sorts of actions gained reward, and what sorts of things were given to those who deserved well, all belong to a bygone age and cannot, like present things, be seen by our eyes or touched with our hands; they can, however, be recognized by great testimonies and reliable evidence, so that no one who looks carefully can doubt them. The best evidence consists of the writings which outstanding minds have left to the memory of posterity; their authority and majesty is so great that no one can fail to trust them. If you should ask my own opinion, their credit is so great, believe me, that I seem somehow to have seen those things that I have read. To my way of thinking, then, it is out of the question that such genuine men could have written anything except the truth, and what they had seen themselves or had accepted from those who were present, or from what they had learned from what was written by great authors—who, I am sure (especially those who were intending to write history, not poems, in which kind of writing perhaps it might be permitted to describe matters otherwise than they were), sought the truth of things above all else and eschewed every falsehood. I am sure that you have diligently read writings of this kind, or certain of the more important ones, and have in many parts of them noted customs and actions of a past Age with some admiration. If you in all fairness compare what we perceive at present with these, you will admit that justice, courage, temperance, and prudence really dwelt more profoundly in their souls, and that they who did great things by the guidance of these virtues were provided with far more worthy rewards. Moreover, proof of this is given by those objects which remain in Rome to this day as testimony to the honors that used to be conferred upon outstanding actions. For although time has consumed many of them—even many of the more magnificent—and only ruins of others appear, which present certain traces of what formerly stood, still, those things that remain, fewer and less magnificent, testify abundantly that those who decreed them must have been of great virtue, and that something great and worthy of praise must have been enacted by those for whom they were being given for their lasting honor and glory. I mean the statues which, either cast in bronze or chiseled in marble, have lasted to the present, and the many fragments of those that have been shattered lying about everywhere, the marble triumphal arches of impressive workmanship and the sculptured columns showing the histories of great deeds, and so many other things of this kind publicly built in honor of men who were distinguished, whether because they had established peace or because they had liberated the fatherland from imminent peril or had extended empire over subjected peoples, as I recall having read in some of them, not without a certain notable pleasure. And you similarly, I suspect, have noticed in passing sometimes and have stopped a little while with some amazement and perhaps have said to yourself, "Surely these are proof of great men." Such proof for such reasons is not forthcoming from our own time. And why, do you think, unless that there are lacking those who should act in such a way as to deserve such rewards, as well as those who would favor men acting in this way, if such there were, by whose means such rewards would be given?

Let us move along to the vigor and effectiveness of minds, in which matter it can be called an abuse rather than a comparison to compare ours with those of the Ancients, since it is clear that they had robust and strong minds, whereas (I would willingly keep still on this theme, but the topic compels me, and truth as well) we should judge the action of ours to be such as to make us think that we have not only weak and feeble minds but none at all. I would not ask that you provide me today with anyone like Coclites, or Curtius, or Scevola, or Regulus, or the two Decii, or innumerable other men, from the citizens of Rome or from foreigners, who either for the safety of their fatherland or its liberty, in order to keep faith, even to the enemy, gave themselves to a certain death with unhesitating mind, having determined to endure it by a sound and deliberate resolution. Nor should I require that you show me leaders like the Scipios or the equal of Cato and many, many others of the Romans, nor of men among the foreigners such as Alexander of Macedonia, Pyrrhus the Epirote, or Hannibal the Carthaginian—who in order to rule others or promote their empires or gain glory for themselves and their followers, would spend either the whole of their lives or the most useful years of them in arms, now storming cities, now rushing the enemy battleline, and who persisted at the cost of much trouble and ceaseless labors, always however with an uncorrupted and unconquered mind. I would not require such minds, since there are none in these days, in which only very rarely do you hear of defenses being stormed and taken, and few attempting it, indeed of those attempting it very few succeeding at all unless by some fraud. And so one should not look for the sort of vigor in us that our ancestors had. Among us you find few who would dare to await the advancing enemy and do so with eagerness. I realize what many people are accustomed to say on this topic, namely, that those deeds which are told of the character of our Ancients were derived rather from rage and imprudence than from virtue, and that they were led to this fury by a desire for empty glory and by ambition for domination. But whatever the truth may be in this matter—that is, whether you say that it is virtuous to choose an undoubted death for such reasons, or whether it should be permitted to invade free and quiet peoples without violating justice and aggressively disturbing them and subjugating them—I do not presently inquire. Nor am I concerned to decide these matters: we ask that you grant only one thing of those mentioned, which cannot be denied, namely, that such great and fearless deeds proceeded from great spirits, and that such difficult attacks could not have been waged with such great perseverance except by more sturdy minds than those which we find in our contemporaries.

Finally, to turn the discussion from character to genius, there can be no one to whom it is not transparently clear, unless he is completely insensitive, that Modern powers of mind have declined from those of the Ancients. Indeed so much so that they be equated in hardly any respect, and indeed in many aspects are overshadowed to the greatest possible degree. For since the minds of men are known through nothing so much as their works, the magnitude of difference between them and us can be shown in no better way than by comparing the works achieved by us respectively. The special achievements of the human mind are the discoveries of the arts and sciences, e.g., of wisdom and the liberal doctrines which are desired as preparation for true wisdom and, needless to say, all writings and literary remains. In addition to these, there are the works of artistry, which are preconceived by the innate genius of reason and by acquired habits of art, and fabricated by the very hands of the artisans from raw materials. Of these works, there is no doubt that the liberal arts or teachings and the other sciences and all of the aspects of wisdom that are humanly derived were first discovered by the Ancients, and once discovered were transmitted by them to posterity in books written with such clear and indubitable principles, with so much order and impregnable method, that they remain to the present day the wonder and veneration of nearly everybody, and are now studied by us still. For it is absurd to ask what sciences are now found out from scratch, they are so meager or non-existent. It is enough and plenty for Moderns if they can just touch the surface of what those Ancients treated in the greatest depth. So that if by chance some Modern should have the confidence in himself to try to invent something or presume to change what has been handed down before (as in our days some dialecticians have done, as you know), it is sufficiently clear how much their results are worth, and how much has endured. They have scarcely lasted past the age in which they were produced, and have perished along with their authors.

Indeed in order to show more clearly what sort of comparisons can be drawn in this matter between the Ancients and the Moderns, let us adduce the most noble and excellent mind of this Age, the most studious and prolific of all writers, proficient in every kind of speaking and writing. I mean Master Petrarch, whom I think you know and have often seen; but I was on close terms with him and was very much a member of his household, especially in his last years. Speaking boldly and in simple truth, without any regard for friendship, I would put his mind first above all others of our age that I know, and I think it would have had a place among the Ancients if he had lived in that age, and also that it will have in future generations even more consideration and esteem than with his contemporaries. The many published works of this man, some of which you may have seen, will please you considerably if you read any part of them, I am sure. For how could they fail to please, filled as they are with such weighty opinions and composed in such a sweet-sounding style and methodical order? If you read them and re-read them again and again, they will please you still more, which is a sure sign of a great work and author. But if, having laid these aside, you turn to read something from the literary remains of the greater Ancients, you will unquestionably feel, if you apply your mind to it, how much deeper a sound they produce. Once when I myself was doing this, I remembered a statement that I heard on one occasion from the mouth of Petrarch himself while he was still alive. For he had had his own *Bucolicum Carmen* bound in together with Virgil's in one volume. I was present with him when a third person, a nobleman, took this book and held it out to him, and asked what the book was. Petrarch answered, "In this book some grey rags are bound in with scarlet," indicating clearly by this response that his work was considerably surpassed by the Ancients. Thus when so singular and unique a mind among us yields, and admits that it yields, to the Ancients, it follows that we have no more right to contend with the Ancients than a spider with Minerva. And this is truly the case. Our minds are of inferior quality: if we have anything historical from them, it is without a doubt more careless than Livy or Sallust, if oratorical, much inferior to Cicero, if poetical, Maro precedes and Horace and Ovid, if philosophical, Varro outshines and Seneca. Nor are these the only Ancients who excel the Moderns; there are almost innumerable others whom I do not mention. I only adduce a few from all of these because they were together in one age and Augustus saw them before him in Rome. If you even find anyone among us who is at all learned in the divine canon and in the sacred scriptures, you will find that he walks far below Augustine and Jerome and innumerable others of the Ancients. This is so obvious that it would be criminal to prolong our discourse on the subject.

Of the artistic products of ancient genius, few survive. But those that do remain anywhere are eagerly sought and seen and highly prized by those who feel strongly about such things: and if you compare them with those of today, it will soon become obvious that their authors were by nature more powerful in genius and more learned in the mastery of their art. I am speaking about ancient buildings and statues and sculptures, with other things of the sort. When some artists of this time scrutinize the productions of that age carefully, they are struck with amazement. I knew a certain well-known worker in marble who was famous for his ability in that art among those whom Italy had at the time, especially in the creation of figures. I have heard this man tell many times about the statues and sculptures that he had seen at Rome, with such admiration and veneration that he seemed in recalling it to be transported beyond himself from the wonder of the thing. For he used to say that sometimes, passing with his friends by a place where some images of this sort could be seen, he had held back, looking in astonishment at their artistry, and, forgetting his company, had stood still so long that his companions had passed on five hundred steps and more. And when he would tell of the great excellence of these figures, and praise their authors beyond measure, he used to add in the end (in his own words): "If only these images did not lack life, they would be better than living ones," as if to say that nature had been not only imitated by the genius of such artists but even surpassed.

Now go, best master, weigh our humble capabilities, and if you can, defend in any way present times against the former (would that you could!) so that I might stop being indignant and would begin to become reconciled with our times. But I suspect that you will not be able, so manifestly does the opposite appear to all. Nor am I unaware that that outstanding doctor, Augustine, may seem to be a supporter of your cause, particularly in the *City of God*, in which, doing battle for the Christian religion, he shows that ancient pagan times were unhappy and full of much misery. His contemporary and disciple Paulus Orosius also tries to show this in his histories of the times, in the book that he wrote to Augustine against the defamers of Christian times. But actually these most Christian and learned men did not weigh those times as blind and miserable by the cultivation of moral virtues or by their minds and genius, which we have shown to be of great worth. Orosius would not deny this, for he very often admires their deeds in telling them, nor would Augustine, who plainly extolled their genius when he writes in Book 1 that Virgil was a great poet, the most outstanding of all, and in Book 2 he testifies that the ancient philosophers found out great things with divine aid, although, handicapped by their humanity, they mixed certain errors in with the things they found. Indeed in Book 4 he said that Varro was the most acute and learned of men. Obviously they were considering the true religion on whose behalf they wrote, and the knowledge of the true divinity. They refer to it when they say that those who lived before the advent of the Savior clung to deceitful gods and thus wandered astray, and are accordingly to be called miserable and blind. On the other hand, only those who profess the orthodox Catholic faith are to be called truly happy. No doubt every loyal Christian agrees with Augustine and Orosius, which is what I have been claiming from the start. I would concede to Orosius that ancient times had many great calamities; indeed no age was ever completely free from misery and afflictions of this kind, since such is the nature of this temporal life, which is all misery and affliction and seems to demand diseases. I mean the deadly epidemics and lethal pestilences, one of which, very terrible and extensive, many times going and returning, we have experienced in our time, afflicting faithful Christians no less than the territories of the infidels. Moreover, as for famines and deprivations and the destructions of wars and daily killings of men beyond number, I must admit that our age seems not to have them so much or so frequently as others. But the reason is obvious. Those who were aroused by greatness of soul or by strength in arms always acted so that either they should rule the weaker or, unwilling to submit, passionately guard their liberty against others. We, with our failing souls, do not have the force to subject others, and we have learned to submit so easily that we all prefer the foul yoke with its burden and have forgotten liberty. Yet no matter how many multitudes were killed every day in that former age by raging wars (as you have often read), still they always exceeded us by a great number. For at the time of Augustus, the number of Roman citizens was tallied at 9,380,000 persons according to Martinus Polonus, which number the whole of Italy scarcely has today. And in the reign of Claudius, according to the census then repeated, there were found at Rome 6,944,000 persons, on the authority of Eusebius of Caesaria in his book on times. Thus we are lacking, not only in virtues of soul and genius, as I have previously claimed, but in the number of persons as well. We prevail only by a certain sluggishness or inertia, although we are happy in the Christian religion. And so I never cease to wonder and become indignant at the fact that we, brought up and nourished in the light of the true religion, have departed so much from former virtue; we have so ceased to be men that in many respects we are driven almost like sheep. But now I have gone on long enough, indeed too long, from the force of grief. Forgive me, I pray you, best of men, for grief has no measure. I know that I have written too much, inanities badly put together, but indignation drove my pen, and I have acted with you in a friendly and confidential fashion. Farewell.

2
The Social and Economic Structure of Early Renaissance Italy

5. Leon Battista Alberti, *On the Family*

Jakob Burckhardt found in Leon Battista Alberti (b. Genoa, 1404; d. Rome, 1474) the embodiment of the Renaissance "universal man." He was an expert runner, jumper, rider, and swimmer. He wrote treatises on ethics, political philosophy, and aesthetics (*On Painting* and *On Architecture*). He designed the loggia of the Rucellai palace and the facade of the church of Santa Maria Novella in Florence, the immense church of Sant'Andrea in Mantua, and the gracious Malatesta Temple in Rimini. He even tried his hand, although less successfully, at painting. As a young man he attended one of the earliest of the new humanist schools, which is where he picked up many of the ideas about pedagogy later expounded in *On the Family*. In 1428, after he had received a degree in canon law from the University of Bologna, the Florentine Republic lifted the ban that had kept the Alberti family in exile since the 1380s. But after a brief visit to his homeland, Leon Battista moved to Rome, where, notwithstanding his illegitimate birth, he accumulated a number of ecclesiastical benefices and served as advisor to popes Eugenius IV, Nicholas V, and Pius II. It was there, in 1432, that he began writing *On the Family*, which he completed later in Florence while attending the Council of Ferrara-Florence.

The dialogue purports to be a conversation among members of the Alberti family assembled at the deathbed of Leon Battista's father in Padua in 1421; and the conversational style is preserved even to the point of maintaining the frequent repetitions, overloaded superlatives, and in-

From *I Libri della Famiglia*, edited by Ruggiero Romano and Alberto Tenenti (Torino: Einaudi, 1969), pp. 74–77, 82–88, 126–41, 155–64, 170–78, 214–16, 222–26. Translated for this volume by Eric Cochrane.

elegant expressions that might be expected of wise, but unlettered, inter-locutors. In order to appeal to his intended audience, the merchant-patricians of Florence, Leon Battista chose to write not in classical Latin, the normal means of written communication among the first gen-erations of Italian humanists, but in the current spoken idiom of Flor-ence, which he, having spent most of his life abroad, had to learn from his Florentine contemporaries. The great number of surviving manu-scripts suggests that he succeeded in his aim. But after Pietro Bembo's refined fourteenth-century Tuscan—rather than colloquial Florentine— became recognized as the official spoken and written language of Italy in the early sixteenth century (see the introduction to Petrarca in this vol-ume), the work went out of fashion. It was not rediscovered until the mid eighteenth century; and the first complete edition was not published until the nineteenth century.

The present translation follows the text established by Cecil Grayson in the Laterza "Scrittori d'Italia" edition of 1960 as reproduced in the most recent critical edition by Ruggiero Romano and Alberto Tenenti in *I libri della famiglia* (Turin: Einaudi, 1969); but the older Pellegrini-Spongano edition of 1946 is still useful for its explanatory footnotes. The entire text has been translated into English by Renée Neu Watkins as *The Family in Renaissance Florence* (Columbia: University of South Carolina Press, 1969).

Book 1

. . . *Lionardo:* Men of letters, as you know, tell us that nature strives to produce all things as complete, both in inherent strength and in various members, as is fitting and proper, with no defects or imperfection, in such a way that they can maintain themselves during their own lifetime and be of some help to other things in doing the same thing. These same men further show us that every living being has innate in it from its very beginnings enough strength, intelligence, and power (*virtù*) both to get what it needs for its maintenance and repose and to flee from or repulse whatever may oppose or harm it. You can see what I mean when you observe that any man who is not completely stupid will, by what is apparently an innate intelligence, dislike and condemn all vice and dishonesty that he observes in others; indeed you won't find anyone who does not think there is some defect in whoever is given to evil. Thus we ought not to condemn the teach-ings of those who bring forth many other arguments to prove that from nature all things proceed as perfect as they can be, and it seems to me that we can affirm with certainty that all mortals are endowed by nature with the ability to love and to put into practice even the most praised virtue (*virtù*). And virtue is nothing else than nature, properly produced and perfect in itself.[1]

Hence, I think I may be permitted to say that the evil we find in the minds and souls of mortals is essentially [the result of] bad habits and corrupted reason, both of which proceed from erroneous opinions and mental deficiency.[2] I should admit, of course, that men's desires and appetites may sometimes be provoked to some extent by certain natural causes. For example, I once learned that sanguine people, if I remember correctly, are naturally more disposed to love than melancholy people, that the choleric are more subject to anger, the phlegmatic to laziness and sloth, and the melancholy to timidity and suspicion and thus to avarice and niggardliness.[3] Therefore if you find that your children have by nature a good intelligence, a good mind, and a good memory, you should do all that you can to get them to follow the way in which nature has directed them: toward the most elegant and most outstanding branches of learning. If on the other hand you notice that they are strong, proud, willful, and better fitted for military exercises than for the leisure[4] [required by] studies, here also you should follow [the lead of] nature: you should teach them to ride horseback, to bear arms, to shoot arrows, and to do all the other feats praised by men of arms; thus strengthening every good disposition they may have and with the greatest care and attention help them overcome their bad inclinations. Prudent men assure us that it is lustful and immoderate habits or practices rather than any natural appetite or inclination that lead us to vice. All this we can learn from experience; for seldom a day goes by that we do not see some young man who by nature was well-behaved, mild, and modest, become shameless, uncontrolled, and immoderate just because he has been running around in bad company and in bad places. And so in many other cases we can see that an acquired habit can be much more effective in leading us to evil than any natural appetites. It is too much fine food, after all, that fills a man with lust. Hence the ancient proverb: "Without Ceres and Bacchus, Venus grows cold."

Thus we can conclude that misuse will corrupt and contaminate every good thing that nature produces, and that good habits will in time over-

1. Here Alberti uses "nature" in a second sense, not as what produces all things, but the things themselves as they are produced naturally.

2. *Imbecillità di mente*, with no overtones from modern psychology.

3. The four-humor theory, of course, which Alberti as much as admits does not fit with the rest of his argument; but the appearance of philosophical rigor is exactly what he is trying to avoid.

4. *Ozio*. The word is used in several different senses, as will be seen below.

come and correct every unreasonable appetite and every imperfection of the mind. It seems to me, then, that if a father notices his son sinking into laziness, avarice, impetuousness, and the like, he ought to draw him back to virtue by having him work at and practice good and praiseworthy things. And if he sees that his son is already headed along the path that leads to virtue and commendable acts, he ought to support and strengthen him by instruction and by example. And since even a person who is headed along the good straight path to the temple may still waste time by stopping in at the theater,[5] so one can easily get slowed down or get lost on the road to fame and praise even though nature has made it wide and easy to follow. Therefore fathers will be alert and foresighted in studying their sons' characters so that they can help them toward whatever is praiseworthy and turn them away from any dissolute manners or ugly affection. . . .

Adovardo: I don't deny, Lionardo, that fathers who are as diligent as you say they ought to be can in good measure help their sons in acquiring good manners; nor do I deny that fathers can, with care and attention, correct their sons' defects and make them into good men. But I'm afraid that the love most fathers bear their children all too often blinds them to the first signs of evil; when the evil itself at last becomes fully evident, then it's too late. Even you realize that it's pretty hard to uproot a vice that has become a confirmed habit. And even with children who are modest and well-mannered, it seems that fathers rarely know where to begin instilling in them a desire for praise and fame.

Lionardo: As everyone knows, the place to begin is with good letters. Letters are indeed so important that without them one would be considered nothing but a rustic, no matter how much a gentleman [he may be by birth]. I'd much rather see a young nobleman with a book than with a falcon in his hand. I've never had much use for the common saying that all you need to know how to do is sign your name and figure out how much money is left [in your bank account].[6] I prefer the old customs of our family; for as you know, we Alberti have always been men of some learning. . . .

Hence in a family, and especially in one like ours that has always been one of the first in its knowledge of good letters as well as in everything else, I think it's very important to bring up children so that they grow in knowledge as they grow in years, not only for the sake of the many ways learned men can be of use to a family, but also for the sake of keeping up our own ancient traditions. Let our family, then, continue to take inspiration from the example of our ancestors, so that the young will be filled with

5. Augustine, *Confessions*, 8.10.
6. The institution had already been developed in fifteenth-century Italy but the technical word had not yet been coined. Alberti says simply *ritrarre* (withdraw).

the desire to acquire knowledge and refinement, and so that their fathers will take pleasure in seeing their sons become learned and wise. Be diligent, then, you young people, in your studies. Do all you can to learn about the events of the past that are worthy of memory. Try to understand all the useful things that have been passed on to you. Feed your minds on good maxims. Learn the delights of embellishing your souls with good morals. Strive to be kind and considerate [of others] when conducting civil business. Get to know those things human and divine that have been put at your disposal in books for good reason. Nowhere will you find a pleasant and consonant combination of voice and song that can equal the harmony and elegance of a verse of Homer, or Virgil, or of some other excellent poet. You will find no field so delightful or flowering as in one of the orations of Demosthenes, Cicero, Livy, Xenophon, and other such pleasing and perfect orators. No effort is more fully compensated—if indeed what is really entertainment and recreation for the mind and soul can be called effort—as the constant reading and rereading of good things. From such reading you will rise rich in good maxims and good arguments, strong in your ability to persuade others and get them to listen to you; among the citizens you will willingly be heard, admired, praised, and loved.

I need not go on at length—a full recitation would take far too much time—how good letters are not only useful, but absolutely necessary to whoever rules and governs; nor will I describe in detail how important they are to the decor of the commonwealth. Let us put aside momentarily a consideration of the many accomplishments by which our family has made itself useful to the commonwealth and known and loved by our fellow citizens, all of which have been the work of the great number of learned and prudent men who have always and still do flourish in our family as in no other. If there is anything that blends well with gentleness and kindness, if there is anything that embellishes the life of a man, if there is anything that lends grace, authority, and a good reputation to a family, that thing is good letters. Without them there is no true gentility and seldom a really happy life; without them no family can consider itself strong and secure. It is well, Adovardo, that here in your presence I commend good letters to these young people who take such pleasure in the pursuit of them. For I certainly think that as good letters are pleasing to you and to your sons, so they are of great use to everyone and absolutely essential in the life of all men.

Let fathers see to it, then, that their children are assiduous in the study of good letters; let them teach their children how to understand what they read and how to write correctly; and let them not think that their efforts are at an end until their boys have become good readers and writers. There's probably not much difference between knowing something imperfectly and not knowing it at all. Let the children then learn arithmetic (*abaco*) and, at the same time, as much as is useful of geometry; for both these sciences are pleasing and easy for children, who have a certain aptitude for them, and what's more, both will be very useful later in life. Let them then go on to taste the poets, the orators, and the philosophers, under the guidance of attentive masters who will see to it that they learn good morals while they're learning good letters. And I would prefer that they stick to good authors—that they learn grammar from Priscian and from Servius,[7] not from the chartulas and the graechimuses,[8] and that they become the familiar friends of Cicero, Livy, and Sallust. For from these remarkable and polished writers they will, along with the knowledge contained in their writings, pick up from the very first all that is most perfect, elegant, and eloquent in the Latin language. The mind, they say, is like a vase: if you start by pouring in a drop of bad liquid, you'll end up spoiling whatever good liquid you put in afterwards. Stay away, then, from all coarse and rough writers, and follow all those who are sweet and pleasing; keep them always in hand and never tire of reviewing them, reading them out loud, and committing them to memory. Not that I have anything against the doctrine of any learned and copious writer [no matter what his style may be]; but since there are plenty of learned authors who have written with elegance, I would prefer them to those who have written poorly. Learn the Latin language from those who have written it carefully and perfectly; and from the others concentrate only on the sciences they may expound.

Fathers must realize that good letters never do any harm, and that indeed they are always profitable to whoever cultivates them. Of all the members of our family who have been eminent for their learning, none has ever found that his studies got in the way of all the other responsibilities the family has placed upon him. There is no need to prove to you how much letters have been profitable both to our reputation and to our business affairs.[9]

7. Priscian of Cesarea in Mauritania (fl. A.D. 500) and Marius Servius or Servius Honoratus (fl. A.D. 384) were Latin philologists. The first is known chiefly for his *Institutio de arte grammatica*, often called the *Priscianus* after the author, a survey of Latin grammar in eighteen books; the second is known for his massive commentaries on Virgil.

8. *Cartule e gregismi*. These two words mystified all commentators until G. Billanovich and C. Grayson, in two articles published in *Lingua nostra*, figured out that they must refer to two rhymed Latin grammar books widely used during the Middle Ages: the *Auctores octo*, which begins with the words "Chartula nostra tibi portat, Raynalde, salutes," and the *Graecismus*, published by J. Wrobel in 1887. The sense of the passage is, then: use the ancient authorities themselves and not the watered-down, and often inaccurate, textbooks and compendia to which schoolboys have been subjected for the past three centuries. On the significance of the "textbook revolution" of the fifteenth century, see Eugenio Garin, *L'educazione in Europa* (Bari, 1957).

9. *Nella fama e nelle cose*. *Cose* (lit., things) almost always refers in Alberti to *material* things or goods as opposed to intangible or spiritual qualities, like a good mind or, here, fame and reputation.

Don't think, however, that I want fathers to keep their sons chained to their books, Adovardo. Quite the contrary, I think that young boys need considerable recreation—at least enough to restore their forces. But let all their games be manly and virtuous, without any trace of vice or immorality. They ought to stick to those praiseworthy exercises handed down to us by the good ancients. Any game that is played sitting down seems to me hardly conducive to virility. Perhaps for old men such games as chess and the amusements of those with gout are all right; but games that involve no exercise are never permissible for robust youths. Leave sitting down to the lazy and to women; exercise is what the others need, exercise for the whole body and for all of its parts. Let them then take up archery, horseback riding, and other virile and noble sports. The ancients themselves practiced archery; it was considered a great refinement among them to appear in public with a bow and a sheaf of arrows, and praises were written of those who knew how to shoot well. It is said that the emperor Domitian was so good with a bow that he had a boy put out his hand as a target and shot the arrows through the space between his fingers. Our young people also ought to play ball, a very ancient game and one that is most conducive to the agility that is admired among gentlemen. The princes of antiquity often played ball. Julius Caesar himself was very fond of this most worthy game. . . . So were Publius Mutius, Caesar Octavian, Dionysius the King of Siracuse,[10] and so many others that space forbids my mentioning them, all of them princes and noble men, who often took exercise by playing ball. Nor would I be displeased if young people learned the arts of cavalry, how to gallop, turn, and stop on horseback; for in this way they will be able, when called upon, to defend their country against its enemies. In order to accustom their young people to these military exercises, the ancients used to propose to them those Trojan games so well described by Virgil in the *Aeneid*. There were many miraculous horseback riders among the princes of Rome. Caesar, it is said, used to ride as fast as he could with his arms tied behind him. [Even] when he was sixty-two years old Pompey used to throw darts and take his sword out of his scabbard while riding at top speed.[11] Thus while they are learning letters, I would have our small ones

10. These examples come from Suetonius, Macrobius, and Cicero. Publius Mutius Scevola, famous in antiquity for his personal morality and his knowledge of the law, was consul in 133 B.C. and later pontifex maximus and a tacit supporter of the Gracchi. Alberti just assumes that the ball games of antiquity are the same as the rough-and-tumble *gioco di calcio*, a form of soccer, played by Florentines of his day. The same game, revived under government auspices in the mid twentieth century, was abolished in 1981 after one contest turned into a bloody brawl between two of the rival teams and their supporters.

11. This story comes from Plutarch's *Life of Pompey*, 64 (*Lives*, 5.281 in the Loeb edition). Actually Pompey was only 58 at the time.

also learn these noble feats and exercises, which will be both useful and praiseworthy throughout their lives: horseback riding, that is, fencing, swimming, and all such things, which it is indeed often dangerous not to know how to do as adults. And if you reflect a bit on the matter, you will find that these things are also necessary in the life of a citizen in the commonwealth; so much the better that children learn early, while it comes easily, what may well be the first accomplishments required of them as adults. . . .

Book 2

The family becomes populous the same way as do countries, provinces, and the whole world, as anyone with a bit of imagination can see by noting how the multitude of mortals has grown from very few to an almost infinite number: by procreating and bringing up children. And for procreating children, let no one doubt that women are necessary. For the child comes into the world tender and weak; he therefore needs someone to take care of him, to love him, to nourish him, and to protect him from harm. . . . Thus the woman from earliest times remained in the shadow [of a roof] to nurture and care for the child. And since she was busy with the heir, she was not able to search for what she needed for herself and for him; hence the man, by nature more energetic and industrious, went out to find and bring back what was necessary. . . . Thus it seems manifest to me that nature and human reason teach that the conjugal union is necessary to increase and to maintain mankind and to nourish and take care of the young. I will now show how necessary it is to use care and diligence in looking for a partner. And I will also show that the nature of this conjugal union is such that a man may have no more than one woman at a time; . . . for if he had several women and families, he would not be able [to provide for them all]. . . . Thus this union was instituted by nature, the good and divine mistress of all things, with this condition: that a man have but one companion in this life, that he take refuge under a roof with her, that he never leave her, that he bring and order what is necessary and commodious to his family, and that the woman at home [be charged with] conserving what is brought to her. . . .

Perhaps it would be useful to force our young men a bit in this way. Let the fathers command in their wills: "If you at a reasonable age have not yet taken a wife, you will no longer be my heir." On what is a reasonable age, it would take a lot of time to go over all the opinions of the ancients. Hesiod made husbands at 30 years, Lycurgus liked fathers at 37. We moderns think it well to marry at 25 years. All agree that it is unwise to entrust so important a task to those under 25, since the fervent and headstrong character natural to that age is better suited to affirming and strengthening their own persons than to procreating others. Seeds planted in a field that are not whole and mature are also less vigorous, and more fallible. Let us then wait for greater maturity. When that moment arrives, it is the obligation of the older members of the family, and particularly of the mothers, the aunts, and the grandmothers, who know the behavior and character of all the maidens of the town, to choose those who are well born and brought up and to present them to the bridegroom-to-be. Let him then choose which he prefers. And let the older men of the household not refuse any daughter-in-law unless perhaps she may bring scandal or ill-repute into the family. For the rest, let them be content that he is content with her. He in turn should do just what good fathers of families do when they carefully look over a piece of property before they buy it. In every purchase of contract, it is well first fully to inform yourself, to ask the opinion of others, and to be diligent so that you won't be sorry afterwards. So much more diligent must be one who becomes a husband. . . . For he takes a wife for two reasons: first to perpetuate himself in his children, and second, to have a sure, stable companion for the rest of his life.

It is said that in choosing a wife one looks for beauty, good parentage, and wealth. The beauty of a man trained in arms seems to me to consist in his having a fierce presence and a body able to undertake the hardest kind of work. Beauty in an old man I find to reside in prudence, pleasantness, and good sense in words and counsel. Thus I hold that beauty in a woman consists not in a pretty face, but in a body capable of producing many beautiful children. [Yet] the first element of beauty in a woman is a good moral character (*i buon costumi*). . . . Let one thus first look for beauty of the spirit in a bride, that is, morals and virtue. An ancient proverb says: "As you want your children, so choose your wife." And the poets say, "from a good body comes pleasing virtue." The philosophers prefer that the wife not be too thin, but not too fat either; for the first are often subject to frigidity and the second to excessive menstrual discharges and slowness in conception. They also prefer women who are happy, merry, vivacious of blood, and in good spirits. They don't mind brunettes, but they dislike those with too dark a complexion; and they disdain those who are too small, those who are too big, and those who move too quickly. They also prefer girls who are still very young. For at that young age the girls have not yet learned evil ways, they have not yet lost their natural modesty, and they more easily learn to follow the manners and the wishes of their husbands.

Having spoken of beauty, let us now look at parentage. I think that under this heading it would be well to examine carefully the life and manners of all your prospective relatives. For frequently marriages have been, as we hear and read every day, the cause of great ruin to families, for they have become related to litigious, jealous, proud, and ill-willed men. . . . And it often happens that the new relatives, finding their own affairs going badly, or having fallen into misfortune, all move into the house of the young couple. Take care, therefore, that your new relatives are not of vulgar birth, not of low fortunes, not of a vile profession, that they are in all things well governed and modest, and not too much higher than you. I do not want them too inferior to you either, for that might cost you money, just as relatives who are above you might reduce you to servitude. Let them then be equal to you, as I have said, modest and civil.

Now, concerning the dowry, I would prefer that it be modest, certain, and payable immediately (*presente*) than large, doubtful, and payable over a period of time (*a tempo*). Everyone tends, led on by common corrupt usages, to let indulgence make him slow in paying the money he owes, especially when he hopes eventually to get out of paying it at all, as sometimes happens in marriages. For the bride now lives in your house, and during the first year it seems impermissible to do other than strengthen the new family relationship through frequent visits and intercourse. Perhaps you will feel it impolite to bring up the question of payment during festivities, for new husbands generally try not to interfere with the still tender bonds of parentage, and they will accept even a minimal excuse. And if you try to act with more force, they will start lamenting their infinite necessities, their bad fortune, the hardships of the times; . . . and you won't be able to turn down the prayers of those you have just accepted as relatives. Moreover, no matter how harsh you may be toward them, you will not be able to resist the sweet and prayerful requests made by your wife in your own house and chamber on behalf of the fathers and brothers. . . .

Battista: I would not interrupt you if you hadn't already given me permission to do so. But I'd like to pause a moment so I can better fix what you have said in my mind. As I remember, you said we should choose an honest companion of good parentage with a good dowry capable of bearing many children. But don't you think, Lionardo, that these three requirements are very hard to find in one woman, not to mention in the number of women needed in a family as large as ours? I notice in other marriages that a girl from a good family often comes without a dowry; hence it is often said, "If you want a dowry, take an old hag." So that our customs seem to be similar to those they write about in Thrace, where ugly maidens with big dowries bought husbands, and where a certain price was assigned to beautiful maidens according to the judgment of the public tax officials. Do you understand what I'm getting at?

Lionardo: I understand, and I'm happy that you've paid such close attention to what I've been saying. It's true; marriages can't always be what I'd like them to be, and all wives can't be similar to Cornelia, daughter of

Metellus Scipio, who married Publius Crassus, a handsome woman, well educated, and expert in music, geometry, and philosophy, and better yet, what is most praiseworthy in a woman of such intelligence and virtue, one completely free of pride, and a sense of superiority. Do rather what was advised by the servant Birria in Terence [in the *Andria*]: "You can't have what you wish; wish therefore for what you can have." [If you must choose among the three requirements], put having children in first place. . . . Property often turns out to be fragile and hard to keep; relatives will always be relations as long as you treat them as nothing more than relations. . . .

It now remains to be considered how children should be procreated. It might seem better to skip over this subject, and I will touch upon it as briefly as possible, so that whoever doesn't want to hear it can regard it as not said. But it is necessary [to our theme]. The husband should not approach his wife with his spirit perturbed by annoyances, fear, or any other such troubles; for these states of mind weaken and lessen the virile forces, and passions that inflame the spirit disturb and confuse the artifice [i.e., the male semen] that must then construct a human image [i.e., a new human being]. It is thus that we have seen a timid, weak, pallid son born of a passionate, strong, intelligent father, and a headstrong, beast-like son born of a moderate and reasonable father. I must add that copulation should be avoided if the body and all its parts are not well disposed and in good health. Medical doctors have shown with good reason that if fathers and mothers are suffering from excessive drink or bad blood, or if they are lacking in vigor or their pulse is slow [at the moment of conception], so, naturally, will their children be leperous, epileptic, dirty, or physically imperfect, as is often seen; and no one wants to produce children like that. The doctors therefore recommend that this conjunction take place only when one is sober, imperturbed, and as happy as possible, and they counsel its taking place at night after the first digestion, when you are neither empty nor full of harsh foods, and free and unoppressed by sleep. They also praise getting the woman to desire this conjunction ardently. They have many [physical] laws which show that when a seed generated with excessive heat is planted in cold ground it will wait for more temperate air before germinating. But it would take too much time to recite all their precepts, and perhaps I should have greater regard for whom I'm talking to. . . .

Lionardo: That's fine with me; I'll be happy to go on with the argument. But still, I'll be as brief as the matter will allow, for time is growing short. Listen, then: our house is, as we have said, well-populated with young people. We must see to it that they are kept busy and not allowed to be idle and thus grow lazy, for idleness is useless and scarcely praiseworthy among the young, and it is of great danger to the whole family. There's no need for me to stir up an abhorrence of idleness among you, for I see you all very studious and active; I want only to give you still more encouragement to go on as you have already, plunging into all kinds of difficult and laborious undertakings in order to acquire virtue and merit fame. Just reflect a moment: have you ever run into anyone, or could you ever imagine a man, not necessarily desirous of fame but at least to some degree afraid of shame, who did not enormously dislike idleness and inactivity? Have you ever run into one who thought it possible to acquire any virtue or any dignity without ardent application in the most perfect arts, without the most strenuous effort, without much sweat expended in manly and difficult exercises? Certainly anyone who wants to obtain the ornaments of fame and praise must flee from and fight against idleness and inertia as if they were the most deadly and harmful enemies. The bosom of the idle has always been the nest and den of vice; and nothing can be found more pestiferous and harmful to public as well as private affairs as lazy and inactive citizens. From idleness is born lust; from lust is born the disdain of laws; from disobedience to law proceeds the ruin and extermination of the land. Arrogance, pride, and every kind of avarice and rapacious desire will spread through the citizenry the moment it begins to look with contempt upon the ways and customs of the country. The robbers, murderers, and adulterers will know no bounds, and every form of criminal and pernicious license will prevail.

Thus idleness, the cause of such evils, deserves the hatred of all good men. Even if idleness were not, moreover, what everyone knows it to be— the pernicious enemy of good morals and the original fashioner of every vice, is it possible that there be any man in this world, even one of limited intelligence, who would not be anxious to exercise his mind, his body, and his virtues? What difference is there between a man given completely to idleness and a detached limb, a statue, or a putrid cadaver? As far as I'm concerned, anyone incapable of feeling honor and shame, anyone unable to move his body and his mind with a certain prudence and self-consciousness, can hardly be considered fully alive; and I would call not alive at all whoever buries himself in idleness and inertia and who avoided all good studies and works. And I would not consider worthy of life anyone who did not direct all his feelings and motions to the acquisition of virtue and praise. The idle man who gets old in inactivity and inertia without offering anything useful either to his relatives or to his country will certainly be thought of by those of manly character as little more than a worthless tree trunk; for it is obvious that all living things are endowed with movement and sentiments, without which qualities nothing can truly be said to be alive. If you have a pair of eyes and yet keep them closed and do not use them as they are meant to be used, you might just as well have no eyes at all. Similarly whoever does not put into operation those attributes by which the existence of life can be distinguished might just as well be considered devoid of life itself. Look at the grass, the plants, and the trees, how they exert themselves to grow and to offer something pleasing and useful to us. All other animals—fish, birds, and those with four feet—constantly keep themselves busy with some sort of work; they are never idle, and they are forever justifying the existence of life in themselves and their utility to other creatures. And by their very activity they are continually demonstrating that they are alive and are not useless to other creatures. One prepares a nest for its young, another provides food for its offspring; all strive by their very nature as if impelled by the hate of idleness; and all flee from inertia into some kind of good work. So it seems to me that man also is born not to lie down and rot, but to stand up and act.

I certainly don't see how anyone could be so stupid as to suppose that mind, intellect, judgment, memory, spiritual appetites, reason, wisdom, and the other divine forces and powers by which men overcome the power, quickness, and ferocity of all other animals, were not meant to be used frequently. I cannot but dislike the opinion of the philosopher Epicurus, according to whom God's supreme happiness consists in doing nothing. It may well be possible for God to do what is forbidden to mortals, that is, nothing. But I believe that there is nothing more displeasing to God and less permitted to men than inactivity, except for evil itself, of course. I dislike somewhat less the statement of the philosopher Anaxagoras, who, when asked for what reason God had created man, replied: "Man was created to contemplate the heavens, the stars, the sun, and all the other marvelous works of the divinity." And this statement is at least in part confirmed by what we observe in other animals, who are usually curved over with their heads bent toward the earth, intent upon the pasture; while only man stands up straight, with his head and face erect, just as if nature had made him for the sole purpose of observing and noting the various parts of the heavens. The Stoics used to say that nature placed man in the world to be a speculator and an operator. Chrisippus believed that all things were born to be of service to man, and that man was born to provide company and friendship for other men. This opinion is not so different from that of another ancient philosopher, Protagoras, as some people suppose. According to him, man is the measure of all things. Plato, writing to Architas the Tarentine,[12] said that men were born for the sake of men, and that we owe part of ourselves to our country, part to our families, and part to our friends. But it would take a long time to follow up all the opinions of the

12. Architas was a famous statesman and mathematician born in Taranto around 430 B.C. Plato's letter to him, Epistle 9, is usually considered a forgery. All the other references in these paragraphs can be found in the footnotes to the Pellegrini-Spongano edition, pp. 191 ff.

ancient philosophers on this question; and it would take even longer to add the many views of all our own theologians in more recent times. I have mentioned only those who have occurred to me at this moment; but as you see, they all agree in preferring in men not idleness and inactivity, but work and action. And you will be convinced of the truth of this common opinion if you look closely at how man, more than any other animal, exerts himself from earliest infancy through all the ages of his life, so that even those people who will have nothing to do with any good or manly work are at least doing something even when they are amusing themselves in idleness. Whoever, moreover, praises idleness and puts it before the [active] use of the body, mind, and reason is mistaken enough; but he is still more mistaken, so I think anyway, who accepts as true the opinion of the father mourning the death of his daughter—of the father, that is, who consoles himself by saying that we mortals are born to suffer in this life the just penalty for our horrible crimes and sins! I much prefer the opinion of Aristotle, who proposed that man is a mortal god: he is happy because he understands by reason and acts by virtue.

But above all I approve of that most true and sound opinion of those who hold man to be created in order to please God and to discover a first and true principle behind all things—behind the great variety and great differences among animals, for instance, in their beauty, their number, their form, their stature, clothing, and color. They hold man's purpose also to be that of joining the whole of nature to praise God for the so many varied yet consonant harmonies he observes in the sweet voices, verses, and songs of all living things. They say man is meant also to thank God, since he notices how many things are produced in nature that are of use to him for casting out illness and preserving good health. They say he should fear and honor God, for he hears, sees, and understands the sun, the stars, the movements of the heavens, and thunder and lightning, all of which he realizes have been ordered for his sake and created and given to him by God alone. Add to this how much man owes to God and how much he should strive to repay Him by good works for having been given a soul far greater and far more excellent than that of all other living things on earth. Nature, that is, God, has made man partly celestial and divine, and partly an animal, although one much stronger and nobler than any other; He has accorded him form and members perfectly suited to all his movements, as well as the ability to recognize and flee whatever might be harmful to him. He has given him the means of discourse and enough wisdom to learn what is useful and necessary to him; He has endowed him with sufficient motion and feeling, desire and incentive, to follow what is beneficial and flee what is improper and dangerous. He has granted him intelligence, ability to learn, memory, and reason—divine things, these, perfectly fashioned for investigating, distinguishing, and knowing what is to be avoided and what is to be sought out in order to keep himself alive. And to all these numerous and inestimable gifts God has added in the soul and mind of man something quite as precious: a sense of modesty, a fear of shame, and a desire for praise, which serve to moderate cupidity and check excessive appetite. God also has established in the souls of men the firm bond of human society—justice, equity, liberality, and love, by which he may gain the grace and praise of other men and the mercy and clemency of God. God has then placed enough strength in virile breasts [to enable them] to put up with any difficulty, any adversity, and any shock of fortune, to realize even the most difficult enterprises, and to overcome sorrow and the fear of death. He has given us the strength, stability, constancy, power, and disdain for transitory things by which we can honor and serve Him as we ought to—by the practice of justice, that is, by mercy and moderation, and by every other perfect and praiseworthy action. Let us then be persuaded that man is born not to mourn in idleness, but to exert himself in magnificent and great actions by which he can both please and honor God and attain for himself the happiness that comes from the possession of perfect virtue.

It may seem to you that I've gotten a bit far from the subject; but all these considerations have been necessary to convince you of the truth of the point I was making. But let's not argue about which of the opinions I have mentioned is the best and the one we should adhere to. Let us say rather that as far as we are concerned man has been given life in order to be virtuous and happy. For whoever can call himself happy is certainly one who is good to other men; and whoever is good to others is certainly pleasing also to God. Whoever misuses the things of this world is harmful to other men and displeasing to God; and who is displeasing to God certainly cannot consider himself happy. We can assert, then, that man is created in order to make use of the things of nature and is endowed by the same nature with the ability to do so; and that man is born to be happy. But many people do not know of this happiness, or at least come up with many different opinions concerning it. Some think happiness to consist simply in being in a position where they no longer lack anything; and so they chase after riches, power, and possessions. Others suppose happiness to be the absence of troubles, cares, and annoyances; and they abandon themselves to delights and sensual pleasures. Others place happiness on top of a steep mountain, where it is more difficult to reach but where it is at least farther removed from sensual appetites; they place it, that is, in being honored and esteemed by other men, and they undertake great labors and actions and give themselves over to long vigils and virile exercises. Perhaps we might add that happiness is not too much different from exerting oneself virtuously and using things moderately and reasonably. For whoever uses things and himself with temerity and without order inevitably ends up in error, and the misuse of himself and of the gifts of God leads him just as far astray as do vice and impiety.[13] This occurs when an evil man tries to go further in what he has undertaken than is required or permitted by honesty and right reason. Wanting to get rich by tricks from the sole motive of avarice, wanting to get honor through vice, and wanting to sit around free of troubles in sensual idleness seems to me nothing but wanting to misuse the things of this world in order to harm men, to displease God, and to be unhappy and miserable: all of which those of us who are not completely lacking in good sense should avoid, and even more so those of us who wish to bring happiness to our whole family.

Let everyone then first seek happiness for himself and then for his family. Happiness, as I said, cannot be obtained without the constant practice of good, just, and virtuous works. Those works are good and just that not only bring harm to no one, but also are beneficial to many. Those works are virtuous in which there is not the least suspicion of dishonesty; those works are the best which benefit the greatest number; and those works are the most virtuous which are executed with the greatest amount of manliness and honesty. It seems to me that whenever we engage in any manly and honest exercise, we would do well to think out very carefully how far it will procure happiness for us. Not everyone is able to procure happiness with the same facility. Nature did not make all men of the same stamp, of the same mind, or of the same will; nor did she make them all equally suited for or capable of doing the same things. She determined that what I cannot do, you can, and that the ability that is lacking in you can be found in another. Why? So that I will have need of you, you of another, he of still another, and someone else of me again; and so that this need of one man for another will cause us to form among ourselves a bond of public amity. And perhaps this need accounts for the formation of republics and the establishment of laws, much more than . . .[14] fire and water, which are said to have been the cause of union among mortals through law, reason, and custom. . . .

We have pointed out that young people should not sit around doing nothing but should pick out some honest occupation that will keep them busy in manly work, particularly one that will be of the greatest possible use to the family and its good name. Let them choose then an occupation

13. "E tanto più a lungi si truova addutto errando quanto di sé e de' doni d'Iddio peggio meriterà con vizii e impietà": Alberti's sentence is not quite clear.
14. The hiatus appears in all manuscripts.

that is fitting to the nature and the fortune of our family, and let them work at it until the family attains the highest level of excellence in that branch of activity.

Now, then, since wealth, which is the end for which most people work, is of the greatest use in obtaining praise in whatever is undertaken and in acquiring friendship, honor, and fame, it is most appropriate that we give some thought to how wealth is to be acquired and maintained. Wealth, after all, is one of the four things that we have called essential to making the family happy and keeping it so. Let us begin then by accumulating wealth. Perhaps, indeed, this is a good moment to talk about this matter, now that it's getting dark outside.[15] No occupation, for anyone who has an open and liberal mind (*magno e liberale*), seems to me less splendid than those instituted for the purposes of amassing wealth. If you give the matter some thought and consideration and if you try to remember which occupations are suited to making money, you will find that they consist in nothing other than in buying and selling, lending and receiving.[16] It may well be that some of you, even though you are completely free of small-mindedness, may well think that all these occupations aimed solely at earning money are somewhat humble and rather lacking in those qualities that gain praise and authority. Yet, in truth, selling is nothing but an exchange (*cosa mercenaria*): you serve the requirements of the buyer, you are paid for your trouble, and you receive the difference above the price you yourself paid for the object. In this way you are really selling not the commodity itself, but your labor. The commodity has been changed for you into money; for your labor you receive what is paid beyond the wholesale price (*soprapagato*). Lending likewise would be but praiseworthy liberality if you required no compensation (*premio*); but it would not be an occupation for gain.

Some people think that these occupations, which they call pecuniary, are never wholly aboveboard and that they never can be carried on without a good bit of lying and without frequent use of dirty deals and false contracts. So they say all these affairs are ugly and mercenary and ought to be shunned by liberal minds. But those who judge all pecuniary occupations in this manner are wrong, in my opinion. If acquiring wealth is not as

15. This is what sense I make out of the sentence, using Pellegrini-Spongano's *si confarà* instead of Grayson's *s'aconfarà*; but it's still not clear just what the hour has to do with the subject. The remark is purely an aside, at any rate.

16. *Prestare e riscuotere*, i.e., commerce and banking. The generic names had not yet been introduced into the language in Alberti's time, even though the respective institutions were still the foundation of the Italian economy. See Raymond de Roover, *The Medici Bank* (New York University Press, 1948).

glorious as some greater occupations, there is no need to look down upon one whom nature has not given a special aptitude for such magnificent activities and who applies himself to those activities in which he is not incompetent and which everyone admits are most useful to both the commonwealth and the family. Wealth is able to acquire friendship and praise by serving those who need it. Wealth can bring fame and authority by being used for grand and noble things with much largesse and magnificence. And in moments of great need and emergency nothing is more useful to your country than the wealth of private citizens, as we learn from daily experience.[17] It's not always possible to maintain those who defend the liberty and dignity of the country with arms and blood merely with stipends paid from the public treasury, nor can republics grow in authority and dominion without immense expenditure. Indeed, Messer Cipriano Alberti, our ancestor, used to say that the rule over other people is bought from fortune at the price of gold and blood. It seems to me that this statement of so prudent a man can be accepted as true. Certainly the fortunes of private citizens are to be considered of the greatest utility when they are used to fulfill the needs of the country. And, as our Messer Benedetto Alberti used to say, a treasury is full not when it has a great number of loans outstanding and extensive sources of taxation, but when it can count on the affection, the faith, and the justice of the rich citizens.[18]

I don't think then that we need to listen to those who look down on all money-making occupations. Just look at our house of the Alberti: as it excels in all professions, so also in this one, pecuniary though it might be, it has flourished throughout Western Europe (*Ponente*) and in many different parts of the world, always with honesty and integrity; hence we have acquired no little fame among all nations and a preeminence not incommensurate with our merits. For in all our business dealings no one was ever found who would permit even the slightest malpractice. We have always observed the greatest simplicity and the plainest truth in every contract; and thus we have come to be recognized as great merchants both in and outside of Italy, in Spain, in the West, in Syria, in Greece, and in all the ports of the world. And we Alberti have always been most attentive to the

17. Lacking an adequate fiscal structure, the Florentine Republic often resorted to forced loans, laid proportionally on individual citizens according to their property and incomes, rather than to an increase in regular taxes. But Alberti may be thinking of similar circumstances in the Roman Republic. In the following remarks the examples of Rome and Florence are probably both present in his mind, for he does not, like his successor Machiavelli, attempt to distinguish between the two.

18. Machivelli's position on this matter is exactly the opposite of Alberti's: a poor state with rich citizens is on the verge of collapse. Cf. *Discourses*, 3:25.

needs of our country. You'll find that of every thirty-two cents our country paid out in those times [19] at least one was always furnished by us. That's a lot of money; but it is much less than the affection, goodwill, and promptness with which we always served our country. Thus we have acquired a good name, fame, and prestige among all, although admittedly we have earned more love and goodwill among foreigners than we ever have among our fellow citizens.

But this is no time to bewail the misfortunes that have befallen us. Let us rejoice rather in those things we Alberti can justly be proud of. It is fitting, Battista and Carlo, that I speak of this matter to you, who are such excellent and outstanding men—that I recall to your memory the praiseworthy acts of our family, so that you will continue to be, as you are now, full of the longing, the affection, and the will to do all that is in you to magnify still further the dignity, authority, fame, and glory of your house. For it would be shameful not to maintain what has been won by our ancestors. I say our family can be proud that for over two hundred years it was always counted among the richest families of Florence. Neither in the memory of our elders nor in the papers in the family archives will you find a trace of any who were not great, famous, truthful, good, and honest merchants. Nor in the annals of our country will you see wealth so great maintained for so long with so few blemishes. Indeed, I would even venture to assert that in this land of ours none but our Alberti have ever passed on a great fortune to the grandchildren. The fortunes of other families have often gone up in smoke, as the popular saying goes, in but a few days; and others have been left with nothing but poverty, misery,[20] and infamy. I don't want to take time now to point out examples nor to figure out the causes of the wiping out of great fortunes among our fellow citizens. I can think of an infinite number of such cases, which are as horrifying as they are true. Far be it from me to speak with anything but honor and reverence of the victims of such misfortune, however; for it is to be attributed to fate rather than to any moral fault. The Cerchi, the Peruzzi, the Scali, the Spini, the Ricci, and a huge number of other families once great and powerful in our country, and still shining with all the noble virtues, were once possessors of limitless riches; but they have since fallen by a twist of fortune into unhappiness and even into dire need.[21] But no one has ever been able to com-

19. Before the expulsion of the Alberti from Florence in 1387.

20. *Povertà, miseria*: both terms should be rendered by the English term "*poverty*"; but the first included in Italian the connotation of the monastic virtue *povertas*, while the second implied that the same moral virtues are absent. Neither really denotes the purely psychological state implied in the English word *misery*.

21. The reference is to the bank crash of the 1340s, the memory of which was apparently still very much alive in Alberti's day.

plain that he has ever been treated other than justly and kindly[22] by our family, even though we ourselves have been badly treated by fortune. There was never any Alberti who in his business transactions ever broke faith or departed from due honesty; and this worthy custom will always, as far as I can see, be observed among us, as long as we are not avaricious, unjust, or lazy in our business transactions. And it seems to me that the reason that our family continues honestly to expand its wealth[23] is to be found not so much in the prudence and sagacity of its members as in a special reward bestowed by God.[24] Thus God, to whom honesty and justice are pleasing above all, gives us the grace[25] to enjoy the fruits of our virtues in long prosperity.

Why this long discussion? Only to show you that there are a great number of honest and praiseworthy occupations by which you can gain no little wealth. One of these is the work of a merchant, as you have seen. You probably have already guessed that there are other occupations as honest and profitable. What are they? Let's put them all out here before us and then pick out which will make us the wealthiest. Those occupations that do not bring in [any immediate] profit but [in the long run] make you wealthy[26] and those that bring in frequent and large profits, all these are conducive to getting rich. Acquiring wealth honestly by gain alone consists, if I'm not mistaken, in taking in what is gotten by our own industry, not what is given to us by fortune or by the grace or favor of another. On what does getting poor depend then? I'll admit it: on fortune. But when we are talking about industry, we can leave fortune aside. If, then, riches proceed from what we earn, and if earnings are the result of our diligence and hard work, then poverty on the contrary follows from just the opposite qualities—from negligence, laziness, and tardiness: which evils are not to be found in external things, nor in fortune, but in you yourself. Getting poor is also the necessary consequence of too much spending and of a prodigality that amounts to tossing money away. The opposite of spending and negligence, it seems to me, is the careful management of things, in other words, economy.[27] Economy, then, will maintain wealth. So we see that to become

22. *Giuste e benigne*: Alberti uses the Florentine word with the Latin adverbial ending.

23. *Onestamente avanzano*: the emphasis is on the adverb.

24. *Ma veramente premio d'Iddio*.

25. *Grazia*, in the theological, not the aesthetic sense of the word.

26. The meaning is not clear in the original: this is one possible interpretation. Good old Uncle Lionardo, just like Leon Battista and most other humanists, is probably trying to avoid the use of abstract categories and is deliberately obscuring them in chattiness and imprecision. Moreover the language had not yet been endowed with such technical terms as "long-term capital investment."

27. *Masserizia*, not *economia*, which Alberti will use in Book 3 to render Xenophon's term *economy*. Don't confuse Alberti's use of the word with its modern meaning.

wealthy we must first earn money and then save what we've earned by the use of reason and economy.

But let's speak first of gain and then of economy. Gain comes partly from us, partly from things outside us. Our industry, intelligence, and other such virtues placed in our souls make us capable of getting wealth, particularly in such occupations as navigation, architecture, medicine, and the like, which require above all judgment and the functioning of the mind. But the work of the body is also capable of earning money, as in the case of all the mechanical and building occupations, and that of a salesman and of one who works with his hands, where gain is the result of the sweat of the worker. Those occupations are also capable of earning money in which our minds and bodies work together, such as painting, sculpture, playing the cithara, and so forth. All these ways of earning money, which we call *arti*, are those that always remain with us. They cannot perish by shipwreck; indeed, they swim away with the naked survivors, and constantly keep company with the very life that is the nurse and custodian of our praise[28] and fame. Those things outside us that bring us gain are, on the other hand, subject to the rule of fortune, such as finding hidden treasures, coming into an inheritance, receiving donations, etc., which not a few men hope for. Many people make it their business to get the friendship of lords and to make friends with rich citizens solely in the hope of obtaining some money from them: about which more in due season. All those occupations are under the sway of fortune, human industry has nothing to do with them. Our expectations and desires can be fulfilled only by chance and by the general course of things; and our work and judgment can do nothing for us unless fortune decides to be liberal and generous. Outside of us are also placed those earnings that come from things, such as usury, and what we get from oxen, mules, forests, and in Tuscany, from heaths,[29] all of which things bear fruit without much effort or industry. From these [two categories] proceed an almost infinite number of occupations, which depend upon one or another of the elements I have mentioned—soul, body, fortune, and material objects (*cose*). It would take too long, and it would hardly be necessary for me to list all these occupations, since with a bit of intelligence you can figure them all out for yourselves. But since we have them all out here on the table before us, let's pick out those that are the most suitable for a magnificent and honored family like our own.

28. *Le lode*: here as elsewhere *praise* means a quality that can exist within a person as well as a manifestation of the recognition of some quality within him on the part of others. I maintain a literal translation to avoid such clumsy and imprecise expressions as *praiseworthiness*.

29. *Scopeti*—low bushes, the twigs of which are used to make brooms and brushes (*scopa*). Alberti will think somewhat better of agriculture as a source of revenue in Book 3, after he has read Xenophon.

Some say the most praiseworthy occupations are those in which fortune holds no sway whatsoever and in which the mind and body are perfectly free. I've always considered this opinion both manly and correct; for if fortune cannot interfere with these occupations, they will remain yours as long as you like; and since they are subject wholly to your will, they can always be a source of utility and happiness. And I am particularly pleased with the liberty that the holders of this opinion find [in such occupations], for they thus apparently exclude usury, avarice, and all vicious and mercenary gain.[30] As you know, a soul subject to avarice cannot be called free (*libero*), and no mercenary work can be considered worthy of a free (*libero*)[31] and noble soul. But I'm not sure that I can agree that some bit of fortune is not present in all our undertakings. I won't say I'm perfectly sure of myself in this matter, for I want to avoid making mistakes; but I think I can say that there is no famous occupation in which fortune does not play some part, at least in the beginning. In military affairs I believe it can be said that victory is the daughter of fortune. The literary occupations also are found to be subject to a thousand blows of fortune: your father dies, your relatives turn out to be jealous, hard, and inhuman; you are struck by poverty; you fall into some misfortune—so that you can't deny that fortune holds as much dominion over your studies as it does over other human affairs, since you cannot pursue them without the help of a good number of things that in turn are subject to fortune.[32] Thus in all glorious and famous occupations you do well not to exclude fortune but to control it with prudence and wisdom.[33]

You may say, let's then talk about those earnings in which industry and prudence together with attentive care have been effective. All right, but I will not be moved from the opinion [I just expressed] even if I also maintain that insofar as gain is the result of our industry, it will be least where our industry and wisdom are the smallest. Small businesses, no matter how much effort you put into them, will never give you great profits; but small businesses can become large ones as our activities increase with our effort

30. Here *mercenary* (*mercennarii guadagni*) has a pejorative connotation that elsewhere is missing; and *usury* (*usure*) is carefully distinguished from what now is called *interest* and what Alberti would probably call *soprapagato*—though he is doing all he can to avoid the issue. *Liberty* (*libertà*) is here used in secularized version of the Pauline or Augustine sense to indicate freedom from the bond of sin, or as Alberti would say to avoid theological complications, of vice.

31. Here Alberti is apparently mixing up the two meanings of the word: that given in the last note and that implied in the English word *magnanimous*. The latter, as can be observed, is by far the more frequent meaning.

32. This passage is obviously autobiographical, or at least a sharp reminder to his family of the shoddy treatment the author has usually received from them.

33. Cf. Machiavelli, *Prince*, 24–25.

and hard work. In large businesses, then, are to be found large earnings; and large businesses are often subject to the interference of fortune, as in the case of our Alberti, when they brought in at one moment from farthest Flanders all the way to Florence enough wool to furnish all the manufacturers of Florence itself and most of Tuscany besides. There's no need for me to remind you of the many other shipments of goods brought to Florence by our family from the uttermost regions of the world at immense expense, across steep mountains and difficult passes. You certainly don't think that all that wool arrived without being touched by the hand of fortune! How many dangers had to be overcome, how many rivers [had to be crossed], how many difficulties [faced] before the merchandise was finally safe! At every minute it was threatened by thieves, tyrants, wars, negligence, evil agents, and so forth. This is what happens, in my opinion, in all great undertakings and in all the business affairs of so noble and honest a family. Let us be as our ancestors were, and as we Alberti are still and will, I don't doubt, always be in the future. Let them engage in great undertakings and in affairs useful to their country; and let them guard the honor and fame of their family, so that day by day they grow no less in authority and [in the good] grace [of others] than in money and possessions. Let us then do what they have told us to do. In all our affairs, may our souls be free and never enslaved, may our bodies be never subject to any dishonesty or turpitude but always embellished with temperance and modesty; and let us follow in those occupations in which fortune plays, I won't say no part at all, but at least not too great a part. . . .

Book 3

Lionardo: In speaking of economy (*masserizia*), you have so far spoken of the soul and the body. What remains to be discussed is time. And in this matter, Giannozzo, what kind of economy would you propose? Time continually flies away and cannot be retained.

Giannozzo: I have said that economy consists in using things well as well as in preserving them, no? Well then, as far as time is concerned, I would try to use it well and never lose a bit of it. I would use my time as much as possible in engaging in laudable occupations, never in disreputable ones; and I would never spend more time at anything than what is required to do it well. And in order not to lose a second of so precious a thing, I have formulated this rule for myself: I never permit myself any idleness, I shun sleep, I never lie down unless completely overcome with tiredness. For it seems pretty stupid to me to fall down without fighting back or judge yourself defeated without a struggle. This then is what I do: I shun sleep and idleness and I always keep myself busy with something.

And in order not to get one piece of business mixed up with another, in order not to find myself having started several different projects and not finishing any of them, or having done only the least important and having left the more important ones aside, do you know what I do, my sons? Every morning as soon as I get up I think to myself: what will I have to do today? Lots of things. I recall them all and reflect on them, and then I assign a certain time to each one: this one in the morning, that one at midday, and still another in the afternoon. In this way I succeed in doing everything in proper order with the least trouble. Messer Niccolaio Alberti (an alert and busy man if there ever was one) used to say that he had never seen a diligent man who did not walk slowly. Just the opposite may seem to be true; but really, when I think about it, I'm sure he was right. Time flies only for the negligent man. He responds only to his immediate necessity and desires. Having lost the proper moment, he is forced to do in a hurry and with difficulty what he could have done more easily earlier at a more convenient hour. Remember this, my sons: there is no job that is not difficult to do at the wrong time no matter how capable we are of doing it. Grain seed, plants, fruit, flowers—all these things are offered to you at the proper season; outside of the season they cannot be found without great difficulty. Therefore, my sons, observe the time;[34] and according to time distribute your affairs and take them up in sequence without ever losing a single hour. I could point out to you what a precious thing time is; but I will leave this to another who can do it with more polished eloquence, with greater intellectual force, and with more abundant doctrine than I possess. Do then what I do. In the morning I arrange the whole day, during the day I follow out what is required of me, and then in the evening, before I retire, I go over all that I have done during the day. At that moment, if I find that I have neglected something that can be done right away, I do it on the spot. Better to lose sleep than time, that is, the proper time for each matter. Eating, sleeping, and the like I can make up for the next day; but the proper moment for a particular affair [will be lost forever]. As long as I have arranged all my business according to a schedule, and as long as I have not been negligent in attending to it, I very seldom find that I have either left something undone or that I have given something more attention than it deserves. But if I discover some omission that cannot then be remedied, I consider my discovery a lesson and try to figure out how I can avoid a similar waste of time in the future. Thus I do with these three things just as you have heard: I [strive to] use my mind, my body, and my time in one way only, that is, I use them well. I try to conserve them and not waste any of them; and to this

---

34. *Si vuole osservare il tempo*.

task I give all my attention, keeping myself as busy and as alert as I can, for it seems to me that they are very precious possessions and more properly mine than anything else. Riches, power, and political authority are given not by man, no, but by fortune; and they belong to man only insofar as fortune permits him to make use of them. . . .

Lionardo: While listening to you speak, Giannozzo, I seem to find in you that magnificent and powerful will which I have always thought to be greater and worthier of a virile soul than any other kind of human will or appetite. I understand that you think the best life one which is lived by and for one's self[35]—a plan of life worthy of a royal spirit who can live a full life without depending on anyone else and who is satisfied with whatever fortune chooses to share with him. There are some whom I, along with you, would reproach: those who think that spiritual greatness consists in setting out on difficult and hard enterprises and taking on the hardest and most disagreeable works for the sole purpose of getting more property than any other citizen. Of such men there are not a few in our own as in all other countries, particularly those who have grown up amid the ancient liberty of our city or who have filled their hearts with a bitter hatred of all tyranny, and who, not satisfied with the common liberty (of the laws), aspire to more liberty, or license, than is accorded to all others. And it is true, Giannozzo, that he who seeks to sit among the magistrates and judge public affairs, not in order to win the praise and good graces of good men by acts of will and reason but in order to gratify their immoderate appetites by enjoying a position of authority over others, shows himself not to be a good citizen. And I maintain that the good citizen will love tranquillity, not only for himself but also for all other good men; that he will enjoy his own private comfort[36] but will love just as much that of his fellow citizens; that he will desire unity, peace, quiet, and tranquillity in his own house, but he will desire them even more in his country and in the republic. These things cannot be preserved unless those citizens who are rich or wise or noble work harder than the other free but less fortunate citizens. But even the republic itself cannot be maintained where the good citizens are interested only in their own private comfort. Wise men tell us that good citizens must take up public office and suffer the troubles that their country lays on them and overlook the stupidity of other men in order to contribute to public well-being and watch over the good of all the citizens and not yield before evil men, whose improbity would pervert everything if good men were

35. *Vivere a sé stessi*—only the circumlocution can approximate the full meaning of the original.
36. The same word *ozii, ozio*, here used without the pejorative connotation that it always has in the first two books, where it has been rendered as *idleness*.

negligent, and who would make it impossible to carry on either public or private affairs.[37]

So you see, Giannozzo, that this praiseworthy proposal or rule of life of yours, to live alone in privacy and honesty,[38] may be excellent and generous; but it is not wholly to be recommended to those desirous of glory. Fame is born not in the quiet of private life but in the bustle of public affairs; glory arises in the market place; and praise and honor are nourished by words and judgments uttered in the midst of the people. Fame shuns solitude and private retreats; it is seated rather in the theaters and public assemblies, where the name of him shines forth who with much sweat and with the assiduous study of good things draws forth [the public good] from silence and shadows, from ignorance and vice.

Hence I would never reproach anyone who, along with other virtuous works and studies and with a truly religious spirit and the strict observance of good morals, should seek to ingratiate himself with some honest and perfect citizen. Nor would I ever call servitude doing what is expected of me. Young people, after all, are always expected to revere their elders and to seek in them the fame and dignity that have earned them love and respect. Nor would I accuse one of having a tyrannical disposition whose constant occupation lay in laborious and generous enterprises because it is just such enterprises that lead to honor and glory. But perhaps it is because you observe no one among those who occupy positions of political authority in our country who has not a passionate mind and a servile soul— perhaps this is why you condemn those who seek to be numbered among such bad, nay, reprehensible citizens. But this is just what I do desire, Giannozzo: to merit fame, to acquire a good reputation, to find myself honored, loved, and entrusted with authority, and to be the object of the benevolence of the citizens of my country—for all of this I would never try to avoid the enmity of any bad or iniquitous citizen, no matter who he is. And whenever it became necessary to execute some sentence with extreme severity, I would certainly consider it an act of great piety to exterminate thievery and every kind of vice and to stamp out the slightest flame of unjust greed, even at the price of my own blood. But since it is not possible at the moment for us to assume such a position, let us nonetheless continue to aspire to that which you may think to be of little value, but which to me has always been preferable to the best of good fortune: honor, that is, and fame. But, I will add, let us not fix our desires solely upon that which for

37. *Cose . . . publiche . . . private; cose* here has the same meaning as the Latin *res* in the term *res publica*; the English *affairs* is not wholly adequate.

38. *Privata onestà*: a direct translation would be awkward in English; but neither the word nor, alas! even the concept of *privacy* exists in Italian.

the moment we cannot by any amount of work obtain.[39] Let us do as you have taught us: let us await the proper season. Perhaps then our patience and modesty will gain us some reward; and the injustice and iniquity of our evil and passionate enemies, who still take no rest in pursuing us everywhere with imprecations and cruelty, will draw upon them, through God's justice, a worthy and well-deserved vengeance. In the meantime, let us continue, Battista, and you, Carlo, with virtue and study, and with all our skill to deserve praise and fame; let us prepare ourselves for being useful to the republic and to our country so that, when the moment comes, we can offer our services in such a way that neither Giannozzo nor these our temperate and modest elders will be ashamed to see us honored in the first places of the state.

Giannozzo: This is just what I would want you to do, my sons, and just what I hope and expect you will do, for thus you will acquire great honor. But let me remind you that you must never—and I am not speaking here of acquiring honor, because for that purpose it is necessary to leave many things aside—you must never while governing others forget to govern yourselves. And while you are taking care of public affairs, do not forget to take care of your private ones too. I remind you of this because whoever is wanting at home will find himself even more wanting abroad, and the commonwealth will not assist you in your private misfortunes. Honors enjoyed in public do not feed the family at home. Keep a diligent eye on your domestic concerns as much as needs be; and give yourself to public concerns not in accordance with the enticements of ambition and arrogance, but in accordance with your own virtue and with the good graces of your fellow citizens.

Lionardo: You have done well to remind us, Giannozzo, of what is necessary in this matter. We will do as you advise us. . . .

6. Alessandra Macinghi negli Strozzi, *Letters to Filippo degli Strozzi*

Alessandra Macinghi negli Strozzi (b. 1407) was the daughter of Filippo de Niccolò Macinghi, one of the wealthiest citizens of Florence. Her mother, Caterina di Alberto Alberti, died when Alessandra was still a girl and was a descendent of the equally prominent Alberti family. (See the

---

39. Because the family is in exile.

From *Lettere di una gentildonna fiorentina del secolo XVI [sic] ai figliuoli esuli*, edited by Cesare Guasti (Florence: Sansoni, 1877), pp. 33–39, 99–106, 177–83, 547–52. Translated for this volume by Lydia G. Cochrane.

introduction to the selections in this volume from Leon Battista Alberti.)
Nothing is known of Alessandra's childhood, although it is clear from her
correspondence and account books that she learned how to read, write,
and perform rudimentary arithmetic operations—abilities that proved in-
dispensable for widows like Alessandra, who were responsible for administering the domestic household as well as their own patrimony. In 1422
she was married to Matteo di Simone Strozzi, a wealthy wool merchant,
humanist, and member of another of the most wealthy and powerful families in Florence. Since she was only sixteen at the time and Matteo only
twenty-five, this marriage was somewhat atypical. The average age of
marriage for young women in Florence in this period was eighteen; for
men, thirty-two. Similarly, the dowry of 1600 florins accompanying Alessandra to her husband was considerably higher than the 1000 to 1200-
florin dowries characteristic of most upper-class Florentines. But one of
the main purposes of marriage was amply fulfilled. From 1426 to 1436,
Alessandra gave birth almost yearly: Andreoula in 1426, Simone in 1427,
Filippo in 1428, Piero in 1429, Lorenzo in 1430, Caterina in 1432, Alessandra in 1434, Matteo in 1436.

Matteo's fortunes declined in 1434 when he, along with several other
Strozzi, found themselves on the opposite side of the allies of Cosimo
de' Medici. He suffered punitive taxation as well as exile. Alessandra
joined her exiled husband in Pesaro, where they resided in comfort
thanks to the generous hospitality of Archbishop Pandolfo Malatesta.
After his death from plague in 1435, she returned to Florence, pregnant,
with four surviving children, and with few financial resources beyond the
dowry, which legally became hers again after the death of her husband.
Her plight was similar to that of many other contemporary women. The
census of Florence taken in 1427 and known as the *catasto* reveals that
husbands tended to predecease their wives, and that one in four adult
women were widows living in comparative poverty. By law all of a husband's estates went to his surviving sons, except for those portions ear-
marked for his daughters' dowries and special legacies, and except for
that portion equivalent to his wife's dowry. Alessandra's financial hardship
was compounded by the fact that first her sons inherited not their father's
fortune but his tax debts, and second, that when they reached the age of
eighteen they too fell under their father's ban of exile. Supported by their
mother, who liquidated her property to provide them with capital, and by
their relatives, who provided them with commercial opportunities, they
eventually restored their family's lost wealth, and after their readmission
to Florence, its former social position. Indeed the Strozzi Palace in Florence stands as testimony to the vision of grandeur and extraordinary
wealth accumulated by Filippo Strozzi.

The epistolary legacy of the Renaissance includes many letters of wives of merchants and public figures. Alessandra Strozzi's seventy-two letters, written to her sons between 1447 and just before her death in 1471, are an exceptional source for the social history of Renaissance Florence.

Letter 2

To Filippo degli Strozzi in Naples
In the name of God, 4 November 1448

I have had your letter of August 8 in the last few days, and I haven't answered sooner because for a month now I've been suffering from intestinal problems (*la scesa*). Writing bothers me these days, as I'm getting older and am in worse health day by day. But I don't yet have to worry about writing you, for I'm dictating to Matteo to give him practice in letter writing. When he writes slowly and puts his mind on what he's doing, he writes well. Antonio Strozzi[1] said as much, and Marco,[2] when I showed them some pages he had written, said that he writes a proper letter. But when he writes rapidly, you'd say it wasn't the same hand: there's a black and white difference between the two. I keep telling him that he should write more slowly. Mention to him when you write him to keep working on it; it will do him good. And that he should be good and respectful, because he is really impressed (*teme*) when you write him. And do write him often, so he can have a reason to write to you. And when you write Marco, put in a word for Matteo, and the same for Antonio degli Strozzi. That way, both of them will give him good guidance and he will pay more respectful attention to them than he does to me. May God give every one [of you] the grace and virtue I wish for you.

I had a letter today from Lorenzo dated 28 September, brought by Pagolo Salterelli, that tells me Lorenzo was supposed to leave for London on September 21; but the companions with whom he was going to travel left without saying a word to him, so he was left stranded. This is what Lorenzo writes me, adding that he thinks it will be a while before he can find traveling companions. Now we're in winter and he still hasn't left. He could spend all winter waiting to leave, and winter is a poor time for such a long trip on horseback. I don't know how he's going to stay at Vignone until spring, if it comes to that. Besides, I really don't much like the idea of his

---

1. Antonio di Benedetto Strozzi was a distant relative, but close to Alessandra and her sons whom he served as financial advisor.
2. Marco Parenti, who married Caterina Strozzi in 1447, was Alessandra's son-in-law.

going to London if he can be elsewhere, for I hear there's an epidemic (*la moria*) there, and the same for Bruges. According to what Iacopo[3] writes, eight or ten people a day are dying there, so for the moment it's a poor idea. God give him [the wisdom] to make the right decision. Last August Granello Ricasoli[4] was here, and I asked him all about Lorenzo. He finally told me that Lorenzo had the right instincts but that he needed someone to guide him, because that would do him good. I have written Iacopo what I think needs to be said, and when I hear that he (Lorenzo) has left for London, I will write Lodovico[5] and get him to write to Antonio as needs be. A pen never seems so heavy to me as when I have to write something for your good and I don't do it. However, when it was necessary, I have always taken care of your interests and his, and in good time too. So enough of that.

This summer Piero de' Ricci, of whom I'm very fond, came to see me and I asked him about you. He told me you were very thin but well, that you did not have insomnia, as it should be, and that Niccolò[6] was in as good health as you, all of which pleases me. I beg you to be aware of the favors you have received from him and to be obedient to him even more than if he were your father, for you could never do as much good as to merit what he has done for you. So do your utmost not to be ungrateful to the person who made a man of you. May God give me reason to be pleased with you and with the others.

I haven't written you anything about the flax because I was making Matteo write you. It seems to me that if you have a mind to send it, you may have waited too long to buy it and won't have it as cheaply as you would have a month ago. Nor will you have as good a price for whoever ships it to me as a month ago when Favilla, the carter, promised to bring it to me without charge. Now I don't know what we'll do. Let me know how far you've gotten.

I've had letters from Rome from Andrea Bizeri saying he had sent you some fennel. You must have had it by now. Let him know so he can thank the person who sent it to you.

They say the king has returned there (to Naples). Tell me about it. May God send us peace everywhere.

Do write Lorenzo, who tells me it has been a good while since he's had news of you. Just write him a couple of lines, and remind him to do the right thing, because it always gets you farther.

---

3. Iacopo di Lionardo Strozzi was Matteo's second cousin with whom he had business dealings.

4. A friend of the family. Granello's father had been exiled in 1434.

5. Perhaps Lodovico di Francesco di Benedetto Strozzi, a distant relative.

6. Niccolò di Lionardo Strozzi was Matteo's second cousin with whom he had business dealings.

The *morìa* (epidemic) is doing a good deal of harm here, with four or five a day [dying]. The 29th of last month they were saying that eleven had died of the plague (*segno*). This is bad news for us, who have no way to flee. May it please God to provide for our needs.

You should know that a little house belonging to Messer Palla[7] has been sold in the Comune to Niccolò d'Ainolfo Popoleschi. The house abuts our own on two sides: it's on the corner of the back street—that is, between the stables and our own ground floor back room. The wall of the house gives onto our courtyard. On the right as you come into the courtyard there's our old house, next to the back entrance there's our stable, as you know, and on the left there's the wall of that house. Now Niccolò Popoleschi has resold it to Donato Rucellai, Giovanni's brother,[8] and he has advised me that I have to give written consent for him to buy the house since he cannot draw up a contract without my consent because the only contiguous property is mine. I have answered him that I am aware that I have right of first refusal, that I wanted to write to my in-laws and to you, and that what you decide to do we will do. Let me tell you that if I had ready money it wouldn't get out of my hands. On the other hand, if someone else buys it and should decide to build a wall, it would cut off all the light from our ground floor kitchen, our courtyard, and all the land behind. This house would be worth nothing if the courtyard lost its sunlight. This is why I wanted to write you. Please show this part to Niccolò, who will understand better and remember the little house better than you. It should cost around 70 *fiorini* since it gets a rent of six *fiorini*. I can't write you the exact price because he sold it along with the house owned by Monna Maddalena—or rather the Conte di Poppi[9]—so the house has no set price of its own but will be priced in proportion to the rent. And if I am in 1450 as I am in 1448, I wouldn't let it slip out of my hands, but I would pay for it with the money we will have coming from the city. It would improve this house enormously. I don't say this for myself, as I have little time left to live, but for all of you and your children. It wouldn't take much work, and that little house would really improve this one and make it the handsomest house in the neighborhood. I wouldn't have neglected writing you about it for anything in the world. Let me hear your thoughts, and don't forget to show this to Niccolò, who will understand it all better than you. May God grant you his grace. Nothing more for now. God save you from harm. From your Alessandra in Florence.

We are all well, thank God.

7. Messer Palla di Nofri Strozzi, relative, and a leading political figure as well as the wealthiest citizen of Florence before his exile in 1434.

8. The Rucellai were a prominent, wealthy family. Giovanni Rucellai had married Palla Strozzi's daughter in 1428.

9. Francesco de' Conti Guidi was Conte di Poppi, a fortified town in the mountains east of Florence.

Letter 8

To Filippo degli Strozzi in Naples
In the name of God, 6 November 1450

I wrote you the 28th of last month and sent the letter by Bartolommeo Seragli, whom I know will use it well. Since then I have had yours of the 10th of last month. This will be my answer to it, and to several other letters that you wrote me some time ago but that I didn't answer for lack of a trustworthy carrier.

First, I am sending you four shirts, six handkerchiefs, and a towel, all well wrapped as you shall see, by Favilla, the carter, who owes us about 2 *ducati*. The shirts are cut and sewn in our style and the handkerchiefs and the towel are as we do them here. I didn't make any more shirts because I don't know if you will like them, and the same with the other things. If they aren't to your liking, I can use them for my Matteo, and if you do like them, let me know what you want and I'll send it to you. If God gives me another year to live and if Lesandra leaves home [i.e., marries] I'll fill your house with linens and you'll be in fine shape. Really, as long as there are young girls in the house, you do nothing but work for them, so when she leaves I will have no one to attend to but you three. And when I get the house in a little better shape I would love it if you could think about coming home. You would have no cause to be ashamed with what there is now, and you could do honor to any friend who dropped in to see you at home. But two or three years from now it will all be much better. And I would love to get you a wife: you're of an age now to know how to manage the help and to give me some comfort and consolation. I have none, unless it is living in the hope of [consolation] from you and the others. May God in his mercy grant me my wish. When Niccolò was here he told me he wanted you to come back here soon and to have you take a wife. [He said] that they [Niccolò and his brother Iacopo, with whom Lorenzo was living] would help you get started so you could stay here (since they prefer that you work for them than someone else), and that they would do enough for you to make me consider myself very happy. [He said] all sorts of things that showed he loves you dearly, and to be sure, I think that he will do great things for you if you do well in the office (*stanza*) he opened in Barcelona and give him good reason to praise you. God give him grace to do so.

In a letter you wrote me some time ago you said that Messer Giannozzo,[10] who was ambassador there [in Naples], told you he wanted me to give Caterina to Franco's brother and that I was unwilling to do so. This is true; I was advised not to by someone who has our interests at heart. Although he is Franco's brother, he doesn't have half of Franco's qualities,

10. Gianozzo Manetti. A friend of the family and leading humanist.

which I don't have to spell out for you. And when a man puts himself in the hands of the *gran maestri* [roughly, big cheeses] and asks their advice, he had better do what they say, for better or for worse. If you don't, they say what Messer Giannozzo said to you. When Niccolò was here, [Giannozzo] brought someone who doesn't ever spend a penny and does nothing to see me about Lesandra, and he urged me to give her to him. Niccolò can tell you all about it. I know that Giannozzo took it badly, and that's why he told you what he did. I plan to do my very best to give him [i.e., the daughter's eventual husband] a good amount of capital (*capitale*) so that he can accomplish something. I told Giovanni [della] Luna[11] and Antonio degli Strozzi as much; and if we can marry her well, I would be happy to add one or two hundred *fiorini* to the thousand she has in the *Monte*.[12] As long as he's a person who deserves her and who can help her and be good to her. If not, I don't want to spend a penny more than she has. For the moment, there's nothing promising on hand: when there is, you will be notified. May God have good fortune in store for her. When you write to Giovanni della Luna and Antonio Strozzi, put in a word for her, and with Marco too.

I think that if Agnolo can walk that far, old as he is, he will come to see you. He wants to, and I begged him to. If he comes, ask him about our affairs, and he'll be able to tell you everything because he takes care of everything for us. I'm giving him two *fiorini larghi* for his expenses from Rome to Naples, so when he heads back, make sure he has spending money and has good traveling companions. Otherwise he will stay too many days in Rome and come with Favilla. Also through Favilla I'm sending you four pair of lovely *marzolini* [fresh Tuscan sheep cheeses]. I sent you four others the 5th of this month by a carter that Avveduto in the Customs office was sending down. I wasn't told the carter's name, but I'm sure he will give good service. With the sack, they weighed a good fifteen pounds. There's nothing owing for the cartage. Here I gave him one *grosso* for the customs, and I promised to write you to pay him something. Francesco di Batista[13] hasn't come back: I am sending you this *marzolino* for two people so as to avoid paying cartage. I would like you to send me by Favilla, if you have a

11. A prominent family and friends of the Strozzi, the Della Luna lived in Alessandra's neighborhood in Florence.

12. Alessandra is referring to the *Monte delle doti* or dowry fund. Established by the city of Florence in 1425, it provided dowries to girls for whom a premium had been paid into the fund. Payment of the dowry was actually made to the husband only after he had presented proof of consummation of marriage. Lesandra (Alessandra) di Matteo Strozzi was enrolled in the fund in 1438 when she was four years old. In 1450 she was married to Giovanni di Donato Bonsi who received 1,000 florins from the fund in partial payment of Lesandra's dowry.

13. The editors cannot identify this person.

chance, twenty pounds of almonds and ten pounds of capers, if they are ripe there. Favilla will bring me as much as thirty pounds without charge. Do it so I can have them for Lent.

As I told you in another letter, I had 154 pounds of flax (with the sack) from Giovanni Lorini—that is, twenty bunches of the coarse and nine of the finer. To tell you the truth, it was no less expensive than the first batch you sent me, which was 125 pounds and of which I still have several bunches left.

You know that some time ago I bought Cateruccia, our slave, and for several years now, though I haven't laid a hand on her, she has behaved so badly toward me and the children that you wouldn't believe it if you hadn't seen it. Our Lorenzo could tell you all about it. Matteo too, if it please God he come here, will tell you the truth of her behavior with us. I've always suffered it because I can't chastise her, and besides I thought you would come once a month so that we could come to a decision together or she could be brought to better obedience. For several months now she has been saying and is still saying that she doesn't want to stay here, and she is so moody that no one can do a thing with her. If it weren't for love of Lesandra, I would have told you to sell her, but because of her malicious tongue, I want to see Lesandra safely out of the house first. But I don't know if I can hold out that long: mark my words, I'm going to get her out of my sight because I don't want this constant battle. She pays no more attention to me than if I were the slave and she were the mistress, and she threatens us all so that Lesandra and I are both afraid of her. My Zanobi is coming back here with me. She doesn't want him and is having fits, but I have decided that he will stay with me as part of the staff here. Plus, here he has some supervision, for in Antella he was by himself and was having a hard time of it. So I have brought him with me. He's not the man to chastise her. I'd like her to have a good beating, but he wouldn't do it. Thus, seeing how she is, don't be surprised if I make up my mind to it myself, as I will do anything to live in peace. I beg you with all my might that on Niccolò's return you take a leave for two months. I don't say this because of the slave woman, but for my own pleasure, as I think I will die of this yearning to see you. I thought of coming to Rome for the Jubilee [14] and to see you, but now, for Lesandra's sake, I don't want to leave here until she's settled. But be sure that if I had gone to Rome and you hadn't come, I think I would have gone all the way to Naples to see you. So do what you can to get Niccolò to give you leave, and come see me.

14. The practice of celebrating a Jubilee or Holy Year, when pilgrims flocked to Rome with a view to the Jubilee indulgence, began in 1300 with the pontificate of Boniface VIII. Before 1470 the Holy Year was celebrated every fifty years.

You have perhaps heard of Soldo's[15] death—God pardon him—and what a great shame it was. I went to pay a call on his wife, and she asked again and again to be remembered to Niccolò and to you, since you have all of Soldo's papers and account books in your hands and since there's so much money owed him [in Naples] that they would like to collect. She talked and talked. She has named Niccolò as her agent to collect it. Try to help those poor orphans; they're poorly off, and it's a work of charity. Put in a word for her with Niccolò when he gets back, and may God give them a good voyage.

You should know that Macigno di Giovacchino[16] has taken to wife the daughter of Agostino Capponi,[17] Luca Capponi's sister. She's a widow and has had two husbands but she is twenty-four years old with a dowry of a thousand *fiorini*. God give them long life.

Let me know which *marzolino* is best, the little one or the big one, so I'll know which to get for the coming year (and will send you in due time). Nothing else for this time. God save you from harm. From your Alessandra in Florence.

Letter 17

To Filippo degli Strozzi in Naples
In the name of God, 6 September 1459
My dear, sweet son. The 11th of last month I had your letter of 29 July saying that my dear and beloved Matteo was down with some sickness, and not knowing from you what disease it was, the letter much distressed me and I was terribly afraid for him. I called on Francesco, and I sent [for word] through Matteo di Giorgio, and I heard from both of them that he had a tertian fever [usually, malaria]. This relieved me a good deal, since people don't die of a tertian fever unless some other sickness is added to it. Since then, I have been informed by you that his sickness was abating, which relieved my mind a bit, though I still was afraid for him. I heard after that on the 23rd it pleased Him who gave him to me to call him to Himself, in full presence of mind, in good grace, and with all the sacraments required of a good and faithful Christian. This was a bitter blow for me to be deprived of such a son, and I feel I have suffered a great loss in his death in more than his filial love. You, my other two sons, reduced to such a small number as you are, [have suffered just as great a loss]. I praise and

---

15. Soldo di Bernardo Strozzi worked in Naples, where he was associated with Niccolò di Lionardo Strozzi.
16. Macigno di Giovacchino was Alessandra's cousin.
17. The Capponi were a socially and politically prominent family.

thank Our Lord for all that is of His will, and I am sure God took care of the salvation of his soul. I see from what you wrote me how well you are accepting this bitter, hard death, and I have heard as much from letters from others there. Although this has grieved my heart more than anything else ever has, I have taken comfort in two things. The first is that he was close to you, and I am sure that doctors, medicines, and whatever it was possible to do for his salvation as well as all available remedies were tried, and that no stone was left unturned to keep him in life. Nothing could have helped him because this was God's will. The other thought from which I have taken comfort is that Our Lord graced him with the strength, on the point of death, to give up his sins and request confession, communion, and extreme unction. I hear that he did all this with devotion, and all these are signs of hope that God has prepared a good place for him. For this reason, and knowing full well we all have to take that road, we know not how, and cannot be sure of doing so with as much grace as my Matteo (for some die of a sudden death and some are cut to pieces, so many die losing both body and soul), I am at peace when I consider that God could do much worse for me. If by His grace and mercy He leaves me you, my two sons, I will not add to my affliction. My only thought is to hear that you are not taking it too hard. It has undoubtedly been a terrible blow to you. But take care not to grieve to the point that it harms you: we don't want to throw the handle out with the broom. We have nothing to reproach ourselves for as far as his care is concerned. Quite the contrary, it was by the will of God that he left the tribulations of this care-laden world. I can see in your [letter] of the 26th that this has much afflicted both your mind and your body, which has grieved me so much (and still grieves me) that it threatens to do me harm, and I will continue to grieve until I have letters from you [saying] you have been consoled. May it please God that I not live long enough to go through another [sorrowful event] like this one! It seems to me that after having been upset by these bad nights and had the melancholy of his death and of other things, you must not be in very good health. I turn this thought over in my head so much day and night that I can't get any rest. I wish I hadn't asked anyone's advice and instead had done what seemed best to me and what I wanted to do. I would have arrived in time to have seen my dearest son alive and touched him, and I would have consoled him, and you, and taken consolation from him. I want to think it was all for the best. I beg you (if my prayers mean anything to you, as I think they do) to arm yourself with patience for love of me and to look after your health and put aside company business for a while. It would also be a good idea to purge yourself a bit, though with light things and particularly with some medicine, and then get some fresh air if you possibly can. Remember that your health should be dearer to you than material possessions since, as you see, all is left behind! And I, a mother laden with cares, what would I do without you? What does it mean to me to know you are making good money if it ruins your health with all these hardships and cares? It grieves me, my son, that I'm not near you to take some of these troublesome things off your hands. You should have told me the first day Matteo fell sick so I could have jumped on a horse and been there in just a few days. But I know that you didn't do it for fear I would get sick or would be put to trouble. But I have more trouble in my mind than it would have been for my body. Now God be praised for everything, and I will take it as all for the best.

I have been told that in the honors you arranged for the burial of my son you did honor to yourself as well as to him. You did all the better to pay him such honor there, since here they don't usually do anything for those who are in your condition [i.e., in exile]. Thus I am pleased that you did so. Here these two girls, who are unconsolable over the death of their brother, and I have gone into mourning, and because I had not yet gotten the woolen cloth to make a mantle for myself, I have gotten it now and I will pay for it. It will take thirteen *braccia* of cloth for each of them and will cost, in cash, 4¼ *fiorini* the *canna* [roughly 3 meters], or 6½ *canne* in all. I will have this paid to Matteo di Giorgio and you will hear from him about it.

I have seen a copy of his will, and it would be a good idea to carry out [the provisions] for the peace of his soul as quickly as possible. The rest can be done with more leisure. [There is one thing] I beg you to do and to let me know if there is anything I can do here: there is a sister here of the boy-servant you had here who is married but cannot go to her husband because she is in great poverty. I have mentioned her to you in other letters, but have never had an answer. Now that this has happened [e.g., Matteo's death], it would be good to help her and not fail her. [She needs] 15 *fiorini* in all. And in case [Matteo's estate] is less than that, we could take it and add the rest, from my money or from yours, which amounts to the same in any event. Be aware of this, and advise me how much it [Matteo's estate] is and what we can do.

I see that Niccolò was sick with the tertian fever, which added to my sorrow in many ways. May it please God in his mercy to liberate him from it.

I have had a letter from Messer Giannozzo, out of the kindness of his heart exhorting me with great charity to be patient and [citing me] a great number of examples. It has given me great comfort to see the affection and love he bears you. May God reward him for it. I do not feel strong enough (*di tale virtù*) to answer a man as important as he, so I won't, but will you please thank him for me [as warmly] as you can. Let me know, and often, how you feel, and may God grant me what I wish. Although I was used to adversities in the past, these weigh heavily on me. Again, thank Bernardo de' Medici with a letter, because I can't tell you how lovingly he came to pay me a visit and console me and how much our loss and our trials grieve him. I will say no more now to avoid boring you, except that I am waiting for your letters to hear that you are taking comfort and are well. May the blessed Jesus concede us this grace, as I pray. From your poor little mother in Florence.

Letter 65

To Filippo degli Strozzi, in Naples
In the name of God, 11 January 1465
I last wrote you the 4th. I have since [received] yours of the 28th of last month, and I can see that you write me more to give me the happiness of having your letters than out of need to write. This gives me great pleasure, now that I cannot see you in person. I thank God for everything, which is perhaps for the best. To answer your letter:
I told you in my other [letter] what happened about 60,[18] and there's nothing new there. And you have been advised that there is no talk of 59[19] until we have placed the older girl. 13[20] believes we should do nothing further until we can see our way clearly concerning these two and see what way they will go. Considering their age, this shouldn't take too long. It's true that my wish would be to see both of you with a companion, as I have told you many times before. That way when I die I would think you ready to take the step all mothers want—seeing their sons married—so your children could enjoy what you have acquired with enormous effort and stress over the long years. To that end I have done my very best to keep up the little I have had, foregoing the things that I might have done for my soul's sake and for that of our ancestors. But for the hope I have that you will take a wife (in the aim of having children) I am happy to have done so. So what I would like would be what I told you. Since then I have heard what Lorenzo's wants are and how he was willing to take her to keep me happy, but that he would be just as glad to wait two years before binding himself to the lady. I have thought a good deal about the matter, and it seems to me that since nothing really advantageous to us is available, and since we have time to wait these two years, it would be a good idea to leave it at that unless something really unexpected turns up. Otherwise, it doesn't seem to me something that requires immediate thought, particularly considering the stormy times we live in these days, when so many young men on this

18. The daughter of Francesco Tanagli.
19. A nubile woman who was perhaps a member of the Adimari family.
20. Marco Parenti.

earth are happy to inhabit it without taking a wife. The world is in a sorry state, and never has so much expense been loaded on the backs of women as now. No dowry is so big that when the girl goes out she doesn't have the whole of it on her back, between silks and jewels. So we here cannot do him much good. Although I have not written anything to him about it, I am not searching around for anything for him, and we were waiting [to see] whether either of the two possibilities turns out to be for you. If 60 works out well, we could sound out the possibility of the other girl for him. There's good forage there if they were to give her, and at any [other] time it would have been a commendable move. As things are going now, it seems to me better to wait and see a while for him. Furthermore, according to what he writes me in all his letters, he is willing to wait two more years. With luck that will be all, and maybe by then people will have calmed down. This way something may come of it, and they will not offer a wife without money, as people are doing now, since it seems superfluous to those who are giving 50[21] to give her a dowry. 13 wrote you that 60's father touched on the matter with him in the way I wrote you about. He says that you should leave it to us to see to it and work it out. For my part, I've done my diligent best, and I can't think what more I could have done—for your consolation more than my own. My time is short, and yours should by rights be long. May it so please God. Marco is still looking out for you both diligently. May God make it all work out for the best. And tell Lorenzo to put his mind at ease as far as a wife is concerned.

Niccolò has gone out of office (*uscì*), and although he did some good things, they weren't the ones I would have wanted. Little honor has been paid to him or to the other outgoing magistrates, either when they were in office, or now that they have stepped down. Our scrutineer[22] was quite upset about it, as were we, but I feel that what was done will collapse, and it is thought they will start fresh. This Signoria has spent days in deliberations, and no one can find out anything about them. They have threatened to denounce whoever reveals anything as a rebel, so things are being done in total secrecy. I have heard that 58[23] is everything and 54[24] doesn't stand a chance. For the moment, it looks to me as if they will get back to 56[25] in the runoffs (*ne' primi termini*), if things continue to go as now. May God, who can do all, set this city right, for it is in a bad way. Niccolò went in proudly and then lost heart—as 14's[26] brother said, "He went in a lion and he will go out a lamb," and that's just what happened to him. When he saw

21. That is, a woman from an exiled family.
22. *Squittinante:* A member of a committee that periodically determined (scrutinized) the eligibility of candidates for office.
23. The Medici.
24. The Pitti. They were allies of the Medici.
25. The brother of Antonio Pucci. The Pucci were allies of the Medici.
26. Tommaso Soderini.

the votes were going against him, he began to humble himself. Now, since he left office he goes about accompanied by five or six armed men for fear of the counts of Maremma[27] or others. It would have been better for him if [he had never been elected], for he would never have made so many enemies.

You were advised of the 14 *fiorini* I had from the bank 5 November, and you answered me about them that same month.

Tell Giovacchino that on the 4th of this month I received the load of flax for the sisters. It came so late that I had already sealed my letter, so I didn't acknowledge it. I have since undone [the package]: there are 12 bundles. I have given four to that sister from [the convent of] San Domenico, I am waiting for the sister from Santa Marta to send for another four, and another four [are for] the sister from Polverosa. I expect them to send for it at any moment. I haven't weighed it, but each of them gets four bundles. They will let me know the weight. Included here is a letter from the sister from San Domenico. Give it to [Giovacchino], and when the others write I will send him [their letters].

I don't know what else to tell you. You must have heard of the new family alliances (*parentado*): Messer Piero de' Pazzi's daughter and Braccio Martegli and Antonio and Priore Pandolfini. Both girls have two thousand in dowry. Messer Piero's [daughter] has one eye that doesn't see well. I haven't heard a thing about Gianfrancesco's[28] girl [granddaughter] here, but I hear from Pierantonio that she will be given in Mantua to Messer Benedetto Strozzi's son. I don't know where he heard it. Giovanni di ser Francesco told me the same thing when he returned. They should send news of this [to Naples], and if it turns out not to be true, think about having Niccolò Strozzi touch on the matter with Giovanfrancesco for 45,[29] if you think it appropriate. Although I doubt that she would deign [to marry] so low, still, it sometimes happens that you look in places that in other times you wouldn't have dreamed of, by the force of events—deaths or other misfortunes. So think about it. Nothing else for now. God save you from harm. From your Alessandra Strozzi, Florence.

7. Bernardino da Siena, *Sermons*

Born in 1380, the year Catherine of Siena died, Bernardino degli Albizzeschi belonged to an eminent Sienese family. Since he lost both parents before the age of six, he was raised by relatives. Especially influ-

27. The Maremma is a coastal district in southwestern Tuscany.
28. Gianfrancesco Strozzi.   29. Lorenzo, Alessandra's son.

From *Le prediche volgari*, vol. 2, edited by Ciro Cannorozzi (Florence: Typografia E. Rinaldi, 1957), pp. 82–95, 113–28. Translated for this volume by Lydia G. Cochrane.

ential were two devout widows, his cousin Tobia and aunt Bartolommea, who steered Bernardino toward the religious life. Bartolommea was an Augustinian Tertiary (a branch of a religious order, whose members were laymen and women, pursuing the ordinary avocations of secular life) who spent her life in contemplation and prayer. Tobia was a Franciscan Tertiary who devoted her life to nursing the sick and providing alms to the poor. As a boy Bernardino studied grammar, and rhetoric, and later canon law at the University of Siena, perhaps with the idea of becoming a public official. He subsequently decided to enter religious life. In 1403 he joined the Observant branch of the Order of Friars Minor, the branch dedicated to a strict observance of Francis' Rule (see vol. 4, doc. 43) and to a life of austerity, poverty, and mortification. The fame he subsequently acquired as a preacher brought considerable prestige to the Observant branch, of which he eventually became the vicar general. At the time he joined, it consisted of no more than twenty small communities in all Italy. By the time of his death, in 1444, the number had risen to 230.

After being ordained a priest in 1404 and commissioned as a preacher in the following year, Bernardino spent the next twenty-six years tramping from place to place in northern and central Italy preaching. As his prestige and reputation as a holy man increased, he was besieged by crowds captivated by his impassioned oratory, his vivid stories, and his pungent vernacular idiom. He was neither a great theologian nor an original thinker. His sermons contain many passages cited without acknowledgment from the works of theological and juridical authorities. He praised the life of simplicity and moderation, while he directed his sermons against conventional targets: usurers, dishonest shopkeepers and merchants, gamblers, fomenters of civic factionalism, sodomites, vain women, ignorant priests, and heretics. Since these sermons are distinguished by astonishing insights into the private world of ordinary men and women, they constitute a valuable source for the historian of Italy in the early Renaissance.

The sermons presented here were delivered in 1425 in Siena. Unlike the some two hundred or more sermons that Bernardino composed carefully in Latin later in his life and that served as models for other preachers of the age, these sermons delivered in vernacular were never written down by Bernardino himself. They were taken down by auditors in a rudimentary shorthand and subsequently written out with the gaps filled in from the auditors' memory. They thus omit the subtle theological discussions and extensive references to biblical, patristic, and juridical sources in which the Latin sermons abound.

Bernardino was canonized only six years after his death by Pope Nicholas V, the first of the humanist popes of the Renaissance.

"On the Vanity of the World and Especially of Women"

This is the Sermon on Worldly Vanity, Particularly among Women.

Odisti observantes vanitates supervacue:[1] Psalm 30 [Ps. 31:6]. These are the words of David the prophet. In the vernacular they say: "You have hated those who needlessly observe vanities."

What these words mean is that God has always borne a hatred for those men and women who, through vanity, dress better than they should or who [think more about their dress] than about anything else. Oh men! Oh women! When you think about the evil you have committed, you will abstain from it, and in the future you will do no more. Many men and many women think they have done just this. But still God hated them in three ways, and for three reasons God now hates us.

In particular, God abhors:

First, curiosity: *observantes*

Second, the vanity in us: *vanitates*

Third, superfluousness: *supervacue*

First, God abhors us for our curiosity—for example, *observantes*, when men and women turn to new fashions. Don't you know that harlots are the first to have all fashions? Isn't this what David says? *Ibunt in inventione sua* [I left them to follow their own counsels. Ps. 81:12].

However, [the psalmist] says *observantes* [about the] great amounts of cloth that are tossed into sleeves and puffs and ruffles and broad fringes. Or about the *berzi* (elaborate, braided hair styles) on your heads. What is a *berzo*? It is something that will bounce you into hell. You will bounce right in just as a cricket sometimes jumps into the hearthfire. That's why he says *vanitates*. Many women will tell me, "I just do so to please my husband. I don't want him to take it badly if I don't do what he wants, and I'm just trying to keep him happy as best as I can." I answer, "You must help him, but not to ruin himself, and yourself too." And remember that a custom that takes hold of others will seem of great importance. Here is an example: There once was a man who emptied privies: that was his trade and his profession. It happened that once when he was in Venice, he passed by the druggists' shops. Surrounded by these shops and their many perfumes, he unexpectedly fell to the ground in a dead faint. A doctor was sent for right away, but he couldn't tell what was wrong with him. Other doctors were fetched, and finally one of them asked what his trade was. When he heard that the man was a privy cleaner, this doctor said, "Bring in some stable manure or some other stinking stuff." He put it to the man's nose and on his wrists and the man came to immediately because this was what he

---

1. *Supervacuas* in the Vulgate. Bernardino is using *supervacue* as an adverb modifying the participle *observantes*.

was used to. You laugh, but this is something to weep about! This is the stink of the woman who gets all dressed up, and who stinks to her own husband, but still she's never satisfied with him. This is [the stink of] the sodomite, who has no odor only among the dregs of society of sodomy. And I tell you, I am here to admonish you for your sins, men and women alike.

[God's] second abhoration: *supervacue*, [superfluous] assiduously. Take a look at the woman: over and above all her other vices, look at the *cioppe* (overdresses) in her coffers and hanging from her clothes poles, and all the coffers and the poles are groaning under their loads. You can see the poor, naked man, dying of the cold, and you're busy clothing your clothes poles! You will answer to God for this.

Third, [you are] changeable—that is, empty-headed—and there's no way to satisfy you. You're always moving, as the wind moves the leaves, as you can plainly see from your own experience. And look at how many sorts of heads there are: there are full heads, empty heads, and over-empty heads. The full heads are the ones filled with memory; the empty heads are [full of] willfullness; and the over-empty heads are [filled with] intellect. This is what God said: "with all your heart, with all your soul, and with all your might." With faith, with hope, and with charity. Let each one of you understand what you must, for this applies to everyone. All the people we have been talking about have empty heads, and Apocalypse 13 says that the empty-headed shall not come before God—that is, people who ignore the fasts commanded by the holy Church and fast instead on Marian or other feast days. Another empty head: whoever lends money at interest in expectation of profit. He thinks he will never die. And if you rise out of these vices, you will be thinking right, and [acting] with faith, hope, and charity. Your head will also be well filled when you say, "I have indulged in these vices, and in others as well, and I want to mend my ways with right thinking. I also want to fast, follow God's commandments, and do all things that please my husband. And if I fast, I will chase away vain thoughts of singing, playing music, and other dissolute pastimes. And this way I want to draw closer to good and leave off evil." You can see what pleases God and that is to do good works.

Here you have seen the curiosity and blindness of *supervacue*.

Why has God despised people who do these things? Only because this is the task of those who hold office or who chose officeholders, and for that reason I beg you to see to it that your city takes action [in these matters]. These are the reasons—vanity, curiosity, and superfluousness—for God's hatred toward you, because [such behavior] spites heaven, because it harms you yourself, and because it brings harm to your neighbor.

First, because it spites heaven. You will hear the seven reasons why you are all heading for damnation and are an offense to God.

First, by trying to improve on God
Second, by willfully refusing to conform to His will
Third, by buzzing in the temple of God
Fourth, by offending God
Fifth, by besmirching Mary in your praise of her
Sixth, by provoking the angels
Seventh, by setting the archangels against you

First, by trying to improve on God in his good and holy works. I am speaking generally, to men and women, young and old, humble and great, but more particularly to women than to men.

What do you think, woman: is it a sin or an insult to God to make yourself into something that you are not? As Cyprian[2] and Scotus[3] say, according to Augustine in Book 4 of *On Christian Doctrine:*[4] *Si quis pingendi artifex vultum aut speciem* [If an artist had depicted the face and form of a man], etc., if there were a most renowned and skillful master painter who made a portrait of Our Lady, or else a [picture] of her with her son in her arms—beautiful, well composed, pleasing and of pious aspect, and someone of less skill or who didn't know what he was doing attempted to improve upon the portrait by adding something, and if he then took an oven whiskbroom or his bare hands and set about rubbing the face, how much would he be wronging the master who painted [the face]? For He is the first painter and you, who know nothing about painting, are spoiling it. And you set yourself up against the will of God when you make a shame of the face he gave you, spoiling it with your smearings. Where you're white, you make yourself red, where you're red, you make yourself white. Where you're yellow, you color yourself, where you're curly, you make yourself cleanshaven. If you're big you belt yourself in until you burst, and if you're thin you pad yourself with cotton batting, and if you're short, you want high *pianelle* (wooden clogs). Whether you're dark or fair or however you are, you spoil the image that God gave you. And then they tell their confessors, "We do it to please our husbands." You're lying in your throats! And the confessors are fooled by you if they believe it, and they are fooling you by their generosity to you. That's why I beg you—so that you won't have to confess something that seems shameful to you—don't ever dirty up your face, either in your bedroom or in any other place. Don't make yourself appear beautiful in public and ugly at home. Do the opposite and I'll believe that you are trying to please your husband. Be ugly when you're outside your house, and make yourself beautiful at home for love of your

2. Cypr. *De habitu virginum*, c. 15 (*PL* 4, 455ff.).
3. Obviously, Augustine could not have cited an opinion of the fourteenth-century Franciscan theologian Duns Scotus. "Scote" is probably a scribal corruption of Ambrose whose teaching, together with Cyprian's, was cited by Augustine.
4. Lib. 4, c. 21, n. 49 (*PL* 34, 113ff.).

husband, and you will please him and content him in every way. And if you do the contrary, every bit of disgust you raise in him will push him into shame, to the harm and discontent of your soul and his own. When he sees that you get all dressed up to go out, he will immediately become suspicious and think that you aren't faithful to him, and then he'll fall into all the sins of sodomy, etc. This is why David says, *Abstitit regina a dextris tuis in vestitu deaurato, circumdata varietate* [Psalm 45:31. The princess is decked in her chamber with gold-woven robes; in many-colored robes she is led to the king]. Thus every star is in its proper place and often little is better than a lot. You can see that a peppercorn is intrinsically better than a whole heap of dung. I can also tell you that I know of few beautiful women who are loved—and who perhaps also love—or whose husbands are not always suspicious and jealous. So don't make yourself otherwise than the way God made you. If God made you beautiful, God gave you a great misfortune, if you only knew it; but if you know how to behave properly, you will be greatly rewarded in eternal life.

I'm talking about beautiful and ugly women alike. Certainly, God does not care more about the great than the humble, about young women more than the old; God loves without measure all who do his will. So don't try to improve on God. This is what Augustine says (just like Ambrose[5] and Jerome[6]) in Book 4 of *Christian Doctrine* to those who change the face God gave them. How will you dare to appear before God? God won't even recognize you. As Saint Matthew says, *Amen dico vobis, nescio vos*, "truly, I say to you, I do not know you," because you don't have the face I gave you, because you have smeared it and dirtied it up to seem more beautiful than I made you.

Second, not conforming to God's will. When you say the "Our Father," pay attention to the phrase that says, *Fiat voluntas tua*. One woman says, "Thy will be done on earth as it is in heaven." She may say so, but see how she spoils what He has made. *Omnia in sapientia fecisti* [Psalm 104:24. In wisdom hast thou made them all]. Therefore, since you have been made by the will of God, why do your actions contradict what you say you want? Don't you see that in what you say—in the prayer you say that God's will should be done in earth as in heaven—you are twisting that prayer around? So you don't want [God's will] to be done, even in heaven. If your hair is falling out, it is perhaps all right to fix it so you don't look bald. Go ahead and do it, but don't overdo it. If it's the custom to go around with a full head of hair, you don't have to do so. However, don't deceive yourself. And don't change your hair color to gold or white: have the amount of hair and the

5. *De virginibus*, I, c. 6 n. 28 (*PL* 16, 196ff.).
6. *Epist. 54 ad Furiam*, n. 7 (*PL* 22, 553).

kind of hair that looks like your own. And if you have [plenty of] hair on your head, why do you set yourself to making it blond, smearing it with so much stuff, drying your head in the sun, wetting it and drying it, wetting it and drying it? Don't you see how much harm this does? It leads to headaches, deafness, rotted teeth, and bad breath. Be content, like the canary, who may be tiny but still doesn't envy the ass, who is so big. Each of them sings in his own way, too, and the ass doesn't envy the nightingale for his song or the canary either.

Third, you make God hate you for your buzzing about in the temple of God. In church there is so much competition among these women, who are so tense that they seem to have mattress-beaters up their spines, each thinking herself the most beautiful. Oxen go plowing up and down and they all pull together, but each mother is just delighted when her daughter is courted. Oh you mothers! If you behave this way, remember that you will lead this daughter of yours to perdition, and perhaps you have already done so. Now just think how many evils were committed during the three holy days of Holy Week, when everyone ought to be weeping, and you were glowering at one another. Oh, how embarrassed I was! It seemed that these things were going on to spite God. You will say, "I wanted to show off my daughter." [Listen to this] example. There is in the world a city in which barefooted women are displayed and measured against a wall to see how tall they are. A man once came to take [a wife] there, and everybody measured her as was the custom, and when he had seen her, they asked him if she pleased him. He answered that he would think about it. At this point the woman said, "So this man says he'll think about it? He can just go and think about it all he wants, for I have thought about it and I don't want him, since he looks first and then thinks about it." To be sure, he was a short man, and she was half a *braccio* [roughly, an arm's length] taller than he.

Another man was interested in marrying his sister to someone, so he brought her to him so he could see her. Her charms were artificial (*lei era falsificata*), and when he realized it, he drew a knife and killed her.

Oh woman! You have already killed hundreds of souls with your face smearings, perhaps thousands. When will you ever repent? You there, you've sucked in perhaps a hundred young men; when will you repent? Solomon in chapter 7 says of the woman dressed like a harlot that she is wily of heart [Prov. 7 : 10] and lies in wait [Prov. 7 : 12], just as the Church attracts souls: *Ad capiendas animas*. She snared men like nightingales and chaffinches. And it doesn't even bother your conscience.

Fourth, don't you believe that Christ, the son of God, loves his father? Oh, when he sees so many great offenses to his magnificence, don't you think that grieves him? Why should that grieve God? Just because it is an offense to the Father. [Christ] came into this world to make peace between you and God, and you do just the opposite. You have been the cause of many shameful sins: usury, homicides, fornications, adulteries, and so forth.

Fifth, offense to the Virgin Mary if you have ever [profaned] a church or any other sanctified place: cathedrals, hospitals, etc. Don't you see that a church is [the same thing as] the saint to which the church is dedicated? Some who have been in the Holy Land say that no woman ever enters into a Saracen's temple while a man is inside, and when the men have left, the women come in. And all the men go barefoot and the women with their faces covered so they cannot be seen. And they pray to the devil with so much faith that they are sometimes off the ground in contemplation. When they hear of our ways they burst out laughing, and they're not far wrong. For my part, I think that more evil is committed in the cathedral on a solemn feast day than in a public place the whole week long. However, the minute they enter into the church, the Virgin Mary gives them her malediction when they act this way. It's the same for you, woman, when you enter the church with vanity: Mary immediately curses you. And let me warn you, don't ever go to a convent to amuse some nun, because when you leave the convent, she will swear at you and curse father, mother, and herself. For this reason, it's better not to go. Furthermore, you shouldn't put anyone into a convent who isn't eighteen years old; and if someone [younger] were put there, you should pay a certain amount [of dowry] for her. I don't want you meddling in these matters. Don't lay your hands on other people's forage, for it belongs to God. Leave to God what is God's, and you be master of your own affairs. Furthermore, I beg you, when country people come here, don't have them arrested for their debts. They come to the sermons to hear the word of God, and you have them hauled away for their debts! Be merciful!

Sixth, the angels despise you. Everyone has a guardian angel to watch over his soul, and when you do so much evil, your angel curses you. [All the angels] leave you and go away from you, and they curse the woman who was the cause of your bad actions as well. Souls are snared just like pigeons and doves, and the angels are just as sad about it as they are joyful over good [actions].

God, the saints, the apostles, and the angels all curse you for opposing the will of God; it is just as in this world when people love one another and one of them is hurt and they all despise the one who did the harm.

[My] second principal part [speaks of] you yourself. Now I want to give you the real medicine; what you have had so far is syrup. Regarding yourself, you will see seven ills.

First, the soul as the chamber of sins. If a woman is vain, she is a chamber of haughty superiority. Oh, how long they look at themselves before they leave the house! If she is haughty, it leads to the sin of vainglory as she preens and plucks herself. When she sees that someone else is more beautiful than she, envy is born, and if she cannot rival her beauty, she is bitter. Then she wants more clothes than she has, and if she doesn't get them, she gets angry. Thus she wears herself out, and she loses weight because she doesn't get to the [social] rank she would like. Then she stimulates [her appetite] with things to eat and drink, she warms up to the idea, and then comes gluttony. One thing follows another and every sin is born in her.

Second, the waste of time. If you thought of how much time is wasted and put that much effort into the salvation of your soul, you would be better off than Mary Magdalen. Saint Paul says, *Dum tempus habemus, operemur in bonum*, "while we have time, let us do good" [Gal. 6:10]. Job says, *Breves dies hominis sunt*, "Brief are men's days" [Job 14:5]. He has but a short time to be saintly and good.

[Take the] example of a holy father who was observing the vanity of a woman and, seeing his own vanity (that is, his efforts had been in vain), began to cry out, Alas! Alas! Alas!, and said that she had gotten further in spreading evil than he had in doing good. When another woman who had been good became wicked, another holy father said of her: "How much time she spent in the good that she did, and now it is of no use whatsoever to her soul."

Third, you lose every prayer that you say. Every church office, every psalm, and every mass. Paul says to Timothy, *Non in tortis crinibus et vestitu pretioso* [1 Tim 2:9. Women should adorn themselves modestly and sensibly in seemly apparel, not with braided hair, or gold, or pearls, or costly attire]. All Lombardy has borrowed the custom of curly hair from Siena. Oh, woe to the person who started this fashion!

Fourth, you get yourselves all excited. Just like a bitch—when a bitch needs a dog, all the dogs come following along behind her. And when she doesn't, they don't. This is like a woman who can be known by her eyes, and you had better get it straight that more can be understood by acts than by words. David the prophet says of this, *Illi maledicent et tu benedices* [they will curse and you will bless]. [For] example, when you want to sell a horse in the piazza, you put straw on his head. This seems crazy to someone who sees this sign but asks "Is that horse for sale?" Someone who understands it will ask how much you want for the horse. This is what happens when a woman dresses in finery and adorns herself: she is for sale to lovers. Sometimes it's the mother who beautifies her and dresses her up, and that beautifying is what arouses love in the girl's lover. And the mother is a procuress for having beautified her that way.

Fifth, when a woman is vain, what you should do is think about providing a dowry, not satisfy her [wishes] with all the clothes she wants. And if her husband has only meager earnings, he won't be able to eat except by her dowry, if it's a good one. So if she keeps all her dowry in her clothes chests, she may force her husband to enter into unfavorable contracts, because she has pushed him to spend beyond his capabilities.

Sixth, vanity often makes your will vacillate, for often it's like the blow-fly that flies into a lamp and buzzes around and around. That's what a lover does: he buzzes around the vain woman until he finally makes her fall by promising, "I'll take you to wife; I love you so; you're the one I'm yearning for," etc. So don't ever believe anyone, because they'll all trick you and then tell everyone about it. And if in any way you give in, everywhere you go you'll be ashamed. Don't listen to a single word, for he will say, "I'll keep it a secret," but it won't be true. As it has been said, *Nichil occultum quod non reveletur*, "There is no secret that will not be revealed" [Luke 12:2]. There are many mothers who'll be happy with their daughters [when this happens] because then they will be married.

There was once a man who wanted to take a wife, but he wanted to trick her because she was rich. Every third day he changed an item of clothing [in the trousseau], until finally he went to see her to conclude the negotiations. When he saw her, he asked, "What do you know how to do?" She was a widow, and she answered, "I know how to spin, sew, and cut [clothes] as all women do." Then he said, "Do you know how to do anything else?" She answered that she knew how to run a household, supervise the children, sweep, etc. So he said, "Do you know how to do anything else?" She told him, "Oh, I know how to make bread." He said, "I'm satisfied; I'll take you." And so it was done. When he led her [to his house], he pawned enough things to buy a *soma* [91.2 litres] of flour. When the flour was finished, the woman said, "Go buy some flour because there isn't any left." He said, "Don't break our contract." She said, "How's that?" He answered that she had given him to understand that she knew how to make bread. She said, "That's why I'm telling you, buy some flour to make bread and I'll make it!" Then the man said, "Oh, I could have found fifteen women that I could have taken to wife if I had provided the flour. Even the baker would have made it for me." And for this reason, he rejected her.

There will even be some who say, "I will take you to wife" and will give you a ring. You can never dissolve such a marriage; if it is consummated, you cannot dissolve it. And if either of them ever wants to marry again, it will not be a legitimate marriage but adultery. Thus, you will have sought misfortune and you will have brought it on yourself. What does Jeremiah say? "That if this happens to you, it serves you right because you brought it on yourself" [Jer. 4:18]. God's mercy permits this. God says, [Ps. 83:16] "Fill their faces with shame." Why? For your vanity. And David says, *Dixit Dominus: Ex Basan convertam; convertam in profundum maris* [Ps. 68:22.

The Lord said, I will bring them back from Bashan, I will bring them back from the depths of the sea]—that is, with greatest shame.

Another woman may decide, "I want to remain honest." The devil will tempt her, but she will resist and be determined to do good. Jeremiah says, chapter 2, "I am desperate" [Jer. 2:25], and I want to eliminate every evil thought.

The third principal part is out of respect for your neighbor, and it concerns your husband's soul. [God] says, "I will make him a helper fit for him" [Gen. 2:18] and he put [Adam's] body to profit. This is what happens when a man loves [his wife] too much. Likewise, you will see a woman is beautiful, but she is [as sharp] as Solomon's [two-edged] sword in Proverbs [5:4]. Thus she doesn't make up for the sin of not giving a good example. Thus she contaminates the other women with her scandal, for when one sees another wearing some new exaggeration, she immediately gets one for herself, just like a sheep.

[For] example, a man had to take some sheep across the sea, and when they had been far from land for quite a few days [the ship] arrived at a port. As they were approaching the port the sheep saw the land, and as ill luck would have it, one of them gave a jump and fell into the sea. All the others followed along behind and they were all drowned. This is what females do: if one could not do just what another does, she would die.

If you have loved your wife, she may say to you, "This is what I want! That's what so-and-so has! You don't love me! Now I see where your mind is! She's this and she's that! I'm prettier than she is! What kind of beauty do you call that? Now we'll see if what I've heard is true: don't you have enough troubles at home? You'd be a fine match for her! Now I'll just see what you think of me and if you love me!"

Similarly, if someone has stolen because of a woman, the woman who caused it all will have her share in the punishment. Do you know why? Because of those wide sleeves, without which you wouldn't dream of going out. And do you know what the devil says? He says, "I made him steal to make broad sleeves for my woman here." Another devil says, "I'll hold him fast so he won't give it back. Just leave it to me!"

Women's vanity is the destruction of a city, ruined by velvets and woolens, for if the same money were put into merchandise it would turn a good profit. But you keep it in your coffers along with your pearls, your other jewelry, your silver, and so forth. You know I speak the truth. Whole families are undone by the inordinate dowries that are given and that men taking a wife demand; if the dowry is not to their liking, they refuse to take her. This is why they give themselves over to the vice of sodomy, some to one kind of ribaldry, some to another, and every sort of vice is practiced. In this way, the population shrinks little by little. And in this way you lose your soul, your body, and your goods, as you have seen. This is why David says, "Odisti observantes vanitates supervacue."

So, my brothers, work for the common good and for the welfare of our city, so that you will have grace here and glory in eternal life. Amen.

"On Usury"

This is the Sermon on Usury.

Thesaurizat et ignorat cui congregabit ea: Psalm 38 [Ps. 39:5].

These are the words of David the prophet. In the vernacular they say: "He hoards [his wealth] and does not know to whom it will go." I want to continue with what I started. Today, just as you have been hearing for the last three mornings, I will talk about the great judgment against usury and about the bitter justice dealt out to those who will not mend their ways. This will perhaps strike many of you, but let it strike whom it will. I rebuke the sin, not the sinner, for man is tethered with reason as the ox is with ropes.

Thus we will see three holy mysteries in what I have to say, shown to us by the Holy Spirit through the mouth of David in the very words you have just heard.

First [is] the mystery of the observance *amirazione* of prudent men: *Thesaurizat*. Second, that of the condition of avaricious men: *et ignorat*. Third, that of the malediction of the avaricious: *cui congregabit ea*. First I will speak of the mystery of prudent men. If we want to see this, [we can look to] the image of the Apocalypse in the third chapter [of Revelation], at the fourth seal, *Cum apparuit* Jesus Christ. The eagle screams, "'Come!' and behold, a pale horse, and its rider's name was Death, and Hades followed him; and they were given power over a fourth of the earth" [Rev. 6:7]—that is, war, hunger, pestilence, and wolves that devour children. Let us return to the first [mystery], that of the observance of prudent men. Anyone with good sense knows that he has little time to live, and the miser becomes more miserly every day. The prudent man carefully watches out in four ways: he looks to the past, to the present, and to the future; and thus he is always vigilant. The greedy usurer does nothing of the sort. Now that we have knocked down the field corporal, we will win the battle. So let's go rush this corporal, who is the usurer, and beat him up in detestation of his sin. If I reprimand him and someone gets hurt, I warn him not to complain of me, but complain of his own defect.

Thus we shall see, first, that the horse stands for usury, and we will see the foresight and the malediction of the wise.

John is talking of *amirazione*: "Come and see"; [you are] the amazement of Tuscany, oh you painstaking women who have married your daughters through usury and you men who have done the same.

And he says, "Come and see" the eagle, the first of four animals:

The first animal is a lion, which stands for justice.

The second is a young ox, which stands for strength.

The third has a face like a man, which signifies temperance.

Man must be temperate—that is, a man who is not greedy. Take this example: if a child were fed a mouthful that was too hot, he would spit it out even if it were worth ten *fiorini*. The avaricious man would swallow it.

You also have the example of the ass who when he has drunk what he needs will drink no more, no matter how you try to force him.

The fourth [animal], the eagle, stands for prudence, for with this virtue the three ages are born—that is, past, present, and future.

Look at the usurers' lives. Their lives are total folly, for they lost their souls for possessions, and then they leave their goods to strangers. There are four arguments for prudence and against usury and the usurer.

First, the argument of nature.

Second, that of Scripture.

Third, that of grace.

Fourth, that of [the law of] the holy Church.

It would take too long to consider the argument of nature, so we'll leave it aside.

Second, the argument of Scripture. You have God's commandment that says "Thou shalt not steal" and he therefore says that it is a sin. And Job, chapter 18, [Ezek. 18:10–13] says that often a good man will have an evil son, a usurer who will lend money and then say, "Give me as interest,[7] firewood, or whatever else you want," as they will agree. He acts like a man with a lot of *fiorini* who cries, "Who wants any? One *denaio* a day apiece!" Scripture says that a man will die spiritually if he even is the cause of someone else's usurious loan, since this is not licit for any Christian. At the beginning of Psalm 14 the Psalmist says, *Domine, quis habitabit in tabernaculo tuo?* [Ps. 15:1. Who will inhabit your tabernacle? tent?] He answers, *Qui iurat proximo suo, et non decipit; qui pecuniam suam non dedit ad usuram* [he who swears to his neighbor and does not deceive him; who does not put out his money at interest]. And elsewhere, in Psalm 54, the Psalmist says, *Et non defecit de plateis eius usura et dolus* [Ps. 55:11. Usury and fraud do not depart from its marketplace].

7. The term translated as "interest" is *merito*, which connoted licit profit. The Latin word *interesse* was a legal term which did not mean interest in the modern sense, but compensation paid by a debtor to a creditor who has suffered damages; for example, because the debtor failed to pay back a loan within an agreed period.

And in many other places the ancient law [i.e., the law of the Old Testament] says the same thing.

Many, many arguments from the Law of Grace say that Christ did not come to break the old law, but to fulfill it. Saint Luke says, chapter 6 [Luke 6:35], "lend freely hoping for nothing thereby." The lender says, "Oh! If I lend, shouldn't I be paid interest?" He says that he's doing a service and [the other] is returning it. It is illicit for you to lend [money] on a house or a shop so that you earn profit from it, and if you do so, you should deduct from the sum the profit you earn.

God has commanded us, "See that you serve others when they are in need" [cf. Matt. 25:34–40].

[Next], the argument [of the law] of the Holy Church. The Decretals, from the fortieth distinction;[8] in the fourth, fifth, and sixth books,[9] and many other books speaks of this. Also in the Decretals, in the chapter *Super eo*,[10] our Sienese [pope] Alexander III, says that by both the Old and the New Laws, it is not permitted to any pope (and he cannot do what is not permitted) to decree that it is licit for any man to lend at usury for any motive without [falling into] mortal sin. If you borrow money at usury to get someone out of prison, the interest is still illicit. [Pope] Urban [III] says two things:[11] If you want to arrange a loan without a contract and the lender expects some interest, even though there is no contract, it is a mortal sin.

Even if someone sells on credit rather than for cash, he sins mortally, for you must give back all the surplus—that is, [you must] give it for God. The Clementine decrees also say that anyone giving help or credence to any usurer is excommunicated.[12] And whoever is to blame, everyone is responsible for restitution.

I tell you that usury is progressing! It has gotten worse now that there is the interdict. And I, frate Bernardino, I would not say mass outside the church if I didn't have permission from the pope to say it in the marketplace and in other honest places. And you can see that many curse God and say, "There's no alternative." God does not command you to do what you cannot do.

You will hear the argument of nature another time. You have heard the three [parts], so that finishes *amirazione*.

8. Gratian, D. XL, *Pars prima*.

9. X. 4. 20. 7, *Per vestras*; X. 5. 19 (*De usuris*); VI. 5. 5 (*De usuris*).

10. X. 5. 19. 4. Alexander III served as pope from 1159 to 1181. In *Super eo* he determined that the church cannot dispense from the prohibition against usury, even to raise money for such a worthy cause as the ransoming of Christian captives from the Saracens.

11. X. 5. 19. 10, *Consuluit*. Urban III served as pope from 1185 to 1187.

12. *Clem*. 5. 5. 1, *Ex gravi*. For the translation of this decree see vol. 4, doc. 54. Pope Clement V served from 1302 to 1316.

Second part of the [usurer's] condition—that is, the mystery, *et ignorat*. There are three [sorts of] fools.

First, [there is] the one who does not see God; [then] the one who is against his neighbor; [and then] the one who is for himself alone. Because [John] says, *Sequebatur infernum* [Rev. 6:8, and Hades followed him]. As you can see, the usurer, represented by the horse, never looks up. Scripture says that the more the usurer looks at gold, the more beautiful it seems to him. The usurer loves a *quattrino* more than a *danaio*, a *grosso* more than a *quattrino*, the *fiorino* more than the *grosso* and all wealth more than God. His wife can't think of anything without having him say, "and somebody earns something from it"! They are like those who gaze lovingly at money as if it were something holy and good. You have the example of Saint Anthony of Padua.[13] Preaching about a usurer who had died, he said that his heart lay with his money: *Ubi est thesaurus tuus, ibi est cor tuum* [where your treasury is, there also is your heart]. His heart was found in with his money, for when he died, no heart was found in his body. And you can see that although the usurer goes to mass or to a sermon, he never believes in anything, for if he believed, he would leave off his vices. When one was asked, "Do you believe in the Crucifix?" he said no. He said, "I adore you but I don't believe in you."

Here's an example: Another [usurer] went to confession, and the priest, as he was preparing to absolve him, told him to give back [his profits]. The usurer said, "Absolve me of the other [sins] and leave usury on my head. It's not on my conscience; absolve me."

The usurer sells the grace of God, because what is God's grace—whoever lends gives grace—should not be sold in charity, but in charity you should do service to one another. You can see that God has made all the days of the year and that they are the same for everyone, and then you sell God's time, which is for everyone, for usurious profit.

But [Revelation] says that [usury] is a beast. *Pallidus* (the pale horse, e.g., the usurer) is not a hypocrite in relation to his neighbor, however; by usury they become hypocrites. The usurer fasts, and he still is not good; he gives alms, and he still is not good because he is made like a horse covered with false gold, full of hypocrisy. And the usurer is called the litigant. People also say, "So-and-so has done me a service," and they don't say, "He has drained my guts little by little." Where the cash box has usurer's money in it, the wife spins and the usurer owns the money. Thus the man works and the usurer takes the earnings, and thus God's wrath comes down on them both. Thus, for these usurers merchants make fraudulent sales and drain one another dry. Moreover, some citizen should be elected to set

13. A great Franciscan preacher of the thirteenth century.

everything to rights and to provide for all these things and to get everything back to normal. Then we can put an end to these credit contracts (*termini*), because the man who is a usurer turns into a thief.

There are thieves of more than one kind—that is, [there are] domestic and wild [thieves] just as there are wild animals and domestic animals. If I call the lion, he runs away at once; if I call the wolf, he runs away at once; if I call the cat, saying, "Here cat, here cat!" he runs away at once. That's the way you call the usurer, and because he is a domesticated beast, he will not run away. And when someone is a thief and you call, "Thief! Thief!" he will run away at once. The usurer will not run away when you call him a thief because he is a domesticated thief. Saint Matthew says in the Gospel that Christ chased them out of the temple with rope whips, which means that they deserve the gallows like thieves. And he drove them from the temple, and in his zeal for God he threw their money on the ground.

Furthermore, the usurer uproots charity (*la carità*) and hounds you (*usa la canità*). Many people say, "We can't prevent them from lending money." I know for a fact that there is a place, in Savoy, where loans are never made because they don't permit anyone to make loans. The moral of this is that people need one another: do a man a service, and he will do one for you. This way love grows between you.

[Here is an example from my own] experience: if you give alms, the more you give, the more you feel like giving. When I was at Monte Amiata, I went begging, at times in Monte Giuovi, at times to Monte Nero, and at times in other of the surrounding towns.[14] And the more often we went, the more we had. And if we went rarely, we had little. This was because of habit: the more people gave, the more they felt like giving. If you did the same, you would do much good. I know many who say, "I don't want to take charity from anyone; I want to pay my way." Another might say, "I would rather sell [something] first!" And it is better to sell than to go begging for a usurious loan, for the usurer will little by little draw everything [you have] to himself. But there's something worse, and that's pawning things. Here he gets everything for practically nothing, whereas if you had sold it, you would have done some good, first to yourself, then to the townsman who buys or resells it, and everyone would have earned something from it. Therefore, think about these things, and keep in mind that the usurer will carry away everything. You can see that this does harm temporally, corporally, and spiritually, without the least charity.

Furthermore, the usurer commits evil and he goes to the house of the Devil on account of possessions, and you lose your belongings as well. Moreover, the usurer hates his own children, his wife, and anyone who

14. All localities in southern Tuscany.

wears out his possessions, and you can't eat a mouthful without his count-ing it. Amos the prophet says, chapter 9, that whoever goes to dine with the usurer goes to dine with the Devil. And the usurer is the ruination of the poor: the poor man needs him [Amos 2:8], and all the help he gets is to have his neck broken. So don't get mixed up with them, because their money has long teeth to gnaw your bones. This is what I say about some-one who has something to pawn in his hands, since there is a saying refer-ring to someone who pawns something: "So-and-so is gnawing my bone little by little." Job says [30:17], "Those who gnaw at me never sleep." And this is why it says that death is riding the horse: *Erat mors super eo.* And death will dig his spurs into him again and again.

The first prick of death's spurs is to be blinded, because if you give what you have, you haven't satisfied your debts, since the food you put into your mouth wasn't your own. Know that by human nature, you only lack what you desire. Do you desire money, for example? If you do, that's what you lack. Do you yearn for pompous display? If so, that's what you lack. Do you want possessions? You lack them. But someone who lives a life of pov-erty doesn't lack either money or possessions, because he does not seek them and does not desire them. And remember that when the usurer grows old, he goes around with his mouth turned down, and this means that he will never be filled, because you can see that if you try to fill a vase with the mouth turned down, it will never fill up. So go around with your mouth turned up as you should. *Sursum corda* [lift up your hearts].

[Here's an] example: [there was] a man who lent at usury, and at that time a loan was made to some priests. And let me warn you that whoever in any way is responsible for money being taken from a church, for reasons of study or for any other reason, is obligated to restore what has been taken; for that is a most grievous sin. Now, this priest had to pay [a debt of] five *fiorini*. He looked all through the church, but he didn't find anything to pawn. He looked in the sacristy, and there was a chalice of gilded tin and other things of little value, save for a cross with a silver crucifix worth enough to pledge for his five *fiorini*. He took this cross, and he said, "My Lord, I'm doing this against my will, for I have no other way out. I will put you up as security for this money!" So he went off to the usurer's. The usurer was old and had left off the lending business because he was near-sighted and people had been giving him more money than they ought to, and for this reason he had handed it over to one of his sons so he could take over the business. Finally the priest went to this old man, who was holding a couple of rosary beads in his hands, praying away loudly with them to appear good. The priest tells him his errand, and how he needs five *fiorini*. "Do you have security?" asks the old man. He answers, "Yes." "Show it to me." So the priest unwraps the cross. The usurer exclaims, "Alas! Accursed man, [do you think] I would ever lend money on my Lord Jesus Christ! Oh God, have mercy on me! For some years now I have not lent money, and have given it back, and I have cleared my conscience, so I don't lend any more." Then the priest wrapped up the cross again and went off on his business, but when he had gone a little way, the usurer sent a child after him and the priest came back. Then the usurer said to him, "I see that you are in need, and I have taken pity on you, so go to my son who makes loans." So he went to him, and the money was lent to him on the cross. There you have the first prick of death's spurs.

The second way the usurer feels [death's] spurs is that he is always harried, day and night, sleeping and waking. If you think about it, you won't find many usurers who don't do crazy things while they are asleep, and they get up at night to be sure their money is safe. In the daytime, [the usurer] always goes where the poor are. Like the lion in the bush hunting prey for his lion cubs, the usurer is always on the prowl to see if someone needs his money. At home, he's still on the lookout: if he sees someone eating a bite, he says, "Nobody does anything but eat around here. Who could possibly provide so much!" He counts how many mouthfuls of bread his wife eats, and his children. He figures it up: so-and-so much is consumed in a year, and every mouthful seems to him a piece taken out of his own flesh. His wife, on the other hand, never has any money from him. She has to sell dried meat, grain, flour, flax, or other household goods in secret to have a few *denai* for her own needs. But as Proverbs, chapter 11 says, avarice always upsets a house [Prov. 11:29].

The third prick of the spurs is that [the usurer's] possessions will always seem as nothing to him. This avaricious greed generates four things:

First, usurious goods
Second, pledged goods
Third, certain goods
Fourth, much goods

First, usurious goods—that is, the usurer has to make a continual profit. If he eats, he's earning; if he drinks, he's earning; if he sleeps, he's earning; if he hears mass, he's earning; if he listens to a sermon, he's earning. Even if it's Easter or a solemn feast day, whether it rains or the wind is blowing, he is always earning. The poor man's earnings all go [to pay] the interest. So let me warn all notaries that if they ever make a usurious contract, they are responsible for the repayment if the first signer doesn't pay it back.

Second, pledged goods, for security is always required so that [the usurer] cannot lose money.

Third, certainly, he wants to be sure of not running short, and every day he sells something to keep up his money supply. However, the holy Church says that a usurer who has no one to leave [his money] to often leaves it to someone whom he previously wanted to see damned. This happened to one usurer, who at the point of death left his possessions to a nephew whom he had always mortally detested. The nephew inherited everything, and the usurer went to the Devil's house for the sake of this nephew who had been his enemy.

Fourth spur prick: he clings to his possessions, for not a one of them ever dies contented, and they die with great suffering. I was once in a convent when the following occurred. A usurer was at the point of death, and after he had confessed, he wanted to take communion, promising first to give back or leave orders to give back all the interest he had ever received, and finally, after he had received communion, he died of his disease. The night following his burial, the Devil went to the sacristan's cell and knocked. The sacristan gets up and the Devil says, "Don't be afraid; come with me." The sacristan didn't want to go, but the Devil said, "If you don't come, I'll make sure you won't live long." So he went. The devil led the sacristan to the sacristy and said, "Take a chalice and come with me." Which he did. He took a chalice and followed the Devil. The Devil led him to where this usurer was buried, and he said to the sacristan, "Take away this stone." The priest refused. Finally he agreed to remove the stone. The Devil said to him, "Go on in." He went in with great fear. Then he said to him, "Weigh this dead man's head." He weighed it. When he had weighed it, the sacred host popped right out and fell into the chalice. Since the priest had the host, the Devil grabbed the body and carried it away.

Another usurer dreamed one night that the Devil was carrying him off in flesh and bones. The next morning he awakened with this vision, and dressed in ragged clothes, he went to a monastery where he hid in a corner of the church. His wife went looking for him but couldn't find him. Everyone looked for him so hard that finally he was found in this church, and relatives brought him back home, apparently out of his wits. As they were returning to his house, they had to cross a large bridge over the water. When the usurer got to the top of this bridge, he saw a boat full of devils coming, and as it approached the bridge the devils said to the usurer, "Come on down." He threw himself into the boat and the devils carried him away.

Another usurer had taken it into his head to fill a box with *fiorini*. One night when it was almost full, the Devil began to strangle him. The man shouted out, but he couldn't get out of his grip. When he felt his throat being squeezed so hard, he let out a shout and said, "The Devil take me." Then, choked as he was, the Devil strangled him all the way and carried his soul off to hell.

Another fell sick, and when the priest went to try to hear his confession, warning him to look to his soul and [telling him] he should give back his usurious earnings, he told him that he was willing to do so. He sent for the notary and for witnesses and he made his will, the first item of which said, "I leave this priest to the Devil to be carried away, because he has always told me that all I had to do was to repent of my wrongdoing. I leave all of my goods to the lord of the earth, and may he enjoy them, and my soul I leave to the Devil to carry away." And thus he died.

Another usurer, at the point of death, called all his children and his wife to him, and he had them bring him all his money, all his beautiful belongings, and a stunning horse. And when all these things stood before him, he began to wail, saying, "*Oime!* (Alas!) *Oime*, my wife! *Oime* my *denari!* *Oime* my dear children! *Oime* my horse! *Oime*, for I am leaving you!" And as he was saying this, he bit into a cup and choked to death, and his soul left his body and the Devil carried it off to hell.

Another lived in Città di Castello. One day when a brother of our order was at the house of a usurer who was sick, he attempted to direct his conscience. The usurer called for a basin and had his money, which he kept under his pillow, put into it. Then, while he was holding his money, the friar told him to look to his soul. He couldn't stop saying, "Oh, my money, oh, my money!" And this is the way he died.

The fifth prick of [death's] spurs is that the usurer plays the good-for-nothing; he's a loafer because he looks after his own advantage alone. If a man is a soldier, someone benefits from it; if he's a wool merchant, someone benefits from it, and every trade does good to someone. Except for the usurer, who does good to no one, and anything a poor man earns comes to him. Some help others, but they're just working for the usurer; some sell grain futures for the usurer; oil is sometimes sold in the olive and wine in the vine. Thus everything comes into his hands by haggling, and all he does is haggle and he never thinks of anything else.

The sixth prick of the spurs is that this is a shameless trade. [I'll give you an] example. A preacher said in his sermon that he could give indulgences, and when he came to give them, first he called, "Doctors, come to me!" They went. Then, "Judges, come to me for an indulgence!" They went. "Knights, come along!" They went. "Priests, come!" They went. Merchants, and so forth. Last, "Usurers, come for an indulgence!" Not a one went. You see, they were called by name and they did not respond. Look, if you call the wolf, he will come to you if he is tame. If you call your sheep, "Whitey!" she will come to you. There is no animal that doesn't respond to its name. But if I say, "Here cat, here cat," it will run away at once. That's what the usurer does, he runs away at once. I think there are some people here who would love not to have come to this sermon, and if they could, they would pay me with a big rock.

The seventh spurring: [the usurer] is desperate, and more than desperate. He takes in goods, and someone else enjoys them. Oh, women, if your husbands are usurers, warn them to stop doing these dastardly things before God. There are many usurers who will say, when you talk to them about this, "What? If I give back [my earnings] I'll be left poor, and my children will have to go begging, and so will I and my wife. And if I give it back and don't do so willingly, I'll still go to the Devil's house. And if I don't give it back, I still will live. So I'd rather throw myself on the mercy of God." But I tell every usurer that neither his wife nor any of his children will ever do his suffering for him in the other world.

The eighth spur prick: the usurer is the worst villain. He never has just one vice, unaccompanied by other vices. First, he has lost his shame before the world and he has no love of God, and these two vices will be with him always. And I promise you, if you really want to mend your ways, take good strong medicine, and if you do so, it will do your soul good. Show a little virility; don't have just a woman's heart.

The ninth spur prick is that the usurer is always occupied by evil, since he is continually warring with God. He sins when he sleeps, he sins when he eats; if he goes to mass he sins, if he goes to hear preaching he sins, if he prays he sins, if he gives alms he sins. He sins in everything he does; he knows no truce with God, just war.

The tenth spur prick is that the usurer is all tangled up by the Devil, struggling and protesting just like a fly entangled in a spider's web. This is what the usurer does. He is always protesting to one man or another because the Devil embroils him in this world's *denari*, and he always talks about money and is never at peace.

The eleventh prick of [death's] spurs comes when the usurer dies, for everyone is happy. His wife is secretly happy, saying, "God be praised, for he will no longer lend at interest here below." And his sons are happy, saying, "God be praised, for now we will handle the money." And his kin are happy, saying, "Now we won't have this shame any longer." And his neighbors rejoice, saying, "Now the Devil won't live in this neighborhood anymore." And priests and monks will go about singing. In the old days, when people met a usurer, they said, "There's the Devil." If they came on his wife, they said, "There's the Devil's wife." The soldier rejoices in his death, saying, "I wish he had died several years ago, when he held my armbands for security, for now I have an arm wound that I wouldn't have had." Marriageable girls rejoice over the usurer's death, saying, "Has he left us anything out of charity?" And when a usurer dies, it is just like when a hog dies since everyone makes a party of it. Some want the bristles to sew their shoes; some want the tail, some the bladder, some the chitterlings, and everyone finds joy in his death. And when he was alive no one rejoiced and now everyone is glad.

The twelfth spur prick comes when he is on the point of death. Although he thinks, "I have done evil!" he is still gnawing at himself, and he still won't give [anything] back out of fear. And thus, as long as he lives he is always harried.

The thirteenth spur prick comes when he is dead. God calls Mammon, who is a devil, and says, "Take this one away to your house!" The Virgin Mary also says, "Take him away!" And Mammon stands before them and says, "What are your commands?" And Saint Catherine says, "Take him away!" So does Saint Lucy, and so does every choir of martyrs, confessors, etc. Then a multitude of devils get ready and they put his soul in hell, from which [we pray that] Christ liberate us, who is blessed *in secula seculorum*. Amen.

3
Humanist Culture and Problems of Political Order in Renaissance Florence

8. Leonardo Bruni, *On the Constitution of the Florentines*

Leonardo Bruni (c. 1370–1444), or Lionardo Aretino, as he was generally known in his own time after his birthplace, Arezzo, fell under the
spell of the first generation of Florentine Petrarchists soon after his arrival in Florence as a young law student. He quickly mastered the classical Latin restored by Petrarca, and he was among the first students of
Manuel Chrysoloras, the first official teacher of ancient Greek in the West
for almost a millenium. So proficient did he become in the new language,
indeed, that he translated a considerable number of previously unknown
Greek texts and retranslated many of those known only in imperfect medieval translations, including Aristotle's *Politics*. He adapted still other
texts to contemporary circumstances. His *Laudatio Florentinae Urbis*
(*Praise of the City of Florence*) of 1403–4 is based on Aristides' pane-
gyric of Athens (Aristides' *Rome* appears in vol. 2 of this series); his
eulogy of the Florentine patrician Nanni degli Strozzi often paraphrases
Pericles' Funeral Oration. From 1427 until his death he served as chancellor (permanent executive secretary) of the Florentine Republic, a
position similar to the one held by Machiavelli before 1512. The most
extensive of his many writings is his *History of the Florentine Peoples*,
which set the standards for all subsequent humanist historiography. He
was one of the formulators (along with Leon Battista Alberti in the work
published in this volume) of the new ethic that Hans Baron has described
as "civic humanism."

From *Peri tes ton Phlorentinon politeias*. Translated by Athanasios Moulakis and based
on his critical edition of Bruni's work, forthcoming in *Rinascimento*. Mr. Moulakis is a professor of political science at the European University Institute in Florence.

On the Constitution of the Florentines was written in Greek as a guide book for the Greek scholars and theologians who arrived in the city when the Council of Ferrara was transferred there in January 1439. It is dedicated to one of them, Georgos Amiroutzes. It was first translated into Latin, as a schoolboy exercise, by Piero de' Medici, the son and heir of Lorenzo the Magnificent.

Since you wish to know about the constitution of our city, of what sort it is and how it was put together, I will try to set it forth for you in writing as clearly as possible. The constitution of the Florentines is neither entirely aristocratic nor entirely democratic, but a mixture of the two. This is clear from the fact that some very prominent families, prominent because of the number of dependents and the wealth that they enjoy, are excluded from holding public office in this city: that is contrary to [the principle of] aristocracy.[1] On the other hand, the city does not receive into the commonwealth menials and the lowest classes of the populace: and that is contrary to [the principle of] democracy. Thus avoiding extremes, the city inclines toward the middle way, or rather toward the best and the richest [among the residents] but not toward the excessively powerful.

The assembly of the people is held very rarely in this city, because everything is arranged for beforehand, and the magistrates and councils have such powers over public affairs that calling an assembly is necessary only if a great change should occur in the constitution[2] and the commonwealth is badly shaken up. Then, the whole people is called together, and the assembly has the supreme power. But as we said, this happens very rarely.

The highest office in the city is that of the nine magistrates whom we

---

1. Bruni is referring to the *Magnati*, descendants of noble families of feudal origin. All but minor offices were reserved for members of the guilds (*arti*), who were called, in contrast, *Popolani*. In order to gain the right to hold office, which was the chief mark of citizenship, a "Magnate" had to be elected to membership in a guild—which of course could happen only if the totally "popular" membership consented to it. Bruni later uses the terms "people" (*demos*) and "the best" (*aristoi*) in a very different sense; there is further inconsistency in his use of the term *plythos* ("multitude" or "mob").

2. The editor follows the translator in rendering *politeia* either as "constitution" (a word that with its modern connotation came into usage only in the eighteenth century) or as "commonwealth" (the Ciceronian *Res Publica*; Italian: *Repubblica*). Here both meanings are superimposed upon the same word, and the editor has taken the liberty of rending asunder what Bruni (and Moulakis) united. These assemblies were called the *parlamento*: see the text of Luca Landucci published in this volume on how it actually functioned. Bruni refers to those who attended as the *demos*; but see n. 1.

call *priori*. Of these, only two are *popolari* of the [lesser] guilds; all the rest are drawn from the best and the richest citizens [of the major guilds].[3] First among these is the standard-bearer of justice (*gonfaloniere di giustizia*), who is chosen only from those prominent in honors and lineage. These nine magistrates are assisted by other men who act as advisors and assistants. They are twenty-eight in number; they do not always reside in the public palace[4] but are summoned by the Nine whenever some common concern must be acted upon. These men are called *colleghi*, as if one would say "councillors." Now, the nine *priori*, together with the said *colleghi*, have great powers, of which the greatest is that nothing can be referred to the great councils that has not first been resolved upon by the Nine and the Councillors.

There are two great councils in this city, one of the people with three hundred members, the other of the most prominent citizens, with two hundred. Those matters that come up are first considered carefully by the Nine and the Councillors and voted upon by them. They are then referred to the Council of the People; if they are approved there, they are brought before the Council of the Prominent (= of the Commune).[5] If they are passed by this council as well, they are then put into effect; having been put through in this manner, we say they have the force [of law]. [This is the procedure followed in matters] concerning war and peace, the conclusion and dissolution of alliances, the rendering of accounts by public officials, exemptions from public burdens, the performance of public duties, and all that regards the affairs of the city. If, however, the Council of the People does not accept the deliberations and decisions of the Nine and the Councillors, these are invalid and cannot be referred to the other council. If the Council of the People consents but the Council of the Prominent does not approve, the deliberations are equally null and void. Thus three votings are necessary: first, the one taken by the Nine and the Councillors; second, the one taken by the Council of the People; and third, the one taken by the Council of the Prominent.

You now see, I believe, something of the form of this commonwealth.

3. The *Priori* later came to be called *Signori*, and collectively as the *Signoria*, which is what Landucci calls them. The editor has incorporated into the text the explanation Moulakis gives in a note of the peculiar (and inconsistent) sense given to the terms *arti* and *popolari* in this passage.

4. Bruni: *en to prytaneio* = Palazzo dei Signori (Landucci: *Palagio*), now the Palazzo Vecchio.

5. With this otherwise unknown, but descriptive, name, Bruni is probably referring not to the recent and extraordinary Council of the Two Hundred, but to the *Consiglio del Comune* (Council of the Commune).

The great councils are like an assembly of the people, while the Nine and the Councillors are like a council, so that it is permissible to say of laws approved in this manner, as we are accustomed to do, that they have been "decreed by the Council and the People of the Florentines."

Since the magistrates do all these things, let us now see how and from what kinds of persons they are chosen. Every five years, elections are held in this manner: the nine *Priori* and the Councillors and some others gather in the Palace and scrutinize all the citizens, voting separately on each one. Whoever receives two-thirds of the votes is declared elected, not in order to assume office at that time, but as one who has been found worthy to assume it should he be chosen by lot. The name of each of those voted upon and deemed worthy is written down separately and placed in purses according to the part of the city [in which he resides]. This city is divided into four parts, which we call quarters. There are therefore that many purses in which are kept the names of those who have been deemed worthy of office. When the time arrives to choose new magistrates, the names are taken by lot from the purses, that is, two for each part of the city. Separate purses are kept in each quarter for the election of the standard-bearer (*gonfaloniere*) since this honor passes from one quarter of the city to another and is a sort of hegemony in which the whole city ought to participate. The selection of the two kinds of Councillors occurs in the same manner as that of the *Priori*. Some are leaders of the companies and are chosen according to their company.[6] There are sixteen companies in the city, and each one has its own leader. The others are the so-called "Good Men" (*Buoni Uomini*) and are chosen not according to company, but according to quarter, that is to say, three from each of the quarters. There thus result twenty-eight men who are advisors and counsillors of the nine *Priori*.

We have said that there are two great councils in the city, one of the people and one of the best (*aristoi*). These also are chosen by lot [from among those who have been] first scrutinized and deemed worthy [to hold office] and have had their names put in purses according to their company. For others than these, elections are held not every five years, but as often as is needed. It is common to all the above-mentioned magistrates to be chosen by lot after having been put to a vote and deemed worthy of holding office. But they are not chosen if [they are found to have] some impediment or obstacle. There are many such impediments: first, age; second, parentage; third, time; fourth, failure to pay taxes. Age is an impediment for the

---

6. Bruni translates *compagnia del popolo*, a relic of the old militia organization of the population, with the Greek term *phylé*, which the Romans rendered as *tribus* in describing the similar divisions of their own people for electoral purposes (see Quintus Cicero's *Handbook on Canvassing* in vol. 2 of this series).

young, for no one under thirty years of age can be among the Nine or the Councillors; nor can he be a standard-bearer if he is under forty-five or a member of the great councils if he is under twenty-five. Parentage often prevents one from taking office. If my brother or father or son or relative holds office, I cannot do so; for the law forbids two members of the same family being in office at the same time. Time is an impediment to those who have previously been magistrates. They may not take office again before three years have elapsed; nor can a relative do so before six months have passed. There is also another impediment: if someone has not paid the taxes for which he has been assessed, or even if he is a debtor of the public treasury.

These magistrates, chosen in this manner, conduct the city's public affairs. There are different courts, laws, and magistrates for private affairs. These [magistrates] are not citizens, but foreigners. Well-known and well-born men from other cities are chosen for this and given salaries from public funds to serve as judges in our city.[7] They judge according to the laws and punish the violent and evil men. There are two of these magistrates. One has jurisdiction over civil cases, contracts, and other such things; the other has the authority to chastise and punish criminals. Their term of office is six months; at the end of their terms, they are examined, and they give account of their actions in office before departing. Foreigners are chosen for these duties out of a desire to prevent hatred from being generated among the citizens. He who has been condemned generally hates him who condemned him and bears him a grudge, either rightly or wrongly. Moreover, a foreigner is more likely than a citizen to punish correctly and impartially. The death and blood of the punished somehow taints the judge; and it appears to be more offensive in a free city [where citizens are] equals when one citizen kills another. [Finally,] a foreigner will be more afraid than a citizen of the consequences of acting contrary to the law.

It would now be fitting to speak of the laws of the city; but that matter would have to be treated at length. We shall say this much at present: the city follows the laws of the Romans, of whom it was a colony.[8] Indeed, Sulla the dictator led the colony here and populated it with Roman nobles. Thus we have the same laws as the metropolis except in those cases where something has been changed in accordance with changed times.

Since the constitution, as we have said, is of mixed nature, it understandably has some elements that tend more to democracy and others more

7. This, of course, is the *podestà*, on which see John of Viterbo in vol. 4 of this series.

8. That was the new thesis put forth by Bruni in his *Florentine Histories*, where he claims that Florence was founded not by Julius Caesar, but by Sulla's veterans (and therefore under a "republican," rather than a "monarchical," regime, as previous Florentine mythology proposed).

to aristocracy. The provision that the terms of offices be short is democratic. The highest of them, that of the Nine, does not extend beyond two months; and of the Councillors, some have a term of three, others of four months. Instituting short tenures of office tends more toward equality. Democratic also is the high respect we show, in word and in deed, for liberty, which we hold to be the end and purpose of the entire constitution. The choosing of magistrates by lot without regard for the wealth [of the candidate] is also democratic, but many elements of the constitution tend toward aristocracy. The provision that all matters be deliberated beforehand and that nothing be referred to the people that has not been previously decided [by the chief magistrates] is aristocratic. Aristocratic also, it seems to me, is the provision that the people have no power of amendment but may only assent or dissent.

This city has experienced some changes, as I believe other cities have, leaning now more toward the multitude, now more toward the best. In former times, when the people were still accustomed to bear arms and fight their own battles, the city destroyed almost all of its neighbors, in part also because it was so populous. Then the strength of the city lay mainly in the multitude; and for that reason the people was preminent—to the point, indeed, of almost excluding the old nobility from the citizen body. With the passage of time, however, the task of waging war was transferred to foreign mercenaries. Thereafter the strength of the city seemed to lie [no longer] in the multitude, but in the best and the richest, for they contributed the most to the public good, albeit with counsel rather than with arms. The power of the people thus quietly[9] dissolved, and the constitution assumed the shape that it now bears.

9. Luca Landucci, *Florentine Diary*

All that is known about Luca Landucci (b. 1436) is what he says about himself in the *Diary*. The diary is very similar in form to many diaries kept by other Florentine merchants (and often continued by their descendants) in the fifteenth and sixteenth centuries. The standard (and only) edition of the original is the one by Isidoro del Badia (Florence: Sansoni, 1883). But the German translation by Marie Herzfeld (Jena: Eugen

---

9. Bruni has quietly forgotten the not-so-quiet uprising of the Ciompi in 1378 and the equally violent restoration of the oligarchy in 1381.

From *Diario fiorentino*, edited by Iodoco Del Badia (Florence: Sansoni, 1888), pp. 1–4, 6–9, 9–11, 70–80, 166–72, 176–78, 244–51, 322–31. Translated for this volume by Lydia G. Cochrane.

Diedrerichs, 1912) is well supplied with explanatory notes and identifications; and the editor has turned to it frequently in attempting to interpret Landucci's vernacular, often imprecise, and literate but hardly literary prose.

I note, on this fifteenth day of October 1450, that I, Luca d'Antonio di Luca Landucci, Florentine citizen and approximately fourteen years of age, went to learn bookkeeping (*abaco*) with a master whose name is Calandro. And I learned it, God be praised.

1 January 1452: I went to work in an apothecary's shop (*speziale*) with Francesco di Francesco at the [sign of the] Ladder, in the Mercato Vecchio ["the Old Market"].

8 February 1453: The mother of my father, Antonio, died and was buried in San Piero Maggiore.

3 November 1454: Antonio, my father, came into his mother's inheritance, for which we have papers, and he took over all her possessions and goods, both in the country and in Florence; among others, a house of which she and Antonio enjoyed lifetime use. An agreement was made through Messer Otto Niccolini that the monks of Cestello, who inherited it, would give Antonio 23 *lire* a year for his lifetime, [after which] they would take the house; and as long as Antonio lived they paid us this sum.

March 1450: The tax called Castato was decreed; and the decree was adopted in the Pope's Chamber [at the monastery of Santa Maria Novella].

And during these times the lantern of the dome of [the cathedral of] Santa Maria del Fiore was begun, as well as the palace of Cosimo de' Medici, San Lorenzo, Santo Spirito, the Badia on the way to Fiesole, and many houses inside the walls near San Barnaba and Santo Ambrogio, and in other places.

During these times there lived the following noble and worthy men: the archbishop Antonino, a monk from San Marco who always dressed in the habit of the order of Saint Dominic, for which he is called blessed; Messer Bartolomeo dei Lapacci, bishop and preacher excellent above all others of our days; master Pagolo [Paolo dal Pozzo Toscanelli], medical doctor, philosopher, astrologer, and of holy life; Cosimo di Giovanni de' Medici, whom everyone called "the great merchant" and who did business all over the city (there was no higher compliment than to say: "you seem to be Cosimo de' Medici," as if to say that no one richer or more famous than he existed); Donatello, the sculptor, who made the tomb of Messer Lionardo d'Arezzo[1] in Santa Croce; and Disidero [Desiderio da Settignano], sculp-

---

1. The same Leonardo Bruni whose *On the Constitution of the Florentines* appears in this volume.

tor, who made the tomb of Messer Carlo d'Arezzo, also in Santa Croce.
After them came il Rossellino [Antonio Gamberelli], a very small man but
a great sculptor, who made the tomb of the cardinal in San Miniato, in the
chapel on the left hand side; master Antonio [Squarcialupi], an organist,
who surpassed all in his day; master Antonio di Guido, improvisational
singer, who surpassed all in this art; master Andreino degli Inpiccati [An-
drea del Castagno], painter; master Domenico da Vinegia [i.e., of Venice],
a rising painter; master Antonio and his brother Piero, who was called del
Pollaiuolo, goldsmiths, sculptors, and painters; master Mariano, who
taught bookkeeping; and Calandro, a master bookkeeping teacher and a
very good, well-mannered man, who was my teacher.

4 September 1462: I left Francesco di Francesco, apothecary at [the
sign of] the Sun, who gave me, in the sixth year, a salary of 50 *fiorini*. I
formed a company with Ispinello di Lorenzo; the hope of higher gains
made me give up sure earnings. We opened the Apothecary at the Sign of
the King in the Mercato Vecchio in what had formerly been a second-hand
goods shop with low ceilings. We raised the roof and spent a fortune
(though it was far from my wishes to spend so much) and did everything,
not counting the expense for the furnishings—one storage closet cost 50
gold *fiorini*! Considering the high expenses, and seeing that Spinello had
no money and was in some difficulty, and since I had already spent 200
gold *fiorini* of my own and he nothing [even though] we had agreed to split
the costs, I made up my mind to back out of the enterprise as soon as I
possibly could. On 27 July 1463, we agreed to separate, and I said to him,
"I would like to leave you the whole shop, credits and debits, without any
further review of the accounts, and I would like 50 gold *fiorini* per year for
the time I am in on the deal and to have you give me back the money I have
already put in." And we did all this without the help of an intermediary. He
said, "So be it, but you will have to give me a few months' time." I agreed
when he gave me enough security—200 gold *fiorini*—paid to me by his
brother Lorenzo and master Lorenzo, son of master Lionardo. I pulled out
on 10 December 1463, and went to work in a shop at San Pulinari. When
we failed to reach an agreement, I fell back on [working for] Giovanni da
Bruscoli, who was opening the shop of the Agnusdei ["Lamb of God"],
and he gave me 36 *fiorini* a year, enough so that I bought [a shop] at the
[Canto de'] Tornaquinci on 1 September 1466. . . .

12 January 1465: The Arno flooded at night without a drop of rain (the
snows melted all at once) and it invaded Florence and flooded all the way
up to the Canto a Monteloro [now the corner of via degli Alfani and Borgo
Pinti]. The water made the sermon benches float from Santa Croce all the
way to Monteloro. The water rose in the Piazza del Grano [now via dei
Neri at via del Proconsolo] halfway up the door of the druggists' shop and
even beyond the Palagio del Podestà [now the Bargello]. The Arno over-

flowed its banks across from Messer Bongianni [Gianfigliazzi]'s house [near the Santa Trinità bridge], and it filled the Prato and via della Scala. Many mules and horses died in their stables, and all the wine barrels floated off, particularly near the Arno. It came without warning. . . .

24 May 1466: I took to wife a daughter of Domenico di Domenico Pagni, named Salvestra, on Saturday, the vigil of Pentecost. I had received a dowry of 400 *fiorini* in the Monte, in the name of God.

5 July 1466: I gave her the ring on Sunday evening, [the contract having been] drawn up by ser Giovanni di Francesco di Neri.

27 July 1466: I took her to wife on Sunday evening in the house of the said Domenico. I had [*ebbi*] as bridal goods:

1 pale blue *sacco* (surcoat) with tight sleeves, embroidered with pearls
1 purple *gamurra* (dress) with brocade sleeves
1 *gamurrino* (undergown)
24 homespun handkerchiefs
6 cotton towels
24 kerchiefs (*bende da lato*)
8 shirts, new, with a scalloped pattern
12 *cuffie* (bonnet-like coifs)
1 white *fetta* (sash) with silver decorations
3 caps of several sorts
1 small green purse with silver beading
1 watch, with pearls (*ogaraiuolo*)

These were appraised by two clothes dealers at 38 *fiorini di suggello*.
Now I will record my own expenses:

1 length of cloth for the girdle, plus silver and gilded decorations, in all:	Lire	—	—	—
for 1 ounce of pearls, for *fruscoli* (dangling headdress decorations), worth 6 gold *fiorini*:	L.	27	—	—
1 *brocchetta* (small pitcher), worth 3 gold *fiorini*:	L.	16	16	—
1 pair small knives, 2 gold *fiorini*:	L.	11	4	—
1 pearl *frenello*, (headdress chain for forehead) 10 gold *fiorini*, 5 *soldi*:	L.	45	5	—
1 *vezzo* (necklace) of 120 pearls, *fiorini*:	L.	40	4	—
for 6 *denari* of pearls, 1 *fiorino*, 10 *soldi*:	L.	6	2	—
for notions for the *fruscoli*:	L.	1	15	—
for 6 *denari* of pearls, 1 *fiorino*, 15 *soldi*:	L.	6	7	—
for *rascia* (woolen cloth) for the *giornea*, (sleeveless overdress):	L.	17	15	—
for *boccaccino* (cotton cloth) for the *giornea*:	L.	—	12	—

for 1 ounce of pearls for the *giornea*, 5 *fiorini*, 15 *soldi*:	L.	26	—	—
for 1 ounce of gold thread, for the *giornea*:	L.	5	5	—
for a ribbon to wind in the hair:	L.	2	14	—
for 6 *denari* of pearls:	L.	3	8	—
for a piece of ribbon:	L.	1	—	—
for silk for the *giornea*:	L.	—	6	—
for *panno* (woolen felt) for the *giornea*:	L.	1	4	—
for notions for the *giornea*:	L.	—	9	—
for *drappo* (heavy woolen) for collars:	L.	1	12	—
for silver and silk, for the *giornea*:	L.	—	15	—
for *drappo*, for the crimson *cotta* (overdress) of *zetani* (heavy silk), 26 gold *fiorini*, 6 *soldi*:	L.	151	10	—
for *valescio* (cotton cloth) for the *cotta*:	L.	5	8	—
for gold made into *brucioli* (decorative dangles) for the *giornea*:	L.	1	15	—
for the making of the *canpanelle* (eyelets):	L.	2	—	—
for azure silk and a piece of leather:	L.	—	7	—
for *guarnello* (lining) for the *cotta*:	L.	—	18	—
for the making of the *cotta*, to Lorenzo, tailor:	L.	5	12	—
for enamel [beads] to string on a necklace:	L.	2	3	—
for *maglie* (hooks) for the *cotta*:	L.	1	2	—
for gold ribbon for the *cotta*:	L.	1	13	—
for the lining of the *cotta*:	L.	—	15	—
for linen cloth for the *cotta*:	L.	1	13	—
for *banbagia* (cotton wool) for the *cotta*:	L.	—	2	—
for red *valescio* (cotton cloth) for the *cotta*:	L.	—	9	—
for a small gold medal for the *cotta*:	L.	2	—	—
for fine cording for the *cotta*:	L.	—	10	—
for *grillo* (braided trim) for the *giornea*:	L.	1	10	—
for 1 *balascio* (spinel ruby) for a pendant:	L.	1	5	—
for azure silk for the *giornea*:	L.	—	6	—
				—
for azure fringes for the tassels of the *giornea*:	L.	—	7	—
for ermine tails for the *gharzo* of the *cotta*:	L.	8	—	—
for fringed edging for the *cotta*:	L.	2	16	—
for fringed edging for the *giornea*:	L.	4	4	—
for fine cording for the *cotta*:	L.	—	2	—
for edging ribbon for the *giornea*:	L.	—	4	—
for 7 gold *brucioli* (bugles) for fasteners:	L.	1	12	—
for buckles for the closings of the *giornea*:	L.	4	17	—

for *senseria* (broker's fee) to Tommaso di				
Currado:	L.	12	14	—
for a diamond, 2 gold *fiorini* and 2 *fiorini*				
grossi:	L.	11	15	—
for a sapphire, 2½ gold *fiorini*:	L.	13	19	—
for a ruby, 1½ gold *fiorini*:	L.	8	8	—
for a ring that broke, loss:	L.	1	3	—
to Lorenzo, tailor:	L.	1	—	—
for setting the pendant:	L.	—	14	—

My wife and dear companion mentioned above, good and virtuous beyond compare, died. In the 48 years she was with me she never once roused me to anger. She had twelve children; and now she leaves me four males and three females, one a nun at Foligno and two at home. God be praised.

There were in my days the following popes, though I do not have the day of their creation:

Pope Eugenius [IV], who left Florence around 1440, when I was four.

Pope Nicholas [V] came after him. At the time of Eugenius, Felix [V] was made pope . . . by the council, and they remained . . .[2]

Pope Calixtus [III] came after him.

Pope Pius [II] of Siena.

Pope Paul [II].

1 September 1466: I bought the druggist's shop at the Canto de' Tornaquinci; and on September 4 I had the keys. . . .

23 November 1466: I led my wife to my house.

12 July 1467: I returned to the house of Domenico, my father-in-law.

27 April 1468: There was news around the fifteenth hour (11 A.M.) that peace had been made. There was celebration with fireworks, and the shops were closed.

15 July 1468: A tax called the Ventina was levied: it wasn't continued for long. Later they levied the Catasto, [in] 1469.

17 September 1468: Eight men were carried in a cart and hanged because they tried to betray Castiglione di Marradi.

15 April 1470: Fifteen men who tried to betray Prato were taken [prisoner] and were hanged.

26 May 1471: I bought some of the first sugar from Madera that ever

2. Pope Eugenius was in Florence in part because he had been chased out of Rome by the last of the late medieval uprisings of the Romans, in part to participate in the Council of Ferrara-Florence, which ended by decreeing the reunion of the Greek and the Latin churches. The Council of Basel had been summoned previously in accordance with the decree *Frequens* of the Council of Constance. After making arrangements with the Greeks, Eugenius transferred it to Ferrara. The majority of the fathers at Basel refused to move; they declared Eugenius deposed and elected Duke Amedeo of Savoy as (anti-)pope in his stead.

came here. This island was conquered a few years ago by the king of Portugal, who began to make sugar there—and I had some of the first that came here.

Monday, 27 May 1471: The gilded copper ball was hoisted to the top of the lantern on top of the dome of Santa Maria del Fiore.

30 May: They placed the cross on the ball, and the canons and many people went up there to sing the *Taddeo* (Te Deum). . . .

21 September 1494: News arrived that the king of France[3] had entered into Genoa, and that the Genoese had shown him great honor, decorating the entire city and even removing the doors at the city gates to add to the magnificence and safety of the king. But later it turned out not to be true that the king went there, although it was true that preparations had been made and that they expected him. It was said that he was skeptical about coming into [the city].

4 October 1494: A second embassy of the king of France came to Florence and went to the Signoria, but the response they received was unclear and confused. Both embassies left Florence indignantly the ninth of the same month, and returned to the king without an invitation to enter the city. The king was rumored to have sworn to turn Florence over to his men to be sacked. For this reason, it seemed to everyone stupid and dangerous not to offer free entry voluntarily.

23 October 1494: News arrived that the Duke of Calabria[4] had died in Naples of a natural death, perhaps of melancholia. People marveled that both father and son should die one right after the other when the state was in so much danger of being lost. Truly he had come to the fullness of [his] time when the hand of God touched him. [In such moments] we begin to believe and to abandon all our pride; for so it will be for all of us. Messer Francesco,[5] of what use is it to subjugate other countries? God forgive us and our sins.

26 October 1494: Piero de' Medici[6] left here and set off on the road to Pisa to meet the king of France, and when he reached the king, he arranged to have the keys to Sarzana and Pietrasanta[7] given to him and also prom-

---

3. Charles VIII crossed the Alps in the Autumn of 1494 at the invitation of Ludovico Sforza, soon to become duke of Milan, for the ostensible purpose of making good a claim to the Kingdom of Naples (and then of going on to destroy the Ottoman Empire, reconquer the Holy Land, etc., etc.).

4. That's not true. The Duke of Calabria succeeded his father Ferrante I as King Alfonso II of Naples in January of 1494. In February 1495, as the army of Charles VIII prepared to invade his kingdom, he abdicated in favor of his son, Ferrante, or Ferdinando II, who fled upon the arrival of the French and then returned shortly after their departure.

5. It is not clear whom Landucci is referring to as "Francesco."

6. Piero succeeded his father Lorenzo the Magnificent as head of the Medici family in 1492. He died in 1503.

7. Possessions of Florence in the northwest corner of Tuscany.

ised him money. The king wanted to make sure that he truly had been commissioned to make this offer, and Lorenzo di Giovanni Tornabuoni, who had gone with Piero de' Medici, came here and went to the Signoria to ask them to give him this commission; they refused to do so. And Lorenzo, somewhat consternated, did not go back there. For this Piero was somewhat criticized. [But] he behaved like a young man, and perhaps it turned out for the good, because we thus remained friends with the king, God be praised.

29 October 1494: The French took Fivizzano by force and sacked it.

4 November 1494: The Signoria decreed that everyone had to show his house for the billeting of the French, and they commanded that nothing in the house be touched or taken away. This displeased many people because they [thought that the Signoria] was showing more fear than necessary and that it was up to [the French] to be afraid if they started anything, even if we would get the worst of it. But God's hand was not lifted from our heads—nor is it now—for he heard the tears, sighs, and prayers of his faithful, who walk in truth and who pray to him throughout the day to show favor to the good and the right-hearted, who hold the honor and the glory of God dearer than all else, who praise him in adversity as in prosperity, and whose only wish and desire is to fulfill the will of God.

5 November 1494: Emissaries of the king of France came to Florence and went through the city picking the houses that they liked best. They went right into the houses and through all the rooms, marking them for this lord or that baron.

In fact, there were not hundreds but thousands of them, so that the entire city was completely occupied, even the houses that were not marked, for when the cavalry and the infantry arrived, they filled all the streets and *borghi* inside the city walls in a twinkling, shouting, "Open up there!" with no thought for whether [the house] was rich or poor. They intimated that they would pay, but there were few who did. And if they did pay something, they paid for the horns and ate the ox. Even worse, few people sent their women away from the house, except for young girls, who were sent to the monasteries or to relatives, where no soldiers were billeted. To tell the truth, [the French] behaved well; not one of them made a dishonest remark to the women. Secretly, they were very much afraid, for all day long they would ask how many troops Florence could muster, and they were told that at the sound of the bells, Florence [could call up] a hundred thousand men from both inside and outside [the walls]. The truth was that they had come with their minds set on sacking Florence, as the king had promised them, but they soon saw that the game wasn't even on the table, let alone won. And this all was the work of the omnipotent Lord.

5 November 1494: Five ambassadors were appointed. They were, first Fra Girolamo [Savonarola], a preacher of the Order of Saint Dominic who

lives in San Marco and comes from Ferrara. We hold him to be a prophet, and he does not deny this in his sermons but always says "da parte del Signore" (from the Lord), and he predicts many things. The second was Tanai de' Nerli, the third was Pandolfo Rucellai, the fourth was Giovanni Cavalcanti, and the fifth was Piero Soderini,[8] all citizens of Florence. And they went on the sixth day of the same month to the king of France, who was in Pisa.

On that day a great number of French (the king's advance guard) arrived to lodge in the houses that had been assigned them and marked with chalk.

That evening around the second hour (10 P.M.), the bell of the Palagio [Palazzo] began to ring. Thinking it was a call to parliament,[9] people immediately filled the piazza, and all were excited and frightened, expecting great things to happen at any moment.

8 November 1494: Piero de' Medici returned here to Florence from the king of France in Pisa. When he reached his house, he tossed out sweetmeats, attempting to increase his popularity, and gave out a goodly amount of wine to the people. He claimed to have reached an agreement with the king, and he appeared of excellent cheer.

And on the same day the Signori decreed that as long as the king remained in Florence no *gabella* (excise tax) would be collected on firewood or green vegetables, and that everyone could sell food and drink as taverns do.

Sunday, 9 November 1494: At about the twentieth hour (4 P.M.), as the bells were ringing for vespers, Piero di Lorenzo de' Medici attempted to go to the Signoria in the Palagio, bringing his armed men with him. When the Signoria refused to admit anyone other than himself, unarmed, he decided not to enter alone, turned back, and returned to the piazza. At this, people began to gather in the piazza, and in an instant people in the Palagio began shouting *Popolo e libertà* ("The People and Liberty") and ringing the bell for summons ringing to parliament and shouting *Popolo e libertà* from the windows. Immediately the *gonfalone* [the head of the militia in one quarter of the city] of the Ox (*Bue*) appeared in the piazza, and behind him came Francesco Valori and some other citizens on horseback, all of them shouting *Popolo e libertà*. He was the first *gonfalone* to come to the piazza; but in no time—less than an hour—all of the *gonfaloni* and all the citizenry

8. The same Soderini who became gonfaloniere-for-life in 1502: see below, n. 17.

9. The *Palagio*, or Palazzo dei Signori, since the mid sixteenth century known as the Palazzo Vecchio ("Old Palace"), was the seat of the government. It faces onto Piazza dei Signori, or della Signoria (the *Signoria* being the chief magistracy of the republic); Luca consistently refers to it simply as the *piazza* (and so does the translator). The parliament (*parlamento*) was an extraordinary assembly of all the citizens called in emergencies for the purpose of changing the constitution—or, more properly, for ratifying the results of another coup d'etat. It usually voted by acclamation to transfer all constitutional powers to an extraordinary *Balià*, which actually did the work.

were in the piazza, which was filled with arms and loud shouts of *Popolo e libertà*. Although it was not clear among the people what these developments meant, still not many citizens went to Piero de' Medici's house. The Tornabuoni and a few other citizens did go there, armed. They stood in the street before his doors with a good number of their soldiers shouting *Palle!* ["balls"—the Medici crest]. Piero then mounted his horse to come to the piazza with his men, starting out and stopping several times. I think he saw that not too many citizens were with him, and he must also have been told that the piazza was full of citizens in arms. Meanwhile, his brother, the cardinal,[10] left his house with many soldiers and the citizens who were with him, and he came down the Corso as far as Orto Sa' Michele (Orsanmichele), shouting *Popolo e libertà* like the others to show he had split with Piero. But what happened was the piazza surged toward him with their weapons pointed at him and shouting, rejecting him and calling him a traitor. He turned back, not without peril. And a decree immediately went out, to be proclaimed at the Canto della Macina and then at the via de' Martegli (Martelli), near the Chiassolino, that all foreigners were to put down their arms, on pain of being hanged, and that no one, also on pain of being hanged, give aid or support to Piero de' Medici.

At this point quite a few could be seen abandoning Piero de' Medici and putting down their arms. They slipped away one at a time, until he was left with only a few. At this, Piero left and went in the direction of Porta a San Gallo, which he had charged Giuliano, his brother, to keep open, with the help of many outside soldiers. And outside [the gates] signor Pagolo Orsini was [waiting] to come in, armed and with horsemen. It seemed to him a poor time to do so; he waited for Piero, and they decided to take off, along with Giuliano. The poor young cardinal was left at home, and I saw him at his windows on his knees with his hands joined, praying to God for mercy. I was very touched when I saw him, and I judged him to be a good and sensible young man. They say that when he saw Piero leave, he disguised himself as a monk and he too took off. In the meantime, it was proclaimed in the piazza that anyone who killed Piero de' Medici would earn two thousand *ducati*, and anyone who killed the cardinal, one thousand.[11] Also, many soldiers left the piazza with Jacopo de' Nerli and went to the house of

10. Cardinal Giovanni dei Medici (1475–1521), elected Pope Leo X in 1512. The Giuliano frequently mentioned in the *Diary*, brother of Cardinal Giovanni and son of Lorenzo the Magnificent, was the lay representative of the Medici in Florence (and therefore effective ruler) after the departure of Cardinal Giovanni in 1512. It was to him that Machiavelli dedicated the first draft of *The Prince* (see Machiavelli's letter of 10 December 1513, in this volume).

11. Actually the decrees, not of December 9 but of December 20, offered monetary rewards for delivering alive Piero and his two chancellors rather than rewards for killing the cardinal.

ser Giovanni di ser Bartolomeo and sacked it. The mob then turned, and crying "Antonio di Bernardo!" they sacked [his house] as well, as they also sacked [the house of] the Bargiello [police captain]. More of the soldiers and the people went robbing every moment. This all occurred before the twenty-fourth hour (8 P.M.), and all within four hours from when it began. Then the Signoria sent out a decree forbidding the further pillaging of houses, on pain of the gallows.

After this, the *gonfaloni* spent the rest of the night going through the streets of Florence by torchlight to maintain order, still crying *Popolo e libertà*, so that no further harm was done, except for the killing in the piazza of one of the Bargiello's servants, who shouted *Palle*! Meanwhile, Girolamo di Marabotto Tornabuoni, Pierantonio Carnesecchi, and others of that party reversed their stand and cried *Popolo e libertà* like the others; but when they tried to enter the piazza, they were met with the points of advancing weapons, and only their breastplates saved them, so they left the city. To be sure, Girolamo Tornabuoni was stripped of his breastplate in Orto Sa' Michele, but when he begged for mercy, his life was spared. Also, Giovan Francesco Tornabuoni was badly wounded in the throat and returned to his house. In the beginning of all this, some of the French who were lodged in Florence took Piero's side and went about shouting *Francia*! I believe that they were told that [the quarrel] was between two groups of citizens and were warned that it would be a mistake to attack the Palagio, so they acted accordingly, going to their lodgings and [afterwards] going about the city without arms.

Monday, 10 November: The citizens returned to the piazza with their arms, and from time to time people were sent for and arrested. Antonio di Bernardo was taken and imprisoned, as were ser Giovanni di ser Bartolomeo, ser Simone from Staggia, ser Ceccone di ser Barone, ser Lorenzo of the customs office, Lorenzo di Giovanni Tornabuoni, and Piero Tornabuoni. The Signoria sent out a decree banishing, under pain of the gallows, anyone who had or who knew anyone who had goods belonging to Piero de' Medici, to his brother the cardinal, or to ser Giovanni, ser Simone, and ser Piero, who resided in the house of the Medici, or to Antonio di Bernardo or ser Lorenzo of the customs office. Then they published another decree calling together all those eligible for membership in the Council. Many citizens went. This same morning, the cardinal's house in Santo Antonio di Firenze was sacked and [the Council] sent the *mazzieri* (macebearers; city functionaries) there to make those engaged in the sack to leave there the last remaining things.

Tuesday, 11 November: Someone came to the piazza from outside the Porta alla Croce and said that he had passed horsemen and foot soldiers of Piero de' Medici's on their way toward Florence. Immediately everyone began to cry *Popolo e libertà*, and in less than a half hour the entire city was up in arms and running in all haste to the piazza. Never have so many, great and small, shown such unity, or cried *Popolo e libertà* so lustily. I think that even if the entire world had attacked them, it could not have broken a unity like this. Thus the Lord gave this people a chance to be tested in this perilous time of the French, who continued to flow into Florence with the evil intention of sacking the city. When they saw the people so united, however, they lost heart. As soon as it was learned, around dinnertime, that no soldiers were coming, a decree went out to lay down arms. Nevertheless, the *gonfaloni* remained on watch day and night with a good number of armed men, and soldiers of the king of France continued to arrive on horse and on foot. The Signoria had the gates of Porta di San Friano [San Frediano] opened wide. That night the king of France stayed in Empoli, and more than six thousand persons preceded him, as many accompanied him, and another six thousand followed behind. The same day the *gabelle* were lowered and a good number of [convicted persons] were granted pardons.

Wednesday, 12 November: Lorenzo di Piero Francesco de' Medici [12] returned to the city and dined at his house at the Gora; and that evening he went to meet the king, who was staying in Legniaia at the house of Piero Capponi. The same day the Bargiello (police captain) was taken [prisoner] in the church of the Servites. [13] More Frenchmen than usual arrived on that day, and they filled every house in the city, even those of the poor, even all of Camaldoli.

Thursday, 13 November: News arrived that the Pisans had overrun their city, taken it back, and pulled down a marble *marzocco*, [14] dragged it through the whole city, and thrown it into the Arno, shouting *Libertà*! News then arrived that Piero de' Medici and his brothers were in Bologna, while here so many French and Swiss and such rabble were coming into [the city] that everything was in confusion, and people of every condition were seized with fear and suspicion. Think what it was like, with that rabble in our houses, from which nothing had been removed, not even the women, and to have to serve their every need, to everyone's great discomfort!

Friday, 14 November: Lorenzo di Piero Francesco de' Medici and his

12. Lorenzo il Popolano ("of the People") (1463–1503) was related to Piero through a common descent from the same great-great grandfather. He had never taken part in the Medici regime under Lorenzo and had been banished by Piero. His son was also called Pierfrancesco (or Piero Francesco) like his father.

13. The church of the Annunziata (Our Lady of the Anunciation) on the first Renaissance piazza designed by Brunelleschi, is the mother house of the Servites (the Servants of Mary). The fugitive was attempting to take advantage of the immunity of churches from civil jurisdiction—an immunity apparently observed at the time more in the breach.

14. A sitting lion holding a shield: one of the symbols for the Republic of Florence.

brother came back into the city along with some others who had been banished or exiled because the bann had been lifted for all those who had been exiled since 1434. Note that their chief hopes, Lorenzo de' Medici and his brother, were pardoned. And every house was already full.

Saturday, 15 November 1494: People were still pouring into [the city] and preparations were under way to pay great honor to the king.

Sunday, 16 November: The house of Piero de' Medici was extravagantly decorated for the king, particularly the doors of the palace. Two tall columns were set up at either side of the outer entry, with more decorations and ornaments bearing the French royal arms than you could count. It was truly a triumphal affair, as every detail was grandiose and well made. I can tell you nothing about the decoration of the interior. People on stilts dressed as spirits and giants and triumphal floats went through the streets, and a stage set was constructed at the Annunziata, and all Florence [was decorated] with pennants and the arms of France. The royal crest was also displayed over the door to the Palagio de' Signori, large, magnificent, and richly ornamented.

17 November 1494: The king of France entered Florence at the twenty-second hour (6 P.M.). He arrived at the San Friano gate and went toward the piazza, and they all went so slowly that it was the twenty-fourth hour (8 P.M.) when he got to Santa Maria del Fiore [the cathedral]. He dismounted at the stairs and went to the high altar, with so many torches on either side that they formed a double line from the door to the high altar, leaving a space free of people between them for him and his barons and countrymen to go up to the high altar, and to more tumultuous shouts of *Viva Francia* than were ever heard in this world. Think of it: all of Florence was there, in church and out. Everyone was shouting—humble and great, old and young—all with true feeling and without flattery. When they saw him standing, the people thought less of him than from his reputation, for to tell the truth, he was a very short man. Nevertheless, there was no one who didn't love him wholeheartedly and sincerely. It was thus easy to prove to him that we all had our bodies covered with lillies,[15] that we all truly supported him, and that he should show us his particular love and trust us in all things. This is true, and he will see in future how faithful the Florentines are. When he came out of the church, he mounted his horse again and went on and dismounted at the house of Piero de' Medici, still to cries of *Viva Francia*! Never was so much or such sincere joy shown and such uncounterfeited honor paid, since all our hopes for peace and tranquillity were placed in him. In the long run, things turned out differently. He took

15. The red lily (*giglio*) is another symbol for Florence; the white lily is a symbol for France (*fleur-de-lys*).

Pisa away from us and gave it to the Pisans, which he had no right to do and should not have done, since it wasn't his to give away. . . .

26 [March 1498]: Some people said that Florence had been placed under interdict (which was not true) and that the interdict was being kept secret. Nevertheless, the Frate [Girolamo Savonarola] was holding processions in San Marco and leading prayers, holding a crucifix and weeping and praying mightily, for a good number of townspeople, who slipped in, unseen by the others in the city.

27 March 1498: In a sermon, fra Domenico da Pescia, also a monk of San Marco, challenged a Santa Croce preacher who had been preaching against fra Girolamo to go through fire [to prove] the truth [of his allegations], and several citizens went to Santa Croce as his emissaries.

28 March: Fra Domenico, preaching in San Marco, declared himself willing to go through fire, adding that many of his fellow monks would do the same. Then, turning to the women, he said that some of these women would do so as well, and he was so filled with the spirit that many of them got to their feet to declare, "I am one of them."

On this same day, the preacher at Santa Croce accepted the invitation, declaring from the pulpit that he was willing to go through fire but adding, "I firmly believe that I will burn, but I am happy to [do so] to liberate this people." He also said, "If he does not burn, believe him to be a true prophet."

29 March 1498: Several monks of San Marco and several from Santa Croce went to the Palagio, bringing the decisions of the two chapters on how the trial should be conducted, and it was agreed that a Franciscan, [fra Giuliano] de' Rondinegli would participate and, for San Marco, fra Mariano Ughi.

1 April 1498: Fra Mariano Ughi, the monk of San Marco who had declared his willingness to walk through the fire, preached in [the cathedral of] Santa Maria del Fiore. He reaffirmed what he had said that evening, kneeling before the Crucifix in the pulpit, solemnly promising to go through fire for the truth and fervently praying that whoever was charged with arrangements for it would see them through. And these things he said publicly and from the pulpit.

2 April 1498: Fra Girolamo led a procession inside San Marco of all his monks and many townspeople. They came out into the cloister, continued around the entire piazza, and then returned to the church, fra Girolamo carrying the Crucifix in his hands and leading off the psalms.

6 April 1498: Fra Girolamo began to preach in San Marco, saying that he was prepared to send some of his monks through fire for the truth he had preached; and not just some of his monks, but all proclaimed themselves ready, and several thousand lay men, women, and children did the same, so

that in the middle of his sermon all the people rose to their feet, shouting and offering their lives for this truth.

7 April: A platform 50 *braccia* ("arms' lengths") long, 10 *braccia* wide, and 4 *braccia* high was ordered erected in Piazza de' Signori. It was anchored by wooden trusses, and on top of it a low wall of rough bricks was built on all sides one half *braccio* high, and in the middle they put gravel and cinders to cover the platform so that the fire could not reach the boards and timbers. All along the two side edges of this platform they put big unhewn logs two and a half *braccia* high, leaving a space of 4 *braccia* free of logs at either end, so that the timbers were 40 *braccia* long on either side. This way they left two *braccia* of space in the middle for [the monks] to walk through, but both outside and inside these logs many broom trees and large branches were piled up, so that there was one *braccio* of space left to walk. Also, oil, *acqua arzente* (alcohol), and turpentine were thrown on [the wood] to make it burn better. And at the appointed hour—the seventeenth—(1 P.M.) of the appointed day, the monks of San Marco and of Saint Francis who were to undergo the trial by fire, as they had agreed and promised, were to present themselves in the Piazza. Fra Domenico da Pescia was entered for San Marco, and for the Franciscans, fra Giuliano de' Rondinegli of the Observants. At the stipulated hour, the Franciscans arrived and took their places under the Loggia dei Signori, which had been divided in half with a fence, and they waited in silence at the side nearest San Piero Scaraggio [Scheraggio]. Then came a large number of monks from San Marco—about 250 of them—walking two by two with a great show of devotion and followed by fra Domenico holding a crucifix and by fra Girolamo with the Body of Christ in his hands. Behind them came an enormous crowd of people holding torches or candles, singing and chanting psalms with great devotion. When they arrived at the Loggia, where they had prepared an altar, they celebrated a sung mass. Then the people [began to] await this great spectacle. After a few hours, however, they began to wonder. The reason [for the delay] was that a disagreement had arisen. The Franciscans wanted fra Dominico to take off his clothes down to his drawers, saying that he was enchanted, which he agreed to do. Then they insisted that he not walk holding the Host, so that you could see that the Franciscans wanted to avoid the trial. Between going up into the Palagio and coming back, the controversy continued until evening. Finally the Franciscans broke off [negotiations] and left. Then the San Marco monks left, with the result that the people were extremely upset and nearly lost their faith in the Prophet. There was much discussion about all this. In particular, one group of *Compagnacci* took heart and began to abuse, revile, and scoff at all those who believed in the work of the Frate, calling them *piagnoni* (wailing psalm-singers), *pinzocheroni* (bigots), and insults of the sort, with the result that none of the Frate's followers could say a word.

8 April, which was Palm Sunday: The order that had been achieved began to break down. In Santa Maria del Fiore, just before vespers, as the people—a goodly number of men and women—were seated for the sermon and as the priests were preparing to sing vespers, some people—perhaps at the instigation of these *compagnacci*—started to say that the sermon should not be given. Then they began to bang the women's backrests and shout things like "Andatevi con Dio piagnonacci!" (Get out, you whimpering psalm-singers!). Consequently, many rose from their seats, there was considerable confusion in the church, and anyone who found his way to the doors was lucky. When some tried to stand up to them, these people treated them with utter arrogance and started a brawl, drawing forth the arms they were wearing. Many of the Frate's followers fled by the via del Cocomero but were attacked and some wounded, which meant that within a few hours the entire city was up in arms—[at least] all of those against the Frate and this company of the *compagnacci*—and flying toward San Marco shouting, "A' frati, a' frati, a San Marco!" (To the monks, to the monks, to San Marco!). People and youngsters came running with stones, so that many men and women who were in San Marco could not leave for [fear of] the stones. I happened to be there, and if I hadn't gotten out through the cloister and gone in the direction of Porta di San Gallo, I would perhaps be lying there dead. Everyone was arming himself, in fact. From the Palagio came the decree that anyone who captured or brought in fra Girolamo would have 1,000 *ducati*. The entire city was turned upside down, and none of the Frate's supporters dared speak out for fear of being killed. Before the twenty-second hour (6 P.M.) had arrived, several of the *Gonfaloni*, almost all *compagnacci*, arrived armed in the piazza, crying *popolo*! Then they began to say and to shout, "To Francesco Valori's house! Sack it!" They ran there, set fire to the door, then entered and looted everything. During this time Francesco Valori left San Marco and passed incognito through the vegetable garden and along the walls. He was seized by two base men and brought to his house. That evening he was taken from his house by the *mazzieri* of the Signori, but he was promised that his life would be spared. They were leading him to the Palagio when, near San Procolo, at the corner where there is that image of the Virgin Mary, someone came up behind him and hit him on the head two or three times with a pruning hook, and he died on the spot. During the sack of his house his wife was wounded and died, his daughters and their nurses were wounded, and everything was stolen.

Andrea Cambini's house was sacked, as was a modest house on via Larga, belonging to a poor man who threw roof tiles into the street from his windows. During this time there was fighting at San Marco, and the crowd there was constantly growing. Three *passavolanti* (long cannons) were brought to via Larga and via del Cocomero, and many people were wounded or killed. It is said that in the two streets about fifteen to twenty were killed and around one hundred wounded.

Around the sixth hour of the night (2 A.M.) they set fire to the doors to both the church and the cloister of San Marco, and there was fighting when they entered the church. Finally, when the Frate was in the choir singing the office, two monks came out and said, "We will give over the Frate to you if you will deliver him safely to the Palagio." This was promised, and at the seventh hour (3 A.M.) they gave them the Frate, fra Domenico, and fra Salvestro, and they took him away to the Palagio, insulting him terribly as they went. People say that they kicked them and said, "Va là, tristo" ("Take that, you wicked man"). They put his legs in irons and handcuffed him, fettering him as tightly as a great criminal; and he was insulted and covered with abuse.

9 April 1498: No new events occurred: people put down their arms but not their tongues, and it seemed as if hell had opened up. They were insatiable with their *ladro* and *traditore* (thief; traitor). No one dared to speak up for the Frate for fear of being killed; they scoffed at the townspeople, calling them *piagnoni* and *pinzocheroni*.

10 April 1498: At the twenty-first hour (5 P.M.), the Frate was carried to the Bargello seated on a stool (because his legs were in irons and his wrists handcuffed), along with fra Domenico. They laid hands on him and strung him up by his hands three times, and fra Domenico four times. Then fra Girolamo said, "Let me down and I will write my whole life for you." You may believe that when men who had every desire to live but who believed in him heard that he had been put to the rope, they did not hold back their tears, for he had taught them to pray: "Fac bene bonis et rectis corde" ("Do well to the good and the just of heart"). All this was done with tears, grief, and fervent prayers to God. . . .

19 May 1498: A representative [*mandatario*—envoy?] of the pope and the General [of the Dominicans] of San Marco arrived in Florence to examine fra Girolamo.

Sunday, 20 May: The pope's representative had him put to the rope, and before they had put him on his feet again, this man asked him if the things he had confessed were true. He answered and said no and said he was sent and commissioned by God. They put him to the rope again, after which he confessed that he was a sinner, as he had said before.

22 May 1498: They reached the decision to put him to death and decided to burn him alive. That afternoon a small platform was erected covering all of the balcony in front of Palagio de' Signori and extending from the lion out toward the middle of the piazza in the direction of the Tetto de' Pisani. Here a sturdy pole many *braccia* high was erected, with a large, round platform around it. A board was nailed crosswise to this pole, and when

they saw it the men said, "They're going to crucify him!" When these mut-
terings about a cross were heard, the board was sawn off so it wouldn't look
like a cross.

Wednesday morning, 23 May 1498: The sacrifice of these three monks
took place. They were taken from the Palagio and brought to the platform
built over the balcony. [The magistrates of] the Otto [the Eight], the Collegi, the envoy of the pope and the general, and many canons, priests, and
monks of various orders were there, as well as Bishop [Cristoforo] de'
Pagagliotti [Pagagnotti], who was charged with defrocking the three
monks. This ceremony was performed on the balcony: [the three monks]
were dressed in full vestments, which were then removed one by one, with
words appropriate to the degradation. Fra Girolamo was called a heretic
and schismatic again and again, and for this reason condemned to the fire.
Then their heads and hands were shaved, as is customary. When this was
done, [the ecclesiastics] turned over the monks into the hands of the Eight,
who immediately sentenced them to be hanged and burned, and indeed
they were led right to the platform with the cross-like pole.

The first [to be executed] was fra Silvestro, and he was hanged on one of
the branches of the crosspiece of this pole. He didn't have far to drop, and
the rope did not pull tightly nor slip properly, so he lasted a good while,
saying *Giesù*! many times while he was hanging. The second was fra
Domenico da Pescia, who also called out *Giesù*!, and the third was the
Frate called a heretic, who did not cry out but spoke softly to himself and
thus he was hanged. Not one of them spoke out, which was held to be a
great miracle, particularly since all were expecting to see signs that what
he had been telling the people was true—all, but particularly the good
people, who desired the glory of God and the beginning of the life of righteousness, the renovation of the Church, and the conversion of the infidels.
It was a bitter moment for them. He did not make the least excuse, nor did
any one of them. Many lost their faith. And when all three of them were
hanged there facing the Palagio, with fra Girolamo in the middle, the platform over the balcony was finally removed and used to make a sort of hut
on top of the round platform. They put in gunpowder and set fire to the
powder, and thus the hut burned, to the din of exploding rockets and fire-
crackers, and in a few hours [the three monks] were burned and their legs
and arms fell off little by little. When only part of the trunks remained
attached to the chains, stones were thrown at them to make them fall, for it
was feared that they would be taken by the people. The hangman and his
helpers took down the pole and burned it to the ground, bringing a good
deal more wood and stirred the fire on top of the bodies to make sure every
least bit, every relic, was consumed. Then, so that nothing of them would
remain, they brought carts and, accompanied by the *massiere*, carried

every speck of dust to the Arno at the Ponte Vecchio. And still, some good people's faith was so strong that they picked up the ashes that were floating away, but with great secrecy and even in fear, since this could not be talked about or even mentioned without fearing for your life, because [the authorities] wanted to wipe out every possible relic of him.

26 May: Some women were found kneeling in prayer on the spot in the piazza where they had been burned. . . .

10 June: The meadows of the Servites and the Tiratoio were covered with black caterpillars eating the plum trees, leaving the trees stripped clean and white. Less than four days later the caterpillars turned gold, and the children caught them, crying, "These are fra Girolamo's caterpillars." . . .

21 June 1502: News came that Valentino[16] had killed the boy [Astorre III Manfredi] who was lord [*signore*] of Faenza, who was with him in Rome, along with three other young men. He had them strangled and thrown into the Tiber when [Astorre], who was still a boy, was playing ball with his young companions. I think his motive was jealousy: he saw that Astorre was beloved of the people and, like a diabolical man, he envied his sway over them.

22 June 1502: News arrived that the king of France had sent an envoy to protest, [declaring] himself an enemy to anyone who offended the Florentines.

23 June 1502: News arrived that Valentino had taken Urbino and then Città del Castello. Furthermore, the French who were coming to our aid reached the Mugello this same day. Then it was said that Vitellozzo had taken Cortona. So much was happening!

24 June 1502: The *palio* (a horse race) was not held, for fear of bringing crowds together.

26 June 1502: News came that Valentino had sent word inviting us to enter into a league with him and threatening to attack us if we refused. He gave us four days' time [to reply].

27 June 1502: Five of the city gates of Florence were closed: San Giorgio, San Miniato, la Giustizia, Porta Pinti, and the Porticciuola al Prato by the mills. This was done for fear that persons and letters might be introduced. The houses along the Arno were ordered not to let down ladders to anyone in the river.

2 July 1502: We heard that Borgo [San Sepolcro] had rebelled, that Anghiari had surrendered on terms, and that things looked bad at [Castello della] Pieve. Thus it seemed that the Florentines had their guts in a basin

---

16. I.e., Cesare Borgia (1475–1507), son of Rodrigo Borgia (Pope Alexander VI), was given the title of duke of Valentinois (*Ital.*: Valentino) to justify his marriage to the sister of the king of Navarre. He is the hero of Machiavelli's *The Prince*.

[i.e., they were scared witless]. Everyone around was laughing at the Florentines.

The French arrived here that same day and were billetted all the way from Sesto to here at the Porta San Gallo and Porta a Faenza.

3 July 1502: News came that Cortona was back under Florentine control.

4 July 1502: There was a muster of the 250 infantrymen enrolled in the last few days. All this week, processions and sermons were ordered held every morning in every quarter of the city.

At seven the same night (3 A.M.), the French troops went off toward Ancisa [Incisa]. There were 100 horsemen and a great many foot soldiers.

That night, gallows and opprobrious things were painted on the houses of the Gonfaloniere, Piero Soderini,[17] and of madonna Selvaggia Strozzi by men who either have no fear of God or are unaware of their responsibility for restoring our reputation, or else who are damned souls. God save us from them.

5 July 1502: News came that the enemy was camped at Poppi and at Chiusi: it looked as if we were trapped.

6 July 1502: News came that the king of France had sworn on his crown to avenge all of the injuries done to the Florentines and to do great things for us, and that he was coming to Italy and was already at the frontier.

7 July 1502: News came that the enemy had broken camp at Poppi and retreated, that our army had arrived at Ponte a Sieve on its way to the Casentino, and that the French felt it was taking a thousand years to confront the enemy.

During this time, the Pistoians were robbing all over these plains as far as Campi.

11 July 1502: Our men who had been held prisoner in Arezzo returned to Florence in exchange for their men whom we were holding in accordance with an exchange arranged in Siena. Among them were Guglielmo de' Pazzi and his son, the bishop, while we sent back to Arezzo the son-in-law of Bernardino d'Arezzo.

14 July 1502: A *bargiello* (police captain) was named here for Pistoia and another for the Valdinievole, along with many mounted crossbowmen. During the night there was an earthquake in Florence around the third hour of the night (11 P.M.), but it didn't amount to much.

16 July: The captain of the French troops came to Florence with a few horsemen, and the troops who were with him continued on to the Mugello

17. Piero Soderini (1452–1522), elected gonfaloniere-for-life (lifetime president) of the republic in 1502 (see below, August 26), by whose government Machiavelli was employed as a "secretary" for foreign and military affairs.

and to Dicomano. The captain lodged with the Pazzi, and after dining there he went to call on the Signoria.

The same day news came that Vitellozzo had fled.

17 July 1502: The French troops reached our other camp at Ponte a Sieve.

18 July 1502: The French captain left here, and the artillery was loaded up and sent to the camp in the Arno valley.

21 July: News arrived that the French captain had gone to Arezzo to talk with them [i.e., the citizens of Arezzo, who were in rebellion against the Florentine government].

25 July 1502: News arrived that the French captain had arranged that we would get back all our holdings in the direction [of Arezzo] except for Arezzo itself. The people thought this not very good news; in fact, [the arrangement] seemed totally unreasonable.

28 July 1502: News came that the king of France had summoned three men; Vitellozzo, Valentino, and Pandolfo Petrucci of Siena.

30 July 1502: 150 persons were slaughtered in Pistoia—men, women, and children. Nothing has ever worked with them!

30 July 1502: News arrived that Vitellozzo had sacked Arezzo.

31 July 1502: News arrived that Valentino had [turned] against Vitellozzo.

7 August 1502: A young boy, one of the Vettori, hanged himself in his house.

9 August 1502: Commissioners [Piero Soderini and Luca degli Albizi] were sent to Arezzo to take possession of the holdings of ours that had been lost.

11 August 1502: A decree went out summoning fifty Pistoians from one faction and fifty from the other. They had four days to appear or be declared rebels and have all their property confiscated.

12 August 1502: The French who were in Arezzo and in those other territories were wreaking havoc. In Arezzo they took away [the Aretines'] arms and forbade them to leave Arezzo without their permission, demanding 200 *fiorini* of anyone who wanted to leave. One man did pay them, and he loaded up nine asses and started off. When he arrived at the gates, however, eight of the animals were taken away from him and he was sent off with just one. See what a fine example for others these crazy actions are!

15 August 1502: 100 Pistoians appeared here and were not permitted to leave [Florence], while our soldiers were sent there. Grain at this time was worth 40 *soldi*.

22 August 1502: A Frenchman arrived here as a representative of the king of France to get our things back for us, and on the 24th he left with our commissioners.

26 August: News arrived that they had retaken Arezzo, and that the leading Aretines had gone off to Siena and elsewhere.

26 August 1502: The Consiglio Maggiore (Great Council) voted to have a Doge according to Venetian usage.

27 August 1502: The Pistoians reached an agreement and the *gabelle* were removed for them, so they gained from their follies.

2 September: Lightning struck a live oak at my country place, only about fifty steps from my house, totally stripping its bark and searing it to its roots. It never recovered.

8 September 1502: The French left Arezzo and went through the Valdelsa, causing great damage.

20 September: The French were still in San Miniato al Tedesco, destroying everything wherever they went. They seem unwilling to leave our territory.

21 September: The image of Our Lady of Santa Maria of Impruneta was sent for in the hope that God would give us a good and wise Doge.

22 September 1502: The Council met and chose a *gonfaloniere* for life, who was Piero di Messer Tommaso Soderini. More than 150 names were put up as candidates, but only three remained after the first drawing: Messer Antonio Malegonnelle, Giovacchino Guasconi, and this same Piero. In the final vote Piero di Messer Tommaso Soderini won, God be praised. They immediately sent for him in Arezzo, where he had been all through the war. He was the one who went to Milano [to meet] the king's troops and who led them here like a valiant and good man. How good it was that he took on this office, and what a wise choice the Great Council made! This was truly the work of God.

7 October 1502: Piero Soderini, who had been in Arezzo, as I have said, came to Florence.

12 October: News arrived that the pope in Rome was quarreling with the Orsini and their allied houses, so he had fled to Castel Sant' Agnolo [Sant' Angelo]. In Bologna troops were being enrolled in fear of the pope, and the Venetians were doing the same in Ravenna.

16 October 1502: A league was formed against the pope and Valentino that included Messer Giovanni Bentivoglio, Vitellozzo, and the Orsini, and they retook Urbino and its fortress.

24 October 1502: News arrived that many towns in the Romagna—Camerino and others—had risen in rebellion against Valentino.

31 October: Cardinal [Federico di Roberto] San Severino entered [Florence] with many horsemen, and much honor was paid him.

1 November 1502, Tuesday: Piero Soderini, gonfaloniere for life, entered into the Palagio along with the Signoria. All Florence was in the

piazza, since this was something that had never before been done in Florence. It was apparent that everyone had high hopes of living well.

13 December 1502: At night, the roof of the butchers' shops in the Mercato Vecchio burned, but no damage was done to the shops [nearby]. . . .

25 August 1512: It was decreed to have [the image of] Our Lady St. Mary brought here from Impruneta.

During these days a great number of men—all comers were accepted— were enrolled as men of arms horse and infantrymen, and supplies were gathered from all about. More attention was paid to Prato than to any other place, so that no assistance was sent to the Mugiello [Mugello]. They[18] took Scarperia and Borgo [San Lorenzo]. Not too much damage was done in the Mugello, but they [the invaders] were in need of provisions.

26 August 1512: Ambassadors from the Viceroy[19] asked three things of the Signoria: that we join the League; that the Medici be brought back to Florence; and that the Gonfaloniere leave his office and go home.

27 August 1512: Six Spaniards who had been taken by our foot soldiers in the Mugello were imprisoned in Florence. Everywhere people were expecting to have to abandon everything at any moment. It was not so much that the peasants were afraid; when they saw the city dwellers acting in this manner, the poor peasants caught their fear. Those who understood, however, saw that in reality there was no point in being so afraid. It was up to them (e.g., the enemy) to be afraid, because they would be in a bad fix if they came down here to the plains. This is how all who understood the situation judged it. So many battalions had been formed, and the men of arms are all eager to go meet the enemy and kill every one of them. As of today, our troops number 17,000 men, between [infantry] batallions and cavalry.

That same day they [the Spanish] descended [to the plain] and took Campi without resistance; they entered [the town], wiped out a whole group of men, and robbed whatever they could carry. They burned [stores of] flax and other things and carried off many prisoners, although four of their own were killed and [others] wounded. They took the town so easily because some [of the townspeople] had opened one of the gates in order to escape, which they failed to do, for all were taken. Then they [the Spanish] entered, and when they had taken all they wanted, they went out again, left the city, and went off in the direction of Prato.

29 August 1512, the feast of (the Decollation of) Saint John the Baptist:

18. The Spanish army that had just been defeated by the French at the Battle of Ravenna—a Pyrrhic victory, for the French commander had died in battle and the army was forced to retreat.

19. Of the Kingdom of Naples on behalf of the nonresident king, Ferdinand the Catholic, also king of Aragon, and after the death of his wife Isabella, of Castille.

At about the eighteenth hour (2 P.M.), the Spanish took Prato by mortar bombardment and hand to hand battle. That they took so fortified a city in one day was astonishing, [particularly since] there were 4,000 foot soldiers [in the city]. Moreover, many peasants from the surrounding countryside had brought goods and their women and children there, fleeing from the entire surrounding territory, so there was treasure galore. It was surprising that they all turned into mice and couldn't hold out for even one day. There were two reasons for the besiegers' boldness: first, they had gone for two days without provisions, and second, they knew of the treasures, although there was an even greater reason, which was that the help that could easily have been sent from here was not sent. Who was responsible for this negligence I do not know, but here I saw troops being held at one gate or another while no one lifted a finger to send them off, and all this time you could hear the mortars booming. This made many wonder about this delay. When the cruel *Marrani* [Christian converts from Islam] and infidels had entered [Prato], they murdered everyone they met; not satisfied with having such a great booty, they refused to spare anyone. And when someone was left alive, they seized him and held him—whether he was rich or poor—for an exorbitant ransom, and whoever could not raise payment was tortured in the most abominable ways. Furthermore, they sacked the monasteries and butchered women and children with every imaginable cruelty and shame, and it is said that five thousand persons were killed. It must be by divine will that our leaders acted so slowly: we had more troops than they, since we had 18,000 men. We had already prevented supplies from getting to them, so they couldn't have lasted more than three or four days without dying of hunger. They all would have been killed or taken prisoner. Furthermore, they were not very prudent in sending so many soldiers and munitions to Prato, for such was their fury, almost impossible [to resist], that they took Campi on the 27th and Prato on the 29th. All this happened because of our sins. And now the traitors had so many provisions that they could have resisted as long as they wanted; they were all getting rich on such booty, and we lost all hope of defeating the Pistoians in any fashion.

30 August 1512: The Pistoians brought the keys [of Pistoia] to the Spanish camp and drew up an agreement with them, and the same happened at Pescia. The Signoria then sent two of our citizens to negotiate with the Viceroy, and after several trips back and forth, they drew up an agreement with the Viceroy that we would enter the League, paying 60,000 *fiorini*, that the Gonfaloniere-for-life would resign, and that the Medici would be reinstated.

31 August: The emissaries returned, and all [the terms] were accepted. As soon as they got back, [the Council] went to the Palagio, around the eighteenth hour (2 P.M.), and they dismissed the Gonfaloniere (who was

named Piero Soderini). He went peacefully and of his own accord, saying that he did not want to be a scandal to his own people and would accept anything that was God's will. Thus we remained without a Gonfaloniere. Later he left the city, as did many citizens, some going to Siena, others to various places, seeking greater safety.

1 September 1512: Giuliano de' Medici entered Florence, and the new Signoria came into the Palagio with no Gonfaloniere, while all the citizens who considered themselves friends of the Medici, fully armed, gathered at the doors to the Palagio and in the Piazza and blocked the streets leading to it. But the Viceroy was still not satisfied with the original agreement: he picked a quarrel and said that he wanted 120,000 *fiorini* in three payments. And still he would not leave, but continued to demand ransom for the poor Pratesi they had taken, doing many cruel and shameful things to them. They were not satisfied with having killed them and stripped them of everything; now they also wanted ransoms for those who remained alive.

3 September 1512: Lightning struck the palace of the Strozzi here and killed a master mason who had built its walls and was at the time paying a call at the house. This was just his bad luck: he who so often braved danger in the building of the house died when those dangers did not exist, as it pleased God. He was a good man.

These days, Spaniards have been coming to sell things taken in from Prato. One of them came with a cartload of clothes. When he got near the Piazza de' Signori, the populace looted the clothes and he barely escaped being killed. Elsewhere others were seized and killed, for example, at the [church of the] Servites, when a priest recognized one who happened there as the man who had killed his father in Prato and had him killed near the church. Another had his hand cut off at the Croce al Trebbio. [The people] wanted to kill all three of them who were together and they barely escaped by being taken into the houses.

4 September 1512: [A Spaniard] was killed at Piazza di Madonna, then dragged by Santa Maria Novella and through the via de' Fossi, and finally thrown into the Arno. It was thus necessary to decree, on pain of hanging, that they not be bothered, obstructed, or harmed. These things are done by ignorant people who just goad [the Spanish] and push them to even greater cruelty. They bring us even greater harm, for when word of this reached [Prato], they tortured the poor prisoners who were in their hands and dug in even more firmly. They even did their utmost to harry the poor contado of Prato in every possible way, and everywhere they went they carried off what they could and burned the rest.

Meanwhile, our batallions were all leaving, and another gonfaloniere still had not been chosen. According to rumor, the citizens were in some disagreement about how they should be governed. The most important problem, however, was to collect the money that had been promised, since the Spanish still refused to leave Prato [without it] and since the Cardinal [Giovanni dei Medici] still had not yet arrived. Among their other cruelties, these accursed *Marrani* held prisoner anyone they had not killed, demanding exorbitant ransoms for them and subjecting them to innumerable tortures. It was much more reprehensible than killing while prey to fury to continue the looting all the time they were there, to take more prisoners, and demand ransom from those they had stripped clean. But I believe the Viceroy and whoever could have put a stop to it will pay dearly for it eventually. We should have demanded as part of the agreement that an end be put to all this, particularly to the keeping of prisoners.

6 September 1512: The Signori, with the Collegi and the (Council of the) Eighty, adopted a decree to limit the powers of the Great Council.

8 September: The Council elected a gonfaloniere for a term of fourteen months, who was Giovan Battista Ridolfi.

11 September 1512: A Spaniard was killed in Piazza di Santa Maria Novella and dragged to the Arno, others were chased, and others had their horse or their money taken. Decrees did no good, and such happenings only brought on worse troubles.

12 September 1512: The money was carried to the Spanish. This same day perhaps twenty Spaniards passed through on their way toward Rome, and out of fear they got one of the Signoria's trumpeters to accompany them. This did them little good, for they were attacked on the other side of San Casciano on the road to Rome and were hijacked and killed. It was rumored that they were carrying several thousand *fiorini* and even letters of change for Spain for money that they were sending there. It also was rumored that their assailants were masked and were not recognized. In the meantime, those left in Prato and everywhere else continued to sow disaster: they continued to take prisoners, refused to respect treaties and alliances, sold everything they had taken from Prato and Campi—grain, oats, household goods, and whatever they found to sell—and claimed they would burn whatever was left.

Thursday, 16 September 1512: At about the nineteenth hour (3 P.M.), Giuliano de' Medici and his men went into the Palagio de' Signori, arms in hand, and took the Palagio, since they met with no resistance. A parliament[20] then had to be called, and at about the twenty-first hour (5 P.M.) the bell rang, the Signoria all came down to the balcony, and the articles of the agreement were read. They were as follows: twelve men per quarter were to be chosen to represent the people of Florence for one year, with power to create or abolish every magistracy of the city [government]. They pub-

20. See n. 9 above.

lished a decree that anyone could come to the piazza if he were unarmed; however, the whole Piazza was full of armed men, with armed horsemen everywhere, all the streets and outlets to the Piazza were barricaded, and everyone was shouting *Palle*! (the Medici "Balls")—inside the Palagio as well and all the way up the bell tower—and some of the people who had entered the Piazza made it known that they were satisfied with the parliament and the new government. God be praised. Everyone must be satisfied with what divine goodness permits, since all states and all governing bodies [signorie—rule?] are from God; and if in these changes of state the people suffer some degree of penury, harm, expense, or discomfort, we must think it for our sins and in view of some higher good.

18 September 1512: They began to dismiss the [members of the Magistracy of the] Eight who had served up to that time, and they created *Capitani di Parte* and another Eight. On this same day the Viceroy came to Florence with some fifty horsemen and went about visiting the city and the churches. He wanted to go up to the top of the dome of Santa Maria del Fiore to take a look, and a good number of citizens went with him, my Benedetto among them. He left on the same day, returned to Prato, and ordered [the Spanish soldiers there] to depart.

19 September: The Spanish left [Prato] and went to Calenzano, taking the unransomed prisoners with them. With this, our peasants who had taken refuge in Florence began to return home, although with some fear. The Cardinal left here and went to find the Viceroy to pay him a call on his departure.

20 September 1512: They who were more cruel than the Devil himself left Calenzano, they left Campi, and they left from everywhere else, and they went off on the road by which they had come. They camped at Barberino. And many peasants left here and returned to their own houses with their poor belongings.

21 September 1512: They left Barberino, burning houses and doing all sorts of damage, and we gave them several pieces of artillery.

22 September 1512: The first brace for the roof of Santa Croce was hoisted up in place, and it was hauled up in one piece and many people were needed because it was a difficult and dangerous task.

24 September: The second [roofbrace] was hoisted up.

26 September 1512: The image of Our Lady came to us from Santa Maria of Impruneta, because we had been granted the grace that our city was not sacked, because we had run a tremendous risk, with eighteen thousand of our people inside [the walls] and as many outside and everything continually tottering.

On the same day another twelve men were added to the forty-eight of the *Balìa* [the body charged with reforming the constitution]. The same day fifty men per quarter were added to these sixty, making a total of 260 citizens, and they had total powers. This decree went out from the Signoria and from the men of the *Balìa*.

2 October 1512: The Medici had their arms repainted on their palace, on the Nunziata, and in many other places, and they had the Gonfaloniere's statue (i.e., Soderini's) removed from the Nunziata of the Servites.

5 October 1512: It was decreed that anyone who had Medici property should declare it, on pain of the gallows, and many things were recovered.

13 October 1512: The Eight (*Otto*) banished Piero Soderini, past and deposed life-term Gonfaloniere, to Raugia [Ragusa—modern Dubrovnik] for five years, stipulating that if he left there he would be declared a rebel. They also exiled his brothers for three years, one to Rome, one to Naples, and one to Milan, on pain of being declared rebels if they crossed the borders.

Furthermore, they added men to the *Balìa* to make a total of five hundred men, by vote of the *Balìa* itself.

10. Bartolomeo Scala, *Dialogue on Laws and Judgments*

Between 1465 and 1494 Bartolomeo Scala held his predecessor Leonardo Bruni's post as first chancellor of the Florentine Republic. Like Bruni, he was a master of both the Greek and Latin languages; and in his official capacity he delivered a number of formal, and much admired, Latin orations. Like Alberti, he wrote a series of fables in imitation of Lucian and Aesop. He wrote his dialogue *On Laws and Legal Judgments* in 1483. This work reflects his study of Plato's *Minos*, which had just been translated into Latin by the leader of the then dominant school of Florentine Platonism, Marsilio Ficino, and the recent discussions of the codex of Justinian's *Digest* of Roman law, which the Florentines brought to Florence after the surrender of Pisa in 1406, and which Scala's friend Angelo Poliziano was the first scholar to examine critically. Like Bruni before him and Machiavelli after, Bartolomeo dedicated the last years of his life to composing a *History of the Florentine People*, which was interrupted at the year 1268 by his death in 1497. For full biographical information, see Alison Brown, *Bartolomeo Scala, 1430–1497: The Humanist as Bureaucrat* (Princeton University Press, 1979).

From "Dialogus de legibus et iudiciis," edited by L. Borglia, *Bibliofilia* 42 (1940): 252–82. Translated by Alison Brown.

There are some who think the sacred profession of jurisprudence and law concerns the art of winning an argument, not the art of revealing the truth and defending justice: it is they who make all the lawcourts now resound and echo with discordant noise and clamor. It is worthwhile to visit instead the libraries or offices of certain lawyers involved in litigation, to see the mountainous piles of books spreading everywhere—some on rotating stands, some on shelves or in cupboards against the walls, always open and ready for use. The readers stand in the middle, approaching now these books, now those, according to the diversity and obscurity of their cases. For they think they will be able to confirm what they want more easily and more readily impress their clients with their wisdom by the display of so many books.

You knew Pandolfo Collenuccio, orator [ambassador] here of the Lord of Pesaro, Florence's military captain, a serious man who excels in every branch of knowledge. The other day he told me an amusing story when by chance we met at the Archbishop's palace as I was on my way to the court, where he was also going. *En route* he embarked on the subject of our present discussion, which I suggested to him in order to prove his opinion. He used to visit the library of a certain bombastic and very mean man who wished to be considered extremely learned in the law. There he saw three rows of books. When he had carefully investigated what distinguished them, he discovered for himself that there were as many rows of books as there were parties to the dispute. Those that supported the case were all together in one place, those against in another, and elsewhere those arguing for a suspended judgment on account of its complexity. After he had agreed to undertake a lawsuit and had received, as is customary, a gold piece as the first payment for the suit he had accepted, he used to lead his client into the tripartite library so that he could see the rows of books and understand that the whole outcome of the trial lay in his hands: you may prefer to weaken your opponent's case and strengthen your own, or to make the judge uncertain and in a state of suspension.

Such I like to think was the judicial role played by Minos, Aeacus or Rhadamantus long ago, whom the Greeks charmingly invented as judges of the shades in the underworld. Certainly, as Homer says, Minos was the son of Jupiter; and during the nine years he ruled Crete, he often spoke with his father, that is, with reason and nature (for what else is Jupiter?), from whom he learnt the precepts of government. Whence "he who bears the golden sceptre" (as the poet says in the *Odyssey*)[1] is the judge of those who when they leave this world are thought to go to join the shades beneath the earth. He sits alone (as Plato says in the *Gorgias*)[2] and ponders the

1. *Odyssey* 19.178–79; cf. Plato, *Minos*, 319B, *Laws* 1.624B.
2. *Gorgias*, 524B.

judgments of Aeacus and Rhadamantus. Surely the same function was performed by Aristides, called the Just, or Cato, who is famous with us for his severity and justice. According to Xenophon in the *Cyropaedia*,[3] Persian boys were sent to masters to learn justice and spent their time pleading cases; and whoever happened to be convicted of a crime or who accused someone falsely paid a penalty. They wished to stimulate the seeds of nature and reason, which are the foundations of justice in our minds, and to induce in their young people habits of mind thanks to which they might make better judgments than by using the confused writings which the poet in his *Satire*[4] on Laws calls enigmas.

The Merchants' Court in our city, where less complicated suits are normally tried and speedily judged, finds it easy to distinguish between the judgments of nature and the heart, as they say, and those of laws. They select six men who are not experts in law but who are naturally shrewd and good. These men hear the disputes that frequently arise between traders and decide what seems equitable and right. Moreover, it is not permitted to appeal from their judgments. "The home of equity and truth" is inscribed above the door of their court, so that those who enter may understand that nothing has more weight with these judges than zeal for demonstrating the truth. The Florentine Merchants' Court enjoyed enormous fame even among foreign nations; and complicated cases were brought there from almost the whole world, just as people used to go long ago to consult the oracles at Dodona, Delphi, and Delos when in doubt about their affairs. The decisions of the six men were taken home and venerated like oracles. I think we lost our reputation as judges from the moment at which formulas of civil-law litigation began to creep in even here. I always find it very upsetting that once passed, laws cannot change so much as a syllable, for whatever reason or cause, however good or equitable.

Thus we see so many things happening every day, human affairs being overturned by so many chance events and so many different situations arising daily, in which one may rightly require less restricted powers and greater freedom of judgment. For it is scarcely possible in nature that a legislator can mentally comprehend every single type of thing that can come under one decree. If the law has faults, time will reveal them: which is why philosophers are accustomed to call it "most wise." For it uncovers and brings to light many things that without the help of time no amount of skill, study, energy or application can achieve. When a fault has come to light, you must either refuse to obey the law, which you may think is the most detestable thing to do, or else do something of the kind that the Roman people disapproved of in the case of Brutus, the author of their liberty [namely, sentence his own sons to death]. For just as we find any irregu-

---

3. Xenophon, *Cyropaedia*, 1.22.14.   4. Juvenal, *Satires*, 8.50.

larity in buildings naturally displeasing, so our minds naturally abhor cruel judgements; and whatever does not seem consonant with reason and nature, which ought to rule our minds, is thought wicked and shameful.

In short, how much better it would be to live according to the arbitration of a good man and good judge given by the light of Nature (who is always free and independent of any outside ordinances and supplies herself with abundant grounds for decision appropriate to the time, the facts, the nature of the case and the circumstances) than according to a necessity that men have imposed on themselves, which willy-nilly has to be obeyed, and often in matters in which a different decision would be highly advantageous. For this reason I do not entirely agree with the opinion that I think originated with you lawyers and that is thought to have been pronounced by certain wise men: that laws either should not be passed or, if they are, that they should surely be inviolably and religiously obeyed. It would perhaps be wiser, if laws have to be passed, to obey them only in so far as they do not contravene the laws of nature, which Nature herself instituted in us unchanging and everlasting. For it is Nature alone who educates correctly without teachers, who reveals uncertainties without dispute, who recognizes the truth and is infallible, who judges rightly and is refuted by no one. If anyone dares to depart from her, too confidently forgetting himself, or rather resisting himself and his very nature, he will inevitably fall into inextricable and most destructive errors. For just as sailors without their captain are borne hither and thither at random and often perish, dashed against the rocks or engulfed by waves, or are driven by gusts of wind to regions from which return by any human means is impossible; just as sheep are scattered if the shepherd of the flock is killed; just as soldiers, deprived by some accident of their commanding officer, are overcome by confusion and exposed to all kinds of dangers, including death: so, if you neglect, scorn and reject nature, the ruler, the guardian and the leader of all human affairs and actions, everything that mankind is rightly accustomed to fear and avoid will be yours to dread, to look forward to, and to suffer.

11. Niccolò Machiavelli, *Letters*

Machiavelli (1469–1527) entered the Florentine civil service as "second chancellor" (a position similar to those held previously by Leonardo Bruni and Bartolomeo Scala) in June of 1498, shortly after the fall of Savonarola. After 1502 he became one of the chief advisors to the lifetime *gonfaloniere*, Pier Soderini, particularly for military and foreign

From *Letters*, edited by Franco Gaeta (Milan: Feltrinelli, 1961), pp. 239–40, 275–81. Translated for this volume by Eric Cochrane.

affairs. He conducted several important diplomatic missions abroad, as far as France and Germany, and he organized the rural militia that was sent first to Pisa, still in rebellion against Florentine rule, and then, with still more unpleasant results, to Prato (all described in Luca Landucci's *Diary*, in this volume). It was during these years that he acquired the "long experience of modern events" to which he refers in the dedication to *The Prince* and in the introduction to the *Discourses*, and he learned to combine what he observed with "a constant study of the past" in such a way, as is evident from his official reports to his political superiors, as to emphasize the general rules governing particular political phenomena.

The reestablishment of a Medici regime in 1512 deprived him of his office, and after a brief imprisonment, he was confined to his small estate just south of the city (where the tavern he describes in the letter of 10 December 1513 has recently been converted into a very fashionable *spuntino* café). He thereupon collected what he had learned during his years in the chancery into the first twenty-five chapters of *The Prince*, as he recounts in the same letter, in the hope that it would be passed on to Giuliano de' Medici, since the election of Pope Leo X in 1512 the lay head of the Medici family and effective ruler of Florence. When Francesco Vettori, to whom he sent it, failed to deliver it, Machiavelli turned to other distractions—in particular, to a rather serious love affair and to much more extensive reading in the historians of antiquity and in the poets and chroniclers of Medieval and Renaissance Italy. He then joined the circle of Florentine men of letters that met regularly in the gardens of the Rucellai family; it was for them that he composed, and read aloud, between 1515 and 1516, the *Discourses*, which with some additions to bring them up to date he dedicated to two of his associates in 1517.

Meanwhile, in the first months of 1516, Pope Leo's twenty-two-year-old nephew Lorenzo succeeded the deceased Giuliano as lay head of the Medici family, and after failing to carve out one secular state for him in northern Italy, Pope Leo presented him with the Duchy of Urbino, which he had just conquered at great expense from the Della Rovere family of his predecessor, Pope Julius II. Suddenly the particular political situation (*occasione*) that had pertained at the time of Cesare Borgia and Pope Alexander VI reappeared: three states in central Italy were united under the rule of a single family. Machiavelli forthwith exhumed his copy of *The Prince*, inserted an introductory phrase to chapter 2 ("I will not speak here of republics") for the benefit of his colleagues in the Rucellai gardens, and added the final chapter (26). What had been a manual of political wisdom thus became an exhortation to use that wisdom for the purpose of ridding Italy of what he now perceived as the immediate cause of all its ills, non-Italian armies.

Unfortunately, Lorenzo showed no signs of possessing the strength of character (*virtù*) necessary to take advantage of the favorable turn of *for-tuna*, and Machiavelli turned to literary pursuits: his first comedy, *La Mandragola*, was recognized as a classic of Italian dramatic literature as soon as it was first performed in 1518. He then returned to political concerns at the invitation of Cardinal Giulio de' Medici, the successor of Lorenzo as effective ruler of the city. In the same year in which Cardinal Giulio became Pope Clement VII (1523–34), he was commissioned to write, like his predecessors Bruni and Scala, his *Florentine Histories*. He died, possibly of disappointment at not being given a responsible job, soon after the coup d'état of 1527 that once again threw out the Medici and restored an oligarchical regime.

Most of Machiavelli's writings circulated widely in manuscript during his lifetime; and the dedication to the first edition was accepted with pleasure by Pope Clement VII in 1531. Even though the establishment of the principate in Florence after 1537 (chronicled in detail in the selection from Ammirato in this volume) ruled out any immediate application of the constitutional formulae set down in the *Discourses*, and even though all the works appeared on the Indexes of Paul IV and of the Council of Trent ("until corrected"), Machiavelli's methods continued to dominate the theoretical discussion of politics in Italy at least through the age of Giovanni Botero (as can be seen in the selections included in this volume); and they continued to be influential elsewhere in Europe for another two centuries thereafter.

No. 124.

Florence, 9 April 1513. To the Magnificent Orator [of the Florentine Republic] to the Supreme Pontiff,[1] Francesco Vettori,[2] in Rome.
    Magnificent Sir Orator:

    1. Pope Leo X, born Giovanni de' Medici, the second son of Lorenzo the Magnificent (1475–1523), elected pope on 15 March of this same year, 1513.
    2. (1474–1539). Vettori became a close friend of Machiavelli during his first embassy, to Emperor Maximilian I, in 1507, and like Machiavelli suffered for his close association with the Soderini regime after its fall in 1512. He was nonetheless chosen ambassador first to Pope Julius II and then to Leo X. In 1515 he arranged the French marriage that seemed to him, as to Machiavelli, to portend the elevation of the pope's nephew, Lorenzo Duke of Urbino, as an incarnation of Machiavelli's *Prince*. After 1530 he became a close counselor to Duke Alessandro de' Medici and was largely responsible for the election of Cosimo as his successor in 1537 (all described in the selections from Ammirato's *History* published in this volume). He was also a distinguished writer of histories, biographies, and political reflections, all of which have been published in his *Scritti storici e politici*, edited by Enrico Niccolini (Bari: Laterza, 1972).

And I, becoming aware of the color of his face,
Said to him: How shall I proceed, who am usually
Comforted by you in my troubles,
When I see that you are afraid?[3]

This letter of yours has scared me more than the rack, and I'm sorry that you think I am angry—not for my sake, now that I am set on no longer desiring anything passionately, but for yours. I pray you to imitate others who get ahead more with persistence and craft than with intelligence and prudence. With regard to that story about Totto, if it displeases you, it displeases me. Anyway, I won't bother about it further; and if you can't enroll him, turn him over. I'm telling you once again: don't take the least trouble for anything I may ask of you, for I'll never get annoyed.

If you have tired of talking about political affairs after having seen them turn out just the opposite of what is said and understood about them, I don't blame you. The same thing has happened to me. Still, if I could talk to you, I would not be able to refrain from filling your head with castles. For fortune has decreed that, since I can't talk either about the silk business, or about the wool business, or about profits and losses, it's fitting that I talk about politics; and I must either make up my mind to shut up altogether or talk about that. If I could get out of Florentine territory, I too would come right down there to see if the pope is at home. Among the many favors he has bestowed upon other Florentines, the ones I expected seem to have been lost in the shuffle, probably because of my own negligence. I'll wait until September.

I hear that Cardinal Soderini[4] has a lot of business with the pope. Please give me some advice. Should I write him a letter asking that he recommend me to His Holiness, or should I let you do this for me by word of mouth when you see the cardinal? Or should I do neither the one nor the other? I await your response.

As for the horse, you make me laugh reminding me of it: you'll have to pay me for it whenever I get around to remembering it and not a moment sooner.

Our archbishop[5] must by now be dead. God take his soul and the souls of all his family. Farewell.

---

3. Dante, *Inferno*, 6:16–18.
4. Francesco Soderini (1453–1524), brother of the *gonfaloniere* Piero, bishop of Volterra; made cardinal in 1503.
5. Cosimo de' Pazzi; hence, a relative of Francesco de' Pazzi, the chief architect of the infamous Pazzi Conspiracy of 1478 and one of the murderers of Lorenzo's brother, Giuliano de' Medici.

No. 135.

Sant'Andrea in Percussina, 10 August 1513. To the Magnificent Orator to the Supreme Pontiff, Francesco Vettori, his [Machiavelli's] Patron:

Mr. Orator: You don't want this poor king of France [Louis XII] to have Lombardy, and I do. I think that your wanting and my not wanting have the same foundation: a natural affection and passion that make you say yes and me no. You back up your "no" by showing that it would be more difficult to bring about a peace if the king returned to Lombardy. I have shown, in order to back up my "yes," that the truth is quite otherwise, and that peace established according to the plan I put forth will be more certain and lasting.

Coming again to particulars in response to your letter of the 5th, I say that I'm with you [in your opinion] that it will always seem strange to the king of England [Henry VIII] to have come into France with such a big show and then to have retreated; yet this retreat must be shown to rest upon some necessity. I judged that a great enough necessity would be that to which he had been driven by Spain [King Ferdinand the Catholic] and the pope; and I judged, and still do judge, that if he realized the difficulties of the expedition on one hand and realized the opposition of Spain and the pope to it on the other, he could be easily persuaded [to get out of France]. If he should remain discontent, so much the better; for, caught between the English and the Swiss, both of them hostile toward and suspicious of him, the king of France would be weakened; he would not be able to think about occupying others' territories but would have to think about getting others to protect his territory for him. Thus the king of Spain would realize his objective: for I believe that besides protecting his own states, he is figuring out how his armies can remain the cock of Italy. That indeed is what they would be; for France, caught between the suspicions of England and the hostility of the Germans, could not send a large army into Lombardy; and he will have to depend upon the Spanish army [to stay there].

Nor do I see how the Swiss alone can force the English to yield, for I do not believe that they can want to serve France in any other way than as mercenaries. They are poor and do not have a common border with England. Hence, it is well that France pay them and pay them well. He can also hire *Landsknechten*[6] and get much the same service out of them, since England is afraid of them [as of the Swiss]. If you tell me that England can get the Swiss to attack France in Burgundy, I say that this is a way of hurting France; and if you want England to withdraw, you have to find a way of hurting him as well. I don't want Spain and the pope to attack him either: I

6. Mercenary soldiers recruited in southern Germany.

want the first to abandon him and the second to show that the real reason for making war on France was out of respect for the Church, and now that France has stopped bothering the Church, the Church need no longer bother him. I think that England is about to retreat without stronger medicine, as I've said many times, since he has before and has now again found that such an expedition is dangerous. England must consider that if he gets involved in a battle and loses it, he may lose his own kingdom as well as France. And if you tell me: "He'll send a lot of money to the Germans and get France attacked from the other side," I reply with my opinion that he has always, out of pride and for the sake of glory, preferred to spend his money on his own men. Moreover, whatever money he might send to the emperor would be thrown away, and the Swiss would want more than he has to give.

I also believe that good relations can be easily established between France and Spain, for it doesn't suit Spain to destroy France in this way. France has already seen an example of this [policy], for in the midst of his greatest dangers, Spain withdrew his army. And France would be all the more likely to place his trust in Spain if through Spain's efforts he were given back Lombardy. For new benefits generally make one forget past injuries. On the other hand, Spain would have nothing to fear from an old, worn-out, sickly king caught between the English and the Germans, the first suspicious and the second hostile. Nor would he need to defend himself solely with help from the pope: all he'd have to do is nourish this hostility. Hence, I do not see any greater difficulty in bringing about peace in the way I proposed than in the way you proposed. Indeed, if there's any advantage to one rather than the other, it's in mine. Moreover, I see no certainty in your plan, whereas I do in mine—at least as much certainty as can be had in these times.

To find out whether a peace is to be either certain or lasting, one must among other things see who remains discontent with it and what will come of his discontent. Considering your plan for peace, then, I see that England, France, and the emperor will remain discontent, for none of them will have realized his objectives. In my plan, England, the Swiss, and the emperor will remain discontent for the same reasons. Discontent in your case can easily cause the ruin of Italy and Spain; for as soon as this peace is made, even though it is approved by France and it is not rejected by England, both of the latter will change their aims and their plans. Whereas France until now has wanted to return to Italy and England to dominate France, they will both turn for revenge against Italy and Spain. For reason would oblige them to make a second accord among themselves; and once that is done, they will have no difficulty whatever in achieving whatever they want as soon as France is willing to reveal himself. With the support of England and France, the emperor will leap off to Castille the very next day, then move on Italy, and finally let France come along with him. Thus, in no time at all three powers together can upset and ruin everything. Neither the Spanish, nor the Swiss armies, nor the money of the pope will be enough to stop them, for they together would have too many troops and too much money. It is reasonable that Spain see this danger and that he try in every way to avoid it. For in this peace of yours France has no reason to love Spain and many reasons for wishing to harm him—reasons which France would never be able to disregard. Hence, if Spain has an eye for seeing distant things, he will neither consent to such a peace nor carry it out, but rather stir up an even greater and more dangerous war. On the other hand, making a peace the way I wrote you about, with only England, the emperor, and the Swiss among the malcontents, none of the latter, either separately or together, can easily harm the other signatories, for France both on this and on the other side of the mountains [the Alps] would act as a barrier against them and, with the help of the others, would see to it that the other signatories remain safe and that the discontented ones avoid embarking on an obviously dangerous enterprise. The various signatories would then have no reason for fearing each other, since, as I have often written you, all of them will have realized their aims and will stay chained together through fear of such dangerous and powerful enemies.

Notice this other grave danger for Italy in your plans: every time a weak duke is left in Milan, Lombardy really belongs not to the duke but to the Swiss. And although the three discontented parties let pass a thousand occasions for acting, I think this proximity of the Swiss is extremely important and should be pondered more carefully than it usually is. For I don't think, as you do, that they'll stay quiet, either out of respect for France, or out of fear of having all Italy against them, or else because they're interested only in raking up what they can get and then going home. First, because France, as I said above, will want to take revenge; after having been injured by all Italy, he will want to ruin all Italy in return. He will therefore pass money under cover to the Swiss and is thus more apt than not to light a fire. As to the union of the other Italians, you make me laugh. First a union is never achieved for the purpose of doing good. Even if the heads of the states came together, they couldn't do anything, because except for the Spanish their armies aren't worth a penny; and the Spanish are too few to do anything alone. The tails are not tied to the heads; and the moment that nation [the Swiss] makes the slightest motion, everyone will rush to join sides with them.

As far as the Swiss grabbing what they can and then leaving, I beg you not to swallow nor to get others to swallow such an idea. Consider the affairs of men and how the powers of this world grow, particularly republics.

You will see that at first men are content with defending themselves and not letting others dominate them. They then go on to injure others and try to dominate them. The Swiss were at first content to defend themselves against the dukes of Austria, and their defense gave them a lot of self-esteem. Then they were content with defending themselves against Duke Charles [the Bold, duke of Burgundy, whom they beat at the Battle of Granson in 1477] and that gave them a reputation abroad. They were then content to be paid by others, which kept their young men accustomed to arms and got them honor as well. Their reputation has thus grown still further in many provinces and among many men and has made them still more audacious; and this experience has also put into their minds a desire to fight [not just for others but] for themselves as well. Pellegrino Lorini once told me that when they came with Beaumont to Pisa, they frequently talked to him about the strength (*virtù*) of their militia. They said it was similar to the Roman militia and gave reasons for its not being able to do one day what the Romans had done. They boasted about having given France all its victories up to that time and wondered why they would not be able someday to fight for themselves. The occasion for their doing just that has now arisen, and they have seized it: they have entered Lombardy with the excuse of restoring the duke [Francesco II Sforza], whereas in fact it is they who are the duke. At the first opportunity (*occasione*) they'll take it in name as well as in fact, wiping out the ducal family and all the nobility of the state. At the next opportunity they'll overrun all Italy, doing the same thing there. Hence I conclude that they're not going just to make a raid and then go home. Rather, we have good reason to be very much afraid of them.

I'm aware that this opinion of mine runs contrary to a natural defect of all men: first, wanting to live from day to day and not believing that anything can occur that has not already been, and second, making calculations about someone always in the same way. Thus there's no one who advises throwing the Swiss out of Lombardy and bringing the French back in, because no one wants to run the risks that would be necessary and because no one wants to think about future ills or is ready to trust France. My good friend, this German river is so full of water that it can be controlled only by very high dikes. Even if France had never come into Italy, and if you did not have fresh in mind his insolence, insatiable greed, and extortions, which are what bother you the most in this deliberation, you would probably have run straight off to France to beg him to come into Lombardy; because the remedy for this flood must be adopted now, before [the Swiss] sink roots too deeply in that state and begin to realize the delights of dominion. If they settle down there, all Italy will be swept away, because all the discontents in Italy will side with them and become a ladder for their greatness and for the ruin of others. I'm afraid of them alone, and not of them [in alliance] with the emperor, as Casa wrote you. Of course, it would be easy for them to unite with him. For he is perfectly happy to see them sack Lombardy and become lords of Milan, even though no one would ever have thought him to be so for the very reasons that you wrote to me. Thus, notwithstanding those reasons, they can be happy to have him make some progress in Italy.

I'm writing you, Mr. Ambassador, more to give you satisfaction than [to show that] I know what I'm talking about. Please, then, let me know in your next letter how the world's going and what is done, hoped for, and feared [in Rome] if you want me to come up with better arguments in these grave matters. Otherwise you'll be stuck with a donkey's will and testament or with one of those things like Biancaccino. I commend myself to you.

Nicholaus Machiavellus in villa.

No. 140.

Florence, 10 December 1513.
To the magnificent Florentine Orator to the Supreme Pontiff, and his bene-factor, Francesco Vettori.
Noble Ambassador:

"Divine blessings were never late." [7] I say this because I appear to have, I do not say lost, but mislaid your favor, since you have been so long a time without writing to me, and I did not know what the cause possibly could be. I paid little attention to all the reasons for it that came into my head except when the fear came to me that you had refrained from writing to me because somebody had written to you that I was not a good guardian of your letters; and I knew that except for Filippo and Pagolo,[8] nobody, so far as I am concerned, had seen them. The last letter I had from you was that of the twenty-third of the past month, from which I learn with great plea-sure how regularly and quietly you carry on the business of your public office, and I encourage you to continue so, because a man who gives up his own comfort for that of others loses his own, and the others feel no grati-tude to him. And since Fortune wishes to do everything, she wishes you to let her alone, and remain quiet, and not give her trouble, and wait for the time when she will let men do something; and then it will be good for you to undergo more labor, and stir things up more, and for me to leave my farm and say: Here I am. Therefore, though I wish to do you an equal favor, I cannot tell you in this letter anything else than what my life is, and if you judge that you would like to swap it for yours, I am ready to make the exchange.

7. Petrarch, *Triumph of the Divinity* (with word order altered).
8. Paolo Vettori, Francesco's brother.

I am living on my farm, and since my last troubles I have not been in Florence twenty days, putting them all together. Up to now I have been setting snares for thrushes with my own hands. I get up before daylight, prepare my birdlime, and go out with a bundle of cages on my back, so that I look like Geta when he came back from the harbor with the books of Amphitryo,[9] and catch at the least two thrushes and at the most six. So I did all of September; then this trifling diversion, despicable and strange as it is, to my regret failed. What my life is now I shall tell you.

In the morning I get up with the sun and go out into a grove that I am having cut; there I remain a couple of hours to look over the work of the past day and kill some time with the woodsmen, who always have on hand some dispute either among themselves or among their neighbors. And as to this grove I could tell you a thousand good things that have happened in my dealings with Frosino da Panzano and others who wanted some firewood from it. Frosino in particular sent for several cords of wood without saying anything to me about them, and when he paid for them he wished to keep back ten lire, which he said he won from me four years ago when he beat me at *cricca* in the house of Antonio Guicciardini. I began to raise the devil, and was intending to accuse the drayman who had come for the wood of theft, but Giovanni Machiavelli stepped in between us and got us to agree. Batista Guicciardini, Filippo Ginori, Tommaso del Bene and certain other citizens each agreed to take a cord of wood when the north wind was blowing. I promised all of them and sent a cord to Tommaso, which turned out half a cord at Florence, because his wife, the servants, and his children were all there to pile it up; they looked like Gabburra when on Thursday he and his servants club an ox. Hence, having seen who was getting the profit, I told the others I had no more wood, and all of them have got angry about it, and especially Batista, who puts this in the same class as his losses at the sack of Prato.

When I leave the grove, I go to a spring, and from there into my aviary. I have a book in my pocket, either Dante or Petrarch or one of the minor poets, as Tibullus, Ovid, and the like. I read about their tender passions and their loves, remember mine, and take pleasure for a while in thinking about them. Then I go along the road to the inn, talk with those who pass by, ask the news of their villages, learn various things, and note the varied tastes and different fancies of men. It gets to be dinner time, and with my troop I eat what food my poor farm and my little property permit. After dinner, I return to the inn where I usually find the host, a butcher, a miller, and two furnace-tenders. With these fellows I sink into vulgarity for the rest of the day, playing at *cricca* and *trich-tach*; from these games come a thousand quarrels and numberless offensive and insulting words; we often

9. In the popular fifteenth-century novella, *Geta e Birria*.

dispute over a penny, and all the same are heard shouting as far as San Casciano. So, involved in these trifles, I keep my brain from getting moldy and express the perversity of Fate, for I am willing to have her drive me along this path to see if she will be ashamed of it.

In the evening, I return to my house and go into my study. At the door I take off the clothes I have worn all day, mud spotted and dirty, and put on regal and courtly garments. Thus appropriately clothed, I enter into the ancient courts of ancient men, where, being lovingly received, I feed on that food which is mine alone and which I was born for; I am not ashamed to speak with them and to ask the reasons for their actions, and they courteously answer me. For four hours I feel no boredom and forget every worry; I do not fear poverty, and death does not terrify me. I give myself completely over to the ancients. And because Dante says that there is no knowledge unless one retains what one has read,[10] I have written down the profit I have gained from their conversation and composed a little book *De principatibus*, in which I go as deep as I can into reflections on this subject, debating what a principate is, what the species are, how they are gained, how they are kept, and why they are lost. If ever any of my trifles can please you, this one should not displease you; and to a prince, and especially a new prince, it ought to be welcome. Hence I am dedicating it to His Magnificence Giuliano.[11] Filippo Casavecchia has seen it; he will be able to tell you something about the thing itself and the talks I have had with him, though I am all the time enlarging and repolishing it.

You wish, Honorable Ambassador, that I give up my present life and come to enjoy yours with you. I shall do so in any case, but what tempts me now is a certain affair of mine that I can finish inside of six weeks. What makes me hesitate is that the Soderini are there, and if I went to Rome I should be obliged to visit them and talk with them.[12] I fear that at my return I could not hope to dismount at home, but should dismount at the Bargello,[13] because, even though this government has very strong foundations and great security, yet it is new and therefore suspicious, and there are plenty of wiseacres who, to appear like Pagolo Bertini, would seat others at the dinner table and let me think about paying the bill. I pray you to settle this doubt for me, and then I surely shall come to visit you within the time I have set.

I have debated with Filippo about this little work of mine, whether it was wise to give it or not to give it, and if it were wise to give it whether it

10. *Paridiso*, 5: 41–42.

11. Giuliano de' Medici, duke of Nemours, and brother of Pope Leo X. After Giuliano's death in 1516, Machiavelli dedicated the final version of *The Prince* (now complete with the last chapter) to his nephew, and heir as secular head of the Medici family, Lorenzo.

12. See n. 4 above.   13. Then the city prison; now a museum.

would be wise to carry it myself or to send it to you. If I do not give it, I fear that, to say the least, it will not be read by Giuliano, and that this Ardinghelli would get honor from this last labor of mine. The pressure of necessity inclines me to give it, because I am wearing myself out and cannot remain long in my present state without getting so poor that I shall be despised. Then there is my hope that these Medici lords will begin to employ me, even if they begin by making me roll a stone, because if I did not then gain them over to me, I would have only myself to blame. This thing I have written, if it came to be read, would show that I have not been asleep or playing for the fifteen years that I have devoted to the study of the art of the state. Anybody should be glad to get the services of one who has had a great deal of experience at the expense of others. They should not hesitate over my faith because, since I have always kept my faith, I am not likely to learn how to break it now. He who has been faithful and good for forty-three years, as I have, is hardly able to change his nature, and my poverty is a testimony to both my faith and my goodness.

I hope, then, that you will write to me giving your opinion on this matter, and I present my respects. I wish you success.

10 December 1513. Niccolò Machiavelli in Florence.

12. *Discourses on the First Ten Books of Titus Livius*

Niccolò Machiavelli to Zanobi Buondelmonti and Cosimo Rucellai,[1] Greetings.

I am sending you a gift which, even though it may not match the obligations I have to you, is, without a doubt, the best that Niccolò Machiavelli can send to you; in it I have expressed all I know and all that I have learned from long experience and continuous study of worldly affairs. And since it is not possible for you or anyone else to ask more of me, you cannot complain if I have not given you more. You may very well complain about the poverty of my wit when my arguments are weak, and about the fallacious quality of my judgment if, in the course of my reasonings, I often manage to deceive myself. This being the case, I do not know which of us should be less obliged to the other: whether I should be so to you, who have encouraged me to write what I never would have written by myself, or you to

From *The Portable Machiavelli*, edited and translated by Peter Bondella and Mark Musa (New York: Penguin Books, 1979), pp. 168–71, 175–81, 193–96, 200–213, 281–90. © 1979 by Viking Penguin, Inc. Some footnotes deleted. Reprinted by permission of Viking Penguin, Inc.

1. Associates of Machiavelli in the city's chief literary circle in the Rucellai Gardens; they were implicated in a plot against the Medici regime in 1523.

me, since I may have written without satisfying you. Take this, then, as you would accept something from a friend: there one considers the intention of the sender more than the quality of the thing which is sent. And rest assured that in this venture I have one consolation, for I believe that although I may have deceived myself in many of its particulars, in one matter I know that I have not made an error; that is, to have chosen you above all others to whom I should dedicate these *Discourses* of mine, both because in so doing I believe that I have shown my gratitude for the benefits I have received and because I felt that I had departed from the common practice of those who write and always address their works to some prince and, blinded by ambition and by avarice, praise him for all his virtuous qualities when they ought to be blaming him for all his bad qualities. So, to avoid this mistake, I have chosen not those who are princes but those who, because of their numerous good qualities, deserve to be princes; not those who might shower me with offices, honors, and wealth, but those who, although unable, would like to do so. If men wish to judge correctly, they must esteem those who are generous, not those who are potentially generous; and, in like manner, they must esteem those who know how to rule a kingdom, not those who, without knowing how, have the power to do so. Thus, historians praise Hiero the Syracusan[2] more when he was a private citizen than they do Perseus of Macedonia[3] when he was king: for Hiero lacked nothing to be prince save a kingdom, while the other had no attribute of a king except his kingdom. Therefore, enjoy this good or bad work which you yourselves have requested; and if you persist in erroneously finding pleasure in my opinions, I shall not fail to follow this with the rest of the history, as I promised you in the beginning. Farewell.

Book 1

Introduction

Because of the envious nature of men, it has always been no less dangerous to discover new methods and institutions than to explore unknown oceans and lands, since men are quicker to criticize than to praise the deeds of others. Nevertheless, driven by that natural desire I have always felt to work on whatever might prove beneficial to everyone, I have determined to enter a path which has not yet been taken by anyone. Although it may bring me worry and difficulty, yet I may find my reward among those who study kindly the goal of these labors of mine. And if my feeble intelligence, my limited experience of current events, and my weak knowledge of ancient

2. King of Syracuse (Sicily), 265–215 B.C.
3. The last king of Macedon (179–168 B.C.), son of Philip V.

ones[4] should make this attempt of mine defective and of little use, it may, at least, show the way to someone with more ability, more eloquence, and more judgment who will be able to fulfill my intention; so that if I do not earn praise, I should not receive blame.

When we consider, then, how much honor is attributed to antiquity, and how many times (leaving aside numerous other examples) a fragment of an ancient statue has been bought at a great price so that the buyer may have it near him to decorate his house or to have it imitated by those who take pleasure in that art; and when we see, on the other hand, the powerful examples which history shows us that have been accomplished by ancient kingdoms and republics, by kings, captains, citizens, and legislators who have exhausted themselves for their fatherland, examples that have been more often admired than imitated (or so much ignored that not the slightest trace of this ancient ability remains), I cannot but be at the same time both amazed and sorry. And I am even more amazed when I see that in civil disputes which arise among citizens, or in sicknesses that break out, men always have recourse to those judgments or remedies which were pronounced or prescribed by the ancients. For civil law is nothing other than the judgments given by ancient jurists which, organized into a system, instruct our jurists today. Nor is medicine anything other than the experiments carried out by ancient doctors on which the doctors of today base their diagnoses. Nevertheless, in instituting republics, maintaining states, governing kingdoms, organizing the army and administering a war, dispensing justice to subjects, and increasing an empire one cannot find a prince or a republic that has recourse to the examples of the ancients.

This, in my opinion, arises not so much from the weakness into which the present religion has brought the world or from the harm done to many Christian provinces and cities by an idle ambition as from not possessing a proper knowledge of histories, for in reading them we do not draw out of them that sense or taste that flavor which they have in themselves. Hence it happens that an infinite number of people read them and take pleasure in hearing about the variety of incidents which are contained in them without thinking to imitate them, for they consider imitation not only difficult but impossible; as if the heavens, the sun, the elements, and men had varied in their motion, their order, and their power from what they were in ancient times. Wishing, therefore, to free men of this erroneous way of thinking, I deemed it necessary to write about all those books by Livy which the malignity of time has not taken from us; I wish to write what I, according to my knowledge of ancient and modern affairs, judge necessary for a better understanding of them, so that those who read these statements of mine

4. A paraphrase of the corresponding passage in the dedication to *The Prince*.

may more easily draw from them that practical knowledge one should seek from an acquaintance with history books. And although this undertaking is difficult, nevertheless, aided by those who have encouraged me to shoulder this burden, I believe I can carry it in such a manner that only a short distance will remain for another to bring it to the destined goal.

Chapter 2. Of How Many Kinds of Republics There Are and of What Kind the Roman Republic Was

I wish to put aside a discussion of those cities which, at their beginnings, were subject to others; and I shall speak about those which have had their beginnings far from any foreign servitude and have been governed from the beginning by their own judgment, either as republics or as principalities, and which have had different laws and institutions just as they have had different origins. Some of them, either at their start or after very little time, were given laws by a single man and at one time, as Lycurgus did with the Spartans; others acquired their laws by chance, at different times and according to circumstances, as occurred in Rome. A republic can, indeed, be called fortunate if it produces a man so prudent that he gives it laws organized in such a manner that it can live securely under them without needing to revise them. And it seems that Sparta observed its laws more than eight hundred years without corrupting them or without any dangerous upheaval. Unfortunate, on the contrary, is the city which is forced to reorganize itself, not having chanced to encounter a prudent organizer. And of these cities, the one which is the furthest from order is the most unfortunate; and that one is furthest from it which in its institutions is completely off the straight path which could lead it to its perfect and true goal, because for those who find themselves in this state it is almost impossible that by any happening they can be set on the right path again. Those other cities that have had a good beginning and are capable of becoming better, even if they have not had a perfect constitution, can, by means of an unexpected course of events, become perfect. But it is very true that institutions are never established without danger; for most men never agree to a new law that concerns a new order in the city unless a necessity demonstrates to them that it is required; and since this necessity cannot arise without danger, the republic may easily be destroyed before it is brought to a perfection of organization. The Republic of Florence testifies to this: reorganized after what occurred at Arezzo in 1502, it was disorganized by what occurred at Prato in 1512.[5]

Since I wish to discuss what the institutions of the city of Rome were and the circumstances which led to their perfection, let me say that those

5. Cf. Luca Landucci, *Diary*, in this volume, pp. 162–66 and 166–71.

who have written about republics declare that there are in them three kinds of governments, which they call principality, aristocracy, and democracy; and that those who organize a city most often turn to one of these, depending upon whichever seems more appropriate to them. Others—and wiser men, according to the judgment of many—are of the opinion that there are six types of government: three of these are very bad; three others are good in themselves but are so easily corruptible that they, too, can become pernicious. Those which are good are the three mentioned above; those which are bad are three others which depend upon the first three, and each of them is, in a way, similar to its good counterpart, so that they easily jump from one form to another. For the principality easily becomes tyrannical; aristocrats can very easily produce an oligarchy; democracy is converted into anarchy with no difficulty. So that if a founder of a republic organizes one of these three governments in a city, he organizes it there for a brief period of time only, since no precaution can prevent it from slipping into its contrary on account of the similarity, in such a case, of the virtue and the vice.

These variations of government are born among men by chance: for in the beginning of the world, when its inhabitants were few, they lived at one time dispersed and like wild beasts; then, when their numbers multiplied, they gathered together and, in order to defend themselves better, they began to search among themselves for one who was stronger and braver, and they made him their leader and obeyed him. From this sprang the knowledge of what things are good and honorable, as distinct from the pernicious and the evil: for if someone were to harm his benefactor, this aroused hatred and compassion among men, since they cursed the ungrateful and honored those who showed gratitude; and thinking that the same injuries could also be committed against themselves, they made laws to avoid similar evils and instituted punishments for transgressors. Thus, the recognition of justice came about. The result was that, later on, when they had to elect a prince, they did not select the bravest man but rather the one who was most prudent and most just. But when they began to choose the prince by hereditary succession rather than by election, the heirs immediately began to degenerate from the level of their ancestors and, putting aside acts of valor, they thought that princes had nothing to do but to surpass other princes in luxury, lasciviousness, and in every other form of pleasure. So, as the prince came to be hated he became afraid of this hatred and quickly passed from fear to violent deeds, and the immediate result was tyranny.

From this there came next the destructions, the conspiracies, and the plots against princes, carried out not by those who were either timid or weak but by those who surpassed others in generosity, greatness of spirit, wealth, and nobility: these men could not stand the disreputable life of such a prince. The masses, therefore, following the authority of these powerful men, took up arms against the prince, and after he had been eliminated they obeyed those men as their liberators. And since those men hated the very idea of a single ruler, they constituted for themselves a government, and in the beginning, since they remembered the past tyranny, they governed according to the laws instituted by themselves, subordinating their own interests to the common good, and they managed and maintained both their private and public affairs with the greatest of care. When this administration later passed to their sons, who did not understand the changeability of Fortune, had never experienced bad times, and could not be satisfied with equality among citizens, they turned to avarice, ambition, and the violation of other men's women, and they caused a government of the aristocrats to become a government of the few, with no regard to any civil rights; so that in a short time they experienced the same fate as the tyrant, for as the masses were sick of their rule, they assisted, in any way they could, anyone who might plan to attack these rulers, and thus there soon arose someone who, with the aid of the masses, destroyed them. And since the memory of the prince and of the injuries received from him was still fresh, they turned to a democratic form of government, having destroyed the government ruled by a few men and not wishing to return to that ruled by a prince; and they organized it in such a way that neither the few powerful men nor a prince might have any authority whatsoever in it. And because all governments are, at the outset, respected, this democratic government was maintained awhile, but not for a long time, particularly after the generation that organized it passed away; it immediately turned to anarchy, where neither the individual citizen nor the public official is feared; each individual lived according to his own wishes, so that every day a thousand wrongs were done; and so, constrained by necessity, either because of the suggestion of some good man or in order to flee such anarchy, it returned again to the principality; and from that, step by step, the government moved again in the direction of anarchy, in the manner and for the reasons just given.

And this is the cycle through which all states that have governed themselves or that now govern themselves pass; but rarely do they return to the same forms of government, for virtually no state can possess so much vitality that it can sustain so many changes and remain on its feet. But it may well happen that while a state lacking counsel and strength is in difficulty, it becomes subject to a neighboring state which is better organized; but if this were not the case, then a state might be liable to pass endlessly through the cycle of these governments.

Let me say, therefore, that all the forms of government listed are defective: the three good ones because of the brevity of their lives, the three bad ones because of their inherent harmfulness. Thus, those who were prudent in establishing laws recognized this fact and, avoiding each of these forms in themselves, chose one that combined them all, judging such a government to be steadier and more stable, for when there is in the same city-state a principality, an aristocracy, and a democracy, one form keeps watch over the other.

Among those who have deserved great praise for having established such constitutions is Lycurgus, who organized his laws in Sparta in such a manner that, assigning to the king, the aristocrats, and the people their respective roles, he created a state which lasted more than eight hundred years, to his everlasting credit, and resulted in the tranquillity of that city. The contrary happened to Solon, who organized the laws in Athens: for in organizing only a democratic state there he made it of such a brief existence that before he died he saw arise the tyranny of Pisistratus; and although forty years later the latter's heirs were driven away and Athens returned to its freedom, having reestablished the democratic state according to the institutions of Solon, it did not last more than a hundred years. In spite of the fact that many laws which were not foreseen by Solon were established in Athens in order to restrain the insolence of the upper class and the anarchy of the populace, nevertheless Athens lived a very brief time in comparison to Sparta, because Solon did not mix democracy with the power of the principality and with that of the aristocrats.

But let us come to Rome. In spite of the fact that she never had a Lycurgus to organize her at the beginning so that she might exist free for a long time, nevertheless, because of the friction between the plebeians and the senate, so many circumstances attended her birth that chance brought about what a lawgiver had not acomplished. If Rome did not receive Fortune's first gift, she received the second: for her early institutions, although defective, nevertheless did not deviate from the right path that could lead them to perfection. Romulus and all the other kings passed many good laws in accordance with a free government; but since their goal was to found a kingdom and not a republic, when that city became free she lacked many institutions which were necessary to organize her under freedom, institutions which had not been set up by those kings. And when it happened that her kings lost their power for the reasons and in the ways described earlier, nonetheless those who drove them out, having immediately established two consuls in place of the king, drove out only the title of king and not royal power; so that, as there were in that republic the consuls and the senate, it came to be formed by only two of the three above-mentioned elements, that is, the principality and the aristocrats. There remained only to make a place for the democratic part of the government. When the Roman nobility became insolent, for the reasons that will be listed below, the people rose up against them; in order not to lose everything, the nobility was forced to concede to the people their own share; and on the other hand, the senate and the consuls retained enough authority so that they could maintain their rank in that republic. And thus there came about the creation of the tribunes of the plebeians, after which the government of the republic became more stable, since each of the three elements of government had its share. And Fortune was so favorable to Rome that even though she passed from a government by kings and aristocrats to one by the people, through those same steps and because of those same reasons which were discussed above, nevertheless the kingly authority was never entirely abolished to give authority to the aristocrats, nor was the authority of the aristocrats diminished completely to give it to the people; but since these elements remained mixed, Rome was a perfect state; and this perfection was produced through the friction between the plebeians and the senate, as the two following chapters will demonstrate at greater length.

Chapter 7. How the Right to Bring Public Charges Is Necessary for a Republic to Preserve Its Liberty

No more useful and necessary authority can be granted to those who are appointed to preserve a city's liberty than the capacity to bring before the people or before some magistrate or council charges against citizens who sin in any manner against the freedom of the government. This institution produces two very useful results in a republic: first, for fear of being accused, the citizens do not attempt anything against the government, or, if they do, they are immediately suppressed without regard to their station; second, it provides an outlet for those hatreds which grow up in cities, in whatever manner, against some particular citizen: and when these hatreds do not find a legal means of expression, they have recourse to illegal means, which cause the eventual ruin of the entire republic. And so, nothing makes a republic so stable and strong as organizing it in such a way that the agitation of the hatreds which excite it has a means of expressing itself provided for by the laws. This can be demonstrated by many examples, and especially by that which Livy brings forth concerning Coriolanus,[6] where he says that since the Roman nobility was angered at the plebeians because they felt that the plebeians had assumed too much authority as a result of the creation of the tribunes, who were to defend them, and since it happened that Rome then suffered a great scarcity of provisions and the senate had sent to Sicily for grain, Coriolanus, enemy of the popular faction, advised that the time had come to punish the plebeians by keep-

6. Livy, 2.33–35.

ing them hungry and not distributing the grain, and by taking away from them the authority which they had usurped from the nobility. When this advice reached the ears of the people, they were so angry at him that he would have been murdered by the crowd as he left the senate if the tribunes had not called him to appear before them in his own defense. What was said above can be applied to this event—that is, that it is useful and necessary for republics to provide with their laws a means of expression for the wrath that the multitude feels against a single citizen, for when these legal means do not exist the people turn to illegal ones, and without a doubt the latter produce much worse effects than do the former.

For, when a citizen is legally oppressed, even if this be unjust to him, little or no disorder in the republic follows; for the execution of the act is done without private or foreign forces, which are the ones that destroy free government; but it is done with public forces and institutions which have their specific limits—nor do they transcend these limits to damage the republic. And as for corroborating this opinion with examples, that of Coriolanus from the ancients should suffice. Everyone should observe how much evil would have resulted for the Roman republic if he had been put to death by the crowd, for this would have created private grievances, which generate fear, and fear seeks defenses for which partisans are recruited, and from partisans are born the factions in cities, and from factions the ruin of the city. But since the matter was handled by those who had the authority to do so, all those evils which might have arisen by using private power were avoided.

We have witnessed in our own times what changes occurred in the Republic of Florence when the people were not able to vent their wrath legally against one of its citizens, as was the case when Francesco Valori[7] was almost like the prince of that city. He was regarded by many as ambitious, a man who would transgress lawful government because of his audacity and hot temper; and since there was no means within the republic's existing institutions of resisting him without establishing a rival party, it came about that he set out to enlist partisans, not fearing anything but illegal methods; on the other hand, since those who opposed him had no legal way to suppress him, they turned to illegal methods and eventually resorted to arms. Given the proper legal institutions, he might have been opposed and his authority destroyed, harming only himself, but because he had to be destroyed unlawfully, this resulted in harm not only to him but also to many other noble citizens. One could also cite, in support of the above conclu-

7. The head of the pro-Savonarola party in the Florentine government between 1495 and 1498. The events mentioned below are described in detail in the *Diary* of Luca Landucci in this volume.

sion, the incident which happened in connection with Piero Soderini, which came about entirely from the absence in that republic of any means of bringing charges against the ambition of powerful citizens. For it is not enough to accuse a powerful citizen before eight judges in a republic; there must be many judges, for the few always act in favor of the few. If these methods had existed in Florence, either the citizens would have accused him if his conduct was bad—by this means, without calling in a Spanish army, they would have vented their anger—or, if his conduct was not bad, they would not have dared to act against him for fear that they themselves might be accused; and thus, in either case the appetite for conflict, which was the cause of the quarrel, would have vanished.

The following conclusion can be drawn: whenever one finds foreign forces being called in by one faction of men living in a city, it may be taken for granted that the bad ordinances of that city are the cause, for it does not have an institution that provides an outlet for the malignant humors which are born among men to express themselves without their resorting to illegal means; adequate provision for this is made by making a number of judges available before whom public indictments may be made; and these accusations must be given proper importance. These means were so well organized in Rome that during the many conflicts between the plebeians and the senate neither the senate nor the plebeians nor any private citizen ever attempted to use outside forces; for they had a remedy at home and there was no need to search for it outside. And although the above examples are more than sufficient to prove this, I nevertheless wish to use another taken from Livy's history: there he relates how in Chiusi, a city which in those times was one of the most noble in Tuscany, a certain Lucumones raped the sister of Aruntes; unable to revenge himself because of the power of the rapist, Aruntes went to meet with the Gauls, who at that time ruled in the area which is now called Lombardy, and persuaded them to come with troops to Chiusi, showing them how they would profit by avenging the injustice he had suffered; Livy further explains how Aruntes would not have sought barbarian troops if he had seen a way to avenge himself through the city's institutions. But just as public accusations are useful in a republic, so false accusations are useless and harmful, as the discussion in the next chapter will show.

Chapter 9. How a Man Must Be Alone in order to Found a New Republic or to Reform Completely Its Ancient Institutions

It may appear to some that I have gone too far along in Roman history without mentioning the founders of that republic or those institutions which are concerned with her religion and her militia; therefore, no longer wishing to keep the minds that wish to hear about this matter in suspense, let me say that many will perhaps judge it to be a bad example for a founder of a constitutional state, as Romulus was, to have first murdered his brother and then to have consented to the death of Titus Tatius, the Sabine, whom he had elected as his companion in his rule. Judging from this, the citizens might, out of ambition and a desire to rule, follow the example of their prince and oppress those who are opposed to their authority. This opinion might be correct, were we not to consider the goal that led Romulus to commit such a murder.

And this should be taken as a general rule: it rarely or never happens that a republic or kingdom is well organized from the beginning, or completely reformed, with no respect for its ancient institutions, unless it is done by one man alone; moreover, it is necessary that one man provide the means and be the only one from whose mind any such organization originates; therefore, a prudent founder of a republic, one whose intention it is to govern for the common good and not in his own interest, not for his heirs but for the sake of the fatherland, should try to have the authority all to himself; nor will a wise mind ever reproach anyone for some extraordinary action performed in order to found a kingdom or to institute a republic. It is, indeed, fitting that while the action accuses him, the result excuses him; and when this result is good, as it was with Romulus, it will always excuse him: for one should reproach a man who is violent in order to destroy, not one who is violent in order to mend things.

The founder should be so prudent and able-minded as not to bequeath the authority he has taken to his heir; for, since men are more apt to do evil than good, his successor might use for ambitious ends what the founder had employed virtuously. Besides this, though one man alone is fit for founding a government, what he has founded will not last long if it rests upon his shoulders alone; it is lasting when it is left in the care of many and when many desire to maintain it. As the many are not fit to organize a government, for they cannot recognize the best means of doing so because of the diversity of opinion among them, just so, when they have realized that they have it they will not agree to abandon it. And that Romulus was among those who deserve to be pardoned for the death of his brother and his companion, and that what he did was for the common good and not for private ambition, is demonstrated by the fact that he immediately organized a senate with whom he would consult and whose opinions he deliberated; and anyone who would examine carefully the authority that Romulus reserved for himself will see that all he kept for himself was the power to command the army during wartime and to convoke the senate. Later, when Rome became free as a result of the expulsion of the Tarquins, we can see that the city was not given any new institutions by the Romans besides their ancient ones, except that in place of a permanent king there were two yearly consuls: this testifies to the fact that all the original institutions were more suitable to a free, self-governing state than to one which was absolutist and tyrannical.

Numerous examples could be cited in support of what I have written above, such as Moses, Lycurgus, Solon, and other founders of kingdoms and republics who were able to form laws for the common good because they had taken sole authority upon themselves, but I shall omit them since they are well known; instead, I shall present only one example, not so well known but worthy of examination by those who wish to be the organizers of good laws, and the example is: Agis, King of Sparta, who wished to return the Spartans to the bounds within which the laws of Lycurgus had enclosed them, for he felt that, having departed from them, his city had lost much of its former ability and, as a result, much of its strength and empire; but at the start of his efforts he was assassinated by the Spartan Ephors as a man who wanted to become a tyrant. But when Cleomenes succeeded him on the throne, the same desire, after a time, arose in him as a result of reading the memoirs and writings of Agis which he had discovered, wherein he saw what his real intentions were, and he realized that he could not do this good for his country if he did not possess sole authority; for it seemed impossible, on account of man's ambition, for him to be able to help the many against the wishes of the few; so, when the right occasion arose he had all the Ephors killed and anyone else who might oppose him; then he completely restored the laws of Lycurgus. This action might have been enough to revive Sparta and to give Cleomenes the same reputation that Lycurgus had if it had not been for the power of the Macedonians and the weakness of the other Greek republics; for, after such institutions had been established, Cleomenes was attacked by the Macedonians, and when he discovered he was weaker in numbers and had nowhere to go for help, he was defeated.[8] This plan of his, no matter how just and praiseworthy it might have been, was not carried out.

Considering all these matters, then, I conclude that it is necessary to be alone in establishing a republic; and that, concerning the death of Remus and Titus Tatius, Romulus deserves to be excused, not blamed.

Chapter 10. Those Who Found a Republic or a Kingdom Deserve as Much Praise as Those Who Found a Tyranny Deserve Blame

Among all praiseworthy men, the most praiseworthy are those who were leaders and founders of religions; next come those who founded either republics or kingdoms; after these the most celebrated men are those who, commanding armies, have increased either their own kingdom or that of

8. 222 B.C.

their native land; next to these may be placed men of letters, who, since they are of various types, are each praised according to their merits. To other men, whose number is infinite, some portion of praise may be attributed according to the skill they possess in their art or profession. On the other hand, men who have destroyed religions, wasted kingdoms and republics, and have been enemies of virtue, letters, and every sort of profession that brings gain and honor to the human race—such as the impious, the violent, the ignorant, the useless, the lazy, and the wicked—are considered infamous and detestable; and no one will ever be so mad or so wise, so sorry or so good that, given the choice between the two kinds of men, he will not praise those who merit praise and blame those who deserve blame.

Nevertheless, in the end nearly all men, deceived by a false appearance of good and a false sense of glory, allow themselves, either by their own choice or through their ignorance, to join the ranks of those who deserve more blame than praise; and while they have the possibility of establishing, to their perpetual honor, either a republic or a kingdom, they turn instead to tyranny, not realizing how much fame, glory, honor, security, tranquillity, and peace of mind they are losing by such a decision and, on the other hand, how much infamy, vituperation, blame, danger, and unrest they incur.

And if they read histories and make use of the records of ancient affairs, it is impossible for those who have lived as private citizens in a republic or who have become princes either because of Fortune or ability not to wish to live, if they are private citizens, in their native land like Scipio rather than like Caesar and, if they are princes, to live like Agesilaus, Timoleon, and Dion rather than like Nabis, Phalaris, and Dionysius;[9] for they would see how the latter are soundly condemned while the former are praised most highly; they would also see how Timoleon and the others had no less authority in their native lands than Dionysius and Phalaris had, and that they enjoyed, by far, greater security for a longer time.

Nor should anyone be deceived by Caesar's glory, so very celebrated by historians, for those who praised him were corrupted by his good fortune and amazed by the duration of the empire which, ruled in his name, did not allow writers to speak freely about him. But anyone who wishes to know what free historians would say about him should examine what they say about Catiline. And Caesar is even more blameworthy, just as a man who has committed an evil deed is more to be blamed than one who has only wished to do so; moreover, let the reader see how Brutus is so highly

9. Agesilaus (400–c. 360 B.C.) was a king of Sparta; Timoleon and Dion overthrew the tyranny of Dionysius II, who had invited Plato to Syracuse; Nabis (206–192 B.C.) and Phalaris (570–555 B.C.) were tyrants respectively of Sparta and Agrigento.

praised, as though, unable to criticize Caesar because of his power, they praise his enemy instead.[10]

Furthermore, let any man who has become a prince in a republic consider how much more praise those emperors deserved who lived under the laws and as good princes after Rome had become an empire than those who lived the opposite way, and he will see how Titus, Nerva, Trajan, Hadrian, Antoninus [Pius], and Marcus [Aurelius] had no need of Praetorian guards nor a multitude of legions to defend themselves, for their customs, the goodwill of the people, and the love of the senate protected them; the prince will also see how the Eastern and Western armies were not sufficient for Caligula, Nero, Vitellius, and other evil emperors to save themselves from the enemies that their wicked customs and evil lives had created for them. And if the history of these men were studied carefully, it would serve as an excellent lesson to show any prince the path to glory or to censure, to his security or to his peril, for of the twenty-six emperors between Caesar and Maximinus, sixteen were murdered and ten died a natural death; and if among those who were murdered there were several good men, like Galba and Pertinax, they were killed by the corruption which their predecessors had left behind in their soldiers; and if among those who died a natural death there was a wicked man, like Severus, this was the result of his very great fortune and ability—a combination of two things which few men enjoy. A prince will also observe, through the lesson of this history, how one can organize a good kingdom: for all the emperors who assumed the imperial throne by birth, except for Titus, were bad, and those who became emperors by adoption were all good, as were the five from Nerva to Marcus; and when the empire fell into hereditary succession, it returned again to its ruin.

Therefore, let a prince examine the times from Nerva to Marcus [Aurelius], and let him compare them with those which came before and afterward, and then let him choose during which period he would wish to be born or in which period he would like to be made emperor. In the times when good emperors governed, he will see a ruler secure in the midst of his secure citizens, and a world of peace and justice; he will see a senate with its full authority, the magistrates with their honors, the rich citizens enjoying their wealth, the nobles and ability exalted, and he will find tranquillity and well-being in everything; and on the other hand, he will see all rancor, licentiousness, corruption, and ambition extinguished; he will see a golden age in which a man can hold and defend whatever opinion he wishes. He will, in the end, see the world rejoicing: its prince endowed with respect and glory, its peoples with love and security. If next he studies carefully the

10. The opposite judgment in *The Prince*, 16.

times of the other emperors, he will see them full of the atrocities of war, the conflicts of sedition, and the cruelties of both peace and war, so many princes put to death by the sword, so many civil wars, so many foreign wars, all of Italy afflicted and full of previously unknown adversities, and her cities ruined and sacked. He will see Rome burned, the Capitoline destroyed by her own citizens, her ancient temples desolate, her rituals corrupted, and the cities full of adulterous conduct; he will see the seas covered with exiles and the earth stained with blood. He will find countless cruelties in Rome and discover that nobility, wealth, past honors, and especially virtue are considered capital crimes. He will see the rewarding of those who accuse falsely, the turning of servants against their masters and freedmen against their former owners, and he will see those who, lacking enemies, are oppressed by their friends. And then he will well understand how many obligations Rome, Italy, and the world owe to Caesar!

And the prince, without a doubt, if he is a man, will be frightened away from any imitation of the bad times and will burn with an ardent desire to follow the ways of the good times. If a prince truly seeks worldly glory, he should hope to possess a corrupt city—not in order to ruin it completely as Caesar did but to reorganize it as Romulus did. And the heavens cannot truly bestow upon men a greater opportunity for obtaining glory than this, nor can men desire a greater one. And if a man who wanted to reorganize a city well had, of necessity, to renounce the principality in order to do so, he might merit some excuse if he did not reform it in order not to lose his rank; but if he were able both to retain his principality and to reform it, he would deserve no excuse whatsoever.

In conclusion, then, let those to whom the heavens grant such opportunities observe that there are two paths open to them: one allows them to live securely and makes them famous after death; the other makes them live in continuous anxiety and, after death, allows them to leave behind an eternal reputation of infamy.

Chapter 11. The Religion of the Romans

Even though Rome found its first institution builder in Romulus and, like a daughter, owed her birth and her education to him, nevertheless, as the heavens judged that the institutions of Romulus would not suffice for so great an empire, they inspired the Roman senate to elect Numa Pompilius as Romulus's successor so that those matters not attended to by Romulus could be seen to by Numa. Numa found the Roman people most undisciplined, and since he wanted to bring them to civil obedience by means of the arts of peace, he turned to religion as an absolutely necessary institution for the maintenance of a civic government, and he established it in such a way that for many centuries never was there more fear of God than in that republic—a fact which greatly facilitated any undertaking that the senate or those great Romans thought of doing.

Anyone who examines the many actions of the Roman people as a whole and of many individual Romans will discover how these citizens were more afraid of breaking an oath than of breaking the laws, since they respected the power of God more than that of man: this is most evident in the examples of Scipio and of Manlius Torquatus. After the rout inflicted upon the Romans by Hannibal at the battle of Cannae, many of the citizens assembled and, despairing for their native land, agreed to abandon Italy and to go to Sicily; when Scipio heard about this, he went to them, and with his bare sword in hand he forced them to swear not to abandon their fatherland. Lucius Manlius, the father of Titus Manlius (afterward called Torquatus), was accused of a crime by Marcus Pomponius, tribune of the plebeians; before the day of the trial arrived Titus went to Marcus and threatened to kill him if he did not swear to remove the indictment against his father; and when Marcus swore to do so, he withdrew the charge out of fear.

In this manner, those citizens whose love for the fatherland or its laws could not have kept them in Italy were restrained by an oath which they were forced to take; and that tribune set aside the hatred he had for the father and the injury he had suffered from the son and his own honor in order to obey the oath he had taken—all this came about from nothing other than the religion which Numa had introduced into that city.

Thus, anyone who examines Roman history closely will discover how much religion helped in commanding armies, encouraging the plebeians, keeping men good, and shaming the wicked. And so, if one were to argue about which prince Rome was more indebted to—whether Romulus or Numa—I believe that Numa would most easily be first choice; for where there is religion it is easy to introduce arms, but where there are arms without religion the latter can be introduced only with difficulty. It is evident that Romulus did not find divine authority necessary to found the senate and other civil and military institutions, but it was necessary for Numa, who pretended to have a relationship with a nymph who advised him what to say to the people; the reason was that he wanted to establish new and unfamiliar institutions in the city, and he doubted that his own authority would be sufficient to do so.

Actually, there never existed a person who could give unusual laws to his people without recourse to God, for otherwise such laws would not have been accepted: for the benefits they bring, although evident to a prudent man, are not self-explanatory enough to be evident to others. Therefore, wise men who wish to avoid this difficulty have recourse to God. Lycurgus did this, as did Solon and many others who had the same goal.

Since the Roman people were amazed at the goodness and the prudence of Numa, they yielded to his every decision. It is, of course, true that those times were very religious ones and that the men with whom he had to deal were unsophisticated, thereby giving him a great deal of freedom to follow his own plans and to be able to impress upon them easily any new form he wished. And, without any doubt, anyone wishing to establish a republic in our present day would find it easier to do so among mountaineers, where there is no culture, than among men who are accustomed to living in cities where culture is corrupt; in like manner, a sculptor can more easily carve a beautiful statue out of a rough piece of marble than he can from one poorly blocked out by someone else.

Having considered everything, then, I conclude that the religion introduced by Numa was among the most important reasons for the success of that city, for it brought forth good institutions, and good institutions led to good fortune, and from good fortune came the felicitous successes of the city's undertakings. And as the observance of religious teaching is the reason for the greatness of republics, in like manner the disdain of the practice is the cause of their ruin; for where the fear of God is lacking a kingdom must either come to ruin or be sustained by the fear of a prince who makes up for the lack of religion. And since princes are short-lived, it is most likely that a kingdom will fail as quickly as the abilities of its prince fail; thus, kingdoms which depend upon the ability of a single man cannot last long, for such ability disappears with the life of the prince; and only rarely does it happen that this ability is revived by a successor, as Dante prudently declares:

> Not often in a family tree does virtue
> rise up to all its branches. This is what
> the Giver wills, that we may ask Him for it.[11]

The well-being, therefore, of a republic or a kingdom cannot rest upon a prince who governs prudently while he is alive, but rather upon one who organizes the government in such a way that it can be maintained in the event of his death. And, while it is true that uncultured men can be more easily persuaded to adopt a new institution or opinion, it is not, however, for this reason impossible to persuade cultured men or men who do not consider themselves uncultured to do the same. The people of Florence do not consider themselves ignorant or uncultured; nevertheless, they were persuaded by Brother Girolamo Savonarola that he spoke with God. I do not wish to judge if this were true or not, for of such a man as this one must speak with respect; but I do say that very many people believed him with-

11. *Purgatorio*, 7.122–23.

out ever having seen anything out of the ordinary to make them believe him, and this was the case because his life, his doctrines, and the topics about which he chose to preach from the Bible were enough to persuade them to have faith in him. No one, therefore, should despair of being able to accomplish what others have accomplished, for men—as I said in my preface—are born, live, and die always in the same way.

Chapter 12. How Much Importance Must Be Granted to Religion, and How Italy, Without Religion, Thanks to the Roman Church, Has Been Ruined

Princes or republics that wish to maintain themselves without corruption must, above all else, maintain free of corruption the ceremonies of their religion and must hold them constantly in veneration; for there is no greater indication of the ruin of a country than to see its religious worship not respected. This is easy to understand when one realizes upon what basis the religion of the place where a man was born is founded, because every religion has the foundation of its existence in one of its main institutions. The essence of the religion of the pagans resided in the responses of oracles and upon a sect of fortune-tellers and soothsayers: all their ceremonies, sacrifices, and rites depended upon these, for it was easy for them to believe that the god who could predict your future, good or evil, could also bring it about for you. From these arose their temples, their sacrifices, their supplications, and every other ceremony used in venerating them; from this arose the oracle of Delos, the temple of Jupiter Ammon, and other famous oracles which filled the world with admiration and devotion. Then, later, as these oracles began to speak on behalf of the powerful, their falsity was discovered by the people and men became unbelievers and were willing to upset every good institution.

Therefore, it is the duty of the rulers of a republic or of a kingdom to maintain the foundations of the religion that sustains them; and if this is done it will be easy for them to keep their republic religious and, as a consequence, good and united. And they must favor and encourage all those things which arise in favor of religion, even if they judge them to be false; the more they do this the more prudent and knowledgeable in worldly affairs they will be. And because this practice has been followed by wise men, there has arisen the belief in miracles that are celebrated even in false religions; for, no matter how they originated, men always gave them greater importance than they deserved, thus causing everyone to believe in them. There were many such miracles in Rome, among them the one that happened while the Roman soldiers were sacking the city of Veii: some of them entered the temple of Juno and, approaching the image of the goddess, asked: "Do you wish to come to Rome?" [12] It seemed to some that she nodded her head as if to say "yes" and to others that she actually replied that she did. Since these men were deeply religious (this Livy demonstrates, for he describes them entering the temple without a sound, devout and full of reverence), perhaps it seemed to them that they heard the reply to their question which they had expected from the start; this opinion and belief was carefully encouraged and cultivated by Camillus and the other leaders of the city. If the rulers of Christian republics had maintained this sort of religion according to the system set up by its founder, Christian states and republics would be more united and happier than they are at present. Nor can there be another, better explanation of its decline than to see how those people who are closer to the Roman church, the head of our religion, are less religious. And anyone who examines the principles upon which it was based and sees how different present practice is from these principles would conclude, without a doubt, that it is drawing near either to calamity or a scourge.

And since there are many who are of the opinion that the well-being of the Italian cities comes from the church of Rome, I wish to present some of my beliefs against such an opinion, very powerful ones which, I feel, cannot be refuted. The first is that because of the bad examples of that court of Rome this land has lost all its devotion and religion; this, in turn, brings about countless evils and countless disorders: for just as one takes for granted that all goes well where there is religion, just so, where religion is lacking one supposes the contrary. We Italians owe this first debt to the church and to the priests—we have become irreligious and wicked; but we owe them an even greater debt still, which is the second reason for our ruin: that the church has kept, and still keeps, this land of ours divided. And, in truth, no land is ever happy or united unless it is under the rule of one republic or one prince, as is the case with France and Spain. And the reason why Italy is not in the same condition and why she, too, has neither one republic nor one prince to govern her, lies solely with the Church: for although the Church possesses temporal power and has its seat in Italy, it has not been powerful enough nor has it possessed sufficient skill to be able to tyrannize Italy and make itself her ruler; and it has not been, on the other hand, so feeble that, when in fear of losing its control of temporal affairs, it has been unable to bring in a foreign power to defend itself from those Italian states which have become too powerful. There are many instances of this in ancient times: when, with Charlemagne's aid, the Lombards—who were in control of almost all of Italy—were driven out; and when, in our

12. Latin in the original, quoting from Livy, 5.22.

own day, the Church took power away from the Venetians with the aid of France, and then when it drove out the French with the help of the Swiss. Therefore, since the Church has not been strong enough to take possession of Italy, nor has she permitted anyone else to do so, Italy has not been able to unite under one ruler. Rather, Italy has been under many rulers and lords, and from this has come so much disunity and so much weakness that she has continued to be at the mercy not only of powerful barbarians but of anyone who might attack her. This is the debt we Italians owe the Church and no one else! And anyone who might wish to see the truth of this borne out by actual experience need only have sufficient power to send the Roman court, with the authority it possesses in Italy, to live in the lands of the Swiss, who are today the only peoples living under both religious and military institutions organized according to ancient practices; and he would see that in a short time the wicked customs of that court would create more disorder in that land than any other event occurring at any time could possibly cause there.

Chapter 58. The Masses [13] Are Wiser and More Constant Than a Prince

Nothing can be more unreliable and more inconstant than the masses, as our own Livy declares and as all other historians affirm. In the recounting of the actions of men, we often read that the masses condemn someone to death and then repent later, wishing that he were still alive, as is evident in what the Roman people did with Manlius Capitolinus, whom they first condemned to death and then wished to have back alive. And the words of the author are these: "As soon as he ceased to represent a danger, the people immediately were seized by remorse." And elsewhere, when he is explaining the events in Syracuse after the death of Hieronymus, the grandson of Hiero, he declares: "Such is the nature of the masses—either to obey humbly or to rule arrogantly." [14]

I do not know whether, in undertaking to defend an argument which, as I have mentioned, all writers have attacked, I may not be taking on a task so difficult and so full of problems that I shall either have to abandon it in shame or follow it with great pains. But be that as it may, I do not, nor shall I ever, think it wrong to defend an opinion with reasons without employing either authority or force. Let me say, therefore, that all men, and especially princes, can be accused individually of that fault for which writers blame the masses: for anyone not regulated by law will make the same errors that

13. The Italian word is *moltitudine* which perhaps would be better rendered by the word multitude.—Ed.
14. Latin in the original, from Livy, 6.20 and 24.25.

the uncontrolled masses will make. And this is obvious, for there are, and have been, many princes who have been able to break the bounds that could restrain them; nor shall we count among these the kings who arose in Egypt when, in that ancient time, the province was ruled by laws, nor those who arose in Sparta, nor those in our own times who arose in France, a kingdom more regulated by laws than any other kingdom that we have any knowledge of in our own day. The kings who arose under such constitutions are not to be considered among those whose individual nature we ought to consider here in order to see if it resembles that of the masses, for they should be compared to the masses regulated by laws in the same fashion as they are; and we shall find in the masses that same goodness we discover in such kings and shall see that the masses neither obey humbly nor rule arrogantly. The Roman people were like this, for while the Roman republic endured without corruption, it never obeyed humbly nor ruled arrogantly; on the contrary, it held its position honorably through its institutions and magistrates. And when it was necessary to band together against some powerful man, as in the case of Manlius, the decemvirs, and others who sought to oppress it, it did so; when it was necessary to obey the dictators and the consuls for the public welfare, it did so. And if the Roman people regretted the death of Manlius Capitolinus, it is not surprising, for they regretted the loss of his virtues, which were such that the memory of them aroused everyone's compassion; and it would have had the power to produce the same effect in a prince, since all writers declare that ability is praised and admired even in one's enemies. If Manlius had been resurrected because of such an opinion, the people of Rome would have pronounced upon him the same sentence that they did when they had him removed from prison and shortly thereafter condemned him to death; nevertheless we see princes, reputed to be wise, who have had someone executed and then wished him returned to life, as Alexander did in the case of Clitus and his other friends and as Herod did with Mariamne. But when our historian speaks of the nature of the masses, he does not mean those who are regulated by law, as the Romans were; he speaks of the uncontrolled masses, like those of Syracuse, which committed crimes typical of undisciplined and infuriated men, as did Alexander the Great and Herod in the instances mentioned. But the nature of the masses is no more to be condemned than that of princes, for both err when there is nothing to control them. There are many examples of this, in addition to the ones I have mentioned, both among the Roman emperors and other tyrants and princes; and in them we witness as much lack of stability and variation of behavior as may ever be found in any multitude.

Therefore, I come to a conclusion contrary to the common opinion, which declares that when the people hold power they are unstable, change-

able, and ungrateful; I affirm, rather, that the people are no more suscep-
tible to these sins than are individual princes. And if one were to blame
both the people and princes alike, he might be telling the truth, but if princes
are to be excluded from this charge, then he would be deceiving himself, because a people which have power and are well organized will be no less
stable, prudent, and grateful than a prince. In fact, they may be more so,
even though the prince is thought wise; and, on the other hand, a prince
freed from the restraint of law will be more ungrateful, changeable, and
imprudent than the people. And the changeability of their behavior does
not arise from a different nature, for it is the same in all men, and if there is
one better than the other, it is the people; it comes, rather, from having
greater or lesser respect for the laws under which they both live. And anyone who considers the Roman people will see that they were opposed to the
very title of king for four hundred years and were lovers of the glory and
the common good of their city; and he will see many examples that testify
to both characteristics. If anyone should cite, to the contrary, the ingratitude that the people showed toward Scipio, I would make the same reply I
did earlier on this subject, where I showed that the people are less ungrateful than princes. But, concerning prudence and stability, let me say
that the people are more prudent, more reliable, and have better judgment
than a prince does. And it is not without reason that the voice of the people
is likened to that of God: for it is evident that popular opinion has marvelous power in predicting, so much so that it would appear to foresee its
own good and evil fortune through some occult ability. As for its judgment
in various matters, when the people hear two equally able speakers, each
arguing different opinions, only very rarely does it happen that they do not
choose the better opinion and are incapable of understanding the truth of
what they hear. And if they err in matters of courage or profit, as was mentioned above, a prince will often err because of his own passions, which
are much stronger than those of the people. It is also evident that the people
make better choices in electing magistrates than does a prince, for one can
never persuade the people that it is good to elect to public office an infamous man of corrupt habits—something that a prince can easily be persuaded to do in a thousand ways; and when the people begin to feel an
aversion for something, we see them persist in this aversion for many
years—something we do not observe in a prince. For both of these characteristics I find it sufficient to cite the Roman people as evidence, for in so
many hundreds of years, in so many elections of consuls and tribunes, the
people did not make even four elections which they were forced to regret.
And, as I have said, they so hated the very name of king that no amount of
meritorious service rendered by one of their citizens seeking to gain the
title could persuade the people to forget the just penalties he deserved for

this ambition. Furthermore, it is evident that cities in which people are the rulers increase their territories in a very short time, much more so than cities which have always been under a prince, just as Rome did after the expulsion of the kings and Athens did after she freed herself of Pisistratus. This is the result of nothing other than the fact that government by the people is better than government by princes. Nor do I wish everything that our historian says in the aforementioned passage and elsewhere to be cited against this opinion of mine, for if we were to discuss all the faults of the people and all those of princes, all the glories of the people and all those of princes, it would be evident that the people are far superior in goodness and in glory. And if princes are superior to the people in instituting laws, forming civic communities, and establishing statutes and new institutions, then the people are so much more superior in maintaining the things thus established that they attain, without a doubt, the same glory as those who established them.

And, in short, to conclude this subject, let me say that just as the states of princes have endured for a long time, so too have the states of republics; both have needed to be regulated by laws, for a prince who is able to do what he wishes is mad, and a people that can do what it wishes is not wise. If, therefore, we are talking about a prince obedient to the laws or a people restricted by them, we shall observe more ability in the people than in the prince; if we are discussing either one or the other as being free from these restrictions, we shall observe fewer errors in the people than in the prince; moreover, they are less serious ones and easier to remedy. For a licentious and unruly people can be spoken to by one good man and can easily be brought back to the right path; however, with an evil prince there is no one who can speak to him and no other remedy than the sword. From this fact one can draw a conclusion concerning the seriousness of their respective maladies: if words are enough to cure the malady of the people and the sword to cure that of the prince, there will never be anyone who will not conclude that the greater the faults, the greater the attention required. When a people is unrestrained, neither its mad actions nor the evil at hand need be feared, but rather the evil that may arise from them, since a tyrant may emerge from so much confusion. But with an evil prince the opposite happens: present evil is feared and one hopes for the future, since men persuade themselves that ending his evil life can result in an era of freedom. So you see the difference between the two: one concerns things as they are and the other concerns things that will be. The cruelties of the masses are directed against anyone who they fear might act against the public welfare; those of the prince are directed against anyone who he fears might act against his own interests. But the prejudice against the people arises because everyone speaks ill of them freely and without fear, even when they rule; one always speaks ill of princes only with great fear and apprehension. And this seems not to be beside the point, since this subject leads me ahead to discuss, in the following chapter, whether one may place more trust in alliances made with a republic or those made with a prince.

Book 2

Introduction

Men always praise ancient times and condemn the present, but not always with good reason; they are such advocates of the past that they celebrate not merely those ages which they know only through the memory of the historians but also those that they, now being old, remember having seen in their youth. And when this opinion of theirs is mistaken, as it is most of the time, I am persuaded that there are several reasons which lead them to make this mistake. First, I believe that we do not know the complete truth about antiquity; most often the facts that would discredit those times are hidden and other matters which bestow glory upon them are reported magnificently and most thoroughly. Most writers submit to the fortune of conquerors, and in order to render their victories glorious they not only exaggerate what they have ably achieved but also embellish the deeds of their enemies in such a way that anyone born afterward in either of the two lands—that of the victor or that of the vanquished—has reason to marvel at those men and those times and is forced to praise them and to love them to the greatest degree. Besides this, since men hate things either out of fear or envy, two very powerful reasons for hatred of things in the past are eliminated, for they cannot hurt you or give you cause for envy. But the contrary applies to those things you deal with and observe: they are known to you in every detail, you see in them what is good as well as the many things that displease you, and you are obliged to judge them most inferior to things of the past; while, in truth, those of the present may deserve even more glory and fame—I am not speaking of things pertaining to the arts here, for in themselves they possess so much brilliance that the times take away from them little and cannot bestow upon them much more glory than they intrinsically merit; I am speaking rather of those matters pertaining to the lives and customs of men, about which we do not witness such clear evidence.

I repeat, then, that this aforementioned custom of praising the old and condemning the new does exist, but it is not always wrong. Sometimes such a judgment has to be correct since human affairs are always in motion, either rising or declining. And so, one city or province can be seen to possess a government that was well organized by an excellent man; and for a time it may keep improving because of the ability of the founder. Anyone, then, who is born in such a state and praises ancient times more than modern times deceives himself, and his deception is caused by those things mentioned above. But those who are born afterward in that city or region, at the time of its decline, do not, then, deceive themselves. As I reflect on why these matters proceed as they do, I believe that the world has always been in the same state and that there has always been as much good as evil in it; but this evil and this good changes from country to country, as we can see from what we know of ancient kingdoms that were different from each other according to the differences in their customs, while the world remained the same as it always had been. There is only this difference: the world's talents first found a home in Assyria, then moved to Media, later to Persia, and, in time, came into Italy and Rome; and if, after the Roman empire, no succeeding empire has lasted, nor has there been one where the world has retained all its talents in one place, nevertheless we can still see them scattered among many nations where men live ably, as in the kingdom of the Franks, the Turks—that of the Sultan—and today among the peoples of Germany; earlier there was that Turkish group which achieved so many grand things and seized so much of the world once it had destroyed the Eastern Roman Empire. In all these lands, then, after the Romans came to ruin, and in all those groups of people, such talents existed and still exist in some of them where they are desired and truly praised. And anyone who is born there and praises past times more than present ones may be deceiving himself, but anyone who is born in Italy or Greece and has not become an Ultramontane in Italy or a Turk in Greece has reason to condemn his own times and to praise others, for in them there were many things that made them marvelous, but in the present ones there is nothing to be seen but utter misery, infamy, and vituperation. There is no observance of religion, laws, or military discipline; all is stained with every kind of filth. Furthermore, these vices are the more detestable as they are found among those who sit on tribunals, command others, and expect to be worshiped.

But, returning to our subject, let me say that if the judgment of men is unfair in deciding which is better—the present age or the past—the latter of which, because of its antiquity, men cannot have as perfect a knowledge of as they can of their own times, this should not corrupt the judgment of old men in assessing the time of their youth and their old age, since they have known and observed both one and the other equally well. This would be true if men were all of the same opinion and had the same desires in all phases of their lives; but since these desires change, and the times do not, things cannot appear to men to be the same, since they have other desires, other pleasures, and other concerns in their old age than they had in their youth. For as men grow older they lose in vigor and gain in judgment and prudence, and the things that seemed acceptable and good to them in their youth become, later on, as they grow older, intolerable and bad; and although they should place the blame for this on their own judgment, they blame the times instead. Besides this, human desires are insatiable, for we are endowed by Nature with the power and the wish to desire everything and by Fortune with the ability to obtain little of what we desire. The result is an unending discontent in the minds of men and a weariness with what they possess: this makes men curse the present, praise the past, and hope in the future, even though they do this with no reasonable motive. I do not know, therefore, if I deserve to be considered among those who deceive themselves if, in these discourses of mine, I am too lavish with my praise of ancient Roman times and condemn our own. And certainly, if the excellence that existed then and the vice that rules now were not clearer than the sun, I would speak more hesitantly for fear that I might fall into the same error of which I accuse others. But since the matter is clear enough for all to see, I shall boldly declare in plain terms what I understand of those ancient times and of our own times, so that the minds of young men who read these writings of mine may be able to reject the present and prepare themselves to imitate the past whenever Fortune provides them with an occasion. For it is your duty as a good man to teach others whatever good you yourself have not been able to do, either because of the malignity of the times or because of Fortune, in order that—since many will thus be made aware of it—someone more beloved by Heaven may be prepared to put your truth into action.

In the discourse of the preceding book I have discussed the decisions the Romans made in matters concerning their internal affairs; now, in this one, I shall discuss what it was that the Roman people did concerning the expansion of their empire.

13. Scipione Ammirato, *The Florentine Histories*

Scipione Ammirato was born in 1531 at Lecce, on Italy's heel, where he grew up under the influence of one of the "model bishops" of the Tridentine Reformation, Braccio Martelli. After various literary peregrinations from Naples to Rome and Venice, he settled in Florence, as the protégé of then Cardinal and later Grand Duke Ferdinando de' Medici and with a commission from the then reigning Grand Duke Cosimo to write the history of Florence, of which selections are published here. He soon became

From *Istoria fiorentina* (Florence: V. Batelli, 1846–49), pp. 225–32, 270–71, 381–87, 393–94, 397, 399, 435–36. Translated for this volume by Lydia G. Cochrane.

a leading light in the Florentine cultural world as mentor of the literary Accademia degli Apatisti—without cutting his ties with his old friends in Naples, for whom he composed a genealogical history and edited an anthology of poetry. His major contribution to the debates in the Apatisti were his *Discourses on Cornelius Tacitus*, a response to Machiavelli's *Discourses on Titus Livius* similar to Giovanni Botero's *Reason of State* (of which selections are printed in this volume) and equally faithful to Machiavelli's form and method. But he also wrote a number of orations, one comedy, and several short stories (*novelle*) and poems; and he supplemented his honorarium from the grand duke by composing (or inventing) genealogical trees for rising patrician families. Only later in life did he finally complete his *Histories*, a "definitive" history of Florence from the earliest times to the death of Cosimo which represents, together with the several other "definitive" histories then being written about other states and cities of the peninsula, the final expression of Renaissance humanist historiography. The books covering the centuries until the mid fifteenth were published in 1600, the year before his death. The other books were published by his adopted heir, Scipione Jr., in 1641.

For more complete biographical and bibliographical information, see Book 2 of Eric Cochrane's *Florence in the Forgotten Centuries* (University of Chicago Press, 1973).

Book 31

The next day—the third after the death of [Duke] Alessandro [de' Medici] [1]—had already arrived when Cardinal [Innocenzo] Cybo, having called the Council of the Forty-Eight together in his apartment, disclosed to them with carefully chosen words the villainous deed that Lorenzino de' Medici [2] had committed in killing a prince [Alessandro] from whom—aside from being of his own blood—he had received so many honors and favors. However, [he went on], by the grace of almighty God the [Medici] family in-

1. 6 January 1537. Alessandro (b. 1510) was the illegitimate son of the same Lorenzo duke of Urbino to whom Machiavelli dedicated the final draft of the *The Prince* and hence the last surviving descendent of Lorenzo the Magnificent. His great uncle, Pope Clement VII, brought him to Florence with the title of hereditary "duke of the republic" after the collapse of the last "republican" regime in 1530.

2. Lorenzino (or Lorenzaccio) (b. 1514) was the second cousin of Cosimo, whose assassins finally caught up with him in 1548; Cardinal Cybo of the powerful Ligurian family of that name was a grandson of Lorenzo the Magnificent (1449–92) through his mother and the unofficial representative of Pope Clement in Florence until Clement's death in 1534. The Forty-Eight was the upper house of the two-house (but "rubber stamp") legislative council established by the constitution of the Florentine principate in 1532.

cluded Cosimo, son of the valorous Giovanni de' Medici[3] and already an adult; to him, according to the dictates of Caesar [Emperor Charles V], the government of Florence should legitimately fall. [The Cardinal] did not propose Cosimo because of any special affection or interest of his own, since he was no more intimately acquainted with the young man than were any of them. He did so—aside from the fact [this proposal] did not run counter to the emperor's declared wishes, which deserved serious consideration—because he thought it of great importance that Cosimo was the son of such a famous father, and that through his maternal line, he brought with him a kinship not only with the Salviati, but also with the very Medici who in the past had been heads of the Republic.[4] For his mother, born of a sister of Pope Leo, happened to be a first cousin of duke Lorenzo.[5] That made Cosimo a second cousin of Duke Alessandro, who was Lorenzo's son.

It was fortunate for [the future] Grand Duke Cosimo[6] that the senators were of different opinions; for their differences made it clear ever thereafter that his election had been a free one, one in which everyone was permitted to say what was on his mind. [For example,] Giovanni Canigiani, either because his family had been intimate servants of the late duke, or because he truly deemed it to be the right course, proposed that Alessandro be succeeded by his son Giulio. Palla Rucellai then rose and, declaring his great love for his fatherland, proclaimed passionately that he would not be induced even by the sight of an executioner's axe before his eyes to admit that a duke or a prince ever again be created in Florence; he insisted instead that the city be given back its liberty and be governed according to its ancient customs. Francesco Vettori[7] first reprimanded Canigiani for having spoken against the emperor's express wishes and for proposing [as prince] a bastard, particularly one who, not having passed the age of three years, needed to have a nurse more than to govern Florence. He turned to Rucellai and sought more patiently to persuade him to desist from making anymore fuss over his vote than was absolutely necessary. He then spoke briefly about the difficult times in which the Florentines found themselves, with two fortresses [poised] over their heads, with Alessandro Vitelli's[8] troops

3. The *condottiere* (general of a privately owned army), usually called Giovanni delle Bande Nere, who was killed while trying to block the advance of the Imperial army that sacked Rome in 1527.

4. Maria Salviati was the granddaughter, through her mother, Lucrezia, of Lorenzo the Magnificent.

5. The same Duke Lorenzo mentioned above in n. 1.

6. Cosimo's first titles were "duke of the republic" and then "duke of Florence." The title "grand duke of Tuscany" was bestowed upon him by Pope Pius V in 1570.

7. The same Vettori to whom many of Machiavelli's letters were addressed.

8. Alessandro Vitelli, lord (*signore*) of Città di Castello in Umbria, was a *condottiere* in Florentine service and the son of the Paolo Vitelli who had been executed by a previous Florentine government for treachery during the siege of Pisa.

in their midst, and with the emperor opposed (because of the pro-French proclivities of some of them) to their living in a free state. Above all, he revealed his fear that the government fall into the hands of the *Arrabbiati*,[9] or worse, into the hands of the Ciompi and the lowest orders of society, as it had been long ago.[10] He then proclaimed it to be a supreme gift of God that, amid so many disasters, there should be living a son of Giovanni de' Medici who, although young, was still old enough to govern, one who could be expected to accept, with certain honorable conditions and limitations, the governance of the city. Cosimo, he said, had been raised without a father and had arrived at an age fraught with the greatest risks without ever having shown the least sign of vanity or of giddiness. He had accompanied Duke Alessandro, his lord, to Bologna, Genoa, and Naples. He had been brought up in Rome with the nephews of [Pope] Clement [VII].[11] He had, one might say, run the gauntlet as a boy in Venice, when he barely escaped from the hands of certain adversaries. It could thus truly be said that he had become, not a young man, but a man wise and mature beyond his years.

Book 32

Once Cosimo had in this manner been made head and prince of the Republic, once the tumults that usually take place at the creation of new princes had died down, and once, orders having been given that everyone refrain from further activities [of this nature], perfect tranquility had been reestablished, Cosimo—of his own initiative and to make clear his intentions—published an edict that restored citizenship and civic honors to all citizens living in exile, [in the hope] that they would foreswear their ancient hatreds and willingly embrace the fortunes of the new regime.

At this point, he was very much upset by the occurrence of an unexpected incident. Thanks to the ineptitude of Pagolo Antonio da Parma, the commander, Alessandro Vitelli seized control of the fortress.[12] Vitelli had persuaded Pagolo, on the pretext of strengthening the guard, to allow Captain Meldola to enter the fortress with a good many soldiers several times.

9. "The Angry Ones": the anti-Savonarola faction of the 1590s that reemerged during the "republican" period between 1527 and 1530.

10. Who had seized control of the city in the revolution of 1378.

11. E.g., the later Duke Alessandro and Cardinal Ippolito, son of the Giuliano to whom Machiavelli dedicated the first draft of *The Prince* (see above, p. 153, n. 10, and pp. 184–85), and until his death in 1535 the other surviving heir of Lorenzo the Magnificent. They were removed from Florence as a consequence of the anti-Medici coup d'état in 1527.

12. The Fortezza da Basso, one of the first of the new cannonproof fortresses built by Antonio da San Gallo on the northwest edge of the city in 1534–35, on which see J. R. Hale, *Renaissance Fortification: Art or Engineering?* (London: Thames & Hudson, 1977).

When the moment came, Pagolo was powerless to get rid of them. Furthermore, it was discovered that the wife of the late duke[13] had retired to the fortress with all the family jewels and with her most intimate servants. Obviously, it would be difficult indeed to get her back. Nevertheless, judging this to be no time for quarrels, not only did Cosimo give no sign of his displeasure when Vitelli told him that he had acted in the interests of the state; he even modestly commended him for it.

Still graver disturbances then arose outside the borders. It was learned that those Florentines who for business or other reasons lived in Rome—among them the Florentine cardinals Salviati, Ridolfi, Pucci, and Gaddi, and the Tuscan cardinal Del Monte—did not approve of what had taken place in the city. A rumor went out that they were on their way to Florence to see whether they could use their authority for the purpose of settling the affairs of the Republic in accordance with their own views. This did nothing but spread new seeds of discord. It was also rumored that Filippo Strozzi,[14] having been informed by the assassin himself of the death of Duke Alessandro, had gone to Bologna, where another exile, Salvestro Aldobrandini, was in charge of the government [during the absence of] the governor. There [Filippo] went in order to be nearer to Florence and to be able, thanks to his reputation and his money, to be of help during the discussion of what ought to be done.

Meanwhile, serious tumults were taking place in Pistoia, in accordance with the habits of that city. The faction of the Panciatichi, incited by Baccio Bracciolini, who had left Florence right after the election of the new prince, took up arms, descended upon the streets, and publicly attacked and killed fourteen of the members of the Cancellieri faction in the twinkling of an eye, beginning with Desiderio Tonti.[15] The Cancellieri, taken unaware, tried to save themselves by fleeing and hiding, but they were unable to prevent the killing of three more of their number in the very house, and almost in the arms of, the police chief (*bargello*) of the city, who was in charge of the administration of justice. Nor were things quiet in the Romagna [Fiorentina].[16] It too, like Pistoia, was divided into factions, all of which were quick to react to the news from the capitol.

13. Margherita of Austria, illegitimate daughter of Emperor Charles V, later married to Ottavio Farnese, grandson of Pope Paul III and second duke of Parma and Piacenza, and subsequently governor of the Netherlands for King Philip II.

14. Successor to the Medici as head of the largest banking concern in Europe; he was married to the daughter of Piero, the son of Lorenzo the Magnificent. Captured by Vitelli on the morrow of the Battle of Montemurlo (August 1, 1537), in which Cosimo defeated an army of exiles, he remained a prisoner in the Fortezza da Basso (see above, n. 12) until, just one year later, he committed suicide.

15. Cf. Machiavelli, *The Prince*, xvii.

16. That part of Florentine territory that extended north and east of the crest of the Appenines.

To settle these matters as well as possible, Ridolfo Baglioni and Federigo da Montauto went to Pistoia, the first with his company of horsemen and the second with a company of foot soldiers, in order to aid Giovan Francesco de' Nobili, the commissioner, in reestablishing order in that city. Francesco della Stufa was sent to the Romagna with the charge of doing everything possible, with the aid of two hundred infantrymen under Valerio da Pescia, to keep order in that province. Alamanno de' Pazzi was sent to meet Cardinals Salviati, Ridolfi, and Gaddi (since the other two, when they heard that things had quieted down in Florence, decided not to trouble themselves further), who were already making their way, unarmed, toward Florence along with Giuliano Soderini, bishop of Santes, Baccio Valori, and several other citizens. Alamanno was soon joined by Matteo Niccolini and Luigi Ridolfi, who were sent as ambassadors not only in order to honor [the cardinals] and, in accordance with the ancient usage of the city, to receive them, all at public expense, but also to find out in what spirit and for what purposes they were coming to the city, so that everything might be settled peacefully and to the satisfaction of all concerned. Finally, when they had arrived in the vicinity of the city, the prince himself went out to meet them; and his name and praises were joyfully shouted by the common people of Florence as he returned with them. This did not detract from the determination of those who were intent upon stirring up trouble. But it so upset Cardinal Ridolfi—as if the honors shown to others were aimed at shaming him—that without a word to anyone, he turned off at San Niccolò and followed the Via del Fondaccio and the Via de' Bardi in order to dismount at his family's palace in the Via Maggio.

The cardinals had no other choice but to put into effect the plan they had worked out; and after they had been assiduously visited by the greater part of the nobility, they began, the next day and during the following days, to make clear the reasons why they had come home: none other, they said, than for the purpose of promoting the welfare of their common homeland. If everyone only would concur in this aim, there was no doubt that the state would have a form of government that would satisfy them all. If they could not so agree, they ran the danger of seeing their homeland fall prey to barbarians. In order to give greater weight to their advice, they made use of the name of the pope, whose approval they claimed to have for their enterprise. Furthermore, they skillfully let it be known that, since their followers were massed in the Valdichiana under the command of Ruberto Strozzi, one of Filippo's sons, of Bandino, the lord of Castello alla Pieve, and of Balduvino Dal Monte, they were perhaps strong enough to force their desires upon anyone who dared oppose them.

When the ministers of the new prince heard of these proceedings, they answered in soft words, meanwhile making provision for their defense. As soon as the army [supporting the cardinals] was removed from the Valdichiana,[17] they would surely be able to reach some sort of agreement, since it did not seem to be honorable to take orders from armed men. This led Cardinal Salviati, whose authority was recognized by all the others and who wanted things to be settled without recourse to arms for other reasons, to go to seek out Ruberto and to persuade him to release his troops. In this way, he pointed out, their aims could be realized much better. Discovering, however, on his return, that this stratagem was less easy than he had been given to suppose, learning of still other difficulties that had arisen, and realizing that he had been cleverly held at bay, he and his companions decided that he should speak in private with his nephew (Cosimo being his sister's son), hoping that, with his authority as a cardinal and in consideration of the young man's tender age, he would be able, either by force of reason or by pointing out the great dangers that awaited his nephew, to lead Cosimo gently toward the solution they desired.

It is widely believed that when Cardinal Salviati went to visit Cosimo at his house, he said something like this:

"If you were not my close kin, I would have to go to much more trouble to persuade you that what I am about to tell you is all for your own good. For what greater pride and satisfaction could I have than to see my sister's son as the greatest prince of Christendom, next to the crowned kings? But since the high position in which you newly find yourself is fraught with dangers, and since I cannot see how you can possibly maintain yourself in it for long, I believe that both for your personal safety and for the glory that will come to you for having liberated your country from dire servitude, you would be wiser to give up virtuously what you have in hand than to hold on obstinately to what you cannot keep. The [fate of the] late prince has shown you what perils come to anyone who lives in such a manner and who reduces a free country to servitude. Nothing—neither having the emperor for a relative, nor being armed, nor possessing the fortresses that were then being erected, nor being supported by the many faithful men who continually surrounded him—none of these saved him from being butchered like an animal by only two men. You may say, 'I will handle myself and live in such a way that no one will ever plot against me in this manner.' But I need only point to examples in our own history. Lorenzo and Giuliano de' Medici were attacked in full daylight, in church, during the sacrifice of the Mass. Moreover, they were not alone but accompanied by a great number of friends. None of this prevented one of them from being wounded and the other from being killed.[18] Although a memorable revenge was visited upon

17. The valley that runs north and south through eastern Tuscany from Lake Trasimeno to the bend in the River Arno near Arezzo.
18. The reference is to the Pazzi Conspiracy of 1478.

the assailants, it did not restore Giuliano to life, nor did it bring great honor to Lorenzo, since it became clear to everyone that his fellow citizens had sought to destroy him, looking upon him not as a supporter and benefactor of his fatherland, which was how he wanted them to think of him, but as a tyrant. It would take too long to recount all the plots that were hatched against the father and the grandfather of these two men and against their sons and grandsons. Finally, we have all seen where all their quests for grandeur have ended: in offenses against God, in the abasement of their fellow citizens, and in their own ruin. Someone may say to me that they simply fell short of achieving their objectives, just as all human undertakings fail in one way or in another. But the avidity with which they constantly oppressed their fatherland will never be erased from human memory; and it has cast a deep shadow over their many brilliant accomplishments, which otherwise would be illustrious and glorious throughout all ages."

"How much better, then, will it be, now that the line of Cosimo the Elder, who began the process of subjugating his country, has become extinct—how much better, I say, will it be that a new Cosimo, a hundred years later, restore its liberty under happier and more honorable auspices in our own time? There is no doubt whatever that your election, as we can see through the glory that has come to Andrea Doria,[19] surpasses all the great works that any living person can achieve either in war or in peace. Since that election has brought us honor and security, I know of no better or more beautiful opportunity that a nobly born person could imagine in this life; and since it has been offered to us by fortune, why should it not be embraced with all haste and with alacrity?"

It is said that Cosimo listened to these and other similar arguments with spellbound attention. Then, when he saw that the cardinal had come to the end of his speech, he asked him whether he had said these things in truth or rather for the purpose of tempting him. When the cardinal affirmed that he had expressed sincerely and with the purest and best intentions what he had on his mind, Cosimo is said to have answered in this manner:

He had no intention of speaking of his Medici predecessors except to state his belief that, whatever else they may have been, many of them had undeniably been ornaments of their homeland and of Italy. Of this, he and his companions were very much aware, since they had received the grandeur and splendor they now enjoyed from none other than the house of Medici. As for himself, not with arms, not with money, not with machinations had he risen to govern and rule his country; rather, he had been sum-

---

19. Andrea Doria was the "proprietor" of the largest Mediterranean fleet in the service of Emperor Charles V. In 1528 he expelled the French from his native Genoa and instituted an oligarchy of which he remained the effective "protector," though without title.

moned to this position by his fellow citizens, each one of whom had been free to nominate other persons, propose other solutions, and do all that is customarily done by free persons in free countries. That they had turned to him he attributed principally to the hand of God, since it was not a work of man that a young man, bereft of all assistance, innocent of all human striving and artifice, and not born into the ruling house should in an instant be raised to such high estate. Not wishing to oppose divine will in this matter but wishing rather to collaborate with it, he had determined to live in such a manner and to adhere to such rules of action that no one would ever have reason to harm him. If, however, something unexpected occurred, he was firm in his resolve that it was better to die a prince than a private citizen. There was more glory awaiting him for having supported his homeland, no longer able to maintain its freedom except with the help of the just reins of a principality,[20] than there would be if, under the false pretext of an apparent freedom, he left it prey to the inveterate and bloody rivalries and discords among its citizens. . . .

Enjoying this respite from external troubles, and realizing that the emperor would not only defend himself heartily against the French but would also give them a good fight led Cosimo, at the beginning of the new year 1543, to turn, as was his inclination, to internal affairs. He was well aware that good letters were not only an ornament of the city but also an excellent way to keep it pacified. For when men are busily occupied with the study of letters, they are less eager for novelties; and that was a state of affairs very useful in new states. He bent all his efforts to reviving the university at Pisa, which had been generally neglected during the troubles of the preceding years. He offered generous salaries in order to attract famous teachers in all the sciences, and through their reputations, to attract students from all nations. To these prospective students he guaranteed all the privileges customarily granted students in the other celebrated universities of Italy. One initiative of singular benefit to the less well-off students of the country was the founding and endowing (with the property confiscated from rebels) of a college capable of giving room and board to forty young men; and he appointed a director (*provveditore*) whom he charged with taking care of everything. The illustrious professors who inaugurated the long-neglected university were Matteo da Core and Boldone in medicine, Brando in philosophy, and the learned Vegio in law.[21]

---

20. I insert *che* in the following phrase to avoid having it suggest the opposite of what Ammirato obviously means: "non più atta a mantenersi libera *che* sotto il giusto freno . . ."

21. Matteo da Corte (not *Core*), having previously been physician to Pope Clement VII, died at the age of seventy the year after his arrival at Pisa in 1543. Niccolò Boldone remained at Pisa, like Matteo as professor of theoretical medicine, until 1554 when King Philip II made

The work in which I am engaged would be a foolish enterprise if for each of the years during which the wars between the emperor and the king of France continued I had to give an account of everything that was thought of them in Florence and all the provisions that were consequently adopted, gracelessly reiterating the same things time after time to the scarce delight, less profit, of the reader—both things deserving of regard. The writer of this history must note the things that occurred, [but] not every minimal thought that passed through others' minds. I will therefore not hesitate to leave out those matters that I deem not worthy of being remembered. But the acts of this state (its prince having thrown his fortunes in with those of the emperor) cannot be understood properly if the acts from which they took their beginnings are not made clear. I now turn, therefore, to these latter concerns, since they open the way to the acts that concern us here, and not the other way around.

Book 35

In the year 1561 Duke Cosimo instituted the religious order of the Knights of Santo Stefano, so named after its patron because of the protection of that glorious pontiff and martyr whose feast day the Church celebrates on the second day of August (the day on which the duke, so fortunately come into the principate from his own house, defeated the rebels at Montemurlo).[22] It followed the rule of Saint Benedict, and [took as its symbol] a cross similar in form to that of the Knights of Malta, but red in color and edged in gold. Cosimo chose himself to be the grand master and decreed that no one but the princes, his successors, could succeed to this post. He ordained that no person was to be admitted to the order without first having given proof of his nobility. Those aspiring to such an honor but unable to offer such proofs had to establish an endowment (*commenda*) sufficiently large to permit them to live from it nobly. The obligations he imposed upon the knights were conjugal fidelity, charity in coming to the aid of needy neighbors, and obedience to the grand master. He assigned moneys to establish endowments for the support of members of advanced age and for arming ships to fight against corsairs. He built and endowed a church and a monastery building for the knights at Pisa, and he obtained many privileges for them

him royal *protomedicus* and called him back to Pavia; he was subsequently elected a member of the Senate of Milan. Brando Borrus (1487–1571) was an orthodox Aristotelian who resigned on the arrival of the not-so-orthodox Simone Porzio of Naples. Giovan Francesco Vegius (or Veggi) (1489–1554) was professor of civil law. All of them were Milanese in origin.

22. Above, n. 14.

from the pope—among them, the right to draw income from ecclesiastical benefices.

That same year, the territory of Montepulciano was raised to the dignity of a bishopric, thanks to the efforts of Giovanni Riccio, a citizen of that city and at the time cardinal of San Vitale. The bishopric was given to Spinello Benci, also a native of that city; and the duke increased its revenues by granting it several benefices. Not long after, word arrived that the pope [Pius IV] had promoted eighteen persons to the cardinalate, among them, to the great pleasure of the duchess of Florence,[23] Francesco Pacecco, who was promoted to that dignity after her brother, don Luigi, had declined to accept it in order to marry. There were some persons, however, who thought this display of generosity toward so many meritorious men was a cover-up by the pope for the severity with which he had treated the nephews of his predecessor. These men were thought to have deserved death for their many wicked acts. Nevertheless, the very city of Rome that had been so mistreated by them seemed to be not in the least pleased to see the Duke of Paliano slaughtered on the bridge with Count d'Alisi on one side of him and don Lionardo di Cardine on the other. Nor was the city pleased to see the drowned body of Cardinal Carafa lying in the Transpontina bereft of the slightest sign of honor.[24]

Thus are men unhappy at the sight of such extreme changes in fortune. For they recognize in the example of persons of highest degree how easy it is for those of lesser condition to be the victims of a similar fate.

News reached the duke that the citizens of Pitigliano, no longer willing to tolerate the tyranny of Count Niccola Orsini, had admitted into their fortress Inglesco Calafati, the captain of the duke's contingent at Soana,[25] and had let it be known that they wished to be subject to no other prince than the duke of Florence. The duke immediately sent Chioppino Vitelli to that city in order to prevent the outbreak of even greater disturbances.

No sooner had news of this reached Rome, however, than both the Imperial and the French ambassadors lodged complaints. The latter did so because the duke had interfered in the affairs—which were none of his busi-

---

23. Eleanora da Toledo, daughter of Pedro de Toledo, viceroy of Naples since 1532, married Cosimo in 1539.

24. Giovanni Carafa, count of Montorio and duke of Paliano, had been the commander of the papal armed forces for his uncle, Pope Paul IV (1555–59) (born Gian Pietro Carafa, of Naples). Ferrante Count of Alife was his brother-in-law. Cardinal Diomede Carafa, bishop of Ariano (b. 1511) perished along with several other members of the pope's family in the violent reaction that followed the pope's death in 1559.

25. Pitigliano was the center of a small feudal domain belonging to the Orsini family of Rome on the border between Tuscany and the Papal State in Latium. It was finally annexed to the Grand Duchy of Tuscany in 1608.

ness—of count Niccola, who was an ally of his king and a member of the king's own [military] order. The former did so because he claimed that the territory of Pitigliano was a feudal dependency of the Empire, and he judged it to be the right of the emperor, not of anyone else, to concern himself with these matters. For his part, the duke was aware that Count Niccola's grandfather had put himself under the protection of the Republic of Siena: since the duke had now succeeded to the rights of that republic, he [claimed to have] a right to interfere in this case.[26] Then Count Niccola's father, Giovanni Francesco, who fifteen years earlier had been chased from his domain by his son, betook himself to Florence; and so earnestly did he plead his case, dwelling at length upon the troubles and calamaties he had suffered (to be sure, he had often been without the necessities of life), that the duke reinstated him, subject to certain conditions, even though he remained dissatisfied with such vassals. Soon afterwards he removed the contingent he had placed in charge of the fortress, for he heard that the emperor, as the supreme feudal lord of that domain, disapproved of its being there.

About this same time, the duke sent Antonio degli Albizzi as resident ambassador to the Republic of Venice. But seeing that the Senate would not condescend to grant the ambassador the rights of precedence over [the ambassador of the duke of] Ferrara that the duke thought belonged to him, he recalled him, not wanting the honor he demanded of others to be turned to his discredit. Still, he did not wish to put off having his son, Prince [Francesco],[27] whom he had determined to send to the court of Spain, first stop [in Rome] to kiss the pope's feet. The pope received [the prince] in the Hall of Constantine with all the honors customarily reserved for kings and kings' sons. Indeed, he was accompanied at the presentation by Cardinal Borromeo[28] and the cardinal chamberlain. He was lodged in the very same rooms of the papal palace in which his father had been received the previous year. He dined at the pope's table; and after completing the ceremonies commonly expected in the company of cardinals, he returned to Florence, leaving behind a very good opinion of himself at the papal court.

Meanwhile, [Prince Francesco's] father had honored with election to the Magistracy of the Forty-Eight Pandolfo della Stufa, Tommaso Soderini,

26. Cosimo captured the city of Siena in the name of the emperor after a long siege in 1554–55; he acquired all the former Sienese territory except the coastal fortresses by the Treaty of Cateau-Cambrésis in 1559, thus justifying the change of his title, in 1570, from "duke of Florence" to "grand duke of Tuscany" (cf. n. 6 above).

27. Cosimo turned over the control of internal affairs to his first son, Francesco (b. 1541) in 1564, and Francesco succeeded his father as grand duke in 1574.

28. The same Carlo Borromeo who is the hero of the Diary of Giovan Battista Casale published in this volume.

Giovanni Ugolini, Jacopo Guadagni, and Giovanni Battista Strozzi.[29] The talent of the latter, a man of letters and an excellent poet, as a writer of madrigals was clear to all, not so much for the originality of his conceits as for the discrimination he showed in choosing and combining his words, for which, in many people's opinion, he was gifted above all the others who have thus far written this sort of poetry. Being a man of wealth, and very rich, and much occupied in beautifying his little villa near Montoliveto, not far from the city, [Strozzi] thanked the prince copiously and humbly begged him, since he had deigned to confer this responsibility upon him, to permit him not to exercise it, arguing both his advanced age and the other interests that took him away from such cares. This the prince not only graciously conceded to him, but he went several times for his own pleasure to see him at his villa.

Then, when the year 1562 had begun and the Council of Trent had opened[30] for the purpose of correcting the erroneous ways of the Christian Republic and of resolving several uncertain points concerning religion, the duke sent Giovanni Strozzi to that holy gathering, and he made sure that all of the bishops of his domain went there too. But he soon encountered that old stumbling block, the precedence question—the same question that so troubled almost all Christian princes at the time. The Florentine ambassador refused to yield his place, which was also claimed by the ambassador of the duke of Bavaria, to the ambassador of the Swiss. The pope begged the duke of Florence to back down in order not to alienate the Swiss in matters of such importance. As it happened, the [duke of] Bavaria had been given the most prominent place; but since [Bavaria] was a principality within the [Holy Roman] Empire [rather than an independent state], the Swiss declared that they would no longer attend the meetings. Once Strozzi had delivered his protests, he was free to drop his suit.

Peace in Italy enabled the duke to enjoy much of the tranquillity that had been so sorely lacking during the preceding wars. Free at last of both the worries and the enormous expenses that war brings on, like a voracious wild beast that feeds on all sorts of foods, this year he was finally able to do what he had long desired to do: send his son to the court of Spain. He sent with him a truly regal entourage, knowing well how all-important appearances were to the Spanish and how highly that court esteemed any display of superior riches and pomp. In reply to a request from the queen of

29. A selection of Strozzi's (1505–71) madrigals was published in 1593. Many others of them have been confused with those of his better known nephew, Giovan Battista Strozzi the Younger, sponsor of the Accademia degli Alterati and hence a close friend of Ammirato.

30. I.e., reconvened, having been transferred from Trent to Bologna in 1547, suspended in 1548, reconvened at Trent in 1551 and suspended again in 1552. See the introduction to the *Canons and Decrees* of the Council published in this volume.

France[31]—that kingdom being beset by religious wars, the Catholics having taken up arms against the heretics who were now known by the new name of Huguenots—he lent her one hundred thousand ducats. Upon learning that the Most Catholic King [Philip II of Spain] was about to give the command of twenty galleys to the pope's nephew, Federigo Borromeo, whom the pope desired to magnify, the duke gave him two of his own as well.

[The duke] was not wholly free from having to make provisions for the military, however. Since the corsairs were doing considerable damage in the seas around Italy, he decided to give some attention to the navy in the hope of being able to purge his seacoasts of this pestilence. To this effect, he named Baccio Martelli captain of his fleet and commanded him to take the four galleys that had borne the prince to Spain, to make every effort to track down the pirates, and to do them whatever harm he could. In the seas of Syria [Martelli] seized a ship that was sailing from Alexandria to Constantinople, from which he learned what a fierce enemy of the Christian name we are dealing with. For on the ship, which belonged to the Turks, he found many Ethiopian blacks, along with a golden cross and a great string of noses that a Turkish captain was sending to his lord as a sign of his victory over Ethiopia. Ethiopia, under the rule of Prester John, a most powerful Christian ruler in those parts, was being attacked by the Turks, even though it was very distant from the nerve center of the Ottoman forces. He captured another ship with ease; then, after many hardships and three months of nearly constant sailing, and after his expenses began to outrun the value of his booty, he returned to Livorno.

There domestic calamities had struck the duke's family severely: he had remained at length in the Sienese Maremma to attend to the needs of that state and to plan fortifications for Grosseto. Either because of the air there, which is reputed to be bad,[32] or because it so pleased the will of God, two of his sons, Cardinal don Giovanni and don Garzia, became so sick that they died, one after the other, all the doctors' knowledge being of no avail. The death of these dear ones was closely followed by that of his valorous wife, who, long subject to stomach troubles, was unable to withstand the violence of this new grief. Submitting peacefully to the will of God, she made provision for the building of a monastery for noble virgins, which is the one we now see in the Via della Scala, called the New Monastery.

Duke Cosimo stood firm against these many blows and neglected not one of the responsibilities that the rule of his peoples required. He made

31. Caterina de' Medici, daughter of Duke Alessandro's father, Lorenzo duke of Urbino (hence a distant relative of Cosimo), married to King Henry II and regent for her sons after the king's death.

32. Indeed, the word *malaria* is the Italian word for "bad air" (*mal aria*).

Giovanni Paolo Pucci, Lodovico Ridolfi, Benedetto Machiavelli, and Giovan Batista Tedaldi members of the Forty-Eight. He was somewhat consoled by the news of the victory in France of the Duke de Guise over the
Huguenot heretics, a victory which, since it regarded the well-being of the
Christian Republic, brought singular satisfaction to every good prince who
held dear the honor of God. However, during the procession in Paris to give
thanks to almighty God for such a boon, the usual quarrels over precedence
did not fail to take place—in this case between the duke's ambassador,
Niccolò Tornabuoni, called del Borgo, and the ambassador of Ferrara.

At nearly the same time another similar altercation occurred in Spain in
the king's chapel between [the duke's] son, the prince, and the prince of
Parma. The latter, who had until then yielded before [Prince Francesco],
both because of the greater size of [his father's] domain and because of the
greater antiquity of his title,[33] suddenly tried to alter the precedence, urged
on, it was believed, either by his mother or by Fra Giuliano Ardinghelli, a
knight of Malta, who was at his side. But Pope Pius, who was very much
devoted to the duke, did not hesitate, in the midst of such misfortunes in
[the duke's] domestic affairs, to apply the remedies he deemed most opportune. Without the duke's even having requested it, not only were all of the
ecclesiastical revenues of his late son confirmed and passed on to Don Ferdinando (fourth in order of the duke's sons and also stricken with grave
sickness), but toward the end of the first month of the year 1563, when
Ferdinando had not yet even passed his sixteenth year, he was promoted to
cardinal.[34]

In the meantime, the duke had sent Aurelio Fregoso to Emperor Ferdinand to congratulate him on the election, at the end of November of the
previous year, of his son Maximilian (already the king of Bohemia) as king
of the Romans.[35] The duke now sent a similar congratulatory embassy to
Maximilian himself, offering to [both the emperor and the king] the support of all the power of his state in whatever occasion they might have need
of it. This state was now, thanks to its ruler's good government, flourishing
much more than it ever had in the past. So much so, indeed, that one
person sought to become a subject of its moderate regime. This person
was Sampiero of Corsica, who, when that island had revolted against the
Genoese, twice requested the duke's protection, promising to turn the is-

33. Pierluigi Farnese had been installed in the duchy of Parma and Piacenza carved for
him out of the papal domains in Emilia by his father, Pope Paul III, in 1545.

34. Cosimo's fourth son (1549–1609) resigned his title as cardinal to succeed his brother
Francesco (see above, n. 27) as grand duke in 1587.

35. Charles V resigned his imperial title in 1556 to his brother Ferdinand, to whom he had
long before entrusted the administration of his German domains. Ferdinand's son Maximilian
II succeeded him as emperor in 1564.

land over to him in accordance with what he had learned to be the desires of the islanders. But the duke did not wish to risk disturbing the peace that then reigned in Italy by yielding to the temptation of dubious hopes. He saw clearly that he would bring down upon his head an enormous amount of envy if he added Corsica—even if he could succeed in doing so—to his recent acquisition of Siena. Therefore, he not only turned a deaf ear to such proposals, but did everything in his power to keep things as they were and to prevent disorders from arising from any quarter. This was what had induced him, up to this moment, to tolerate the occupation of Soana by Count Niccola [Orsini], even though, according to the statutes, it should have been restored to him. But when he heard that the count had complained of him in the court of France, saying that it was he who had engineered his expulsion from Pitigliano, the duke decided to wait no longer to make the count see the error of his ways. He sent six pieces of artillery and five thousand foot soldiers to Soana; and with very little effort he took the city back.

In the midst of the greatest peace and tranquillity that Italy had ever known (unless we go back to the most ancient times and compare it to that of Augustus), it appeared to the duke that all the dangers that might thereafter threaten it could arise only from the power of the Turk. But even this was most unlikely to occur as long as the states of the king of Spain in Italy were governed with such prudence and equity. The peoples were not sucked dry by continual taxation and hence had no reason to rebel. The king was not burdened with unbearable expenses and so had no occasion to give his subjects any trouble. Quite the contrary: he was rich and wealthy,[36] and he was prepared to show his face to the enemy whenever the need might arise. . . .

These were the events that took place in the year 1564, to which I am not ashamed to add the pompous funeral ceremonies that the members of the Accademia del Disegno[37] offered in Florence for Michelangelo Buonarroti, the greatest painter, the greatest sculptor, and the greatest architect of his times. For since I am writing in particular of the things that took place in Tuscany, I think it not unworthy to take this occasion to mention one of the major glories of this, its capital city. Moreover, this event was one worthy of being remembered if only for the excellence and the mastery of the many craftsmen [who took part in it]. This is the same Michelangelo whom the major rulers of Christendom honored, who revived in our times the achievements of ancient times, whose genius was so supremely com-

36. The pleonasm is in the original: *danaioso e ricco*.

37. Founded in 1563 by Giorgio Vasari and several Florentine men of letters for the purpose of giving instruction in the arts.

mendable, and in whom, having lived for ninety years, no one ever found
the slightest stain or any blemish of behavior, notwithstanding the passage
of such a long span of time and the presence of so many occasions for sin.

The new members of the Forty-Eight created this year were Giulio da'
Ricasoli, Piero Niccolini, Agostino del Nero (the proprietor of the houses
of the Neri nobly built [by Michelangelo] on the road to Rome just beyond
the Rubaconte bridge), and Lotto Salviati.

The year 1565 had already begun when the duke, intent upon taking full
advantage of the great peace Italy was then enjoying (a peace that, thanks
to divine goodness, still endures), decided to found a new town near Cas-
trocaro on the border of the territory of Forlì in the State of the Church.
While the priest, according to the usual ceremonies of the Church, was
about to pose the first stone, the sky, which had been totally covered with
clouds, cleared enough to leave only the place where the new town was to
be founded in sunshine. This sign was interpreted to auger well, and the
town was named Città del Sole (City of the Sun). He founded another town
at the confines of Urbino near Sestine and the Pieve di Santo Stefano,
where a marvelous site for a fortress was discovered. This one he named,
putting aside elegant titles, Sasso di Simone (Simon's Rock), which is what
the inhabitants of the area had called the site.

[The duke also] made an inventory of all the artillery and munitions in
his fortresses; and he gave orders that others should continually be manufactured, knowing that in time of war it is better to use things that are already made than to make new ones. He diligently drew up a balance sheet
of all his revenues and expenditures, ordinary and extraordinary, so that he
could know at a glance how much his income surpassed his debts or his
income—just like an astute sailor who knows in all weathers how much
water he is drawing. But he was above all persuaded that the greatest ornament of provinces and kingdoms lay not in the walls, garrisons, and other
works we could call dead, but in the splendor and nobility of their great
men. When he heard that the pope was about to create a number of cardinals, in order to discourage the designs of some who, were no creations
made, might be said to have the papacy in their hands, he arranged for
Agnolo Niccoli, doctor of laws and, thanks to the duke's influence, already
archbishop of Pisa, to be honored with that dignity.

Meanwhile, the king of Spain was gathering a great fleet in the hope of
arriving in time to succor the island of Malta, toward which it was believed
the Turk was sending a very powerful force in order to take revenge on that
religious order [of Malta] which was constantly harassing his peoples.
Being unaware that Malta was the chief outpost in the line of defense of
Sicily and the Kingdom of Naples, he [delayed his attack] while waiting for
ten of his galleys to be put in shape to assist his undertaking. While some

of these ships were rounding Elba and Pianosa, a single one of the galleys of the lord of Piombino met a Turkish warship and took it prisoner after a valorous resistance, liberating eighty Christians from the oars.

It is not my intention to write about the War of Malta, because that would suggest that I had forgotten my purpose to write about the events of Florence and that I was writing instead about the events of all Christendom. But this war was carried on with the participation of the forces of the duke of Florence—both of his galleys (by the end of the war nine of them had been engaged) and his ships and of the many soldiers recruited in Tuscany with his permission under the command of Vincenzio Vitelli. Moreover, Prince Francesco had foreseen the danger and had already sent a good quantity of powder to the grand master of the order. Suffice to say, this was one of the most glorious defenses ever undertaken by Christians against the forces of the Turk. If we marvel at the histories of the ancient Greeks, and if it seems to us extraordinary that all Greece joined together to block the enormous army of Xerxes, it is a matter far more worthy of admiration that against the tremendous forces of the Turks, which if not in number certainly in valor and in the quality of their weapons must be considered superior to the ancient Persians, an island like Malta not only defended itself, but inflicted such notable losses upon the Turks and thus brought down their pride and vainglory. The ancients had the good fortune to encounter the noblest writers, whose mastery and beauty of speech added much strength and vigor to their accomplishments. But if we weigh things for what they are really worth, we will not let ourselves be dazzled by appearances; and the famous battles of Salamis and Marathon will yield, in all fairness, to the defense of Malta. It also seems to me part of my task not to omit mention of those knights about which I am writing who shed their blood on that island or suffered cruel servitude for the faith of Christ and for the honor shared by all who go by his name. . . .

In the meantime the princess[38] was proceeding toward Florence; and out to meet her went four thousand foot soldiers and five hundred horsemen, arrayed just as if they were about to do battle. Duke Cosimo also went out to meet her, accompanied by his son the cardinal [Ferdinando] and his other son don Pietro, by Ferdinand, son of the duke of Bavaria, by the apostolic nuncio, and by other ambassadors of princes. After passing through the Porta al Prato under a canopy that fifty young men of the highest nobility of Florence, all richly dressed, took turns carrying, a royal crown was placed on her head by the archbishop-elect of Siena and the bishop of Arezzo. And everywhere she went from here to the Duomo, where she stopped to do reverence to the Sacrament, then from the Duomo

38. Joanna (Giovanna) of Austria, daughter of Emperor Ferdinand I.

to the ducal palace [i.e., Palazzo Vecchio], she found the streets decorated with arches, statues, paintings, and other magnificent prospectives representing the actions and the faces not only of the great men of the house of Medici, but of other citizens famous in arms, in letters, or in some other excellent and noble art.

So no one will think that I am excessively indulging in minutia, let me say that I speak of such things because, like the ancient Greeks, the Tuscans of our days—and particularly the Florentines—excel in the art of drawing, so that they can easily do what could not possibly be done elsewhere for infinite amounts of gold. Moreover, since they are shrewd when it comes to spending, they, more than [anyone] elsewhere, have plenty of gold readily available [when the occasion demands it], as can be seen in the festivities that followed. Among these, besides balls, displays of horsemanship, wild-animal hunts, musical concerts, and similar entertainments, two were held to be [particularly] astonishing spectacles: the masque of the ancient and fabulous gods, which was the subject of a long and learned book, and the presentation of a comedy and of *intermezzi* between the acts that to the eyes of all present seemed equally ingenious and stupendous.[39]

It was the opinion of many men of letters that after the decline of the Roman Empire Italy had never seen the like of these festivities. For not only the end of this year but the beginning of the year 1566 were most happy times in Florence. There was equal joy in Rome for the election of the new pope, who, beginning as a poor and humble monk of Saint Dominic, was created cardinal by Paul IV in recognition of his rigorous life, and then served in the office of high inquisitor. He chose the name of Pius V; and he turned out to be one of the best and most worthy popes to direct the Church of God in many years. Nor did he hesitate to initiate good works, assigning to the building of a new fortress at Malta five thousand *scudi* per month until it was finished. He highly praised the duke of Florence who, following his usual zeal for providing his just share for the needs of Christianity, contributed fifteen thousand *scudi* to that good work; for the pope knew that the duke's galleys stood ready to respond to the call of the king of Spain on behalf of the needs and the convenience of the Christian religion. [The pope and the duke] agreed to lay aside any rivalries over their respective jurisdictions, which in many places lay side by side. They also agreed to permit each other to penetrate the state of the other whenever it was necessary to pursue outlaws, and to turn over the vassals of the other freely at the request of officers of justice.

39. The masque was planned by Vincenzo Borghini; the costumes and chariots were designed by Vasari; Baccio Baldini wrote the published description here referred to: *Discorso sopra la mascherata della geneologia degl'iddei de' gentili* (Florence: Giunti, 1565).

The pope [then] sent the master of the holy palace to Florence to ask that Piero Carnesecchi, previously interrogated by the inquisition on charges of heresy, be handed over to him; and this was done expeditiously, even though, as a longtime servant of [Pope] Clement and of the House of Medici, [Carnesecchi] had been protected by the duke in other such occasions. If there ever was a courtier in Rome whom the people admired and acclaimed for the favor he enjoyed from princes and for his gracious manners, this was surely monsignor Carnesecchi. He was far from ignorant of good letters. He had been born a noble in his homeland. He was endowed with all the benefits of fortune. Above all, he was a prudent man, always amiable and courteous toward everyone he met. If he had not persisted in the perverse opinions of the heretics, which even when faced with the terror of death he refused to retract, he would have not obscured all of his other good qualities by his miserable end. Not content to lose his life in such an ugly manner, he cared nothing about leaving by the loss of his soul an odious and abominable memory of himself to posterity, bringing great harm to his family and his country. . . .

The rest of the year [1573] passed without other new events, except for the creation, on the nomination of the grand duke, of the following members of the Forty-Eight: Alamanno da Filicaia, Alessandro Gianfigliazzi, Lorenzo del Vigna, Marabotto Rustici, Carlo de' Medici, Luigi Altoviti, and Bartolommeo Orlandini. The grand duke's illness, however, grew worse at the beginning of the year 1574; and no longer being able to resist it, on the twenty-first day of April he departed this life. Grand Duke Cosimo was a man of handsome body and clear complexion, but of fierce looks; and he did not willingly cast his eyes on other persons. He was a man of few but serious words and of acute pronouncements filled with fine phrases. He always had works of history read to him. He wrote much in his own hand. He kept secrets and was diligent above all other princes of his age. No ruler ever entered into his kingdom, because of the nature of the times, with greater [effusion of] blood; nor was there any who, at his death, was more desired [by his subjects]. He erected many buildings and reduced much land to cultivation. He never wavered before the magnitude or difficulty of any enterprise he undertook once he had taken it firmly to heart. He was just, and he loved men for whatever quality they might have; tolerating their vices, he made use of their virtues. He was extremely fond of hunting, but even fonder of fishing. In his time, he was held to be an oracle among princes; and by his good sense and hard work he made himself lord of Siena. If he had not in his very last years cast a shadow on the brilliance of his many virtues with two acts, one of incontinence and the other of cruelty, very few princes of the most highly praised centuries could be compared favorably with him.

14. Giovanni Botero, *The Reason of State*

Giovanni Botero was born near Cuneo in Piedmont in 1544. From 1560
until 1580, when he was granted an "honorable discharge," he served the
Society of Jesus as a teacher of grammar and rhetoric in various cities of
Italy and France. He then became an enthusiastic follower and assistant
of Carlo Borromeo, the Tridentine archbishop of Milan (whose activities
are chronicled in Casale's *Diary* published in this volume), and then mentor and secretary of Federigo Borromeo, Carlo's nephew, and later successor as archbishop of Milan. From 1598 until his death in 1617 he
served the duke of Savoy as a diplomat and as a preceptor to his sons.
Above all, Botero was a prolific and very successful writer. He published
a large number of sermons, orations, and theological and religious treatises. His *On the Causes of the Greatness and Magnificence of Cities*
(1588—enlarged edition, 1590) was almost immediately translated into
Spanish, Latin, and English; although an independent work, it was usually published thereafter as an appendix to the *Reason of State* (and so it
appears in this translation). His *Relazioni universali* (1591) appeared in
over one hundred editions—and even in a Polish translation—and was
used as a textbook of geopolitics by the ruling classes of all Europe. *The
Reason of State* was first published in 1589, then in an enlarged edition in
1590 and frequently thereafter.

I:15. On Justice Between One Subject and Another

It is the responsibility of the prince to make sure that justice is observed in
all his subjects' dealings with each other. This means keeping both country
and city free from violence and fraud. Violence comes from outlaws,
thieves, assassins, and murderous men, who must be kept in check by vigorous laws and by terror: it does little good to keep enemy arms and armies
far away as long as there is no want of persons who do even worse things at
home. Fraud, although it causes less commotion, does no less harm: it alters weights and measures; it falsifies wills, contracts, and the value of
money; it subjects commerce to monopolies; it makes foodstuffs disappear;
and it does other things of the sort that undermine peace and concord. If
the prince can solve these problems, he is sure to earn the affection and win
the everlasting love of his people, just as the people of France called [King]

From *Della Ragion di Stato* (Venice: Gioliti, 1598). Translated for this volume by Lydia
G. Cochrane.

Louis XII [1498–1515] "father" for the trouble he took and the solicitude he showed in aiding and defending them against the oppression of powerful lords.

But there is nothing more worthy of his attention than usury, for usury is nothing but robbery. In fact, it is much worse [than robbery] since, as Cato writes, the ancients sentenced the usurer to pay back fourfold if he took more than twelve percent, whereas the thief was condemned to pay only double.[1] This pestilence often brought confusion to the republic of Athens and the city of Rome, and the extreme poverty to which the usurers reduced both these peoples led them into great danger ("the curse of usury was indeed of old standing . . . and a most frequent cause of sedition and discord").[2] More than once it forced the kings of France to banish the Italian bankers.[3] Furthermore, of what use is it to the prince to keep his vassals' taxes down if he lets them be swallowed up by the avarice of the usurers who, without the least effort and doing nothing profitable for the republic, consume the wealth of private citizens?

But what am I saying, private citizens! Usury is the destruction of the public treasury and of public revenues. Excise taxes and customs fees bring in considerable revenue when actual goods circulate, enter, and leave your states, collecting tolls at seaports, river crossings, city gates, and other appropriate places. Now, goods cannot circulate without the use of money. Who does not know that those who try to get rich through usury— leaving commerce because it necessarily involves the risk of one's possessions and because it requires hard work for mind and body—multiply their money with loan contracts, selling both time and the use of the cash, and get fat in leisure on others' toil? They are like certain large, lazy, and worthless wasps who break into bees' hives to bother the bees and devour the fruit of their industry and labor. This is the way of the world: because everyone likes to make money effortlessly, the marketplace is deserted, the trades are abandoned, commerce is interrupted, the artisan leaves his shop and the peasant his plow, the noble sells his inheritance and puts the proceeds into ready coin, and the merchant, whose trade makes him travel indefatigably from one country to another, turns into a homebody. Meanwhile, cities lose what made them worthy and beautiful, customs fees fall off, the customs office goes bankrupt, and the state treasury runs dry. The people, reduced to miserable poverty and desperation, will demand a

1. Cicero, *De Officiis*, 2.25.

2. Tacitus, *Annales*, 6.16; all the passages quoted in the text are in the original language. I follow the English version by Alfred John Church and William Jackson Brodribb (Modern Library) except when a more literal rendition better fits the meaning Botero derives from, or imposes on, the passage quoted.

3. Nonsense. It gave Philip the Fair a chance to extract a large donation from them.

change in government. Asia twice submitted to Mithridates amidst an enormous slaughter of Romans because they [the Romans] had wasted the province like harpies with their endless usury. Solon was much admired for eliminating usury, or at least for moderating interest rates, in Athens.[4] Lucullus did the same in Asia and Caesar in Spain. The wealth of a prince depends upon the wealth of private citizens; this wealth in turn consists of goods and of the real exchange of the fruits of the soil and of industry—revenues, expenditures, and the transportation [of goods] from one place to another within one kingdom or among several countries. Not only does the usurer do none of these things, but by drawing money fraudulently to himself, he prevents others from engaging in commerce. We have in Italy two highly flourishing republics, Venice and Genoa. Of the two, Venice is undeniably the greater in both territory and grandeur. If we ask why, we will find this reason: because the Venetians, occupying themselves with commerce in real goods, have become moderately rich as individuals but infinitely wealthy in common; while the Genoese, to the contrary, concerning themselves exclusively with financial transactions, have immoderately increased private wealth, but have greatly diminished public revenues.

II:6. Some Prudent Advice

Take it as a fact that in the deliberations of princes, it is interest that always wins: you should never put your trust in friendship, kinship, alliances, or any other bond than that of the interest of the person who is negotiating with the prince. Polybius says that by their nature princes have neither friends nor foes, but that they measure amity and enmity by interest; and Plutarch says that kings use the words "peace" and "war" as they do coins—as they have need of them.[5] Sally forth in full strength at the first sign of a problem, because with time troubles grow and intensify. Remember the words of Otho: "There is no room for delay in a business which can only be approved when it is done."[6] But when troubles outstrip your strength, throw time in the breach, because things shift and change character with time, and he who has time has life.

Do not permit anything to be deliberated that would bring the slightest change or innovation to the state, because anything that is discussed or negotiated increases in credence and reputation, no matter how strange or pernicious it might be. The ruin of France and Flanders began with two

---

4. See the selection from Solon published in vol. 1 of this series.

5. Polybius, *Historiae*, 2.47.5; Botero here attempts to quote Plutarch from memory; this exact passage does not occur in any original text.

6. Tacitus, *Historiae*, 1.38.

petitions, the one that Gaspard de Coligny presented to Francis II and the one that [Baron] de Brederode presented to Madame of Parma.[7]

Do not ignore small disturbances, because all bad things begin as small things; but as time progresses, they grow bigger and bring on ruin, as we can see when imperceptible vapors gradually give rise to storms and terrible tempests.

Do not think that in your deliberations you can eliminate all disadvantages; for since it is impossible in this world that one thing be generated from another without corruption, some element of disorder is joined to all order: "There is some injustice in every great precedent which, though injurious to individuals, has its compensation in the public advantage."[8]

Do not take on many important undertakings at once: he who embraces much holds little. Mohammed I [i.e., II] carried on three wars at once—with the Mamelukes, at Rhodes, and at Otranto. He was defeated by the Mamelukes, suffered heavy losses at Rhodes, and failed to keep Otranto. He would have had sufficient forces for one of these undertakings, but not for all.[9]

Stand firm after a conquest and be sure of it before you attempt anything else. Tacitus praises Publius Ostorius: "It was his fixed purpose not to undertake any fresh enterprise till he had consolidated his previous successes."[10] Thus a wise king will avoid taking on new enterprises in the first years of his reign. For this reason Ariosto inadvertently accuses King Francis [I] of imprudence while intending to praise him, saying that he took on the conquest of Lombardy, "In the first year of his successful reign, / the crown yet ill secure upon his front.[11] Pyrrhus, king of Epirus, lost the cities and kingdoms he had conquered out of greed for new conquests. The same happened to King Demetrius. Ladislao, son of Charles III, king of Naples, went off to take possession of the kingdom of Hungary, to which he had been called, before having brought his father's kingdom firmly under his foot. As soon as he arrived in Zara, however, he learned that the Hun-

7. Henry Baron de Brederode (1531–68) presented the *Request* along with three hundred armed supporters on 5 April 1566. Margaret (Margherita) of Parma (1522–86) is the same illegitimate daughter of Emperor Charles V and wife first of Duke Alessandro de' Medici and then of Duke Ottavio Farnese of Parma and Piacenza about whom Scipione Ammirato speaks at length in the selection published in this volume.

8. Tacitus, *Annales*, 14.44.

9. Mohammed II, the conqueror of Constantinople, laid siege to Rhodes for three months in 1470 (the Knights of Rhodes, who became the Knights of Malta after their departure, ceded it on terms to his successor in 1522) and occupied Otranto on the heel of Italy between August 1480 and September 1481.

10. Tacitus, *Annales*, 12.32.

11. Ariosto, *Orlando Furioso*, 26.44.1–2, here in the William Steward Rose translation (Bobbs-Merrill, 1968).

garians, having changed their minds, had enthroned Sigismund, king of Bohemia, [instead], and that the barons of the Kingdom [of Naples] had risen in revolt.[12]

Avoid clashes with those more powerful than you, and do not get involved in more than one war at a time: "Not even Hercules fought against two at once."[13] The Romans studiously kept their eyes fixed on this truth, as do the Turks.

Dissimulate the injuries of those more powerful than you and crimes that cannot be punished. A wise man now and then yields occasionally to the times and [avoids] major confrontations; for the best shelter in an insurmountable storm is to furl your sails. Philip of Macedon excelled in this: toward the beginning of his reign, when a great number of enemies descended upon him, he chose to reach an accomodation, even on terms unfavorable to himself, with the most powerful of them. He then made war on the weaker of them, thus raising his followers' morale and showing courage to his enemies. The Venetians, who saved their cause by wisely yielding when Louis king of Hungary and his allies declared war on them, found themselves on the verge of total ruin when they refused to yield in their war against Louis XII of France and his confederates.[14] As Tacitus puts it so well: "Prudent rather than vigorous counsels insure the maintenance of power."[15]

There is nothing more unworthy of an astute prince than to put himself at the mercy of fortune and chance, as Tiberius Caesar's firmness illustrates: "In opposition to these remonstrances, Tiberius remained firm in his resolve not to quit the center of affairs and give himself over to chance."[16] Among modern generals, the same could be said of Prospero Colonna and Duke Francesco Maria of Urbino, to say nothing of Fabius Maximus and other ancient leaders. But the one whose firmness is incomparable is Philip [II] of Spain.[17]

---

12. Ladislao of Durazzo, son of King Carlo (Charles) III, and after the death of Giangaleazzo Visconti in 1402, the most successful pretender to the hegemony of all Italy, was indeed crowned king of Naples in 1390; but thanks to the rebellion referred to here by Botero, it was not until 1399 that he was able finally to enter his capital city.

13. *Phaedo*, 37.89, quoted in Marsilio Ficino's Latin translation.

14. In the War of the League of Cambrai.

15. Tacitus, *Annales*, 11.29.

16. Tacitus, *Annales*, 1.47. Here I substitute my own translation for the Modern Library translation in order to preserve the concept of "chance" (*in casum dare*) omitted by the translator.

17. Prospero Colonna (d. 1523) was one of the chief generals in the service of Emperor Charles V in Italy; Guicciardini (*History of Italy*, 15, 8) compares his strategy (*cunctator*) with that of the architect of Rome's victory over Carthage, Fabius Maximus. Francesco Maria duke of Urbino took much of the blame for permitting and then not putting an end to the Sack

A prince who has neighbors more powerful than he should do everything to keep them at peace with one another. For if they go to war and he helps one of them, he offends the other; if he serves both of them, he spends his own money and obligates neither of them; if he fails them both, he makes two enemies.

Make no sudden changes. For suddenness smacks of violence, and violence rarely succeeds and never produces durable effects. When Charles Martel, who had been majordomo to the king, aspired to the crown of France, he refused to usurp the title of king immediately, but first had himself called prince of the French nobility. In this way his son Pepin easily took on both the name of king and the kingdom. The Caesars began as perpetual dictators, then acquired tribunitian powers, then became princes and finally emperors and absolute rulers.

When you are ready for some undertaking, do not delay; because in this case waiting is more apt to upset it than do anything else: "to defer brings harm to him who is ready." [18]

Prefer the old to the new and calm to turbulence; for thus you put certainty before uncertainty and safety before danger. Emperor Maximilian II [19] excelled in this: he directed all his thoughts toward peace and public tranquillity.

Keep in mind what Demetrius Phalereus said to Ptolemy Philadelphus: that he would find many beautiful secrets in books that no one would dare tell him.

Do not pick a quarrel with powerful republics unless superior advantage makes you sure of victory, because love of liberty is so intense and so well rooted in the souls of those who have for some time enjoyed it that it is difficult to conquer and nearly impossible to extirpate. The actions and the counsels of princes die with them; the projects and the deliberations of free cities are nearly immortal. Similarly, do not pick a quarrel with the Church; it is unlikely that your cause will be just, and it will always appear to be impious and nothing will be gained by it. The experience of the dukes of Milan, the Florentines, the kings of Naples, and the Venetians are instructive in this regard: their wars with the popes were very costly and got them nowhere.

In selecting ministers, choose men who are equal, not superior or in-

---

of Rome in 1527; only pressure from the Venetians got him restored to his domains after the revival of the Papal State in 1530. Philip II succeeded his father Charles V as direct sovereign first of his states in Italy (Naples, Sicily, and Milan), and then, after Charles's abdication in 1555–56, of Spain and the Netherlands.

18. Lucan, *Pharsalia*, 1.281.

19. See Ammirato, in this volume, n. 35.

ferior, to the task you set before them: this rule was diligently observed by
Tiberius. For those who feel themselves worthy of greater things will disdain your task, and lesser men will be incapable of carrying it out.

Do not let a war with your neighbors drag on, because it will make them
warlike and bellicose. When Agesilaus was wounded by the Thebans, he
was told that he was getting what he deserved from people who learned
how to use weapons in his continual wars with them. The Turk has used
this technique with Christian princes. He has never carried on a long war
with any one of them. Instead, he has moved against first one and then the
other, taking an important fortress from one and a kingdom from the other.
Then, not to give them time to practice the art of war, he has made a truce
and turned elsewhere. He has not given the people time to take heart and
gather their courage to continue a war, but has easily agreed to peace or a
truce after taking a few states or cities from them. Hence the Turkish armies have always been made up of veterans and our own of raw recruits,
since the Turk has perpetually been at war with someone and none of our
princes has consistently been at war with him. Meanwhile, he has secured
his conquests.

It is even less wise to drag out a war with your subjects, particularly
with those of your own country. For that will exacerbate their resistance
and increasingly alienate them from you; and if at the beginning they
merely express their resentment, in the long run they will be driven to open
rebellion. This is what happened to King Sigismund in the Bohemian war
and to the Catholic King [Philip II] in the war in Flanders. No people has
the temerity to rebel openly against its ruler at the very first moment, since
the very words felony and rebellion provoke sentiments of infamy and hatred. But once their swords have tasted blood, the veil is rent and the obligation to justify their proceedings vanishes, and the matter ends in total
rupture and revolt. Alexander [Balas] king of the Jews had warred with his
subjects for six years, during which some fifty thousand persons were
killed. Seeing no end to the conflict, he finally asked his subjects what
could be done to arrive at an equitable peace. "Only by your death," was
their answer. In the end he did what he should have done at the beginning.

Do not put so much trust in peace that you disarm, for an unarmed
peace is a weak peace. Constantine the Great disbanded his border troops
because he thought them unnecessary once universal peace had been established. He thus opened the gates to the barbarians.

Be persuaded that speed is much more important than strength in any
undertaking, because speed wounds unexpectedly whereas strength can be
discerned beforehand. Speed throws the enemy into disorder; but strength
crushes him; and it is easier to sow discord and then crush an enemy than to
crush an enemy among whom order reigns. Caesar set off the civil war with

[only] three hundred horsemen and five thousand foot soldiers. But he baffled his enemies with his incredible swiftness. He left them no time to enroll new troops or to assemble the old ones; and in sixty days he occupied all of Italy.

Hold it also certain that more enterprises succeed through a long-term effort than through a sudden onslaught, because a sudden assault forces the issue with violence, whereas a long-term effort weakens the enemy [by allowing you to take advantage of] time and favorable occasions. It is easier to weaken an enemy and then strike him down than to overwhelm him all at once.

Learn to choose the right moment for an undertaking or a piece of business, and then seize upon it; for nothing is more important than [being able to determine] that critical, opportune moment in time, which is nothing other than a concourse of circumstances that make an enterprise easier for us than it would have been before and would be afterward. What Livy says is true: "Often the most important things are decided in an instant." [20] Philip I of Macedon excelled at this: he made admirable use of the weakness and the discord among the Greek cities in carrying his own designs to a happy conclusion. Amurath I, king of the Turks, was no less clever. He enlarged his empire in Europe by making good use of the Greek princes' quarrels. In the long run, might and cunning are not worth much if they are not seconded and even guided by good timing. Probus says of Epaminondas: "He made good use of the times." [21]

Do not admit to councils of state anyone who is a dependent of another prince. The advice of someone who has ties of interest with someone else cannot be sincere; for there is nothing that more frequently and more subtly enters into the consultations of princes and other persons than interest.

Do not give responsibility for the execution of an enterprise to someone who argued against it while it was being deliberated: the will cannot be effective where the intellect is not inclined. During the Battle of Lepanto,[22] Ulug Ali, who had been opposed to engaging in the battle, fled from it.

Discuss an undertaking thoroughly, but do not prescribe how to execute it. Execution depends largely on finding an appropriate time and opportunity; and since these vary continually, prescribing the execution of a decision does nothing but fetter the executer and cripple the undertaking. This is what happened to Ranieri Vasco in the war against the king of Hun-

20. Where Livy might have said such a thing, no previous editor has been able to discover.

21. This is not Probus, but Cornelius Nepos, and in the life not of Epaminondas, but of Alcibiades (7, 1).

22. The allied Spanish, Papal, Neapolitan, and Venetian fleets destroyed the Ottoman navy at the Battle of Lepanto (Greek: Naupactos) in 1571 (actually the battle took place just outside, not inside, the mouth of the Gulf of Corinth).

gary. "One should deliberate slowly, but execute rapidly what has been deliberated";[23] and nothing is more contrary to this rapidity than too narrowly defined commissions. Therefore employ cautious men in your deliberations, but ardent men for the execution of your plans.

Do not think you can avoid difficulties and dangers by fleeing them, but go meet them and then pursue them. For if you flee them, they will follow after you and grow on you. But if you meet them head on, they will retreat and dissolve into nothing.

Be careful not to show more partiality toward the nobility than toward the people, or the other way around. In either way you will become the leader of a party, not the prince of all.

Put no trust in anyone who has been or who believes himself to have been offended by you, because a desire for vengeance is tenacious and will reawaken whenever it has a chance, as is shown by examples of Count Giuliano and Charles of Bourbon.[24]

Ministers who are in your presence will look out for themselves. Pay attention to those who are absent, for they will usually accomplish more and work harder than the others.

Do not oppose the multitude directly, because you will not easily overcome them and, if you do, you will lose their love. Like a good sailor, tack when you cannot run before the wind, and make a show of wanting and giving what you cannot prevent or take away: "Crimes gain by hasty action, better counsels by delay."[25]

I:16. Ways to Propagate Religion

Religion gives so much strength to governments that without it any other foundation of a state will give way. Thus almost all those who have sought to found new empires have either introduced new sects or given new life to the old ones, as shown by the examples of Ismail, king of Persia, and the Sharif of Morocco. But of all religions, none prescribes laws more favorable to princes than the Christian religion; for it places under them not only the bodies and the possessions of the subjects, as is proper, but also their souls and their consciences; it binds not only their hands, but their affection and their thoughts as well. It requires obedience to reckless princes as well as to moderate ones, and it demands that they suffer anything rather than disturb the peace.

23. Botero seems to be quoting some proverb or current saying (in Latin).
24. Charles of Bourbon, offended by his feudal overlord, King Francis I, entered the service of Francis's chief enemy, Emperor Charles V; he died as the army he commanded (as best he could) was breaking through the walls of Rome in 1527.
25. Tacitus, *Historiae*, 1.32.

Furthermore, nothing releases a subject from due obedience to the prince unless [what he commands] runs counter to the laws of nature or of God; and [even] in these cases, [the Christian religion] insists that everything be done [to reach an accommodation] before arriving at an open break. Of this, the Christians in the primitive Church gave a great example. Even though they were persecuted and cruelly tormented in every imaginable way, still we do not read that they ever rebelled against the Empire or revolted against their princes: they suffered the wheel, iron, fire, and the bestiality and rage of tyrants and executioners, all for [the sake of] public peace. We must not think that this happened because they lacked the power [to do otherwise]; for entire legions threw down their arms and let themselves be cruelly torn to pieces. Even more astonishing, with all this they still prayed to God daily for the preservation of the Roman Empire. In our own times we have seen Catholics persecuted by the heretics everywhere: in Scotland, England, France, Flanders, and many parts of Germany. This shows the truth of the proposition that the Catholic faith makes subjects obedient to their prince, binds their consciences, and makes them desirous of peace and enemies of tumult and scandals. But Luther and Calvin and the rest, straying from the truth of the Gospels, everywhere sow discord and [bring about] revolutions in states and the ruin of kingdoms.

Now, since religion is so important for felicitous government and the tranquillity of states, the prince should encourage it and do his best to favor its spread; for, as Duke [Carlo] Emanuele of Savoy used to say, people dedicated to religion and to piety live much more obediently than those who govern themselves according to chance. First of all, he must avoid the extremes of simulation and superstition. The one, as I have already said, cannot be kept up, and when it is discovered, it totally discredits the simulator. The second arouses scorn. Be solidly religious in combating simulation and wisely pious in combating superstition. God is truth, and he wants to be adored in truth and sincerity.

Starting from this foundation, pay due honor to the vicar of Christ and likewise to the ministers of holy things. Make yourself an example to others, persuading them that nothing is more foolish, and nothing more betrays baseness of spirit, than picking quarrels with the pope and religious persons: if you honor them out of respect for God, whom they represent, you are impious when you do not yield to them; if you honor them not out of respect for God but for some quality of their own, you are foolish. "The highest civil authority yields to religion," says Valerius Maximus.[26] Henry II, king of France, after his triumphal entry, gave a magnificent banquet for the nobles of the realm, as custom prescribes. When a dispute arose be-

26. Valerius Maximus, *Dicta et facta memorabilia*, 1.1.2.

tween ecclesiastics and laymen, he put an end to it with these noble words: "Long ago I gave and dedicated my right hand to the Church." Hernando Cortez, the conqueror of New Spain, cannot be praised enough in this connection for the incredible reverence he showed toward priests and monks. He raised the Christian faith and the Christian religion to a position of highest prestige in those lands, and his example was so influential that even today the clergy is not more respected nor the religious more revered anywhere in the world than in New Spain. No one can possibly hold religion in high esteem if he does not venerate the clergy: how can you honor religion, which you cannot see, if you do not respect the clergy, whom you have before your eyes?

Choose religious men of excellent learning and virtue, and do all you can to strengthen their reputation among the people by hearing them often if they are preachers, making use of their prudence if they are persons of great experience, attending divine offices in churches that are served by exemplary ministers, honoring them occasionally at your table, asking their advice on some matter, occasionally submitting to them memoranda or petitions that pertain to questions of conscience, aid to the poor, or other good works, and giving them the possibility and the opportunity to use their talents for the common good. Since so large a part of the spiritual life of the people depends upon preachers, make every effort to have many of them. Do not commend those who, making use of flowery and decorative, but fruitless and vain, forms of speech, act the role more of entertainers than of preachers. Give credit rather to those who, scorning such pompous and impudent ways of speaking, breathe into and infuse with their preaching the souls of their hearers the spirit and the truth—those who flay vices, abhor sin, enflame souls with the love of God, and in a word, preach not themselves but Jesus Christ, "and him crucified." [27]

Do not permit the clergy to be scorned for their beggarliness, for there is nothing that abases religion and the worship of God more in the eyes of the common people than need and poverty among its ministers. Give generously to the building of churches, and hold it more worthy of a Christian prince to restore old churches than to build new ones, because restoration will always be a work of piety, whereas vanity often hides in new buildings and nests there. Mieczylow, king of Poland, increased the faith in his realm enormously by founding and endowing churches and enriching and adorning God's cult; and his son Boleslas followed his example. Finally, encourage the worship of your Creator in every way you can. Even in the midst of wars, David brought together all that was needed for building a magnificent temple; he worked for the improvement of the tabernacle service; and he

27. 1 Cor. 2:2.

added both instruments and voices to divine offices. Charlemagne brought excellent musicians all the way from Rome for holy services and gave orders to search out diligently the sermons of the Church Fathers and the lives of the ancient martyrs. He also made it possible for Paul the Deacon to write his *Acts of the Saints* and Usuard to write his *Martyrology*. Constantine the Great brought glory to religion by ordering that the books scattered during previous persecutions be gathered together at his expense in well-stocked libraries.

With regard to matters of government, leave freely to the prelates the judgment of matters of doctrine and morals, and leave them all the jurisdiction that the proper direction of souls requires and that canon and civil law allow them. (In a suit over an episcopal appointment, the emperor Aurelian, although not a Christian, ordered that the church of Samosata be given to the nominee of the Roman pope.) Furthermore, you should promote the carrying out of their decisions by all possible means—by your authority, your power, your money, and your acts—because the better your subjects behave and the more fervently they follow the ways of God, the more tractable and obedient they will be to their prince. When a suit involving pope Symmachus was brought before Theodoric, king of the Goths, he put the entire matter into the hands of a synod of bishops, adding that "he had nothing to do with ecclesiastical affairs, except to give them due reverence." [28]

IV:7. On the Poor

Those who have no interest in public tranquillity are also a menace to it— that is, those who are in great poverty and wretchedness. For having nothing to lose, they are easily aroused by any new turn of events and are quick to embrace any opportunity to rise through the ruin of others. Thus in Rome the poor, who made up the fifth class, were not usually enrolled in the militia except for service at sea, which was always held to be less honorable than service on land. Livy writes that in Greece, when rumors arrived of a war between King Persius and the Romans, the poor, hoping to see the world turned upside down, sided with Persius, while the good people, who had a stake in things remaining as they were, sided with the Romans. [29] When Catiline wanted to set off disturbances in the republic, he made use of those of low life or fortune, because, as Sallust says, "to anyone who aspires to power, the poorest man is the most helpful, since he has

28. The text from *Acta Synodi Romani sub Symmacho* is in Cesare Baronio, *Annales Ecclesiastici*, 14.502.
29. Livy, 42.30.

no regard for his property, having none, and considers anything honorable for which he receives pay."[30] And Caesar, aspiring to the rule of his country, lent a hand to all who had fallen into dire need, either through debts, bad management, or other accidents. Since they had no reason to be happy with the present state of things, he thought them ripe for use in his project of overturning the republic. If there were some whose poverty was such that he could not help them, he said publicly that they had need of a civil war.

All those who have deprived their country of its liberty have made use of such people, because, as Sallust says, "in every community those who have no means envy the good, exalt the base, hate what is old and established, long for something new, and from disgust with their lot desire a general upheaval."[31] Among all the poor, those who are quickest to turn to evil are the ones who were once rich and are now in need, and extreme poverty is as dangerous in a person of authority and reputation as extreme wealth. When David was fleeing the anger of Saul, "there came to join him all those who found themselves in narrow straits, those tormented by debts, the malcontents."[32] All the troubles in France, about which we have heard all the way here [in Italy], arose among just this sort of people. Since the nobles had gone deeply into debt and since many had fallen into poverty because of the great expenses incurred during the wars between the Most Christian king [of France] and the Catholic king [of Spain], and since the soldiers no longer had the possibility of living and spending as they were accustomed, they all decided to enrich themselves with the wealth of the church, which in that kingdom had revenues of more than six million *scudi*. Using the excuse of heresy—which they call the new religion—they took up their arms and reduced that once flourishing realm to extreme poverty. As Alienus Cecina said, "they decided to hide their own wounds in the wounds of the State."[33]

A king must therefore protect himself from the poor. He will do so in one of two ways: either by chasing them from his state, or by giving them an interest in keeping it at peace. They can be gotten rid of by sending them off to colonies, as the Spartans did to the Partheniae: fearing that they might cause trouble, they sent them to Tarentum. Or they can be sent off to war, as the Venetians did with the many mercenaries that then filled their city: they used the Cyprus war to get rid of them. Or they can simply be chased out, as the Gypsies were when King Ferdinand of Spain [i.e., Aragon] gave them sixty days to leave. They can be given an interest [in the state] by obliging them to do something, such as take up agriculture, a

30. *De Bello Jugurthino*, 86.3. Loeb translation.
31. *De Catilinae Coniuratione* ("The Conspiracy of Catiline" in vol. 1 of this series), 37. Loeb translation.
32. 1 Kings 22:2.
33. A very rough paraphrase of Tacitus, *Historiae*, 1.53.

trade, or some other occupation that will bring them enough to live on. Amasis, king of Egypt, made a law that obliged every subject to present himself before the provincial governors and account for how he lived and what he lived on. Anyone unable to do so was sentenced to death. In Athens, the Council of the Areopagus severely punished loafers without a trade, and Solon said that any son whose father neglected to give him a trade should not have to take care of his father. The laws of China stipulate that a son must learn and practice his father's trade.

Two good things come of this: first, the trades are brought to perfection; second, everyone can learn a trade to live on in his own home. Loafers and idlers are in no way tolerated. The blind and the crippled are given work appropriate to their capabilities; and only the totally incapacitated are admitted to the hospitals. Vopiscus says of Alexandria that it was "a prosperous, rich, and fruitful [city], and in it no one is idle. . . . the lame have their occupations, . . . the blind have theirs, and not even those whose hands are crippled are idle." [34] King Wu Ti, who gave to China a good part of the rules by which it maintains itself, decreed that women carry on the trade of their fathers, or at least that they keep busy with a distaff and needle. Augustus Caesar "brought up his daughter and his granddaughters to be accustomed to spinning wool." [35] In order to involve their people in the defense of the republic as much as possible, the kings of Rome saw to it that every one of them owned property: the love of their farms, [they believed,] would lead them to love and defend the established order. Lycurgus, as Nabis said to Quintus Flaminius, "thought that equality of wealth and dignity would make many willing to bear arms on behalf of the republic." [36]

However, since not everyone can own land or practice a trade—for [the maintenance of] human life requires that there also be others [who do not] [37]—the prince must provide, either himself or through others, a means by which the poor can earn a living. Dionysius of Halicarnassus says that nothing is more dangerous for princes than the idleness of the plebeians. [38] To this end Augustus Caesar built extensively and exhorted the principal

34. Flavius Vopicus of Syracuse is the author of the lives of Produs and Bonosus included in *Scriptores Historiae Augustae*. The passage here quoted is in 29.8 according to the system used in most editions, but in vol. 2, p. 401, of the Loeb edition, which uses another system. Botero alters a few words and omits much of the passage—e.g., the part on eunuchs. In these sections, I translate *arte* as "trade"; that is the nearest modern English can come to a combination of "craft," "manufacturing," "art," "profession"—and anything else that requires the imposition of human ingenuity and rewards that imposition with a fee or a salary.

35. Suetonius, *De Vita Caesarum*, 2.64.

36. A paraphrase of Livy, 34.31.

37. That is what he says: "Perché alla vita umana vi bisognano anco degli altri"; even though it would make more sense in the context to say: "since it is in the nature of human life that there always be some who do not. . . ."

38. Dionysius Hallicarnassus, *Antiquitates Romanae*, 4.44.

citizens to do the same, and in this way he kept the plebeian poor quiet. To an engineer who proposed to him a way of putting up on the Capitoline some enormous columns at little expense, Vespasian responded that he liked the invention very much, and he paid him for it, but that he wished to be free to provide a livelihood for the lower classes of the people. He thus let it be known that he would willingly spend money to enable those to live whom the engineer would have left unemployed.[39] Finally, you will make sure to entrust public affairs[40] only to those to whom peace and tranquillity are important and who would be endangered by unrest and innovation. Quintus Flaminius, wanting to reorganize the cities of Thessaly, raised to power that party which stood most to gain from the security and peace of the republic.

VIII:1. Two Ways to Increase the Population and the Power [of the State]

The population and the power of the state are augmented in two ways: by increasing your own, and by attracting others' to you. You can increase your own through agriculture and the arts, by encouraging the education of children, and with colonies. You can attract others' by absorbing your enemies, destroying nearby cities, bestowing citizenship [upon foreigners], concluding alliances, raising armies, establishing marriage bonds, and doing other similar things such as we will explain briefly one by one.

2. On Agriculture

Agriculture is the foundation of population growth. I call agriculture any work that is concerned with or that depends upon the soil in any way. The first kings of Rome, particularly Ancus Martius, were very clever and diligent in agriculture. King Dionysius [Diniz] of Portugal called farmers the sinews of the republic. Isabella, queen of Castile, used to say that in order to make sure that Spain abounded in all things, it ought all to be given to the fathers of St. Benedict, since they take such marvelous care of their own lands.

Thus the prince must favor and promote agriculture and show that he values people who improve the fertility of their lands and whose farms are exceptionally well cultivated. It will be his duty to initiate and direct every-

39. I translate *ingegno* here as if it were *ingegniere*, since the same person is meant, and since the change of wording may represent nothing more than another case of Botero's overhaste in writing and proofreading. Still, the engineer's quality ("brilliance of mind") could also be justified, even though it would be less elegant.

40. The sentence makes sense only if *republica* here is given its root meaning rather than that of "commonwealth," which is far more common in sixteenth century prose.

thing that belongs to the public good of his land: drying up swamps, uprooting useless or excess forests and reducing the land to cultivation, and helping and encouraging those who undertake such works. Thus Massinissa, king of Africa, by his efforts made Numidia and the Mediterranean part of the Barbary coast, which before had been uncultivated and barren, very productive and abundant in all goods. Tacitus writes of Tiberius Caesar that, with all diligence and solicitude, and without sparing either expense or hard work, he resolved the problem of the sterility of the soil: he "endeavored to overcome the problem of barren soils and stormy seas with every resource of wealth and foresight."[41] Because humidity and heat are the causes of generation and abundance, it is also the prince's duty to help nature by creating rivers and lakes in his territory. Here we cannot praise too highly the prudence of the former lords of Milan, who enriched that happy land beyond belief by building one canal from the Ticino and another from the Adda. The poets tell us that Hercules, in single combat with the river Achelous, broke one of his horns. But they hid the truth behind the story: that he really changed the bed and diverted the course of the river because it was gravely damaging the fields (the poets call "horns" the branching mouths of rivers as they flow into the sea).

It is up to the prince, then, to make provisions for such inconveniences and, finally, to support all means for making sure that his country abounds and is fecund in all things he knows it to be capable of producing. If plants or seeds are not to be found in his state, it is his duty to see that they are brought in from elsewhere. Thus the Romans brought cherries and peaches from the remotest parts of Asia, jujube from Africa and, little by little, other fruits. The cotton plant, once native to Egypt, can now be found in Cyprus, Malta, and a thousand other places. In Portugal you can find growing excellent ginger brought from India; and I can remember having eaten ginger grown in Paris. What I say of trees and fruits is also true of animals. Buffalos, unknown in Pliny's time, were [subsequently] introduced into Italy: no wonder that what he writes about them is so far from the truth.[42]

Further, the prince should not permit lands to be employed uselessly or for such things as parks (England is full of parks, to the great displeasure of the people, who complain that because of them they suffer shortages of grain and other things). Nor should he shrink from the expenses involved in most of these works, because they can be done during the winter and by using slaves or those condemned to the galleys, if he has any. If he does not have any, he can put to work those who otherwise would deserve to be sent to the galleys or to death. The Romans sent such men to mine metals or cut

41. Tacitus, *Annales*, 6.4; I modify slightly the Modern Library translation.
42. Pliny, *Naturalis Historia*, 8.15 and 11.90.

marble. If even these are insufficient, there will always be Gypsies, vaga-
bonds, and rootless people who are better employed for the public good
than left to go begging. In China, an extremely well-governed province,
begging is not permitted: everyone is employed as his forces allow. The
blind, if they have no livelihood of their own, are hired to turn hand mills;
the crippled do what work they can; and only the totally incapacitated are
admitted to the public hospitals. The Romans accomplished this sort of
works by putting soldiers to work on them when they were not otherwise
occupied, as is attested by the Mariane canals in Provence, the Drusine
canals in Ghelderland, and the Via Emilia and the Via Cassia [in Italy].
When Augustus Caesar saw that the canals which carried water from the
Nile to nearby fields were stopped up and filled in, he had his army clean
them out and redig them. The Swiss use local people in such projects: the
communities themselves build levees for the rivers, level heights, divert
streams, or build roads, accomplishing major works in little time.

Over and above these things, the prince must do his best to prevent
money from leaving his state needlessly. Even if things that are needed are
expensive within the state, the money spent on them will still remain
within the country or return to the treasury in the long run in customs
charges and taxes. Once the money leaves the state, however, both it and
the profits it would have earned are lost. For some years now, many formerly barren areas in Italy have been brought under cultivation, such as the
Pontine marshes, which not only occupied uselessly a great stretch of land
from which is now extracted a considerable profit, but which also so in-
fected the air that Rome itself was unhealthy. The Venetians too have made
enormous improvements in the Polesine of Rovigo, as have the Grand
Duke [of Tuscany] in the countryside of Arezzo and of Pisa and the duke
of Ferrara in the *valli* (marshes) of Comacchio, where grain enough to feed
a large city is now grown. The same could be done in many other areas, if
the princes paid attention to such matters and were not so enamoured of
immediate profit that they neglect future gain.

3. Of Industry

There is nothing more important for enlarging a state and for assuring it a
multitude of population and of all kinds of goods than the industry of its
people and the quantity of its trades (*arti*).[43] Some of these are necessary,
and others commodious, for civil life. Still others are desirable for the de-

43. See above, n. 34. *Industria* more generally means "the application of human effort,"
with much less connotation of "skill," as in *arte*. Here Botero uses it also to mean "manufacturing," as opposed to "agriculture," which is the main sense of the word today. In order to
avoid confusion, or rather, to respect Botero's lexical confusion, I always translate *industria*
as "industry," while varying the translation of *arte* according to the context.

lectation and amusement of people of leisure. They attract money, and they attract the people who make or traffic in manufactured goods, who provide materials to the workers, and who buy, sell, or transport the products of man's hands and ingenuity from one place to another. Selim I, emperor of the Turks, brought to Constantinople several thousand excellent craftsmen in order to increase both the population and the reputation of that city, first from the royal city of Tauris, then from the great city of Cairo. The Poles also understood this, for when they elected Henry, duke of Anjou,[44] to be their king, they asked him, among other things, to bring one hundred families of craftsmen to Poland with him.

Since art (*arte*) rivals nature, some may ask whether fertile soil or man's industry is more important for enlarging and populating an area. Industry, undoubtedly. In the first place, the things produced by a man's skilled hand are far superior in quantity and value than things generated by nature. Nature provides the matter and the subject; but the subtlety and the art of a man produces an indescribable variety of forms. Wool is a simple and crude product of nature; but how many lovely things art makes of it, how varied, and how multiform they are! Think of all the earnings drawn from wool by the industry of those who card it, warp it, set up the looms, weave it, dye it, cut it, sew it, form it in a thousand ways, and transport it from one place to another! Silk is a simple product of nature; but how many varieties of graceful cloth are fashioned from it by art! It is through industry that the excrement of a lowly worm comes to be prized by princes, appreciated by queens, and desired by everyone.

Moreover, many more people live from their industry than from rents.[45] Many cities in Italy can attest to this, but principally Venice, Florence, Genoa, and Milan, whose size and magnificence we need not dwell on, and where almost two thirds of the inhabitants live by the silk and the wool trades. Furthermore, to pass from cities to provinces [i.e., whole countries], people who have carefully calculated the wealth of France say that the annual rents (*frutti*) of that realm amount to fifteen million *scudi* for a population they estimate at something more than fifteen million souls. Even if we suppose the population to be no more than fifteen million, this means an annual per capita income of one *scudo*. So all the rest comes from industry.

---

44. Subsequently King Henry III of France (1574–89), the last of the Valois kings and the last surviving son of King Henry II and Catherine de' Medici.

45. *Entrate*: the same notion that is conveyed in the French term *rentier*, one who lives from an inheritance or investments that he does not personally administer (modern "coupon clippers"). The same concept is rendered by the term *frutti* (the "fruits" of such investment) below, while *entrate* is transferred to income produced by means of industry. Botero's vocabulary in economic matters is very irregular—but for very good reasons.

But who cannot see that this is true in all matters? The earnings from iron mines are not enormous. But a great many people live on profits from processing and exchanging this iron: those who mine it, who refine it, who smelt it, who sell it at wholesale and retail, who use it to make war machines and arms for defense and offense and innumerable tools for use in agriculture, architecture, and all sorts of crafts, for daily needs and for the innumerable necessities of life, to which iron is as important as bread. Thus if you compare what the owners earn from the iron mines with the profits made by the craftsmen and the merchants through their industry—which also greatly enrich the prince through customs fees—you will find that industry far surpasses nature. Compare raw marble with statues, colossi, columns, friezes, and the infinite numbers of works made from it. Compare timber with galleys, galleons, ships, and other vessels of every sort—warships, freighters, and pleasure craft—or with statues, household objects, and all the innumerable things that are made with the plane, the chisel, and the lathe. Compare colors with paintings, and the price of the one with the value of the other, and you will see how much more valuable labor is than material. (Zeuxis, an excellent painter, used to give away his works, generously saying that they could not be bought at any price.) You will also see how many more people live by their trades than from the immediate benefits of nature.

Industry is so powerful that no silver mine or gold mine in New Spain and in Peru can compare with it, and the customs revenues of Milan bring in more to the Catholic King than all the mines of Zacatecas or Jalisco. Italy is a province in which, as I have said before, there are no gold or silver mines of any importance, as there are none in France. Nevertheless, money and wealth abound in both, thanks to industry. Flanders too has no metal deposits; yet when it was at peace it had nothing to envy the mines of Hungary or Transylvania, thanks to its many, varied, and admirable products, manufactured there with inestimable skill (*arte*) and subtlety. There was no European country that was more splendid, more wealthy, or more populous, nor was there any part of Europe or the world in which there were cities so numerous, so great, and so attractive to foreigners. Some rightly called those countries His Majesty's Indies from the incomparable wealth that the emperor Charles got from them. Nature imposes its forms onto raw materials, and human industry uses these natural compounds to make artificial forms without end, since nature is to the craftsman what raw material is to the natural agent.

Thus the prince who seeks to increase the population of his city must bring in all sorts of industry and crafts. He will do this by bringing excellent craftsmen from other countries and assuring them employment and appropriate facilities, by showing his consideration for ingenious men and his appreciation of inventions and singular or unusual works, and by proposing prizes for perfection and excellence. Above all it is necessary that he not allow raw materials to be taken out of his state—wool, silk, timber, metals, and other such things. For craftsmen will leave when the materials do. Many more people can live on the trade of finished goods than on that of raw materials, and the prince's revenues are by far higher because of the exportation of [finished] products than because of the exportation of raw materials. Velvet, for example, brings in more than silk, *rascie* (rough woolens) more than raw wool, linen cloth more than flax, and cordage more than hemp. When the kings of France and England realized this some years ago, they prohibited the exportation of wool; and the Catholic King later did the same. But these ordinances could not at all be put into effect so soon. For those countries produce an incredible quantity of the highest grade wool, and there were not enough workmen to process it all. It is therefore probable that the above-mentioned princes adopted these measures simply because [they were aware that] the income and the taxes to be realized from woolen cloth are much greater than what can be had from raw wool. Nevertheless, these measures are also effective means to increase the population of the country, since many more people can live on manufactured wool than on raw wool. From this results an increase in the wealth and the greatness of the king; for the multitude of peoples make the soil productive and, with hand and skill, give a thousand forms to the matter provided by nature.

On the Causes of the Greatness and the Magnificence of Cities

9. On Having in One's Possession Some Important Item of Trade

It will also be very useful in attracting people to our city for it to have some important item of trade. Some such items are made wholly from what is naturally produced on the land around the city, like cloves in the Moluccas, incense in Sheba, balsam in Palestine or elsewhere. Others are made in large part from the natural products of the land, like the pepper of Calcutta and the cinnamon of Ceylon. Still others are the result wholly of human ingenuity (*eccellenza*), like salt in Cyprus, sugar in Madeira, and wool in some of the cities of Spain and England. Superior manufacturing also makes one place more successful than another, either through the quality of the water, the keen intelligence of the inhabitants, some occult secret known only to them, or some similar reason. Examples of this are the armaments of Damascus and Shiraz, the tapestries of Arras, the *rascia* woolens of Florence, the velvets of Genoa, the brocades of Milan, and the scarlet woolens of Venice. Let me also mention that in China nearly all the arts have been brought to the highest degree of excellence, among other reasons, because sons must take up their fathers' trade. Thus, because children are practically born with their mind formed in the paternal trade—the father hiding nothing from them and teaching them with all possible affection, assiduity, diligence, and solicitude—manufactured products reach the highest degree of beauty and completion that one could desire, as we can see in the few works that are carried from China to the Philippines, from the Philippines to Mexico, and from Mexico to Seville. But let us return to our subject.

Some other cities are masters of certain items not because the raw material is native to their land or is worked by their inhabitants, but because they hold dominion over a particular territory or over the seas that give access to it. Seville holds dominion over New Spain and Peru; and that is where the infinite riches of those countries end up. Lisbon holds dominion over the seas; and it draws to itself the pepper of Cochin, the cinnamon of Ceylon, and the other riches of India, which can only be shipped by them or with their safe-conduct. In somewhat the same way, Venice was the mistress of the spice trade ninety years ago. Before the Portuguese occupied India, spices were shipped via the Red Sea to Suez and from there on camelback to Cairo, then by the Nile to Alexandria, where they were bought by the Venetians, who sent their huge galleys to that great city; and they made incredible profits distributing the spices throughout most of Europe. Now almost all of this trade has been shifted to Lisbon, where every year the Portuguese ship spices, the control of which they have seized from the Moors and the Turks, by a new route; and they sell them to the Spanish, the French, the English, and all of northern Europe. This Indies trade is so sizable that it alone has enriched Portugal and given it an abundance of all goods.

Some other cities are masters of certain merchandise and its commerce because they are conveniently situated so as to serve as storehouses and warehouses for other nations. Such is the case with Malacca and Hormuz in the East, Alexandria, Constantinople, Messina, and Genoa in the Mediterranean, Antwerp, Amsterdam, Danzig, and Narva in the northern ocean [sic], and Frankfurt and Nürnberg in Germany. Many great merchants keep warehouses in these cities, and nearby peoples come there to get what they need, attracted by the ease of shipment—that is, by the size and security of the ports, good bays and inlets, navigable rivers that come right into a city or flow nearby, lakes and navigable canals, and level and safe roads. Speaking of roads, we might mention that over the ages the kings of Cuzco (which was called Inca in their language) built two roads that were two thousand miles long, roads so pleasant and broad, so level and straight, that they are unequaled even by Rome's great achievements. There one can see that precipitous mountains have been leveled, deep valleys filled in, and horrible boulders cut in two. Rows of trees are planted on either side, offering the traveler the ineffable delights of their restoring shade and the twittering of the ever-present birds. Nor are there lacking lodgings filled with every necessity, nor palaces built on high ground that seem to rival one another in their joyous display of their excellence, nor enchanting cities and pleasant countrysides and a thousand other delights to charm the eye with their variety and fill the soul with wonder at the infinite effects of both nature and human industry.

But to return to our subject: the prince will do well to understand the natural advantages of [his city's] site and to work to increase them judiciously. For example, he will see that breakwaters are built to make the port safer and to facilitate loading and unloading merchandise. He will make sure that the sea is kept free of pirates, that the rivers are made navigable, that appropriate warehouses capacious enough for any quantity of goods are built, and that roads will be made and maintained both on the plains and in the mountains. The kings of China deserve the highest praise for this. At incredible expense they have paved all of the roads in that famous realm, made stone bridges over immense rivers, cut down mountains of inestimable height and ruggedness, and paved the plains with impermeable stones so that winter and summer you can easily travel them on foot or on horseback and carry merchandise in carts or by beasts of burden. Some Italian princes have much to learn in this respect. In their lands during the wintertime, horses drown and wagons sink into the mud, so that transporting goods becomes enormously difficult; and a trip that should take a day is sometimes made, and with great effort, in three days and more. The roads are just as much of a hazard in many parts of France—in the regions of Poitou, Saintonge, and the Beauce, in Burgundy, for example. But this is no place to censure such famous provinces. Let us pass on to other matters.

4
Arts and Letters

15. Giorgio Vasari, *Life of Michelangelo*

Giorgio Vasari (1511–74) studied painting under Michelangelo as a young man and remained one of his most faithful disciples and admirers thereafter. Vasari spent much of his life traveling up and down Italy on various commissions as one of the most fashionable and prolific painters of his age; and in the course of his travels he managed to collect the vast amount of specific information incorporated into the first edition of his *Lives of the Artists* in 1550. In 1554 he was appointed chief architect to the duke of Florence, Cosimo de' Medici, for whom he built one of the greatest monuments of late Renaissance building and city planning, the Palace of the Uffizi ("government offices"). In 1566 he made another research trip around Italy in preparation for the second, and much expanded, edition of the *Lives* (1568); and he died while busily working on one more grandiose project, the decoration of the inside of the dome on the cathedral in Florence. The definitive edition of the *Life of Michelangelo* is by Paola Barocchi (Ricciardi, 1962), whose interminable footnotes all but bury the original text.

Michelangelo Buonarotti (1475–1564) was launched into an artistic career through the patronage of Lorenzo de' Medici, virtual master of Florence until his death in 1492. Michelangelo had already established his reputation as a sculptor (e.g., the *Pietá*, 1501) when he was commissioned by Piero Soderini, elected permanent president of the Florentine Republic under the constitutional reform of 1502 (see introductory note

From *Lives of the Artists*, rev. ed., translated by George Bull (Baltimore: Penguin Classics, 1971), pp. 325–26, 337–39, 349–57, 364–69, 378–83. © 1965 by George Bull. Some footnotes deleted. Reprinted by permission of Penguin Books Ltd.

to Machiavelli), to do the *David*. In 1505 he was called to Rome to design a future tomb for Pope Julius II (1502–13), of which the *Moses* is one of the best known elements, and to begin painting the ceiling of the Sistine Chapel (1509). After 1513 he spent most of his time in Florence, where he designed the sacristy ("Medici Chapel") and the library of San Lorenzo and directed the fortification of Florence in preparation for the siege of 1529–30. In 1534 he moved to Rome, where Pope Paul III commissioned him to paint the *Last Judgment* behind the altar of the Sistine Chapel. In 1547 he was put in charge of the construction of the basilica of St. Peter's—a task that kept him busy up to the moment of his death and prevented him from retiring to the house he had bought for himself and his family in Florence. Besides mastering (or "bringing to perfection," in Vasari's judgment) all three branches of the fine arts, Michelangelo was also a talented poet, although his poems were not published until early in the following century.

Enlightened by what had been achieved by the renowned Giotto[1] and his school, all artists of energy and distinction were striving to give the world proof of the talents with which fortune and their own happy temperaments had endowed them. They were all anxious (though their efforts were in vain) to reflect in their work the glories of nature and to attain, as far as possible, perfect artistic discernment or understanding. Meanwhile, the benign ruler of heaven graciously looked down to earth, saw the worthlessness of what was being done, the intense but utterly fruitless studies, and the presumption of men who were farther from true art than night is from day, and resolved to save us from our errors. So he decided to send into the world an artist who would be skilled in each and every craft, whose work alone would teach us how to attain perfection in design (by correct drawing and by the use of contour and light and shadows, so as to obtain relief in painting) and how to use right judgment in sculpture and, in architecture, create buildings which would be comfortable and secure, healthy, pleasant to look at, well-proportioned and richly ornamented. Moreover, he determined to give this artist the knowledge of true moral philosophy and the gift of poetic expression, so that everyone might admire and follow him as their perfect exemplar in life, work, and behaviour and in every endeavour, and he would be acclaimed as divine. He also saw that in the

---

1. 1276–1336. Among his most famous works were the fresco cycles in the Arena Chapel at Padua and in the Basilica of St. Francis at Assisi and the bell tower (*campanile*) of the cathedral of Florence.

practice of these exalted disciplines and arts, namely, painting, sculpture, and architecture, the Tuscan genius has always been preeminent, for the Tuscans have devoted to all the various branches of art more labour and study than all the other Italian peoples. And therefore he chose to have Michelangelo born a Florentine, so that one of her own citizens might bring to absolute perfection the achievements for which Florence was already justly renowned.

So in the year 1474 in the Casentino,[2] under a fateful and lucky star, the virtuous and noble wife of Lodovico di Leonardo Buonarroti gave birth to a baby son. That year Lodovico (who was said to be related to the most noble and ancient family of the counts of Canossa) was visiting magistrate at the township of Chiusi and Caprese near the Sasso della Vernia (where St. Francis received the stigmata) in the diocese of Arezzo. The boy was born on Sunday, 6 March, about the eighth hour of the night; and without further thought his father decided to call him Michelangelo,[3] being inspired by heaven and convinced that he saw in him something supernatural and beyond human experience. This was evident in the child's horoscope which showed Mercury and Venus in the house of Jupiter, peaceably disposed; in other words, his mind and hands were destined to fashion sublime and magnificent works of art.

David

Then some of his friends wrote to him from Florence urging him to return there as it seemed very probable that he would be able to obtain the block of marble that was standing in the Office of Works. Piero Soderini, who about that time was elected gonfaloniere for life,[4] had often talked of handing it over to Leonardo da Vinci, but he was then arranging to give it to Andrea Contucci of Monte Sansovino, an accomplished sculptor who was very keen to have it. Now, although it seemed impossible to carve from the block a complete figure (and only Michelangelo was bold enough to try this without adding fresh pieces) Buonarroti had felt the desire to work on it many years before; and he tried to obtain it when he came back to Florence. The marble was eighteen feet high, but unfortunately an artist called Simone da Fiesole had started to carve a giant figure, and had bungled the work so badly that he had hacked a hole between the legs and left the block completely botched and misshapen. So the wardens of Santa Maria del

2. The valley formed by the headwaters of the Arno river, north of Arezzo and east of Florence, inside the Florentine territorial dominion.

3. I.e., for the archangel Michael.

4. All recounted by Luca Landucci in the diary published in this volume.

Fiore (who were in charge of the undertaking) threw the block aside and it stayed abandoned for many years and seemed likely to remain so indefinitely. However, Michelangelo measured it again and calculated whether he could carve a satisfactory figure from the block by accommodating its attitude to the shape of the stone. Then he made up his mind to ask for it. Soderini and the wardens decided that they would let him have it, as being something of little value, and telling themselves that since the stone was of no use to their building, either botched as it was or broken up, whatever Michelangelo made would be worthwhile. So Michelangelo made a wax model of the young David with a sling in his hand; this was intended as a symbol of liberty for the Palace, signifying that just as David had protected his people and governed them justly, so whoever ruled Florence should vigorously defend the city and govern it with justice. He began work on the statue in the Office of Works of Santa Maria del Fiore,[5] erecting a partition of planks and trestles around the marble; and working on it continuously he brought it to perfect completion, without letting anyone see it.

As I said, the marble had been flawed and distorted by Simone, and in some places Michelangelo could not work it as he wanted; so he allowed some of the original chisel marks made by Simone to remain on the edges of the marble, and these can still be seen today. And all things considered, Michelangelo worked a miracle in restoring to life something that had been left for dead.

After the statue had been finished, its great size provoked endless disputes over the best way to transport it to the Piazza della Signoria.[6] However, Giuliano da Sangallo, with his brother Antonio, constructed a very strong wooden framework and suspended the statue from it with ropes so that when moved it would sway gently without being broken; then they drew it along by means of winches over planks laid on the ground, and put it in place. In the rope which held the figure suspended he tied a slipknot which tightened as the weight increased: a beautiful and ingenious arrangement. (I have a drawing by his own hand in my book showing this admirable, strong, and secure device for suspending weights.)

When he saw the *David* in place Piero Soderini was delighted; but while Michelangelo was retouching it he remarked that he thought the nose was too thick. Michelangelo, noticing that the gonfaloniere was standing beneath the Giant and that from where he was he could not see the figure

5. *Opera del Duomo*, the magistracy charged with keeping up and commissioning work for the cathedral of Santa Maria del Fiore (St. Mary of the Flower, referring to the supposed etymology of the name of the city, *Fiorenza*, or *Firenze*).

6. The main square of the city, facing the government palace (Palazzo dei Signori, today Palazzo Vecchio). A copy of the statue stands in the same place today; the original is protected against the elements in the museum of the Accademia.

properly, to satisfy him climbed on the scaffolding by the shoulders, seized hold of a chisel in his left hand, together with some of the marble dust lying on the planks, and as he tapped lightly with the chisel let the dust fall little by little, without altering anything. Then he looked down at the gonfaloniere, who had stopped to watch, and said:

"Now look at it."

"Ah, that's much better," replied Soderini. "Now you've really brought it to life."

And then Michelangelo climbed down, feeling sorry for those critics who talk nonsense in the hope of appearing well informed. When the work was finally finished he uncovered it for everyone to see. And without any doubt this figure has put in the shade every other statue, ancient or modern, Greek or Roman. Neither the Marforio in Rome, nor the Tiber and the Nile of the Belvedere, nor the colossal statues of Monte Cavello can be compared with Michelangelo's *David*, such were the satisfying proportions and beauty of the finished work. The legs are skilfully outlined, the slender flanks are beautifully shaped and the limbs are joined faultlessly to the trunk. The grace of this figure and the serenity of its pose have never been surpassed, nor have the feet, the hands, and the head, whose harmonious proportions and loveliness are in keeping with the rest. To be sure, anyone who has seen Michelangelo's *David* has no need to see anything else by any other sculptor, living or dead.

The *David* (for which Piero Soderini paid Michelangelo four hundred crowns) was put in position in the year 1504. It established Michelangelo's reputation as a sculptor and he went on to make for the gonfaloniere a very fine *David* in bronze, which Soderini sent to France.

Pope Julius' Funeral Monument; Sistine Ceiling

Meanwhile, the Pope had returned to Rome while Michelangelo remained in Bologna to finish the statue. In his absence Bramante was constantly plotting with Raphael of Urbino to remove from the Pope's mind the idea of having Michelangelo finish the tomb on his return. Bramante did this (being a friend and relation of Raphael and therefore no friend of Michelangelo's) when he saw the way his holiness kept praising and glorifying Michelangelo's work as a sculptor. He and Raphael suggested to Pope Julius that if the tomb were finished it would bring nearer the day of his death, and they said that it was bad luck to have one's tomb built while one was still alive. Eventually they persuaded his holiness to get Michelangelo on his return to paint, as a memorial for his uncle [Pope] Sixtus [IV], the ceiling of the chapel that he had built in the Vatican. In this way Bramante and Michelangelo's other rivals thought they would divert his energies from sculpture, in which they realized he was supreme. This, they argued, would make things hopeless for him, since as he had no experience of colouring in fresco he would certainly, they believed, do less creditable work as a painter. Without doubt, they thought, he would be compared unfavourably with Raphael, and even if the work were a success, being forced to do it would make him angry with the Pope; and thus one way or another they would succeed in their purpose of getting rid of him. So when Michelangelo returned to Rome he found the Pope resolved to leave the tomb as it was for the time being, and he was told to paint the ceiling of the chapel. Michelangelo, being anxious to finish the tomb, and considering the magnitude and difficulty of the task of painting the chapel, and his lack of experience, tried in every possible way to shake the burden off his shoulders. But the more he refused, the more determined he made the Pope, who was a wilful man by nature and who in any case was again being prompted by Michelangelo's rivals, and especially Bramante. And finally, being the hot-tempered man he was, his holiness was all ready to fly into a rage.

However, seeing that his holiness was persevering, Michelangelo resigned himself to doing what he was asked. Then the Pope ordered Bramante to make the ceiling ready for painting, and he did so by piercing the surface and supporting the scaffolding by ropes. When Michelangelo saw this he asked Bramante what he should do, when the painting was finished, to fill up the holes. Bramante said: "We'll think of it when it's time." And he added that there was no other way. Michelangelo realized that Bramante either knew nothing about the matter or else was no friend of his, and he went to the Pope and told him that the scaffolding was unsatisfactory and that Bramante had not known how to make it; and the Pope replied, in the presence of Bramante, that Michelangelo should do it himself in his own way. So he arranged to have the scaffolding erected on props which kept clear of the wall, a method for use with vaults (by which many fine works have been executed) which he subsequently taught to various people, including Bramante. In this instance he enabled a poor carpenter, who rebuilt the scaffolding, to dispense with so many of the ropes that when Michelangelo gave him what was over he sold them and made enough for a dowry for his daughter.

Michelangelo then started making the cartoons for the vaulting; and the Pope also decided that the walls that had been painted by previous artists in the time of Sixtus should be scraped clean and that Michelangelo should have fifteen thousand ducats for the cost of the work, the price being decided through Giuliano da Sangallo. Then being forced reluctantly, by the magnitude of the task, to take on some assistants, Michelangelo sent for help to Florence. He was anxious to show that his paintings would surpass the work done there earlier, and he was determined to show modern artists how to draw and paint. Indeed, the circumstances of this undertaking encouraged Michelangelo to aim very high, for the sake both of his own reputation and the art of painting; and in this mood he started and finished the cartoons. He was then ready to begin the frescoes, but he lacked the necessary experience. Meanwhile, some of his friends, who were painters, came to Rome from Florence in order to assist him and let him see their technique. Several of them were skilled painters in fresco, and they included Granaccio, Giuliano Bugiardini, Jacopo di Sandro, the elder Indaco, Angelo di Donnino, and Aristotile. Having started the work, Michelangelo asked them to produce some examples of what they could do. But when he saw that these were nothing like what he wanted he grew dissatisfied, and then one morning he made up his mind to scrap everything they had done. He shut himself up in the chapel, refused to let them in again, and would never let them see him even when he was at home. So, when they thought the joke was wearing thin, they accepted their dismissal and went back ashamed to Florence.

Thereupon, having arranged to do all the work by himself, Michelangelo carried it well on the way to completion; working with the utmost solicitude, labour, and study he refused to let anyone see him in case he would have to show what he was painting. As a result every day the people became more impatient.

Pope Julius himself was always keen to see whatever Michelangelo was doing, and so naturally he was more anxious than ever to see what was being hidden from him. So one day he resolved to go and see the work, but he was not allowed in, as Michelangelo would never have consented. (This was the cause of the quarrel described earlier, when Michelangelo had to leave Rome as he would not let the Pope see what he was painting.) Now when a third of the work was completed (as I found out from Michelangelo himself, to clear up any uncertainty) during the winter when the north wind was blowing several spots of mould started to appear on the surface. The reason for this was that the Roman lime, which is white in colour and made of travertine, does not dry very quickly, and when mixed with pozzolana, which is a brownish colour, forms a dark mixture which is very watery before it sets; then after the wall has been thoroughly soaked, it often effloresces when it is drying. Thus this salt efflorescence appeared in many places, although in time the air dried it up. When Michelangelo saw what was happening he despaired of the whole undertaking and was reluctant to go on. However, his holiness sent Giuliano da Sangallo to see him and explain the reason for the blemishes. Sangallo explained how to remove the moulds and encouraged him to continue. Then, when the work was half finished, the Pope who had subsequently gone to inspect it several times (being helped up the ladders by Michelangelo) wanted it to be thrown open to the public. Being hasty and impatient by nature, he simply could not bear to wait until it was perfect and had, so to say, received the final touch.

As soon as it was thrown open, the whole of Rome flocked to see it; and the Pope was the first, not having the patience to wait till the dust had settled after the dismantling of the scaffolds. Raphael da Urbino (who had great powers of imitation) changed his style as soon as he had seen Michelangelo's work and straight away, to show his skill, painted the prophets and sibyls of Santa Maria della Pace; and Bramante subsequently tried to persuade the Pope to let Raphael paint the other half of the chapel. When Michelangelo heard about this he complained of Bramante and revealed to the Pope, without reserve, many faults in his life and in his architectural works. (He himself, as it happened, was later to correct the mistakes made by Bramante in the fabric of St. Peter's.) However, the Pope recognized Michelangelo's genius more clearly every day and wanted him to carry on the work himself; and after he had seen it displayed he was of the opinion that Michelangelo would do the other half even better. And so in twenty months Michelangelo brought the project to perfect completion without the assistance even of someone to grind his colours. Michelangelo at times complained that because of the haste the Pope imposed on him he was unable to finish it in the way he would have liked; for his holiness was always asking him importunately when it would be ready. On one of these occasions Michelangelo retorted that the ceiling would be finished "when it satisfies me as an artist."

And to this the Pope replied: "And we want you to satisfy us and finish it soon."

Finally, the Pope threatened that if Michelangelo did not finish the ceiling quickly he would have him thrown down from the scaffolding. Then Michelangelo, who had good reason to fear the Pope's anger, lost no time in doing all that was wanted; and after taking down the rest of the scaffolding he threw the ceiling open to the public on the morning of All Saints' Day, when the Pope went into the chapel to sing Mass, to the satisfaction of the entire city.

Michelangelo wanted to retouch some parts of the painting *a secco*, as the old masters had done on the scenes below, painting backgrounds, draperies, and skies in ultramarine, and in certain places adding ornamentation in gold, in order to enrich and heighten the visual impact. The Pope, learning that this ornamentation was lacking, and hearing the work praised so enthusiastically by all who saw it, wanted him to go ahead. However, he lacked the patience to rebuild the scaffolding, and so the ceiling stayed as it was. His holiness used to see Michelangelo often and he would ask him to have the chapel enriched with colours and gold, since it looked impoverished. And Michelangelo would answer familiarly:

"Holy Father, in those days men did not bedeck themselves in gold and those you see painted there were never very rich. They were holy men who despised riches."

For this work Michelangelo was paid by the Pope three thousand crowns in several instalments, of which he had to spend twenty-five on colours. He executed the frescoes in great discomfort, having to work with his face looking upwards, which impaired his sight so badly that he could not read or look at drawings save with his head turned backwards; and this lasted for several months afterwards. I can talk from personal experience about this, since when I painted five rooms in the great apartments of Duke Cosimo's palace[7] if I had not made a chair where I could rest my head and relax from time to time I would never have finished; even so this work so ruined my sight and injured my head that I still feel the effects, and I am astonished that Michelangelo bore all that discomfort so well. In fact, every day the work moved him to greater enthusiasm, and he was so spurred on by his own progress and improvements that he felt no fatigue and ignored all the discomfort.

The painting on the ceiling of the chapel is arranged with six pendentives on either side and one in the centre of the walls at the foot and the head; and on these Michelangelo painted prophets and sibyls, twelve feet high. In the middle of the vault he depicted from the Creation up to the Flood and the Drunkenness of Noah; and in the lunettes he showed all the Ancestors of Jesus Christ. For the foreshortenings in these compartments he used no consistent rule of perspective, nor is there any fixed point of view. He accommodated the various compartments to the figures, rather than his figures to the compartments, for he was resolved to execute both the draped figures and the nudes so that they should demonstrate the perfect quality of his draughtsmanship (*disegno*). There is no other work to compare with this for excellence, nor could there be; and it is scarcely possible even to imitate what Michelangelo accomplished. The ceiling has proved a veritable beacon to our art, of inestimable benefit to all painters, restoring light to a world that for centuries had been plunged into darkness. Indeed, painters no longer need to seek new inventions, novel attitudes, clothed figures, fresh ways of expression, different arrangements, or sublime subjects, for this work contains every perfection possible under those headings. In the nudes, Michelangelo displayed complete mastery: they are

7. The same Palazzo dei Signori mentioned in the preceding note; Vasari remodeled the interior as a residence for Duke Cosimo; about whom, see the account given in the selections from Ammirato's *History of Florence* published in this volume.

truly astonishing in their perfect foreshortenings, their wonderfully rotund contours, their grace, slenderness, and proportion. And to show the vast scope of his art he made them of all ages, some slim and some full-bodied, with varied expressions and attitudes, sitting, turning, holding festoons of oakleaves and acorns (to represent the emblem of Pope Julius and the fact that his reign marked the golden age of Italy, before the travail and misery of the present time). The nudes down the middle of the ceiling hold medallions painted like gold or bronze with subjects taken from the Book of Kings. Moreover, to show the perfection of art and the greatness of God, in the histories Michelangelo depicted God dividing Light from Darkness, showing him in all his majesty as he rests self-sustained with arms outstretched, in a revelation of love and creative power.

In the second history, with beautiful judgment and skill he showed the Creation of the Sun and the Moon, depicting God, supported by many *putti*, in an attitude of sublime power conveyed by the strong foreshortening of his arms and legs. In the same scene Michelangelo showed the Almighty after the Blessing of the Earth and the Creation of the Animals, when he is seen on the vaulting in the form of a foreshortened figure, flying through the air, which turns and changes direction as one walks about the chapel. The same happens in the next history, where God is dividing the Waters from the Earth. And both these figures are beautiful forms and refinements of genius that only the inspired hands of Michelangelo could create. Then he went on to the Creation of Adam, where he showed God being borne by a group of nude angels of tender age who appear to be bearing up not one figure alone but the weight of the world; and this effect is achieved by the venerable majesty of the Divine Form and the way in which he moves, embracing some of the *putti* with one arm, as if to support himself, while with the other he stretches out his right hand towards Adam, a figure whose beauty, pose, and contours are such that it seems to have been fashioned that very moment by the first and supreme creator rather than by the drawing and brush of a mortal man. Beyond this in another scene he showed God taking our mother Eve from the side of Adam; and here we see the two nude figures, one so enslaved by sleep that it seems dead, and the other awakened to life by the divine benediction. The brush of this wonderfully ingenious craftsman arrestingly reveals the difference that there is between sleep and wakefulness and how the divine majesty can be portrayed in the firm and tangible terms that humans understand.

After this comes the scene when Adam, at the persuasion of a figure half woman and half serpent, brings death upon himself and upon us through the apple; and there again we see Adam and Eve, now being driven from Paradise by the angel who appears in sublime grandeur to execute the commands of a wrathful Lord. Adam displays his remorse at having sinned and his fear of death; and the woman also shows her shame, abasement, and desire for forgiveness, as she covers her breasts with her arms, pressing her hands palm to palm and sinking her neck on to her bosom, and turns her head towards the angel, showing more fear of the justice of God than hope of divine mercy. No less beautiful is the scene showing the sacrifice of Cain and Abel, where there are some figures bringing the wood, some bending down and blowing the fire, and others cutting the throat of the victim; and this Michelangelo executed as carefully and judiciously as the others. He displayed similar art and judgement in the history of the Flood, where there are depicted some dying men who are overwhelmed by terror and dismay at what has happened and in various ways are striving their utmost to find safety. For in the heads of these figures one sees life in prey to death, along with fear, dismay, and hopelessness. Michelangelo also showed the pious actions of many people who are helping one another to climb to safety to the top of a rock. Among them is a man who has clasped someone who is half dead and is striving his utmost to save him; and nothing better than this could be seen in living nature. Nor can I describe how well expressed is the story of Noah, who is shown drunk with wine and exposed, in the presence of one son who is laughing at him and two others who are covering him up: a scene of beautiful artistry that sets its own standards. Then, as if Michelangelo's genius were emboldened by what he had already done, it soared even higher and achieved even more in the five sibyls and seven prophets that are painted on the ceiling. These figures, each ten feet or more in height, are shown in varied attitudes, wearing a variety of vestments and beautiful draperies; they are all executed with marvellous judgment, and invention, and they appear truly inspired to whoever studies their attitudes and expressions.

Thus, Jeremiah can be seen with his legs crossed, holding one hand to his beard and resting an elbow on his knee; the other hand rests on his lap, and the manner in which he inclines his head clearly expresses his melancholy and anxious reflection, and the bitterness forced on him by his people. Equally fine are the two *putti* and the first sibyl beyond him, in the direction of the door. In this figure Michelangelo was anxious to express the spirit of old age itself; she is enveloped in draperies, to suggest that her blood had frozen with the passing of time. And since her sight has failed, Michelangelo has depicted her holding the book she reads very close to her eyes. Beyond this figure follows the prophet Ezekiel, an old man, full of movement and grace, and holding in one hand a roll of prophecies while he raises the other and, as he turns his head, prepares to utter words of lofty significance. Behind him there are two *putti* holding his books. . . .

The Sacristy and Library of San Lorenzo

To go back to Michelangelo's own life: from Carrara he returned to Florence where he wasted a great deal of time now on one thing and now on another. Then for the Medici Palace he made a model for the windows with supporting volutes that belong to the apartments at the corner. Giovanni da Udine decorated the room in stucco and painting, with results that are greatly admired; and Michelangelo gave the goldsmith Piloto instructions to make the shutters of perforated copper, which are certainly very impressive.

Michelangelo devoted many years of his life to quarrying marble, although it is true that while the blocks were being excavated he also made wax models and other things for the facade. But the project was delayed so long that the money the Pope assigned to it was spent on the war in Lombardy, and when Leo died the work was left unfinished, nothing having been accomplished save the laying of a foundation in front to support the facade and the transportation of a large column of marble from Carrara to the Piazza di San Lorenzo.

The death of Leo was a fearful blow to the arts and those who practised them, both in Florence and Rome; and while Adrian VI was Pope, Michelangelo stayed in Florence giving his attention to the tomb of Julius. Then Adrian died and was succeeded by Clement VII,[8] who was no less anxious than Leo and his other predecessors to leave a name glorified by the arts of architecture, sculpture, and painting. It was at that time, in 1525, that Giorgio Vasari was taken as a young boy to Florence by the cardinal of Cortona and placed with Michelangelo as an apprentice. However, Michelangelo was called to Rome by Pope Clement, who was ready to have a start made on the library of San Lorenzo and the new sacristy, in which he intended to place the marble tombs he was having built for his ancestors. Before leaving, Michelangelo decided that Vasari should go to work with Andrea del Sarto until he was free again himself, and in person he took Vasari along to Andrea's workshop to introduce him.

He then left for Rome in a hurry, harassed once again by Francesco Maria, duke of Urbino, the nephew of Pope Julius, who complained that Michelangelo had received sixteen thousand crowns for the tomb and yet stayed in Florence amusing himself, and who threatened him angrily that if he did not attend to the work he would make him regret it. After Michelangelo had arrived in Rome, Pope Clement, who wanted to make use of his services, advised him to settle his account with the duke's agents, for the

8. Giulio de' Medici, son of Giuliano, the brother of Lorenzo the Magnificent; Pope Clement VII (1523–34). For the other members of this family mentioned below, see the introduction to the selections from Machiavelli in this volume.

Pope believed that in view of all he had done Michelangelo was a creditor rather than a debtor; and that was how matters were left. After the Pope and Michelangelo had discussed many things together, they resolved to finish completely the sacristy and the new library of San Lorenzo at Florence.

So Michelangelo again left Rome and raised the cupola of the sacristy as we see it today. He designed it in a composite style and asked the goldsmith Piloto to make for it a very beautiful ball with seventy-two facets. It happened that while the cupola was being raised Michelangelo was asked by some of his friends:

"Shouldn't you make your lantern very different from that of Filippo Brunelleschi?" [9]

"Certainly I can make it different," he replied, "but not better."

Michelangelo made in the sacristy four tombs to hold the bodies of the fathers of the two Popes: namely, the elder Lorenzo and his brother Giuliano, and those of Giuliano, the brother of Leo, and of Duke Lorenzo, Leo's nephew. He wanted to execute the work in imitation of the old sacristy made by Filippo Brunelleschi but with different decorative features; and so did the ornamentation in a composite order, in a style more varied and more original than any other master, ancient or modern, has ever been able to achieve. For the beautiful cornices, capitals, bases, doors, tabernacles, and tombs were extremely novel, and in them he departed a great deal from the kind of architecture regulated by proportion, order, and rule which other artists did according to common usage and following Vitruvius and the works of antiquity but from which Michelangelo wanted to break away.

The licence he allowed himself has served as a great encouragement to others to follow his example; and subsequently we have seen the creation of new kinds of fantastic ornamentation containing more of the grotesque than of rule or reason. Thus all artists are under a great and permanent obligation to Michelangelo, seeing that he broke the bonds and chains that had previously confined them to the creation of traditional forms.

Later Michelangelo sought to make known and to demonstrate his new ideas to even better effect in the library of San Lorenzo: namely, in the beautiful distribution of the windows, the pattern of the ceiling, and the marvellous entrance of the vestibule. Nor was there ever seen such resolute grace, both in detail and overall effect, as in the consoles, tabernacles, and cornices, not any stairway more commodious. And in this stairway, he made such strange breaks in the design of the steps, and he departed in so many details and so widely from normal practice, that everyone was astonished. . . . Meanwhile, he continued the work in the sacristy of San

9. Brunelleschi (1377–1446), the founder of Renaissance architecture; among his many major works is the dome and the lantern on the Florence cathedral.

Lorenzo, in which there were seven statues which were left partly finished and partly not. Taking these and the architectural inventions of the tombs into account, it must be confessed that he surpassed all others in practice of the three arts. To be sure, the marble statues to be seen in San Lorenzo, which he blocked out or finished, provide convincing evidence for this claim. Among them is the figure of Our Lady, seated with her right leg crossed over the left and one knee placed on the other, while the child, with his thighs astride the leg that is uppermost, turns in a most enchanting attitude, looking for his mother's milk; and Our Lady, holding him with one hand and supporting herself with the other, leans forward to give it to him. Although this statue remained unfinished, having been roughed out and left showing the marks of the chisel, in the imperfect block one can recognize the perfection of the completed work. Michelangelo's ideas for the tombs of Duke Giuliano and Duke Lorenzo de' Medici caused even more astonished admiration. For here he decided that Earth alone did not suffice to give them an honourable burial worthy of their greatness but that they should be accompanied by all the parts of the world; and he resolved that their sepulchres should have around and above them four statues. So to one tomb he gave Night and Day, and to the other Dawn and Evening; and these statues are so beautifully formed, their attitudes so lovely, and their muscles treated so skilfully, that if the art of sculpture were lost they would serve to restore to it its original lustre.

Then among the other statues there are the two captains in armour: one, the pensive Duke Lorenzo, the embodiment of wisdom, with legs so finely wrought that nothing could be better; the other, Duke Giuliano, a proud figure, with the head, the throat, the setting of the eyes, the profile of the nose, the opening of the mouth, and the hair made with such inspired craftsmanship, as are the hands, the arms, the knees, the feet, and indeed every detail, that one's eyes can never be tired of gazing at it. One has only to study the beauty of the buskins and the cuirass to believe that the statue was made by other than human hands. But what shall I say of the Dawn, a nude woman who is such as to arouse melancholy in one's soul and throw sculpture into confusion? In her attitude may be seen the anxiety with which, drowsy with sleep, she rises up from her downy bed; for on awakening she has found the eyes of the great duke closed in death, and her eternal beauty is contorted with bitter sorrow as she weeps in token of her desperate grief. And what can I say of the Night, a statue not only rare but unique? Who has ever seen a work of sculpture of any period, ancient or modern, to compare with this? For in her may be seen not only the stillness of one who is sleeping but also the grief and melancholy of one who has lost something great and noble. And she may well represent the Night that covers in darkness all those who for some time thought, I will not say to surpass, but even to equal Michelangelo in sculpture and design. In this statue Michelangelo expressed the very essence of sleep. And in its honour various erudite people wrote many Latin verses and rhymes in the vernacular, of which the following, by an unknown author, is an example:

> The Night that you see sleeping in such loveliness was by an angel carved in this rock; and by her sleeping she has life; wake her, if you disbelieve, and she will speak to you.

To this, speaking in the person of Night, Michelangelo replied:

> Dear to me is sleep, and dearer to be of stone while wrongdoing and shame prevail; not to see, not to hear, is a great blessing: so do not awaken me; speak softly.

To be sure, if the enmity that exists between fortune and genius, between the envy of the one and the skill of the other, had allowed this work to be completed, then art would have demonstrated that it surpassed nature in every way. However, in 1529, while Michelangelo was labouring with intense love and solicitude on these works, Florence was besieged,[10] and this decisively frustrated their completion. Because of the siege Michelangelo did little or no more work on the statues, because he had been given by the Florentines the task of fortifying both the hill of San Miniato and, in addition, as I said, the city itself. After he had lent a thousand crowns to the Republic and found himself elected one of the Nine of the Militia (a council appointed for the war) Michelangelo turned all his thoughts and energies to the job of perfecting the fortifications. . . .

The *Last Judgment*

Since he could hardly do otherwise, Michelangelo resolved to enter the service of Pope Paul,[11] who wanted him to continue with the work commissioned by Pope Clement without changing anything in the inventions and general conception of what had been decided, such was the Pope's respect for his great talents. Indeed, Pope Paul felt for Michelangelo such reverence and love that he always went out of his way to please him. For example, his holiness wanted to have his own coat-of-arms painted under the Jonah in the chapel, in place of the arms of Pope Julius; but when this suggestion was put to Michelangelo, not wanting to make changes that would

10. By a joint papal and imperial army bent upon restoring the Medici, expelled in the coup d'etat of 1527, to the city. The anti-Medici regime surrendered in August 1530; in 1532 Pope Clement's nephew Alessandro was installed as duke.

11. Alessandro Farnese, Pope Paul III from 1534 to 1549; on whom, see the Bull of Convocation of the Council of Trent, in this volume.

do wrong to Pope Julius and Pope Clement, he would not agree, saying that his coat-of-arms would not look well there. And his holiness, to avoid offending him, accepted his decision. To be sure, the Pope fully appreciated Michelangelo's excellence and realized that he always did what was just and honourable, without any adulation or respect of persons: something which rulers rarely come across.

For the wall of the chapel, overhanging about a foot from the summit, Michelangelo then had carefully built a projection of bricks, which had been especially chosen and baked, to prevent any dust or dirt from settling on the painting. I shall not dwell on the details of the inventions and composition of the *Last Judgment*, since so many copies of all sizes have been printed that there is no call to waste time describing it. It is enough for us to understand that this extraordinary man chose always to refuse to paint anything save the human body in its most beautifully proportioned and perfect forms and in the greatest variety of attitudes, and thereby to express the wide range of the soul's emotions and joys. He was content to prove himself in the field in which he was superior to all his fellow craftsmen (*artefici*), painting his nudes in the grand manner and displaying his great understanding of the problems of design. Thus he has demonstrated how painting can achieve facility in its chief province: namely, the reproduction of the human form. And concentrating on this subject he left to one side the charm of colouring and the caprices and noble fantasies of certain minute and delicate refinements that many other artists, and not without reason, have not entirely neglected. For some artists, lacking Michelangelo's profound knowledge of design, have tried by using a variety of tints and shades of colour, by including in their work various novel and bizarre inventions (in brief, by following the other method of painting) to win themselves a place among the most distinguished masters. But Michelangelo, standing always firmly rooted in his profound understanding of the art, has shown those who can understand how they should achieve perfection.

To return to the *Last Judgment*: Michelangelo had already finished more than three-fourths of the work when Pope Paul went to see it. On this occasion Biagio da Cesena, the master of ceremonies and a very high-minded (*scrupulosa*) person, happened to be with the Pope in the chapel and was asked what he thought of the painting. He answered that it was most disgraceful that in so sacred a place there should have been depicted all those nude figures, exposing themselves so shamefully, and that it was no work for a papal chapel but rather for the public baths and taverns. Angered by this comment, Michelangelo determined he would have his revenge; and as soon as Biagio had left he drew his portrait from memory in the figure of Minos, shown with a great serpent curled round his legs, among a heap of devils in hell; nor for all his pleading with the Pope and Michelangelo could Biagio have the figure removed, and it was left, to record the incident, as it is today.

It then happened that Michelangelo fell no small distance from the scaffolding in the chapel and hurt his leg; and in his pain and anger he refused to be treated by anyone. Now at this time there lived a certain Florentine called Baccio Rontini, a friend and admirer of Michelangelo's and an ingenious physician. Feeling sorry for Michelangelo, one day he went along to see him at home; when he received no answer to his knocking, either from Michelangelo or the neighbors, he made his way up by a secret way from room to room until he found Buonarroti, who was in a desperate condition. And then Baccio refused to go away or leave his side until he was better. After he was cured, Michelangelo returned to the chapel and worked continuously until everything was finished. And the paintings he did were imbued with such force that he justified the words of Dante: "Dead are the dead, the living truly live . . ." We are shown the misery of the damned and the joy of the blessed.

When the *Last Judgment* was revealed it was seen that Michelangelo had not only excelled the masters who had worked there previously but had also striven to excel even the vaulting that he had made so famous; for the *Last Judgment* was finer by far, and in it Michelangelo outstripped himself. He imagined to himself all the terror of those days and he represented, for the greater punishment of those who have not lived well, the entire Passion of Jesus Christ, depicting in the air various naked figures carrying the cross, the column, the lance, the sponge, the nails, and the crown of thorns. These were shown in diverse attitudes and were perfectly executed with consummate facility. We see the seated figure of Christ turning towards the damned his stern and terrible countenance in order to curse them; and in great fear Our Lady draws her mantle aroud her as she hears and sees such tremendous desolation. In a circle around the figure of Christ are innumerable prophets and apostles; and most remarkable are the figures of Adam and St. Peter, included, it is believed, as being respectively the original parent of the human race that is now brought to Judgment and the first foundation of the Christian Church. At the feet of Christ is a most beautiful St. Bartholomew, who is displaying his flayed skin. We see also the nude figure of St. Lawrence, and in addition an endless number of male and female saints and other figures of men and women around Christ, near or distant, who embrace each other and rejoice, because they have won everlasting beatitude by the grace of God and as a reward for their good deeds. Beneath the feet of Christ are the Seven Angels with the Seven Trumpets as described by St. John the Evangelist; as they sound the call to Judgment they cause the hair of those who are looking at them to stand on end at the terrible wrath of their countenances. Among the rest are two angels with the Book of Life in their hands; and near them on one side, depicted with perfect judgment, may be seen the seven mortal sins in the form of devils, assailing and striving to drag down to hell the souls that are flying towards heaven, all striking the most beautiful attitudes and wonderfully foreshortened. Nor did Michelangelo hesitate to show to the world, in the resurrection of the dead, how they take to themselves once more bones and flesh from the same earth and how, with the help of others already alive, they go soaring towards heaven, where again they are assisted by the souls of those already blessed; and all this was painted with the appropriate judgement and consideration. Throughout the painting may be seen exercises and studies of various kinds, the perfection of which is clearly illustrated by a notable detail showing the bark of Charon. In an attitude of frenzy, Charon is striking with his oar the souls being dragged into his bark by the demons. Here, Michelangelo was following the description given by his favourite poet, Dante, when he wrote: "Charon, his eyes red like a burning brand, / Thumps with his oar the lingerers that delay, / And rounds them up, and beckons with his hand."

Michelangelo painted the heads of his demons with such marvellous force and variety that they are truly like monsters out of hell. And in the figures of the damned we can see the presence of sin and the fear of eternal punishment. Apart from the beauty of its every detail, it is extraordinary to see how this painting produces in its finished state an impression of such harmony that it seems to have been executed all in one day, and even so with a finish unrivalled by any miniature. To be sure, the awesomeness and grandeur of this painting, with its vast host of figures, are so overwhelming that it defies description; for in it may be seen marvellously portrayed all the emotions that mankind can experience. The discerning eye can easily distinguish the proud and the envious, the avaricious, the lustful, and other sinners of various kinds; for in this painting Michelangelo observed all the rules of decorum, and gave his figures the appropriate expressions, attitudes, and settings. This was a great and wonderful achievement; but it was all the same well within his powers, because he was always shrewd and observant and he had seen a lot of mankind, and thus he had acquired by contact with the day-to-day world the understanding that philosophers obtain from books and speculation. To any discerning critic the *Last Judgment* demonstrates the sublime force of art and Michelangelo's figures reveal thoughts and emotions that only he has known how to express. Moreover, anyone in a position to judge will also be struck by the amazing diversity of the figures which is reflected in the various and unusual gestures of the young and old, the men and the women. All these details bear witness to the sublime power of Michelangelo's art, in which skill was combined with a natural inborn grace. Michelangelo's figures stir the emotions even of people who know nothing about painting, let alone those who understand. The foreshortenings that appear to be in actual relief; the way he blended his colours to produce a mellow softness and grace; and the delicate finish he gave to every detail: these serve to show the kind of picture that a good and true artist should paint. In the contours of the forms turned in a manner no other artists could have rivalled Michelangelo showed the world the true Judgment and the true Damnation and Resurrection.

The *Last Judgment* must be recognized as the great exemplar of the grand manner of painting, directly inspired by God and enabling mankind to see the fateful results when an artist of sublime intellect infused with divine grace and knowledge appears on earth. Behind this work, bound in chains, follow all those who believe they have mastered the art of painting; the strokes with which Michelangelo outlined his figures make every intelligent and sensitive artist[12] wonder and tremble, no matter how strong a draughtsman he may be. When other artists study the fruits of Michelangelo's labours, they are thrown into confusion by the mere thought of what manner of things all other pictures, past or future, would look like if placed side by side with this masterpiece. How fortunate they are, and what happy memories they have stored up, who have seen this truly stupendous marvel of our times! And we can count Pope Paul III as doubly fortunate and happy, seeing that, by allowing this work to come into existence under his protection, God ensured future renown for his holiness and for Michelangelo. How greatly are the merits of the Pope enhanced by the genius of the artist! The birth of Michelangelo was indeed a stroke of fortune for all artists of the present age, for his work as a painter, a sculptor, and an architect has with its brilliance illuminated every problem and difficulty.

Michelangelo laboured for eight years on the *Last Judgment*, and he threw it open to view, I believe, on Christmas Day in the year 1541, to the wonder and astonishment of the whole of Rome, or rather the whole world. That year, I went to Rome myself, travelling from Venice, in order to see it; and I along with the rest was stupefied by what I saw.

16. Jacopo Pontormo, *Letter to Benedetto Varchi*

Jacopo Pontormo (1494–1556) was a disciple of the chief resident "High Renaissance" painter in Florence in the 1510s, Andrea Del Sarto. While

---

12. *Trema e teme ogni terribile spirito*: Vasari does not use, here or elsewhere, the word *artist* ("artista"). The term translated here as "draughtsman" is *disegno* in the original, one of the most important in Vasari's aesthetic vocabulary.

From *Scritti d'arte del Cinquecento*, vol. 3, edited by Paola Barocchi (Turin: Einaudi, 1978), pp. 504–7. Translated for this volume by Lydia G. Cochrane.

completing Andrea's cycle in the portico of the Annunziata (the head-quarters of the Servites, frequently mentioned by Luca Landucci in the selections published in this volume), he initiated in Florence what Giorgio Vasari called a "maniera nuova," and what later came to be called the mannerist style. Similar experiments with High Renaissance standards at the hands of other artists—Perin del Vaga in Rome, Giulio Romano in Mantua, Parmigianino in Emilia, Tintoretto in Venice, the Campi in Cremona and Milan—soon made mannerism the first Italian "national" art style, one which became international when Rosso Fiorentino and Primaticcio carried it to Fontainebleau in France.

Mannerism neither responded to, nor developed, a full theoretical program. In an effort to find out why the artists of his day were doing what he observed, the poet and historian Benedetto Varchi (1503–65), best known today for his popularization of Aristotelian science and his *History of Florence*, conducted a "poll" of the Florentine artists. Varchi's questionaire was formulated in accordance with the current format for discussions about aesthetics: a debate about which of the major art forms is the best. The results were published in Varchi's *Lezzione . . . nella quale si disputa della maggioranza delle arti* (Florence: Torrentino, 1549).

To the Very Magnificent and Honorable M. Benedetto Varchi:

The pleasure that I know you take, most excellent[1] M. Benedetto, in a beautiful painting or sculpture and the love that you bear the men of these professions must be, it seems to me, what has moved your most keen intellect to investigate the [comparative] nobility and guiding principles of these two arts—a question of dispute that is no doubt admirable, highly difficult, and a proper ornament to your rare genius. Although I was so kindly asked about these principles in your recent letter, I [fear that] I will not be able, with words or in ink, to give a full explanation of the labors of those who actually perform such work. Still, restricting myself simply to two or three arguments and examples, I will tell you what occurs to me [on this subject], without arriving at any final conclusions.

The question is so intrinsically difficult that it is impossible to debate it, let alone resolve it. For there is one thing alone that is noble and that is fundamental to the question, and that is drawing:[2] all other criteria are feeble in comparison to this one. (Think about it: anyone who has [mastered] this skill is good in both [art forms].) Furthermore, if all other inferences are

1. *Magnifico*—a term of honor reserved a half century earlier for Lorenzo dei Medici and more recently for Lorenzo Duke of Urbino (in Castiglione's *Book of the Courtier*); by now it has become a common title of respect.
2. *Disegno*: a key word in Vasari's aesthetic vocabulary.

by comparison feeble and petty, how can you use [skill in drawing] as an argument, except to put it aside, since it has no equal, and to produce other weaker, aimless, and inconclusive arguments. Take as an example a sculpted figure, worked in the round, fully realized on all sides and finished all over using chisels and other toilsome instruments. The hard stone may be carefully finished, even in places seemingly impossible for tools to reach, in ways that would be laborious and difficult even in soft clay, not to speak of the difficulty of [making] an arm [raised] in the air with something held in its hand, which requires work and skill to achieve without breaking it. Besides this, there is truly no way to remedy [the mistake] if you have placed it a little too high. (This indeed is the truth.) Moreover, you can make [your statue] perfectly harmonious on one side and then not be able to finish the other sides, either because there isn't enough stone somewhere, or because of the enormous difficulty in getting the proportions of all the parts properly coordinated all the way around. For you never can really see the way [a piece] ought to be until it is finished, so that when [the problems] are more than minimal, there is no way to fix it. Someone without a good foundation in drawing, however, will run into overly evident errors and inadvertances, but minute things are hard to avoid in both [painting and sculpture]. There are also various materials to work in, such as marble, bronze, and various kinds of stone, stucco, wood, clay, and many other materials, all of which require considerable labor, even apart from the physical exertion, which is far from negligable. But this keeps the sculptor healthier and gives him a good complexion. For the painter the opposite is true: his body is made ill-disposed by the hard labor of his art. This [ill-disposition] consists more in troubles of the mind than in an increase of life.[3] He is overly bold and ambitious (*ardito*) and strives with his colors to imitate all the things nature has made, in order that [what he paints] appears to be those same things, or even better than they are; and [he strives] to make his work rich and full of various things—what shall I say?—splendors, nighttime fires or other lights, air, clouds, towns far off or nearby, houses in a variety of perspectives, animals of so many sorts and with such a variety of colors and so many other things that it is possible that in one painting[4] he might do he may introduce what nature has never made, as well as—as I was saying above—improvements upon [nature's works], giving them grace[5] through art, adjusting them, and placing them

3. *Aumento di vita*: the expression is not clear in the original either.
4. *Storia*, or narration: a work of art was always supposed to have a "historical" subject, political, religious, or mythological; hence, it could be referred to simply as a *storia*, as if the thing or action represented was the same as the thing or the action itself, where today we would speak of "a work of art" or "a painting."
5. *Grazia*: a key word frequently used by mannerist artists in justifying their innovations.

where they seem best [to him].[6] Furthermore, there are various media to work in: affresco, oils, tempera, and with glue, so that all in all you need great practice in manipulating all the various colors, in getting to know what effects when mixed in various ways—in chiaroscuro, in light and shade, in reflexions, and in infinitely many other ways. But what I meant by overly bold—and this is of great importance—is [that the painter] goes beyond nature by wanting to infuse a spirit into a figure and to make it seem alive. And to do so on one plane! For if he had at least considered that when God made man, he made him in the round because that way it was easier to put life into him, he would never have chosen an object of his endeavors (*soggetto*) so dependent upon artifice and even miraculous and divine.

I will say further, among the examples that could be brought forth, that Michelangelo could not have demonstrated the full depth of his drawing and the greatness of his divine genius [solely] in the stupendous figures that he made in relief. He did so rather in his miraculous works of painting, with their great variety of figures, their beautiful [representations of actions], and their foreshortenings (*scorci*). He always loved [painting] and preferred it as the more difficult [art form] and the one more suited to his supernatural genius. He was aware that his greatness and everlasting [fame] might have been assured by his sculpture, which is so praiseworthy and everlasting. But to longevity, the marble quarries of Carrara[7] contributed more than the strength (*virtù*) of the craftsman (*artifice*), because the material (*soggetto*) is superior; and thus in the hands of great masters, this art form, sculpture, is the cause of great rewards and much fame and other forms of recompense for such praiseworthy virtue. I can compare this to clothing: [sculpture] is like fine wool felt because it lasts longer and costs more; painting [is like] back-combed winter felt, which lasts a short time and costs little, because when its nap has rubbed off no one pays any further attention to it. But even though all things must come to an end, they are not longlasting in the same way.

Much more could be said about this; but please excuse me if I lack the courage to force this pen to write anything more, except to repeat my main point in this entire letter, which is to show you that I am your obsequious [servant] and stand ready to [satisfy] your wishes. I see that [my pen] has sprung back to life, and an entire notebook would not satisfy it—let alone these few pages—now that it has drunk deep. But to avoid cloying ceremonials and to keep from boring you, I will no longer dip it into the ink, except to note the date, which is 18 February.

Your

Jacomo, at home

6. I.e., and not where he would ever have observed them in nature.
7. Where Carrara marble still comes from.

17. Marguérite de Navarre, *The Heptameron*

The *Heptameron* ("Eight Days") is a collection of stories in a "frame"
written in imitation (as is admitted in the Prologue) of what was hailed in
the Renaissance as the "classic" of the genre, the *Decameron* ("Ten
Days") of Giovanni Boccaccio (1313–1375), a friend, contemporary, and
compatriot of Petrarca. A new French translation was made by a member
of the court of King Francis I and first published in 1545. The great
differences of content among the first editions and the many contemporary manuscripts make it all but impossible to establish the authorship of
the various stories. The work was probably a collective endeavor of the
literary entourage of Marguérite d'Angouleme (1492–1549), the sister
of King Francis I (1494–1547; king from 1515), who became queen
of Navarre (or rather, of that portion of the old kingdom of Navarre
lying north of the crest of the Pyrenees—in what is today called the Pays
Basques). She spent most of her life thereafter between the peripatetic
court of her brother and her own "capital" at Nérac. If she did not actually write the stories, she at least supervised their composition and
probably reviewed and edited them; hence they are not incorrectly attributed to her.

This translation follows the text established by Michel François in the
Classiques Garnier edition. The whole work is available in the translation
of P. A. Chilton (Penguin Books, 1984).

Prologue

On the first day of September, when the baths of the Pyrenees mountains
begin to come into their full powers, a number of persons from both France
and Spain were at Cauterets, some to drink the waters, others to take the
baths, and still others for the mud baths, all such marvelous things that
patients for whom doctors have given up all hope return from them completely cured. My aim, however, is not to describe these baths to you or to
explain their virtues, but only to say as much about them as I need for the
matters about which I intend to write. All the patients at these particular
baths remained for more than three weeks, until they knew by their improvement that they could return home. But when the moment came for
their return, there came rains so extraordinary and so prodigious that it

From *The Heptameron*, edited by Michel François (Paris: Editions Garnier, 1950), pp.
1–10, 18–22. Translated for this volume by Lydia G. Cochrane.

seemed that God had forgotten his promise to Noah never again to destroy the earth by water. All the bathhouses and the lodgings at Cauterets were so filled with water that they were uninhabitable. Those who had come from the Spanish side returned over the mountains as best they could, and the ones who knew the trails well were the ones who fared the best. The French lords and ladies, however, thinking they could return to Tarbes as easily as they had come, found the little brooks so swollen that they could hardly ford them. And when they came to cross the Gave de Pau, which on their way there was not even two feet deep, they found it so high and so swift that they turned aside to look for a bridge, but since the bridges were only wooden, they had been swept away by the fury of the water. Some of them, thinking they could break the force of the current by crossing together, were so swiftly carried off that the others intending to follow them lost all desire and courage to do so. Upon this, both to search for a new route and because they were of several opinions, they parted company. Some crossed over the mountains and, passing through Aragon, went to the county of Roussillon and from there to Narbonne; others went straight to Barcelona, where some went by sea to Marseille and some to Aigues-Mortes.

One widowed lady of long experience named Oisille[1] decided to put aside all her fear of the bad roads and push on to Our Lady of Sarrance.[2] Not that she was superstitious enough to think that the glorious Virgin would leave her seat at the right hand of her son to come live in that deserted spot, but merely out of a desire to see the holy place about which she had heard so much. Moreover, she was sure that if there were a way to escape danger, the monks would find it. And she did indeed get there, passing through places so strange and so steep that even her age and her weight could not spare her from doing the greater part of the route on foot. But the greatest pity of it was that most of her people and their horses died along the way, so that she arrived at Sarrance, where she was charitably received by the monks, with only one man and one woman.

There were also among the French two gentlemen who had gone to the baths more to accompany the ladies whose *serviteurs* they were than for any ill health. When these gentlemen saw the company part ways and saw that the husbands of their ladies were taking them off on their own, they decided to follow them at a distance without making their presence known. One night around midnight, however, when the two married gentlemen and their wives were stopping at the house of a man more bandit than peasant, the two young gentlemen, who were lodged with a farmer nearby, heard an

1. An anagram for Louise of Savoy (b. 1476), Marguérite's mother.
2. An ancient abbey, and a stop on the pilgrim road to St. James of Compostella.

enormous racket. They got up, roused their serving men, and asked their host what this tumult was all about. The poor man, who was as startled as they, told them that it was [being caused by] some evil men who had come to claim their share of the prey lodged with their fellow bandit. At this, the gentlemen immediately grabbed their arms and, with their servants, rushed to the aid of the ladies, for they felt they would rather die than face life without them. When they arrived at the house, they found the outside door broken in and the two gentlemen and their servants defending themselves valiantly. But because the bandits outnumbered them, the gentlemen [inside] were sorely wounded, and having already lost most of their servants, they began to give ground. Looking in through the windows, the two gentlemen [outside] saw the ladies weeping and wailing; and pity and love so increased their courage that, like two wild bears down from the mountains, they struck the bandits with such fury, killing many of them, that the rest chose not to await their turn but fled to their hideout. When the gentlemen had routed these outlaws, the host lay among the dead, and when they were told that his wife was even worse than her husband, they dispatched her with one sword thrust. Then, going into a lower room, they found one of the married gentlemen about to give up the ghost. The other was unhurt, except that his clothing was all ripped by their knives and his sword was broken. The poor gentleman, seeing that the two had saved him, embraced them, thanked them, and begged them not to abandon him—a request they willingly agreed to. Then, after the dead gentleman had been buried and they had comforted his wife as best they could, they started off again, leaving the choice of route to God, as they had no idea of which way to go.

If it would please you to know the name of the three gentlemen, the married man's name was Hircan[3] and his wife's name Parlamente;[4] the young widow's was Longarine, and the names of the two gentlemen were Dagoucin and Saffredent.[5] Toward evening, after riding all day on horseback, they saw a church tower and they made their way to it with considerable effort and difficulty. They were received humanely by the abbot and the monks. The abbey was named Saint-Savin.[6] The abbot, who came of an excellent family, lodged them honorably, and as he was leading them to their rooms he inquired about their adventures. When he had heard the truth of the matter, he told them that they were not the only ones in such a predicament, for in another room there were two young ladies who had es-

3. This may be Marguérite's husband, Henri d'Albret.

4. This one, therefore, is Marguérite herself (the one, after all, who is supposedly "talking"—*parle*—in the Prologue).

5. There is no agreement about the historical identity of these other participants.

6. Another place that really did, and does, exist (near Argelès, in the modern Department of Hautes-Pyrénées.

caped as great a danger, or even a greater one, since it involved beasts, not men. These poor ladies had encountered a bear coming down the mountain half a league from Pierrefitte, and they had fled so fast before him that their horses had dropped dead beneath them at the gates to the abbey. Two of their women, who arrived some time later, reported that the bear had killed all their serving men. When the two ladies and the three gentlemen came into their room, they found them crying, and they saw that they were Nomerfide and Ennasuite. When they all had embraced the ladies and they had told what had happened to them, they began to cheer up, at the exhortation of the good abbot, at the thought of all being reunited. And the next morning they all heard mass with great devotion, praising God for having escaped their many perils.

While they were all at mass, a man in shirt sleeves came running into the church calling for help, as if someone were chasing him. Immediately, Hircan and the other gentlemen ran to him to see what the matter was, and they saw two men coming for him with drawn swords. When these men saw such a large company, they turned to flee, but Hircan and his companions hotly pursued them and left them lifeless. When Hircan returned, he found that the man in shirt sleeves was a companion of theirs named Geburon. He told them that as he lay in bed in a cottage near Pierrefitte, three men had arrived, and even though he was wearing only his shirt and had no weapon but his sword, he wounded one of them so badly that he fell on the spot. As the two others were occupied with picking up their companion, he decided, seeing that he was undressed and they were armed, that flight was the only way to get the better of them, since he had the advantage of being less encumbered with clothing. He praised God [for his escape] and thanked his rescuers.

After they had heard mass and had dined, they sent off to find out if it were possible to cross the Gave de Pau, and when they learned that it was still impassable, they were panic stricken, even though the abbot repeatedly offered them hospitality until the waters subsided, which they agreed to for that day. That evening as they were going off to bed an old monk arrived. He went to Sarrance every year for the [feast of the] Nativity of Our Lady in September. When they asked him for news of his trip, he said that because of the flooding he had come through the mountains and by the worst roads he had ever traveled, but that he had seen a truly piteous sight. He had met a gentleman named Simontault who, tired of waiting for the river to subside, had decided to force his way across, trusting to his excellent horse. He had put all of his serving men around him to break the force of the water, but when they reached the main current, those with weaker mounts were swept away in spite of all their efforts—men and horses, all downstream, never to return. The gentleman, finding himself alone, turned back his horse, but not soon enough to prevent it being swept out from under him. But, by God's will, he was so close to the bank that after swallowing a good deal of water he dragged himself out on all fours onto the solid rocks, so weak and weary that he could not stand. That evening a shepherd happened by, bringing in his sheep, and found him sitting among the rocks, soaking wet and not much happier than his servants, whom he had seen lost before his eyes. The shepherd, who understood his plight as much by what he saw as by what he heard, took him by the hand and led him to his poor house, where he kindled a few sticks to dry him off as best he could. That same evening God brought this good monk to the shepherd's hut, and he showed Simontault how to get to Our Lady of Sarrance. He assured him that he would be better lodged there than anywhere else and that he would find there an elderly widow named Oisille who had had her own adventures. When the assembled company heard the names of the good lady Oisille and the gentle knight Simontault, they were filled with inestimable joy, praising the Creator who, satisfied with taking the servants, had saved the masters and mistresses. Of all the ladies Parlamente in particular praised God with all her heart, for Simontault had long been her most affectionate *serviteur*. They inquired eagerly about the route to Sarrance, and although the good old man said it was difficult indeed, nothing could deter them from making the trip. They set off that very day in fine order and lacking for nothing, for the abbot had furnished them with wine and plenty of food and with agreeable companions to guide them safely through the mountains, traveling more on foot than on horseback. They finally arrived, weary and bathed in perspiration, at Our Lady of Sarrance, where the abbot, a rather bad man, did not dare to refuse them lodging, since he knew they were good friends with the Lord of Béarn. Like the hypocrite he was, he put on the best face he could and led them to see the good lady Oisille and the gentleman Simontault.

Joy was so great among this company miraculously reunited that the night, which they spent in the church praising God for the grace He had shown them, seemed all too short. Toward morning, after a little rest, they all went to hear mass and to receive the holy sacrament of union in which all Christians are joined in one, and they prayed to God, whose goodness had brought them together, to bring their voyage to a fitting end for his glory's sake. After dinner they sent to find whether the waters had subsided, and on finding that instead the river had risen and that crossing in safety would be impossible for some time, they decided to build a bridge at a point where two rock outcrops stand close to one another (where you can still see some boards that people coming from Oleron use to cross the river if they do not want to go by the ford). The abbot was delighted at their offer to pay for this work, knowing that the number of pilgrims would increase, and he provided them with workmen. He was so miserly, though, that he did not put up a single penny. Then, because the workmen said that they could not possibly finish the bridge in less than ten or twelve days, boredom threatened to settle in among the company, men and women alike. At this Parlamente, Hircan's wife, who was never idle or melancholy, begged her husband's permission to speak and said to the elderly lady Oisille, "Madame, I am surprised that you, who have such long experience and to whom we women look as to a mother, have not suggested some pastime to lighten the hardships that we must bear during our long wait, for if we do not have some amusing and virtuous occupation, we may easily fall sick." Longarine, the young widow, added, "But even worse, we will become sad, and that is an incurable disease, for there is not one of us, man or woman, who does not have cause for deepest sorrow if he thinks of what he has lost." Ennasuite answered her laughingly, saying, "We haven't all lost a husband, like you, and the loss of servants is no reason to despair, for it's easy enough to get more. Still, I agree that we should have some entertaining exercise to pass the time, or we'll be dead in a day!"

The gentlemen seconded these thoughts and they all begged lady Oisille to decide what they should do. "My children," she replied, "you are asking something of me that I find extremely difficult: to find you a pastime that will deliver you from your troubles. All my life I have searched for such a remedy and have found only one—the reading of Holy Scripture. That brings true and perfect joy to the spirit and leads to the repose and health of the body. And if you ask my recipe for keeping joyful and healthy in my old age, it is that the minute I get up I take up the Holy Scripture and I read. When I see and contemplate the goodness of God, who for our sake sent His son to earth to preach this holy word and the good news by which He offers us remission of all sins and satisfaction of all debts by His gift to us of His love, His passion, and His merits, this thought gives me such joy that I take up my psalmbook and, as humbly as I can, my heart sings and my mouth pronounces the beautiful psalms and canticles that the Holy Spirit put into the hearts of David and the other authors. The contentment that this gives me makes all the ills that come to me that day seem blessings, since by faith my heart is filled with Him who has borne them for me. In the same way, I retire before supper to nourish my soul with a little reading, and in the evening I think over all I have done during the day to ask forgiveness for my errors and give thanks for His mercy. Then, in love and fear of Him and in peace I take my rest, safe from all ills. By this, my children, you can see the pastime I have fixed on after having long searched in all the others and not found peace of mind. It seems to me that if you agreed to devote an hour to reading in the morning and then during mass said your prayers devoutly, you would find in this wilderness beauty equal to that of any city, for he who knows God sees all things beautiful in Him, and ugly without Him. So, I beg you, take my advice if you would live joyously."

Hircan then spoke up. "My lady," he said, "anyone who has read the Holy Scriptures, as I believe we all have, will confess that what you say is all true. But you must also be aware that we are still in poor enough condition that we need some pastime and some bodily exercise. When we are at home we take to hunting and falconry to distract us from a thousand foolish cares, and the ladies have their household duties, their handiwork, and occasional dances in which to take honest exercise. This leads me to say, speaking for the men, that you, who are the eldest, should read to us in the morning of the life of our lord Jesus Christ and of the great and admirable works he accomplished for us. For after dinner until vespers, we need to choose some pastime that is not harmful to the soul and is pleasurable to the body, and in that way we will pass the day joyfully."

Dame Oisille replied that she had made such an effort to forget all vanities that she feared she might make a poor choice. Other opinions on the matter should be heard, she continued, and she begged Hircan to be the first to give his. "For my part," he said, "my opinion would be quickly given if I thought that my choice of pastime were as agreeable to someone else in this company as it is to myself. But for the moment I will keep still and will go along with what the others say." His wife Parlamente flushed, thinking he was speaking about her, and she replied, partly in anger and part laughing, "Hircan, perhaps the lady you have in mind, who should be the most offended [by your suggestion], might have a way to find compensation if she cared to. But let us leave aside pastimes in which two alone can take part and talk of one that we all can share." Hircan then turned to all the ladies and said, "Since my wife has so well understood my meaning and a private pastime is not to her liking, I think she will know better than anyone else how to find one to give everyone pleasure, and I say right now that I will accept her opinion as if it were my very own." To this all the company agreed.

Parlamente, seeing that it had fallen to her lot to speak, began thus: "If I felt equal to the ancients, who discovered the arts, I would invent some pastime or game to fulfill the responsibility you have given me. But I know that my own learning and my powers [are so slight that] I can scarcely recall the clever things others have done, so I will be content with imitating those who have already answered your request. For one, I think there is no one here who has not read Boccaccio's hundred tales, recently translated into French from Italian.[7] King Francis I, monseigneur the Dauphin,

---

7. That gives one *terminus ante quem non* for the composition of the Prologue (see the introduction to this text). The translation by Antoine Le Maçon was licenced in November

madame the Dauphine, and madame Marguerite are so fond of them that if Boccaccio could hear them he would rise from the dead to hear such persons praise him. I have recently heard that the two ladies mentioned, along with others of the court, decided to imitate Boccaccio, but with one difference, which was to write no tale not based on a true story. These ladies, together with monseigneur the Dauphin, promised to provide ten stories each and to gather together as many as ten people whom they thought best qualified for storytelling. They excluded those who had studied and were men of letters, for monseigneur the Dauphin did not want their art mixed into it and feared that the beauty of rhetoric would take something from the tales' truth.

However, the important affairs that subsequently engrossed the king—the peace [treaty] between him and the king of England,[8] the confinement of madame the Dauphine,[9] and several other things worthy of the attention of the court—made them completely forget this undertaking, which we could complete in the ten days we must wait for our bridge to be finished. And if it pleases you, we could go every day from noon to four o'clock to the lovely meadow beside the Gave, where the trees are so leafy that the sun cannot pierce their cool shade. There, comfortably seated, each of us can tell some story that he has seen himself or heard from some trustworthy person. At the end of ten days we will have our hundred tales, and if God wills that our labor is found worthy of the eyes of the lords and ladies I have named, we can present it to them on our return from this voyage instead of [holy] images or beads. Of course, if someone finds a more agreeable occupation than the one I have suggested, I will bow to his opinion."

The entire company answered that nothing better could possibly be suggested and that they could hardly wait for the morrow to get started.

The rest of the day was spent joyously as they reminded one another of what they had seen during their lives. As soon as morning came they went to madame Oisille's room, where they found her already at her prayers. They listened to her read for a good hour and then devoutly heard mass; they went to dine at ten, and afterward they retired, each to his room, to do whatever they wanted. At noon they gathered eagerly in the meadow, as they had decided, and it was so lovely and so pleasing that we would need a Boccaccio to paint a true picture of it. Suffice it to say that never was there

---

1544 and published in 1545. The *Dauphin* mentioned hereafter is the future King Henry II; the *Dauphine* is his wife, Catherine (or Caterina) dei Medici (on whom see the notes to the selection from Scipione Ammirato in this volume).

8. The Treaty of Ardres, signed on 7 June 1546: still another *terminus ante quem non.*

9. With Princess Elizabeth, the future wife (after the death of Queen Mary Tudor of England) of King Philip II of Spain.

a meadow more lovely. When all the group was seated on the green grass—so noble and delicate that they needed neither cushions nor carpet—Simontault spoke up first: "Who will be the first among us?" Hircan replied, "Since you have been first to speak, why don't you command us, for we are all equal in this game." "May God grant," said Simontault, "that no better gift come to me in this world than to command all those of this company!" At this Parlamente, who knew very well just what he meant, began to cough so that Hircan did not notice the color rising to her cheeks. He invited Simontault to begin, which he then did.

The First Day

During the first day a group of tales were told of the bad tricks women have played on men and men on women. . . .

"My ladies, I have been so badly repaid for my long service that in order to take my revenge on love and on the lady who is so cruel to me, I will try to tell you of all the bad turns that women have played on we poor men, and I will say nothing but the pure truth. . . ."

. . . Parlamente, pretending not to understand that he was saying this for her sake, replied, "Since hell is as agreeable as you say, you must have no fear of the Devil, who has put you there." But he answered her sharply, "If my Devil turned as black as her cruelty, it would be just as frightening to this company as she was pleasurable for me to look at. But the fire of love makes me forget the fires of this hell and, to say no more, I pass the word to madame Oisille to tell us the second tale, for I am sure that if she were willing to say what she knows of women, she would back me up." At this, the entire company turned toward [Oisille], begging her to begin. She agreed and began with a laugh.

The Second Tale

A mule driver's wife from Amboise preferred a cruel death at the hand of his valet to assenting to his evil desires.

In the town of Amboise, there was once a mule driver in the service of the Queen of Navarre, the sister of King Francis I, who was then at Blois for the birth of a son. This mule driver had gone to Blois to collect his quarterly pay, while his wife remained in Amboise in a house on the other side of the bridges. Now, for some time one of her husband's serving men had loved her desperately, and one day he could not help speaking to her of his love. But she, a truly virtuous woman, reprimanded him so severely, threatening to have her husband beat him and send him away, that he did not dare speak of it again or make any similar move. So he kept this fire hidden in his heart, until one day, when his master was out of town and his mistress had gone to vespers at Saint Florentin, the castle church, far from their house. When he was left alone, the idea came to him that he might be able to take by force what no prayers or services had gotten him. He broke through a partition between the room in which he slept and his mistress's bedroom. Because the curtains of the master's bed on one side of the wall and the servant's on the other covered the wall so that the opening was invisible, his evil act was not noticed until his mistress was in bed, along with a little girl eleven or twelve years old. When the poor woman had fallen asleep, the man came through the hole he had broken in the wall and got into bed with her, dressed in nothing but his shirt, with bare sword in his hand. As soon as she felt him next to her, she jumped out of bed, remonstrating with him as vehemently as a virtuous woman possibly could. Then he, who knew only bestial love and would have understood the language of his mules better than her honest arguments, proved himself more bestial than the beasts with whom he had so long lived. When he saw her determined to keep the table between them so that he could not grab her— she was strong enough to have struggled out of his grasp twice—he gave up all hope of taking her alive and ran his sword into the small of her back, thinking that pain would make her surrender where fear and force had failed. But just the opposite took place, for just as a good soldier who sees his own blood is all the more determined to avenge himself on his enemies and to acquire honor, her chaste courage redoubled, and she kept running to stay out of reach of the wretch's hands. She reasoned with him as best she could and tried to find some way to bring him to his senses; but he was in such a flaming fury that he could in no way listen to reason. He hit her again and again with his sword while she ran as long as her legs could carry her to avoid his thrusts. When she had lost so much blood that she sensed death near, she raised her eyes to heaven and, joining her hands in prayer, gave thanks to God. She called Him her strength, her virtue, her patience and her chastity, and she prayed Him to accept the blood that she was shedding to keep his commandment in reverent homage to the blood of his Son, in whom she firmly believed all her sins would be washed away and wiped from His wrathful memory. Then, saying, "Lord, receive this soul redeemed by your goodness," she fell face down to the ground. The wretch then stabbed her several more times and when she had lost all speech and bodily strength, the miserable brute took her defenseless body by force.

When he had satisfied his evil lust, he fled with such haste that he has never been found in spite of all pursuits. The girl who had been sleeping with the mule driver's wife was so terrified that she had hidden under the bed, but when she saw that the man had left she ran to her mistress. Finding her without speech or movement, she ran to the window and shouted to the neighbors for help. They came immediately, since she was as beloved and esteemed as any woman of the town, and they brought surgeons with them, who found she had twenty-five mortal wounds in her body. They did what they could to help her, but in vain. Nevertheless, she lingered on an hour, unable to speak but making signs with her hands and her eyes that showed she had not lost all understanding. Interrogated by a man of the church concerning the faith in which she was dying and her hopes of salvation through Jesus Christ alone, she responded by signs so clear that words could not have expressed her intentions any better. Thus, with joy on her face and her eyes raised to heaven, this chaste body gave up its soul to its Creator. No sooner had her body been removed, wrapped in a shroud, and placed at the door to await the burial procession, than her poor husband arrived. He had had no word of all this, so when he laid his eyes on the body of his wife laid out before his house and inquired what had happened, he had double reasons for grief. He mourned so deeply that he nearly died himself. Thus was this martyr to chastity buried in the church of Saint Florentin, where no good woman of the town failed in her duty to pay her all possible honor, holding herself fortunate to live in a city in which such a virtuous woman had lived. Foolish and wanton women, seeing the honor paid to her corpse, vowed to change their lives for the better.

"So, my ladies," [Oisille concluded,] "there you have a true story that should encourage you to respect the beautiful virtue of chastity. We who are of good families should die of shame for the worldly feelings in our hearts—feelings that this poor mule driver's wife had the courage to flee by such a cruel death. And who can call herself a proper woman if she has never shown she can resist to the bitter end, like this woman? This is why we must humble ourselves; for God's graces are not granted to men for their nobility and wealth, but as it pleases His goodness. He does not look to the person, but chooses according to His will; and His elect honor Him by their virtues. He often chooses lowly things to confound those whom the world honors and holds in high esteem. As He says Himself, 'Let us not rejoice in our virtues, but rejoice that we are inscribed in the Book of Life, from which Death, Hell, and Sin cannot erase us.'" [10]

There was not one lady in the company who did not have tears in her eyes out of compassion for the mule driver's wife in her piteous and glorious death. Each of them thought to herself that if fortune brought her anything of the sort, she would do her best to follow her to martyrdom. But when lady Oisille realized that time was slipping by in their praises of this deceased woman, she turned to Saffredent and said, "If you cannot say

10. This passage echoes the Revelation of John; but it is not an exact quotation.

something to make the company laugh, no one here can make up for my error of making everyone cry. So I give you my vote to tell the third tale." Saffredent, who was eager to say something pleasing to the company—and to one among them in particular—protested that this would be unjust, since some among them had longer experience than he and by rights should speak before him. But, he added, since luck would have it so, he was happy to take his turn, for the more they heard from those who knew how to speak well, the worse his own tale would seem.

18. Montaigne, *Essays*

Michel Eyquem de Montaigne (he subsequently dropped the surname) was born in 1533 on his father's estates in the Dordogne, in southwestern France. After a thoroughly humanist education, and after a relatively unhappy marriage, he closed himself up in a tower of his chateau to read and to meditate. As he explains it himself in the first of them, he began writing the essays, a form of literature he himself invented, as a way of keeping track of what he read; but the surprising editorial success of the first edition of the first two books (Bordeaux, 1580) encouraged him to revise and add to them; and a complete edition was published at Paris in 1588. Upon his return from a tour of Italy in 1580, Montaigne was persuaded by King Henry III to accept the position of mayor of the city of Bordeaux; but after one term, the hardships and the trouble of the religious wars then raging in the area led him to return to his retreat; and he died there in 1592.

"Of Cannibals" constitutes Montaigne's reflections, some fifteen years later, upon his meeting, in Rouen in 1562, with a cannibal who had been brought to France by the French explorer Villegagnon. "Of Books" was also written sometime between 1578 and 1580.

"Of Cannibals"

When King Pyrrhus passed over into Italy, after he had reconnoitered the formation of the army that the Romans were sending to meet him, he said: "I do not know what barbarians these are" (for so the Greeks called all foreign nations), "but the formation of this army that I see is not at all

From *The Complete Essays of Montaigne*, translated by Donald M. Frame (Stanford: Stanford University Press, 1958), pp. 150–59, 296–306. © 1958 by the Board of Trustees of the Leland Stanford Junior University. Some footnotes deleted. Reprinted with permission of the publishers, Stanford University Press.

barbarous." [1] The Greeks said as much of the army that Flaminius brought into their country, and so did Philip, seeing from a knoll the order and distribution of the Roman camp, in his kingdom, under Publius Sulpicius Galba. Thus we should beware of clinging to vulgar opinions, and judge things by reason's way, not by popular say.

I had with me for a long time a man who had lived for ten or twelve years in that other world which has been discovered in our century, in the place where Villegagnon landed, and which he called Antarctic France. [2] This discovery of a boundless country seems worthy of consideration. I don't know if I can guarantee that some other such discovery will not be made in the future, so many personages greater than ourselves having been mistaken about this one. I am afraid we have eyes bigger than our stomachs, and more curiosity than capacity. We embrace everything, but we clasp only wind.

Plato brings in Solon, telling how he had learned from the priests of the city of Saïs in Egypt that in days of old, before the Flood, there was a great island named Atlantis, right at the mouth of the Strait of Gibraltar, which contained more land than Africa and Asia put together, and that the kings of that country, who not only possessed that island but had stretched out so far on the mainland that they held the breadth of Africa as far as Egypt, and the length of Europe as far as Tuscany, undertook to step over into Asia and subjugate all the nations that border on the Mediterranean, as far as the Black Sea; and for this purpose crossed the Spains, Gaul, Italy, as far as Greece, where the Athenians checked them; but that some time after, both the Athenians and themselves and their island were swallowed up by the Flood. [3]

It is quite likely that that extreme devastation of waters made amazing changes in the habitations of the earth, as people maintain that the sea cut off Sicily from Italy—" 'Tis said an earthquake once asunder tore / These lands with dreadful havoc, which before / Formed but one land, one coast" [4]—Cyprus from Syria, the island of Euboea from the mainland of Boeotia; and elsewhere joined lands that were divided, filling the channels between them with sand and mud: "A sterile marsh, long fit for rowing, now / Feeds neighbor towns, and feels the heavy plow." [5] But there is no great likelihood that that island was the new world which we have just discovered; for it almost touched Spain, and it would be an incredible result of a flood to have forced it away as far as it is, more than twelve hundred leagues; besides, the travels of the moderns have already almost revealed

---

1. Plutarch, *Life of Pyrrhus*, 8.
2. Villegagnon landed in Brazil in 1557.
3. *Timaeus*, 22–25.
4. Virgil, *Aeneid*, 3.414.
5. Horace, *Ars Poetica*, 65.

that it is not an island, but a mainland connected with the East Indies on one side, and elsewhere with the lands under the two poles; or, if it is separated from them, it is by so narrow a strait and interval that it does not deserve to be called an island on that account.

It seems that there are movements, some natural, others feverish, in these great bodies, just as in our own. When I consider the inroads that my river, the Dordogne, is making in my lifetime into the right bank in its descent, and that in twenty years it has gained so much ground and stolen away the foundations of several buildings, I clearly see that this is an extraordinary disturbance; for if it had always gone at this rate, or was to do so in the future, the face of the world would be turned topsy-turvy. But rivers are subject to changes: now they overflow in one direction, now in another, now they keep to their course. I am not speaking of the sudden inundations whose causes are manifest. In Médoc, along the seashore, my brother, the sieur d'Arsac, can see an estate of his buried under the sands that the sea spews forth; the tops of some buildings are still visible; his farms and domains have changed into very thin pasturage. The inhabitants say that for some time the sea has been pushing toward them so hard that they have lost four leagues of land. These sands are its harbingers; and we see great dunes of moving sand that march half a league ahead of it and keep conquering land.

The other testimony of antiquity with which some would connect this discovery is in Aristotle, at least if that little book *Of Unheard-of Wonders*[6] is by him. He there relates that certain Carthaginians, after setting out upon the Atlantic Ocean from the Strait of Gibralter and sailing a long time, at last discovered a great fertile island, all clothed in woods and watered by great deep rivers, far remote from any mainland; and that they, and others since, attracted by the goodness and fertility of the soil, went there with their wives and children, and began to settle there. The lords of Carthage, seeing that their country was gradually becoming depopulated, expressly forbade anyone to go there any more, on pain of death, and drove out these new inhabitants, fearing, it is said, that in course of time they might come to multiply so greatly as to supplant their former masters and ruin their state. This story of Aristotle does not fit our new lands any better than the other.

This man I had was a simple, crude fellow—a character fit to bear true witness; for clever people observe more things and more curiously, but they interpret them; and to lend weight and conviction to their interpretation,

---

6. Montaigne is following not Aristotle, but the contemporary geographer Girolamo Benzoni (b. 1519) in his *La historia del mondo* (Venice, 1565), who attributes this account to Aristotle.

they cannot help altering history a little. They never show you things as they are, but bend and disguise them according to the way they have seen them; and to give credence to their judgment and attract you to it, they are prone to add something to their matter, to stretch it out and amplify it. We need a man either very honest, or so simple that he has not the stuff to build up false inventions and give them plausibility; and wedded to no theory. Such was my man; and besides this, he at various times brought sailors and merchants, whom he had known on that trip, to see me. So I content myself with his information, without inquiring what the cosmographers say about it.

We ought to have topographers who would give us an exact account of the places where they have been. But because they have over us the advantage of having seen Palestine, they want to enjoy the privilege of telling us news about all the rest of the world. I would like everyone to write what he knows, and as much as he knows, not only in this, but in all other subjects; for a man may have some special knowledge and experience of the nature of a river or a fountain, who in other matters knows only what everybody knows. However, to circulate this little scrap of knowledge, he will undertake to write the whole of physics. From this vice spring many great abuses.

Now, to return to my subject, I think there is nothing barbarous and savage in that nation, from what I have been told, except that each man calls barbarism whatever is not his own practice; for indeed it seems we have no other test of truth and reason than the example and pattern of the opinions and customs of the country we live in. *There* is always the perfect religion, the perfect government, the perfect and accomplished manners in all things. Those people are wild, just as we call wild the fruits that Nature has produced by herself and in her normal course; where really it is those that we have changed artificially and led astray from the common order, that we should rather call wild. The former retain alive and vigorous their genuine, their most useful and natural, virtues and properties, which we have debased in the latter in adapting them to gratify our corrupted taste. And yet for all that, the savor and delicacy of some uncultivated fruits of those countries is quite as excellent, even to our taste, as that of our own. It is not reasonable that art should win the place of honor over our great and powerful mother Nature. We have so overloaded the beauty and richness of her works by our inventions that we have quite smothered her. Yet wherever her purity shines forth, she wonderfully puts to shame our vain and frivolous attempts: "Ivy comes readier without our care; / In lonely caves the arbutus grows more fair; / No art with artless bird song can compare."[7] All our efforts cannot even succeed in reproducing the nest of the tiniest little bird,

7. Propertius, 1.11.10.

its contexture, its beauty and convenience; or even the web of the puny spider. All things, says Plato,[8] are produced by nature, by fortune, or by art; the greatest and most beautiful by one or the other of the first two, the least and most imperfect by the last.

These nations, then, seem to me barbarous in this sense, that they have been fashioned very little by the human mind, and are still very close to their original naturalness. The laws of nature still rule them, very little corrupted by ours; and they are in such a state of purity that I am sometimes vexed that they were unknown earlier, in the days when there were men able to judge them better than we. I am sorry that Lycurgus and Plato did not know of them; for it seems to me that what we actually see in these nations surpasses not only all the pictures in which poets have idealized the golden age and all their inventions in imagining a happy state of man, but also the conceptions and the very desire of philosophy. They could not imagine a naturalness so pure and simple as we see by experience; nor could they believe that our society could be maintained with so little artifice and human solder. This is a nation, I should say to Plato, in which there is no sort of traffic, no knowledge of letters, no science of numbers, no name for a magistrate or for political superiority, no custom of servitude, no riches or poverty, no contracts, no successions, no partitions, no occupations but leisure ones, no care for any but common kinship, no clothes, no agriculture, no metal, no use of wine or wheat. The very words that signify lying, treachery, dissimulation, avarice, envy, belittling, pardon—unheard of. How far from this perfection would he find the republic that he imagined: *Men fresh sprung from the gods.*[9] "These manners nature first ordained." [10]

For the rest, they live in a country with a very pleasant and temperate climate, so that according to my witnesses it is rare to see a sick man there; and they have assured me that they never saw one palsied, bleary-eyed, toothless, or bent with age. They are settled along the sea and shut in on the land side by great high mountains, with a stretch about a hundred leagues wide in between. They have a great abundance of fish and flesh which bear no resemblance to ours, and they eat them with no other artifice than cooking. The first man who rode a horse there, though he had had dealings with them on several other trips, so horrified them in this posture that they shot him dead with arrows before they could recognize him.

Their buildings are very long, with a capacity of two or three hundred souls; they are covered with the bark of great trees, the strips reaching to the ground at one end and supporting and leaning on one another at the top,

8. *Laws*, 10.   9. Seneca, *Epistle* 90.
10. Virgil, *Georgics*, 2.20.

in the manner of some of our barns, whose covering hangs down to the ground and acts as a side. They have wood so hard that they cut with it and make of it their swords and grills to cook their food. Their beds are of a cotton weave, hung from the roof like those in our ships, each man having his own; for the wives sleep apart from their husbands.

They get up with the sun, and eat immediately upon rising, to last them through the day; for they take no other meal than that one. Like some other Eastern peoples, of whom Suidas tells us, who drank apart from meals, they do not drink then; but they drink several times a day, and to capacity. Their drink is made of some root, and is of the color of our claret wines. They drink it only lukewarm. This beverage keeps only two or three days; it has a slightly sharp taste, is not at all heady, is good for the stomach, and has a laxative effect upon those who are not used to it; it is a very pleasant drink for anyone who is accustomed to it. In place of bread they use a certain white substance like preserved coriander. I have tried it; it tastes sweet and a little flat.

The whole day is spent in dancing. The younger men go to hunt animals with bows. Some of the women busy themselves meanwhile with warming their drink, which is their chief duty. Some one of the old men, in the morning before they begin to eat, preaches to the whole barnful in common, walking from one end to the other, and repeating one single sentence several times until he has completed the circuit (for the buildings are fully a hundred paces long). He recommends to them only two things: valor against the enemy and love for their wives. And they never fail to point out this obligation, as their refrain, that it is their wives who keep their drink warm and seasoned.

There may be seen in several places, including my own house, specimens of their beds, of their ropes, of their wooden swords and the bracelets with which they cover their wrists in combats, and of the big canes, open at one end, by whose sound they keep time in their dances. They are close shaven all over, and shave themselves much more cleanly than we, with nothing but a wooden or stone razor. They believe that souls are immortal and that those who have deserved well of the gods are lodged in that part of heaven where the sun rises, and the damned in the west.

They have some sort of priests and prophets, but they rarely appear before the people, having their home in the mountains. On their arrival there is a great feast and solemn assembly of several villages—each barn, as I have described it, makes up a village, and they are about one French league from each other. The prophet speaks to them in public, exhorting them to virtue and their duty; but their whole ethical science contains only these two articles: resoluteness in war and affection for their wives. He prophesies to them things to come and the results they are to expect from their undertakings, and urges them to war or holds them back from it; but this is on the condition that when he fails to prophesy correctly, and if things turn out otherwise than he has predicted, he is cut into a thousand pieces if they catch him, and condemned as a false prophet. For this reason, the prophet who has once been mistaken is never seen again.

Divination is a gift of God; that is why its abuse should be punished as imposture. Among the Scythians, when the soothsayers failed to hit the mark, they were laid, chained hand and foot, on carts full of heather and drawn by oxen, on which they were burned. Those who handle matters subject to the control of human capacity are excusable if they do the best they can. But these others, who come and trick us with assurances of an extraordinary faculty that is beyond our ken, should they not be punished for not making good their promise, and for the temerity of their imposture?

They have their wars with the nations beyond the mountains, further inland, to which they go quite naked, with no other arms than bows or wooden swords ending in a sharp point, in the manner of the tongues of our boar spears. It is astonishing what firmness they show in their combats, which never end but in slaughter and bloodshed; for as to routs and terror, they know nothing of either.

Each man brings back as his trophy the head of the enemy he has killed, and sets it up at the entrance to his dwelling. After they have treated their prisoners well for a long time with all the hospitality they can think of, each man who has a prisoner calls a great assembly of his acquaintances. He ties a rope to one of the prisoner's arms, by the end of which he holds him, a few steps away, for fear of being hurt, and gives his dearest friend the other arm to hold in the same way; and these two, in the presence of the whole assembly, kill him with their swords. This done, they roast him and eat him in common and send some pieces to their absent friends. This is not, as people think, for nourishment, as of old the Scythians used to do; it is to betoken an extreme revenge. And the proof of this came when they saw the Portugese, who had joined forces with their adversaries, inflict a different kind of death on them when they took them prisoner, which was to bury them up to the waist, shoot the rest of their body full of arrows, and afterward hang them. They thought that these people from the other world, being men who had sown the knowledge of many vices among their neighbors and were much greater masters than themselves in every sort of wickedness, did not adopt this sort of vengeance without some reason, and that it must be more painful than their own; so they began to give up their old method and to follow this one.

I am not sorry that we notice the barbarous horror of such acts, but I am heartily sorry that, judging their faults rightly, we should be so blind to our own. I think there is more barbarity in eating a man alive than in eating him dead; and in tearing by tortures and the rack a body still full of feeling, in roasting a man bit by bit, in having him bitten and mangled by dogs and swine (as we have not only read but seen within fresh memory, not among ancient enemies, but among neighbors and fellow citizens, and what is worse, on the pretext of piety and religion), than in roasting and eating him after he is dead.

Indeed, Chrysippus and Zeno, heads of the Stoic sect, thought there was nothing wrong in using our carcasses for any purpose in case of need, and getting nourishment from them; just as our ancestors, when besieged by Caesar in the city of Alésia, resolved to relieve their famine by eating old men, women, and other people useless for fighting. "The Gascons once, 'tis said, their life renewed / By eating of such food." [11] And physicians do not fear to use human flesh in all sorts of ways for our health, applying it either inwardly or outwardly. But there never was any opinion so disordered as to excuse treachery, disloyalty, tyranny, and cruelty, which are our ordinary vices.

So we may well call these people barbarians, in respect to the rules of reason, but not in respect to ourselves, who surpass them in every kind of barbarity.

Their warfare is wholly noble and generous, and as excusable and beautiful as this human disease can be; its only basis among them is their rivalry in valor. They are not fighting for the conquest of new lands, for they still enjoy that natural abundance that provides them without toil and trouble with all necessary things in such profusion that they have no wish to enlarge their boundaries. They are still in that happy state of desiring only as much as their natural needs demand; anything beyond that is superfluous to them.

They generally call those of the same age, brothers; those who are younger, children; and the old men are fathers to all the others. These leave to their heirs in common the full possession of their property, without division or any other title at all than just the one that Nature gives to her creatures in bringing them into the world.

If their neighbors cross the mountains to attack them and win a victory, the gain of the victor is glory, and the advantage of having proved the master in valor and virtue; for apart from this they have no use for the goods of the vanquished, and they return to their own country, where they lack neither anything necessary nor that great thing, the knowledge of how to enjoy their condition happily and be content with it. These men of ours do the same in their turn. They demand of their prisoners no other ransom than that they confess and acknowledge their defeat. But there is not one in a

11. Juvenal, *Satires*, 15.93.

whole century who does not choose to die rather than to relax a single bit, by word or look, from the grandeur of an invincible courage; not one who would not rather be killed and eaten than so much as ask not to be. They treat them very freely, so that life may be all the dearer to them, and usually entertain them with threats of their coming death, of the torments they will have to suffer, the preparations that are being made for that purpose, the cutting up of their limbs, and the feast that will be made at their expense. All this is done for the purpose of extorting from their lips some weak or base word, or making them want to flee, so as to gain the advantage of having terrified them and broken down their firmness.[12] For indeed, if you take it the right way, it is in this point alone that true victory lies: "It is no victory / Unless the vanquished foe admits your mastery."[13]

The Hungarians, very bellicose fighters, did not in olden times pursue their advantage beyond putting the enemy at their mercy. For having wrung a confession from him to this effect, they let him go unharmed and unransomed, except, at most, for exacting his promise never again to take up arms against them.

We win enough advantages over our enemies that are borrowed advantages, not really our own. It is the quality of a porter, not of valor, to have sturdier arms and legs; agility is a dead and corporeal quality; it is a stroke of luck to make our enemy stumble, or dazzle his eyes by the sunlight; it is a trick of art and technique, which may be found in a worthless coward, to be an able fencer. The worth and value of a man is in his heart and his will; there lies his real honor. Valor is the strength, not of legs and arms, but of heart and soul; it consists not in the worth of our horse or our weapons, but in our own. He who falls obstinate in his courage, *if he has fallen, he fights on his knees*.[14] He who relaxes none of his assurance, no matter how great the danger of imminent death; who, giving up his soul, still looks firmly and scornfully at his enemy—he is beaten not by us, but by fortune; he is killed, not conquered.

The most valiant are sometimes the most unfortunate. Thus there are triumphant defeats that rival victories. Nor did those four sister victories, the fairest that the sun ever set eyes on—Salamis, Plataea, Mycale, and Sicily—ever dare match all their combined glory against the glory of the annihilation of King Leonidas and his men at the pass of Thermopylae.

Who ever hastened with more glorious and ambitious desire to win a battle than Captain Ischolas to lose one?[15] Who ever secured his safety

12. Cf. Jean de Léry, *Histoire d'un voyage fait en la terre du Brésil, dite Amérique* (1578).
13. Claudian, *On the Sixth Consulship of Honorius*, 248.
14. Seneca, *On Providence*, 2.   15. Diodorus Siculus, 15.16.

more ingeniously and painstakingly than he did his destruction? He was charged to defend a certain pass in the Peloponnesus against the Arcadians. Finding himself wholly incapable of doing this, in view of the nature of the place and the inequality of the forces, he made up his mind that all who confronted the enemy would necessarily have to remain on the field. On the other hand, deeming it unworthy both of his own virtue and magnanimity and of the Lacedaemonian name to fail in his charge, he took a middle course between these two extremes, in this way. The youngest and fittest of his band he preserved for the defense and service of their country, and sent them home; and with those whose loss was less important, he determined to hold this pass, and by their death to make the enemy buy their entry as dearly as he could. And so it turned out. For he was presently surrounded on all sides by the Arcadians, and after slaughtering a large number of them, he and his men were all put to the sword. Is there a trophy dedicated to victors that would not be more due to these vanquished? The role of true victory is in fighting, not in coming off safely; and the honor of valor consists in combating, not in beating.

To return to our story. These prisoners are so far from giving in, in spite of all that is done to them, that on the contrary, during the two or three months that they are kept, they wear a gay expression; they urge their captors to hurry and put them to the test; they defy them, insult them, reproach them with their own cowardice and the number of battles they have lost to the prisoners' own people.

I have a song composed by a prisoner which contains this challenge, that they should all come boldly and gather to dine off him, for they will be eating at the same time their own fathers and grandfathers, who have served to feed and nourish his body. "These muscles," he says, "this flesh and these veins are your own, poor fools that you are. You do not recognize that the substance of your ancestors' limbs is still contained in them. Savor them well; you will find in them the taste of your own flesh." An idea that certainly does not smack of barbarity. Those that paint these people dying, and who show the execution, portray the prisoner spitting in the face of his slayers and scowling at them. Indeed, to the last gasp they never stop braving and defying their enemies by word and look. Truly here are real savages by our standards; for either they must be thoroughly so, or we must be; there is an amazing distance between their character and ours.

The men there have several wives, and the higher their reputation for valor the more wives they have. It is a remarkably beautiful thing about their marriages that the same jealousy our wives have to keep us from the affection and kindness of other women, theirs have to win this for them. Being more concerned for their husbands' honor than for anything else, they strive and scheme to have as many companions as they can, since that is a sign of their husbands' valor.

Our wives will cry "Miracle!" but it is no miracle. It is a properly matrimonial virtue, but one of the highest order. In the Bible, Leah, Rachel, Sarah, and Jacob's wives gave their beautiful handmaids to their husbands; and Livia seconded the appetites of Augustus, to her own disadvantage; and Stratonice, the wife of King Deiotarus, not only lent her husband for his use a very beautiful young chambermaid in her service, but carefully brought up her children, and backed them up to succeed to their father's estates.

And lest it be thought that all this is done through a simple and servile bondage to usage and through the pressure of the authority of their ancient customs, without reasoning or judgment, and because their minds are so stupid that they cannot take any other course, I must cite some examples of their capacity. Besides the warlike song I have just quoted, I have another, a love song, which begins in this vein: "Adder, stay; stay, adder, that from the pattern of your coloring my sister may draw the fashion and the workmanship of a rich girdle that I may give to my love; so may your beauty and your pattern be forever preferred to all other serpents." This first couplet is the refrain of the song. Now I am familiar enough with poetry to be a judge of this: not only is there nothing barbarous in this fancy, but it is altogether Anacreontic.[16] Their language, moreover, is a soft language, with an agreeable sound, somewhat like Greek in its endings.

Three of these men, ignorant of the price they will pay some day, in loss of repose and happiness, for gaining knowledge of the corruptions of this side of the ocean; ignorant also of the fact that of this intercourse will come their ruin (which I suppose is already well advanced: poor wretches, to let themselves be tricked by the desire for new things, and to have left the serenity of their own sky to come and see ours!)—three of these men were at Rouen, at the time the late King Charles IX[17] was there. The king talked to them for a long time; they were shown our ways, our splendor, the aspect of a fine city. After that, someone asked their opinion, and wanted to know what they had found most amazing. They mentioned three things, of which I have forgotten the third, and I am very sorry for it; but I still remember two of them. They said that in the first place they thought it very strange that so many grown men, bearded, strong, and armed, who were around

16. The reference is to the Greek love and drinking songs circulated in the early Roman Empire under the name of the sixth to fifth century B.C. poet Anacreon. They were first published by Henri Estielle in 1554.

17. 1562–74, the second son of Henry II and Catherine de' Medici, who was, when this event took place in 1562, the regent for her still minor son.

the king (it is likely that they were talking about the Swiss of his guard) should submit to obey a child, and that one of them was not chosen to command instead. Second (they have a way in their language of speaking of men as halves of one another), they had noticed that there were among us men full and gorged with all sorts of good things, and that their other halves were beggars at their doors, emaciated with hunger and poverty; and they thought it strange that these needy halves could endure such an injustice, and did not take the others by the throat, or set fire to their houses.

I had a very long talk with one of them; but I had an interpreter who followed my meaning so badly, and who was so hindered by his stupidity in taking in my ideas, that I could get hardly any satisfaction from the man. When I asked him what profit he gained from his superior position among his people (for he was a captain, and our sailors called him king), he told me that it was to march foremost in war. How many men followed him? He pointed to a piece of ground, to signify as many as such a space could hold; it might have been four or five thousand men. Did all his authority expire with the war? He said that this much remained, that when he visited the villages dependent on him, they made paths for him through the underbrush by which he might pass quite comfortably.

All this is not too bad—but what's the use? They don't wear breeches.[18]

"Of Books"

I have no doubt that I often happen to speak of things that are better treated by the masters of the craft, and more truthfully. This is purely the essay of my natural faculties, and not at all of the acquired ones; and whoever shall catch me in ignorance will do nothing against me, for I should hardly be answerable for my ideas to others, I who am not answerable for them to myself, or satisfied with them. Whoever is in search of knowledge, let him fish for it where it dwells; there is nothing I profess less. These are my fancies, by which I try to give knowledge not of things, but of myself. The things will perhaps be known to me some day, or have been once, according as fortune may have brought me to the places where they were made clear. But I no longer remember them. And if I am a man of some reading, I am a man of no retentiveness.

Thus I guarantee no certainty, unless it be to make known to what point, at this moment, extends the knowledge that I have of myself. Let attention be paid not to the matter, but to the shape I give it.

Let people see in what I borrow whether I have known how to choose

18. *Haut de chausses*, not *cullottes*.

what would enhance my theme. For I make others say what I cannot say so well, now through the weakness of my language, now through the weakness of my understanding. I do not count my borrowings, I weigh them. And if I had wanted to have them valued by their number, I should have loaded myself with twice as many. They are all, or very nearly all, from such famous and ancient names that they seem to identify themselves enough without me. In the reasonings and inventions that I transplant into my soil and confound with my own, I have sometimes deliberately not indicated the author, in order to hold in check the temerity of those hasty condemnations that are tossed at all sorts of writings, notably recent writings of men still living, and in the vulgar tongue, which invites everyone to talk about them and seems to convict the conception and design of being likewise vulgar. I want them to give Plutarch a fillip on my nose and get burned insulting Seneca in me. I have to hide my weakness under these great authorities. I will love anyone that can unplume me, I mean by clearness of judgment and by the sole distinction of the force and beauty of the remarks. For I who, for lack of memory, fall short at every turn in picking them out by knowledge of their origin, can very well realize, by measuring my capacity, that my soil is not at all capable of producing certain too rich flowers that I find sown there, and that all the fruits of my own growing could not match them.

For this I am obliged to be responsible: if I get myself tangled up, if there is vanity and faultiness in my reasonings that I do not perceive or that I am not capable of perceiving when pointed out to me. For faults often escape our eyes; but infirmity of judgment consists in not being able to perceive them when another reveals them to us. Knowledge and truth can lodge in us without judgment, and judgment also without them; indeed the recognition of ignorance is one of the fairest and surest testimonies of judgment that I find.

I have no other marshal but fortune to arrange my bits. As my fancies present themselves, I pile them up; now they come pressing in a crowd, now dragging single file. I want people to see my natural and ordinary pace, however off the track it is. I let myself go as I am. Besides, these are not matters of which we are forbidden to be ignorant and to speak casually and at random.

I should certainly like to have a more perfect knowledge of things, but I do not want to buy it as dear as it costs. My intention is to pass pleasantly, and not laboriously, what life I have left. There is nothing for which I want to rack my brain, not even knowledge, however great its value.

I seek in books only to give myself pleasure by honest amusement; or if I study, I seek only the learning that treats of the knowledge of myself and instructs me in how to die well and live well: "This is the goal toward which my sweating horse should strain." [19]

If I encounter difficulties in reading, I do not gnaw my nails over them; I leave them there, after making one or two attacks on them. If I planted myself in them, I would lose both myself and time; for I have an impulsive mind. What I do not see at the first attack, I see less by persisting. I do nothing without gaiety; continuation and too strong contention dazes, depresses, and wearies my judgment. My sight becomes confused and dispersed. I have to withdraw it and apply it again by starts, just as in order to judge the luster of a scarlet fabric, they tell us to pass our eyes over it several times, catching it in various quickly renewed and repeated glimpses.

If this book wearies me, I take up another; and I apply myself to it only at the moments when the boredom of doing nothing begins to grip me. I do not take much to modern books, because the ancient ones seem to me fuller and stronger; nor to those in Greek, because my judgment cannot do its work with a childish and apprentice understanding.

Among the books that are simply entertaining, I find, of the moderns, the *Decameron* of Boccaccio, Rabelais, and *The Kisses* of Johannes Secundus, if they may be placed under this heading, worth reading for amusement. As for the Amadises [20] and writings of that sort, they did not have the authority to detain even my childhood. I will also say this, whether boldly or rashly, that this heavy old soul of mine no longer lets itself be tickled, not merely by Ariosto, [21] but even by the good Ovid: his facility and inventions, which once enchanted me, hardly entertain me at all now.

I speak my mind freely on all things, even on those which perhaps exceed my capacity and which I by no means hold to be within my jurisdiction. And so the opinion I give of them is to declare the measure of my sight, not the measure of things. When I feel a distaste for Plato's *Axiochus* as a work without power considering such an author, [22] my judgment does not trust itself: it is not so stupid as to oppose itself to the authority of so many other famous ancient judgments, which it considers its tutors and masters, and with which it is rather content to err. It blames and condemns itself either for stopping at the outer bark, not being able to penetrate to the

19. Propertius, 4.1.70.

20. *Amadis des Gaules*: a fourteenth-century Portuguese romance based on the Round Table legends translated into French between 1540 and 1548. Johannes Everaerts (1511–36) wrote Latin poetry, including the rather sexually explicit poem referred to here in imitation of Catullus.

21. Ludovico Ariosto, author of the romantic epic *Orlando furioso* (1516–1531), one of the great classics of Renaissance Italian literature—on the same level, in the history of Italian literature, as Boccaccio's masterpiece of the fourteenth century.

22. It was recognized as apocryphal even by the philologists of Montaigne's generation.

heart, or for looking at the thing by some false light. It is content with simply securing itself from confusion and disorder; as for its weakness, it readily recognizes and admits it. It thinks it gives a correct interpretation to the appearances that its conception presents to it; but these are weak and imperfect.

Most of Aesop's *Fables* have many meanings and interpretations. Those who take them allegorically choose some aspect that squares with the fable, but for the most part this is only the first and superficial aspect; there are others more living, more essential and internal, to which they have not known how to penetrate; this is how I read them.

But, to pursue my path, it has always seemed to me that in poetry Virgil, Lucretius, Catullus, and Horace hold the first rank by very far, and especially Virgil in his *Georgics*, which I consider the most accomplished work in poetry; in comparison with it one can easily recognize that there are passages in the *Aeneid* which the author would have brushed up still a little more if he had had the chance. And the fifth book of the *Aeneid* seems to me the most perfect. I also love Lucan and enjoy his company, not so much for his style as for his own worth and the truth of his opinions and judgments. As for the good Terence, the very refinement and charm of the Latin language, I find him admirable at representing to the life the movements of the soul and the state of our characters; at every moment our actions throw me back to him. I cannot read him so often as not to find in him some new beauty and grace.

Those who lived near Virgil's time used to complain that some compared Lucretius to him. I am of the opinion that that is in truth an unequal comparison; but I have much to do to confirm myself in this belief when I find myself fixed on one of the beautiful passages in Lucretius. If they were stung by this comparison, what would they say of the barbarous brutishness and stupidity of those who nowadays compare Ariosto to him? And what would Ariosto himself say? "O foolish and dull-witted age!"[23]

I think the ancients had still more reason to complain of those who compared Plautus to Terence (the latter savors much more of the gentleman) than of those who compared Lucretius to Virgil. It does much for the esteem and preference of Terence that the father of Roman eloquence has him, and him alone of his class, so often in his mouth; and also the verdict that the first judge among the Roman poets gives of his fellow.

It has often struck my mind how in our time those who set themselves to write comedies (like the Italians, who are rather happy at it) use three or four plots from Terence or Plautus to make one of their own. They pile up in a single comedy five or six stories from Boccaccio. What makes them so

23. Catullus, 43.8.

load themselves with material is the distrust they have of being able to sustain themselves by their own graces; they have to find a body to lean on; and not having enough of their own to detain us, they want the story to amuse us. It is quite the contrary with my author: the perfections and beauties of his style of expression make us lose our appetite for his subject. His distinction and elegance hold us throughout; he is everywhere so delightful, "Clear flowing and most like a crystal stream," [24] and so fills our soul with his charms, that we forget those of his plot.

This same consideration draws me on further. I observe that the good ancient poets avoided the affectation and the quest, not only of the fantastic Spanish and Petrarchian flights, but even of the milder and more restrained conceits that are the adornment of all the poetic works of the succeeding centuries. Yet there is no good judge who misses them in those ancients, and who does not admire incomparably more the even polish and that perpetual sweetness and flowering beauty of Catullus' epigrams than all the stings with which Martial sharpens the tails of his. This is for the same reason that I was stating just now, as Martial says of himself: *he had less need for the labor of wit, since his subject matter took the place of wit.* [25] The former, without getting excited and without goading themselves, make themselves sufficiently felt: they have matter enough for laughter everywhere, they don't have to tickle themselves. The latter need outside help: the less wit they have, the more body they need. They mount on horseback because they are not strong enough on their legs.

Just as at our balls these men of low condition who keep dancing schools, not being able to imitate the bearing and fitness of our nobility, seek to recommend themselves by perilous leaps and other strange mountebank's antics. And the ladies can more cheaply show off their carriage in the dances where there are various contortions and twistings of the body, than in certain other formal dances where they need only walk with a natural step and display a natural bearing and their ordinary grace. As I have also seen excellent clowns, in their ordinary dress and usual face, give us all the pleasure that can be derived from their art, while the apprentices and those who are not so highly skilled need to flour their faces, dress up, and counterfeit wild movements and grimaces in order to make us laugh.

This idea of mine is easier to recognize in the comparison of the *Aeneid* and the *Orlando furioso* [26] than anywhere else. We see the former on outspread wings in lofty and sustained flight always pursuing his point; the latter fluttering and hopping from tale to tale as from branch to branch, not

---

24. Horace, *Epistles*, 2.2.120.   25. Martial, Preface to *Epigrams*, 8.
26. See above, n. 21.

trusting his wings except for a very short hop, and alighting at every turn for fear his breath and strength should fail: "He tries his wings in short excursions." [27] These, then, in this sort of subjects, are the authors I like best.

As for my other reading, which mingles a little more profit with the pleasure, and by which I learn to arrange my humors and my ways, the books that serve me for this are Plutarch, since he exists in French, and Seneca. They both have this notable advantage for my humor, that the knowledge I seek is there treated in detached pieces that do not demand the obligation of long labor, of which I am incapable. Such are the *Moral Essays* of Plutarch and the *Epistles* of Seneca, which are the finest part of his writings, and the most profitable. I need no great enterprise to get at them, and I leave them whenever I like. For they have no continuity from one to the other.

These authors agree in most of the opinions that are useful and true; and so were their fortunes similar: they were born at about the same time, each tutored a Roman Emperor, both came from foreign countries, both were rich and powerful. Their teaching is the cream of philosophy, and presented in simple and pertinent fashion. Plutarch is more uniform and constant, Seneca more undulating and diverse. The latter labors, strains, and tenses himself to arm virtue against weakness, fear, and vicious appetites; the other seems not to esteem their power so much, and to disdain to hurry his step or stand on guard for them. Plutarch's opinions are Platonic, mild, and accomodated to civil society; the other's are Stoic and Epicurean, more remote from common use, but in my opinion more suitable for private life and more sturdy. In Seneca it seems that he concedes a little to the tyranny of the emperors of his time, for I hold it for certain that it is by a forced judgment that he condemns the cause of those high-minded murderers of Caesar; Plutarch is free throughout. Seneca is full of witty points and sallies, Plutarch of things. The former heats you and moves you more; the latter contents you more and pays you better. He guides us, the other pushes us.

As for Cicero, the works of his that can best serve my purpose are those that treat of philosophy, especially moral. But to confess the truth boldly (for once you have crossed over the barriers of impudence there is no more curb), his way of writing, and every other similar way, seems to me boring. For his prefaces, definitions, partitions, etymologies, consume the greater part of his work; what life and marrow there is, is smothered by his longwinded preparations. If I have spent an hour in reading him, which is a lot for me, and I remember what juice and substance I have derived, most of

27. Virgil, *Georgics*, 4.194.

the time I find nothing but wind; for he has not yet come to the arguments that serve his purpose and the reasons that properly touch on the crux, which I am looking for.

For me, who ask only to become wiser, not more learned or eloquent, these logical and Aristotelian arrangements are not to the point. I want a man to begin with the conclusion. I understand well enough what death and pleasure are; let him not waste his time anatomizing them. I look for good solid reasons from the start, which will instruct me in how to sustain their attack. Neither grammatical subtleties nor an ingenious contexture of words and argumentations are any use for that. I want reasonings that drive their first attack into the stronghold of the doubt; his languish around the pot. They are good for the school, for the bar, and for the sermon, where we have leisure to nap and are still in time a quarter of an hour later to pick up the thread of the discourse. It is necessary to speak thus to judges, whom we want to win over rightly or wrongly, to children, and to the common herd, to whom we have to say everything to see what will carry.

I do not want a man to use his strength making me attentive and to shout at me fifty times "*Or oyez!*" in the manner of our heralds. The Romans used to say in their religion "*Hoc age*," as we say in ours "*Sursum corda*": these are so many words lost on me.[28] I come fully prepared from my house; I need no allurement or sauce; I can perfectly well eat my meat quite raw; and instead of whetting my appetite by these preparations and preliminaries, they pall and weary it.

Will the license of the times excuse my sacrilegious audacity in considering that even Plato's dialogues drag and stifle his substance too much, and in lamenting the time put into these long vain preliminary interlocutions by a man who had so many better things to say? My ignorance will excuse me better in that I have no perception of the beauty of his language. In general I ask for books that make use of learning, not those that build it up.

The first two, and Pliny, and their like, have no *Hoc age*; they want to have to do with men who themselves have told themselves this; or if they have one, it is a substantial *Hoc age* that has a body of its own.

I also like to read the *Letters to Atticus*, not only because they contain a very ample education in the history and affairs of his time, but much more because in them I discover his personal humors. For I have a singular curiosity, as I have said elsewhere, to know the soul and the natural judgments of my authors. We must indeed judge their capacity, but not their character nor themselves, by that display of their writings that they expose on the

28. "Hear now!"; "Do thus"; "Lift up your hearts" (from the preface of the Roman Mass).

stage of the world. I have regretted a thousand times that we have lost the book that Brutus had written on virtue: for it is a fine thing to learn the theory from those who well know the practice. But since the preachings are one thing and the preacher another, I am as glad to see Brutus in Plutarch as in a book of his own. I would rather choose to know truly the conversation he held in his tent with some one of his intimate friends on the eve of a battle than the speech he made the next day to his army; and what he was doing in his study and his chamber than what he was doing in the public square and in the Senate.

As for Cicero, I am of the common opinion, that except for learning there was not much excellence in his soul. He was a good citizen, of an affable nature, as all fat jesting men, such as he was, are apt to be; but of softness and ambitious vanity he had in truth a great deal. And moreover I do not know how to excuse him for having considered his poetry worth being published. It is not a great imperfection to write verses badly; but it is a lack of judgment in him not to have felt how unworthy they were of the glory of his name. As for his eloquence, it is entirely beyond comparison; I believe that no man will ever equal him.

The younger Cicero,[29] who resembled his father only in name, while commanding in Asia, had several strangers at his table one day, and among others Cestius, seated at the lower end, as people often push in to the open tables of the great. Cicero inquired who he was of one of his men, who told him his name. But like a man whose thoughts were elsewhere and who kept forgetting what they answered him, he asked him that again two or three more times. The servant, in order not to have the trouble of repeating the same thing so often to him, and to make him know him by some circumstance, said to him: "It is that Cestius of whom you were told that he sets no great store by your father's eloquence in comparison with his own." Cicero, suddenly stung by this, ordered them to lay hold of this poor Cestius and had him very soundly whipped in his presence. That was a discourteous host!

Even among those who, all things considered, esteemed this eloquence of his as incomparable, there were some who did not fail to note some faults in it; thus the great Brutus, his friend, used to say that it was a broken and weak-loined eloquence, *fractam et elumbem*.[30] The orators who lived near his time also reprehended in him his sedulous care for a certain long cadence at the end of his periods, and noted the words *esse videatur*[31] which he uses so often. As for me, I prefer a cadence that falls shorter, cut into iambics. To be sure, he does sometimes mix up his rhythms roughly,

29. Marcus Cicero (Jr.), a lieutenant in the army of Brutus.
30. Cf. Tacitus, *On Orators*, 18.   31. Ibid., 23.

but rarely. My ears have noted this passage: "Ego vero me minus diu senem esse mallem, quam esse senem, antequam essem." [32]

The historians come right to my forehand. They are pleasant and easy; and at the same time, man in general, the knowledge of whom I seek, appears in them more alive and entire than in any other place—the diversity and truth of his inner qualities in the mass and in detail, the variety of the ways he is put together, and the accidents that threaten him. Now those who write biographies, since they spend more time on plans than on events, more on what comes from within than on what happens without, are most suited to me. That is why in every way Plutarch is my man. I am very sorry that we do not have a dozen Laertiuses, [33] or that he is not either more receptive or more perceptive. For I consider no less curiously the fortunes and the lives of these great teachers of the world than the diversity of their doctrines and fancies.

In this kind of study of history we must leaf without distinction through all sorts of authors, both old and new, both gibberish and French, in order to learn in them the things of which they variously treat. But it seems to me that Caesar singularly deserves to be studied, not only for the knowledge of history, but for himself, so much perfection and excellence he has above all the others, although Sallust is one of their number. Indeed I read this author with a little more reverence and respect than one reads human works: now considering him in himself by his actions and the miracle of his greatness, now the purity and inimitable polish of his language, which surpassed not only all the historians, as Cicero says, but perhaps Cicero himself. With so much sincerity in his judgments when speaking of his enemies, that except for the false colors with which he tries to cover his evil cause and the filthiness of his pestilential ambition, I think the only fault that can be found in him is that he has been too sparing in speaking of himself. For so many great things cannot have been performed by him without much more of himself having gone into them than he sets down.

I like historians who are either very simple or outstanding. The simple, who have not the wherewithal to mix in anything of their own, and who bring to it only the care and diligence to collect all that comes to their attention and to record everything faithfully without choice or discrimination, leave our judgment intact to discern the truth. Such, for example, among others, is the good Froissart, [34] who has gone along in his undertaking with such frank simplicity that having made a mistake he is not at all afraid to recognize it and correct it at the spot where he has been made

32. "As for me, I would prefer to be old for a shorter time than be old before I am old": Cicero, *On Old Age* (*De Senectute*), 10.

33. Diogenes Laertius, author of *Lives of the Philosophers*.

34. Jean Froissart, author of a chronicle of the Hundred Years' War (fourteenth century).

aware of it; and who presents to us even the diversity of the rumors that were current and the different reports that were made to him. This is the material of history, naked and unformed; each man can make his profit of it according to his understanding.

The really outstanding ones have the capacity to choose what is worth knowing; they can pick out of two reports the one that is more likely. From the nature and humors of princes they infer their intentions and attribute appropriate words to them. They are right to assume the authority to regulate our belief by their own; but certainly this privilege belongs to very few people.

Those in between (which are the commonest sort) spoil everything for us. They want to chew our morsels for us; they give themselves the right to judge, and consequently to slant history to their fancy; for once the judgment leans to one side, one cannot help turning and twisting the narrative to that bias. They undertake to choose the things worth knowing, and often conceal from us a given word, a given private action, that would instruct us better; they omit as incredible the things they do not understand, and perhaps also some things because they do not know how to say them in good Latin or French. Let them boldly display their eloquence and their reasonings, let them judge all they like; but let them also leave us the wherewithal to judge after them, and not alter or arrange by their abridgments and selection anything of the substance of the matter, but pass it on to us pure and entire in all its dimensions.

Most of the time, especially in these days, people are selected for this work from among the common herd for the sole consideration of knowing how to speak well; as if here we were trying to learn grammar! And having been hired only for that and having put on sale only their babble, they are right accordingly to care chiefly only about that part. Thus with many fine words they go and cook up a fine concoction of the rumors they pick up in the city squares.

The only good histories are those that have been written by the very men who were in command in the affairs, or who were participants in the conduct of them, or who at least have had the fortune to conduct others of the same sort. Such are almost all the Greek and Roman histories. For when several eyewitnesses have written about the same subject (as it happened in those days that greatness and learning usually met), if there is a mistake, it must be very slight, and on a very doubtful incident. What can you expect of a doctor discussing war, or a schoolboy discussing the intentions of princes? If we want to note the scruples the Romans had in this, we need only this example. Asinius Pollio[35] found in the histories even of Cae-

---

35. Caius Asinius Pollio (76 B.C.–4 A.D.), a friend of Virgil and author of a lost history of the civil wars of Rome.

sar some mistake into which he had fallen through not having been able to keep his eyes on every part of his army and having believed individuals who often reported to him things insufficiently verified; or else through not having been carefully enough informed by his lieutenants about what they had done in his absence. We can see by this example whether this quest of truth is delicate, when we cannot trust the commander's knowledge of a battle his soldiers have fought, or the soldiers' knowledge of what happened near them, unless, in the manner of a judicial inquiry, we confront the witnesses and hear the objections about the evidence in the slightest details of each incident. Truly, the knowledge we have of our own affairs is much looser. But this has been sufficiently treated by Bodin,[36] and according to my way of thinking.

To compensate a little for the treachery and weakness of my memory, so extreme that it has happened to me more than once to pick up again, as recent and unknown to me, books which I had read carefully a few years before and scribbled over with my notes, I have adopted the habit for some time now of adding at the end of each book (I mean of those that I intend to use only once) the time I finished reading it and the judgment I have derived of it as a whole, so that this may represent to me at least the sense and general idea I had conceived of the author in reading it. I want to transcribe here some of these annotations.

Here is what I put some ten years ago in my Guicciardini[37] (for whatever language my books speak, I speak to them in my own): "He is a diligent historiographer from whom, in my opinion, one can learn the truth about the affairs of his time as exactly as from any other: and indeed in most of them he was an actor himself, and of honorable rank. There is no appearance that through hatred, favor, or vanity, he disguised things; which is attested by the free judgments he gives of the great, and especially of those by whom he had been advanced and employed in responsibilities, like Pope Clement VII. As for the part he seems to want to make most of, which is his digressions and discourses, there are some good ones and enriched with fine traits, but he is too fond of them. For by not wanting to leave anything unsaid, having a subject so full and ample and almost infinite, he becomes diffuse and smacking a bit of scholastic prattle. I have also noted this, that of so many souls and actions that he judges, so many motives and plans, he

36. Jean Bodin (1530–96), one of the greatest political philosophers of the age, author of *Six Books on the Republic*. Montaigne's reference here is to his *Method for the Easy Comprehension of History* (1576).

37. Francesco Guicciardini (1482–1540), a friend and correspondent of Machiavelli, and author of the classic *History of Italy* from 1492 to 1534, written in the literary Tuscan that, in the sixteenth century, became the official literary language of Italy.

never refers a single one to virtue, religion, and conscience, as if these qualities were wholly extinct in the world; and of all actions, however fair in appearance they may be of themselves, he throws the cause back onto some vicious motive or some profit. It is impossible to imagine that among the infinite number of actions that he judges there was not a single one produced by the way of reason. No corruption can have seized men so universally that someone would not escape the contagion. This makes me fear that his taste was a bit corrupted; and it may have happened that he judged others by himself."

In my Philippe de Commines [38] there is this: "Here you will find the language pleasant and agreeable, of a natural simplicity; the narrative pure, and the author's good faith showing through it clearly, free from vanity in speaking of himself, and of partiality or envy in speaking of others; his ideas and exhortations accompanied more by good zeal and truth than by any exquisite capacity; and, throughout, authority and gravity, representing the man of good background and brought up in great affairs."

On the *Memoirs* of Monsieur du Bellay: [39] "It is always a pleasure to see things written by people who have experienced how they should be conducted; but it cannot be denied that there is clearly revealed in these two lords a great falling off from the frankness and freedom of writing that shine forth in the ancients of their class, such as the sire de Joinville, intimate friend of Saint Louis; [40] Eginhard, chancellor of Charlemagne; and, of more recent memory, Philippe de Commines. This is rather a plea for King Francis against the Emperor Charles V, than a history. I will not believe that they have changed anything in the main facts; but as for turning the judgment of events to our advantage, often contrary to reason, and omitting everything that is ticklish in the life of their master, they make a practice of it: witness the disgrace of Messieurs de Montmorency and de Brion, which are forgotten; indeed the very name of Madame d'Etampes is not to be found. One may cover up secret actions; but to be silent about what all the world knows, and about things that have led to public results of such consequence, is an inexcusable defect. In short, to get a complete knowledge of King Francis and the events of his time, a man should turn elsewhere, if he takes my advice. The profit one can make here is from the detailed narrative of the battles and exploits of war at which these gentlemen were

38. c. 1445–1509, author of a chronicle of his times from 1464 to 1498.

39. Guillaume du Bellay, diplomat, historian, and viceroy of Piedmont during the French occupation after 1534.

40. Jean de Joinville, a vassal and counsellor of King Louis IX of France, wrote a chronicle of his reign.

present; some private words and actions of certain princes of their time; and the dealings and negotiations carried on by the seigneur de Langey, in which there are plenty of things worth knowing, and ideas above the ordinary."

19. Vincenzo Galilei, *Dialogue on Ancient and Modern Music*

Vincenzo Galilei (c. 1533–91), the father of the more famous natural philosopher Galileo, studied music theory with Gioseffo Zarlino, one of the first proponents of the application of humanist methods to music. He became the musical mentor of the informal group of players and dilettantes who met in the *Camerata* of the wealthy Florentine patrician Giovanni de' Bardi for the purpose of experimenting with new forms of music that might appeal not only to the ears, but above all, in accordance with humanist rhetorical principles, to the emotions. Galilei was also an expert lute and viola player, and he published a number of his own compositions, including musical settings for passages from Dante's *Divine Comedy*, in order to demonstrate the effectiveness of these experiments. The discovery by the Florentine philologist Girolamo Mei of several fragments of ancient musical scores appeared to confirm what the theorists had deduced from extant literary sources: that ancient music had achieved the effects ascribed to it because it was monodic, not polyphonic, and because it reinforced, rather than distracted from, the words to which it was set. The musical revolution proposed in Galilei's *Dialogue*, published in 1581, was soon carried out in practice; and a new art form was born, the *dramma in musica*, or "opera," of which the earliest extant score is that of *Euridice* by Galilei's disciple Jacopo Peri, first performed in Florence in 1600.

Music was numbered by the ancients among the arts that are called liberal, that is, worthy of a free man, and among the Greeks its masters and discoverers, like those of almost all the other sciences, were always in great esteem. And by the best legislators it was decreed that it must be taught, not only as a lifelong delight but as useful to virtue, to those who were born to acquire perfection and human happiness, which is the object of the state. But in the course of time the Greeks lost the art of music and the other

"The Renaissance," in *Source Readings in Music History*, edited and translated by Oliver Strunk (New York: W. W. Norton, 1965), pp. 112–32. © 1965, 1950 by W. W. Norton & Company, Inc. Some footnotes deleted. Reprinted by permission of W. W. Norton & Company, Inc.

sciences as well, along with their dominion. The Romans had a knowledge of music, obtaining it from the Greeks, but they practiced chiefly that part appropriate to the theaters where tragedy and comedy were performed, without much prizing the part which is concerned with speculation; and being continually engaged in wars, they paid little attention even to the former part and thus easily forgot it. Later, after Italy had for a long period suffered great barbarian invasions, the light of every science was extinguished, and as if all men had been overcome by a heavy lethargy of ignorance, they lived without any desire for learning and took as little notice of music as of the western Indies. And they persisted in this blindness until first Gafurius and after him Glareanus and later Zarlino[1] (truly the princes in this modern practice) began to investigate what music was and to seek to rescue it from the darkness in which it had been buried. That part which they understood and appreciated, they brought little by little to its present condition, but from what can be learned from countless passages in the ancient histories and in the poets and philosophers, it does not seem to any who are intelligent that they restored it to its ancient state, or that they attained to the true and perfect knowledge of it. This may have been owing to the rudeness of the times, the difficulty of the subject, and the scarcity of good interpreters.

Nonetheless, these writers deserve the highest praise and the world owes them a perpetual debt; if for nothing else, at least for having given to many the occasion to devote greater labor to the subject, trying to discover how to bring it to perfection. This it seems, but only so far as pertains to theory, has been attained in our times by Girolamo Mei,[2] a man of worth, to whom all musicians and all men should give thanks and honor, and afterwards, in our own city, by the very illustrious Signor Giovanni Bardi de' Conti di Vernio,[3] who having long studied music, and finding great delight

1. Franchino Gafori was one of the first humanists to take a special interest in Greek texts about music; his *On the Harmony of Musical Instruments* was published in Milan in 1518. Heinrich Glareanus (named after his native Swiss canton of Glarus), a friend of Erasmus and a historian and poet as well as a music theorist. His most important work is the *Dodecachordon* of 1547; but he also prepared an edition of Boethius, published posthumously in 1570. Gioseffo Zarlino, a disciple of the Flemish-Venetian musician Adrian Willaert and his successor as choirmaster at San Marco in Venice, was in turn the teacher of Galilei, who eventually turned against him. Among his works: *Istituzioni armoniche* (1558) and *Dimostrazioni armoniche* (1571).

2. A well born pupil of the great Florentine philologist Pier Vettori who, after settling in Rome, discovered several fragments of ancient musical notation in the Vatican Library.

3. A descendant of the ancient Florentine family of the Bardi, the chief private patron of music in Florence until his departure for Rome in 1592, convenor of the informal group of humanists and performing musicians known as the Camerata, and author of a *Discourse on Ancient Music* very similar to Galilei's.

in it as in all the other sciences, has greatly ennobled it and made it worthy of esteem, having by his example incited the nobles to the same study, many of whom are accustomed to go to his house and pass the time there in cultivated leisure with delightful songs and laudable discussions.

Being therefore under great obligation to the courtesy of this most gracious gentleman, and consequently desiring to show him by some outward sign my inward wish to serve him, I have judged that I could not spend the time to better profit than by devoting my energies to this subject, since I hoped by so doing to give him some sign of gratitude and to aid the world not a little to escape from the darkness in which it has been enveloped since the above-mentioned loss. Be this, however, said without arrogance and with all respect for those who from Guido Aretino[4] down to our times have written on this subject; although if I should attribute to myself some little glory in this action, I might perhaps not merit rebuke, since the inclination for these liberal studies given to me by nature, and the continual diligence I have employed for many years in preparing them, would with great reason justify my discussing them. But let the judgment of this be strictly reserved to those versed in the subject.

For this reason, apart from the one previously mentioned, and in order that I may not defraud the world of any benefit it might receive from my efforts, it has pleased me to publish some thoughts of mine on ancient music and that of our times, which until this day have been (in my opinion) little understood by any who have discussed them, a thing that without further testimony from me may serve as clear evidence of the difficulty of the subject. I therefore desire of the reader that he be prepared to pass judgment and to compare my writings with those of the other moderns with the greatest attention and with his mind free from any human passion, for it is clear that whoever has not wholly freed his mind from passion cannot form a perfect judgment of anything. I shall receive with pleasure every suggestion that is given to me by an understanding man and lover of truth and shall be obliged to him for it without being ashamed to learn from one who understands better than myself.

And now, since long continuous speaking, flowing on like a torrent, seems not to have that force and vigor in concluding sentences and arguments which dialogue has, I have judged it most to the purpose to treat my present discourses in that manner, and this I can easily believe to have been one of the potent causes that induced Plato to treat the subjects of divine philosophy in this way. I have accordingly chosen to discuss this subject the very illustrious Signor Giovanni Bardi, mentioned a little while ago, and

---

4. The most important music theorist of the Middle Ages, author of *Micrologus de disciplina artis musicae*.

with him Signor Piero Strozzi, as being both most zealous for the true music and great lovers of such speculations as these and moreover qualified to sustain this or even a weightier argument. . . .

Strozzi: May it please you to give me some further particulars, so that I may escape from my ignorance and also learn how to answer the practical musicians of today, who maintain that the music of the ancients was in comparison with their own a thing to be laughed at, and that the astonishment they caused with it in men's minds had no other source or origin than their coarseness and rudeness, but being proud of it, they afterwards made a great to-do over it in their books.

Bardi: Observe how bold they are, these men who laugh at the effects of a thing without knowing what it was, or what its nature and properties were, or how its effects could have been produced! What better argument do you wish, in order to convince them, than the miracles, to give them that name, that this music performed, miracles related to us by the worthiest and most famous writers, outside the profession of music, that the world has ever had?

But, leaving this to one side, let us turn to a clear and reasonable example, which will be this: from what I have been able to gather, it is certain that the present manner of singing several airs together has not been in use for more than a hundred and fifty years, although I do not know that there exists an authoritative example of the modern practice that is that old or that anyone wishes to have one. And all the best practical musicians agree in saying and believing that between that time and this, music has reached the highest perfection that man can imagine, indeed that since the death of Cipriano Rore,[5] a musician truly unique in this manner of counterpoint, it has rather declined than advanced. Now if in the hundred years, or a little more, that it has been practiced in this manner by people who are commonly of little or no worth, of unknown birthplace and parentage, so to speak, having no gifts of fortune, or else few, and hardly able to read, it has reached the pitch of excellence that they say, how much more astonishing and marvelous it must have been among the Greeks and Romans, where it lasted for centuries and centuries, continually in the care of the wisest, most learned, most judicious, and most wealthy men and of the bravest and most princely commanders that the world has ever had! . . .

For all the height of excellence of the practical music of the moderns, there is not heard or seen today the slightest sign of its accomplishing what ancient music accomplished, nor do we read that it accomplished it fifty or a hundred years ago when it was not so common and familiar to men. Thus neither its novelty nor its excellence has ever had the power, with our mod-

5. Another of Willaert's students (1516–65), best known for his madrigals.

ern musicians, of producing any of the virtuous, infinitely beneficial and comforting effects that ancient music produced. From this it is a necessary conclusion that either music or human nature has changed from its original state. But what ancient music was, and what modern music is, and how this change could come about, this I shall show at the proper time.

Strozzi: I take such pleasure in hearing these novelties which you advocate with such reasonable and living arguments, that if you are content, I shall be glad to hear all that you may wish to say further on the subject and shall not interfere with the order in which you have proposed to yourself to discuss the material.

Bardi: If that is your pleasure, it shall be mine as well, the more so because, having gone over it in advance, I shall not have to repeat the same thing several times. Let us then determine how much of the proposed material we can truly perceive, without fearing (since our only desire is for the public benefit) any imputation that may be cast on us for having been the first to dare to break this ice, so hard, thick, and plentiful. But observe this: if the practice of music—I mean now the true music which, as Polybius says,[6] is useful to all men, and not that music which, according to Ephorus, was invented to delude and deceive them—if the practice of music, I say, was introduced among men for the reason and object that all the learned concur in declaring, namely, if it arose primarily to express the passions with greater effectiveness in celebrating the praises of the gods, the genii, and the heroes, and secondarily to communicate these with equal force to the minds of mortals for their benefit and advantage, then it will be clear that the rules observed by the modern contrapuntists as inviolable laws, as well as those they often use from choice and to show their learning, will be directly opposed to the perfection of the true and best harmonies and melodies. It will not be difficult to prove and demonstrate this to them convincingly, for when they recall all that has thus far been said on this subject, they will set aside their own interest and their envy, wrong practice, and ignorance.

As the foundation of this subject, then, I shall briefly mention only two topics as principal and important, promising to explain them comprehensively a little further on. I say accordingly that the nature of the low sound is one thing, that of the high sound another, and that of the intermediate sound different from either of these. I say likewise that fast movement has one property, slow movement another, and that intermediate movement is far from either. Now if these two principles are true, and they most certainly are, it may easily be gathered from them, since truth is a unity, that singing in consonance in the manner that the modern practical musicians

6. Polybius, *Histories*, 4.20.

use is an absurdity, for consonance is nothing but a mixture of high and low sound which (as you know already) strikes the ear inoffensively, or delightfully, or very sweetly.

For if we find this contrariety of passion between the extreme sounds of the simple consonances, how much more the extended and composite consonances will have, by reason of the greater distance between their extremes, and how much more than these the consonances that are several times extended and composite, which because of their greater distance from their origin are less pure, less perceptible to the ear, and less comprehensible to the intellect! Nonetheless, the modern practical musicians go industriously seeking them out on the artificial and natural instruments. And if the diapason and diapente are as we have described them, and if the extreme sounds of each of these are perfectly combined, particularly those of the least multiple interval, which because of their mutual correspondence seem to be almost the same and to unite in a single term, how much more will the extremes of the imperfect consonances differ in nature, and how much more than these the dissonances of which their music is full! And if such diversity is found between only two parts which together sound a single interval, whether simple or composite, how much greater diversity there will be among four or six or more, often composite and of different natures, sounded together at the same time, as for the most part and to the greater ruin of true music is the custom of the contrapuntists in their *canzoni*!

After these impediments, caused by the diversity of sounds and the variety of voices, those that arise from the unequal movement of the parts are no less important, and these are that the soprano part often hardly moves because of the slowness of its notes, while on the contrary the bass part flies and those of the tenor and alto walk with leisurely pace, or while one of these fairly flies, the bass is proceeding at a walk and the soprano is almost motionless. Thus while the nature of the movement and sound made by one of the parts would be attracting the listener, and the more so when combined with words conforming to this movement and sound, the other part, as its contrary, would be repelling him, not otherwise than would happen to a column, everywhere set evenly upon its base, if anyone, to overthrow it, were to attach two or more equal ropes to its capital, each pulled in an opposite direction from an equal distance with an equal force. For it would not move at all from its place, for all the effort expended, unless perhaps it was somewhat weakened by some imperfection of its own, since the force on one side would counteract the opposite force. But if someone else were to attack it with the same appliances and the same forces, pulling from one side only, it would not be wonderful, to my thinking, if all that effort were strong enough to make it fall. . . .

The present way of composing and singing several airs in consonance at the same time was derived, unless I am mistaken, from stringed instruments similar to the epigonion and the simicion, or from these very ones. Seeing that the strings of these were in their number and arrangement and in the manner of their stretching such as has been shown above, the cithara players of those times began—either for the purpose of somehow surpassing those who sang to the cithara or of escaping the need of always having a singer with them for the sake of the perfection of the melody that his voice and their instrument produced—they began, I say, with that little knowledge of music which they had and with no regard for the laws of Terpander or of any other approved and authoritative legislator, to seek a way of somehow delighting the ear with the mere sound of the instrument, without the aid of the voice. And they decided that the variety of consonances and harmonies would be an effective means of coloring this design. Before this time the use of these for the purpose we have mentioned had not been approved by anyone of sound mind, but greatly and with just cause abhorred, for it was well known that consonance had the power of arousing discord in listeners whose minds were well-ordered. . . .

Thus the cithara players, wishing to make up for their defect, introduced upon the artificial instruments this way of playing several airs together in consonance. Long practicing these, and looking always toward the prescribed end, they began, by long experience, to distinguish in them what displeased, what caused annoyance, and finally what delighted the ear. And to have a broader and more spacious field, they introduced not only the use of imperfect consonances (discreetly so called to make it seem rather that they were consonances) but also that of dissonances, seeing that with only the five consonances that the ancients esteemed (those now called perfect), the matter became tedious and difficult to manage. . . .

The practical players of those times therefore began to form, upon the instruments that I have mentioned to you above, their rules and laws. The first of these was, that when not more than two strings were sounded at once, it was forbidden to take, one after another, two of those consonances that are today called perfect, when these were of the same species and genus. For this there was no other reason than that with two strings only, these consonances, because of the simplicity of their extreme sounds, do not completely delight the ear, for hearing, like all the other senses, takes pleasure in the diversity of its proper objects. On the other hand they admitted two and three imperfect consonances as less simple and more varied, not because of the difference of the major or minor tone that is found between them, as some make bold to say, but because of the variety of their extremes, which do not blend so well in this respect as those of the perfect consonances. And it is clear that this rule of not taking two or more perfect consonances one after another under the conditions mentioned above was enacted by the legislators only for the situation in which two strings and not more were sounded at the same time, for when three, four, or more strings were sounded upon the artificial instruments, they allowed them, just as they are allowed today, without offense to the ear.

I am well aware that some pedants of our time (I know no politer name to call them by) make bold to say, to those simpler than themselves who listen to them as miracles, that on the keyboard instruments of which they make profession, changing the fingers conceals the two perfect consonances from the sight and not the hearing of those who observe them attentively. Notice, please, what unheard-of folly this is, to wish to make sight a competent judge of the different quality of sounds, which is equivalent to saying that hearing has a share in discerning the differences of colors.

It was from this way of playing in consonance, I say then, that practical musicians, a little before our grandfathers' time, derived the belief that it was also possible to compose and to sing in this manner, for the ancient and learned manner had been lost many, many years before as a result of wars or other circumstances. Of this ancient manner we shall speak a little further on, and we shall throw upon it, in addition to the light we have already thrown, the greatest light possible to our feeble powers, with the sole object of inciting great and virtuous minds to labor in so noble a science and to see to bringing it back to its first and happy state. This I do not consider impossible, knowing that it was not revealed by the stars to those who first discovered it and brought it to the height of perfection, but of a certainty acquired by industrious art and assiduous study. The ancient music, I say, was lost, along with all the liberal arts and sciences, and its light has so dimmed that many consider its wonderful excellence a dream and a fable.

After its loss they began to derive from the stringed and wind instruments and also from the organ, which was in use in those times, although somewhat different from ours, rules and a norm for composing and singing several airs together, just as they had played them on the instruments. And they adopted as laws the same practices that the cithara players and organists had previously been observing, excepting that of not using two perfect consonances of the same species when four or more voices were singing together; perhaps to make the matter more difficult, or to show that they had a more refined and delicate ear than their predecessors, or actually believing that the same conditions which govern the relations of two voices singing together also govern those of four or six or more.

This way of composing and singing, by the novelty which it introduced, along with the ease of quickly becoming a musician, pleased the generality of people, as usually happens, thanks to their imperfection and the little knowledge they always have of what is good and true, and gave opportunities for the artisans to indulge in wild fancies and to introduce further novel doctrines, for the latest comers were unwilling to follow in the footsteps of their predecessors and wholly to approve their work, lest they should seem to be almost confessing by silent consent their inferiority to them in industry and talent; all this with the aim of bringing music to the ruin in which we find it. For this reason they added to the rule that it was permissible to use two imperfect consonances, that these must necessarily be of different species, and further, that in proceeding from imperfect to perfect consonance the progression should always be to the nearest, always meaning in compositions for two voices.

Now you see how, little by little, lured by ambition, they went on without at all perceiving it, making reason subject to sense, the form to the material, the true to the false. Not content with this, men of our time have added to the way of proceeding from imperfect to perfect consonance and from imperfect to imperfect, the rule that one must take into consideration and indeed avoid the relations of the tritone and semidiapente which may arise between the one part and the other, and they have therefore decreed that when a third follows a major sixth, it should always be minor (because the parts have changed position by contrary motion), and that when the major third is followed by a sixth, it should always be minor, and vice versa. They decreed further that when four or more parts are singing together, the lowest part should never be without its third and fifth (or instead of the fifth, the sixth) or one of their extensions.

There is no one who does not consider these rules excellent and necessary for the mere delight the ear takes in the variety of the harmonies, but for the expression of conceptions they are pestilent, being fit for nothing but to make the concentus varied and full, and this is not always, indeed is never suited to express any conception of the poet or the orator. I repeat, therefore, that if the rules in question had been applied to their original purpose, those who have amplified them in modern times would deserve no less praise than those who first laid them down, but the whole mistake is that the purpose today is different, indeed directly opposed to that of the first inventors of this kind of music, while what the true purpose is has long been evident. It was never the intention of the inventors that these rules should have to serve for the use of those harmonies that, combined with words and with the appropriate passion, express the conceptions of the mind; they were to serve for the sound of the artificial instruments alone, both stringed and wind, as may be gathered from what we have said thus far of their first authors. But the matter has always been understood in the opposite way by their successors, and this belief has endured so long that I think it will be most difficult, if not impossible, to remove and dispel it from men's minds, especially from the minds of those who are mere practitioners of this kind of counterpoint, and therefore esteemed and prized by the vulgar and salaried by various gentlemen, and who have been informing others about this practice, by them called music, down to the present day.

For if anyone wished to persuade such men as these that they were ignorant of the true music, he would need, not the rhetoric of Cicero or Demosthenes, but the sword of the paladin Orlando,[7] or the authority of some great prince who was a friend to truth and who might abandon the vulgar music to the vulgar, as suited to them, and persuade the noble, by his example, to devote themselves to the music suited to them. This is the music that Aristotle calls honest and used with dignity, for in the well-ordered state, as he says in his Eighth Book [of the *Politics*], those forms of music that are like the vulgar, corrupt and removed from the true form, are conceded to the vulgar, as are those so much admired and prized by them today, for each naturally seeks his like. But of this, enough said.

Consider each rule of the modern contrapuntists by itself, or, if you wish, consider them all together. They aim at nothing but the delight of the ear, if it can truly be called delight. They have not a book among them for their use and convenience that speaks of how to express the conceptions of the mind and of how to impress them with the greatest possible effectiveness on the minds of the listeners; of this they do not think and never have thought since the invention of this kind of music, but only of how to disfigure it still more, if such a thing be possible. And that in truth the last thing the moderns think of is the expression of the words with the passion that these require, excepting in the ridiculous way that I shall shortly relate, let it be a manifest sign that their observances and rules amount to nothing more than a manner of modulating about among the musical intervals with the aim of making the music a contest of varied harmonies according to the rules stated above and without further thought of the conception and sense of the words. And if it were permitted me, I should like to show you, with several examples of authority, that among the most famous contrapuntists of this century there are some who do not even know how to read, let alone understand. Their ignorance and lack of consideration is one of the most potent reasons why the music of today does not cause in the listeners any of those virtuous and wonderful effects that ancient music caused. . . .

If the object of the modern practical musicians is, as they say, to delight the sense of hearing with the variety of the consonances, and if this property of tickling (for it cannot with truth be called delight in any other sense)

7. The reference is to the Renaissance epic romance *Orlando furioso* by the poet of Ferrara, Ludovico Ariosto.

resides in a simple piece of hollow wood over which are stretched four, six, or more strings of the gut of a dumb beast or of some other material, disposed according to the nature of the harmonic numbers, or in a given number of natural reeds or of artificial ones made of wood, metal, or some other material, divided by proportioned and suitable measures, with a little air blowing inside them while they are touched or struck by the clumsy and untutored hand of some base idiot or other, then let this object of delighting with the variety of their harmonies be abandoned to these instruments, for being without sense, movement, intellect, speech, discourse, reason, or soul, they are capable of nothing else. But let men, who have been endowed by nature with all these noble and excellent parts, endeavor to use them not merely to delight, but as imitators of the good ancients, to improve at the same time, for they have the capacity to do this and in doing otherwise they are acting contrary to nature, which is the handmaiden of God.

Judicious and learned men, when they regard the various colors and shapes of objects, do not find satisfaction, like the ignorant multitude, in the mere pleasure that sight affords, but in investigating afterwards the mutual appropriateness and proportion of these incidental attributes and likewise their properties and nature. In the same way, I say that it is not enough merely to take pleasure in the various harmonies heard between the parts of a musical composition unless one also determines the proportion in which the voices are combined, in order not to be like the herbalist who in his simplicity knows nothing about simples except their names—and such are most of those who pass for musicians today among the vulgar.

Among their absurdities and novelties is also numbered that of sometimes transposing music originally composed according to natural, singable, and usual movements up or down to strange pitches that are unsingable, altogether out of the ordinary, and full of artifice (just as skilled organists are accustomed to transpose for the convenience of the chorus, using accidental signs, by a tone, a third, or some other interval), and this only in order to vaunt themselves and their achievements as miracles before those more ignorant than themselves. Add to this that among the more famous there are and always have been those who have first put notes together according to their caprice and have then fitted to them whatever words they pleased, not minding at all that there was the same incongruity between the words and their notes as that which has been said to exist between the dithyramb and the Dorian harmony, or a greater one, for even men of worth are amazed that most modern compositions sound better when well played than when well sung, failing to perceive that their purpose is to be communicated to the hearer by means of artificial instruments and not of natural ones, since they are artifice itself and not at all natural. And to diminish still further their amazement and my trouble in so often reciting the words of others, let them read in this connection the tenth problem in Aristotle's Nineteenth Book, which will dispose of them.

Beyond the beauty and grace of the consonances, there is nothing ingenious or choice in modern counterpoint excepting the use of the dissonances, provided these are arranged with the necessary means and judiciously resolved. For the expression of conceptions in order to impress the passions on the listener, both of them are not merely a great impediment, but the worst of poisons. The reason is this: the continual sweetness of the various harmonies, combined with the slight harshness and bitterness of the various dissonances (besides the thousand other sorts of artifice that the contrapuntists of our day have so industriously sought out to allure our ears, to enumerate which I omit lest I become tedious), these are, as I have said, the greatest impediment to moving the mind to any passion. For the mind, being chiefly taken up and, so to speak, bound by the snares of the pleasure thus produced, is not given time to understand, let alone consider, the badly uttered words. All this is wholly different from what is necessary to passion from its nature, for passion and moral character must be simple and natural, or at least appear so, and their sole aim must be to arouse their counterpart in others.

Strozzi: From what you have said thus far may be gathered, it seems, among other important things, that the music of today is not of great value for expressing the passions of the mind by means of words, but is of value merely for the wind and stringed instruments, from which the ear, it appears, desires nothing but the sweet enjoyment of the variety of their harmonies, combined with the suitable and proportioned movements of which they have an abundance; these are then made manifest to the ear by some practiced and skilled performer.

Bardi: What you say would always be the case if the various harmonies of the artificial instruments were fit only to divert and tickle the ears, as you say, and if the contrapuntists of our time were content to disfigure only the part of music that pertains to the expression of conceptions. But they have not been content with this and have treated no better the part having to do with the harmonies of the artificial instruments in themselves and concerned with the pleasure of the sense without going on to that of the mind. This too they have reduced to such estate that if it were to get the least bit worse, it would need rather to be buried than to be cured. . . .

Finally I come as I promised to the treatment of the most important and principal part of music, the imitation of the conceptions that are derived from the words. After disposing of this question I shall speak to you about the principles observed by the ancient musicians.

Our practical contrapuntists say, or rather hold to be certain, that they have expressed the conceptions of the mind in the proper manner and have imitated the words whenever, in setting to music a sonnet, *canzone*, *romanzo*, madrigal, or other poem in which there occurs a line saying, for example: "Bitter heart and savage, and cruel will,"[8] which is the first line of one of the sonnets of Petrarch, they have caused many sevenths, fourths, seconds, and major sixths to be sung between the parts and by means of these have made a rough, harsh, and unpleasant sound in the ears of the listeners.

The sound is indeed not unlike that given by the cithara of Orpheus in the hands of Neantius, the son of Pittacus, the tyrant of the Greek island of Lesbos, where flourished the greatest and most esteemed musicians of the world, in honor of whose greatness it had been deposited there, we read, after the death of the remarkable cithara player Pericletus, the glorious winner in the Carneian festival of the Lacedaemonians. When this Neantius played upon the cithara in question, it was revealed by his lack of skill that the strings were partly of wolf-gut and partly of lamb-gut, and because of this imperfection—or because of the transgression he had committed in taking the sacred cithara from the temple by deceit, believing that the virtue of playing it well resided in it by magic, as in Bradamante's lance that of throwing to the ground whomsoever she touched with it—he received, when he played it, condign punishment, being devoured by dogs.[9] This was his only resemblance to the learned poet, sage priest, and unique musician who as you know was slain by the Bacchantes.

At another time they will say that they are imitating the words when among the conceptions of these there are any meaning "to flee" or "to fly"; these they will declaim with the greatest rapidity and the least grace imaginable. In connection with words meaning "to disappear," "to swoon," "to die," or actually "to be extinct" they have made the parts break off so abruptly, that instead of inducing the passion corresponding to any of these, they have aroused laughter and at other times contempt in the listeners, who felt that they were being ridiculed. Then with words meaning "alone," "two," or "together" they have caused one lone part, or two, or all the parts together to sing with unheard-of elegance. Others, in the singing of this particular line from one of the sestinas of Petrarch: "And with the lame ox he will be pursuing Laura,"[10] have declaimed it to staggering, wavering, syncopated notes as though they had the hiccups. And when, as sometimes happens, the conceptions they have had in hand made mention of the rolling of the drum, or of the sound of the trumpet or any other such instrument, they have sought to represent its sound in their music, without

8. Petrarca, *Canzoniere*, 265.
10. *Canzoniere*, 239.
9. *Orlando furioso*, 8.17; 30.15.

minding at all that they were pronouncing these words in some unheard-of manner. Finding words denoting diversity of color, such as "dark" or "light" hair and similar expressions, they have put black or white notes beneath them to express this sort of conception craftily and gracefully, as they say, meanwhile making the sense of hearing subject to the accidents of color and shape, the particular objects of sight and, in solid bodies, of touch. Nor has there been any lack of those who, still more corrupt, have sought to portray with notes the words "azure" and "violet" according to their sound, just as the stringmakers nowadays color their gut strings. At another time, finding the line: "He descended into hell, into the lap of Pluto," they have made one part of the composition descend in such a way that the singer has sounded more like someone groaning to frighten children and terrify them than like anyone singing sense. In the opposite way, finding this one: "This one aspires to the stars," in declaiming it they have ascended to a height that no one shrieking from excessive pain, internal or external, has ever reached. And coming, as sometimes happens, to words meaning "weep," "laugh," "sing," "shout," "shriek," or to "false deceits," "harsh chains," "hard bonds," "rugged mount," "unyielding rock," "cruel woman," and the like, to say nothing of their sighs, unusual forms, and so on, they have declaimed them, to color their absurd and vain designs, in manners more outlandish than those of any far-off barbarian.

Unhappy men, they do not perceive that if Isocrates or Corax or any of the other famous orators had ever, in an oration, uttered two of these words in such a fashion, they would have moved all their hearers to laughter and contempt and would besides this have been derided and despised by them as men foolish, abject, and worthless. And yet they wonder that the music of their times produces none of the notable effects that ancient music produced, when, quite the other way, they would have more cause for amazement if it were to produce any of them, seeing that their music is so remote from the ancient music and so unlike it as actually to be its contrary and its mortal enemy, as has been said and proved and will be proved still more, and seeing that it has no means enabling it even to think of producing such effects, let alone to obtain them. For its sole aim is to delight the ear, while that of ancient music is to induce in another the same passion that one feels oneself. No person of judgment understands the expression of the conceptions of the mind by means of words in this ridiculous manner, but in another, far removed and very different.

Strozzi: I pray you, tell me how.

Bardi: In the same way that, among many others, those two famous orators that I mentioned a little while ago expressed them, and afterwards every musician of repute. And if they wish to understand the manner of it, I shall content myself with showing them how and from whom they can learn with little pain and trouble and with the greatest pleasure, and it will be thus: when they go for their amusement to the tragedies and comedies that the mummers act, let them a few times leave off their immoderate laughing, and instead be so good as to observe, when one quiet gentleman speaks with another, in what manner he speaks, how high or low his voice is pitched, with what volume of sound, with what sort of accents and gestures, and with what rapidity or slowness his words are uttered. Let them mark a little what difference obtains in all these things when one of them speaks with one of his servants, or one of these with another; let them observe the prince when he chances to be conversing with one of his subjects and vassals; when with the petitioner who is entreating his favor; how the man infuriated or excited speaks; the married woman, the girl, the mere child, the clever harlot, the lover speaking to his mistress as he seeks to persuade her to grant his wishes, the man who laments, the one who cries out, the timid man, and the man exultant with joy. From these variations of circumstance, if they observe them attentively and examine them with care, they will be able to select the norm of what is fitting for the expression of any other conception whatever that can call for their handling.

Every brute beast has the natural faculty of communicating its pleasure and its pain of body and mind, at least to those of its own species, nor was voice given to them by nature for any other purpose. And among rational animals there are some so stupid that, since they do not know, thanks to their worthlessness, how to make practical application of this faculty and how to profit by it on occasion, they believe that they are without it naturally.

When the ancient musician sang any poem whatever, he first considered very diligently the character of the person speaking: his age, his sex, with whom he was speaking, and the effect he sought to produce by this means; and these conceptions, previously clothed by the poet in chosen words suited to such a need, the musician then expressed in the tone and with the accents and gestures, the quantity and quality of sound, and the rhythm appropriate to that action and to such a person. For this reason we read of Timotheus, who in the opinion of Suidas[11] was a player of the aulos and not of the cithara, that when he roused the great Alexander with the difficult mode of Minerva to combat with the armies of his foes, not only did the circumstances mentioned reveal themselves in the rhythms, the words, and the conceptions of the entire song in conformity with his desire, but in my opinion at least, his habit, the aspect of his countenance, and each particular gesture and member must have shown on this occasion that he was burning with desire to fight, to overcome, and to conquer the enemy. For

11. The early Byzantine collector of ancient biographical lore. The reference is to the biography of Timotheus in his *Lexicon*.

this reason Alexander was forced to cry out for his arms and to say that this should be the song of kings. And rightly, for provided the impediments have been removed, if the musician has not the power to direct the minds of his listeners to their benefit, his science and knowledge are to be reputed null and vain, since the art of music was instituted and numbered among the liberal arts for no other purpose. . . .

Strozzi: I have only one remaining doubt, Signor Giovanni, which by your leave will serve as a seal for our discussion, and it is this: how does it happen that the compositions of many who are generally reputed to be great players, both of the lute and of the keyboard instruments, do not succeed when they play them on these instruments, and that other players, also of repute, have left no other memory than their names? And that on the other hand there are some of little repute with the general public who have succeeded excellently in writing in their chosen profession? And that other musicians are very learned and erudite, and for all that, on the practical side, their compositions have not been at all satisfactory when performed? And that others will hardly know how to read, and will have very little knowledge of practical matters, especially in music, and for all that they will succeed marvelously in counterpoint? And finally, which of these are to be more reputed and esteemed, and which less, and why?

Bardi: Properly to clear up your doubts, I should need your permission to speak freely (for at the beginning of our discussion you said that this befitted those who seek the truth of things), but since according to the flatterers of today it is ill-bred to name anyone and reproach him with reason in order that he may learn his error and mend his ways, I shall go over them in whatever random order occurs to me and say what I think of them with the greatest modesty at my command, not because what could be said of any is not pure truth, but in order not to be considered slanderous (even with complete injustice) by the envious and malicious.

I say then that in our times there have been and are many excellent players, both of the lute and of the keyboard instruments, among whom some have indeed known how to play well and how to write well, or let us say how to compose well, for their instrument, as for the keyboard instrument an Annibale Padovano and for the lute a Fabrizio Dentice, noble Neapolitan.

Others there have been and are who . . . will know how to write and to show their knowledge excellently and who will observe every slightest particular detail that is needed for good playing and good composition, but apart from this the imagination of one is so lacking in invention, and the fingers and hands of another, either from some natural defect, or from having exercised them little, or from some other circumstance, are so weak or so unskilled in obeying the commands given to them by reason, that he is unable to express the passions with them as he understands them and has engraved them in his thought; these are the reasons why neither the one nor the other gives entire satisfaction in what he does and why they give up the attempt, still seeking, like the orator, to remedy this defect with the pen, with which some of them have been remarkably successful.

Others there have been and are who will play well on one or the other instrument and yet will write badly. Of these a part, being more prudent, have never taken the pains to show their knowledge to the world with the pen, and if they have composed or written anything, have not published it, well aware that it was of little or no worth and that it would thus have brought discredit on them if it had come into the hands of this or that man of understanding.

There are others who have not known how to do the one thing or the other; none the less they have been and are reputed by many to be men of worth. And the same thing that has happened to players has likewise happened (as you will understand) to simple contrapuntists.

5
The Religious Reformation

20. Martin Luther, *Letter to Pope Leo X*

Luther (1483–1546) was an Augustinian canon and professor of Holy
Scriptures at the University of Wittenberg in Saxony, which bestowed
upon him the degree of doctor of theology in 1512. His theological inves-
tigations and meditations suddenly attracted widespread public attention
when, on 31 October 1517, he responded to the current campaign to
encourage the purchase of indulgences (the remission of penalties merited in the next world for sins committed, but absolved in the Sacrament
of Penance) in a typically academic manner: by posting ninety-five theses
for debate upon the door of the cathedral. The ensuing controversy, described in this letter, led him further to clarify his position, and to expound it in the three major treatises of 1520, *To the Christian Nobility of
the German Nation*, *On the Babylonian Captivity of the Church*, and *A
Treatise on Christian Liberty*. The *Letter to Pope Leo* was intended as a
cover letter for the latter. Needless to say, it did not reach its destination:
the pope excommunicated him in January 1521, and the princes of the
Holy Roman Empire agreed to enforce the excommunication bull at the
imperial diet of the following April.

After a year in hiding (at the *Wartburg*), Luther launched a vigorous
campaign on behalf of his theological doctrines. These doctrines were
summarized in definitive form in the Augsburg Confession of 1530,
which was promulgated as the official creed of the Lutheran churches by
a large number of German princes. They thereafter collaborated with

From *Works of Martin Luther*, translated by W. A. Lambert (Philadelphia: Muhlenberg
Press, 1915), pp. 301–11. Some footnotes deleted.

Luther in reorganizing the ecclesiastical institutions under their political jurisdictions in accordance with those doctrines.

To Leo the Tenth, Pope at Rome: Martin Luther wishes thee salvation in Christ Jesus our Lord. Amen.

In the midst of the monsters of this age with whom I am now for the third year waging war, I am compelled at times to look up also to thee, Leo, most blessed Father, and to think of thee; nay, since thou art now and again regarded as the sole cause of my warfare, I cannot but think of thee always. And although the causeless raging of thy godless flatterers against me has compelled me to appeal from thy See to a future council, despite those most empty decrees of thy predecessors Pius and Julius,[1] who with a foolish tyranny forbade such an appeal, yet I have never so estranged my mind from thy Blessedness as not with all my heart to wish thee and thy See every blessing, for which I have, as much as lay in me, besought God with earnest prayers. It is true, I have made bold almost to despise and to triumph over those who have tried to frighten me with the majesty of thy name and authority. But there is one thing which I cannot despise, and that is my excuse for writing once more to thy Blessedness. I understand that I am accused of great rashness, and that this rashness is said to be my great fault, in which, they say, I have not spared even thy person.

For my part, I will openly confess that I know I have only spoken good and honorable things of thee whenever I have made mention of thy name. And if I had done otherwise, I myself could by no means approve of it, but would entirely approve the judgment others have formed of me, and do nothing more gladly than recant such rashness and impiety on my part. I have called thee a Daniel in Babylon, and every one who reads knows with what zeal I defended thy notable innocence against thy defamer, Sylvester.[2] Indeed, thy reputation and the fame of thy blameless life, sung as they are throughout the world by the writings of so many great men, are too well known and too high to be assailed in any way by any one man, however great he may be. I am not so foolish as to attack him whom everyone praises: it has rather been, and always will be, my endeavor not to attack

1. Pius II (Enea Silvio Piccolomini, 1405–64) had originally supported the Council of Basel (1431–49) in its conflict with Pope Eugenius IV; after he became pope, he issued the bull *Execrabilis*, which forbade appeals from papal decisions to a future council. Julius II (on whom see the selections in this volume from Luca Landucci, Machiavelli, and Vasari's *Life of Michelangelo*) summoned the Fifth Lateran Council at Rome in 1512 in response to the anti-papal council called with the backing of King Louis XII the year before, first at Pisa, then at Milan.

2. The Dominican Sylvester Prierias, Master of the Sacred Palace, to whom Leo X turned over Luther's writings for a judgment on their orthodoxy in 1519.

even those whom public report decries; for I take no pleasure in the crimes of any man, since I am conscious enough of the great beam in my own eye, nor could I be he that should cast the first stone at the adultress.

I have indeed sharply inveighed against ungodly teachings in general, and I have not been slow to bite my adversaries, not because of their immorality, but because of their ungodliness. And of this I repent so little that I have determined to persevere in that fervent zeal, and to despise the judgment of men, following the example of Christ, Who in His zeal called His adversaries a generation of vipers, blind, hypocrites, children of the devil. And Paul arraigned the sorcerer as a child of the devil full of all subtlety and mischief, and brands others as dogs, deceivers, and adulterers. If you will allow those delicate ears to judge, nothing would be more biting and more unrestrained than Paul. Who is more biting than the prophets? Nowadays, it is true, our ears are made so delicate by the mad crowds of flatterers that as soon as we meet with a disapproving voice we cry out that we are bitten, and when we cannot ward off the truth with any other pretext we put it to flight by ascribing it to a fierce temper, impatience, and shamelessness. What is the good of salt if it does not bite? Or of the edge of the sword if it does not kill? Cursed be he that doeth the work of the Lord deceitfully.

Wherefore, most excellent Leo, I pray thee, after I have by this letter vindicated myself, give me a hearing, and believe that I have never thought evil of thy person, but that I am a man who would wish thee all good things eternally, and that I have no quarrel with any man concerning his morality, but only concerning the Word of truth. In all things else I will yield to any man whatsoever: to give up or to deny the Word I have neither the power nor the will. If any man thinks otherwise of me, or has understood my words differently, he does not think aright, nor has he understood what I have really said.

But thy See, which is called the Roman Curia, and of which neither thou nor any man can deny that it is more corrupt than any Babylon or Sodom ever was, and which is, as far as I can see, characterized by a totally depraved, hopeless, and notorious wickedness—that See I have truly despised, and I have been incensed to think that in thy name and under the guise of the Roman Church the people of Christ are mocked. And so I have resisted and will resist that See, as long as the spirit of faith shall live in me. Not that I shall strive after the impossible or hope that by my lone efforts anything will be accomplished in that most disordered Babylon, where the rage of so many sycophants is turned against me; but I acknowledge myself a debtor to my brethren, whom it is my duty to warn, that fewer of them may be destroyed by the plagues of Rome, or at least that their destruction may be less cruel.

For, as thou well knowest, these many years there has flowed forth from Rome, like a flood covering the world, nothing but a laying waste of men's bodies and souls and possessions and the worst possible examples of the worst possible things. For all this is clearer than the day to all men, and the Roman Church, once the most holy of all, has become the most licentious den of thieves, the most shameless of all brothels, the kingdom of sin, death and hell; so that even Antichrist himself, should he come, could think of nothing to add to its wickedness.

Meanwhile thou, Leo, sittest as a lamb in the midst of wolves, like Daniel in the midst of the lions, and, with Ezekiel, thou dwellest among scorpions. What canst thou do single-handed, against these monsters? Join to thyself three or four thoroughly learned and thoroughly good cardinals: what are even these among so many? You would all be poisoned before you could undertake to make a single decree to help matters. There is no hope for the Roman Curia: the wrath of God is come upon it to the end; it hates councils, it fears a reformation, it cannot reduce the raging of its wickedness, and is meriting the praise bestowed upon its mother, of whom it is written, "We have cured Babylon, but she is not healed: let us forsake her."[3] It was thy duty, indeed, and that of thy cardinals, to remedy these evils, but that gout of theirs mocks the healing hand, and neither chariot nor horse heeds the guiding rein. Moved by such sympathy for thee, I have always grieved, most excellent Leo, that thou hast been made pope in these times, for thou wert worthy of better days. The Roman Curia has not deserved to have thee or men like thee, but rather Satan himself; and in truth it is he more than thou who rules in that Babylon.

O would that thou mightest lay aside what thy most mischievous enemies boast of as thy glory and wert living on some small priestly income of thine own or on thy family inheritance! To glory in that glory none are worthy save the Iscariots, the sons of perdition. For what dost thou accomplish in the Curia, my dear Leo? Only this: the more criminal and abominable a man is, the more successfully will he use thy name and authority to destroy the wealth and the souls of men, to increase crime, to suppress faith and truth and the whole Church of God. O truly, most unhappy Leo, thou sittest on a most dangerous throne; for I tell thee the truth, because I wish thee well. If Bernard pitied his Pope Eugene at a time when the Roman See,[4] although even then most corrupt, yet ruled with better prospects, why should not we lament who have for three hundred years had so great an increase of corruption and worthlessness? Is it not true that under yon vast expanse of heaven there is nothing more corrupt, more pestilential, more

---

3. Jer. 51:9.

4. Bernard of Clairvaux addressed a book *De Consideratione* on the dangers of the papal office to Pope Eugenius III (1145–53).

hateful than the Roman Curia? It surpasses the godlessness of the Turks beyond all comparison, so that in truth, whereas it was once a gate of heaven, it is now an open mouth of hell, and such a mouth as, because of the wrath of God, cannot be shut; there is only one thing that we can try to do, as I have said: perchance we may be able to call back a few from that yawning chasm of Rome and so save them.

Now thou seest, my Father Leo, how and why I have so violently attacked that pestilential See: for so far have I been from raging against thy person that I even hoped I might gain thy favor and save thee, if I should make a strong and sharp assault upon that prison, nay that hell of thine. For thou and thy salvation and the salvation of many others with thee will be served by every thing that men of ability can contribute to the confusion of this wicked Curia. They do thy work, who bring evil upon it; they glorify Christ, who in every way curse it. In short, they are Christians who are not Romans.

To go yet farther, I never intended to inveigh against the Roman Curia, or to raise any controversy concerning it. For when I saw that all efforts to save it were hopeless, I despised it and gave it a bill of divorcement and said to it, "He that is filthy, let him be filthy still, and he that is unclean, let him be unclean still."[5] Then I gave myself to the quiet and peaceful study of holy Scripture, that I might thus be of benefit to my brethren about me. When I had made some progress in these studies, Satan opened his eyes and filled his servant John Eck, a notable enemy of Christ, with an insatiable lust for glory, and thereby stirred him up to drag me at unawares into a disputation, laying hold on me by one little word about the primacy of the Roman Church which I had incidentally let fall. Then that boasting braggart, frothing and gnashing his teeth, declared that he would venture all for the glory of God and the honor of the holy Apostolic See, and, puffed up with the hope of misusing thy power, he looked forward with perfect confidence to a victory over me. He sought not so much to establish the primacy of Peter as his own leadership among the theologians of our time; and to that end he thought it no small help if he should triumph over Luther. When that debate ended unhappily for the sophist, an incredible madness overcame the man: for he feels that he alone must bear the blame of all that I have brought forth to the shame of Rome.

But permit me, I pray thee, most excellent Leo, this once to plead my cause and to make charges against thy real enemies. Thou knowest, I believe, what dealings thy legate, Cardinal of St. Sixtus,[6] an unwise and un-

5. Rev. 22:11.
6. Cajetan, or Gaetano (from his birthplace, Gaeta), was the Dominican theologian Tommaso de Vio made a cardinal by Leo X in 1518 and sent as his legate to the Diet of Augsburg for the purpose of overcoming resistence in Germany to the imposition of a crusade tax.

fortunate, or rather, unfaithful man, had with me. When, because of reverence for thy name, I had put myself and all my case in his hand, he did not try to establish peace, although with a single word he could easily have done so, since I at that time promised to keep silent and to end the controversy, if my opponents were ordered to do the same. But as he was a man who sought glory and was not content with that agreement, he began to justify my opponents, to give them full freedom and to order me to recant, a thing not included in his instructions. When the matter was in a fair way, his untimely arbitrariness brought it into a far worse condition. Therefore, for what followed later Luther is not to blame; all the blame is Cajetan's, who did not suffer me to keep silent and to rest, as I then most earnestly asked him to do. What more should I have done?

Next came Carl Miltitz,[7] also a nuncio of thy Blessedness, who after great and varied efforts and constant going to and fro, although he omitted nothing that might help to restore that status of the question which Cajetan had rashly and haughtily disturbed, at last with the help of the most illustrious prince, Frederick the elector, barely managed to arrange several private conferences with me. Again I yielded to your name, I was prepared to keep silent, and even accepted as arbiter either the archbishop of Trier or the bishop of Naumburg. So matters were arranged. But while this plan was being followed with good prospects of success, lo, that other and greater enemy of thine, Eck,[8] broke in with the Leipzig Disputation which he had undertaken against Dr. Carlstadt.[9] When a new question concerning the primacy of the pope was raised, he suddenly turned his weapons against me and quite overthrew that counsel of peace. Meanwhile Carl Miltitz waited: a disputation was held, judges were selected; but here also

7. Carl Miltitz was a Saxon nobleman (hence Luther's compatriot) and a papal chamberlain whom Leo X sent as an emissary to Duke Frederick of Saxony in 1518. The next year he met with Luther in an unsuccessful effort to persuade him to be reconciled with the Roman Church.

8. Johann Eck (1486–1541) was born Hans Maier in Egg (hence his surname) in Swabia. He received a doctorate in 1510 and thereafter taught theology at the University of Ingolstadt in Bavaria (i.e., his career was parallel to Luther's). His knowledge of Greek and Hebrew and of the Church fathers made him a formidable debator; and it was largely he, during the Leipzig debates of July 1519, who forced Luther into several of his more radical theological positions. Thereafter he became the principal champion of Catholicism in Germany. The best known of his many works in the *Enchiridion Locorum Communium* ("Handbook of Commonplaces"). It went through some ninety editions during the sixteenth century and has recently been translated into English by Ford Lewis Battles (Grand Rapids: Baker Book House, 1979).

9. Andreas Carlstadt (Bodenstein), the dean of the theological faculty at Wittenberg who conferred Luther's doctoral degree on him. He was largely responsible for introducing a new liturgy in the church of Wittenberg in 1521. He represented Luther in the first sessions of the Leipzig debates of 1519.

no decision was reached, and no wonder: through the lies, the tricks, the wiles of Eck everything was stirred up, aggravated, and confounded worse than ever, so that whatever decision might have been reached, a greater conflagration would have resulted. For he sought glory, not the truth. Here also I left nothing undone that I ought to have done.

I admit that on this occasion no small amount of corrupt Roman practices came to light, but whatever wrong was done was the fault of Eck, who undertook a task beyond his strength, and, while he strove madly for his own glory, revealed the shame of Rome to all the world. He is thy enemy, my dear Leo, or rather the enemy of thy Curia. From the example of this one man thou canst learn that there is no enemy more injurious than a flatterer. For what did he accomplish with his flattery but an evil which no king could have accomplished? Today the name of the Roman Curia is a stench throughout the world, and papal authority languishes, ignorance that was once held in honor is evil spoken of; and of all this we should have heard nothing if Eck had not upset the counsel of peace planned by Carl and myself, as he himself now clearly sees, and is angry, too late and to no purpose, that my books were published. This he should have thought of when, like a horse that whinnies on the picket line, he was madly seeking only his own glory and sought only his own gain through thee at the greatest peril to thee. The vainglorious man thought that I would stop and keep silent at the terror of thy name; for I do not believe that he trusted entirely to his talents and learning. Now, when he sees that I have more courage than that and have not been silenced, he repents too late of his rashness and understands that there is One in heaven who resists the proud and humbles the haughty, if indeed he does understand it at last.

Since we gained nothing by this disputation except that we brought greater confusion to the cause of Rome, Carl Miltitz made a third attempt; he came to the fathers of the Augustinian Order assembled in their chapter, and asked counsel in settling the controversy which had now grown most confused and dangerous. Since, by the favor of God, they had no hope of being able to proceed against me with violence, some of the most famous of their number were sent to me, and asked me at least to show honor to the person of thy Blessedness, and in a humble letter to plead as my excuse thy innocence and mine; they said that the affair was not yet in the most desperate state if of his innate goodness Leo the Tenth would take a hand in it. As I have always both offered and desired peace that I might devote myself to quieter and more useful studies and have stormed with so great fury merely for the purpose of overwhelming by volume and violence of words, no less than of intellect, those whom I knew to be very unequal foes: I not only gladly ceased, but also with joy and thankfulness considered it a most welcome kindness to me if our hope could be fulfilled.

So I come, most blessed Father, and, prostrate before thee, I pray, if it be possible do thou interpose and hold in check those flatterers, who are the enemies of peace while they pretend to keep peace. But that I will recant, most blessed Father, let no one imagine, unless he prefer to involve the whole question in greater turmoil. Furthermore, I will accept no rules for the interpretation of the Word of God, since the Word of God, which teaches the liberty of all things else, dare not be bound. Grant me these two points, and there is nothing that I could not or would not most gladly do or endure. I hate disputations; I will draw out no one; but then I do not wish others to draw me out; if they do, as Christ is my Teacher, I will not be speechless. For, when once this controversy has been cited before thee and settled, thy Blessedness will be able with a small and easy word to silence both parties and command them to keep the peace, and that is what I have always wished to hear.

Do not listen, therefore, my dear Leo, to those sirens who make thee out to be no mere man but a demigod, so that thou mayest command and require what thou wilt. It will not be done in that fashion, and thou wilt not succeed. Thou art a servant of servants, and beyond all other men in a most pitiable and most dangerous position. Be not deceived by those who pretend that thou art lord of the world and allow no one to be a Christian unless he accept thy authority; who prate that thou hast power over heaven, hell, and purgatory. These are thy enemies and seek thy soul to destroy it; as Isaiah says, "O my people, they that call thee blessed, the same deceive thee." They err who exalt thee above a council and above the Church universal. They err who ascribe to thee alone the right of interpreting Scripture; for under cover of thy name they seek to establish all their own wickedness in the Church, and alas! through them Satan has already made much headway under thy predecessors. In short, believe none who exalt thee, believe those who humble thee. For this is the judgment of God; "He hath put down the mighty from their seat, and hath exalted the humble." [10] See, how unlike His successors is Christ, although they all would be His vicars. And I fear that most of them have indeed been too literally His vicars. For a vicar is a vicar only when his lord is absent. And if the pope rules while Christ is absent and does not dwell in his heart, what else is he but a vicar of Christ? But what is such a Church except a mass of people without Christ? And what is such a vicar else than antichrist and an idol? How much more correctly did the Apostles call themselves servants of the present Christ and not vicars of an absent Christ!

Perhaps I am impudent, in that I seem to instruct so great, so exalted a personage, from whom we ought all to learn, and from whom, as those

10. Luther quotes from the Magnificat, Luke 1:52.

plagues of thine boast, the thrones of judges receive their decisions. But I am following the example of St. Bernard in his book *de consideratione ad Eugenium*,[11] a book every pope should have by heart. For what I am doing I do not from an eagerness to teach, but as an evidence of that pure and faithful solicitude which constrains us to have regard for the things of our neighbors even when they are safe and does not permit us to consider their dignity or lack of dignity, since it is intent only upon the danger they run or the advantage they may gain. For when I know that thy Blessedness is driven and tossed about at Rome, that is, that far out at sea thou art threatened on all sides with endless dangers, and art laboring hard in that miserable plight, so that thou dost need even the slightest help of the least of thy brethren, I do not think it is absurd of me, if for the time I forget thy high office and do what brotherly love demands. I have no desire to flatter in so serious and dangerous a matter, but if men do not understand that I am thy friend and thy most humble subject, there is One that understandeth and judgeth.

Finally, that I may not approach thee empty-handed, blessed Father, I bring with me this little treatise published under thy name as an omen of peace and of good hope. From this book thou mayest judge with what studies I would prefer to be more profitably engaged, as I could be if your godless flatterers would permit me, and had hitherto permitted me. It is a small thing if thou regard its bulk, but, unless I am deceived, it is the whole of Christian living in brief form, if thou wilt grasp its meaning. I am a poor man, and have no other gift to offer, and thou hast no need to be made rich by any other than a spiritual gift. With this I commend myself to thy Fatherhood and Blessedness. May the Lord Jesus preserve thee forever. Amen.

Wittenberg, 6 September 1520.

21. *The Twelve Articles* and *Admonition to Peace*

The Peasants' War of 1525 was the last and most extensive of the numerous rural uprisings that had occurred periodically in Germany (they were to continue in France through the seventeenth century) since the late fourteenth century. Among the various lists of demands drawn up by the insurgents, the most complete and the most diffused is the *Twelve Ar-*

11. See above, n.4.

From *The Twelve Articles and Luther's Admonition to Peace*, translated and edited by Robert C. Schultz, in *Luther's Works*, vol. 46, edited by Jaroslav Pelikan and Helmut T. Lehrmann (Philadelphia: Fortress Press, 1967), pp. 8–43. © 1967 by Fortress Press. Footnotes deleted. Used by permission.

ticles adopted at Memmingen between January and February of 1525. Luther wrote his reply, the *Admonition to Peace*, during a trip through Thuringen in early April. A month later he wrote the much more virulent treatise *Against the Robbing and Murdering Hordes of Peasants*, which put him squarely behind the violent (and effective) repression carried out in the succeeding months.

The current authority on the subject is Peter Blickle, in his *The Revolution of 1525*, translated by Thomas A. Brady and E. C. Erik Midelfort (Johns Hopkins University Press, 1981).

The Twelve Articles of the Peasants

The basic and chief articles of all the peasants and subjects of spiritual and temporal lords, concerning the matters in which they feel they are being denied their rights.

To the Christian reader: Peace and the grace of God through Christ.

Many antichrists [I John 2:18] have recently taken advantage of the assembling of the peasants and used it as an excuse to speak scornfully about the Gospel. They say, "Is this the fruit of the new Gospel? Will no one be obedient anymore? Will the people rebel everywhere, revolt against their lords, gather and organize in crowds, and use their power to overthrow their spiritual and temporal authorities? Indeed they may even kill them." The following articles are our answer to these godless and blasphemous critics. Our intention is twofold: first, to remove this calumny from the word of God and, second, to excuse in a Christian way the disobedience and even the rebellion of the peasants.

First, the Gospel does not cause rebellion and disturbance, because it is a message about Christ, the promised Messiah, whose words and life teach nothing but love, peace, patience, and unity. And all who believe in this Christ become loving, peaceful, patient, and agreeable. This is the basis of all the articles of the peasants (as will clearly appear), and they are basically concerned with hearing the word of God and living according to it. On what basis, then, can these antichrists call the Gospel a cause of revolt and violence? That some antichrists and enemies of the Gospel resist these demands and requests is not the fault of the Gospel, but of the devil, the Gospel's deadliest enemy, who by means of unbelief arouses opposition in his own. Through this opposition the word of God, which teaches love, peace, and unity, is suppressed and taken away.

Second, on this basis the conclusion is obvious that the peasants cannot properly be called disobedient and rebellious. For, as these articles indicate, they desire this Gospel [to be the basis of] their teaching and life.

Now if God wills to hear the peasants' earnest and fervent prayer that they may live according to his word, who will criticize the will of God? Who will meddle in his judgment? Who indeed will resist his majesty? Did he not hear the children of Israel when they cried to him and release them out of the hand of Pharaoh; and can he not today deliver his own? Yes, he will deliver them, and will do so quickly [Ps. 46:5]! Therefore, Christian reader, read the following articles carefully and then decide.

The First Article

First, we humbly ask and request—in accordance with our unanimous will and desire—that in the future the entire community have the power and authority to choose and appoint a pastor. We also desire the power to depose him, should he conduct himself improperly. The pastor whom we thus choose for ourselves shall preach the holy Gospel to us clearly and purely. He is to add no teaching or commandment of men to the Gospel, but rather is always to proclaim the true faith and encourage us to ask God for his grace. He is to instill and strengthen this true faith in us. For if the grace of God is not instilled in us, we remain mere flesh and blood. And mere flesh and blood is useless, as Scripture clearly says, for we can come to God only through true faith and can be saved only through his mercy. That is why we need such a leader and pastor; and thus our demand is grounded in Scripture.

The Second Article

Second, since the tithe is prescribed in the Old Testament, although it is fulfilled in the New, we are willing to pay the just tithe of grain, but it must be done in a proper way. Since men ought to give it to God and distribute it to those who are his, it belongs to the pastor who clearly proclaims the word of God, and we desire that in the future this tithe be gathered and received by our church provost, appointed by the community. With the consent of the whole community the pastor, who shall be chosen by an entire community, shall receive out of this tithe a modest, sufficient maintenance for him and his; the remainder shall be distributed to the poor and needy in the same village, according to the circumstances and with the consent of the community. Anything that then remains shall be kept, so that if the needs of the land require the laying of a war tax, no general tax may be laid upon the poor, but it shall be paid out of this surplus.

If it should happen that there were one or more villages that had sold their tithes to meet certain needs, they are to be informed that he who has [bought] the tithes from a whole village is not to be deprived of them without compensation; for we will negotiate with him, in the proper way, form, and manner, to buy them back from him on suitable terms and at a suitable time. But in case anyone has not bought the tithes from any village, and his forbears have simply appropriated them to themselves, we will not, we ought not, nor do we intend to pay him anything further, but will keep them for the support of the aforesaid, our chosen pastor, and for distribution to the needy, as the Holy Scriptures [command]. It does not matter whether the holders of the tithes be spiritual or temporal lords. The small tithe we will not pay at all, for God the Lord created cattle for the free use of men, and we regard this tithe as an improper one which men have invented; therefore we will not give it any longer.

The Third Article

Third, it has been the custom for men to hold us as their own property. This situation is pitiable, for Christ has redeemed and bought us all with the precious shedding of his blood, the lowly as well as the great, excepting no one. Therefore, it agrees with Scripture that we be free and will to be so. It is not our intention to be entirely free. God does not teach us that we should desire no rulers. We are to live according to the commandments, not the free self-will of the flesh; but we are to love God, recognize him in our neighbor as our Lord, and do all (as we gladly would do) that God has commanded in the Lord's Supper; therefore, we ought to live according to his commandment. This commandment does not teach us to disobey our rulers; rather to humble ourselves, not before the rulers only, but before everyone. Thus we willingly obey our chosen and appointed rulers (whom God has appointed over us) in all Christian and appropriate matters. And we have no doubt that since they are true and genuine Christians, they will gladly release us from serfdom, or show us in the Gospel that we are serfs.

The Fourth Article

Fourth, it has been the custom that no poor man has been allowed to catch game, wild fowl, or freshwater fish, which seems to us altogether improper and unbrotherly, selfish, and not according to the word of God. In some places the rulers keep the game to our vexation and great loss, because the unreasoning animals wantonly devour our crops which God causes to grow for man's use; and we have to put up with this and keep quiet about it, though it is against God and neighbor. When God the Lord created man, he gave him authority over all animals, over the birds of the air, and over the fish in the water. Therefore it is our request that if anyone has waters, he offer satisfactory documentary evidence that the waters have been intentionally sold to him. In that case we do not wish to take them from him by force; on the contrary, for the sake of brotherly love, Christian consideration must be shown. But whoever cannot offer sufficient proof shall surrender these waters to the community in a proper manner.

The Fifth Article

Fifth, we also have a grievance about wood cutting, for our lords have appropriated all the forests solely to themselves, and when the poor man needs any wood, he must buy it at a double price. In our opinion the forests held by spiritual or temporal lords who have not bought them should revert to the entire community. This community should be free, in an orderly way, to allow anyone to take home what he needs for firewood without payment, and also to take for nothing any that he needs for wood-working: this is to be done with the approval of a supervisor appointed by the community. If there are any forests which have not been thus honestly purchased, a brotherly and Christian agreement should be reached about them; but if the property had first been expropriated and afterward sold, an agreement shall be made in accordance with the facts of the case, and according to brotherly love and the Holy Scriptures.

The Sixth Article

Sixth, we are grievously oppressed by the free labor which we are required to provide for our lords. The amount of labor required increases from day to day and [the variety of services required] increases from day to day. We ask that an appropriate investigation be made of this matter and that the burdens laid upon us not be too heavy. We ask that we be dealt with graciously, just as our ancestors were, who provided these services according to the word of God.

The Seventh Article

Seventh, in the future we will not allow ourselves to be further oppressed by the lords. Rather, a man shall possess his holding according to the terms on which it has been granted, that is, according to the agreement between the lord and the peasants. The lord shall not in any way put pressure on the peasant, or force him to render more services, or demand anything else from him without payment, so that the peasant may use and enjoy his property unburdened and in peace; but if the lord needs more services, the peasant shall be obedient, and willing to perform them. However, he is to do so at a time when the peasant's own affairs do not suffer, and he shall receive a fair wage for this labor.

The Eighth Article

We are greatly aggrieved because many of us have holdings that do not produce enough to enable us to pay the rents due on them. As a result, the peasants bear the loss and are ruined. We ask that the lords have honorable men inspect the said holdings, and fix a fair rent, so that the peasant shall not labor for nothing; for every laborer is worthy of his hire.

The Ninth Article

We are aggrieved by the great wrong of continually making new laws. Punishment is inflicted on us, not according to the facts in the case, but at times by great ill-will, at times by great partiality. In our opinion we should be punished by the ancient written law, and the cases dealt with according to the facts, and not according to partiality.

The Tenth Article

We are aggrieved because some have expropriated meadows from the common fields which once belonged to a community. We would take these back again into the hands of our communities, unless they have been honestly purchased. If they have been improperly purchased, we should come to a kindly and brotherly agreement about them, according to the facts of the case.

The Eleventh Article

We would have the custom called death tax entirely abolished. We will not tolerate it or allow widows and orphans to be so shamefully robbed by those who ought to guard and protect them, as now happens in many places and under many forms, contrary to God and honor. They have disgraced and cheated us, and although they had little authority, they have taken what was left after that. God will no longer permit it; it shall be entirely done away with. Henceforth no man shall be required to pay any of this tax, whether large or small.

The Twelfth Article

Twelfth, it is our conclusion and final opinion that if one or more of the articles set forth here is not in agreement with the word of God (though we think this is not the case), and this disagreement is shown to us on the basis of Scripture, we shall withdraw such an article—after the matter is explained to us on the basis of Scripture. If some of our demands are granted and it is afterward found that they were unjust, they shall be null and void from that hour. Similarly, if additional articles are found to be properly based on Scripture and more offenses against God and our neighbor be revealed thereby, [they will be added to these articles]. We, for our part, will and have determined to use forbearance and will discipline ourselves in all Christian doctrine and practice. We will pray to God the Lord for this; for he, and no one else, can give it to us. The peace of Christ be with us all.

Martin Luther, *Admonition to Peace*

A Reply to the Twelve Articles of the Peasants in Swabia

The peasants who have now banded together in Swabia have formulated their intolerable grievances against the rulers in twelve articles, and have undertaken to support them with certain passages of Scripture. Now they have published them in printed form. The thing about them that pleases me most is that, in the twelfth article, they offer to accept instruction gladly and willingly, if there is need or necessity for it, and are willing to be corrected, to the extent that it can be done by clear, plain, undeniable passages of Scripture. And it is indeed right and proper that no one's conscience should be instructed or corrected except by Holy Scripture.

Now if that is their serious and sincere meaning—and it would not be right for me to interpret it otherwise, because in these articles they come out into the open and do not shy away from the light—then there is good reason to hope that things will be well. Since I have a reputation for being one of those who deal with the Holy Scriptures here on earth, and especially as one whom they mention and call upon by name in the second document, I have all the more courage and confidence in openly publishing my instruction. I do this in a friendly and Christian spirit, as a duty of brotherly love, so that if any misfortune or disaster comes out of this matter, it may not be attributed to me, nor will I be blamed before God and men because of my silence. But if this offer of theirs is only pretense and show (without a doubt there are some people like that among them for it is impossible for so big a crowd all to be true Christians and have good intentions; a large part of them must be using the good intentions of the rest for their own selfish purposes and seeking their own advantage) then without doubt it will accomplish very little, or, in fact, it will contribute to their great injury and eternal ruin.

This, then, is a great and dangerous matter. It concerns both the kingdom of God and the kingdom of the world. If this rebellion were to continue and get the upper hand, both kingdoms would be destroyed and there would be neither worldly government nor word of God, which would ultimately result in the permanent destruction of all Germany. Therefore it is necessary for us to speak boldly and to give advice without regard to anyone. It is also necessary that we be willing to listen and allow things to be said to us, so that we do not now—as we have done before—harden our hearts and stop our ears, and so that God's wrath not run its full course. For the many terrible signs that are seen both in heaven and earth point to a great disaster and a mighty change in Germany. Sad to say, however, we care little about it. Nevertheless, God goes on his way, and someday he will soften our hardheadedness.

To the Princes and Lords

We have no one on earth to thank for this disastrous rebellion, except you princes and lords, and especially you blind bishops and mad priests and monks, whose hearts are hardened, even to the present day. You do not cease to rant and rave against the holy Gospel, even though you know that it is true and that you cannot refute it. In addition, as temporal rulers you do nothing but cheat and rob the people so that you may lead a life of luxury and extravagance. The poor common people cannot bear it any longer. The sword is already at your throats, but you think that you sit so firm in the saddle that no one can unhorse you. This false security and stubborn perversity will break your necks, as you will discover. I have often told you before to beware of the saying, in Psalm 107 [:40], "*Effundit contemptum super principes*," "He pours contempt upon princes." You, however, keep on asking for trouble and want to be hit over the head. And no warning or exhortation will keep you from getting what you want.

Well, then, since you are the cause of this wrath of God, it will undoubtedly come upon you, unless you mend your ways in time. The signs in heaven and the wonders on earth are meant for you, dear lords; they bode no good for you, and no good will come to you. A great part of God's wrath has already come, for God is sending many false teachers and prophets among us, so that through our error and blasphemy we may richly deserve hell and everlasting damnation. The rest of it is now here, for the peasants are banding together, and, unless our repentance moves God to prevent it, this must result in the ruin, destruction, and desolation of Germany by cruel murder and bloodshed.

For you ought to know, dear lords, that God is doing this because this raging of yours cannot, will not, and ought not be endured for long. You must become different men and yield to God's word. If you do not do this amicably and willingly, then you will be compelled to do it by force and destruction. If these peasants do not compel you, others will. Even though you were to defeat them all, they would still not be defeated, for God will raise up others. It is his ill to defeat you, and you will be defeated. It is not the peasants, dear lords, who are resisting you; it is God himself, to visit your raging upon you. Some of you have said that you will stake land and people on exterminating the Lutheran teaching. What would you think if you were to turn out to be your own prophets, and your land and people were already at stake? Do not joke with God, dear lords! The Jews, too, said, "We have no king" [John 19:15], and they meant it so seriously that they must be without a king forever.

To make your sin still greater, and guarantee your merciless destruction, some of you are beginning to blame this affair on the Gospel and say that it is the fruit of my teaching. Well, well, slander away, dear lords! You did not want to know what I taught or what the Gospel is; now the one who will soon teach you is at the door, unless you change your ways. You, and everyone else, must bear witness that I have taught with all quietness, have striven earnestly against rebellion, and have energetically encouraged and exhorted people to obey and respect even you wild and dictatorial tyrants. This rebellion cannot be coming from me. Rather the murder-prophets, who hate me as they hate you, have come among these people and have gone about among them for more than three years, and no one has resisted and fought against them except me.

Therefore, if God intends to punish you and allows the devil through his false prophets to stir up the people against you, and if it is, perhaps, God's will that I shall not be able to prevent it any longer, what can I or my Gospel do? Not only have we suffered your persecution and murdering and raging; we have also prayed for you and helped to protect and maintain your rule over the common people. If I desired revenge, I could laugh up my sleeve and simply watch what the peasants are doing or even join in with them and help make matters worse; may God keep me from this in the future as he has in the past.

Therefore my dear lords—whether you are my enemies or friends—as a loyal subject I humbly beg you not to despise my faithfulness, though I am a poor man. I beseech you not to make light of this rebellion. It is not that I think or fear that the rebels will be too strong for you or that I want you to be afraid of them for that reason. Rather fear God and respect his wrath! If he wills to punish you as you have deserved (and I am afraid that he does), then he will punish you, even though the peasants were a hundred times fewer than they are. He can make peasants out of stones and slay a hundred of you by one peasant, so that all your armor and your strength will be too weak to save you.

If it is still possible to give you advice, my lords, give way a little to the will and wrath of God. A cartload of hay must give way to a drunken man—how much more ought you to stop your raging and obstinate tyranny and not deal unreasonably with the peasants, as though they were drunk or out of their minds! Do not start a fight with them, for you do not know how it will end. Try kindness first, for you do not know what God will do to prevent the spark that will kindle all Germany and start a fire that no one can extinguish. Our sins are before God [Ps. 90:8]; therefore we have to fear his wrath when even a leaf rustles [Lev. 26:36], let alone when such a multitude sets itself in motion. You will lose nothing by kindness; and even if you did lose something, the preservation of peace will pay you back ten times. But if there is open conflict you may lose both your property and your life. Why risk danger when you can achieve more by following a different way that is also the better way?

The peasants have just published twelve articles, some of which are so fair and just as to take away your reputation in the eyes of God and the world and fulfil what the Psalm [107:40] says about God pouring contempt upon princes. Nevertheless, almost all of the articles are framed in their own interest and for their own good, though not for their best good. Of course, I would have formulated other articles against you that would have dealt with all Germany and its government.

I did this in my book *To the German Nobility*, when more was at stake; but because you made light of that, you must now listen to and put up with these selfish articles. It serves you right for being a people to whom nothing can be told.

In the first article they ask the right to hear the Gospel and choose their pastors. You cannot reject this request with any show of right, even though this article does indeed make some selfish demands, for they allege that these pastors are to be supported by the tithes, and these do not belong to the peasants. Nevertheless, the basic sense of the article is that the preaching of the Gospel should be permitted, and no ruler can or ought to oppose this. Indeed, no ruler ought to prevent anyone from teaching or believing what he pleases, whether it is the Gospel or lies. It is enough if he prevents the teaching of sedition and rebellion.

The other articles protest economic injustices, such as the death tax. These protests are also right and just, for rulers are not appointed to exploit their subjects for their own profit and advantage, but to be concerned about the welfare of their subjects. And the people cannot tolerate it very long if their rulers set confiscatory tax rates and tax them out of their very skins. What good would it do a peasant if his field bore as many gulden as stalks of wheat if the rulers only taxed him all the more and then wasted it as though it were chaff to increase their luxury, and squandered his money on their own clothes, food, drink, and buildings? Would not the luxury and the extravagant spending have to be checked so that a poor man could keep something for himself? You have undoubtedly received further information from the peasants' tracts, so that you are adequately aware of their grievances.

To the Peasants

So far, dear friends, you have learned only that I agree that it is unfortunately all too true that the princes and lords who forbid the preaching of the Gospel and oppress the people unbearably deserve to have God put them down from their thrones [Luke 1:52] because they have sinned so greatly against both God and man. And they have no excuse. Nevertheless, you, too, must be careful that you take up your cause justly and with a good conscience. If you have a good conscience, you have the comforting advantage that God will be with you, and will help you. Even though you did not succeed for a while, or even suffered death, you would win in the end, and you would preserve your souls eternally with all the saints. But if you act unjustly and have a bad conscience, you will be defeated. And even though you might win for a while and even kill all the princes, you would suffer the eternal loss of your body and soul in the end. For you, therefore, this is no laughing matter. The eternal fate of your body and soul is involved. And you must most seriously consider not merely how strong you are and how wrong the princes are, but whether you act justly and with a good conscience.

Therefore, dear brethren, I beg you in a kindly and brotherly way to look carefully at what you are doing and not to believe all kinds of spirits and preachers [I John 4:1]. For Satan has now raised up many evil spirits of disorder and of murder, and filled the world with them. Just listen attentively, as you offer many times to do. I will not spare you the earnest warning that I owe you, even though some of you have been so poisoned by the murderous spirits that you will hate me for it and call me a hypocrite. That does not worry me; it is enough for me if I save some of the goodhearted and upright men among you from the danger of God's wrath. The rest I fear as little as they despise me much; and they shall not harm me. I know One who is greater and mightier than they are, and he teaches me in Psalm 3 [:6], "I am not afraid of ten thousands of people who have set themselves against me round about." My confidence shall outlast their confidence; that I know for certain.

In the first place, dear brethren, you bear the name of God and call yourselves a "Christian association" or union, and you allege that you want to live and act according to divine law. Now you know that the name, word, and titles of God are not to be assumed idly or in vain, as he says in the second commandment, "Thou shalt not take the name of the Lord your God in vain," and adds, "for the Lord will not hold him guiltless who takes his name in vain" [Deut. 5:11]. Here is a clear, plain text, which applies to you, as to all men. It threatens you, as well as us and all others, with God's wrath without regard to your great numbers, rights, and terror. God is mighty enough and strong enough to punish you as he here threatens if his name is taken in vain, and you know it. So if you take his name in vain, you may expect no good fortune but only trouble. Learn from this how to judge yourselves and accept this friendly warning. It would be a simple thing for God, who once drowned the whole world with a flood [Gen. 7:17–24] and destroyed Sodom with fire [Gen. 19:24–28], to kill or defeat so many thousands of peasants. He is an almighty and terrible God.

Second, it is easy to prove that you are taking God's name in vain and putting it to shame; nor is there any doubt that you will, in the end, encounter all misfortune, unless God is not true. For here is God's word, spoken through the mouth of Christ, "All who take the sword will perish by the sword" [Matt. 26:52]. That means nothing else than that no one, by his own violence, shall arrogate authority to himself; but as Paul says, "Let every person be subject to the governing authorities with fear and reverence" [Rom. 13:1].

How can you get around these passages and laws of God when you boast that you are acting according to divine law, and yet take the sword in your own hands, and revolt against "the governing authorities that are instituted by God?" Do you think that Paul's judgment in Romans 13 [:2] will not strike you, "He who resists the authorities will incur judgment"? You take God's name in vain when you pretend to be seeking divine right, and under the pretense of his name work contrary to divine right. Be careful, dear sirs. It will not turn out that way in the end.

Third, you say that the rulers are wicked and intolerable, for they will not allow us to have the Gospel; they oppress us too hard with the burdens they lay on our property, and they are ruining us in body and soul. I answer: The fact that the rulers are wicked and unjust does not excuse disorder and rebellion, for the punishing of wickedness is not the responsibility of everyone, but of the worldly rulers who bear the sword. Thus Paul says in Romans 13 [:4] and Peter, in I Peter 3 [2:14], that the rulers are instituted by God for the punishment of the wicked. Then, too, there is the natural law of all the world, which says that no one may sit as judge in his own case or take his own revenge. The proverb is true, "Whoever hits back is in the wrong." Or as it is said, "It takes two to start a fight." The divine law agrees with this, and says, in Deuteronomy 32 [:35], "Vengeance is mine; I will repay, says the Lord." Now you cannot deny that your rebellion actually involves you in such a way that you make yourselves your own judges and avenge yourselves. You are quite unwilling to suffer any wrong. That is contrary not only to Christian law and the Gospel, but also to natural law and all equity.

If your cause is to prosper when the divine and Christian law of the Old and New Testaments and even the natural law are all against you, you must produce a new and special command of God, confirmed by signs and wonders, which commands you to do these things. Otherwise God will not allow his word and ordinance to be broken by your violence. On the contrary, because you boast of the divine law and yet act against it, he will let you fall and be punished terribly, as men who dishonor his name. Then he will condemn you eternally, as was said above. For the word of Christ in Matthew 7 [:3] applies to you; you see the speck in the eye of the rulers, but do not see the log in your own eye. The word of Paul in Romans 3 [:8] also applies, "Why not do evil that good may come? Their condemnation is just." It is true that the rulers do wrong when they suppress the Gospel and oppress you in temporal matters. But you do far greater wrong when you not only suppress God's word, but tread it underfoot, invade his authority and law, and put yourselves above God. Besides, you take from the rulers their authority and right, indeed, everything they have. What do they have left when they have lost their authority?

I make you the judges and leave it to you to decide who is the worse robber, the man who takes a large part of another's goods, but leaves him something, or the man who takes everything that he has, and takes his life besides. The rulers unjustly take your property; that is the one side. On the other hand, you take from them their authority, in which their whole property and life and being consist. Therefore you are far greater robbers than they, and you intend to do worse things than they have done. "Indeed not," you say, "we are going to leave them enough to live on." If anyone wants to believe that, let him! I do not believe it. Anyone who dares to go so far as to use force to take away authority, which is the main thing, will not stop at that, but will take the other, smaller thing that depends upon it. The wolf that eats a whole sheep will also eat its ear. And even if you permitted them to keep their life and some property, nevertheless, you would take the best thing they have, namely, their authority, and make yourselves lords over them. That would be too great a robbery and wrong. God will declare you to be the greatest robbers.

Can you not think it through, dear friends? If your enterprise were right, then any man might become judge over another. Then authority, government, law, and order would disappear from the world; there would be nothing but murder and bloodshed. As soon as anyone saw that someone was wronging him, he would begin to judge and punish him. Now if that is unjust and intolerable when done by an individual, we cannot allow a mob or a crowd to do it. However, if we do permit a mob or a crowd to do it, then we cannot rightly and fairly forbid an individual to do it. For in both cases the cause is the same, that is, an injustice. What would you yourselves do if disorder broke out in your ranks and one man set himself against another and took vengeance on him? Would you put up with that? Would you not say that he must let others, whom you appointed, do the judging and avenging? What do you expect God and the world to think when you pass judgment and avenge yourselves on those who have injured you and even upon your rulers, whom God has appointed?

Now in all this I have been speaking of the common, divine, and natural law which even the heathen, Turks, and Jews have to keep if there is to be any peace or order in the world. Even though you were to keep this whole law, you would do no better and no more than the heathen and the Turks do. For no one is a Christian merely because he does not undertake to function as his own judge and avenger but leaves this to the authorities and the rulers. You would eventually have to do this whether you wanted to or not. But because you are acting against this law, you see plainly that you are worse than heathen or Turks, to say nothing of the fact that you are not Christians. What do you think that Christ will say about this? You bear his name, and call yourselves a "Christian association," and yet you are so far from being Christian, and your actions and lives are so horribly contrary to his law, that you are not worthy to be called even heathen or Turks. You are much worse than these, because you rage and struggle against the divine and natural law, which all the heathen keep.

See, dear friends, what kind of preachers you have and what they think of your souls. I fear that some prophets of murder have come among you, who would like to use you so they can become lords in the world, and they do not care that they are endangering your life, property, honor, and soul, in time and eternity. If, now, you really want to keep the divine law, as you boast, then do it. There it stands! God says, "Vengeance is mine; I will repay" [Rom. 12:19], and, "Be subject not only to good lords, but also to the wicked" [I Pet. 2:18]. If you do this, well and good; if not, you may, indeed, cause a calamity, but it will finally come upon you. Let no one have any doubts about this! God is just, and will not endure it. Be careful, therefore, with your liberty, that you do not run away from the rain and fall in the water. Beware of the illusion that you are winning freedom for your body when you are really losing your body, property, and soul for all eternity. God's wrath is there; fear it, I advise you! The devil has sent false prophets among you; beware of them!

And now we want to move on and speak of the law of Christ, and of the Gospel, which is not binding on the heathen, as the other law is. For if you claim that you are Christians and like to be called Christians and want to be known as Christians, then you must also allow your law to be held up before you rightly. Listen, then, dear Christians, to your Christian law! Your Supreme Lord Christ, whose name you bear, says, in Matthew 6 [5:39–41], "Do not resist one who is evil. If anyone forces you to go one mile, go with him two miles. If anyone wants to take your coat, let him have your cloak too. If anyone strikes you on one cheek, offer him the other too." Do you hear this, O Christian association? How does your program stand in light of this law? You do not want to endure evil or suffering, but rather want to be free and to experience only goodness and justice. However, Christ says that we should not resist evil or injustice but always yield, suffer, and let things be taken from us. If you will not bear this law, then lay aside the name of Christian and claim another name that accords with your actions, or else Christ himself will tear his name away from you, and that will be too hard for you.

In Romans 12 [:19] Paul says, "Beloved, never avenge yourselves, but leave it to the wrath of God." In this same sense he praises the Corinthians for gladly suffering if someone hits or robs them, II Corinthians 11 [:20]. And in I Corinthians 6 [:1–2] he condemns them for going to court for the sake of property rather than suffering injustice. Indeed, our leader, Jesus Christ, says in Matthew 7 [5:44] that we should bless those who insult us, pray for our persecutors, love our enemies, and do good to those who do evil to us. These, dear friends, are our Christian laws.

Now you can see how far these false prophets have led you astray. They still call you Christians, although they have made you worse than heathen. On the basis of these passages even a child can understand that the Christian law tells us not to strive against injustice, not to grasp the sword, not to protect ourselves, not to avenge ourselves, but to give up life and property, and let whoever takes it have it. We have all we need in our Lord, who will not leave us, as he has promised [Heb. 13:5]. Suffering! suffering! Cross! cross! This and nothing else is the Christian law! But now you are fighting for temporal goods and will not let the coat go after the cloak, but want to recover the cloak. How then will you die and give up your life, or love your enemies and do good to them? O worthless Christians! Dear friends, Christians are not so commonplace that so many can assemble in one group. A Christian is a rare bird! Would to God that the majority of us were good, pious heathen, who kept the natural law, not to mention the Christian law!

I will give you some illustrations of Christian law so that you may see where the mad prophets have led you. Look at St. Peter in the garden. He wanted to defend his Lord Christ with the sword, and cut off Malchus' ear [John 18:10]. Tell me, did not Peter have great right on his side? Was it not an intolerable injustice that they were going to take from Christ not only his property, but also his life? Indeed, they not only took his life and property, but in so doing they entirely suppressed the Gospel by which they were to be saved and thus robbed heaven. You have not yet suffered such a wrong, dear friends. But see what Christ does and teaches in this case. However great the injustice was, he nevertheless stopped St. Peter, bade him put up his sword, and would not allow him to avenge or prevent this injustice. In addition, he passed a sentence of death upon him, as though upon a murderer, and said, "He who takes the sword will perish by the sword" [Matt. 26:52]. This should help us understand that we do not have the right to use the sword simply because someone has done us an injustice and because the law and justice are on our side. We must also have received power and authority from God to use the sword and to punish wrong. Furthermore, a Christian should also suffer it if anyone desires to keep the Gospel away from him by force. It may not even be possible to keep the Gospel from anyone, as we shall hear.

A second example is Christ himself. What did he do when they took his life on the cross and thereby took away from him the work of preaching for which God himself had sent him as a blessing for the souls of men? He did just what St. Peter says. He committed the whole matter to him who judges justly, and he endured this intolerable wrong [I Pet. 2:23]. More than that, he prayed for his persecutors and said, "Father, forgive them, for they know not what they do" [Luke 23:34].

Now, if you are genuine Christians, you must certainly act in this same way and follow this example. If you do not do this, then give up the name of Christian and the claim that Christian law is on your side, for then you are certainly not Christians but are opposing Christ and his law, his doctrine, and his example. But if you do follow the example of Christ, you will soon see God's miracles and he will help you as he helped Christ, whom he avenged after the completion of his passion in such a way that his Gospel and his kingdom won a powerful victory and gained the upper hand, in spite of all his enemies. He will help you in this same way so that his Gospel will rise with power among you, if you first suffer to the end, leave the case to him, and await his vengeance. But because of what you are doing, and because you do not want to triumph by suffering, but by your fists, you are interfering with God's vengeance and you will keep neither the Gospel nor your fists.

I must also give you an illustration from the present. Pope and emperor have opposed me and raged against me. Now what have I done that the more pope and emperor raged, the more my Gospel spread? I have never drawn a sword or desired revenge. I began neither conspiracy nor rebellion, but so far as I was able, I have helped the worldly rulers—even those who persecuted the Gospel and me—to preserve their power and honor. I stopped with committing the matter to God and relying confidently at all times upon his hand. This is why God has not only preserved my life in spite of the pope and all the tyrants—and this many consider a really great miracle, as I myself must also confess—but he has made my Gospel grow and spread. Now you interfere with what I am doing. You want to help the Gospel and yet you do not see that what you are doing hinders and suppresses it most effectively.

I say all this, dear friends, as a faithful warning. In this case you should stop calling yourselves Christians and stop claiming that you have the Christian law on your side. For no matter how right you are, it is not right for a Christian to appeal to law, or to fight, but rather to suffer wrong and endure evil; and there is no other way, I Corinthians 6 [:1–8]. You yourselves confess in the preface to your articles that "all who believe in Christ become loving, peaceful, patient, and agreeable." Your actions, however, reveal nothing but impatience, aggression, anger, and violence. Thus you contradict your own words. You want to be known as patient people, you who will endure neither injustice nor evil, but will endure only what is just and good. That is a fine kind of patience! Any rascal can practice it! It does not take a Christian to do that! So again I say, however good and just your cause may be, nevertheless, because you would defend yourselves and are unwilling to suffer either violence or injustice, you may do anything that God does not prevent. However, leave the name Christian out of it. Leave the name Christian out, I say, and do not use it to cover up your impatient, disorderly, un-Christian undertaking. I shall not let you have that name, but so long as there is a heartbeat in my body, I shall do all I can, through speaking and writing, to take that name away from you. You will not succeed, or will succeed only in ruining your bodies and souls.

In saying this it is not my intention to justify or defend the rulers in the intolerable injustices which you suffer from them. They are unjust, and commit heinous wrongs against you; that I admit. If, however, neither side accepts instruction and you start to fight with each other—may God prevent it!—I hope that neither side will be called Christian. Rather I hope that God will, as is usual in these situations, use one rascal to punish the other. If it comes to a conflict—may God graciously prevent it!—I hope that your character and name will be so well known that the authorities will recognize that they are fighting not against Christians but against heathen; and that you, too, may know that you are not fighting Christian rulers but heathen. Christians do not fight for themselves with sword and musket, but with the cross and with suffering, just as Christ, our leader, does not bear a sword, but hangs on the cross. Your victory, therefore, does not consist in conquering and reigning, or in the use of force, but in defeat and in weakness, as St. Paul says in II Corinthians 1 [10:4], "The weapons of our warfare are not material, but are the strength which comes from God," and, "Power is made perfect in weakness" [II Cor. 12:9].

Your name and title ought therefore to indicate that you are people who fight because they will not, and ought not, endure injustice or evil, according to the teaching of nature. You should use that name, and let the name of Christ alone, for that is the kind of works that you are doing. If, however, you will not take that name, but keep the name of Christian, then I must accept the fact that I am also involved in this struggle and consider you as enemies who, under the name of the Gospel, act contrary to it, and want to do more to suppress my Gospel than anything the pope and emperor have done to suppress it.

I will make no secret of what I intend to do. I will put the whole matter into God's hands, risk my neck by God's grace, and confidently trust in him—just as I have been doing against the pope and the emperor. I shall pray for you, that God may enlighten you, and resist your undertaking, and not let it succeed. For I see well that the devil, who has not been able to destroy me through the pope, now seeks to exterminate me and swallow me up by means of the bloodthirsty prophets of murder and spirits of rebellion that are among you. Well, let him swallow me! I will give him a bellyful, I know. And even if you win, you will hardly enjoy it! I beg you, humbly and kindly, to think things over so that I will not have to trust in and pray to God against you.

For although I am a poor, sinful man, I know and am certain that my concern in this matter is right and just, for I fight in behalf of the name Christian and pray that it not be put to shame. I am sure, too, that my prayer is acceptable to God and will be heard, for he himself has taught us to pray, in the Lord's Prayer, "Hallowed be thy name" [Matt. 6:9], and in the second commandment he has forbidden that it be put to shame [Deut. 5:11]. Therefore I beg you not to despise my prayer and the prayer of those who pray along with me, for it will be too mighty for you and will arouse God against you, as St. James says, "The prayer of the righteous man who prays persistently has great effects, just as Elijah's prayer did" [James 5:16–17]. We also have many other comforting promises of God that he will hear us, such as John, "If you ask anything in my name I will do it" [John 14:14], and, "If we ask anything according to his will he hears us" [I John 5:14]. You cannot have such confidence and assurance in prayer because your own conscience and the Scriptures testify that your enterprise is heathenish, and not Christian, and, under the name of the Gospel, works against the Gospel and brings contempt upon the name Christian. I know that none of you has ever once prayed to God or called upon him in behalf of this cause. You could not do it! You dare not lift up your eyes to him in this case. You only defiantly shake your fist at him, the fist which you have clenched because of your impatience and unwillingness to suffer. This will not turn out well for you.

If you were Christians you would stop threatening and resisting with fist and sword. Instead, you would continually abide by the Lord's Prayer and say, "Thy will be done," and, "Deliver us from evil, Amen" [Matt. 6:10, 13]. The psalms show us many examples of genuine saints taking their needs to God and complaining to him about them. They seek help from God: they do not try to defend themselves or to resist evil. That kind of prayer would have been more help to you, in all your needs, than if the world were full of people on your side. This would be especially true if, besides that, you had a good conscience and the comforting assurance that your prayers were heard, as his promises declare: "God is the Savior of all men, especially of those who believe," I Timothy 4 [:10]; "Call upon me in the day of trouble, I will deliver you," Psalm 50 [:15]; "He called upon me in trouble, therefore I will help him," Psalm 91 [:15]. See! That is the Christian way to get rid of misfortune and evil, that is, to endure it and to call upon God. But because you neither call upon God nor patiently endure, but rather help yourselves by your own power and make yourselves your own god and savior, God cannot and must not be your God and Savior. By God's permission you might accomplish something as the heathen and blasphemers you are—and we pray that he will prevent that—but it will only be to your temporal and eternal destruction. However, as Christians, or Evangelicals, you will win nothing. I would stake my life a thousand times on that.

On this basis it is now easy to reply to all your articles. Even though they all were just and equitable in terms of natural law, you have not been putting this program into effect and achieving your goals by patiently praying to God, as Christians ought to do, but have instead undertaken to compel the rulers to give you what you wanted by using force and violence. This is against the law of the land and against natural justice. The man who composed your articles is no godly and honest man. His marginal notes refer to many chapters of Scripture on which the articles are supposed to be based. But he talks with his mouth full of nothing, and leaves out the passages which would show his own wickedness and that of your cause. He has done this to deceive you, to incite you, and to bring you into danger. Anyone who reads through the chapters cited will realize that they speak very little in favor of what you are doing. On the contrary, they say that men should live and act like Christians. He who seeks to use you to destroy the Gospel is a prophet of discord. May God prevent that and guard you against him!

In the preface you are conciliatory and claim that you do not want to be rebels. You even excuse your actions by claiming that you desire to teach and to live according to the Gospel. Your own words and actions condemn you. You confess that you are causing disturbances and revolting. And then you try to excuse this behavior with the Gospel. You have heard above that the Gospel teaches Christians to endure and suffer wrong and to pray to God in every need. You, however, are not willing to suffer, but like heathen, you want to force the rulers to conform to your impatient will. You cite the children of Israel as an example, saying that God heard their crying and delivered them [Exod. 6:5–7]. Why then do you not follow the example that you cite? Call upon God and wait until he sends you a Moses, who will prove by signs and wonders that he is sent from God. The children of Israel did not riot against Pharaoh, or help themselves, as you propose to do. This illustration, therefore, is completely against you, and condemns you. You boast of it, and yet you do the opposite of what it teaches.

Furthermore, your declaration that you teach and live according to the Gospel is not true. Not one of the articles teaches anything of the Gospel. Rather, everything is aimed at obtaining freedom for your person and for your property. To sum it up, everything is concerned with worldly and temporal matters. You want power and wealth so that you will not suffer injustice. The Gospel, however, does not become involved in the affairs of this world, but speaks of our life in the world in terms of suffering, injustice, the cross, patience, and contempt for this life and temporal wealth. How, then, does the Gospel agree with you? You are only trying to give your unevangelical and un-Christian enterprise an evangelical appearance; and you do not see that in so doing you are bringing shame upon the holy Gospel of Christ, and making it a cover for wickedness. Therefore you must take a different attitude. If you want to be Christians and use the name Christian, then stop what you are doing and decide to suffer these injustices. If you want to keep on doing these things, then use another name and do not ask anyone to call you or think of you as Christians. There is no other possiblilty.

True enough, you are right in desiring the Gospel, if you are really serious about it. Indeed, I am willing to make this article even sharper than you do, and say it is intolerable that anyone should be shut out of heaven and driven by force into hell. No one should suffer that; he ought rather lose his life a hundred times. But whoever keeps the Gospel from me, closes heaven to me and drives me by force into hell; for the Gospel is the only means of salvation for the soul. And on peril of losing my soul, I should not permit this. Tell me, is that not stated sharply enough? And yet it does not follow that I must rebel against the rulers who do me this wrong. "But," you say, "how am I supposed to suffer it and yet not suffer it at the same time?" The answer is easy. It is impossible to keep the Gospel from anyone. No power in heaven or on earth can do this, for it is a public teaching that moves about freely under the heavens and is bound to no one place. It is like the star that went in the sky ahead of the Wise Men from the east and showed them where Christ was born [Matt. 2:9].

It is true, of course, that the rulers may suppress the Gospel in cities or places where the Gospel is, or where there are preachers; but you can leave these cities or places and follow the Gospel to some other place. It is not necessary, for the Gospel's sake, for you to capture or occupy the city or place; on the contrary, let the ruler have his city; you follow the Gospel. Thus you permit men to wrong you and drive you away; and yet, at the same time, you do not permit men to take the Gospel from you or keep it from you. Thus the two things, suffering and not suffering, turn out to be one. If you occupy the city for the sake of the Gospel, you rob the ruler of the city of what is his, and pretend that you are doing it for the Gospel's sake. Dear friend, the Gospel does not teach us to rob or to take things, even though the owner of the property abuses it by using it against God, wrongfully, and to your injury. The Gospel needs no physical place or city in which to dwell; it will and must dwell in hearts.

This is what Christ taught in Matthew 10 [:23], "When they persecute you in one town, flee to the next." He does not say, "When they persecute you in one town, stay there and take over the town by force and rebel against the ruler of the town—all to the praise of the Gospel," as men now want to do, and are teaching. However, Jesus says, "Flee, flee straightaway into another, until the Son of man shall come." And in Matthew 23 [:34] he says that godless men will drive his evangelists from town to town. And in II Corinthians 4 [I Cor. 4:11] Paul says that we are homeless. And if it does happen that a Christian must, for the sake of the Gospel, constantly move from one place to another, and leave all his possessions behind him, or even if his situation is very uncertain and he expects to have to move at any moment, he is only experiencing what is appropriate for a Christian. For because he will not suffer the Gospel to be taken or kept from him, he has to let his city, town, property, and everything that he is and has be taken and kept from him. Now how does your undertaking comform to this? You capture and hold cities and towns that are not yours, and you will not let them be taken or kept from you; though you take and keep them from their natural rulers. What kind of Christians are these, who, for the Gospel's sake, become robbers, thieves, and scoundrels, and then say afterward that they are evangelicals?

On the First Article

"The entire community should have the power and authority to choose and appoint a pastor." This article is just only if it is understood in a Christian sense, even though the chapters indicated in the margin do not support it. If the possessions of the parish come from the rulers and not from the community, then the community cannot give these possessions to one whom they choose, for that would be robbery and theft. If they desire a pastor, let them first humbly ask the rulers to give them one. If the rulers are unwilling, then let them choose their own pastor, and support him out of their own possessions; they should let the rulers keep their property, or else secure it from them in a lawful way. But if the rulers will not tolerate the pastor whom they chose and support, then let him flee to another city, and let any flee with him who want to do as Christ teaches. That is a Christian and evangelical way to choose and have one's own pastor. Whoever does otherwise, acts in an un-Christian manner, and is a robber and brawler.

On the Second Article

The pastor "shall receive out of this tithe . . .; the remainder shall be distributed to the poor and needy." This article is nothing but theft and highway robbery. They want to appropriate for themselves the tithes, which are not theirs but the rulers', and want to use them to do what they please. Oh, no, dear friends! That is the same as deposing the rulers altogether. Your preface expressly says that no one is to be deprived of what is his. If you want to give gifts and do good, use your own possessions, as the wise man says [Prov. 3:9]. And God says through Isaiah, "I hate the offering that is given out of stolen goods" [Isa. 61:8]. You speak in this article as though you were already lords in the land and had taken all the property of the rulers for your own and would be no one's subjects, and would give nothing. This shows what your intention really is. Stop it, dear sirs, stop it! It will not be you who puts an end to it! The chapters of Scripture which your lying preacher and false prophet has smeared on the margin do not help you at all; they are against you.

On the Third Article

You assert that no one is to be the serf of anyone else, because Christ has made us all free. That is making Christian freedom a completely physical matter. Did not Abraham [Gen. 17:23] and other patriarchs and prophets have slaves? Read what St. Paul teaches about servants, who, at that time, were all slaves. This article, therefore, absolutely contradicts the Gospel. It proposes robbery, for it suggests that every man should take his body away from his lord, even though his body is the lord's property. A slave can be a Christian, and have Christian freedom, in the same way that a prisoner or a sick man is a Christian, and yet not free. This article would make all men equal, and turn the spiritual kingdom of Christ into a worldly, external kingdom; and that is impossible. A worldly kingdom cannot exist without an inequality of persons, some being free, some imprisoned, some lords, some subjects, etc.; and St. Paul says in Galatians 5 that in Christ the lord and the servant are equal. My good friend Urbanus Rhegius has written more adequately on this subject. If you want to know more, read his book.

On the Other Eight Articles

The other articles, which discuss the freedom to hunt game animals and birds, to catch fish, to use wood from the forest, their obligation to provide free labor, the amount of their rents and taxes, the death tax, etc., are all matters for the lawyers to discuss. It is not fitting that I, an evangelist, should judge or make decisions in such matters. I am to instruct and teach men's consciences in things that concern divine and Christian matters; there are books enough about the other things in the imperial laws. I said above that these things do not concern a Christian, and that he cares nothing about them. He lets anyone who will rob, take, cheat, scrape, devour, and rage—for the Christian is a martyr on earth. Therefore the peasants ought properly to stop using the name Christian and use some other name that would show that they are men who seek their human and natural rights rather than their rights as Christians. For obtaining their rights as Christians would mean they should keep quiet about all these matters and complain only to God when they suffer.

Dear friends, this is the instruction that you asked me to give you in the second document. Please remember that you have gladly offered to receive instruction on the basis of Scripture. So when this reaches you, do not be so ready to scream, "Luther flatters the princes and speaks contrary to the Gospel." First read and examine my arguments from Scripture. For this is your affair; I am excused in the sight of God and the world. I know well the false prophets who are among you. Do not listen to them. They are surely deceiving you. They do not think of your consciences; they want to make Galatians of you. They want to use you to gain riches and honor for themselves. Afterward, both you and they will be damned eternally in hell.

Admonition to Both Rulers and Peasants

Now, dear sirs, there is nothing Christian on either side and nothing Christian is at issue between you; both lords and peasants are discussing questions of justice and injustice in heathen, or worldly, terms. Furthermore, both parties are acting against God and are under his wrath, as you have heard. For God's sake, then, take my advice! Take a hold of these matters properly, with justice and not with force or violence and do not start endless bloodshed in Germany. For because both of you are wrong, and both of you want to avenge and defend yourselves, both of you will destroy yourselves and God will use one rascal to flog another.

Both Scripture and history are against you lords, for both tell how tyrants are punished. Even the heathen poets say that tyrants seldom die a dry death, but are usually slain and perish in their own blood. Because, then, it is an established fact that you rule tyrannically and with rage, prohibit preaching of the Gospel, and cheat and oppress the poor, you have no reason to be confident or to hope that you will perish in any other way than your kind have always perished.

Look at all the kingdoms that have come to their end by the sword—Assyria, Persia, Israel, Judah, and Rome. In the end they were all destroyed in the same way they destroyed others. Thus God shows that he is Judge upon earth and that he leaves no wrong unpunished. Therefore nothing is more certain than that this same judgment is breathing down your necks, whether it comes now or later, unless you reform.

Scripture and experience are also against you peasants. They teach that rebellion has never had a good end and that God always keeps his word exactly, "He that takes the sword will perish by the sword" [Matt. 26:52]. You are certainly under the wrath of God, because you are doing wrong by judging your own case and avenging yourselves and are bearing the name Christian unworthily. Even though you win and destroy all the lords, you will finally start tearing the flesh from one another's bones, like wild beasts. For because flesh and blood, not spirit, prevails among you, God will soon send an evil spirit among you, as he did to the men of Shechem and to Abimelech [Judg. 9:22–57]. See the end that finally comes to rebellion in the story of Korah, Numbers 16 [:31–35], and of Absalom [II Sam. 18:14–15], of Sheba [II Sam. 20:22], Zimri [I Kings 16:18], and others like them. In short, God hates both tyrants and rebels; therefore he sets them against each other, so that both parties perish shamefully, and his wrath and judgment upon the godless are fulfilled.

As I see it, the worst thing about this completely miserable affair is that both sides will sustain irreparable damage; and I would gladly risk my life and even die if I could prevent that from happening. Since neither side fights with a good conscience, but both fight to uphold injustice, it must follow, in the first place, that those who are slain are lost eternally, body and soul, as men who die in their sins, without penitence and without grace, under the wrath of God. Nothing can be done for them. The lords would be fighting to strengthen and maintain their tyranny, their persecution of the Gospel, and their unjust oppression of the poor, or else to help that kind of ruler. That is a terrible injustice and is against God. He who commits such a sin must be lost eternally. The peasants, on the other hand, would fight to defend their rebellion and their abuse of the name Christian. Both these things are great sins against God, and he who dies in them or for them must also be lost eternally, and nothing can prevent it.

The second injury is that Germany will be laid waste, and if this bloodshed once starts, it will not stop until everything is destroyed. It is easy to start a fight, but we cannot stop the fighting whenever we want to. What have all these innocent women, children, and old people, whom you fools are drawing with you into such danger, ever done to you? Why do you insist on filling the land with blood and robbery, widows and orphans? Oh, the devil has wicked plans! And God is angry; he threatens to let the devil loose upon us and cool his rage in our blood and souls. Beware, dear sirs, and be wise! Both of you are equally involved! What good will it do you intentionally to damn yourselves for all eternity and, in addition, to bequeath a desolate, devastated and bloody land to your descendants, when you still have time to find a better solution by repenting before God, by concluding a friendly agreement, or even by voluntarily suffering for the sake of humanity? You will accomplish nothing through strife and violence.

I, therefore, sincerely advise you to choose certain counts and lords from among the nobility and certain councilmen from the cities and ask them to arbitrate and settle this dispute amicably. You lords, stop being so stubborn! You will finally have to stop being such oppressive tyrants—whether you want to or not. Give these poor people room in which to live and air to breathe. You peasants, let yourselves be instructed and give up the excessive demands of some of your articles. In this way it may be possible to reach a solution of this dispute through human laws and agreements, if not through Christian means.

If you do not follow this advice—God forbid!—I must let you come to blows. But I am innocent of your souls, your blood, or your property. The guilt is yours alone. I have told you that you are both wrong and that what you are fighting for is wrong. You lords are not fighting against Christians—Christians do nothing against you; they prefer to suffer all things—but against outright robbers and defamers of the Christian name. Those of them who die are already condemned eternally. On the other hand, you peasants are not fighting against Christians, but against tyrants, and persecutors of God and man, and murderers of the saints of Christ. Those of them who die are also condemned eternally. There you have God's sure verdict upon both parties. This I know. Do what you please to preserve your bodies and souls, if you will not accept my advice.

I, however, will pray to my God that he will either reconcile you both and bring about an agreement between you, or else graciously prevent things from turning out as you intend. Nonetheless, the terrible signs and wonders that have come to pass in these times give me a heavy heart and make me fear that God's wrath has grown too great; as he says in Jeremiah, "Though Noah, Job, and Daniel stood before me, I would have no pleasure in the people." Would to God that you might fear his wrath and amend your ways that this disaster might be delayed and postponed a while! In any case, my conscience assures me that I have faithfully given you my Christian and fraternal advice. God grant that it helps! Amen.

22. Desiderius Erasmus of Rotterdam

Erasmus (1476–1536) was one of the most prolific and influential writers of his day, thanks in part to his skillful use of the greatest technical innovation of the Renaissance, the printing press. His literary accomplishments won him honors and offers of honors from most of the popes, emperors, and kings of his age, most of which he turned down in order not to give up his peripatetic lifestyle. Educated first at Deventer in the Netherlands and then at Paris, he began his career as an editor of ancient Latin and an editor and translator of ancient Greek literature—Cicero, Livy, Aristotle, Demosthenes, Euripides, Xenophon, Plutarch, et al. He was also a popularizer of ancient literature—e.g., in his collection of *Adagia* (sayings and proverbs) and in his *Familiar Colloquies*, which soon replaced medieval grammars as the chief textbook of the Latin language in elementary schools all over Europe. He was an expert satirist— for instance, in his *Praise of Folly* and in the *Julius Exclusus*, a parody of Pope Julius II. But his chief commitment was to the rejuvenation of Christian piety through editions of and commentaries upon its biblical and patristic sources—Jerome, Augustine, Origen—and through such manuals of the good life as the *Enchiridion of the Christian Soldier*. One of the most succinct, although far from complete, statements of this ideal is the *Paraclesis*, first published as a preface to his bilingual (the Greek original with a new Latin translation) edition of the New Testament in 1516. Another is the letter to Henry Bullock published here. It was in defense of this ideal that he eventually broke with Luther over the question of the role of the free will in the process of salvation (*On Free Will*, 1524).

The editors have not identified in the notes most of those proper names that Erasmus himself identifies in the text.

Erasmus, Letter 456 to Henry Bullock. Rochester [22?] August 1516.

Erasmus of Rotterdam to the Distinguished Theologian Henry Bullock

From your letter it is pretty clear that mine, which I left with Thomas More in London, had not yet reached you. Your long-standing feelings for me, my dear Bullock, I gratefully recognize and welcome. I only wish we

From *The Correspondence of Erasmus*, translated by R. A. B. Mynors and D. F. S. Thomson (Toronto: University of Toronto Press, 1977), pp. 43–54. © 1977 by The University of Toronto Press. Reprinted by permission of the publisher.

might one day return to our old way of life together and those common studies which were so perfectly delightful. I expect to spend the winter in Louvain; you must decide meanwhile what suits you best. That the New Testament as my efforts have restored it should be approved in your part of the world by all the best men, indeed by everyone as you put it of sound judgment, is a great joy to me. Though I have heard from trustworthy witnesses that you have one college steeped in theology whose members are regular Areopagites, and who are said to have provided by solemn resolution that no man bring the said volume by horse, boat, wagon or porter within the curtilage of the said college. I ask you, my learned friend, should one laugh or cry? How their zeal has led them astray! Their prejudice and bad temper hurt no one but themselves: they look askance at what would be very good for them. What kind of men are these, so hard to please that they are provoked by kindness which tames even wild beasts, and so implacable that all that one says in one's defence cannot soften them? In fact, what is much more impudent, they condemn and tear in pieces a book which they have not even read and, in any case, would not understand if they did. They have merely heard over their cups or in little gatherings in the marketplace that a new book has come out which tries to peck the crow's eyes out and give all the theologians a taste of their own medicine, and off they go, pursuing with unmixed invective both the author, who has tried with so much nightly toil to be of use to all who wish to learn, and his book, by which they might profit. Is that a way for philosophers or theologians to behave? A noisome thing philosophy must be, if it turns out men like that, and a feeble watered-down thing, if it cannot make such men better.

Then again, they do not refute and put right what they regard as errors in my work, but merely condemn me for committing them. It is unlawful, they say, to attempt anything of the sort, except on the authority of a General Council. What could be more iniquitous than that? They distort the sacred text every day, consulting no authorities but their own ignorance and rashness; and am I not to be allowed to restore what has been corrupted in accordance with the views of the Fathers, unless the whole of Christendom has been summoned to a Council? You see their policy: the man who removes an error is to be treated worse than he who introduces one, and he who serves the public by his industry worse than he whose lack of thought does it a disservice.

But there is one question I should like them to answer. This same version to which they are so much attached, was it undertaken by a translator authorized by a General Council, or was it published first and approved by the Fathers thereafter? Written first, I imagine, and afterwards approved.

But the same thing can happen to this text of mine, not that I desire or demand anything of the kind. Though even that is more than I would concede. It seems to me that it slipped into circulation by being used, and gradually gathered strength as time went by. Otherwise, if it had been approved and handed down by the official decision of a Council, it would have been in general use by everyone. As it is, Ambrose cites one version, Augustine another, Hilary and Jerome others. In fact, there is no general agreement even among copies of our own day.

If, however, they suppose that all is up with Christianity if there is any variation anywhere, we were already exposed to that risk, even if I had kept my eyes shut. "But this is the text," they say, "used by the synods of the Fathers." Ancient synods or modern? Why should the practice of Councils in antiquity carry less weight than modern practice?—especially in a subject such as this. Not but what there is a point they ought to prove: that texts cited in the acts of Councils differ from my emended text. What are we to make of the fact that the acts of most Councils were published in Greek? Again, it may well be that texts therein cited in a different form have been altered by someone to agree with our current version, as we find every day in the commentaries of Jerome and Ambrose. About twenty years ago they were printing in Paris service-books and books of hours according to the usage of Trier. The craftsman, who had a mere tincture of letters, found a great many discrepancies and corrected them all against our current version; so he himself confessed to me, thinking he did something admirable.

In fact, I do not find it absurd that something should escape the attention of a General Council, especially in things not necessary to salvation. It is sufficient that the actual proceedings of a synod should be exempt from criticism. And after all, why are we in greater distress over a difference of reading in Scripture than over a difference of interpretation? At least the risk in both is equal. Yet we see commentators not merely vary but conflict, constantly.

There is another problem, which let them clear up if they can. Do they allow any changes in Holy Writ, or none at all? If they allow any, why not examine in the first place whether it is right or no to make the change? If they do not, what will they make of those passages in which the existence of a corruption is too obvious to be denied or overlooked? Would they rather imitate on this point the mass-priest who refused to change the word *mumpsimus* which he had used for twenty years, when someone told him that *sumpsimus* was what he ought to say? They burst out in horror crying, "O heavens, o earth! This man is correcting the Gospels!" But with how much more justice one would cry out upon the man who fills them with error, "Rank sacrilege! This man corrupts the Gospels!" It is not as though I undermine the modern text; I restore the old one to the utmost of my power, but in such a way as not to weaken their new one. Those who do battle for the new one as though for hearth and altar still have what they are so much attached to; they have lost nothing, and have gained something worth having. The text they love they will henceforward read more accurately and understand more correctly.

Suppose I had expounded all the sacred books by way of a paraphrase, and made it possible to keep the sense inviolate and yet to read them without stumbling and understand them more easily? Would they quarrel with me then? Juvencus was actually admired for his courage in putting the Gospel narrative into verse. Who issues a writ against that excellent divine Gilles van Delft, who versified almost the whole of Scripture? Every day in church they sing the Psalms in the ancient version; and yet we possess not only a revision by St. Jerome but his new translation made from the Hebrew original. The old version is read in choir, the others in universities or in private. Neither interferes with the other. In fact, only the other day Felice da Prato published a new version of the whole Psalter which differs considerably from all its predecessors. Has anyone ever stirred up trouble for him? My friend Jacques Lefèvre d'Etaples some time ago did for St. Paul what I have done for the whole New Testament.[1] Why should certain people wait until now to rise in their wrath as though this were something new? Are they ready to give leave for this to everyone except me? Yet Lefèvre showed rather more enterprise than I did, for he set his new version opposite the old, and did so in Paris, the queen of all universities, while I set up as no more than a reviser, and either correct or explain a few passages only. This I say with no desire to make Lefèvre generally unpopular—he is a distinguished man whose reputation has long outlived any ill will; but I wish to show how unfair some people are who pick on something which has long been done by many men without arousing protests, and protest against it when I do it as a sudden innovation. What have students of Aristotle lost by the appearance of the new edition by Argyropylus, Leonardo Aretino[2] and Theodore of Gaza? Surely no one wants to suppress

1. Of these, the most prominent, and the best known today, was Lefèvre d'Etaples (c. 1460–1536), author of very popular commentaries on Aristotle based on the original Greek and a French translation of the New Testament and the Psalms. His commentary on the Pauline Epistles won him recognition also as a theologian, even though he never received the corresponding academic degree. Many of his writings have recently been published (in the original Latin) by Eugene Rice as *The Prefatory Epistles* (Columbia University Press, 1972).

2. The same Leonardo Bruni who wrote the *Constitution of the Florentines* published in this volume.

their version or do away with it for fear it may look as though there were some things which the older generation of specialists in Aristotelian philosophy did not know? Does that reason deter Guillaume Cop from translating books by Galen and Hippocrates, for fear the world should perceive that earlier physicians mistranslated many passages?

Someone may say, "In secular studies this is expedient; but that it should be done in the Scriptures everywhere and by the first comer is most perilous." To begin with, I do not make changes all up and down; the mass of it remains the same, and discussion is confined to a few passages. Nor is it entirely correct, I think, at least as far as this subject is concerned, to class me as one of the common herd. I show that in some places slips have been made by Hilary, by Augustine, by Thomas; and this I do, as is right and proper, with great respect and with no personal attacks, in such a way that, were they themselves alive today, they would be grateful even to a humble creature like myself for the way in which I put them right. They were very great men, but only men after all. Let my opponents show that they were right, and refute what I say with argument and not abuse; and I shall be much indebted to them. Let those who wish every word that Lyra wrote to be treated as an oracle defend him in the places where I differ from him. For to look in Hugo for passages to criticize I regard as a foolish waste of time; I noted only a few passages that were exceptionally absurd, in order to encourage caution in those who read such writers with complete confidence and no critical sense.

At any rate, let those who attribute all qualities to authors of that sort defend their precious darlings, and show that I am all at sea while they hit the target. But they think it beneath them to descend to these small and schoolmasterly questions; for so they are wont to refer to those who have had a good literary education, regarding it as a great insult to call a man a schoolmaster, as though it would be to the credit of a theologian to be innocent of schooling. Knowledge of grammar by itself is not the making of a theologian, but much less is he made by ignorance of grammar; at the very least, skill in this subject is an aid to the understanding of theology and lack of skill is the reverse. Nor can it be denied that Jerome and Ambrose and Augustine, the principal authorities on whom our theology rests, were all drawn from the teaching profession. For in those days Aristotle was not yet accepted as an authority in the theological schools, and the philosophy current in our universities nowadays was not yet invented. Yet a modest man is glad to be put right by anyone; as Horace puts it, "Though he were blind who shows you where to go, / Yet listen none the less."

Again, even those who reserve this whole matter for authority and not critical judgment have not much to find fault with in me. Everyone knows that it was provided by this last Lateran Council that a book should be pub-

lished after approval by the local bishop or by those to whom he has dele-
gated his functions. But both the writing and the publication of my work
was done with the cognizance and approval of the bishop of the place, and
no ordinary bishop either, but one who besides his venerable years and his
distinguished lineage is remarkable for outstanding sanctity of life and exceptional learning. And he not merely approved, but offered me everything
one could think of if I had been willing to remain with him, and on my
departure showed me such kindness, such generosity (incomparable man
that he is) that I blush to record it. Even this did not content him; of his own
accord he wrote to the archbishop of Canterbury to commend me in most
honourable terms, and to thank him on my behalf. And so my labours have
been approved, if not by a Council, at least in accordance with a conciliar
decision. The authority concerned is such that by himself he ought to be
regarded as the equivalent of many; and his verdict ought to carry even more
weight, inasmuch as it was not obtained by humble requests or services
rendered, but was freely offered to a man who almost tried to avoid it.

If anyone thinks that one man's authority carries too little weight, the
bishop's opinion has been underwritten by two professors of theology, and
those by a long way in the first rank. One is Ludwig Baer, a man by common consent richly supplied with every form of virtue and knowledge and
in the rough and tumble of philosophy of such experience that at Paris he
earned first place on the list of those qualifying for the doctorate. Such
disapproval did he feel for my work that he offered to share with me all his
resources, which are considerable, and of the two prebends which he possesses he handed one over to me of his own accord. Besides him there
is Wolfgang Faber Capito, whose distinguished knowledge of theology
earned him election to the chapter of Basel, where he holds the office of
public preacher. He is a man who besides the other liberal disciplines has
no ordinary proficiency in the three tongues, Greek, Latin and Hebrew, and
is of such integrity, so upright a character that I never saw anything more
invulnerable. These are the men on whose verdict the book was published,
and their judgment would inspire complete confidence in the bishop on any
subject however important, if he mistrusted his own opinion.

But it is not as though my work has been condemned by anyone in the
rest of the theological world. Some merely lamented that they had not
learnt Greek in boyhood, and that the book had appeared too late for them
to use it. I could report what was said of my edition by the venerable prior
of the charterhouse at Freiburg, Gregor Reisch, whose opinion carries the
weight of an oracle in Germany, or by that eminent divine Jakob Wimpfe-
ling; I could produce numberless letters from distinguished men—thanking
me because they have risen from the reading of my works, especially what
I have published on the New Testament, both better men and better schol-

ars—were I not afraid that someone might think I showed more vanity in saying this than regard for the truth. And yet those who have known me well in Germany, and the people in England to whom all my affairs are as familiar as they are to me, are well aware how sparingly I touch on this kind of thing. I am of course reluctant, and for two reasons: one, that I hate nothing so much as boasting, and the other, that I have no wish to cause embarrassment to any of my friends on my account. Not to speak of others, you know, my dear Bullock, what manner of man is that outstanding prelate the bishop of Rochester, chancellor of your university, whether one considers his integrity and true piety or his learning. And are these worthless wretches not ashamed to pursue with their abuse books which so great a man approves and reads?

For that matter, are not these three-halfpenny puppets ashamed to attack as they think fit books which have the approval of the supreme pontiff himself? For unless he approved my work, he could not in any case have said in a letter that he would regard it as a great privilege if I were to offer him the dedication of the whole fruit of my labours. He does more than approve who promises a reward as well. I had set out my plans in a letter to him, enquiring tentatively whether he wished for the dedication. He counterbalanced my single letter at once with two of his own, one a most friendly complimentary scholarly reply to mine, the other a recommendation of me and my learned projects to his serene majesty the English king; with how much emphasis and warmth, you shall judge for yourself, for I enclose a copy of both letters. Both cardinals had replied, Grimani that is, and San Giorgio; but their letters were sent by Andrea Ammonio, who is a particular ornament of your native England, to Richard Pace, the envoy of his king to the Swiss and to Maximilian, for him to hand on to me as I was at that time living in Basel; but up to now they have not yet arrived. Last winter I sent one volume to Leo, to whom it is dedicated, and if it reached him safely, I have no doubt that he will respond to my nights of toil with a handsome reward.

What remains then for them to complain of in me? I am not the first to attempt this enterprise, nor did I do so unadvisedly. I have followed the decision of the Council. I have won the approval of the best judges at least, if not of everyone. If there were anything irreligious in what I have done, religious men would dislike it; if it were unscholarly, scholars would reject it. But none welcome it more than those who are distinguished by unusual holiness of life and more than ordinary erudition. If my critics are more moved by learning, the most learned men approve it; if by virtue, the most virtuous men approve it; if by authority, bishops approve it and archbishops and the supreme pontiff himself. And yet none of these could give me support worth having, if it were known that I had canvassed for the support of any one among them all. Any tributes that have been paid were paid to the facts and not the man.

Many as they are, these considerations do not induce them to wish to unlearn what they have learnt in the wrong way. Are they afraid that if the young are persuaded by them, they themselves will lecture to empty benches? Why do they not rather take into account quite another point? About thirty years ago, nothing was taught in the university at Cambridge except Alexander, what they call the *Parva logicalia*, and the traditional doctrines of Aristotle with Scotistic *questiones*. As time went on the humanities were added; then mathematics; then a new, or at least a new-fangled Aristotle; then the knowledge of Greek; then all those authors whose very names were unknown in the old days even to the brahmins of philosophy Iarcas-like enthroned. And what, pray, was the effect of all this on your university? Why, it flourished to such a tune that it can challenge the first universities of the age, and there are men there compared with whom those earlier scholars are mere shadows of theologians, not the reality. This is not disputed by such of the older men as have an open mind. They rejoice at other people's good fortune, and deplore their own bad luck. Are objectors distressed by the thought that hereafter the writings of evangelists and apostles will be read by more men and read with closer attention? Do they resent that even this space of time should be allotted to the studies to which it would have been proper to devote all their time, and would they prefer to dissipate a lifetime on the puerile niceties of their *questiones*?

Yet on these grounds at least I do not much regret my nightly vigils. It is common knowledge that before now there have been some theologians so unfamiliar with sacred literature that they never even read the *Sentences* or laid a finger to any part of the subject except their riddling *questiones*. Surely it must be right to recall such people to the genuine sources? For my part, my dear Bullock, I could wish that the labours I have undertaken for the general good, which were by no means inconsiderable, might prove to be of general use. For I look for my whole reward from Christ Himself, if I can only do something to deserve it first; but if it is impossible for me to win general approval, I console myself in the meantime with the fact that almost everywhere I am approved by the men who themselves most enjoy universal approval. And I hope that in future what is now accepted by the best judges may prove to be acceptable to the majority. In other things to be new is the way to be popular, but this work of mine has earned ill will by its novelty. And so I think we shall see the opposite result: they lost their popular appeal as they grew older, and I perhaps shall acquire it. One thing at any rate I foresee: my works, such as they are, will get a fairer hearing from posterity. Not that I can complain even of my contemporaries. They think more highly of me, I will not say than I demand but than I either deserve or can live up to. Diverse and hard to please as are the tastes of mortal men, especially in the domain of literature, it remains true that my writings, which are not irreligious, although inadequate in scholarship compared with the books of others, have not yet been attacked except by a handful of men so captious that they approve nothing not of their own making, so stupid as to be quite insensitive, so idle that they do not even read what they criticize, so ignorant as to be incapable of criticism, so starved of reputation and so greedy for it that they carp at other men's labours in hopes of earning a little glory for themselves. There are even men in this group who condemn and spurn in public what they read with approval at home. It may be a kind of modesty to conceal those who have helped you, but it is the modesty of a man mean and ungrateful. To rend in public the reputation of those whose labours are your standby at home is very far from any form of civilized behaviour; though the man who would serve in Christ's army must swallow this too.

You say you are preaching before public audiences; I think this an excellent plan, and am glad that it goes well, especially since you preach Christ unadulterated, and neither magnify nor advertise the petty cleverness of men. What you write about the boy can be answered very briefly; I already have more than I need, so far am I from wishing for any further burdens. Please give my warmest greetings to the friends whom I bear round with me in my heart, Doctor Fawne, the learned John Bryan, that most cultivated John Vaughan, Humphrey kindest of men, and my old host Garrett the bookseller; for Watson I hear is away. Farewell, my most learned Bullock.

Rochester, in the bishop's lodging, [31] August 1516

23. John Calvin, *Institutes of the Christian Religion*

John Calvin (or Cauvin, 1509–64) abandoned the study of law at an early age for the study of Greek and Hebrew. Between 1533 and 1534 he experienced what he called "a sudden conversion" and thereafter devoted himself to theology. He fled from Paris to Basel in 1534 to escape persecution in the wake of the first "Lutheran" uprising, and he there published

From *Institutes of the Christian Religion by John Calvin*, translated by John Allen (Philadelphia: The Presbyterian Board of Christian Educators, 1930), pp. 40–45, 148–50, 410–17, 633–50, 654–57, 660–63. Footnotes deleted.

the first draft of what was to become, in the much revised and expanded definitive edition of 1559, his greatest work, the *Institutes of the Christian Religion*. But Calvin was more than just a theologian. He was invited to settle in the free city of Geneva during a visit there in 1536 in order to help Guillaume Farel (1489–1565) reform the local church in accordance with the theological precepts of the Zurich reformer, Ulrich Zwingli. Expelled from the city the next year, he was invited back in 1541; and he remained there as head of the church in Geneva and as the organizer of missionary enterprises all over Europe until his death. Calvin turned Geneva into a "holy city" very much like the "New Jerusalem" established by Carlo Borromeo shortly afterwards in Milan (see the *Diary* of Casale in this volume). Calvin's theology, and Calvinist ecclesiastical organization, were adopted by the reformed churches of France, Scotland, the United Provinces of the Netherlands, and several of the states of Germany; and they were brought to America by the Puritan founders of Massachusetts.

God's Preservation and Support of the World by His Power, and His Government of Every Part of It by His Providence

To represent God as a Creator only for a moment, who entirely finished all his work at once, were frigid and jejune; and in this it behoves us especially to differ from the heathen, that the presence of the Divine power may appear to us no less in the perpetual state of the world than in its first origin. For although the minds even of impious men, by the mere contemplation of earth and heaven, are constrained to rise to the Creator, yet faith has a way peculiar to itself to assign to God the whole praise of creation. To which purpose is that assertion of an Apostle before cited, that it is only "through faith that we understand the worlds were framed by the word of God"; because, unless we proceed to his providence, we have no correct conception of the meaning of this article, "that God is the Creator"; however we may appear to comprehend it in our minds and to confess it with our tongues. The carnal sense, when it has once viewed the power of God in the creation, stops there; and when it proceeds the furthest, it only examines and considers the wisdom, and power, and goodness of the Author in producing such a work, which spontaneously present themselves to the view even of those who are unwilling to observe them. In the next place, it conceives of some general operation of God in preserving and governing it, on which the power of motion depends. Lastly, it supposes that the vigour originally infused by God into all things is sufficient for their sustentation. But faith ought to penetrate further. When it has learned that he is the Creator of all things, it should immediately conclude that he is also their perpetual governor and preserver; and that not by a certain universal motion, actuating the whole machine of the world, and all its respective parts, but by a particular providence sustaining, nourishing, and providing for every thing which he has made. . . .

But as we know that the world was made chiefly for the sake of mankind, we must also observe this end in the government of it. The Prophet Jeremiah exclaims, "I know that the way of man is not in himself: it is not in man that walketh to direct his steps." And Solomon: "Man's goings are of the Lord: how can a man then understand his own way?" Now, let them say that man is actuated by God according to his own pleasure. If this could be asserted with truth, man would have the free choice of his own ways. That, perhaps, they will deny, because he can do nothing independently of the power of God. But since it is evident that both the Prophet and Solomon ascribe to God choice and appointment, as well as power, this by no means extricates them from the difficulty. But Solomon, in another place, beautifully reproves this temerity of men, who predetermine on an end for themselves, without regard to God, as though they were not led by his hand: "The preparation of the heart in man," says he, "and the answer of the tongue, is from the Lord." It is, indeed, a ridiculous madness for miserable men to resolve on undertaking any work independently of God, whilst they cannot even speak a word but what he chooses. Moreover, the Scripture, more fully to express that nothing is transacted in the world but according to his destination, shows that those things are subject to him which appear most fortuitous. For what would you be more ready to attribute to chance, than when a limb broken off from a tree kills a passing traveller? But very different is the decision of the Lord, who acknowledges that he has delivered him into the hand of the slayer. Who, likewise, does not leave lots to the blindness of fortune? Yet the Lord leaves them not, but claims the disposal of them himself. He teaches us that it is not by any power of their own that lots are cast into the lap and drawn out; but the only thing which could be ascribed to chance, he declares to belong to himself. To the same purpose is another passage from Solomon: "The poor and the deceitful man meet together: the Lord enlighteneth the eyes of them both." For although the poor and the rich are blended together in the world, yet, as their respective conditions are assigned to them by Divine appointment, he suggests that God, who enlightens all, is not blind, and thus exhorts the poor to patience; because those who are discontented with their lot, are endeavouring to shake off the burden imposed on them by God. Thus also another Prophet rebukes profane persons, who attribute it to human industry, or to fortune, that some men remain in obscurity, and others rise to honours: "Promotion cometh neither from the east, nor from the west, nor from the south. But God is the Judge; he putteth down one, and setteth up another." Since God cannot divest himself of the office of a judge, hence he reasons, that it is from the secret counsel of God, that some rise to promotion, and others remain in contempt. . . .

The Proper Application of This Doctrine to Render It Useful to Us

. . . Those who have learned this modesty will neither murmur against God on account of past adversities nor charge him with the guilt of their crimes, like Agamemnon in Homer, who says, "The blame belongs not to me, but to Jupiter and Fate." Nor will they, as if hurried away by the Fates, under the influence of despair, put an end to their own lives, like the young man whom Plautus introduces as saying, "The condition of our affairs is inconstant; men are governed by the caprice of the Fates; I will betake myself to a precipice, and there destroy my life and every thing at once." Nor will they excuse their flagitious actions by ascribing them to God, after the example of another young man introduced by the same poet, who says, "God was the cause: I believe it was the Divine will. For had it not been so, I know it would not have happened." But they will rather search the Scripture, to learn what is pleasing to God, that by the guidance of the Spirit they may strive to attain it; and at the same time, being prepared to follow God whithersoever he calls them, they will exhibit proofs in their conduct that nothing is more useful than a knowledge of this doctrine. Some profane men foolishly raise such a tumult with their absurdities, as almost, according to a common expression, to confound heaven and earth together. They argue in this manner: If God has fixed the moment of our death, we cannot avoid it; therefore all caution against it will be but lost labour. One man dares not venture himself in a way which he hears is dangerous, lest he should be assassinated by robbers; another sends for physicians, and wearies himself with medicines, to preserve his life; another abstains from the grosser kinds of food, lest he should injure his valetudinary constitution; another dreads to inhabit a ruinous house; and men in general exert all their faculties in devising and executing methods by which they may attain the object of their desires. Now, either all these things are vain remedies employed to correct the will of God, or life and death, health and disease, peace and war, and other things which, according to their desires or aversions, men industriously study to obtain or to avoid, are not determined by his certain decree. Moreover they conclude, that the prayers of the faithful are not only superfluous, but perverse, which contain petitions that the Lord will provide for those things which he has already decreed from eternity. In short, they supersede all deliberations respecting futurity, as opposed to the providence of God, who, without consulting men, has decreed whatever he pleased. And what has already happened they impute to the

Divine providence in such a manner as to overlook the person, who is known to have committed any particular act. Has an assassin murdered a worthy citizen? They say he has executed the counsel of God. Has any one been guilty of theft or fornication? Because he has done what was foreseen and ordained by the Lord, he is the minister of his providence. Has a son, neglecting all remedies, carelessly waited the death of his father? It was impossible for him to resist God, who had decreed this event from eternity. Thus by these persons all crimes are denominated virtues, because they are subservient to the ordination of God. . . .

The same persons inconsiderately and erroneously ascribe all past events to the absolute providence of God. For since all things which come to pass are dependent upon it, therefore, say they, neither thefts, nor adulteries, nor homicides, are perpetrated without the intervention of the Divine will. Why, therefore, they ask, shall a thief be punished for having pillaged him whom it has pleased the Lord to chastise with poverty? Why shall a homicide be punished for having slain him whose life the Lord had terminated? If all such characters are subservient to the Divine will, why shall they be punished? But I deny that they serve the will of God. For we cannot say, that he who is influenced by a wicked heart, acts in obedience to the commands of God, while he is only gratifying his own malignant passion. That man obeys God, who, being instructed in his will, hastens whither God calls him. Where can we learn his will, but in his word? Therefore in our actions we ought to regard the will of God, which is declared in his word. God only requires of us conformity to his precepts. If we do any thing contrary to them, it is not obedience, but contumacy and transgression. But it is said, if he would not permit it, we should not do it. This I grant. But do we perform evil actions with the design of pleasing him? He gives us no such command. We precipitate ourselves into them, not considering what is his will, but inflamed with the violence of our passions, so that we deliberately strive to oppose him. In this manner even by criminal actions we subserve his righteous ordination; because, in the infinite greatness of his wisdom, he well knows how to use evil instruments for the accomplishment of good purposes. . . .

Man, in His Present State Despoiled of Freedom of Will, and Subjected to a Miserable Slavery

Since we have seen that the domination of sin, from the time of its subjugation of the first man, not only extends over the whole race, but also exclusively possesses every soul, it now remains to be more closely investigated, whether we are despoiled of all freedom, and, if any particle of it yet remain, how far its power extends. But, that we may the more easily discover the truth of this question, I will first set up by the way a mark, by which our whole course must be regulated. The best method of guarding against error is to consider the dangers which threaten us on every side. For when man is declared to be destitute of all rectitude, he immediately makes it an occasion of slothfulness; because he is said to have no power of himself for the pursuit of righteousness, he totally neglects it, as though it did not at all concern him. On the other hand, he cannot arrogate any thing to himself, be it ever so little, without God being robbed of his honour, and himself being endangered by presumptuous temerity. Therefore, to avoid striking on either of these rocks, this will be the course to be pursued—that man, being taught that he has nothing good left in his possession, and being surrounded on every side with the most miserable necessity, should, nevertheless, be instructed to aspire to the good of which he is destitute, and to the liberty of which he is deprived; and should be roused from indolence with more earnestness, than if he were supposed to be possessed of the greatest strength. The necessity of the latter is obvious to every one. The former, I perceive, is doubted by more than it ought to be. For this being placed beyond all controversy, that man must not be deprived of any thing that properly belongs to him, it ought also to be manifest how important it is that he should be prevented from false boasting. For if he was not even then permitted to glory in himself, when by the Divine beneficence he was decorated with the noblest ornaments, how much ought he now to be humbled, when, on account of his ingratitude, he has been hurled from the summit of glory to the abyss of ignominy! At that time, I say, when he was exalted to the most honourable eminence, the Scripture attributes nothing to him, but that he was created after the image of God; which certainly implies that his happiness consisted not in any goodness of his own, but in a participation of God. What, then, remains for him now, deprived of all glory, but that he acknowledge God, to whose beneficence he could not be thankful, when he abounded in the riches of his favour? and that he now, at least, by a confession of his poverty, glorify him, whom he glorified not by an acknowledgment of his blessings? It is also no less conducive to our interests than to the Divine glory, that all the praise of wisdom and strength be taken away from us; so that they join sacrilege to our fall, who ascribe to us any thing more than truly belongs to us. For what else is the consequence, when we are taught to contend in our own strength, but that we are lifted into the air on a reed, which being soon broken, we fall to the ground. Though our strength is placed in too favourable a point of view, when it is compared to a reed. For it is nothing but smoke, whatever vain men have imagined and pretended concerning it. Wherefore it is not without reason, that the remarkable sentence is so frequently repeated by Augustine, that free will is rather overthrown than established even by its own advocates. It was necessary to premise these things for the sake of some, who, when they hear that human power is completely subverted in order that the power of God may be established in man, inveterately hate this whole argument, as dangerous and unprofitable; which yet appears to be highly useful to us, and essential to true religion. . . .

This being admitted will place it beyond all doubt, that man is not possessed of free will for good works, unless he be assisted by grace, and that special grace which is bestowed on the elect alone in regeneration. For I stop not to notice those fanatics, who pretend that grace is offered equally and promiscuously to all. But it does not yet appear, whether he is altogether deprived of power to do good, or whether he yet possesses some power, though small and feeble; which of itself can do nothing, but by the assistance of grace does also perform its part. Lombard, in order to establish this notion, informs us that two sorts of grace are necessary to qualify us for the performance of good works. One he calls operative, by which we efficaciously will what is good; the other cooperative, which attends as auxiliary to a good will. This division I dislike, because, while he attributes an efficacious desire of what is good to the grace of God, he insinuates that man has of his own nature antecedent, though ineffectual, desires after what is good; as Bernard asserts that a good will is the work of God, but yet allows that man is self-impelled to desire such a good will. But this is very remote from the meaning of Augustine, from whom, however, Lombard would be thought to have borrowed this division. The second part of it offends me by its ambiguity, which has produced a very erroneous interpretation. For they have supposed that we cooperate with the second sort of Divine grace, because we have it in our power either to frustrate the first sort by rejecting it, or to confirm it by our obedience to it. The author of the treatise "On the Vocation of the Gentiles" expresses it thus—that those who have the use of reason and judgment are at liberty to depart from grace, that they may be rewarded for not having departed, and that what is impossible without the cooperation of the Spirit, may be imputed to their merits, by whose will it might have been prevented. These two things I have thought proper to notice as I proceed, that the reader may perceive how much I dissent from the sounder schoolmen. For I differ considerably more from the later sophists, as they have departed much further from the judgment of antiquity. However, we understand from this division, in what sense they have ascribed free will to man. For Lombard at length pronounces, that we are not therefore possessed of free will, because we have an equal power to do or to think either good or evil, but only because we are free from constraint. And this liberty is not diminished, although we are corrupt, and the slaves of sin, and capable of doing nothing but sin.

Then man will be said to possess free will in this sense, not that he has an equally free election of good and evil, but because he does evil voluntarily, and not by constraint. That, indeed, is very true; but what end could it answer to decorate a thing so diminutive with a title so superb? Egregious liberty indeed, if man be not compelled to serve sin, but yet is such a willing slave, that his will is held in bondage by the fetters of sin. I really abominate contentions about words, which disturb the Church without producing any good effect; but I think that we ought religiously to avoid words which signify any absurdity, particularly when they lead to a pernicious error. How few are there, pray, who, when they hear free will attributed to man, do not immediately conceive, that he has the sovereignty over his own mind and will, and is able by his innate power to incline himself to whatever he pleases? But it will be said, all danger from these expressions will be removed, if the people are carefully apprized of their signification. But on the contrary, the human mind is naturally so prone to falsehood, that it will sooner imbibe error from one single expression, than truth from a prolix oration; of which we have a more certain experiment than could be wished in this very word. For neglecting that explanation of the fathers, almost all their successors have been drawn into a fatal self-confidence, by adhering to the original and proper signification of the word. . . .

But I am obliged to repeat here, what I promised in the beginning of this chapter—that he who feels the most consternation, from a consciousness of his own calamity, poverty, nakedness, and ignominy, has made the greatest proficiency in the knowledge of himself. For there is no danger that man will divest himself of too much, provided he learns that what is wanting in him may be recovered in God. But he cannot assume to himself even the least particle beyond his just right, without ruining himself with vain confidence, and incurring the guilt of enormous sacrilege, by transferring to himself the honour which belongs to God. And whenever our minds are pestered with this cupidity, to desire to have something of our own, which may reside in ourselves rather than in God, we may know that this idea is suggested by the same counsellor, who excited in our first parents the desire of resembling "gods, knowing good and evil." . . .

The True Church and the Necessity of Our Union with Her, Being the Mother of All the Pious

. . . Here we must regard both the secret election of God, and his internal vocation; because he alone "knoweth them that are his"; and keeps them enclosed under his "seal," to use the expression of Paul; except that they bear his impression, by which they may be distinguished from the reprobate. But because a small and contemptible number is concealed among a vast multitude, and a few grains of wheat are covered with a heap of chaff, we must leave to God alone the knowledge of his Church whose foundation is his secret election. Nor is it sufficient to include in our thoughts and minds the whole multitude of the elect, unless we conceive of such a unity of the Church, into which we know ourselves to be truly ingrafted. For unless we are united with all the other members under Christ our Head, we can have no hope of the future inheritance. Therefore the Church is called *Catholic*, or universal; because there could not be two or three churches, without Christ being divided, which is impossible. But all the elect of God are so connected with each other in Christ, that as they depend upon one head, so they grow up together as into one body, compacted together like members of the same body; being made truly one, as living by one faith, hope, and charity, through the same Divine Spirit, being called not only to the same inheritance of eternal life, but also to a participation of one God and Christ. Therefore, though the melancholy desolation which surrounds us, seems to proclaim that there is nothing left of the Church, let us remember that the death of Christ is fruitful, and that God wonderfully preserves his Church as it were in hiding-places; according to what he said to Elijah: "I have reserved to myself seven thousand men, who have not bowed the knee to Baal."

This article of the creed, however, relates in some measure to the external Church, that every one of us may maintain a brotherly agreement with all the children of God, may pay due deference to the authority of the Church, and, in a word, may conduct himself as one of the flock. Therefore we add *The Communion of Saints*—a clause which, though generally omitted by the ancients, ought not to be neglected, because it excellently expresses the character of the Church; as though it had been said that the saints are united in the fellowship of Christ on this condition, that whatever benefits God confers upon them, they should mutually communicate to each other. This destroys not the diversity of grace, for we know that the gifts of the Spirit are variously distributed; nor does it disturb the order of civil polity, which secures to every individual the exclusive enjoyment of his property, as it is necessary for the preservation of the peace of society that men should have peculiar and distinct possessions. . . .

Here are three things, therefore, worthy of our observation. First, that whatever holiness may distinguish the children of God, yet such is their condition as long as they inhabit a mortal body, that they cannot stand before God without remission of sins. Secondly, that this benefit belongs to the Church; so that we cannot enjoy it unless we continue in its communion. Thirdly, that it is dispensed to us by the ministers and pastors of the Church, either in the preaching of the gospel, or in the administration of the sacraments; and that this is the principal exercise of the power of the keys, which the Lord has conferred on the society of believers. Let every one of us, therefore, consider it as his duty, not to seek remission of sins anywhere but where the Lord has placed it. Of public reconciliation, which is a branch of discipline, we shall speak in its proper place. . . .

Book 3

Chapter 21

Eternal Election, or God's Predestination of Some to Salvation, and of Others to Destruction

The covenant of life not being equally preached to all, and among those to whom it is preached not always finding the same reception, this diversity discovers the wonderful depth of the Divine judgment. Nor is it to be doubted that this variety also follows, subject to the decision of God's eternal election. If it be evidently the result of the Divine will, that salvation is freely offered to some, and others are prevented from attaining it—this immediately gives rise to important and difficult questions, which are incapable of any other explication, than by the establishment of pious minds in what ought to be received concerning election and predestination—a question, in the opinion of many, full of perplexity; for they consider nothing more unreasonable, than that, of the common mass of mankind, some should be predestinated to salvation, and others to destruction. But how unreasonably they perplex themselves will afterwards appear from the sequel of our discourse. Besides, the very obscurity which excites such dread, not only displays the utility of this doctrine, but shows it to be productive of the most delightful benefit. We shall never be clearly convinced as we ought to be, that our salvation flows from the fountain of God's free mercy, till we are acquainted with his eternal election, which illustrates the grace of God by this comparison, that he adopts not all promiscuously to the hope of salvation, but gives to some what he refuses to others. Ignorance of this principle evidently detracts from the Divine glory, and diminishes real humility. But according to Paul, what is so necessary to be known, never can be known, unless God, without any regard to works, chooses those whom he has decreed. "At this present time also, there is a remnant according to the election of grace. And if by grace, then it is no more of works; otherwise, grace is no more grace. But if it be of works, then it is no more grace; otherwise, work is no more work." If we need to be recalled to the origin of election, to prove that we obtain salvation from no other source than the mere goodness of God, they who desire to extinguish this principle, do all they can to obscure what ought to be magnificently and loudly celebrated, and to pluck up humility by the roots. In ascribing the salvation of the remnant of the people to the election of grace,

Paul clearly testifies, that it is then only known that God saves whom he will of his mere good pleasure, and does not dispense a reward to which there can be no claim. They who shut the gates to prevent any one from presuming to approach and taste this doctrine, do no less injury to man than to God; for nothing else will be sufficient to produce in us suitable humility, or to impress us with a due sense of our great obligations to God. Nor is there any other basis for solid confidence, even according to the authority of Christ, who, to deliver us from all fear, and render us invincible amidst so many dangers, snares, and deadly conflicts, promises to preserve in safety all whom the Father has committed to his care. Whence we infer, that they who know not themselves to be God's peculiar people will be tortured with continual anxiety; and therefore, that the interest of all believers, as well as their own, is very badly consulted by those who, blind to the three advantages we have remarked, would wholly remove the foundation of our salvation. And hence the Church rises to our view, which otherwise, as Bernard justly observes, could neither be discovered nor recognized among creatures, being in two respects wonderfully concealed in the bosom of a blessed predestination, and in the mass of a miserable damnation. But before I enter on the subject itself, I must address some preliminary observations to two sorts of persons. The discussion of predestination—a subject of itself rather intricate—is made very perplexed, and therefore dangerous, by human curiosity, which no barriers can restrain from wandering into forbidden labyrinths, and soaring beyond its sphere, as if determined to leave none of the Divine secrets unscrutinized or unexplored. As we see multitudes everywhere guilty of this arrogance and presumption, and among them some who are not censurable in other respects, it is proper to admonish them of the bounds of their duty on this subject. First, then, let them remember that when they inquire into predestination, they penetrate the inmost recesses of Divine wisdom, where the careless and confident intruder will obtain no satisfaction to his curiosity, but will enter a labyrinth from which he will find no way to depart. For it is unreasonable that man should scrutinize with impunity those things which the Lord has determined to be hidden in himself; and investigate, even from eternity, that sublimity of wisdom which God would have us to adore and not comprehend, to promote our admiration of his glory. The secrets of his will which he determined to reveal to us, he discovers in his word; and these are all that he foresaw would concern us or conduce to our advantage.

II. "We are come into the way of faith," says Augustine, "let us constantly pursue it. It conducts into the king's palace, in which are hidden all the treasures of wisdom and knowledge. For the Lord Christ himself envied not his great and most select disciples when he said, 'I have many things to say unto you, but ye cannot bear them now'. We must walk, we must improve, we must grow, that our hearts may be able to understand those things of which we are at present incapable. If the last day finds us improving, we shall then learn what we never could learn in the present state." If we only consider that the word of the Lord is the only way to lead us to an investigation of all that ought to be believed concerning him, and the only light to enlighten us to behold all that ought to be seen of him, this consideration will easily restrain and preserve us from all presumption. For we shall know that when we have exceeded the limits of the word, we shall get into a devious and darksome course, in which errors, slips, and falls will often be inevitable. Let us, then, in the first place, bear in mind, that to desire any other knowledge of predestination than what is unfolded in the word of God, indicates as great folly, as a wish to walk through unpassable roads, or to see in the dark. Nor let us be ashamed to be ignorant of some things relative to a subject in which there is a kind of learned ignorance. Rather let us abstain with cheerfulness from the pursuit of that knowledge, the affectation of which is foolish, dangerous, and even fatal. But if we are stimulated by the wantonness of intellect, we must oppose it with a reflection calculated to repress it, that as "it is not good to eat much honey, so for men to search their own glory, is not glory." For there is sufficient to deter us from that presumption, which can only precipitate us into ruin.

III. Others, desirous of remedying this evil, will have all mention of predestination to be as it were buried; they teach men to avoid every question concerning it as they would a precipice. Though their moderation is to be commended, in judging that mysteries ought to be handled with such great sobriety, yet, as they descend too low, they have little influence on the mind of man, which refuses to submit to unreasonable restraints. To observe, therefore, the legitimate boundary on this side also, we must recur to the word of the Lord, which affords a certain rule for the understanding. For the Scripture is the school of the Holy Spirit, in which, as nothing necessary and useful to be known is omitted, so nothing is taught which it is not beneficial to know. Whatever, therefore, is declared in the Scripture concerning predestination, we must be cautious not to withhold from believers, lest we appear either to defraud them of the favor of their God, or to reprove and censure the Holy Spirit for publishing what it would be useful by any means to suppress. Let us, I say, permit the Christian man to open his heart and his ears to all the discourses addressed to him by God, only with this moderation, that as soon as the Lord closes his sacred mouth, he shall also desist from further inquiry. This will be the best barrier of sobriety, if in learning we not only follow the leadings of God, but as soon as he ceases to teach, we give up our desire of learning.

IV. Profane persons, I confess, suddenly lay hold of something relating to the subject of predestination, to furnish occasion for objections, cavils, reproaches, and ridicule. But if we are frightened from it by their impudence, all the principal articles of the faith must be concealed, for there is scarcely one of them which such persons as these leave unviolated by blasphemy. The refractory mind will discover as much insolence, on hearing that there are three persons in the Divine essence, as on being told, that when God created man, he foresaw what would happen concerning him. Nor will they refrain from derision on being informed, that little more than five thousand years have elapsed since the creation of the world. They will ask why the power of God was so long idle and asleep. Nothing can be advanced which they will not ridicule. Must we, in order to check these sacrileges, say nothing of the Divinity of the Son and Spirit, or pass over in silence the creation of the world? In this instance, and every other, the truth of God is too powerful to dread the detraction of impious men; as is strenuously maintained by Augustine, in his treatise on the "Perseverance of the Faithful." We see the false apostles, with all their defamation and accusation of the true doctrine of Paul, could never succeed to make him ashamed of it. Their assertion, that all this discussion is dangerous to pious minds, because it is inconsistent with exhortations, shakes their faith, and disturbs and discourages the heart itself, is without any foundation. Augustine admits, that he was frequently blamed, on these accounts, for preaching predestination too freely; but he readily and amply refutes them. But as many and various absurdities are crowded upon us here, we prefer reserving every one to be refuted in its proper place. I only desire this general admission, that we should neither scrutinize those things which the Lord has left concealed, nor neglect those which he has openly exhibited, lest we be condemned for excessive curiosity on the one hand, or for ingratitude on the other. For it is judiciously remarked by Augustine, that we may safely follow the Scripture, which proceeds as with the pace of a mother stooping to the weakness of a child, that it may not leave our weak capacities behind. But persons who are so cautious or timid, as to wish predestination to be buried in silence, lest feeble minds should be disturbed—with what pretext, I ask, will they gloss over their arrogance, which indirectly charges God with foolish inadvertency, as though he foresaw not the danger which they suppose they have had the penetration to discover. Whoever, therefore, endeavours to raise prejudices against the doctrine of predestination, openly reproaches God, as though something had inconsiderately escaped from him that is pernicious to the Church.

V. Predestination, by which God adopts some to the hope of life, and adjudges others to eternal death, no one, desirous of the credit of piety, dares absolutely to deny. But it is involved in many cavils, especially by those who make foreknowledge the cause of it. We maintain, that both belong to God; but it is preposterous to represent one as dependent on the other. When we attribute foreknowledge to God, we mean that all things have ever been, and perpetually remain, before his eyes, so that to his knowledge nothing is future or past, but all things are present; and present in such a manner, that he does not merely conceive of them from ideas formed in his mind, as things remembered by us appear present to our minds, but really beholds and sees them as if actually placed before him. And this foreknowledge extends to the whole world, and to all the creatures. Predestination we call the eternal decree of God, by which he has determined in himself, what he would have to become of every individual of mankind. For they are not all created with a similar destiny; but eternal life is foreordained for some, and eternal damnation for others. Every man, therefore, being created for one or the other of these ends, we say, he is predestinated either to life or to death. This God has not only testified in particular persons, but has given a specimen of it in the whole posterity of Abraham, which should evidently show the future condition of every nation to depend upon his decision.

VII. Though it is sufficiently clear, that God, in his secret counsel, freely chooses whom he will, and rejects others, his gratuitous election is but half displayed till we come to particular individuals, to whom God not only offers salvation, but assigns it in such a manner, that the certainty of the effect is liable to no suspense or doubt. These are included in that one seed mentioned by Paul; for though the adoption was deposited in the hand of Abraham, yet many of his posterity being cut off as putrid members, in order to maintain the efficacy and stability of election, it is necessary to ascend to the head, in whom their heavenly Father has bound his elect to each other, and united them to himself by an indissoluble bond. Thus the adoption of the family of Abraham displayed the favour of God, which he denied to others; but in the members of Christ there is a conspicuous exhibition of the superior efficacy of grace; because, being united to their head, they never fail of salvation. Paul, therefore, justly reasons from the passage of Malachi which I have just quoted, that where God, introducing the covenant of eternal life, invites any people to himself, there is a peculiar kind of election as to part of them, so that he does not efficaciously choose all with indiscriminate grace. The declaration, "Jacob have I loved," respects the whole posterity of the patriarch, whom the prophet there opposes to the descendants of Esau. Yet this is no objection to our having in the person of one individual a specimen of the election, which can never fail of attaining its full effect. These, who truly belong to Christ, Paul correctly observes, are called "a remnant"; for experience proves, that of a great multitude the most part fall away and disappear, so that often only a small portion remains. That the general election of a people is not always effectual and permanent, a reason readily presents itself, because, when God covenants with them, he does not also give them the spirit of regeneration to enable them to persevere in the covenant to the end; but the external call, without the internal efficacy of grace, which would be sufficient for their preservation, is a kind of medium between the rejection of all mankind and the election of the small number of believers. The whole nation of Israel was called "God's inheritance," though many of them were strangers; but God, having firmly covenanted to be their Father and Redeemer, regards that gratuitous favour rather than the defection of multitudes; by whom his truth was not violated, because his preservation of a certain remnant to himself, made it evident that his calling was without repentance. For God's collection of a Church for himself, from time to time, from the children of Abraham, rather than from the profane nations, was in consideration of his covenant, which, being violated by the multitude, he restricted to a few, to prevent its total failure. Lastly, the general adoption of the seed of Abraham was a visible representation of a greater blessing, which God conferred on a few out of the multitude. This is the reason that Paul so carefully distinguishes the descendants of Abraham according to the flesh, from his spiritual children called after the example of Isaac. Not that the mere descent from Abraham was a vain and unprofitable thing, which could not be asserted without depreciating the covenant; but because to the latter alone the immutable counsel of God, in which he predestinated whom he would, was of itself effectual to salvation. But I advise my readers to adopt no prejudice on either side, till it shall appear from adduced passages of Scripture what sentiments ought to be entertained. In conformity, therefore, to the clear doctrine of the Scripture, we assert, that by an eternal and immutable counsel, God has once and for all determined, both whom he would admit to salvation, and whom he would condemn to destruction. We affirm that this counsel, as far as concerns the elect, is founded on his gratuitous mercy, totally irrespective of human merit; but that to those whom he devotes to condemnation, the gate of life is closed by a just and irreprehensible, but incomprehensible, judgment. In the elect, we consider calling as an evidence of election, and justification as another token of its manifestation, till they arrive in glory, which constitutes its completion. As God seals his elect by vocation and justification, so by excluding the reprobate from the knowledge of his name and the sanctification of his Spirit, he affords an indication of the judgment that awaits them. Here I shall pass over many fictions fabricated by foolish men to overthrow predestination. It is unnecessary to refute things which, as soon as they are advanced, sufficiently prove their own falsehood. I shall dwell only on those things which are subjects of controversy among the learned, or which may occasion difficulty to simple minds, or which impiety speciously pleads in order to stigmatize the Divine justice.

Book 4

Chapter 12

The Discipline of the Church; Its Principal Use in Censures and Excommunication

The discipline of the Church, the discussion of which I have deferred to this place, must be despatched in a few words, that we may proceed to the remaining subjects. Now, the discipline depends chiefly on the power of the keys, and the spiritual jurisdiction. To make this more easily understood, let us divide the Church into two principal orders—the clergy and the people. I use the word *clergy* as the common, though improper appellation of those who execute the public ministry in the Church. We shall, first, speak of the common discipline to which all ought to be subject; and in the next place we shall proceed to the clergy, who, beside this common discipline, have a discipline peculiar to themselves. But as some have such a hatred of discipline, as to abhor the very name, they should attend to the following consideration: that if no society, and even no house, though containing only a small family, can be preserved in a proper state without discipline, this is far more necessary in the Church, the state of which ought to be the most orderly of all. As the saving doctrine of Christ is the soul of the Church, so discipline forms the ligaments which connect the members together, and keep each in its proper place. Whoever, therefore, either desires the abolition of all discipline, or obstructs its restoration, whether they act from design or inadvertency, they certainly promote the entire dissolution of the Church. For what will be the consequence, if every man be at liberty to follow his own inclinations? But such would be the case, unless the preaching of the doctrine were accompanied with private admonitions, reproofs, and other means to enforce the doctrine, and prevent it from being altogether ineffectual. Discipline, therefore, serves as a bridle to curb and restrain the refractory, who resist the doctrine of Christ; or as a spur to stimulate the inactive; and sometimes as a father's rod, with which those who have grievously fallen may be chastised in mercy, and with the gentleness of the Spirit of Christ. Now, when we see the approach of certain beginnings of a dreadful desolation in the Church, since there is no solicitude or means to keep the people in obedience to our Lord, necessity itself proclaims the want of a remedy; and this is the only remedy which has been commanded by Christ, or which has ever been adopted among believers.

II. The first foundation of discipline consists in the use of private admonitions; that is to say, that if any one be guilty of a voluntary omission of duty, or conduct himself in an insolent manner, or discover a want of virtue in his life, or commit any act deserving of reprehension, he should suffer himself to be admonished; and that every one should study to admonish his brother, whenever occasion shall require; but that pastors and presbyters, beyond all others, should be vigilant in the discharge of this duty, being called by their office, not only to preach to the congregation, but also to admonish and exhort in private houses, if in any instances their public instructions may not have been sufficiently efficacious; as Paul inculcates, when he says, that he "taught publicly and from house to house," and protests himself to be "pure from the blood of all men," having "ceased not to warn every one night and day with tears." For the doctrine then obtains its full authority and produces its due effect, when the minister not only declares to all the people together what is their duty to Christ, but has the right and means of enforcing it upon them whom he observes to be inattentive, or not obedient to the doctrine. If anyone either obstinately rejects such admonitions, or manifests his contempt of them by persisting in his misconduct; after he shall have been admonished a second time in the presence of witnesses, Christ directs him to be summoned before the tribunal of the Church, that is, the assembly of the elders, and there to be more severely admonished by the public authority, that if he reverence the Church, he may submit and obey; but if this does not overcome him, and he still perseveres in his iniquity, our Lord then commands him, as a despiser of the Church, to be excluded from the society of believers.

III. But as Jesus Christ in this passage is speaking only of private faults, it is necessary to make this distinction—that some sins are private, and others public or notorious. With respect to the former, Christ says to every private individual, "Tell him his fault between thee and him alone." With respect to those which are notorious, Paul says to Timothy, "Them that sin rebuke before all, that others also may fear." For Christ has before said, "If thy brother shall trespass against thee"; which no person who is not contentious can understand in any other sense, than if our Lord had said, "If any one sin against thee, and thou alone know it, without any other persons being acquainted with it." But the direction given by the apostle to Timothy, to rebuke publicly those whose transgressions were public, he himself exemplified in his conduct to Peter. For when Peter committed a public offence, he did not admonish him in private, but brought him forward before all the Church. The legitimate course, then, will be, in correcting secret faults, to adopt the different steps directed by Christ; and in the case of those which are notorious, to proceed at once to the solemn correction of the Church, especially if they be attended with public offence.

IV. It is also necessary to make another distinction between different sins; some are smaller delinquencies, others are flagitious or enormous crimes. For the correction of atrocious crimes, it is not sufficient to employ admonition or reproof; recourse must be had to a severer remedy; as Paul shows when he does not content himself with censuring the incestuous Corinthian, but pronounces sentence of excommunication immediately on being certified of his crime. Now, then, we begin to have a clearer perception how the spiritual jurisdiction of the Church, which corrects sins according to the word of the Lord, is a most excellent preservative of health, foundation of order, and bond of unity. Therefore when the Church excludes from its society all who are known to be guilty of adultery, fornication, theft, robbery, sedition, perjury, false witness, and other similar crimes, together with obstinate persons, who, after having been admonished even of smaller faults, contemn God and his judgment, it usurps no unreasonable authority, but only exercises the jurisdiction which God has given it. And that no one may despise this judgment of the Church, or consider it as of little importance that he is condemned by the voice of the faithful, God has testified that it is no other than a declaration of his sentence, and that what they do on earth shall be ratified in heaven. For they have the word of the Lord, to condemn the perverse; they have the word, to receive the penitent into favour. Persons who believe that the Church could not subsist without this bond of discipline, are mistaken in their opinion, unless we could safely dispense with that remedy which the Lord foresaw would be necessary for us; and how very necessary it is, will be better discovered from its various use.

V. Now, there are three ends proposed by the Church in those corrections, and in excommunication. The first is, that those who lead scandalous and flagitious lives, may not, to the dishonour of God, be numbered among Christians, as if his holy Church were a conspiracy of wicked and abandoned men. For as the Church is the body of Christ, it cannot be contaminated with such foul and putrid members without some ignominy being reflected upon the Head. That nothing may exist in the church, therefore, from which any disgrace may be thrown upon his venerable name, it is necessary to expel from his family all those from whose turpitude infamy would redound to the profession of Christianity. Here it is also necessary to have particular regard to the Lord's supper, that it may not be profaned by a promiscuous administration. For it is certain that he who is intrusted with the dispensation of it, if he knowingly and intentionally admit an unworthy person, whom he might justly reject, is as guilty of sacrilege as if he were to give the Lord's body to dogs. Wherefore, Chrysostom severely inveighs against priests, who, from a fear of the great and the powerful, did not dare to reject any persons who presented themselves. "Blood," says he, "shall be required at your hands. If you fear man, he will deride you; if you fear God, you will also be honoured among men. Let us not be afraid of sceptres, or diadems, or imperial robes; we have here a great power. As for myself, I will rather give up my body to death, and suffer my blood to be shed, than I will be partaker of this pollution." To guard this most sacred mystery, therefore, from being reproached, there is need of great discretion in the administration of it, and this requires the jurisdiction of the Church. The second end is, that the good may not be corrupted, as is often the case, by constant association with the wicked. For, such is our propensity to error, nothing is more easy than for evil examples to seduce us from rectitude of conduct. This use of discipline was remarked by the apostle, when he directed the Corinthians to expel from their society a person who had been guilty of incest. "A little leaven," says he, "leaveneth the whole lump." And the apostle perceived such great danger from this quarter, that he even interdicted believers from all social intercourse with the wicked. "I have written unto you, not to keep company, if any man that is called a brother be a fornicator, or covetous, or an idolater, or a railer, or a drunkard, or an extortioner; with such a one, no, not to eat." The third end is, that those who are censured or excommunicated, confounded with the shame of their turpitude, may be led to repentance. Thus it is even conducive to their own benefit for their iniquity to be punished, that the stroke of the rod may arouse to a confession of their guilt, those who would only be rendered more obstinate by indulgence. The apostle intends the same when he says, "If any man obey not our word, note that man, and have no company with him, that he may be ashamed." Again, when he says of the incestuous Corinthian, "I have judged to deliver such a one unto Satan, that the spirit may be saved in the day of the Lord"; that is, as I understand it, that he had consigned him to a temporal condemnation, that the spirit might be eternally saved. He therefore calls it *delivering to Satan*, because the devil is *without* the Church, as Christ is *in* the Church. For the opinion of some persons, that it relates to a certain torment of the body in the present life, inflicted by the agency of Satan, appears to me extremely doubtful.

VI. Having stated these ends, it remains for us to examine how the Church exercises this branch of discipline, which consists in jurisdiction. In the first place, let us keep in view the distinction before mentioned, that some sins are public, and others private, or more concealed. Public sins are those which are not only known to one or two witnesses, but are committed openly, and to the scandal of the whole Church. By private sins, I mean, not such as are entirely unknown to men, like those of hypocrites—for these never come under the cognizance of the Church—but those of an intermediate class, which are not without the knowledge of some witnesses, and yet are not public. The first sort requires not the adoption of the gradual measures enumerated by Christ; but it is the duty of the Church, on the occurrence of any notorious scandal, immediately to summon the offender, and to punish him in proportion to his crime. Sins of the second class, according to the rule of Christ, are not to be brought before the Church, unless they are attended with contumacy, in rejecting private admonition. When they are submitted to the cognizance of the Church, then attention is to be paid to the other distinction, between smaller delinquencies and more atrocious crimes. For slighter offences require not the exertion of extreme severity; it is sufficient to administer verbal castigation, and that with paternal gentleness, not calculated to exasperate or confound the offender, but to bring him to himself, that his correction may be an occasion of joy rather than of sorrow. But it is proper that flagitious crimes should receive severer punishment; for it is not enough for him who has grievously offended the Church by the bad example of an atrocious crime, merely to receive verbal castigation; he ought to be deprived of the communion of the Lord's supper for a time, till he shall have given satisfactory evidence of repentance. For Paul not only employs verbal reproof against the Corinthian transgressor, but excludes him from the Church, and blames the Corinthians for having tolerated him so long. This order was retained in the ancient and purer Church, while any legitimate government continued. For if anyone had perpetrated a crime which was productive of offence, he was commanded, in the first place, to abstain from the Lord's supper, and, in the next place, to humble himself before God, and to testify his repentance before the Church. There were, likewise, certain solemn rites which it was customary to enjoin upon those who had fallen, as signs of their repentance. When the sinner had performed these for the satisfaction of the Church, he was then, by imposition of hands, readmitted to the communion. This readmission is frequently called *peace* by Cyprian, who briefly describes the ceremony. "They do penance," he says, "for a sufficient time; then they come to confession, and by the imposition of the hands of the bishop and clergy, are restored to the privilege of communion." But though the bishop and clergy presided in the reconciliation of offenders, yet they required the consent of the people; as Cyprian elsewhere states.

VII. From this discipline none were exempted; so that princes and plebeians yielded the same submission to it; and that with the greatest propriety, since it is evidently the discipline of Christ, to whom it is reasonable that all the sceptres and diadems of kings should be subject. Thus Theodosius when Ambrose excluded him from the privilege of communion, on account of a massacre perpetrated at Thessalonica, laid aside the ensigns of royalty with which he was invested, publicly in the Church bewailed his sin, which the deceitful suggestions of others had tempted him to commit, and implored pardon with groans and tears. For great kings ought not to think it any dishonour to prostrate themselves as suppliants before Christ the King of kings, nor ought they to be displeased at being judged by the

Church. As they hear scarcely anything in their courts but mere flatteries, it is the more highly necessary for them to receive correction from the Lord by the mouth of his *ministers*; they ought even to wish not to be spared by the *pastors*, that they may be spared by the Lord. I forbear to mention here by whom this jurisdiction is to be exercised, having spoken of this in another place. I will only add, that the legitimate process in excommunicating an offender, which is pointed out by Paul, requires it to be done, not by the elders alone, but with the knowledge and approbation of the Church: in such a manner, however, that the multitude of the people may not direct the proceeding, but may watch over it as witnesses and guardians, that nothing may be done by a few persons from any improper motive. Beside the invocation of the name of God, the whole of the proceeding ought to be conducted with a gravity declarative of the presence of Christ, that there may be no doubt of his presiding over the sentence.

VIII. But it ought not to be forgotten, that the severity becoming the Church must be tempered with a spirit of gentleness. For there is constant need of the greatest caution, according to the injunction of Paul respecting a person who may have been censured, "lest perhaps such a one should be swallowed up with overmuch sorrow;" for thus a remedy would become a poison. But the rule of moderation may be better deduced from the end intended to be accomplished; for as the design of excommunication is, that the sinner may be brought to repentance, and evil examples taken away, to prevent the name of Christ from being blasphemed and other persons being tempted to imitation—if we keep these things in view, it will be easy to judge how far severity ought to proceed, and where it ought to stop. Therefore, when the sinner gives the Church a testimony of his repentance, and by this testimony, as far as in him lies, obliterates the offence, he is by no means to be pressed any further; and if he be pressed any further, the rigour is carried beyond its proper limits.

24. *The Council of Trent*

The Council of Trent, summoned in the manner and for the purposes set forth here in the Bull of Convocation, was the last of a series of reform councils that had been inaugurated by the Council of Constance in 1414–17. The previous Council of Basel (see above in the notes to Luca Landucci) had ended not in reform but in schism; the Fifth Lateran Council of 1512–18 had been called chiefly to check the threat of an anti-papal

From *Canons and Decrees of the Council of Trent*, edited and translated by H. J. Schroeder (St. Louis, Mo.: B. Herder Book Co., 1941), pp. 319–49. Some footnotes deleted.

Council called in 1511 by King Louis XII of France (Pisa and Milan), and its decrees remained a dead letter. Many of the reform provisions of the Council of Trent, however, were indeed put into practice (see Casale's *Diary* in this volume); and its dogmatic decrees provided the theological basis for what soon became known as the Roman Catholic Church, or churches, ever since. After many interruptions, the Council finally concluded its deliberations in 1562; and the decrees were formally accepted by Pope Pius IV a few months later.

Although it is signed by Pope Paul III (1534–47) (on whom see the selection in this volume from Giorgio Vasari's *Life of Michelangelo*), the Bull of Convocation was actually written by Jacopo Sadoleto (1477–1547), one of the foremost Latin scholars of his day (and an unnamed target of Erasmus' scathing satire on the "Ciceronians"). He served as secretary to Popes Leo X and Clement VII, then escaped from the Sack of Rome in 1527 to anticipate many of the reforms later decreed by the Council in his own diocese of Carpentras, near the former papal court city of Avignon. He is best known today for his open *Letter to the Council and People of Geneva*, which provoked an even more polemical reply by Calvin.

Bull of the Convocation of the Holy Ecumenical Council of Trent under Pope Paul III

Paul, Bishop, servant of the servants of God, for a perpetual remembrance hereof

Recognizing at the very beginning of our pontificate,[1] which the divine providence of Almighty God, not for any merit of our own, but by reason of its own great goodness, has committed to us, to what troubled times and to how many distresses in almost all affairs our pastoral solicitude and vigilance were called, we desired indeed to remedy the evils that have long afflicted and well-nigh overwhelmed the Christian commonwealth; but we also, as men *compassed with infirmity*,[2] felt our strength unequal to take upon ourselves such a burden. For while we realized that peace was necessary to free and preserve the commonwealth from the many dangers that threatened it, we found all filled with hatreds and dissensions, and particularly those princes, to whom God has entrusted almost the entire direction of affairs, at enmity with one another. Whilst we deemed it necessary for

1. 1534. For Pope Paul III (Alessandro Farnese), see the abundant references in Vasari's *Life of Michelangelo* in this volume.
2. Heb. 5:2.

the integrity of the Christian religion and for the confirmation within us of the hope of heavenly things, that there be *one fold and one shepherd*[3] for the Lord's flock, the unity of the Christian name was well-nigh rent and torn asunder by schisms, dissensions and heresies. Whilst we desired the commonwealth to be safe and protected against the arms and insidious designs of the infidels, yet, because of our transgressions and the guilt of us all, indeed, because of the wrath of God hanging over us by reason of our sins, Rhodes had been lost,[4] Hungary ravaged, war by land and sea intended and planned against Italy, and against Austria and Illyria, since the Turk, our godless and ruthless enemy, was never at rest and looked upon our mutual enmities and dissensions as his fitting opportunity to carry out his designs with success. Wherefore, having been called, as we have said, in so great a tempest of heresies, discords and wars and in such restlessness of the waves to rule and pilot the bark of Peter, and not trusting sufficiently our own strength, we first of all *cast our cares upon the Lord*,[5] that He might sustain us and provide our soul with firmness and strength, our understanding with prudence and wisdom. Then, considering that our predecessors, endowed with admirable wisdom and sanctity, had often in the greatest dangers of the Christian commonwealth had recourse to ecumenical Councils and general assemblies of bishops as the best and most suitable remedy, we also decided to hold a general Council. When, on consulting the opinions of the princes whose consent in this matter we deemed particularly useful and expedient, we found them at that time not averse to so holy a work, we, as our letters and records attest, summoned an ecumenical Council and a general assembly of those bishops and fathers, whose duty it is to attend, to be opened in the city of Mantua on the twenty-third of May in the year 1537 of our Lord's Incarnation and the third of our pontificate; entertaining almost the assured hope that when we should be assembled there in the name of the Lord, He would, as He promised, *be in our midst*[6] and in His goodness and mercy dispel with ease by the breath of His mouth all the storms and dangers of the times. But, as the enemy of mankind always plots against pious enterprises, at the very outset, contrary to all our hopes and expectations, the city of Mantua[7] was refused us unless we subscribed to certain conditions which were totally irreconcilable with the ordinances of our predecessors, with the condition of the

3. John 10:16.

4. The Knights of Rhodes left Rhodes on terms after a long siege in 1521 and subsequently settled in Malta, which became another bastion against Turkish expansion in the Mediterranean.

5. Ps. 54:23.   6. Matt. 18.

7. Mantua (between Venice and Milan) was then an independent duchy under the rule of the Gonzaga family.

times, with our own dignity and liberty, and with that of the Apostolic See and the ecclesiastical name, as we have made known in other letters. Wherefore we were obliged to find another place and to choose another city, and since a convenient and suitable one did not immediately present itself, we were constrained to prorogue the celebration of the Council to the following first day of November. In the meantime, the Turk, our cruel and everlasting enemy, having attacked Italy with a powerful fleet, captured, sacked and ravaged several cities on the shores of Apulia and carried off as booty the inhabitants, while we, in the greatest fear and general danger, were occupied in fortifying our shores and in furnishing assistance to the nearest neighboring localities. At the same time, however, we did not neglect to consult and exhort the Christian princes to inform us what in their opinion would be a suitable place to hold the Council, and since their opinions were various and uncertain, and there seemed to be needless delay, we, with the best intention and, we think, with prudence, chose Vicenza, a populous city, which by reason of the valor, esteem and power of the Venetians, who conceded it to us, offered not only free access but also and especially a free and safe place of residence for all. But since time had already far advanced and the choice of the new city had to be made known to all, the proximity of the first of November precluding any announcement of this change, and winter moreover was near, we were again obliged to prorogue the council to the following spring, that is, to the first of the next May. This having been firmly settled and decreed, we considered, while preparing ourselves and everything else to hold and celebrate that Council successfully with the help of God, that it was a matter of prime importance both for the celebration of the Council and for Christendom, that the Christian princes be united in peace and concord, and so we did not fail to implore and beseech our most beloved sons in Christ, Charles, ever august Emperor of the Romans, and Francis, the most Christian King,[8] the two chief props and supports of the Christian name, to come together in a conference with us. Both of them we very often urged by letters, nuncios and legates *a latere* selected from the number of our venerable brethren, to lay aside their jealousies and animosities, to agree to an alliance and holy friendship, and to succor the tottering state of Christendom, for the preservation of which especially did God give them power; and in case of neglect to do this and of failure to direct all their counsels to the common welfare of Christendom, they would have to render to Him a strict and severe account. Yielding at last to our petitions they repaired to Nice,[9] whither we also, for

8. I.e., of France (Emperor Charles V and King Francis II).
9. June 1538; but the two rulers refused to meet in person and negotiated through representatives.

the cause of God and of bringing about peace, undertook a long and, to our advanced age, very fatiguing journey. Neither did we neglect in the meantime, as the time set for the Council, namely, the first of May, approached, to send to Vicenza three legates *a latere*, men of the greatest worth and esteem, chosen from the number of our brethren, the cardinals of the holy Roman Church, to open the Council, to receive the prelates coming from various parts, and to transact and attend to such matters as they should deem necessary, till we ourselves on our return from our journey and mission of peace should be able to direct everything with greater exactness. In the meantime we applied ourselves with all the zeal, love and energy of our soul to that holy and most necessary work, the establishment of peace among the princes. God is our witness, in whose goodness we trusted when we exposed ourselves to the dangers of the journey and of life. Our conscience is witness, and in this matter certainly cannot reproach us with having either neglected or not sought an opportunity to effect a reconciliation. Witnesses are the princes themselves, whom we so often and so urgently implored through our nuncios, letters, legates, admonitions, exhortations and entreaties of every kind to lay aside their jealousies and form an alliance, that with united zeal and action they might aid the Christian commonwealth, already reduced to the greatest immediate danger. Witnesses, moreover, are those vigils and anxieties, those labors and strenuous exertions of our soul by day and night, which we have endured to such large measure in this matter and cause. For all that, our counsels and labors have not yet produced the desired results; for so it pleased the Lord our God, who, however, we trust will yet look more favorably on our wishes. We ourselves have not in this matter, so far as we could, omitted anything pertaining to the duty of our pastoral office. If there be any who interpret our efforts for peace in any other sense, we are grieved indeed, but in our grief we nevertheless give thanks to almighty God who, as an example and a lesson of patience to us, willed that His own Apostles should be *accounted worthy to suffer reproach for the name of Jesus who is our peace*.[10] However, though by reason of our sins a true and lasting peace between the two princes could not be effected in our meeting and conference at Nice, nevertheless, a truce of ten years was agreed upon; and hoping that as a result of this the holy Council might be celebrated more beneficially and thus by its authority peace be permanently established, we urged the princes to come to the Council themselves and to bring with them the prelates who had accompanied them and to summon those absent. On both these points, however, they excused themselves on the grounds that it was necessary for them to return to their kingdoms and that the prelates who had accompanied

10. Acts 5:41; Eph. 2:14.

them, being wearied and exhausted by the journey and its expenses, must recover and recruit themselves, and they besought us to decree yet another prorogation of the time for the opening of the Council. While we were rather unwilling to yield in this, we received in the meantime letters from our legates at Vicenza, announcing that though the day for the opening of the Council had arrived, indeed had long since passed, hardly more than one or two prelates had repaired to Vicenza from foreign nations. Since we saw on receipt of this information that the Council could under no circumstances be held at this time, we yielded to the princes and put off the time for the opening of the council till the following Easter, the feast of the resurrection of the Lord. The decretal letters concerning this our ordinance and prorogation were given and published at Genoa on the twenty-eighth of June in the year of the Incarnation of our Lord 1538. This delay we granted the more readily because each of the princes promised to send ambassadors to us at Rome, that those things which remained for the perfect establishment of peace and which on account of the brevity of time could not be accomplished at Nice, might be considered and negotiated more conveniently in our presence at Rome. And for this reason also both requested that the peace negotiations might precede the celebration of the Council, for with peace established the Council would be much more beneficial and salutary to the Christian commonwealth. It was this hope for peace that moved us always to yield to the wishes of the princes, a hope that was greatly strengthened by the kind and friendly conference between those two princes after our departure from Nice, the news of which, giving us the greatest joy, confirmed us in the good hope, so that we believed God had at last listened to our prayers and received our earnest wishes for peace. This conclusion of peace, therefore, we earnestly desired and urged, and since it was the opinion not only of the two aforesaid princes but also of our most dear son in Christ, Ferdinand, King of the Romans, that the work of the Council ought not to be undertaken till peace had been established, and all urged us by letters and through their spokesmen to decide on a further prorogation of the time, particularly insistent being the most illustrious Emperor, who declared that he had promised those who dissent from Catholic unity that he would consider the matter with us on their behalf to the end that some plan of agreement might be arranged, which could not be done satisfactorily before his return to Germany, and guided throughout by the same hope of peace and the wishes of such powerful princes, and above all, seeing that even on the said feast of the resurrection no other prelates had assembled at Vicenza, we, now avoiding the word prorogation, which has been so often repeated in vain, preferred to suspend the celebration of the general Council during our own good pleasure and that of the Apostolic See. This we therefore did and dispatched letters concerning this suspension to each of the aforesaid princes on the tenth day of June, 1539, as may be clearly seen therein. This suspension having been made by force of circumstances, we looked forward to that more favorable time and to some conclusion of peace that would later bring dignity and numbers to the Council as well as a more immediate safety to the Christian commonwealth. But the affairs of Christendom meanwhile became worse day by day. The Hungarians on the death of their king called in the Turks; King Ferdinand declared war against them; a portion of Belgium was incited to revolt against the Emperor, who, to crush that rebellion, traversed France into Belgium on the most friendly and peaceful terms with the most Christian King and with a great manifestation of mutual good will toward each other.[11] Thence he returned to Germany where he began to hold diets of the princes and cities of Germany with a view to discuss that agreement of which he had spoken to us. But as the hope for peace was already on the wane and that method of providing and establishing unity by means of diets seemed rather adapted to produce greater discord, we were led to return to our former remedy of a general Council, and through our legates, cardinals of the holy Roman Church, proposed this to the Emperor himself, which we also did later and especially in the Diet of Regensburg, at which our beloved son, Gasparo Contarini,[12] Cardinal of St. Praxedes, acted as our legate with great learning and integrity. For since, as we had previously feared, we might be petitioned by a decision of the diet to declare that certain articles maintained by the dissenters from the church be tolerated till they be examined and decided upon by an ecumenical Council, and since neither Christian and Catholic truth, nor our own dignity nor that of the Apostolic See would permit us to yield in this, we chose rather to command that it be proposed openly that a Council be held as soon as possible. Neither did we ever have any other intention and wish than that an ecumenical and general Council should be convened at the earliest opportunity. For we hoped that thereby peace might be restored to the Christian people and integrity to the Christian religion; yet we desired to hold that Council with the good will and favor of the Christian princes. However, while looking forward to this will, while watching for the hidden time, *the time of thy good pleasure, O Lord*,[13] we were at last forced to conclude that all time is pleasing to God when there is question of deliberation on holy

---

11. In 1539.

12. A Venetian patrician and diplomat, author of a treatise on the Venetian constitution, raised to the cardinalate in 1537; he was a member of the pope's committee on the reform of the Church of Rome which produced the famous document, *De Emendanda Ecclesia*. His conversations with Luther's chief theologian, Philip Melanchthon, at the Diet of Regensburg yielded a compromise definition of the doctrine of Grace; but the compromise was thereafter rejected both by Luther and the Roman Curia.

13. Ps. 68:14.

things and on such as pertain to Christian piety. Wherefore, beholding with the bitterest grief of our soul that the affairs of Christendom were daily becoming worse, Hungary oppressed by the Turks, Germany endangered, and all other states overwhelmed with apprehension and grief, we resolved to wait no longer for the consent of any prince, but to look solely to the will of the Almighty God and to the good of the Christian commonwealth. Wherefore, since the city of Vicenza was no longer at our disposal, and we desired in our choice of a new place for holding the Council to have in mind both the common welfare of Christians and the conveniences of the German nation, and seeing that among the various places proposed these desired the city of Trent, we, though of opinion that everything could be transacted more conveniently in cisalpine Italy, nevertheless yielded with paternal charity to their desires. Accordingly, we have chosen the city of Trent as that in which the ecumenical Council is to be held on the following first day of November, selecting that place as a convenient one in which the bishops and prelates from Germany and from the nations bordering on Germany can assemble very easily and those from France, Spain and other more remote provinces without difficulty. In fixing the day for the Council, we considered that there should be time both for the publication of this our decree throughout the Christian nations and to make it possible for all the prelates to arrive. Our reason for not announcing the change of place of the Council one year in advance, as has been prescribed by certain constitutions,[14] was this, that we were not willing that the hope of applying some remedy to the Christian commonwealth, afflicted as it is with so many disasters and calamities, should be delayed any longer, though we know the times and recognize the difficulties, and we understand that what may be looked for from our counsels is a matter of uncertainty. But since it is written: *Commit thy way to the Lord, and trust in him, and he will do it*,[15] we have resolved to trust in the clemency and mercy of God rather than distrust our own weakness, for in undertaking good works it often happens that where human counsels fail the divine power succeeds. Wherefore, relying on the authority of Almighty God, Father, Son, and Holy Spirit, and on that of His blessed Apostles Peter and Paul, which we also exercise on earth, and supported also by the advice and assent of our venerable brethren, the cardinals of the holy Roman Church, having removed and annulled the aforesaid suspension, which by the present we remove and annul, we announce, proclaim, convoke, ordain and decree a holy ecumenical and general Council to be opened on the first day of November of the present year 1542 from the Incarnation of the Lord in the city of Trent, for all nations a commodious, free and convenient place, to be there begun and

14. Council of Constance (1418), *Frequens*.
15. Ps. 36:5.

prosecuted and with the help of God concluded and completed to His glory and praise and the welfare of the whole Christian people; and we summon, exhort and admonish, in whatever country they may be, all our venerable brethren, the patriarchs, archbishops, bishops, and our beloved sons, the abbots, as well as all others who by law or privilege have the right to sit in general Councils and express their sentiments therein, enjoining and strictly commanding them by virtue of their oath to us and to this Holy See, and in virtue of holy obedience and under other penalties that by law or custom are usually imposed and proposed in the celebration of Councils against absentees, that they attend and be present personally at this holy Council, unless they should perhaps be hindered by a just impediment, of which, however, they shall be obliged to give proof, in which case they must be represented by their lawful procurators and delegates. Also the aforesaid Emperor and the most Christian King, as well as the other kings, dukes and princes, whose presence, if ever, would certainly at this time be very salutary to the most holy faith of Christ and of all Christians, we beg and beseech by the bowels of the mercy of God and of our Lord Jesus Christ, the truth of whose faith and whose religion are now so violently assailed both from within and without, that if they wish the Christian commonwealth to be safe, if they feel themselves bound and under obligation to the Lord for His great favors toward them, they will not abandon His cause and interests but will come personally to the celebration of the holy Council, where their piety and virtue would be greatly conducive to the common good, to their own and the welfare of others, temporal as well as spiritual. But if, which we do not wish, they themselves cannot appear, let them at least send distinguished men entrusted with authority, each of whom may represent in the Council with prudence and dignity the person of his prince. But above all, and this is for them an easy matter, let them see to it that the bishops and prelates of their respective kingdoms and provinces proceed to the Council without tergiversation and delay, a favor that God himself and we can in justice claim particularly from the prelates and princes of Germany; for since it is chiefly on their account and at their wishes that the Council has been summoned, and in the very city that they desired, let them not regard it burdensome to celebrate and adorn it with their presence, so that God going before us in our deliberations and holding before our minds the light of His wisdom and truth, we may in the holy ecumenical Council, in a better and easier manner consider, and with the charity of all concurring to one end, ponder, discuss, execute and bring speedily and happily to the desired result whatever things pertain to the purity and truth of the Christian religion, to the restoration of what is good and the correction of bad morals, to the peace, unity and harmony of Christians among themselves, of the princes as well as of the people, and whatever is necessary to repulse those attacks of barbarians and infidels whereby they seek the overthrow of all Christendom. And that this our letter and its contents may come to the knowledge of all whom it concerns, and that no one may plead ignorance as an excuse, particularly since there may not perchance be free access to all to whom it ought to be especially communicated, we wish and command that it be read publicly and in a loud voice by the messengers of our court or by some public notaries in the Vatican Basilica of the Prince of the Apostles and in the Lateran Church,[16] at a time when the people are accustomed to assemble there to hear divine services; and after having been read, let it be affixed to the doors of the said churches, also to the gates of the Apostolic Chancery and to the usual place in the Campo dei Fiori, where it shall hang openly for some time for the perusal and cognizance of all; and when removed thence, copies of it shall still remain affixed in the same places. For by being thus read, published and affixed, we wish that each and all whom our aforesaid letter concerns be, after the interval of two months from the day of being published and affixed, so bound and obligated as if had been read and published in their presence. We command and decree also that an unshaken and firm faith be given to transcripts thereof, written or subscribed by the hand of a notary public and authenticated by the seal of some person constituted in ecclesiastical dignity. Therefore, let no one infringe this our letter of summons, announcement, convocation, statute, decree, command, precept and supplication, or with foolhardy boldness oppose it. But if anyone shall presume to attempt this, let him know that he will incur the indignation of Almighty God and of His blessed Apostles Peter and Paul. Given at Rome at Saint Peter's in the year 1542 of the Lord's incarnation on the twenty-second of May, in the eighth year of our pontificate.

Fourth Session
Celebrated on the Eighth Day of April, 1546

Decree concerning the Canonical Scriptures

The holy, ecumenical and general Council of Trent, lawfully assembled in the Holy Ghost, the same three legates of the Apostolic See presiding, keeps this constantly in view, namely, that the purity of the Gospel may be preserved in the Church after the errors have been removed. This [Gospel], of old promised through the Prophets in the Holy Scriptures, our Lord Jesus Christ, the Son of God, promulgated first with His own mouth, and then commanded it to be preached by His Apostles to every creature as the source at once of all saving truth and rules of conduct. It also clearly perceives that these truths and rules are contained in the written books and in

16. I.e., in St. Peter's and in St. John Lateran.

the unwritten traditions, which, received by the Apostles from the mouth of Christ Himself, or from the Apostles themselves, the Holy Ghost dictating, have come down to us, transmitted as it were from hand to hand. Following, then, the examples of the orthodox Fathers, it receives and venerates with a feeling of piety and reverence all the books both of the Old and New Testaments, since one God is the author of both; also the traditions, whether they relate to faith or to morals, as having been dictated either orally by Christ or by the Holy Ghost, and preserved in the Catholic Church in unbroken succession. It has thought it proper, moreover, to insert in this decree a list of the sacred books, lest a doubt might arise in the mind of someone as to which are the books received by this Council. They are the following: of the Old Testament, the five books of Moses, namely, Genesis, Exodus, Leviticus, Numbers, Deuteronomy; Josue, Judges, Ruth, the four books of Kings, two of Paralipomenon [Chronicles], the first and second of Esdras, the latter of which is called Nehemias, Tobias, Judith, Esther, Job, the Davidic Psalter of 150 Psalms, Proverbs, Ecclesiastes, the Canticle of Canticles, Wisdom, Ecclesiasticus, Isaias, Jeremias, with Baruch, Ezechiel, Daniel, the twelve minor Prophets, namely, Osee, Joel, Amos, Abdias, Jonas, Micheas, Nahum, Habacuc, Sophonias, Aggeus, Zacharias, Malachias; two books of Machabees, the first and second. Of the New Testament, the four Gospels, according to Matthew, Mark, Luke and John; the Acts of the Apostles written by Luke the Evangelist; fourteen Epistles of Paul the Apostle, to the Romans, two to the Corinthians, to the Galatians, to the Ephesians, to the Philippians, to the Colossians, two to the Thessalonians, two to Timothy, to Titus, to Philemon, to the Hebrews; two of Peter the Apostle, three of John the Apostle, one of James the Apostle, one of Jude the Apostle, and the Apocalypse of John the Apostle. If anyone does not accept as sacred and canonical the aforesaid books in their entirety and with all their parts, as they have been accustomed to be read in the Catholic Church and as they are contained in the old Latin Vulgate Edition, and knowingly and deliberately rejects the aforesaid traditions, let him be anathema. Let all understand, therefore, in what order and manner the Council, after having laid the foundation of the confession of faith, will proceed, and who are the chief witnesses and supports to whom it will appeal in confirming dogmas and in restoring morals in the Church.

Decree concerning the Edition and Use of the Sacred Books

Moreover, the same holy Council considering that not a little advantage will accrue to the Church of God if it be made known which of all the Latin editions of the sacred books now in circulation is to be regarded as authentic, ordains and declares that the old Latin Vulgate Edition, which, in use for so many hundred years, has been approved by the Church, be in public lectures, disputations, sermons and expositions held as authentic, and that no one dare or presume under any pretext whatsoever to reject it.

Furthermore, to check unbridled spirits, it decrees that no one relying on his own judgment shall, in matters of faith and morals pertaining to the edification of Christian doctrine, distorting the Holy Scriptures in accordance with his own conceptions, presume to interpret them contrary to that sense which holy mother Church, to whom it belongs to judge of their true sense and interpretation, has held and holds, or even contrary to the unanimous teaching of the Fathers, even though such interpretations should never at any time be published. Those who act contrary to this shall be made known by the ordinaries and punished in accordance with the penalties prescribed by the law.

And wishing, as is proper, to impose a restraint in this matter on printers also, who, now without restraint, thinking what pleases them is permitted them, print without the permission of ecclesiastical superiors the books of the Holy Scriptures and the notes and commentaries thereon of all persons indiscriminately, often with the name of the press omitted, often also under a fictitious press name, and what is worse, without the name of the author, and also indiscreetly have for sale such books printed elsewhere, [this Council] decrees and ordains that in the future the Holy Scriptures, especially the old Vulgate Edition, be printed in the most correct manner possible, and that it shall not be lawful for anyone to print or to have printed any books whatsoever dealing with sacred doctrinal matters without the name of the author, or in the future to sell them, or even to have them in possession, unless they have first been examined and approved by the ordinary, under penalty of anathema and fine prescribed by the last Council of the Lateran. If they be regulars they must in addition to this examination and approval obtain permission also from their own superiors after these have examined the books in accordance with their own statutes. Those who lend or circulate them in manuscript before they have been examined and approved, shall be subject to the same penalties as the printers, and those who have them in their possession or read them, shall, unless they make known the authors, be themselves regarded as the authors. The approbation of such books, however, shall be given in writing and shall appear authentically at the beginning of the book, whether it be written or printed, and all this, that is, both the examination and approbation, shall be done gratuitously, so that what ought to be approved may be approved and what ought to be condemned may be condemned.

Furthermore, wishing to repress that boldness whereby the words and sentences of the Holy Scriptures are turned and twisted to all kinds of profane usages, namely, to things scurrilous, fabulous, vain, to flatteries, detractions, superstitions, godless and diabolical incantations, divinations, the casting of lots and defamatory libels, to put an end to such irreverence and contempt, and that no one may in the future dare use in any manner the words of Holy Scripture for these and similar purposes, it is commanded and enjoined that all people of this kind be restrained by the bishops as violators and profaners of the word of God, with the penalties of the law and other penalties that they may deem fit to impose.

Sixth Session
Celebrated on the Thirteenth Day of January, 1547

Decree concerning Justification

Introduction

Since there is being disseminated at this time, not without the loss of many souls and grievous detriment to the unity of the Church, a certain erroneous doctrine concerning justification, the holy, ecumenical and general Council of Trent, lawfully assembled in the Holy Ghost, the most reverend John Maria, Bishop of Praeneste de Monte, and Marcellus, priest of the Holy Cross in Jerusalem, cardinals of the holy Roman Church and legates Apostolic *a latere*,[17] presiding in the name of our most holy Father and Lord in Christ, Paul III, by the providence of God, Pope, intends, for the praise and glory of Almighty God, for the tranquillity of the Church and the salvation of souls, to expound to all the faithful of Christ the true and salutary doctrine of justification, which the *Sun of justice*,[18] Jesus Christ, *the author and finisher of our faith*[19] taught, which the Apostles transmitted and which the Catholic Church under the inspiration of the Holy Ghost has always retained; strictly forbidding that anyone henceforth presume to believe, preach or teach otherwise than is defined and declared in the present decree.

Chapter 1

The Impotency of Nature and of the Law to Justify Man

The holy Council declares first, that for a correct and clear understanding of the doctrine of justification, it is necessary that each one recognize and confess that since all men had lost innocence in the prevarication of Adam, having become unclean, and, as the Apostle says, *by nature children of wrath*,[20] as has been set forth in the decree on original sin,[21] they were so far *the servants of sin*[22] and under the power of the devil and of death, that

---

17. I.e., Giovan Maria Del Monte and Marcello Cervini, later Pope Marcellus II (1555).
18. Mal. 4:2.   19. Heb. 12:2.
20. Eph. 2:3.   21. Session 5 of the Council of Trent.
22. Rom. 6:17, 20.

not only the Gentiles by the force of nature, but not even the Jews by the very letter of the law of Moses, were able to be liberated or to rise therefrom, though free will, weakened as it was in its powers and downward bent, was by no means extinguished in them.

Chapter 2

The Dispensation and Mystery of the Advent of Christ

Whence it came to pass that the heavenly Father, *the Father of mercies and the God of all comfort, when the blessed fulness of the time was come*,[23] sent to men Jesus Christ, His own Son, who had both before the law and during the time of the law been announced and promised to many of the holy fathers, *that he might redeem the Jews who were under the law*, and *that the Gentiles who followed not after justice*[24] might attain to justice, and that all men might receive the adoption of sons. Him has God *proposed* as a propitiator *through faith in his blood for our sins, and not for our sins only, but also for those of the whole world.*[25]

Chapter 3

Who Are Justified through Christ

But though *He died for all*,[26] yet all do not receive the benefit of His death, but those only to whom the merit of His passion is communicated; because as truly as men would not be born unjust, if they were not born through propagation of the seed of Adam, since by that propagation they contract through him, when they are conceived, injustice as their own, so if they were not born again in Christ, they would never be justified, since in that new birth there is bestowed upon them, through the merit of His passion, the grace by which they are made just. For this benefit the Apostle exhorts us always *to give thanks to the Father, who hath made us worthy to be partakers of the lot of the saints in light, and hath delivered us from the power of darkness, and hath translated us into the kingdom of the Son of his love, in whom we have redemption and remission of sins.*[27]

Chapter 4

A Brief Description of the Justification of the Sinner and Its Mode in the State of Grace

In which words is given a brief description of the justification of the sinner, as being a translation from that state in which man is born a child of the first Adam, to the state of grace and of the adoption of the sons of God

23. 2 Cor. 1:3; Gal. 4:4.   24. Gal. 4:4; Gen. 49:10, 18.
25. Gen. 49:10, 18; Gal. 4:5; Rom. 9:30.
26. 2 Cor. 5:15.   27. Col. 1:12–14.

through the second Adam, Jesus Christ, our Savior. This translation however cannot, since the promulgation of the Gospel, be effected except
through the laver of regeneration or its desire, as it is written: *Unless a man
be born again of water and the Holy Ghost, he cannot enter into the kingdom of God.*[28]

Chapter 5

The Necessity of Preparation for Justification in Adults, and Whence It Proceeds

It is furthermore declared that in adults the beginning of that justification
must proceed from the predisposing grace of God through Jesus Christ,
that is, from His vocation, whereby, without any merits on their part, they
are called; that they who by sin had been cut off from God, may be disposed through His quickening and helping grace to convert themselves to
their own justification by freely assenting to and cooperating with that
grace; so that, while God touches the heart of man through the illumination
of the Holy Ghost, man himself neither does absolutely nothing while receiving that inspiration, since he can also reject it, nor yet is he able by his
own free will and without the grace of God to move himself to justice in
His sight. Hence, when it is said in the sacred writings: *Turn ye to me, and
I will turn to you,*[29] we are reminded of our liberty; and when we reply:
Convert us, O Lord, to thee, and we shall be converted,[30] we confess that
we need the grace of God.

Chapter 6

The Manner of Preparation

Now, they [the adults] are disposed to that justice when aroused and aided
by divine grace, receiving *faith by hearing,*[31] they are moved freely toward
God, believing to be true what has been divinely revealed and promised,
especially that the sinner is justified by God *by his grace, through the redemption that is in Christ Jesus;*[32] and when, understanding themselves to
be sinners, they, by turning themselves from the fear of divine justice, by
which they are salutarily aroused, to consider the mercy of God, are raised
to hope, trusting that God will be propitious to them for Christ's sake; and
they begin to love Him as the fountain of all justice, and on that account are
moved against sin by a certain hatred and detestation, that is, by that repentance that must be performed before baptism; finally, when they resolve
to receive baptism, to begin a new life and to keep the commandments of

---

28. John 3:5.   29. Zec. 1:3.
30. Lam. 5:21.   31. Rom. 10:17.
32. Rom. 3:24.

God. Of this disposition it is written: *He that cometh to God, must believe that he is, and is a rewarder to them that seek him*; and, *Be of good faith, son, thy sins are forgiven thee*; and, *The fear of the Lord driveth out sin*; and, *Do penance, and be baptized every one of you in the name of Jesus Christ, for the remission of your sins, and you shall receive the gift of the Holy Ghost*; and, *Going, therefore, teach ye all nations, baptizing them in the name of the Father, and of the Son, and of the Holy Ghost, teaching them to observe all things whatsoever I have commanded you*; finally, *Prepare your hearts unto the Lord.*[33]

Chapter 7

In What the Justification of the Sinner Consists, and What Are Its Causes

This disposition or preparation is followed by justification itself, which is not only a remission of sins but also the sanctification and renewal of the inward man through the voluntary reception of the grace and gifts whereby an unjust man becomes just and from being an enemy becomes a friend, that he may be *an heir according to hope of life everlasting.*[34] The causes of this justification are: the final cause is the glory of God and of Christ and life everlasting; the efficient cause is the merciful God who *washes and sanctifies*[35] gratuitously, signing and anointing *with the holy Spirit of promise, who is the pledge of our inheritance*;[36] the meritorious cause is His most beloved only begotten, our Lord Jesus Christ, who, *when we were enemies,*[37] *for the exceeding charity wherewith he loved us,*[38] merited for us justification by His most holy passion on the wood of the cross and made satisfaction for us to God the Father; the instrumental cause is the sacrament of baptism, which is the sacrament of faith, without which no man was ever justified; finally, the single formal cause is the justice of God, not that by which He Himself is just, but that by which He makes us just, that namely, with which we being endowed by Him, are *renewed in the spirit of our mind,*[39] and not only are we reputed but we are truly called and are just, receiving justice within us, each one according to his own measure, which the Holy Spirit distributes to everyone as He wills, and according to each one's disposition and cooperation. For though no one can be just except he to whom the merits of the passion of our Lord Jesus Christ are communicated, yet this takes place in that justification of the sinner, when by the merit of the most holy passion, *the charity of God is poured forth by the*

33. Heb. 11:6; Matt. 9:2; Mark 2:5; Eccles. 1:27; Acts 2:38; Matt. 28:19f; 1 Kings 7:3.
34. Titus 3:7.   35. 1 Cor. 6:11.
36. Eph. 1:13f.   37. Rom. 5:10.
38. Eph. 2:4.   39. Eph. 4:23.

Holy Ghost in the hearts[40] of those who are justified and inheres in them; whence man through Jesus Christ, in whom he is ingrafted, receives in that justification, together with the remission of sins, all these infused at the same time, namely, faith, hope and charity. For faith, unless hope and charity be added to it, neither unites man perfectly with Christ nor makes him a living member of His body. For which reason it is most truly said that *faith without works is dead* and of no profit, and *in Christ Jesus neither circumcision availeth anything nor uncircumcision, but faith that worketh by charity.*[41] This faith, conformably to Apostolic tradition, catechumens ask of the Church before the sacrament of baptism, when they ask for the faith that gives eternal life, which without hope and charity faith cannot give. Whence also they hear immediately the word of Christ: *If thou wilt enter into life, keep the commandments.*[42] Wherefore, when receiving true and Christian justice, they are commanded, immediately on being born again, to preserve it pure and spotless, as *the first robe*[43] given them through Christ Jesus in place of that which Adam by his disobedience lost for himself and for us, so that they may bear it before the tribunal of our Lord Jesus Christ and may have life eternal.

Chapter 8

How the Gratuitous Justification of the Sinner by Faith Is to Be Understood

But when the Apostle says that man is justified by faith and freely,[44] these words are to be understood in that sense in which the uninterrupted unanimity of the Catholic Church has held and expressed them, namely, that we are therefore said to be justified by faith, because faith is the beginning of human salvation, the foundation and root of all justification, *without which it is impossible to please God*[45] and to come to the fellowship of His sons; and we are therefore said to be justified gratuitously, because none of those things that precede justification, whether faith or works, merit the grace of justification. For, *if by grace, it is not now by works, otherwise*, as the Apostle says, *grace is no more grace.*[46]

Chapter 9

Against the Vain Confidence of Heretics

But though it is necessary to believe that sins neither are remitted nor ever have been remitted except gratuitously by divine mercy for Christ's sake,

40. Rom. 5:5.   41. James 2:17, 20.
42. Matt. 19:17.   43. Luke 15:22.
44. Rom. 3:24; 5:1.   45. Heb. 11:6.
46. Rom. 11:6.

yet it must not be said that sins are forgiven or have been forgiven to anyone who boasts of his confidence and certainty of the remission of his sins,
resting on that alone, though among heretics and schismatics this vain and
ungodly confidence may be and in our troubled times indeed is found and
preached with untiring fury against the Catholic Church. Moreover, it must
not be maintained, that they who are truly justified must needs, without
any doubt whatever, convince themselves that they are justified, and that
no one is absolved from sins and justified except he that believes with certainty that he is absolved and justified, and that absolution and justification
are effected by this faith alone, as if he who does not believe this, doubts
the promises of God and the efficacy of the death and resurrection of
Christ. For as no pious person ought to doubt the mercy of God, the merit
of Christ and the virtue and efficacy of the sacraments, so each one, when
he considers himself and his own weakness and indisposition, may have
fear and apprehension concerning his own grace, since no one can know
with the certainty of faith, which cannot be subject to error, that he has
obtained the grace of God.

Chapter 10

The Increase of the Justification Received

Having, therefore, been thus justified and made the friends and *domestics
of God*, advancing *from virtue to virtue*, they are *renewed*, as the Apostle
says, *day by day*, that is, *mortifying the members*[47] of their flesh, and pre-
senting them as instruments of justice unto sanctification,[48] they, through
the observance of the commandments of God and of the Church, faith cooperating with good works, increase in that justice received through the
grace of Christ and are further justified, as it is written: *He that is just, let
him be justified still*; and, *Be not afraid to be justified even to death*; and
again, *Do you see that by works a man is justified, and not by faith only?*[49]
This increase of justice holy Church asks for when she prays: "Give unto
us, O Lord, an increase of faith, hope and charity."[50]

Chapter 11

The Observance of the Commandments and the Necessity and
Possibility Thereof

But no one, however much justified, should consider himself exempt from
the observance of the commandments; no one should use that rash state-

47. Eph. 2:19; Ps. 83:8; 2 Cor. 4:16; Col. 3:5.
48. Rom. 6:13, 19.
49. Rev. 22:11; Eccles. 18:22; James 2:24.
50. Collect for the Thirteenth Sunday after Pentecost in the Pre-Vatican II Roman Missal.

ment, once forbidden by the Fathers under anathema, that the observance of the commandments of God is impossible for one that is justified. For God does not command impossibilities, but by commanding admonishes thee to do what thou canst and to pray for what thou canst not, and aids thee that thou mayest be able.[51] *His commandments are not heavy*, and *his yoke is sweet and burden light*.[52] For they who are the sons of God love Christ, but they who love Him, keep His commandments, as He Himself testifies;[53] which, indeed, with the divine help they can do. For though during this mortal life, men, however holy and just, fall at times into at least light and daily sins, which are also called venial, they do not on that account cease to be just, for that petition of the just, *forgive us our trespasses*,[54] is both humble and true; for which reason the just ought to feel themselves the more obliged to walk in the way of justice, for *being now freed from sin and made servants of God*, they are able, *living soberly, justly and godly*,[55] to proceed onward through Jesus Christ, by whom they have access unto this grace. For God does not forsake those who have been once justified by His grace, unless He be first forsaken by them. Wherefore, no one ought to flatter himself with faith alone, thinking that by faith alone he is made an heir and will obtain the inheritance, even though *he suffer* not *with Christ, that he may be also glorified with him*.[56] For even Christ Himself, as the Apostle says, *whereas he was the Son of God, he learned obedience by the things which he suffered, and being consummated, he became to all who obey him the cause of eternal salvation*.[57] For which reason the same Apostle admonishes those justified, saying: *Know you not that they who run in the race, all run indeed, but one receiveth the prize? So run that you may obtain. I therefore so run, not as at an uncertainty; I so fight, not as one beating the air, but I chastise my body and bring it into subjection; lest perhaps when I have preached to others, I myself should become a castaway*.[58] So also the prince of the Apostles, Peter: *Labor the more, that by good works you may make sure your calling and election. For doing these things, you shall not sin at any time*.[59] From which it is clear that they are opposed to the orthodox teaching of religion who maintain that the just man sins, venially at least, in every good work; or, what is more intolerable, that he merits eternal punishment; and they also who assert that the just sin in all works, if, in order to arouse their sloth and to encourage themselves to run the race, they, in addition to this, that above all God may be glorified, have in view also the eternal reward,

51. Augustine, *De Natura et Gratia*, 43.   52. 1 John 5:3; Matt. 11:30.
53. John 14:23.   54. Matt. 6:12.
55. Rom. 6:18, 22; Titus 2:12.   56. Rom. 8:17.
57. Heb. 5:8f.   58. 1 Cor. 9:24, 26f.
59. 2 Pet. 1:10.

since it is written: *I have inclined my heart to do thy justifications on account of the reward*; and of Moses the Apostle says; that *he looked unto the reward.*[60]

Chapter 12

Rash Presumption of Predestination Is to Be Avoided

No one, moreover, so long as he lives this mortal life, ought in regard to the sacred mystery of divine predestination, so far presume as to state with absolute certainty that he is among the number of the predestined, as if it were true that the one justified either cannot sin any more, or, if he does sin, that he ought to promise himself an assured repentance. For except by special revelation, it cannot be known whom God has chosen to Himself.

Chapter 13

The Gift of Perseverance

Similarly with regard to the gift of perseverance, of which it is written: *He that shall persevere to the end, he shall be saved*, which cannot be obtained from anyone except from Him who is able to make him stand who stands,[61] that he may stand perseveringly, and to raise him who falls, let no one promise himself herein something as certain with an absolute certainty, though all ought to place and repose the firmest hope in God's help. For God, unless men themselves fail in His grace, as *he has begun a good work, so will he perfect it, working to will and to accomplish.*[62] Nevertheless, let those who think themselves to stand, take heed lest they fall, and with fear and trembling work out their salvation, in labors, in watchings, in almsdeeds, in prayer, in fastings and chastity. For knowing that they are born again unto the hope of glory, and not as yet unto glory, they ought to fear for the combat that yet remains with the flesh, with the world and with the devil, in which they cannot be victorious unless they be with the grace of God obedient to the Apostle who says: *We are debtors, not to the flesh, to live according to the flesh; for if you live according to the flesh, you shall die, but if by the spirit you mortify the deeds of the flesh, you shall live.*[63]

Chapter 14

The Fallen and Their Restoration

Those who through sin have forfeited the received grace of justification can again be justified when, moved by God, they exert themselves to obtain

---

60. Ps. 118:112; Heb. 11:26.   61. Matt. 10:22, 24:13; Rom. 14:4.
62. Phil. 1:6; 2:13.   63. Rom. 8:12f.

through the sacrament of penance the recovery, by the merits of Christ, of the grace lost. For this manner of justification is restoration for those fallen, which the holy Fathers have aptly called a second plank after the shipwreck of grace lost. For on behalf of those who fall into sins after baptism, Christ Jesus instituted the sacrament of penance when he said: *Receive ye the Holy Ghost, whose sins you shall forgive, they are forgiven them, and whose sins you shall retain, they are retained.*[64] Hence, it must be taught that the repentance of a Christian after his fall is very different from that at his baptism, and that it includes not only a determination to avoid sins and a hatred of them, or *a contrite and humble heart*,[65] but also the sacramental confession of those sins, at least in desire, to be made in its season, and sacerdotal absolution, as well as satisfaction by fasts, alms, prayers and other devout exercises of the spiritual life, not indeed for the eternal punishment, which is, together with the guilt, remitted either by the sacrament or by the desire of the sacrament, but for the temporal punishment which, as the sacred writings teach, is not always wholly remitted, as is done in baptism, to those who, ungrateful to the grace of God which they have received, have grieved the Holy Spirit and have not feared to *violate the temple of God.*[66] Of which repentance it is written: *Be mindful whence thou art fallen; do penance, and do the first works*; and again, *The sorrow that is according to God worketh penance, steadfast unto salvation*; and again, *Do penance, and bring forth fruits worthy of penance.*[67]

Chapter 15

By Every Mortal Sin Grace Is Lost, But Not Faith

Against the subtle wits of some also, who *by pleasing speeches and good words seduce the hearts of the innocent*,[68] it must be maintained that the grace of justification once received is lost not only by infidelity, whereby also faith itself is lost, but also by every other mortal sin, though in this case faith is not lost; thus defending the teaching of the divine law which excludes from the kingdom of God not only unbelievers, but also the faithful [who are] *fornicators, adulterers, effeminate, liers with mankind, thieves, covetous, drunkards, railers, extortioners*,[69] and all others who commit deadly sins, from which with the help of divine grace they can refrain, and on account of which they are cut off from the grace of Christ.

---

64. John 20:22f.   65. Ps. 50:19.
66. Eph. 4:30; 1 Cor. 3:17.
67. Rev. 2:5; 2 Cor. 3:17; Matt. 3:2, 4:17; Luke 3:8.
68. Rom. 16:18.   69. 1 Cor. 6:9f; 1 Tim. 1:9f.

Decree concerning Reform

The same holy Council of Trent, continuing the matter of reform,[70] resolves and ordains that the things following be at present decreed.

Chapter 1

The Negligence of Pastors of Churches in the Matter of Residence Is in Various Ways Restrained. The *Cura Animarum* Is Provided For

Since by divine precept it is enjoined on all to whom is entrusted the *cura animarum* to know their sheep,[71] to offer sacrifice for them, and to feed them by the preaching of the divine word, the administration of the sacraments, and the example of all good works, to exercise a fatherly care in behalf of the poor and other distressed persons and to apply themselves to all other pastoral duties, all of which cannot be rendered and fulfilled by those who do not watch over and are not with their flock, but desert it after the manner of hirelings, the holy Council admonishes and exhorts them that, mindful of the divine precepts and *made a pattern of the flock*,[72] they in judgment and in truth be shepherds and leaders. And lest those things that concern residence which have already been piously and with profit decreed under Paul III,[73] of happy memory, be understood in a sense foreign to the mind of the holy Council, as if in virtue of that decree it were lawful to be absent during five continuous months, the holy Council, adhering to that decree, declares that all who, under whatever name or title, even though they be cardinals of the holy Roman Church, preside over patriarchal, primatial, metropolitan and cathedral churches, are bound to personal residence in their church or diocese, where they are obligated to discharge the office committed to them and from which they may not absent themselves except for the reasons and in the manner subjoined. Since Christian charity, urgent necessity, due obedience, and manifest advantage to the Church or the commonwealth require and demand that some at times be absent, the same holy Council decrees that these reasons for lawful absence must be approved in writing by the most blessed Roman pontiff, or by the metropolitan, or, in his absence, by the oldest resident suffragan

70. After a long suspension; this decree was debated, in the light of subsequent experience, after the council was reconvened in 1561. It represents a compromise between those who insisted that the obligation of residence was by divine right, and that the authority of the bishops was thus independent of the pope, and those who maintained the opposite position, that the bishops were basically delegates of the pope in local churches. The pope at this moment was Pius IV, the uncle of Charles Borromeo (about which see the *Diary* of Casale published in this volume); hence the reference backward in time to his predecessor, Paul III.

71. John 10:1–16, 21:15–17; Acts 20:28.

72. John 10:12f; 1 Pet. 5:3.   73. In Session 6, On Reform, chapters 1–2.

bishop, whose duty it shall also be to approve the absence of the metropolitan; except when the absence is necessitated by some function or office of the state attached to the episcopal dignity, in which cases the absence being a matter of public knowledge and at times unexpected, it will not be necessary to make known to the metropolitan the reasons therefor. To him, however, in conjunction with the provincial Council, it shall pertain to decide concerning the permissions granted by himself or by his suffragans and to see that no one abuses that right and that transgressors are punished in accordance with canonical prescriptions. Moreover, those who are about to depart should remember so to provide for their sheep that as far as possible they may not suffer any injury through their absence. But since those who are absent only for a brief period appear in the sense of the ancient canons not to be absent, because they are soon to return, the holy Council wishes that that period of absence in a single year, whether continuous or interrupted, ought, except for the reasons mentioned above, in no case to exceed two or at most three months, and that consideration be taken that it be made from a just cause and without any detriment to the flock. Whether this be the case, the Council leaves to the conscience of those who depart, which it hopes will be religious and delicate, for hearts are open to God, whose work they are bound at their peril not to do deceitfully. Meanwhile it admonishes and exhorts them in the Lord, that unless their episcopal duties call them elsewhere in their diocese, they are on no account to absent themselves from their cathedral church during the periods of the Advent of the Lord, Quadregesima, the Nativity, Easter, Pentecost and Corpus Christi, on which days especially the sheep ought to be refreshed and to rejoice in the Lord at the presence of the shepherd.

But if anyone, which it is hoped will never happen, shall have been absent in violation of the provision of this decree, the holy Council ordains that in addition to the other penalties imposed upon and renewed against nonresidents under Paul III, and the guilt of mortal sin which he incurs, he can acquire no proprietorship of any fruits in proportion to the time of his absence, and cannot, even though no other declaration follows the present one, retain them with a safe conscience, but is bound, even in his default, through his ecclesiastical superior, to apply them to the treasury of the churches or to the poor of the locality; every agreement or arrangement to which appeal is made for ill-gotten fruits, whereby the aforesaid fruits might be restored to him in whole or in part, being forbidden; any privileges whatsoever granted to any college or treasury to the contrary notwithstanding.

Absolutely the same, as regards the guilt, the loss of fruits, and the penalties, does the holy Council declare and decree with reference to inferior pastors and to all others who hold any ecclesiastical benefice having the *cura animarum*; so however, that should it happen that they are absent for a reason that has first been made known to and approved by the bishop, they shall leave a due allowance of the stipend to a competent vicar to be approved by the ordinary. The permission to go away, which is to be granted in writing and gratuitously, they shall not obtain for a period longer than two months except for a grave reason. In case they shall be summoned, even though not personally, by an edict, and should be contumacious, the ordinaries shall be at liberty to constrain them by ecclesiastical censures, by the sequestration and withdrawal of fruits and other legal means, even deprivation; and no privilege whatsoever, no concession, domestic position, exemption, not even by reason of some benefice, no contract or statute, ven though confirmed by oath or by any authority whatsoever, no custom, even though immemorial, which is to be regarded rather as a corruption, no appeal or inhibition, even in the Roman Curia or by virtue of the constitution of Eugene, shall be able to suspend the execution hereof.

Finally, the holy Council commands that both the decree under Paul III and this present one be published in the provincial and episcopal Councils; for it desires that things which so intimately concern the office of pastors and the salvation of souls, be frequently impressed on the ears and mind of all, so that with the help of God they may not hereafter fall into decay either through the corrosive action of time, the forgetfulness of men or by desuetude.

Chapter 21

In All Things the Authority of the Apostolic See Shall Remain Intact

Lastly, the holy Council declares that each and all of the things which under whatever clauses and words have been established in this holy council in the matter of reform of morals and ecclesiastical discipline, under the supreme pontiffs Paul III and Julius III, of happy memory, as well as under the most blessed Pius IV, have been so decreed that in these matters the authority of the Apostolic See is and is understood to be intact.

25. A Reformation City: *The Diary of Giambattista Casale* (1554–98)

All that is known about the author of this diary comes from the abundant biographical references in the text itself. The external form is identical to

From *Memorie storiche della diocesi di Milano*, vol. 12, edited by Carlo Monacorda (Milano: Biblioteca Ambrosiana, 1965), pp. 209–437. Translated for this volume by Eric Cochrane.

that used by most diarists of the Italian city-states in the late Middle Ages and the Renaissance—although such periodic concepts do not really apply to persons of the social category of the author. The translation follows the original fairly closely at the beginning, including the various spellings of the author's own name, with its irregular orthography, dialectical forms of speech, empty formulas, and incessant repetitions, in order to give the flavor of the prose of an unlearned mind. Thereafter the text is simplified and abbreviated in order to make it somewhat more legible.

The chief hero of this diary, Carlo Borromeo, born of a noble Milanese family in 1538, studied law at the University of Padua, was made cardinal archbishop of Milan at the ripe age of 22 soon after the election of his uncle, Pius IV, in 1559 (February 1560), who kept him in Rome in charge of a great number of important curial offices. He was also one of the most active participants in the debates of the last sessions of the Council of Trent, which is apparently where he picked up his pastoral vocation. After the death of his uncle he moved to his diocese, and homeland, where his work thereafter won him wide acclaim as an often-imitated model of the new kind of pastoral bishop proclaimed in the Tridentine decrees. Indeed, the printed text of his edicts and his provincial and diocesan synods were used as authoritative guides for the reform of local churches by bishops all over the world. His efforts to transform the diocese from a merely administrative unit into a means for the sanctification of all its subjects led him into frequently acrimonious quarrels with papal authorities in Rome and with political authorities in Milan and Madrid—none of which the diarist sees fit to mention.

Having been intermittently under the control of the French or the Swiss or the local Sforza dukes (the situation described in Machiavelli's letters of 1513), the city and Duchy of Milan passed under the direct control of Emperor Charles V in 1534 (formalized in 1537), who ruled through an Italian governor. His son Philip II concentrated much formerly local power in the Council of Italy in Madrid and was represented in Milan by Spanish governors. However, because the governors changed frequently and because they seldom knew much about the country they were sent to govern, much of the control of local government fell to the Senate, composed of Milanese aristocrats, as is evident in the diary. Casale often refers to the governors as "princes," thus associating them with the native dukes who had ruled Milan since the thirteenth century.

YHS Maria 1563

I note (*Memoria come*) that on the 29th of December the two sons of King Maximilian, king of Bohemia,[1] made an entrance into Milan, and that when they made the entrance they were about 10 years of age; and the governor in Milan at that time was the Duke of Sessa; and he went out to meet them, along with the Magistracy and all the lords of Milan. And many great games and tourneys were put on: heaven and hell were represented (in a drama) with great skill and very great expense at court. And on the day of St. Sylvester (December 31), during the feast of said St. Sylvester, the Duke of Sessa commanded by public cryer that all the shops in Milan be opened and that everyone put on display all the most beautiful things he had to offer so that the said two sons might see the beauties of the stores of Milan. And thus it was done; and it was indeed a marvel to behold. And the two sons were accompanied by the Duke and all the lords of Milan and headed for Nice. And they were presented with 120 bundles of goods, that is, salame, cheese, candles, and many other presents; and the festivities cost the commune about five thousand *scudi*.

YHS Maria 1564

I note that I, Ioan Batista da Caxal, was appointed by the general assembly as sub-prior of San Jacobo in Porta Nova, although not worthy, and that Mr. Francesco Renaldi Sperone [was made] prior. And on the 2nd of February the prior general, that Mr. Hieronimo Rabia, a priest, had made for me a writing table six *braccia* long and 1 *braccio* 6 wide with three triple legs so that I could teach writing. And so on the day of Our Lady Holy Mary I began to teach them to write; for I, Ioan Batista, taught writing gratis *et amore Dei* (and for the love of God); and the said table cost a golden *scudo*: and all this for the honor of God and the salvation of souls and the common good. And so on the first day that good table was put in place by the grace and gift of the Holy Spirit and of the glorious Virgin Mary Mother of God our advocate and protector; and it was full all around with men and young men and boys, which was beautiful to behold, for the honor of Our Lord.

YHS Maria 1563[2]

I note that on the 24th of June, I, Ioan Batista da Caxal, gave to the head of the carpenters guild (*paradegho di legname*) *Lire* 4, *soldi*, *danari*, in order

1. Maximilian (II) son of Emperor Ferdinand and nephew of Emperor Charles V was named King of Bohemia in 1549 in order to strengthen the possibility of his succeeding his father. He was crowned King of the Romans in 1562 after giving assurances that he would remain faithful to Catholicism. He became emperor on his father's death in 1564 and died, a doubtful Catholic at the most, in 1576.
2. *Sic*. Another entry out of order.

to be inscribed as a master; and 5 more to the *paradegho* as above, and to balance the rest on account of the *paradegho*, that is, to have myself inscribed as a master, *L.* 3. And on the same day I gave to the said *paradego* as an honorarium *L. soldi* 7, and to a custodian in order that he pass on the order to the *ligatori* of the said *paradego*, *L. s.* 2, *d.* 6. The notary of the said *paradego* was Signor Ioan Batista. I note that on the 5th of July 1563 I, Ioan Batista, was made and inscribed as a master in the *paradego di legname* in Milan, as a maker of cases (*ligator di balle*) to the praise, honor, and glory of the Holy Trinity and of the glorious Virgin Mary and of St. Joseph and all the court of heaven, that I may make a good beginning, better continuation, and still better end, to the honor of God, the salvation of souls, and the common good: *Laus Deo*.

YHS Maria 1564, 29th of August, Feast of Beheading of St. John the Baptist

I note that Signor Nicolò Ormaneto,[3] vicar general, was sent by His Holiness Pope Pius[4] to publish in Milan and in the whole diocese of Milan the decrees of the Holy Council of Trent and to see that they were put into execution up to every *iota*, by order of His Holiness. And thus on the day *ut supra* (as above) he held a meeting of all the priests of the diocese of Milan, that is, provosts, abbots, curates, and all those who had any kind of benefice; and thus on the said day all of them submitted to obedience. And on the said day there was a general procession, [in which] also a multitude of children took part, that is, those who go to the Schools of Christian life, by command of the said vicar; and the procession went on to the cathedral. While the friars returned home, all the priests awaited in the cathedral the benediction of the said vicar; and a review was made one by one of all the priests who were there. At 19 hours the bell rung for supper, [after which] all returned to the cathedral, each in his liturgical vestments. And a barricade was erected in the middle of the cathedral in a place where all could be heard; and a table was placed in the middle, where the said vicar and the heads [of the church] were seated; and there all were registered and com-

---

3. A protegé of the most famous "model bishop" of the pre-Tridentine era, Gian Matteo Giberti, bishop of Verona, Ormaneto became an unofficial "professional reformer" of dioceses according to the prescriptions of the Council of Trent (which were based in part upon the example of Giberti). As "vicar" for nonresident bishops he was the first to introduce the Tridentine reform in several Italian churches before becoming bishop of Padua in his own name in 1570.

4. Giovanni Angelo Medici (1499–1565) of Milan (no direct relationship to the Medici of Florence), elected pope as Pius IV in 1559. He recalled the council to Trent for its final sessions and approved and then promulgated the conciliar decrees (1564). Among his first acts as pope was the elevation of his nephew, Carlo Borromeo, as cardinal.

manded to put into effect all that the Holy Council had ordered; and the cathedral was locked up behind them. And the said assembly (*Concilio*) lasted for three days, that is, it began on Tuesday and finished on Thursday, with great honor to the Lord God; and the reverent father Don Benedetto gave a sermon every time the assembly was opened. And twelve prelates were appointed to settle any disputes that might arise during the meetings. And four doctors were appointed to interrogate the confessors, so that those who were not qualified for [hearing] confessions should not do so under any circumstances, because it is a matter of great importance for the salvation of souls.

YHS Maria 1564 in Milan

I note that on the 10th of December the reverend fathers came to Milan, that is, the priests of [the Society of] Jesus,[5] which said fathers were sent in the number of 30 to Milan by his Holiness our Lord Pope Pius IV to reside in Milan with the spirit and intention of His Holiness and according to the intentions of the Holy Council and also of the most reverent monsignor Cardinal Borromeo, archbishop of Milan, in order that the said fathers establish a seminary to bring together a quantity of clerks and instruct them in the holy apostolic and divine doctrine, so that the said clerks will become good and holy priests. And when any parish priest or curate should die, in their place shall be put one of these clerks, who are more in accord with the times and can serve as examples of good doctrine and good morals, for the edification of the Holy Roman Catholic Church, the honor and glory of God, the salvation of souls, and the common good. And thus on the same day a general procession took place by command of His Holiness to accompany the said fathers to the holy place [selected for] the seminary, which was San Vivo in Porta Decinesa [S. Vito al Carobbio]. And the procession was accompanied also by the most reverend mons. Signor Nicolò Ormaneto, vicar general of all the diocese of Milan, and also the most illustrious prince, Signor Gabriello Cuova, a Spaniard, and all the most illustrious Senate of Milan, with much devotion and honor of the Lord God, and to the joy of all the people, men and women, who followed them; and in the said procession there were also some hundred clerks. And in those days one of these fathers of Jesus by the name of don Benedetto preached in the cathedral of Milan: a man rare in this world and a great preacher. And since for many days hence it had not stopped raining, the goodness of God granted that the day of the said procession was a clear and beautiful day, showing that [what was done] was most pleasing to His Divine Maj-

---

5. The Society of Jesus was founded by the associates of Ignatius of Loyola in 1537 and formally recognized by Pope Paul III in 1540.

esty. And this I, Ioan Batista da Caxal, have wished to write down as a memorial to the world.

YHS Maria 1565

I note that on the 16th of February, I, Ioan Batista da Caxal, introduced a common prayer for all my household; and the composer of this prayer was the Reverend Mr. Hieronimo Rabia, a priest, who in the year 1564 had been prior general of the Confraternity of Christian Life (*Opera de la Vita Christiana*). And I, the above-mentioned Ioan Batista, did this with the permission of Father Catellino da Castello, who 18 years had been my father confessor. He indeed praised this prayer and devotion to the skies as something inspired by the Holy Spirit by the grace of the good Jesus; and he said that prayers like this are what maintain peace, union, and concord in a household and in all households, for where there is the Lord, there is every good thing, all happiness and consolation. The prayer is as follows: I, Ioan Batista, kneel down with all my family, that is, with my wife named Cathelina, my children Zanevera and David, my servant named Ioan Antonio. I say "in nomine Patris et Filii et Spiritus Sancti Amen," then the "Veni Sancte Spiritus," etc., then the grace of the Holy spirit, etc., the "Emitte Spiritum tuum et creabuntur," etc. I pronounce the words and all repeat them after me. We then say three Our Fathers and three Ave Marias, word by word *ut supra*, in honor and reverence for those three holy nails by which our Lord Jesus Christ was borne on the holy wood of the Cross for the love of us, that he might deign for the sake of his holy thoughts, words, and deeds, to be merciful with regard to the wicked thoughts, words, and deeds of this miserable world, and in particular that he deign to be merciful toward all those of our household, and that he not heed our miserable sins but rather that he pardon them through his great mercy and goodness, that he keep it in perfect union and perfect love, us and all of Christendom, and in peace and holiness of soul and body, and that we may persevere until death and that he grant honor and victory in all our undertakings, and that we may do and say everything to the honor and glory of God, the salvation of souls, and the common good. Amen. And all this I make the others say on their knees, word for word.

YHS Maria 1565

I note that in 1565 on the 16th of September was founded the school for small children who on feast days go to learn Christian doctrine and good morals *gratis* in San Michele al Gallo. And it was founded by Mr. Rinaldo di Lanzi and Mr. Ioan Paolo d'Angiera and Mr. Christophoro Robio, with great honor to God and to the amazement of the people. And the Reverend Father Castellino da Catello, founder of this institution, was also present with some of his spiritual sons, that is, Ioan Batista da Caxal and Mr. Ion Antonio di Raymondo. This said father had been for the past 7 years confined to his bed; and on this morning it miraculously pleased the Lord God to give him such strength, in consideration of his good desire to see augmented these holy schools *ut supra*. That morning *ut supra* he went to hear a sermon at the cathedral, then to take communion at San Sepulchro, then after dinner at 18 hours he went to see the foundation of the said school, which was the marvel of all Milan because it was thought that the said father had long been dead, and he was embraced and caressed by many priests and secular persons because he was a great servant of God and well liked and honored by all.

YHS Maria 1565 in Milan

How the entrance of the Cardinal and Archbishop Mons. Carlo Borromeo took place. I note that in 1565 on 23d of September at 20 hours he entered into the city and at 23 hours into the cathedral; for he rested during the three [intervening] hours at Sant' Eustorgio, for he wanted to watch the procession of all the clergy in festive groups according to the usual custom, that is: the priests, the friars, the penitent confraternities, etc. And the said entrance took place on Sunday. And the said clergy began [in procession] from the cathedral and went to Sant' Eustorgio, and followed the street outside Porta Ledovica, and entered into Sant' Eustorgio where our most reverend and illustrious archbishop Borromeo, archbishop of Milan, was waiting, and he was already a cardinal; and having greeted him at the main altar of said church, they returned to the cathedral, accompanied with great honor by all the people, which was certainly something marvelous to behold, and it can be recounted only with great amazement. And the Reverend vicar Niccolò Ormaneto requested of the Company of Christian Doctrine, which teaches Christian doctrine *gratis*, that 24 of the said masters be sent to him, each carrying a red staff bearing on it *la moraia*, that is, the arms of the said archbishop, and that they take on the responsibility of keeping order among all the clergy. And I, Ioan Baptista di Casali, carried the first staff. And also there went out to meet him [the archbishop] the prince of Milan, who was the most excellent lord don Gabriele de la Cuova. And thus by the order of the said Vicar all the bells of Milan were sounded for three days before the feast day, that is la *zobia*; and the following Saturday at the second hour of the night the bells of Milan were rung at length, which was certainly a holy melody to hear. And many, many other things were done that I will not recount in order not to be too prolix. On the following Sunday the archbishop sang Mass in the cathedral. And the said prince was there with much ceremony, all so well arranged that it is impossible to describe, and the cathedral was so full of people that no more could get in. And the said archbishop, after the Gospel, preached in person; and after Mass another sermon was given from the pulpit in the choir by another great, reverend man. At the end [the archbishop] gave his holy benediction to all the people; and everyone who went devoutly to visit the cathedral on the occasion of the said Mass gained a plenary indulgence granted by Pope Pius IV, who was the uncle of the said archbishop. The next Sunday, which was the 7th of October there was a marvellous procession accompanied by said archbishop and by the said prince. This procession was ordered to beseech God's grace that the holy council to be held by His Most Reverent Lordship in the cathedral might dedicate itself solely to the consideration of matters tending to the pure honor of God, the salvation of souls, and the common good. And the same order imposed upon the whole people a three-day fast, that is, the following Wednesday, Friday, and Saturday, and that they confess and communicate the following Sunday. And all who did this would receive an indulgence for all their sins. In this order he (the archbishop) wished to imitate the saying of St. Ambrose, which says that who seeks a grace from the Lord God must undertake these three things: charity, fasting, and prayer. And to give a good example, the said archbishop was the first to do these three things. And thus he had presents given to the poor monasteries of every kind, to those in prison, and to all the poor laymen, and in particular to those who fear God.

YHS Maria 1565

On the 14th of October the said archbishop on commission from Pope Pius IV made a bishop cardinal in the cathedral with much ceremony.[6] And after the Mass a Father Basileo of the Passion in Milano gave a marvellous sermon on the Gospel of the adulterous woman, that is, on mercy and on judgment. And there were present the said archbishop, many honored bishops, the prince, the Senate, the magistracy, and a great number of people, and all listed with attention and great devotion, which was a great example and a matter of joy to all the people, being a rare, unheard of happening.

On the said 15th of October the holy provincial council was convened; and there were present the archbishop and all the bishops he has under him; and (Mass) was sung by the said archbishop with such ceremony, such order, and such devotion and such honor to the Lord Jesus Christ crucified, the only son of the living God, his omnipotent Father and the Paraclite, the Spirit of Truth, and the most glorious Mother ever Virgin Mary and of all the celestial court, and with such consolation and edification of all the

---

6. I.e., he presented him with the signs of the rank to which he had been elevated the previous March. This happens to have been Guido Ferrero, bishop of Vercelli, the son of Borromeo's aunt, formerly Papal nuncio to Venice.

people, who never in our times has ever seen such great things in the said cathedral. And on the said morning all the ordinances of the holy Council of Trent were promulgated and confirmed by the holiness of our Lord Pope Pius IV, who was pope when (the last sessions) the said Council was held. And every day sermons were given in the said cathedral . . . from the day in which the council was opened, by the said Father Basileo . . . ; and on the following Sunday a father of St. Francis, called Franceschino, began preaching.

The first session of the said council began on the 15th of October and lasted until the 23d of the said month. And the second session began then on the 24th of said month in the same way and with the same order and devotion as above. And that morning after the high Mass the Jesuit father Benedetto, for a long time preacher in the cathedral, gave a sermon. And the said second session lasted from the 24th *ut supra* until the following 3d of November, a Saturday. And the (participants) remained in the cathedral from early in the morning until the 1st hour of night without eating, namely, all the bishops, who swore orally and in writing to remain faithful to all that the said council had ordered, with many fine ceremonies and with much praise to God the Father, the Son, and the Holy Spirit, with such edification of all the people that it was marvelous, more marvelous than anything before heard of. . . .

YHS Maria 1568

On the 4th of July 1568 the most reverend Cardinal Carlo Borromeo laid the cornerstone for the restoration of the (church of) San Fidele near the palace of Sig. Thomaso da Marino, which was later occupied by the Jesuits; . . . and the canons of the cathedral and all [the students in] the seminary came along in procession with the said cathedral, as well as the prince of Milan, don Gabriel de la Cuova. . . . After the said cardinal had placed the stone he delivered a marvelous sermon in which he explained the significance of the stone right there next to the stone; . . . and after the sermon he went into the church and said Mass, and he gave communion to a great number of people with his own hand, to the great amazement of all who beheld the service. On the said stone was written the first and the family name and the offices held by the said cardinal, and on the back was a cross. And I, Ioan Baptista da Casalli, was present at what has been described above, *Laus Deo, sit semper.* . . . And (later) that same day he gave a dinner for all the virgins of the Company of Santa Ursula in a garden of the Guastala near San Barnaba, to afford a bit of recreation for the said virgins and to the honor of God.

YHS Maria 1569

On the last day of August there occurred this great event: that the most reverend Carlo Borromeo wishing to conduct a visitation of the church of La Scala in Milan, the canons of the said church did not want him to enter. When the man who was carrying the red flag of his lordship tried to get in, they tore off the reins from the horse he was riding on and threw him out. Amazed, the . . . archbishop . . . ordered the man who carried his cross to proceed toward the church [anyway]; but they [inside] went toward the one who carried the cross and would not let him enter. Noting how little reverence they showed toward the cross, the archbishop dismounted, reverently picked up the cross in his own hand, and headed himself toward the said canons and toward the other seculars who were with them bearing various arms to keep him from getting in; and with the cross in his hand he defended himself like a true knight of God. And it was a sight to cry about, how his sons turned against their loving father, the sheep against their good shepherd, servants against their faithful lord. But it was a great miracle that no one succeeded in injuring [the archbishop, who], not being able to get in, returned to the cathedral and in his own person excommunicated, to the sound of ringing bells, all the said canons and all those who had taken part in the affair; and in the evening he had sung before the Holy Sacrament the lauds in reverence of the cross that begin: "Adoramus te Christe," etc.

YHS Maria

On the 26th of October there occurred this great event concerning the person of the Cardinal. As he was going as usual into his oratory to pray, as he does every evening for an hour after the Ave Maria (for an oratory he uses one of the rooms in his palace, which is the first room to the right after going down two flights of marble stairs, in which he had constructed a wooden partition), suddenly a great rogue, an enemy of God and of the Holy Mother Church, got next to the door through the said partition with a crossbow with a ball inside it; and aiming it at the person of His Reverence, he fired the said crossbow. The ball passed through his garments to his shirt; but except for inflicting a superficial wound in his back, it went no further. Just at that moment the cantors were singing the words of the Lord Jesus Christ "non turbetur cor vestrum," etc., which gave much credence to the word of the Lord, so that those who were present at the prayers hearing the loud noise caused by the crossbow jumped up to grab that rogue. But His Reverence did not want anyone to move from prayer until it was finished. When it was finished he got up and the ball that had been fired at him fell to the ground; and all who were present could not keep from crying from compassion. . . .

YHS Maria 1570

On the 16th of April, a Sunday, at 20 hours, the criminal who shot at the Reverend Cardinal was led into Milan in a cart by seventy Spanish bowmen, sent by the Duke of Savoy, since Pope Pius V [7] had excommunicated all those who knew something of the criminal's whereabouts and did not report it. He was brought in through Porta Tosa. . . . On the 28th the said man was defrocked (deprived of his clerical status). [The ceremony] took place in the bishop's palace, and it was performed by the bishop of Lodi because the said cardinal was absent. All four of the said provosts were turned over to the secular authorities and led to the Captain of Justice.

On the 2d of August the above mentioned four provosts were put to death, that is, the one who shot the crossbow at the cardinal, and the three others: the provost of Verci, the provost of Levate, the provost of Caravazo, and the provost of the Trinita de Porta Comasina, [the latter being] the one who shot the crossbow, and his name was Hieronimo di Dona. . . . Two of them were hung, two of them were beheaded; in addition the one who shot the crossbow had his hand cut off before the great door of the archepiscopal palace where he had committed his crime. . . .

YHS Maria 1567

On the 16th of February, the beginning of the Ambrosian carnival,[8] our Reverend Archbishop decided for the honor and glory of God . . . to get the people of Milan to observe a wholly spiritual and holy carnival . . . He [accordingly] requested through one of the chief members of his household, don Alberto, that the deans of the cathedral and all those who taught Christian doctrine do him the favor of receiving communion every day during carnival in order to give a good example to the people, and that they pray the Lord God to take away the bad things that usually are done in those days. . . . Having heard so holy a request from such a man, we all consented; . . . and the archbishop offered to administer communion to us from his own hands. Having heard the answer of our Company, . . . he instantly sent to invite all the *Disciplini* (penitential confraternities) of

7. Antonio Ghislieri (1504–72), a Dominican and previously head of the Roman Inquisition, was elected as Pius V in 1566 with the support of Borromeo. One of the most energetic reformers of the Roman church and chief organizer of the naval expedition that culminated in the Battle of Lepanto in 1571, mentioned below, at which the Venetian-Papal-Spanish navy destroyed the Ottoman navy. He was canonized in 1712.

8. The Church of Milan inherited a variant of the Latin liturgy established by Ambrose, of which one feature is that Lent begins on the Sunday *after* Ash Wednesday. It is thanks to Borromeo that the Ambrosian liturgy was saved from the centralizing policy of the post-Tridentine Catholic Church and that it still survives today.

Milan to join us in such a holy gathering; and they too were prompt in obeying his request. It was then broadcast to all the people; and by the grace of
God . . . one thousand three hundred souls came to receive communion
from the hand of the cardinal. The number was recorded by the official in
charge of counting the communicants. The first to receive communion
were the members of [the cardinal's] household, religious and secular; then
the senators, preachers, gentlemen and ladies, then merchants, artisans,
and every sort of person. Of the *Disciplini* there were three hundred. The
said cardinal said low Mass at the altar of St. Agnes in the cathedral. The
altar was adorned for the occasion with tapestries, silver vessels, and many
beautiful things . . . Seeing the great humility of their pastor, the people
were particularly reverent. All the male children of the Schools of Christian doctrine were lined up in the cemetary and led in order into the
church, where His Reverence was waiting to give them all his benediction.
All of them were dressed in wings and shirts, and as they returned toward
their respective schools, toward Porta Renza and Porta Romana, it seemed
that through all Milan there was to be seen nothing but angels, as if Paradise had been opened. So edified was the whole of Milan that everyone
forgot about the usual ribald carnival and talked thereafter only of the holy
things of Paradise. "May God ever be praised, Amen." I, Ioan Baptista da
Casal, received communion with all the others *ut supra*.

YHS Maria 1570

On the 1st of January I, Ioan Baptista di Casalli, was made prior of the
School of Christian Life, although unworthy, at Santo Iacobo in Porta
Nova; and as sub-prior Messer Hieronimo de Poleti was chosen; I had been
subprior for five or six years before by the grace of God. May the Lord
make me a worthy worker in this his holy vineyard. . . .

   On the 17th of May at 13 hours a procession took place by order of Pope
Pius V in celebration for the victory of the Venetian navy over the Turks.
And as the said procession left the cathedral, we looked up into the sky;
and all the people saw three suns, one in the middle and the two others at
either side, in the form of a 'C'; and they seemed to be fixed over the city
of Milan. And all were not a little amazed.

The Year 1569 in Milan

I note that in the year 1569 there was a vast and universal famine, *videlicet*
Item: wheat went up to *L*. 30 the *mogio*
Item: rye went up to *L*. 20 the *mogio*
Item: millet *L*. 14 the *mogio*
Item: wheat bread *L*. 40 the *stara*

Item: small loaves (*miche*) went up from 1 *soldo* to 4 apiece

Item: millet bread 9 ounces for 1 *soldo*

Item: rye bread 8 ounces the *soldo* but it was like clay

The retailers of white bread and millet bread will deliver through a window; but who does not arrive there early will not find any at all.

Item: a *botta per botta* in all the *poste de Milano*; of both wheat and millet bread you won't find any at all unless you pay a *scudo*.

Item: foreigners who are residing at the Hosterie delle Volte cannot buy bread at all for their [foreign] currency.

Item: flour could not be bought anywhere except at a storehouse established in Broveto Novo, [and it is well stocked] by Signor don Gabriel de La Cuove, prince of Milan, the Senate, and the Lords of Food Supplies (*Signori di Provisione*); in which storehouse was sold mixed flour, that is, rye and rice and millet and rice together, and no one could buy more than one *staro* at a time. But you had to be signed up one day and then go buy the flour the next, for which reason the Broveto was jammed full of people at all hours of the day, whose cries could be heard as far as the heavens as they held up their hands with their money in the hopes of having a *staro* of wheat. Such was the great confusion. Women in the crowd gave birth, some persons died—it was enough to make stones weep.

Wine sold that year for as much as *lire* 11 *la brente*; but there was also some for lower prices.

Rice 6 *soldi* the *mita*

beans *s*. 4 *d*. 6 the *mita*

chickpeas *s*. 4 *d*. 6 the *mita*

lentils *s*. 6 *d*. 6

lima beans *s*. 5

lasagna and other *pasta* products, *s*. 8 the pound (*lipra*) and they were so expensive because there weren't any to be had and because the bakers used the flour rather to make bread. Everything indeed was turned into bread, even oats—provided that too could be obtained.

Item: the said year outside the city in the meadows were found dead persons with grass or straw in their mouths. Which cannot be told without tears. *Propter peccata veniunt adversa: escam dedit timentibus se* (evil comes because of sin; He gave food to those who fear Him). Therefore let us pray God that such days will never come again if it pleases his Divine Majesty. On the 5th of February 1570 the Reverend Cardinal absolved the 15 canons of the Scala who previously had turned against him with arms when he tried to visit the said Scala. The absolution was given at the door of the cathedral; and after the ceremony all went to the high altar where the cardinal gave a good sermon; he then went to the Scala to consecrate the chapel that had been deconstructed and closed for a year, singing the *Te Deum* as the bells rung, to the great joy of all the people. *Laus Deo sit semper.*

YHS Maria 1571

On the 4th of September my nephew Augustino became a friar of the Order of St. Jerome in Milan, and after a month he came back out [of the monastery] saying that he could not stand having to be continuously at prayer.

In 1572 on October 18 the said Agostino [*sic*] became a friar once again at the Monastery of San Vitore, and he was clothed as a friar on the day of St. Luke and was given the name Friar Luca.

On the 13th of September 1571 Cardinal Borromeo made a procession at midnight in which 500 persons participated dressed as penitents; among them were all sorts of people, gentlemen, merchants, and artisans. They assembled at San Francesco at the palace of Signor Tomaso da Marino; and the archbishop [designated] his archpriest as general of this Company. And they began beating themselves in that place, and they went to the cathedral and back, continuously beating themselves, with marvelous order and devotion, so that it was splendid to behold. The said cardinal waited on the Company in the cathedral have gave them his benediction, one at a time, while prayers were being said that God might defend the Christians from the hand of the Turks because they were now approaching Venice. This procession then took place every Friday night for about two months, all with bare feet and carrying some hundred torches on poles until such time as the Lord God was pleased to give [us] victory over the Turks. . . .

In 1571 on the 7th of October the ineffable Providence of Our Lord God, after such tragedies and troubles for our sins, today deigned, moved by His great goodness and clemency, to visit and favor his Holy Church with the marvelous and unheard of victory won by the most serene John of Austria against the pride and tyranny of the Turks, the enemy of the Christian name, in the gulf of Lepanto—an undertaking truly worthy of such a prince, the son of the invincible Charles V of eternal memory,[9] from which only very important and marvelous effects can be expected. . . . As soon as news of the said victory arrived in Milan, there was a huge celebration with fireworks and artillery fire; and on the day of St. Martin, the 11th of November, there were more fireworks and lamps were lighted in every window until the 3d hour of night, and it was marvelous to behold; and the

9. John was the illegitimate son of Charles V, ruler of Austria, the Netherlands, Castile and Aragon, and Holy Roman Emperor in 1519. On the extinction of the Sforza family, which had ruled Milan off and on since 1450, Charles also became duke of Milan in 1534, a title which he yielded to his son, Philip II of Spain, before his retirement in 1555.

cardinal ordered three days of general processions to thank God for the said victory over the Turks. . . .

YHS Maria 1572

On the 6th of April the cardinal initiated a prayer in which all the people were instructed by preachers to pray in their houses every evening at the ringing of the bell in the cathedral, this he said was the desire of Pope Pius V, who wished to pray God that he give us grace not to offend His Divine Majesty and to protect us against all evil, particularly from the Turk, the great opponent of Christendom. And thus on that day, the first day of Easter, the bell rung at a half hour of the night, and all the people began with great devotion to say the said prayers. . . .

YHS Maria 1575

On the 30th of October all 24 members of the board (*corpo*) of the Congregation of Christian Doctrine with as many other assistants to a total of 48 conducted a visitation for the reformation [of established] schools and the foundation [of new ones], by order of the prior general, the Rev. Mr. Francesco, and with the consent of the whole Congregation—who also commanded that the visitors accept nothing to eat or drink or anything else from [the schools they were visiting]. And all this provided considerable edification for the whole people . . . And I, Giovanni Battista di Casalli, was assigned the area outside of Porta Nova, and among other places I established a school for boys and girls in the church of Santo Martino a Balsamo. *Laus Deo*. . . .

On the 7th of September I . . . was made one of the six visitors of the schools of Christian Doctrine of Milan and I was charged with inspecting all the schools around Porta Nova. And on the same day I was made general chancellor of the congregation.

YHS Maria 1576

On the vigil of Easter at 23 hours the Reverend Bishop of Famagosta arrived in Milan sent by Pope Gregory XIII [10] as visitor general. And he visited all the churches, the monasteries, the schools of the *Disciplini*, and the schools of Christian Doctrine, of which there were 100. And he did nothing but conduct visitations, administer communion, and give sermons wherever he went, with great charity, kindness, and courtesy. As a consequence every-

10. Ugo Boncompagni of Bologna (1502–85), made a cardinal by Pius IV and charged with the reform of canon law. He was elected pope in 1572 and is best known today for authorizing the reformed calendar that still bears his name.

one gladly did all he requested. He remained here until the end of Holy Provincial Council and returned to Rome on May 26, leaving behind a very good reputation, so that all Milan was sorry to see him go. . . .

[Later in the same year] some cases of the plague broke out in the Borgho di Ortolani. According to some, it had been brought to Meregnano by certain renegade Christians from Turkey, and from Meregnano then to Milan. In the said Borgho it spread rapidly, and people collapsed like flies. So that the Lords of Milan were obliged, in order to repair this evil and keep it out of the city, to close up the whole borgho, which lies outside the Porta Comasina. Hence one night at 5 hours the Marchese de l'Aymonde, who was Prince of Milan, went there with all his bowmen, lancemen, and other soldiers to close up the said borgho, for all the inhabitants put up a big defense against being locked inside. The Marchese and his soldiers cleared the streets and threatened with hanging anyone who tried to get out. . . . But because God wished to adopt this plague in order to punish us justly for our enormous sins . . . , He let it come into the city [in spite of the precautions], first along the street to the Porta Comasina; and from there it spread all over the city. Santo Gregorio was opened as a hospital for the stricken. . . . And soon nothing was heard in the city except "here comes the *monato* with the cart" with which to transport the sick and the dead to Santo Gregorio. And seeing that the said illness continued to grow, the said Prince and the Senate put out an order that the schools of human- ities be closed. And yet it continued to grow. They then put out another order that all women and children under 15 were not to leave their houses under any circumstances. . . . These temporal remedies are holy and good, and pleasing to God, particularly those that are ordered by our lords and loving patrons, ever vigilant for the good of the commonwealth. Still more marvelous, such that all creatures would be amazed, was to see the Reverend Cardinal praying and ordering prayers incessantly all over Milan and the diocese—all in the hope that such would be effective in placating the wrath of God through his infinite mercy. And hence public prayers were conducted in all the public squares . . . so that nothing could be seen in Milan but beautiful altars where the people came together every evening for prayer, and Milan looked like one big church with its [side] altars all around. And every evening a great number of people took part in a pro- cession in the cathedral. . . . The archbishop ordered that the holy prayers of the 40 hours be celebrated and that the Holy Sacrament be exposed day and night, and that the same ceremony be observed in all the churches of the city. He further ordered three general processions of friars as well as priests; and on the third day all the holy relics of the city were also carried in procession—including the Holy Nail which passed through the holy flesh [of Christ] into the wood of the Cross, which is kept in the cathedral above the high altar. . . . On the 9th of October, as I was returning home from the devotions, one of the brothers of Christian Doctrine . . . [stopped me] to say: "Giovanni Battista, I am sorry to tell you some bad news: the Lords of the Health (Signori de la Sanita) came to visit some sick persons in your building and judged their illness to be the plague. They immediately locked up the door [of the house] and [of] the shop beneath. Asking where you were, they were told you were following the procession. They are waiting for you and will shut you up too as soon as you go home. . . . Eight days later the officials came to take away the belongings of all those stricken. As they left they perfumed their beds . . . and consequently a fire started about midnight which we then discovered the next morning. None of the neighbors would come help us for fear of the plague, and . . . we had no choice but to throw ourselves upon (God's) infinite mercy and invoke the glorious Virgin Mary and all the saints to intercede for us. . . . We then cried out to our neighbors that they at least [tell] the plague official to come before we were all killed; . . . and they managed finally to put the fire out. . . .

[The discovery of still other cases led the governor to impose a quarantine], closing up all the shops and the doors and forcing everyone to stay inside his house; and no one could go out except to attend the Mass of the Resurrection, which was on April 7 of the said year [1577]. The cardinal ordered other Masses to be said in the streets . . . where the people could follow them from their windows. . . .

YHS Maria 1578

On the 20th of January, the feast of St. Sebastian, the Cardinal ordered a general procession of priests, friars, and all the people . . . to thank God . . . for the liberation of Milan from the plague. . . . The Senate [removed all the restrictions] by the sound of the trumpet because for some two months no further cases of plague had been reported. . . . The Cardinal himself led the procession in pontifical vestments followed by the Prince, the Senate, the magistrates, the Lords of the Provision, and all the nobility, and the Cardinal sung Mass in Santo Sebastiano and again gave a marvelous sermon. After the procession, the Prince and the Senate issued a proclamation declaring the liberation of Milan from the plague and ordering that all the streets be illuminated—that both rich and poor light two lamps at each window, so that Milan would demonstrate its joy in this miraculous grace conceded by the Lord God of having freed all of us from the horrible contagion . . .

YHS Maria 1583

On the 16th of June, Wednesday, I . . . gave my word and hand in good faith to Messer Christophoro de Manara that I give my daughter Zanevera to be his wife. Present were Messer Stephano di Oldroni, Messer Michel di

Recardi, and Messer Agostino Carota . . . And the next Sunday, which was the 19th, the [the banns] were first announced in the church of Santo Protasio, the second time on the day of St. John the Baptist [24th June], and the third on the following Sunday, which was the 26th; and on the 29th, the feast of St. Peter, at 11 hours, she was married to the said Messer Christophoro, and the parish priest [officiating] was the reverent Giovanni Antonio, and the witnesses signing were Messer Paulo d'Angera and Messer Michel di Recardi, the barber. And I promised a dowry of 600 imperial lire, that is lire six hundred, half in cash, half in goods. . . .

YHS Maria 1584

On the 3d of November Cardinal Borromeo died at 3 hours of night between Saturday and Sunday, and he was laid in the oratory in the episcopal palace on top of a high thing (*cosa*) covered with brocade around which were placed four torches, and he was dressed in pontifical vestments with his pastoral staff in hand, and he remained there through the following Wednesday. He was 46 years old plus a month and a day, having been a cardinal for 24 years; and on the 5th of November the office was said for him in the cathedral.

Index of Names

Clement V (pope), 130n12
Clement VI (pope), 25
Clement VII (pope), 176, 211–13, 218n21, 263, 264, 266, 267, 306, 387
Coligny, Gaspard de, 233
Collenuccio, Pandolfo, 172
Colonna, Giacomo. *See* Giacomo (bishop)
Colonna, Prospero, 234
Colonna, Stefano, 42
Colonna, Stefano the Elder, 42n
Colonna, Stefanno the Younger, 42n
Commines, Philippe de, 307
Contarini, Gasparo (cardinal), 392
Contucci, Andrea, 254
Cop, Guillaume, 362
Core, Matteo da. *See* Corte, Matteo da
Corte, Matteo da, 218, 218n21
Cortez, Hernando, 240
Cosimo (grand duke). *See* Medici, Cosimo I de' (grand duke)
Cuova, Gabriel de la, 413, 415, 417, 421
Cybo (family), 211n2
Cybo, Innocenzo (cardinal), 211

Dante, Alighieri, 25n96, 40n, 183–84, 268–69, 308
da Vinci, Leonardo, 254
del Bene, Tommaso. *See* Bene, Tommaso del
Delft, Gilles van, 361
Della Luna (family), 110n11
Della Luna, Giovanni, 110
Della Rovere (family), 175
del Sarto, Andrea, 263, 270–71
Donatello, 145
Donato Bonsi, Giovanni de, 110n12
Dondi, Giovanni, 68
Donnino, Angelo di, 258
Doria, Andrea, 217
Duns Scotus, John, 121

Eck, Johann, 329–31
Egidius of Albornoz. *See* Albornoz, Gil Álvarez Carillo de (cardinal)
Elizabeth of Valois (queen), 281n9
Erasmus, Desiderius, 4, 309n1, 358, 387
Estielle, Henri, 295n16
Etaples, Jacques Lefèvre d', 361
Eugenius II (pope), 328

Eugenius IV (pope), 78, 149, 326n1
Everaerts, Johannes, 298

Farel, Guillaume, 367
Farnese, Alessandro. *See* Paul III (pope)
Farnese, Ottavio (duke), 214n13, 233n7
Farnese, Pierluigi, 224n33
Felix V (pope), 149
Ferdinand (son of the duke of Bavaria), 227
Ferdinand I (emperor), 224, 227n, 391–92, 411n1
Ferdinand I (grand duke of Tuscany), 210, 224, 227
Ferdinand I (king of Naples), 150n4
Ferdinand II (the Catholic), king of Aragon, 166n, 178, 242
Ferdinand II (king of Naples), 150n4
Ferdinand II (king of Spain), 242
Ferrante (count of Alife), 220n24
Ferrante I (king of Naples). *See* Ferdinand I (king of Naples)
Ficino, Marsilio, 171, 234n13
Fieschi, Sinibaldo. *See* Innocent IV (pope)
Fiesole, Simone da, 254–55
Filicaia, Alamanno da, 229
Fiorentino, Rosso, 271
Francesco, Francesco di, 145, 146
Francesco, Giovanni di ser, 117, 221
Francesco Maria (duke), 234, 263
Francis I (king of France), 233, 238n24, 274, 280, 282
Francis II (king of France), 233, 389
Frederick III (duke and elector), 330
Fregoso, Aurelio, 224
Froissart, Jean, 304

Gaddi (cardinal), 214–15
Gaetano. *See* Cajetan (cardinal)
Gafori, Franchino, 309
Galilei, Vincenzo, 4, 308, 309
Galileo, 308
Ghislieri, Antonio. *See* Pius V (pope)
Giacomo (bishop), 38, 40, 42n
Gianfigliazzi, Alessandro, 229
Gianfigliazzi, Bongianni, 147
Giberti, Gian Matteo (bishop), 412n3
Giles of Rome. *See* Romanus, Egidius
Ginori, Filippo, 183
Giorgio, Matteo di, 112, 114
Giotto, 253